ORNAMENTAL
FLOWERING
SHRUBS IN
AUSTRALIA

ORNAMENTAL FLOWERING SHRUBS IN AUSTRALIA

Raymond J. Rowell

PRESS

All photographs and captioned drawings are
by the author except those specifically labelled
by others whose assistance is gratefully
acknowledged.

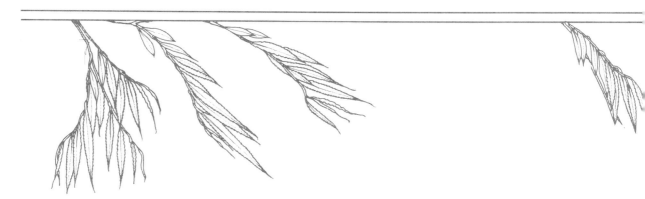

Published by
UNIVERSITY OF NEW SOUTH WALES PRESS
PO Box 1 Kensington NSW Australia 2033
Phone (02) 398 8900
Fax (02) 398 3408

This edition first published in 1991
Reprinted in 1994

National Library of Australia
Cataloguing-in-Publication entry:

Rowell, Raymond J.
Ornamental flowering shrubs in Australia.
Index
Bibliography.
ISBN 0 86840 084 X

1. Flowering shrubs — Australia. I. Title.

635.976'0994

Designed by Diane Quick
Printed in Singapore by Kyodo Printing

Available in North America through
International Specialized Book Services
Portland Oregon 97213–3644
United States of America

Contents

Colour Illustrations

PLATE 1 Acacia cardiophylla; Acacia rotundifolia; Acacia flexifolia; Acacia spectabilis; Acacia rotundifolia; Acacia conferta; Acacia elongata. **PLATE 2** Banksia collina; Breynia disticha 'Roseo-picta'; Berberis thunbergii 'Atropurpurea'; Abelia x grandiflora 'Francis Mason'; Boronia mollis; Acalypha wilkesiana 'Triumphans'; Banksia ericifolia. **PLATE 3** Calliandra haematocephala; Boronia muelleri; Berberis thunbergii 'Atropurpurea Nana'; Boronia heterophylla; Boronia heterophylla; Bauhinia galpinii; Boronia 'Telopea Valley Star'. **PLATE 4** Callistemon phoeniceus; Callistemon 'Candy Pink'; Cassia artemisioides; Callistemon viminalis 'Captain Cook'; Clianthus puniceus; Cassia eremophila; Callistemon 'Harkness'. **PLATE 5** Camellia japonica 'Chandleri'; Camellia reticulata 'Shot Silk' *Photo by Charles Cowell;* Camellia japonica 'C.M. Hovey'; Camellia japonica 'Laurie Bray'. **PLATE 6** Camellia japonica 'Monjisu'; Camellia japonica 'The Czar'; Camellia japonica 'Magnoliaeflora'; Camellia sasanqua 'Setsu Gekka'; Camellia japonica 'Shiro Chan'; Camellia japonica 'Betty Sheffield Supreme'; Camellia hiemalis 'Kanjiro' syn. 'Hiryu'; Camellia sasanqua 'Plantation Pink'. **PLATE 7** Camellia reticulata 'Purple Gown' *Photo by Charles Cowell;* Camellia reticulata 'Cornelian' *Photo by Charles Cowell;* Camellia japonica 'Carter's Sunburst'; Camellia japonica 'Pink Gold'; Camellia reticulata 'Dr Clifford Parks' *Photo by Charles Cowell;* Camellia japonica 'Spring Sonnet'; Camellia japonica 'Lady Loch'; Camellia reticulata 'Valentine Day' *Photo by Charles Cowell.* **PLATE 8** Cassia coluteoides; Ceanothus 'Mountain Haze'; Chamelaucium uncinatum; Chamelaucium uncinatum; Cassia coluteoides; Ceanothus x edwardsii; Coleonema pulchrum 'Sunset Gold'. **PLATE 9** Clianthus formosus; Cotinus coggygria; Crowea saligna *Photo by Bro. P. Stanley;* Correa reflexa *Photo by P.M. Althofer;* Cytisus scoparius var. prostratus; Crotalaria semperflorens; Cytisus x praecox. **PLATE 10** Cotoneaster conspicuus; Catharanthus roseus; Cotoneaster pannosus; Coleonema pulchrum (Red form); Coleonema pulchrum; Cytisus multiflorus; Cotoneaster glaucophyllus f. serotinus; Cotoneaster lacteus. **PLATE 11** Cytisus x spachianus; Duranta erecta 'Variegata'; Epacris purpurascens; Euphorbia pulcherrima 'Annette Hegg'; Daphne cneorum; Euphorbia veneta; Fatsia japonica; Felicia fruticosa. **PLATE 12** Elaeagnus pungens 'Maculata'; Felicia amelloides; Eupatorium megalophyllum; Euphorbia pulcherrima 'Henrietta Ecke'; Erica vestita; Eriostemon australasius; Euonymus europaeus; Erica peziza. **PLATE 13** Fuchsia 'Mission Bells'; Hibbertia astroticha (syn. H. empetrifolia); Greyia sutherlandii; Euphorbia milii; Fuchsia 'Gartenmeister Bonstedt'; Hovea acutifolia; Forsythia x intermedia; Hebe hulkeana. **PLATE 14** Isopogon dubius *Photo by Bro. P. Stanley;* Indigofera australis; Hebe x franciscana 'Blue Gem'; Iboza riparia; Halimium (Cistus) lasianthum ssp. formosum; Hydrangea macrophylla; Hypocalymma robustum. **PLATE 15** Lagerstroemia indica 'Rubra'; Grevillea longifolia; Fremontodendron californicum; Pimelia ferruginea 'Magenta Mist'; Grevillea 'Robyn Gordon'; Grevillea hookerana; Ixora chinensis 'Prince of Orange'; Gardenia augusta. **PLATE 16** Hibiscus 'Golden Bell'; Hibiscus 'Crown of Warringah'; Hibiscus 'Dawn'; Hibiscus 'Celia'; Hibiscus 'Fire Engine' *Photo by Les Beers;* Hibiscus 'Crown of Bohemia'

Photo by Les Beers; Hibiscus 'Catavki' *Photo by Les Beers;* Hibiscus mutabilis 'Plena' *Photo by Les Beers;* Hibiscus mutabilis *Photo by Les Beers.* **PLATE 17** Hibiscus 'Madonna' *Photo by Les Beers;* Hibiscus 'Freddie Brubaker' *Photo by Les Beers;* Hibiscus syriacus 'Hino-maru' *Photo by Les Beers;* Hibiscus 'Surfrider'; Hibiscus syriacus 'Ardens' *Photo by Les Beers;* Hibiscus mutabilis *Photo by Les Beers;* Hibiscus 'Mary Wallace' *Photo by Les Beers;* Hibiscus 'Boondah'; Hibiscus 'Norman Stevens' *Photo by Les Beers.* **PLATE 18** Leptospermum nitidum; Lambertia formosa; Isopogon anethifolius; Hypocalymma angustifolium; Kerria japonica 'Plena'; Kunzea capitata; Prostanthera rotundifolia; Leptospermum squarrosum. **PLATE 19** Murraya paniculata; Nandina domestica; Melaleuca steedmanii *Photo by Bro. P. Stanley;* Pieris formosa var. forrestii 'Wakehurst'; Melaleuca lateritia *Photo by Bro. P. Stanley;* Mahonia bealei; Leptospermum scoparium var. rotundifolium; Kolkwitzia amabilis. **PLATE 20** Mussaenda erythrophylla; Mussaenda frondosa; Heliotropium arborescens 'Aureum'; Leptospermum squarrosum; Leptospermum scoparium var. scoparium 'Martinii'; Pimelia ferruginea; Pieris formosa var. forrestii; Pieris 'Bert Chandler'. **PLATE 21** Prostanthera ovalifolia; Photinia x fraseri 'Robusta'; Photinia glabra 'Rubens'; Pyracantha angustifolia; Prunus glandulosa 'Alba Plena'; Podalyria calyptrata; Ribes sanguineum 'King Edward VII'; Prunus glandulosa 'Rosea Plena'. **PLATE 22** Pyracantha atalantioides; Retama monosperma; Rhododendron Azalea Kurume 'Hinode-giri'; Punica granatum; Pukeiti Rhododendron Trust Garden, New Plymouth, N.Z.; Pyracantha angustifolia; Potentilla fruticosa 'Klondyke'; National Rhododendron Garden, Olinda, Victoria. **PLATE 23** Prostanthera rotundifolia; Rhododendron Azalea Kurume 'Yaye-hiryu'; Rhododendron Azalea Kurume 'Kirin'; Raphiolepis delacourii; Rhododendron Azalea 'Splendens'; Pyracantha fortuneana; Pyracantha fortuneana. **PLATE 24** Rhododendron Azalea Kurume cvs; Rhododendron Azalea 'Agnes Neale'; Rhododendron Azalea 'Exquisite'; Rhododendron Azalea 'Lady Poltimore'; Rhododendron Azalea Kurume 'Omoine'; Rhododendron Azalea Mollis 'Hugo Koster'; Rhododendron Azalea Mollis 'Hortulanus H. Whitte'; Rhododendron Azalea Mollis 'Directeur Moerlands'. **PLATE 25** Raphiolepis x delacourii; Rhododendron Azalea Mollis 'Dr M. Oosthoek'; Rhododendron Azalea Ghent Hybrid; Schefflera venulosa; Sedum praealtum; Senecio petasitis; Syringa x vulgaris 'Katherine Havemeyer'; Streptosolen jamesonii. **PLATE 26** Syringa vulgaris 'Vulcan'; Tibouchina lepidota; Thryptomene saxicola; Telopea speciosissima; Spiraea cantoniensis 'Lanceata'; Tibouchina lepidota; Spartium junceum; Viburnum opulus 'Sterile'. **PLATE 27** Sambucus canadensis 'Aurea'; Viburnum rhytidophyllum; Viburnum tinus; Vitex agnus-castus; Templetonia retusa *Photo by Bro. P. Stanley;* Tibouchina heteromalla; Tetratheca ericifolia *Photo by Bro. P. Stanley;* Verticordia grandis *Photo by Bro. P. Stanley.* **PLATE 28** Weigela florida 'Aureo-variegata'; Viburnum macrocephalum 'Sterile'; Tibouchina macrantha; Tibouchina mutabilis; Weigela 'Styriaca'; Viburnum opulus 'Sterile'; Viburnum plicatum var. tomentosum.

Acknowledgements

Seldom is a project of this kind brought to its conclusion without assistance from other people whose expert knowledge derives from skill and experience in one or more of the many specialised fields of horticulture.

This book is no exception. In the course of its compilation a great number of horticultural institutions such as botanic gardens, national and state parks, public and private gardens, nurseries and exhibitions have been visited to examine plant material at first hand and to glean information from people attached to these places.

Contact with these specialists has been inspirational. Without exception, they have shown a willingness to share their knowledge, to make plant specimens available for drying, pressing, and later study, to allow pictures to be taken and to co-operate in every possible way. I am deeply grateful for their practical help and encouragement.

Special thanks are offered to the following, whose technical assistance far exceeded what would normally have been expected.

The Directors and Staff Members of the following Scientific or Botanical Institutions: The Royal Botanic Gardens, Kew, England, and Edinburgh, Scotland; the Royal Botanic Gardens, Sydney (notably the Horticultural Botanist, Mr A. N. Rodd whose help in the identification of plant material and the verification of its correct nomenclature has been indispensable); National Botanic Gardens, Canberra, ACT, and the Australian Cultivar Registration Authority; Melbourne Botanic Gardens, Victoria; Ballarat Botanic Gardens, Victoria; Adelaide Botanic Gardens, South Australia; National Botanic Gardens of South Africa, Kirstenbosch; Montreal Botanic Gardens, Van Dusen Botanic Gardens, Vancouver, Niagara School of Horticulture, and Butchart Gardens, Victoria in Canada; and the Burrendong Arboretum, Wellington, NSW.

Other Horticultural Authorities for advice on particular plant species: Mr Les Beers, Warriewood, NSW (Hibiscus); Mr Bill Cane, Maffra, Vic. (Eriostemons, Prostantheras and Callistemons); Mr and Mrs Claude Crowe, Berrima, NSW (Malus and Cotoneasters); Mr E. F. K. Denny, Manager of the Bridestowe Estate, Lilydale, Tas. (Lavandulas) Mr and Mrs John Gaibor, Wentworth Falls, NSW (Maples); the late Dr G. H. Hewitt, MBE, Bellingen, NSW (Cassias, Tibouchinas and Tabebuias); Mr A. G. Floyd, Coff's Harbour, NSW (Tabebuias); Mr Leo Hodge, Vic. (Grevilleas); Mrs G. Pike (Poinsettias) and Dr J. J. Wurdack, Curator, Dept of Botany, Smithsonian Institute, Washington DC, USA (Tibouchinas).

Members of the staff of the State Libraries of NSW and South Australia and the University of Sydney, and of the Consulates-General of Denmark, Italy, Sweden, Federal Republic of Germany and The Netherlands for historical

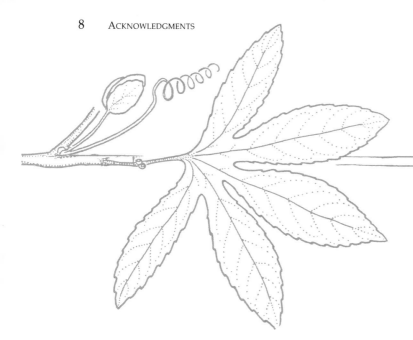

information on botanists and others connected with the origin and derivation of plant names.

In particular, thanks are due to the Head of Division, Teachers, Library and Office Staff and Field Staff at the School of Horticulture, Ryde College of TAFE for their most valuable assistance, as well as the many privileges and courtesies extended to me since my retirement from that institution.

This section would not be complete without an expression of my gratitude for the skilful and ever-willing help given by my wife. Her self-appointed task of pressing and drying the hundreds of plant specimens collected throughout our very lengthy travels was performed with great patience and care. Supported by rough field notes, these herbarium specimens have proved to be of immense value in providing the basis for most of the final descriptions.

R. J. R.

Preface to the Second Edition

The first edition of this book was released in 1980. During these last ten years or so, the work has been very well received. In its primary objective, it appears to have satisfied the demands of the horticultural community for essential information about the trees and shrubs commonly grown in Australia. Nurserymen, in particular, have come to rely upon it as their guide to correct nomenclature and upon its descriptive and graphic detail to verify the identity of their stock. And in the educational field it has been adopted as the standard text and reference book by the horticultural colleges of T.A.F.E. and other relevant organisations throughout the country. An author could ask no more!

The decade has seen changes and advances of considerable importance, especially in the sciences and in horticultural practices. New plants have arrived in ever-increasing numbers, either as direct importations from older countries, or as the product of local selection and plant-breeding activities. The best of these are already finding their place in nursery lists, as well as being included in this edition. In marketing terms, official accreditation by the Australian Cultivar Registration Authority has proved to be of inestimable value to such plants.

Conversely, a few plants have fallen from public favour through their unfortunate suckering or seeding habits, and some have been branded, officially or otherwise, as dangerous because of poisonous fruits or leaves. In balance, rather more new plants are deserving of inclusion than those being deleted. So, in order to keep the book within reasonable limits of size and cost, the best compromise solution appears to be a slight reduction in the botanical content throughout. It might even be argued that this is an improvement.

I am confident that in the skilful hands of Mr Douglas Howie and his Staff at The New South Wales University Press, this new edition will continue to occupy a useful place in the literature of horticulture.

R. J. Rowell
1 January 1990

Explanation of Marginal Captions

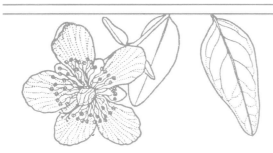

Genus (singular), Genera (plural), Generic (adjectival)

*T*he internationally recognised method of naming plants is by the *binominal system* attributed to the Swedish systematic botanist, Carl Linnaeus.

In his *Species Plantarum*, 1753, Linnaeus, for the purpose of study and comparison, named and classified all the then-known plants into an orderly system of categories or *taxa* (*taxon*—singular).

The lower taxa of *family, genus* and *species* are the fundamental units by which plants are separated and named individually. These taxa form the main basis of taxonomic terminology used here.

Scientific plant names have the same purpose and value as the names of everyday objects in that they facilitate communication of thought or information between people. Material objects are designated by a single name — a noun — and to describe, qualify or specify the kind of object, an adjective is added. Such a combination is a *binomial*.

In plant nomenclature, the first word, a proper noun, relates to the genus; the second is an adjective relating to the species or kind of plant and is called a *specific epithet*.

The genus name then is a Latin word, sometimes derived from another language, referring to a group of closely related species (or to a single species in some cases). Thus, the more than 800 species of *Acacia* are united into a common genus by certain fundamental features such as their alternate, bipinnate leaves, or modified petioles called 'phyllodes', flowers with sepals and petals in fours or fives, and handsome white, cream or yellow stamens of indefinite number, and leguminous fruit containing hard-coated seeds. All *Acacias* have these features. Variations in these and in other respects such as floral perfume, spiny phyllodes and colour and texture of foliage and bark determine the species or kinds of *Acacias*.

Generic names used in binomials are always spelt with an initial capital letter. Some, by popular usage, are sometimes used singly as common names, such as Hydrangea, usually becoming decapitalised in their change of status from proper to common noun.

In more formal writings, it is customary to indicate the name of the author of the genus in abbreviated form after the generic name. Thus, *Cassia* L. cites Linnaeus as the author of the genus, and *Callistemon* R.Br. assigns the Bottlebrush genus to the early British botanist, Robert Brown.

Derivation of the generic name

The main types of generic names or the sources from which they are drawn are:

a) *Commemorative names*, taken from the names of people, usually those making a substantial contribution to botany or to horticulture, e.g. *Banksia*, named for Joseph Banks (later knighted), botanist with Captain James Cook's expedition of discovery of the eastern Australian coast in 1770.

b) *Descriptive names*, derived mainly from the ancient classical languages Greek and Latin, and often drawing attention to a conspicuous feature of the plant, e.g. *Melaleuca*, from the Greek, describing the black and white bark of one of the species.

c) *Vernacular names*, used by ancient races of people to name their local plants, latinised and brought into the botanical language by Linnaeus and other early botanical authors, e.g. *Prunus*, the ancient Latin name of the European Plum.

Common name

The use of common names alone as a means of identification or communication in any serious treatment of plants is unacceptable because of two inherent weaknesses:

a) a single common name may refer to more than one plant, and

b) common names are too vernacular, that is, they are generally understood only by people using the same native language, often in a very limited geographical region.

However, while lacking the precision and universality of the scientific language, common names are useful where more exact terminology is not called for or where ambiguity is unlikely.

Common names do not follow prescribed rules, nor are their creators or users answerable to anyone.

Family

The plant family is the next senior taxon to the genus, consisting of a number of genera (rarely one) united because of similarities in the floral and fruiting organs, e.g. Fabaceae, the Pea family, comprises the plants with 5-petalled flowers having distinctly shaped standard, wing and keel petals and elongate, flat, leguminous fruits in such genera as *Spartium*, *Cytisus* and *Brachysema*.

With few exceptions such as the now superseded Compositae (now Asteraceae) and Cruciferae (now Brassicaceae), family names end in 'aceae'; the substantive part of the name being adapted from one of its principal genera, e.g.

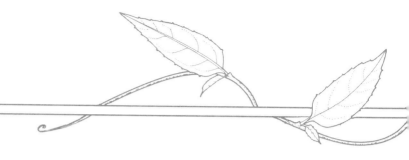

Rosaceae, from the genus *Rosa* and Magnoliaceae from the genus *Magnolia*.

Sub-families are sometimes used to designate major groups within the family but the modern trend is to separate such groups into distinct families with new names.

Families are always spelt with an initial capital letter.

Botanical description of the genus

In general, the objective is to give identity to the genus by listing briefly the main characteristics which distinguish it from others, especially those closely related or of somewhat similar character, e.g. *Acacia* (q.v.).

Special qualities or values which may prove to be useful to the landscape or garden designer are sometimes included here.

Propagation

This lists briefly the principal methods used by professional propagators but for a more comprehensive treatment of the subject of plant propagation techniques, and the structures and equipment used, specialist literature should be consulted.

Cultivation

Here the most favourable conditions of climate, exposure and soil likely to produce normal, healthy growth are set out in condensed form.

Pruning

The need for pruning, its extent, frequency and timing, or conversely, the more urgent need for restraint, are treated briefly here.

Species (singular and plural), Specific (adjectival)

The next subordinate taxon to the rank of genus is the species, comprising plants with the capacity to breed freely amongst themselves and maintain an essential resemblance to each other when grown under similar conditions. Some variations amongst the individuals may be expected to occur in non-essential characters such as colour and size, especially in flowers and foliage.

Subspecies and *variety* are still further subordinate taxa sometimes used to designate lower categories of plants showing variations developed and maintained in geographical separation from the parent species, e.g. *Eucalyptus pauciflora* subsp. *niphophila*, the Alpine Snow Gum, which

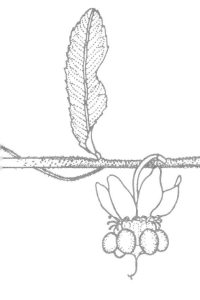

rarely descends below the 2000 m level in alpine regions. *Leptospermum scoparium* var. *rotundifolium*, in its orbicular leaves, is distinct from its lanceolate-leafed parent. The taxon *forma* (pl. *formae*) is also used occasionally where a plant varies from the parent in a relatively minor feature such as hairiness or colour, e.g. *Cotoneaster glaucophyllus* f. *serotinus.*

Specific epithets are drawn from three main areas. They are:

a) *Descriptive* of any plant feature remaining more or less constant, such as plant form, the shape, size, number, texture, hairiness, arrangement or other peculiarities of leaves or flowers, bark, thorns, stipules, etc., or sometimes similarity to other species;

b) *Geographic*, indicating the plant's native habitat by directly naming the place of origin, such as *chinensis*, or sometimes less precisely, such as *alpina* — from mountain regions, or *exotica* — foreign;

c) *Commemorative* of people, honoured for their close connection with the plant concerned, that is, its discovery or its introduction to horticulture, or for their contribution or patronage of botany or horticulture in a less direct manner.

In modern nomenclatural practice, specific names, regardless of their origin, even when drawn from the names of people, places or other plant genera, are always spelt with a small initial letter.

Interspecific hybrids

Plants resulting from the crossing or hybridising of two distinct species within a genus are indicated with a multiplication sign before the name, but otherwise follow the rules relating to species, e.g. *Abelia* x *grandiflora*, the product of crossing *A. chinensis* and *A. uniflora.*

Cultivars

Cultivars occur in many specific and interspecific hybrid groups, originating under cultivation, usually in gardens or nurseries, and differing significantly from their species, subspecies or hybrid parents in one or more minor characters.

The *International Code of Nomenclature for Cultivated Plants* decrees that cultivars developed since 1 January 1959 shall have 'fancy' names (from common languages, English, German, Japanese, etc.) but those of earlier date shall be preserved in their original Latin form.

All are capitalised and either enclosed in single quotation marks or are prefixed by the abbreviation 'cv.', e.g. *Berberis thunbergii* 'Kellers Surprise' and *Berberis thunbergii* cv. Atropurpureum. The former method is preferred here although some authors combine both styles thus *Berberis thunbergii* cv. 'Aurea'.

Derivations

These are quoted wherever known.

Synonyms

These are names once in common use but now superseded by the rule of priority for the correct name, that is, the first name given legitimately by the person who discovered and described the plant. Thus, the earlier valid name *Abutilon megapotamicum* now takes precedence over the later name which is expressed as syn. *A. vexillarium*.

Common names

The most generally used common name(s) of the species are given, especially where such a name differs specifically from that used for the genus as a whole.

Country of origin

This is given, sometimes with details of the geographical region or habitat.

Specific description

This comprises a detailed statement of the plant's: habit of growth and mature dimensions; leaves; flowers and flowering season; fruit and fruiting season; other distinguishing features.

Climatic range

See climatic map of Australia and accompanying notes.

Accent marks

To assist in the pronunciation of scientific plant names, the syllable to be stressed is marked; if with a grave, the vowel sound is long as in 'cape', rather than 'cap', but if with an acute, the vowel sound is short as in 'sit', rather than 'site'.

Australian Climatic Zones

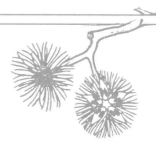

The climate of a place is determined by an interplay of many factors. Latitude, altitude, proximity to the sea, the direction and velocity of its winds, as well as physical features such as high mountains, plains and valleys, all exert a powerful influence.

Small islands in a large sea mass usually enjoy an equable maritime climate with quite narrow thermal extremes, but in the larger land masses of the continents, the variations in climate are much wider.

Australia, lying within the latitudes of 10°S and 43°S, and measuring approximately 4000 km east to west and 3600 km north to south, with elevations ranging up to 2200 m, is relatively flat, and except for about 15 per cent of its area, is the driest of the continents.

Nevertheless, within its boundaries a number of regions with well-defined climatic patterns of horticultural significance are identifiable. The boundaries of the nine zones are independent of State borders but most bear the names of the capital cities. As well, the local conditions of the cities provide the 'type' climates, each more or less representative of the whole of its zone.

The boundaries are by no means absolute. Unless demarked by an abrupt change in elevation as in parts of the coast escarpment of the Great Dividing Range, most zones merge gradually with their neighbours, although here and there, because of irregularities in local landform, fingers of a zone may deeply invade adjoining territory.

In isolated patches, 'microclimates' may show measurable differences from the norm, temperature variations being the most common. The slope of the land, either towards or away from the sun's path, affects temperature directly, or may alter the prevailing wind pattern, to advantage or otherwise. 'Frost pockets' are created where heavy, cold air collects in ground depressions or is dammed into pools by belts of dense trees or other obstructions to its downward flow. Near the coast, extremes of temperature are sometimes modified reciprocally, first in winter by the warmth of the sea mass, then in summer by its cooling sea breezes.

The climatic plan used here is an adaptation of a system originally prepared by the Commonwealth of Australia Meteorological Bureau to assist gardeners in plant selection. In the context of this book, it is considered to be a valid method of expressing, simply and concisely, the climatic range of the plants described. With slight modification in detail, the system is now used, with respectful acknowledgment to the Bureau and all others concerned with its earlier use.

It is hoped that the climatic recommendations given for each species will be taken more as a provisional guide than an arbitrary prescription of its likely hardiness.

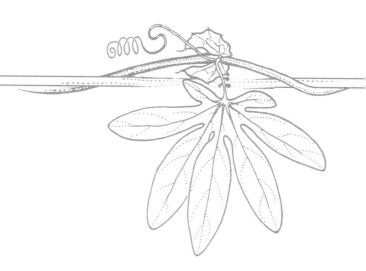

The approximate boundaries are set out diagrammatically on the climatic map of Australia accompanying the summarised descriptions of the zones.

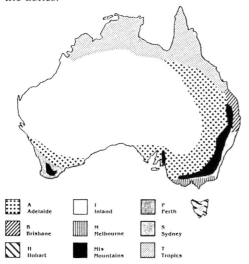

A Adelaide	I Inland	P Perth
B Brisbane	M Melbourne	S Sydney
H Hobart	Mts Mountains	T Tropics

Summarised descriptions of the zones

Adelaide zone (A)
The zone lies mainly between the 375 mm and 750 mm isohyets. Except for the fringe of humid, Mediterranean-type climate near the coast, it has a moderately warm, dry, continental climate.

Summer temperatures are high in the hottest months, with an all-time record maximum of 47°C. Along the coast, sea breezes help to moderate the excessive heat.

Winter temperatures are mild in coastal districts but become more severe inland, especially on elevated land close to the mountains where low readings of –5°C to –7°C are on record, with up to 25 or so sharp frosts each year.

Winds from the interior are hot and dry in summer, causing severe dehydration in tender plants and sometimes complete defoliation. Evaporation levels are high, in places up to 3 to 5 times the annual rainfall, and humidity is low, especially away from the coast. Prolonged droughts are not uncommon.

Where supplementary irrigation is provided, the zone supports a wide range of plants mainly consisting of tough-leafed natives and comparably hardy plants from overseas.

Brisbane zone (B)
This is a narrow strip of coastal land extending from about Coff's Harbour in NSW (30°S) to the Tropic of Capricorn in Queensland (23½°S) and varying in depth from less than 50 km in the south to 100 km or so elsewhere.

For horticultural purposes, the Atherton Tableland of North Queensland, with elevations to 1000 m is included here, the effects of high

altitude and low latitude tending to counterbalance.

Summer temperatures are moderately high, but heat waves are short. Winter temperatures are mild close to the coast but decrease sharply inland, especially in the upper valleys draining the higher land.

Rainfall varies between about 1000 mm and 1500 mm annually, the summers being wet and humid and the winters substantially drier.

The zone is distinguished horticulturally by the abundance and high quality of its subtropical trees and shrubs but it is generally too wet and humid for the continued success of plants from the dry interior.

Hobart zone (H)

Tasmania is divided into roughly equal areas of high country above 300 m, classified here as Mountains zone, and the lower land on the northern and eastern coastal fringes where most of the horticulture is concentrated.

Summer temperatures are lower than those of places with similar altitude on the mainland, because of the higher latitudes (40°–43°S) and the prevailing cool sea winds. Heat wave conditions are rare. Winter temperatures are low, with frosts likely in the colder months. Minimum temperatures of –6°C are on record in coastal towns, decreasing even further inland.

Rainfall is heavy on the west coast due to the prevailing cold, wet winds, the Roaring Forties, and the presence of a high mountain barrier (Zeehan, 2400 mm), but falls away elsewhere to 600 mm at Hobart and 700 mm at Launceston. Serious drought is almost unknown.

The Hobart zone is one of the best for cool-climate plants, and is compared favourably with parts of New Zealand, Great Britain, northern USA and Europe for the wide variety and fine performance of its trees, shrubs and conifers.

Inland zone (I)

The zone comprises the whole of the hinterland area enclosed by the inner boundaries of the Adelaide and Tropics zones, the north-west coast of Western Australia and the strip of Nullarbor Desert on the Great Australian Bight.

Apart from the scattered population centres where additional water is available, little horticulture is practised. Homesteaders hopefully cultivate a few tough, indigenous trees for shade or protection against dust by strictly rationing their meagre water supplies.

Summer temperatures are extremely high. Alice Springs, located roughly in the centre of the continent, has a record maximum of 47°C. Conversely, winter temperatures may be quite low. Alice Springs, at an elevation of 600 m has frequent sharp frosts in the June-August period, with a record minimum of –7°C.

Winds are variable and mostly very dry,

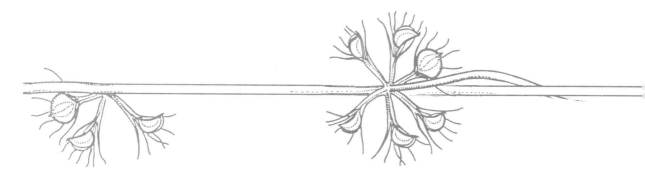

having lost their moisture in passing over high land barriers elsewhere.

Rainfall varies from less than 125 mm in the real desert areas up to 375 mm at the outer edge of the zone. Prolonged droughts are common, some lasting for several years when virtually no rain falls. Evaporation is extremely high.

Water is almost always a critical growth factor. However, besides the hardy local native species which are well adapted to the conditions, a surprising variety of exotic plants are grown, both groups responding favourably to supplementary irrigation.

Melbourne zone (M)

The Melbourne zone has a maritime climate, extending from the NSW border in the east to the South Australian border in the west and adjoining the southern slopes of the Great Dividing Range for most of that distance.

Summer temperatures are moderated by the frequent sea breezes but occasionally soar when heated air from the interior is imported by winds from the north and north-west. Temperatures above 37–38°C are not uncommon.

Winter temperatures are cool, with frequent light to medium frosts which become more severe on the rising land close to the mountains.

Winds from the south to west sector are cold and violent enough in winter to limit the selection of seaside plants to the minimum.

Rainfall varies between about 600 mm and 875 mm, with an even monthly distribution, interrupted only rarely by prolonged drought.

The zone is renowned for its fine parks and gardens. It supports an extensive and flourishing nursery industry mainly located in the sheltered parts of the lower Dandenong Hills.

In inland parts, remote from the destructive salty winds of the coast, mainly dry-climate species are grown, thriving on the well-drained soils and moderate but uniformly distributed rainfall.

Mountains zone (Mts)

In general, the Mountains zone occupies elevated land where low winter temperatures and cold winds are the main limiting factors to plant growth.

Summer day temperatures are mild, only a little cooler and less humid than those of lower levels, but nights are considerably cooler because of the greater heat loss by radiation through the less dense atmosphere. Day temperatures of more than 37–38°C are uncommon, although bushfires sometimes bring about abnormal readings.

Winters are longer and colder than in other zones with frequent heavy frosts likely between early May and November, and a few snow falls on the higher land. Temperatures of –5°C to –8°C are not unusual but the occasional –10°C

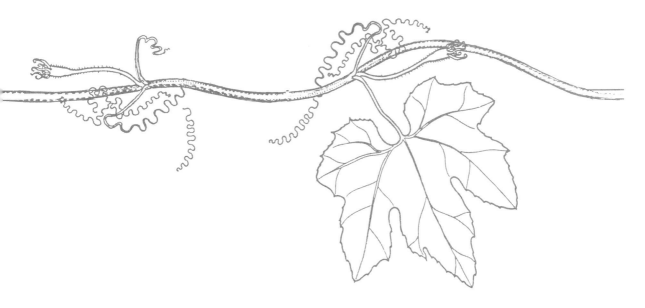

takes heavy toll of all but the most resistant plants.

Winds are variable, increasingly cold when blowing over snow-clad country, or hot and dry in summer when from the heated interior.

Rainfall varies from 500 to 1000 mm along much of the Great Dividing Range, to about double the amount in scattered localities where local topography and frequent moist sea winds exert strong orographic influence. Evaporation and humidity levels are normally moderate.

The selection of plant species is limited by the low temperatures to the hardy kinds only. Tender tropical plants are seen only in conservatories. Conversely, the lower temperatures have a beneficial effect on some ornamentals, especially most of the conifers and fruiting or autumn-foliage plants. Deciduous species from the cool-temperate parts of the Northern Hemisphere are planted extensively, together with a useful range of native evergreen trees and shrubs.

Perth zone (P)

The zone is confined to that part of the coastal plain and hill country in the south-western corner of Western Australia affected by the wet westerly winds. It extends from Esperance Bay in the south to about 200 km north of Perth, varying in depth from 50 km in the drier parts to about 200 km in the wetter, hilly regions.

Summer temperatures are warm, rising to an occasional 37–38°C and a record maximum of 44°C. Sea breezes are frequent near the coast. Winter temperatures are mild near the sea but decrease inland to a minimum of –3°C or –4°C on the higher land where frosts are not uncommon.

Winds from the south and west sector bring the bulk of the rain which varies from 625 mm on the coastal plains up to about 1250 mm on the windward side of the low mountains, then falling away inland where evaporation rates begin to rise steeply.

The range of introduced plants approximates that of Sydney and Adelaide, but greater use is made in gardens of the zone's unique native flora which attracts a large annual pilgrimage from the eastern states and from other countries in spring.

Sydney zone (S)

The Sydney zone extends from the Victorian border in the south to about Coff's Harbour in the north, on the latitude of 30°S. Where the landform changes abruptly from coastal plain to tablelands, the zone abuts the Mountains zone, but in the deeper valleys of the Hawkesbury and Hunter Rivers, the climate closely resembles that of the Adelaide zone.

Summer temperatures are medium to high but 37°–38°C readings average only one or two

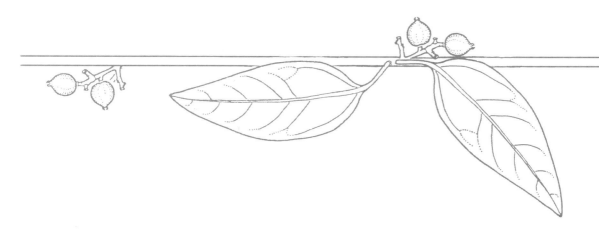

each year. Cool sea breezes are fairly dependable. Winter temperatures are mild, the littoral strip being virtually frost-free but farther inland on the upper slopes and plateaus light frosts are more common between June and August.

On exposed coastal land tender plants are seriously damaged by the salt-laden sea winds.

Rainfall averages 875 mm to 1500 mm but the long term rainfall record at Sydney shows wide annual variations from 575 mm to 2150 mm. Occasional extremely heavy falls of up to 836 mm in one month (Feb. 1990) cause serious plant losses, especially amongst dry-climate species.

The climate is generally congenial, allowing a very broad range of plants to be grown. In wind-sheltered but sunny coastal gardens, some tropical plants thrive. The free-draining sands and gravels of the Hawkesbury sandstone areas, particularly on the higher plateaus, provide the best conditions for the more durable species from drier climates, but artificial drainage and/or raised planting positions are a good insurance against losses by excessive soil saturation.

Tropics zone (T)

The zone includes most of the 'Top End', from the Kimberleys to the Atherton Tableland, the southern margin generally following the 750 mm isohyet, with a narrow coastal strip extending south to the Tropic of Capricorn at Rockhampton.

Summer temperatures are very high, with correspondingly high atmospheric humidity. Winter temperatures are mild, with virtually no frost, except on the few elevated parts or where the river valleys penetrate deeply inland.

Wind is a dominating factor. The south-east trades prevail in summer, bringing heavy rain to the east coast in typical orographic pattern, but pass on over the ranges as a comparatively dry wind. Across the northern region, the north-west monsoon has a similar but weaker effect between December and April. Occasional tropical cyclones cause widespread devastation to plants and severe structural damage.

Rainfall on the Pacific Coast is the highest in Australia with an average of 4206 mm annually and a record annual maximum of 7775 mm in 1950, at Tully, North Queensland. Elsewhere, the annual figure seldom exceeds 1500 mm, with a well-defined difference between the wet summer and dry winter.

Evaporation is moderate on the east coast but often reaches 2250 mm on the peninsulas.

Horticulture is mostly confined to the coastal strip where both the indigenous vegetation and imported material thrives, often providing a luxuriant seasonal display of colour and interest in parks, streets and private gardens.

Descriptive List of Genera

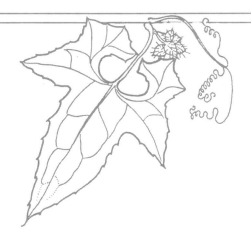

ABÈLIA

Commemorating Dr Clarke Abel, British physician, botanical collector and author of works on the flora of China.

Glossy Abelia; Mexican Abelia; Schumann's Abelia.

Caprifoliaceae, the Honeysuckle family.

Generic description. A small genus of shrubs from Eastern Asia, grown for their mainly evergreen, simple, opposite or sometimes whorled leaves, funnelform or tubulate flowers in axillary or terminal panicles or cymes, with persistent reddish sepals. Well-managed plants are attractive in growth habit, foliage and flowers and are ideal material for foundation, hedge or shrubbery planting.

Propagation. Soft-tip cuttings taken in spring or summer; semi-hardwood cuttings taken at other times; or hardwood nodal cuttings without leaves taken in late autumn or winter. All types are struck in a sand/peat mixture under mist, with bottom heat an advantage in late autumn and winter.

Cultivation. Abelias thrive in well-drained, fertile soils in sunny or lightly-shaded positions, with shelter from the salty winds of the coast. They are hardy in most Australian climates.

Pruning. An essential operation for best results, pruning is best deferred until late winter, when some of the oldest basal shoots should be removed entirely to clear the way for new watershoots. Younger, twiggy stems that have flowered are reduced slightly to remove the faded sepals. The natural arching character of the plant should be preserved, not destroyed by close shearing. Only in hedging or occasionally to control excessive growth is more severe pruning justifiable.

Species and cultivars

Abèlia x *grandiflòra* (Latin 'with large flowers'): the interspecific hybrid of *A. chinensis* and *A. uniflora*: Glossy Abelia.

Habit. An evergreen shrub to 2 m tall and as wide, with many basal stems arching outwards; young stems smooth and reddish-brown; laterals opposite or 3-whorled.

Leaves. Ovate, 2–5 cm long and 1.5–2.5 cm wide; apex acute to acuminate; base obtuse; margin crenate-serrate; glabrous except for the villous midrib and lower main veins beneath; dark lustrous green above, or reddish in winter, paler beneath, some leaves turning orange and red before falling in winter.

Flowers. Borne singly or in small clusters; corolla funnelform-campanulate, to 2 cm long, 5-lobed, white flushed with mauve-pink; stamens 4; calyx with 2–5 brick-red lanceolate sepals, often partly joined; perfume faint; flowers from early December to April; calyces coloured from February to July.

Fruit. Absent.

Other distinguishing features. Old stems become rough and stringy.

'Francis Mason' (syn. 'Aurea' and 'Variegata') is of similar growth habit but with leaves heavily margined and suffused with yellow, the colour more intense under severe conditions of soil quality and exposure to sunlight.

Climatic range. A B H M Mts P S T.

Abèlia floribúnda (Latin 'with abundant flowers'): Mexican Abelia: mountains of southern Mexico.

Habit. An evergreen shrub of somewhat open form to about 2 m tall and as broad.

Leaves. Like those of *A.* x *grandiflora* but slightly smaller and less glossy.

Flowers. Tubulate, 3–5 cm long, in few-flowered pendulous clusters, rosy-carmine, flowering from November to April; calyx with 5 reddish sepals, persisting to July.

Fruit. Not seen.

Other distinguishing features. More tender than other species and best used in a warm sunny position in the shelter of a wall, fence or other plants, especially in marginal climates.

Climatic range. A B M P S T.

Abèlia schùmannii (commemorating Dr Karl M. Schumann, 19th century German botanist) (syn. *A. longituba*) Schumann's Abelia: western and central China.

Habit. A nearly-evergreen shrub to 1.5–2.0 m with a dense form when pruned annually, but partly-deciduous in severe climates. Young stems reddish, pubescent.

Leaves. Broadly ovate to 3 cm long, shallowly crenate, pale at first, becoming dull green, with white hairs on the base of the midrib and lower laterals.

Flowers. Funnelform-campanulate, about 2 cm long, in clusters of 2 to 6, pale rosy-mauve, paling to white at the base, deeper inside with a broad white stripe and some orange spots on the lowest lobe, flowering from November to April; calyx of 2 red oblanceolate sepals to 1 cm long, persisting to July.

Fruit. Not seen.

Climatic range. A H M Mts P S.

Abèlia uniflòra (Latin 'one-flowered'): western and central China.

Habit. An evergreen shrub to 2 m tall and as broad, with more open form than the others, with fewer watershoots from the base.

Leaves. Like those of *A.* x *grandiflora*, but often larger to 5–6 cm long.

Flowers. Campanulate to 3 cm long and across the spreading lobed mouth; solitary or in clusters of 2 or 3, purplish-pink on the upper side, whitish beneath, with a broad orange patch and white hairs inside, flowering from November to April but somewhat less abundantly than other species; sepals red, 2 or 3.

Fruit. Not seen.

Climatic range. A B H M Mts P S.

ABUTILON

Derived from the ancient Arabic vernacular name for a related plant.

Chinese Lantern; Flowering Maple; Brazilian Bell-flower.

Malvaceae, the Mallow family.

Generic description. Attractive evergreen shrubs with alternate, maple-like leaves and variously coloured, pendulous bell-shaped flowers with a prominently-ribbed calyx, broad petals, and an exserted staminal-column. All are useful plants in temperate gardens for their handsome foliage and long flowering season, the variegated-leafed kinds being especially valuable to add variety of colour in a garden.

Propagation. a) Firm tip cuttings from late summer to winter root easily in a sand/peat mixture under mist in a humid glass-house or frame.

b) *A. megapotamicum* and 'Variegatum' are almost self-layering but will root more reliably if the prostrate stems are covered with soil.

Cultivation. Most of the cultivars are strong-growing plants which are best not fed heavily but grown somewhat frugally to reduce their vigour and to promote more abundant flowers. They thrive on any reasonably fertile garden soil, if well drained. Protection from strong or salty winds is desirable, but they enjoy exposure to full sunlight.

Pruning. Pruning is confined to an annual shaping of the bush into globose form in late winter, but if growth is excessive, the removal of the tips of the strong shoots in summer will help to discourage rank growth.

Species and cultivars

Abutilon x *hybridum* (a collective name for a group of plants which cannot be attributed with certainty to any particular species): Chinese Lantern.

Habit. Most of the cultivars are evergreen shrubs to 1.5–2.5 m tall, generally of loose, open habit, but denser and more leafy when pruned annually.

Leaves. Simple, alternate, palmately-lobed, 15–30 cm long and 8–20 cm broad when well grown, with 3 large and sometimes 2 small lobes, the petiole to 5–15 cm long; base cordate, margin dentate; venation palmate-reticulate; roughly hairy on both surfaces; dark green above, paler beneath; stipulate at the base.

Flowers. Mostly solitary in the upper leaf-axils, on long, drooping pedicels; calyx 5-parted, with 10 coarse ribs; corolla cyathiform-campanulate, 6–10 cm across, with 5 broadly obovate petals and a central staminal-column with golden yellow anthers, the flowers in a wide range of colours including white, pale to deep pink, red to deep crimson, cream, yellow, orange, and lilac, flowering abundantly in September to December but also intermittently until winter.

Other distinguishing features. In several cultivars the leaves are handsomely variegated with green and creamy-white, e.g. '**Savitzii**' and '**Souvenir de Bonn**', the latter also flowering well with heavily veined orange flowers. Many cultivars are available from nurseries and the following list represents a good sample of the range.

'**Boule de Neige**' (Ball of Snow) white
'**Carmine**' carmine-pink
'**Eclipse**' (Orange King) orange
'**Emperor**' crimson
'**Golden Fleece**' deep golden-yellow
'**Jubilee**' rose-pink
'**Keiller's Surprise**' red with yellow centre
'**Sydney Belle**' large, pure yellow
'**Tunisia**' salmon-pink
'**Yellow Gem**' soft yellow
Climatic range. A, B, M, P, S, T.

Abùtilon megapotámicum (Greek 'from the big river', the Rio Grande of Brazil) (syn. *A. vexillarium*) Brazilian Bell-flower: Brazil.

Habit. A low bush with prostrate, spreading stems, forming a leafy mound 0.5 m tall but often 1 to 2 m wide.

Leaves. Simple, alternate, ovate-lanceolate, 6–8 cm long, 3 cm wide; petiole 1.5 cm; apex long-acuminate; base cordate; margin crenate; almost glabrous; dark green above, paler beneath.

Flowers. Mostly solitary in the upper leaf-axils; calyx urceolate 1.0–1.5 cm long, with 5 prominent ribs, red, on slender 2 cm pedicels; corolla campanulate, 1.5–2.0 cm long, with 5 pointed yellow petals, streaked dark purple at the base; staminal-column dark purple, shaped like a small tree, 5 cm long; flowers abundant between September and December but then intermittent throughout summer and autumn.

'Variegàtum' is the more popular plant, with green leaves as above, heavily spotted and blotched with pale yellow.

Other distinguishing features. The prostrate stems and attractive flowers and leaves make the cultivar a popular rock-garden or ground-cover plant.

Climatic range. A, B, M, P, S, T.

ACÀCIA

Thought to be derived from the Greek *ake* 'a sharp point', descriptive of the spiny branches of some of the species.

Wattle (various).

Mimosaceae, the Mimosa family.

Generic description. A large genus of some 800 species scattered throughout many of the warm-temperate countries, over 600 indigenous to Australia and found in every part of the country from the well-watered tropics to the arid Centre and cold mountain regions. Some have been spread by man beyond the limits of their native habitats to form new colonies elsewhere, e.g. *Acàcia baileyana*. The genus is characterised by the following main features:

a) Bipinnate foliage, at least in the early seedling stage; in some, the compound character persists into adulthood but in others is soon abandoned, the leaves being reduced to modified petioles called 'phyllodes' which look like leaves and perform their normal photosynthetic role of food manufacture; some are long and flat like gum-leaves, others are modified into sharp spines; in

most cases, one or more glands appear on the rachis or phyllode.

b) Flowers white, cream, or yellow in globular heads of a few to 100 or more, or in cylindrical spikes, set among the upper leaves in axillary racemes or terminal panicles, or singly or in pairs along the younger stems; the sepals and petals are 4- or 5-merous, the stamens of indefinite number with much variation in their length and colour among the species; many species have perfumed flowers.

c) Fruit is a mostly flattened legume containing several to many round or oval, flattened, hard-coated seeds, attached by a curved or coiled funicle, an important identification feature for some species; in some, the legume is curiously twisted and contorted even into close spiral form.

d) Spines are not uncommon, especially in hot or arid regions where many of the local species have adapted successfully to their environment by modifying their leaves or phyllodes to present the smallest possible surface to the sun and wind.

The species described below are some of the more commonly-used shrubby wattles for ornamental or amenity planting. Tree species will be found in the companion volume Ornamental Flowering Trees in Australia.

Propagation. The seed has a very hard coat or testa and is capable of maintaining its viability for long periods, reputedly up to fifty years under good conditions of storage with low temperatures and humidity. Pre-germination treatment is desirable to ensure moisture penetration of the seed coat. Heating or soaking are the usual methods and the most suitable is to soak the seeds in warm water at 40°–45°C for about twelve hours, then sow them immediately. Germination is usually improved considerably. August and September are the best months for sowing to establish the young plants before the commencement of cold weather.

Cultivation. See specific notes below for details.

Pruning. Most wattles, especially the shrubby kinds, benefit from a light pruning after the flowering season to remove the spent inflorescences and to improve growth vigour.

Species and cultivars

Acàcia béckleri (commemorating Dr Herman Beckler, early botanical collector, botanist and surgeon with the Burke and Wills trans-Australian expedition): Barrier Range Wattle: Western Plains of NSW to the Flinders Range in SA, mostly on broken country in the 200–300 mm rainfall zone.

Habit. A stiff, erect bush to 2–3 m tall, branching irregularly to 2 m or so wide, improved in cultivation by moderate pruning while young.

Leaves. Phyllodes lanceolate, 12–15 cm long and 1–3 cm wide, falcate or occasionally straight; apex acute with a small recurved mucro; base slenderly cuneate; margin with 2–4 small glands along the upper edge; stiff and leathery; glabrous; dull blue-green.

Flowers. Heads globose, 12–15 mm across, with 50 or more flowers; heads solitary or in sparse flexuose racemes on a thick pubescent peduncle 5–10 mm long; flowers deep golden yellow between late May and September.

Fruit. A flat legume 8–12 cm long and 5–6 mm wide, slightly falcate, constricted shallowly between the 6–8 black oblong seeds.

Other distinguishing features. Upper twigs round or slightly ribbed, flexuose, glabrous, reddish at first, later blue-green. Probably the largest flowered species of wattle, making it an interesting as well as an attractive subject for a dry-climate garden.

Climatic range. A I M P and on dry or freely-drained sites with sandy or rocky soils in lower Mts and S.

Acàcia boòrmanii (commemorating Joh Luke Boorman, botanical collector of the Royal Botanic Gardens, Sydney): Snowy River Wattle; NSW Southern Tablelands and Snowy River valley Vic.

Habit. A round-headed shrub or small tree to 3–4 m tall, but often 4–5 m wide when old.

Leaves. Phyllodes narrow-linear, 4–8 cm long, 2–4 mm wide, apex hooked, marginal gland indistinct, about 5 mm from the swollen base, margin translucent, silvery blue-green.

Flowers. Inflorescence a dense terminal panicle of many slender racemes to 3–4 cm long, each carrying 15–20 butter-yellow, globose heads about 4–5 mm across, faintly perfumed, flowering from late August to October.

Fruit. Legume linear, 6–10 cm long, 5–6 mm wide, flat, thin, blue-green.

Other distinguishing features. Upper twigs very slender, glaucous-green, glabrous but ridged by the decurrent leaf-bases. One of the most beautiful wattles, deserving wider use in small gardens, especially in cool climates.

Climatic range. H, M, Mts, and on cool, elevated sites in A, P, and S.

Acàcia cardiophýlla (Greek 'with heart-shaped leaves', referring here to the pinnules): Wyalong Wattle: NSW Western Slopes of the Great Dividing Range.

Habit. A large shrub to 3–4 m tall with graceful, arching form, spreading to 3 m or so wide.

Leaves. Bipinnate, the rachis 3.5–4.5 cm long, pubescent, with 8–15 pairs of pinnae 8–10 mm long, pinnules 6–10 opposite pairs, cordate or obliquely oval, 1–2 mm long, pubescent, dark green.

Flowers. In slender racemes 4–6 cm long forming a large terminal panicle; racemes with 12–20 heads of fragrant, bright golden-yellow flowers abundant from late September to mid-October.

Fruit. Legume linear, 7–10 cm long, 5–8 mm wide, nearly straight, dark blue-grey with whitish pubescence.

Other distinguishing features. An extremely attractive wattle with dainty foliage and showy, fragrant flowers, suitable for well-drained soils in the medium-rainfall areas.

Climatic range. A, I, M, Mts, P, and on coarse, open soils in S.

Acàcia confèrta (Latin 'with crowded leaves'): Crowded Wattle: Western Slopes of the Great Dividing Range in NSW and Qld.

Habit. A sparse shrub or small tree in the dry sclerophyll land of its native habitat but more densely foliaged and of compact, hemispherical form to 2 m or so in cultivation.

Leaves. Phyllodes linear, mostly about 7–12 mm long and 1–2 mm wide, closely scattered or sometimes 2- or 3-whorled, straight or slightly falcate with a recurved tip, silky hairy, the margin somewhat thickened; venation indistinct but one vein more prominent, off-centre; grey-green.

Flowers. Heads globular, 7–8 mm across, borne singly on slender 12–15 mm peduncles from the upper axils, deep golden-yellow, flowering profusely in late August and September.

Fruit. Legumes oblong, flat, 4–8 cm long, glaucous, the seeds arranged transversely.

Other distinguishing features. Upper stems slender, silky pubescent, grey-green. An elegant little wattle well suited to the small garden with

a sunny aspect and well-drained soil, preferably sandy or gravelly.
Climatic range. A B M P S and on sheltered sites in Mts.

Acàcia cultrifòrmis (Latin 'shaped like a knife', referring to the phyllodes): Knife-leafed Wattle: NSW and Qld mainly in the 400–600 mm rainfall region on the Western Slopes of the Great Dividing Range.
Habit. A large rounded shrub or small tree to 3–4 m tall with spreading branches forming a broad hemispherical crown.
Leaves. Phyllodes obliquely ovate to triangular to 1.8 cm long, 1.3 cm broad, the inner margin prominently rounded, with a single yellowish gland near the middle; midrib alone distinct, eccentric; glabrous; blue-grey.
Flowers. Inflorescence a terminal panicle to 25 cm long made up of many axillary racemes each 5–6 cm long with 8–20 nearly-globular heads 7–8 mm long and 6–7 mm wide, bright golden-yellow, flowering in late winter and early spring.
Fruit. Legume linear, 5–6 cm long, 8–9 mm wide, flat, glaucous.
Other distinguishing features. One of the most handsome and prolific of the smaller wattles, best suited to sandy or gravelly soils.
'**Australora Cascade**' is a registered cultivar of prostrate form to about 10 cm tall, spreading to about 2 m.
Climatic range. A, M, P, S, and lower slopes of Mts.

Acàcia decòra (Latin 'ornamental'): Western Silver Wattle, Golden Wattle, Showy or Graceful Wattle: Central and Northern Tablelands and Slopes of NSW, also in Qld and Vic, usually in open dry-sclerophyll forests on well-drained hillsides.
Habit. An upright shrub, 2–3 m tall, the short trunk supporting an open, irregular crown.
Leaves. Phyllodes lanceolate, 2–4 cm long, 3–6 mm wide, slightly falcate, the apex a short curved point, a single gland near the middle of the inner margin; midrib distinct; glabrous; pale grey-green.
Flowers. Inflorescence a short terminal panicle composed of several to about 10 racemes to 3–4 cm long extending beyond the foliage; heads 6–8 mm across, with 10–20 bright golden-yellow flowers, mildly fragrant, flowering from late winter to early November.

Fruit. Legume 6–8 cm long, 6–8 mm wide, thin, flat, straight, glaucous-green.
Other distinguishing features. A handsome wattle of fine colour for small gardens with freely drained, sandy or gravelly soils in medium-rainfall zones.
Climatic range. A, M, Mts, P, and on elevated ridges in S.

Acàcia drúmmondii (commemorating James Drummond, one-time Western Australian Government Botanist): Drummond's Wattle.
Habit. A shrub to 1.5–2.0 m tall with spreading branches forming a somewhat open, hemispherical bush about 2 m wide.
Leaves. Bipinnate, finely pubescent, the rachis to 5 mm long with a single large gland at the apex; pinnae 2 pairs, the lower 4–5 mm long, the upper 9–10 mm long; pinnules oblong-linear, 4 mm long, 1–2 mm wide, mostly in 4 pairs; apex obliquely acute; dark green above, paler, glaucescent and warty beneath.
Flowers. Inflorescence a cylindrical spike 2–3 cm long, 7–8 mm broad, in the upper axils forming a racemose spray 12–15 cm long; flowers 50–70 in a spike, golden-yellow, flowering in September and October.
Fruit. Legume 2.5 cm long, 6–8 mm wide, flat, green at first but ripening in summer to chocolate-brown.
Other distinguishing features. Upper stems reddish puberulent, with shallow grooves and ridges.
A fine but uncommon shrubby wattle making an ideal subject for small gardens with moderately fertile soils and shelter from strong winds.
Climatic range. A, B, M, P, S, T, and on the warmer, lower slopes of Mts.

Acàcia elongàta (Latin 'long', referring to the narrow phyllodes): Swamp Wattle: NSW and Qld on heavy soils in swampy localities between the coast and mountains.
Habit. A shrub to 3–4 m tall with slender, slightly pendulous branches forming an open framework about 2 m wide.
Leaves. Phyllodes linear, 8–12 cm long and 3–5 mm wide, falcate, sharply pointed, the single marginal gland 4–5 mm from the base; venation parallel with 3 main and 2 minor veins; bright grey-green.
Flowers. In small clusters or pairs in the axils of the terminal 40–60 cm length of the upper twigs;

heads 7–8 mm across, globular, on whitish-pubescent peduncles with 25–35 flowers in each head, green at first but opening to deep golden-yellow, then to pale yellow, flowering in August and September.

Fruit. Legume linear, about 6 cm long and 5 mm wide, straight or nearly so.

Other distinguishing features. Upper twigs bright green, pubescent and shallowly ridged.

An outstanding shrubby wattle for moist situations, especially in coastal regions.

Climatic range. B, M, P, S, T.

Acàcia fimbriàta (Latin 'fringed', referring to the ciliate leaf-margins): Fringed Wattle: northern half of NSW and southern half of Qld, mostly on the coastal ridges and lower levels of the mountains.

Habit. A dense shrub to 3 m tall, of hemispherical form with pendulous branchlets.

Leaves. Phyllodes linear-lanceolate, 3–5 cm long, 3–5 mm wide, flat or occasionally undulate, a single gland 5–7 mm from the base, grey-green.

Flowers. In a slender raceme 5–7 cm long, the 10–20 globular heads to 7–8 mm across on creamy-yellow peduncles; 20–25 flowers in each head, the very slender filaments lemon-yellow with golden-yellow anthers, sweetly fragrant, flowering from August to October.

Fruit. Legume linear, 4–7 cm long, 4–7 mm wide, thin, straight but slightly constricted between the seeds; blue-green with a whitish bloom.

Other distinguishing features. A prolific and very beautiful wattle, and an ideal choice for small gardens with well-drained, fertile soil.

Climatic range. A, B, H, M, Mts, P, S.

Acàcia flexifòlia (Latin 'with bent leaves'): Bent-leafed Wattle: western NSW, central-western Vic. and southern Qld, usually on sandy soils in the 500–600 m rainfall zones.

Habit. A small shrub to about 1.5 m tall, with spreading branches from the base forming an irregular crown about 2 m across.

Leaves. Phyllodes linear, 1.5–2.0 cm long and 2 mm wide, spreading or erect, then made nearly parallel with the twig by the pronounced bend near the base where a small single gland occurs; apex obtuse with a minute recurved mucro; venation indistinct except for the prominent single vein near the thickened upper margin;

glabrous; somewhat fleshy but leathery; grey-green.

Flowers. Heads single or in pairs in the upper axils, forming racemose sprays to 30 cm long covering the crown of the plant; heads 5–8 mm across, with up to 8 or so lemon-yellow, fragrant flowers from mid-June to late September.

Fruit. Legumes linear, 5–6 cm long and 3–4 mm wide, twisted, slightly constricted between the 5–8 dark brown ovoid seeds.

Other distinguishing features. Upper twigs grey-green with decurrent, translucent ridges. A particularly floriferous wattle, very bright in the late winter landscape and well suited to the smaller gardens in suitable climates.

Climatic range. A H M Mts P and on well-drained soils in B and S.

Acàcia gladiifòrmis (Latin 'sword-shaped', referring to the phyllodes): Sword-leafed Wattle: NSW, along the Central and Western Slopes of the Great Dividing Range, especially abundant in the Warrumbungle National Park.

Habit. An erect shrub to about 2 m tall, with a short trunk supporting an irregular open crown.

Leaves. Phyllodes linear-lanceolate, 6–12 cm long, 8–12 mm wide, curved upwards, the midrib alone prominent; margins slightly thickened, with 1 to several glands on the upper edge; apex acute with a small mucro; base attenuate, but stouter near the stem; glabrous; mid-green.

Flowers. Heads globular, 8–9 mm across, with up to 40 flowers, the heads in flexuose racemes of 4–5 cm from the upper axils forming an erect spray to 35 cm long; flowers golden-yellow, abundant in August-September.

Fruit. Legume linear to 12 cm or so long and 7–8 mm wide, falcate, slightly constricted between the 8–10 blackish, oval seeds.

Other distinguishing features. The base of the plant is inclined to be somewhat sparse. It is an attractive wattle but best used in a rear position with smaller plants in the front.

Climatic range. A H M Mts P S and I where supplementary irrigation is available.

Acàcia iteaphýlla (Greek 'willow-leafed'): Willow-leafed or Port Lincoln Wattle: SA, mainly around the Gulfs and in the Flinders Ranges, in the 250–400 mm annual rainfall areas.

Habit. A tall shrub to 3–4 m with a short trunk

and slender branches forming an attractive pendulous crown.

Leaves. Phyllodes slender-linear, 8–10 cm long, 5–8 mm wide, drooping, finely tapered at base and apex, the tip recurved; margin with a mostly obscure gland; midrib alone distinct; bluish at first, becoming grey-green.

Flowers. Flowers in short racemes of 6–10 heads from the upper axils, the buds enclosed at first in pinkish bracts, opening to butter-yellow, globose heads each with 10–15 flowers, mainly in autumn and winter.

Fruit. Legumes linear to about 10 cm long and 1 cm wide, falcate, silvery-green, slightly constricted between the 8–10 seeds, many bunched together in large drooping clusters.

Other distinguishing features. An unusually attractive wattle for the medium rainfall areas, grown mainly for the interest and beauty of the pendulous legumes.

'Parson's Cascade' is a registered cultivar with pendulous branches, forming a rounded mound of foliage to about 50 cm tall and 3–4 m broad, making it useful as a ground-cover or embankment plant.

Climatic range. A, I, M, P, and on the lower levels of Mts.

Acàcia linifòlia (Latin 'flax-leafed'): Flax-leafed Wattle: NSW, in open sclerophyll forests on the Hawkesbury sandstones along the Central Coast and lower Blue Mountains.

Habit. An erect shrub to 3 m or so, sometimes more or less tree-like with a single main trunk.

Leaves. Phyllodes slenderly linear, 3–4 cm long, 1–3 mm wide, mostly straight but occasionally curved near the acute apex, the prominent midrib often eccentric; margin with one small gland in the lower half, but not always visible; dark green and slightly shiny.

Flowers. Inflorescence an axillary raceme about as long as the phyllodes, with 5–10 heads each with up to about 10 flowers, pale yellow, flowering mainly in summer and autumn, but sporadically in mild winters also.

Fruit. Legume oblong to 6–8 cm and 8–12 mm wide, flat, slightly constricted between the seeds.

Other distinguishing features. The fine-textured, dark green foliage contrasts well with other coarser-leafed plants.

Climatic range. A, M, Mts, P, S, preferably on sandy or gravelly soils in full sunlight or only light shade.

Acàcia longìssima (Latin 'very long', referring to the phyllodes): Long-leafed Wattle: coastal plains and adjacent lower mountain slopes of NSW and Qld, mostly in sheltered gullies.

Habit. A shrub to 3–4 m tall with slender, arching branches forming an open bush with rounded outline.

Leaves. Phyllodes narrowly linear, 20–25 cm long, 3–4 mm wide, flat, straight, the marginal gland not prominent but often merged into the swollen base; venation parallel with distinct midrib; glabrous; bright green.

Flowers. In a cylindrical spike 4–5 cm long and 7–8 mm broad on yellow-green peduncles; spikes mainly in pairs in the upper axils for a length of 40–60 cm of the slender twigs, the flowers 100–120 in close spiral rows, pale yellow to butter-yellow, fragrant, flowering at irregular periods but chiefly in summer.

Fruit. Legume linear, 5–8 cm long, 4–6 mm wide, nearly straight but slightly constricted between the seeds, green at first, ripening to brown.

Other distinguishing features. Young stems yellow-green, smooth and lustrous with a bluish bloom and sparse black lenticels, angled and flexuose between the nodes.

Climatic range. A, B, M, P, S, T.

Acàcia myrtifòlia (Latin 'with leaves like *Myrtus*'): Myrtle-leafed Wattle: widespread in southern and eastern states, especially abundant on sandstone soils and gravels in dry sclerophyll forests and heathlands between the coast and mountains of NSW.

Habit. A shrub to about 2 m, stiff and open in character but improved by occasional pruning.

Leaves. Phyllodes lanceolate or oblanceolate, 4–5 cm long, 1–2 cm wide, slightly falcate, the margin thickened and with a single gland 7–8 mm from the base; translucent midrib prominent; coriaceous; dark green.

Flowers. Flower heads solitary or in short racemes of 8–10 large, pale-yellow heads each with 2–5 flowers giving a dainty but not prolific display from early June to late September.

Fruit. Legume linear, 3–6 cm long, 5 mm wide, falcate, thick, flat but with stout margin; seeds ovoid.

Other distinguishing features. Upper twigs reddish, angular with a sharp red ridge extending below the nodes.

Climatic range. A, B, H, M, P, S, and on lower elevations of Mts.

Acàcia neriifòlia (Latin 'with *Nerium*-like leaves'): New England Silver Wattle: NSW Northern Tablelands and North-western Slopes, usually on coarse granite soils.

Habit. A tall bush to 3–4 m with slender, flexible branches, but sometimes reduced to much smaller size when exposed to a harsh environment.

Leaves. Phyllodes linear, 8–12 cm long, 6–10 mm wide, the base swollen, slightly falcate; marginal gland 4–6 mm from the base with occasionally 1 or 2 others in the upper half; apex with short, thick, recurved point; base attenuate; midrib distinct; grey-green, with a fine white pubescence at least while young.

Flowers. Inflorescence a slender axillary raceme slightly shorter than the phyllodes, the flowers in globular heads of 30 or so, bright yellow, flowering abundantly from late May to early spring.

Fruit. Legume linear, as long as the phyllodes, flattened, slightly constricted between the seeds; glaucous, but ripening to brown.

Other distinguishing features. Upper stems shallowly ridged, yellow-green. A handsome small wattle suitable for screening or specimen planting, especially in areas of low to medium rainfall, grown mainly for its fine-textured foliage and colourful flowers.

Climatic range. A, M, Mts, and on well-drained sites in P, and S.

Acàcia oxycèdrus (from its resemblance to the European Prickly Juniper, *Juniperus oxycedrus*): SA, Vic and NSW in a wide variety of habitats, mostly on stony hillsides with free drainage and commonly seen on the sandstone soils of the Blue Mountains and coastal plateaus.

Habit. A tall stiff shrub to 3 m or so, of irregular form but often improved by annual pruning.

Leaves. Phyllodes linear-lanceolate, 1.5–2.5 cm long and 3–4 mm wide, the apex armed with a sharp, horny spine; base broadly truncate, subtended by a pair of small stipular spines 1–2 mm long; venation prominently tri-nerved; coriaceous and stiff; dark green.

Flowers. Inflorescence a drooping raceme 2.5–3.0 cm long, several together from the upper axils, with 30–50 heads closely arranged resembling a spike, the flowers orange-yellow at first, opening to lemon-yellow, flowering from May to September and occasionally into early summer.

Fruit. Legume elongate, 6–8 cm long, 5 mm

wide, falcate, pubescent and green while young, ripening to brown.

Other distinguishing features. A wattle of some beauty when well grown but because of its strongly armed foliage, particularly useful as a barrier plant.

Climatic range. A, I, M, Mts, P, S.

Acàcia polybótrya (Greek 'with many clusters'): Western Silver Wattle: NSW and Qld, usually on light soils on the Western Slopes of the Great Dividing Range.

Habit. A shrub to 2–3 m with a broad hemispherical crown, the outer branches sweeping the ground when heavy with flower.

Leaves. Bipinnate, the winged rachis 2–3 cm long with 1–4 pairs of pinnae, a single yellowish gland between the lowest pair, the rachis terminating in a 2 mm recurved bristle which soon falls; pinnae straight, angular, 2.5–3.5 cm long; pinnules 6–10 pairs, slenderly oblong-ovate to 7–8 mm long and 2 mm wide, the prominent eccentric midrib closer to the distal margin; apices slightly recurved; all parts thinly pubescent; grey-green.

Flowers. Borne in racemes 5–6 cm long with about 15–20 heads in each, numerous, forming a heavy panicle; flower-heads globose, 5–6 mm across, with about 30 fragrant deep yellow flowers in each during late August and September.

Fruit. Legumes linear, 6–8 cm long and 5–6 mm wide, clearly constricted between the seeds, grey-green at first, ripening to dark brown.

Other distinguishing features. The plant is easily adapted to tree form by early pruning and training. It is one of the most handsome wattles with a spectacular crop of flowers and pleasant foliage.

Climatic range. A, H, I, M, Mts, P but only on well-drained sandy soils in the higher-rainfall climates B and S.

Acàcia pravíssima (Latin 'very crooked', referring to the asymmetrical phyllodes): Ovens Wattle: NSW, ACT and Vic. on the lower slopes of the Great Dividing Range and in its higher valleys, mainly on deep riverine soils often with some overhead shade.

Habit. A bushy shrub to 3–5 m with drooping branches forming a broad-domed mound, but occasionally tree-like when competing for light with other plants.

Leaves. Phyllodes asymmetrically triangular, 8–12 mm long, with two main veins, the lower terminated by a small hooked mucro, the upper directed towards the broadly-curved distal margin with its single recessed gland near the base; dull olive-green.

Flowers. Inflorescence an axillary raceme of 10 cm or so, the 10–12 flower-heads on slender peduncles; flower-heads 5–6 mm across, bearing 10–15 flowers, bright golden-yellow in September and early October.

Fruit. Legumes linear, 6–8 cm long and 5–6 mm broad, straight or curved, flat but slightly constricted between the seeds.

Other distinguishing features. The principal species of wattle in the Ovens River valley, providing a spectacular display on the upper levels above the town of Bright.

'Golden Carpet' is a registered cultivar of prostrate form, about 50 cm tall with a spread of 5–6 m, of special value as a ground cover.

Climatic range. H, M, Mts and on cool, sheltered sites in A, P and S.

Acàcia pulchèlla (Latin 'beautiful, but small and dainty';): Western Prickly Moses: south-west WA, mainly on the forested slopes of the Darling Range and the adjacent sandy heathlands of the coastal plains.

Habit. A small shrub to 1–2 m tall, with an open irregular form, but improved in shape and density by occasional pruning.

Leaves. Bipinnate in opposite pairs from the spined nodes; pinnae 2, 3–5 mm long; pinnules oblong-obovate, 3–5 mm long, in 3– 7 sessile, opposite pairs; glabrous; bright-green to slightly bluish-green.

Flowers. Flower heads globular, 9–10 mm across, one or two from each of the upper nodes on very slender peduncles 7–8 mm long; flowers deep yellow, slightly fragrant, flowering from late June to November, the peak period in early October.

Fruit. Legumes linear, flat, 3–5 cm long and 5–7 mm wide, often slightly falcate.

Other distinguishing features. Spines finely subulate, 6–12 mm long, mostly in pairs from the nodes; upper stems somewhat angular, narrowly ridged, yellowish-green, with scattered white hairs. A handsome little wattle in its fine-textured foliage and large colourful flowers, its sharp spines making it useful as a decorative barrier plant.

Climatic range. A, H, M, P, S and on lower slopes of Mts, preferably on deep, moist, fertile soils.

Acàcia rotundifòlia (Latin 'round', referring to the phyllodes): Round-leafed Wattle: Central Tablelands and Western Slopes of NSW and in similar climates in Vic and SA.

Habit. A shrub of globose form to 2.5 m tall and as wide, with pendulous branchlets, at least when in flower.

Leaves. Phyllodes obovate, mostly 5–10 mm long and 3–6 mm wide, somewhat oblique, the midrib slightly eccentric, a single gland about the middle of the larger side; apex notched and finely mucronate; dull grey-green.

Flowers. Flower heads globular, 5–6 mm across, with 12–15 flowers in each, the heads solitary or in pairs on very slender 8–12 mm peduncles from the upper axils, forming handsome racemose sprays 10–15 cm long; flowers bright golden-yellow, abundant from late September to November.

Fruit. Legume linear, coiled, 3–5 m wide, grey-green, ripening to brown.

Other distinguishing features. One of the most beautiful of the shrubby wattles, extremely dainty, prolific and colourful and an ideal species for the small garden.

Climatic range. A, H, M, Mts, P, and on well-drained, elevated sites in S.

Acàcia rùbida (Latin 'red', referring to the stems and foliage): Red-stem Wattle or Red-leafed Wattle: Qld, Vic. and NSW, found mostly on gravelly soils on the Great Dividing Range and its slopes and coastal ridges.

Habit. An open, rather stiff shrub to 2–3 m tall with a short trunk and irregular head, or less commonly, taller, then somewhat tree-like.

Leaves. Phyllodes lanceolate, 6–12 cm long, 1–2 cm wide, falcate, the midrib and margins thickened, a single gland just below the middle; some bipinnate leaves are often seen among the phyllodes; young leaves or phyllodes reddish-green, becoming dark red when mature, especially in cool climates.

Flowers. In axillary racemes slightly shorter than the upper phyllodes, each with 10–12 or so globular heads; flowers golden-yellow, 10–15 in each head, flowering abundantly from September to November.

Fruit. Legume linear, 8–10 cm long, 6–8 mm wide, flat, straight or slightly falcate.

Other distinguishing features. Upper stems red, angular, with conspicuous ridges, changing to brown-green when older.

An unusual and attractive wattle because of its red stems and foliage, useful in providing variety in the common green colour of a garden.
Climatic range. A, H, M, Mts, P, S.

Acàcia spectábilis (Latin 'spectacular or showy', referring to the floral display): Mudgee Wattle: NSW on the Central Western Slopes of the Great Dividing Range.
Habit. A shrub to about 3 m tall and a little wider, or sometimes seen as a small tree with a short trunk and drooping branchlets, both forms of growth improved by light annual pruning.
Leaves. Bipinnate, the rachis 4–6 cm long with mostly 4 pairs of pinnae, a single swollen gland below the lowest pair; pinnae curved, from 1 cm in the lowest pair to 2 cm in the top pair; pinnules oblong to obovate, 1 cm long, 5 mm wide, in 3–8 sessile pairs, glabrous, glaucous-green.
Flowers. In racemes 10–15 cm long in the upper axils, forming a heavy terminal panicle, with 35–45 globose heads in each raceme; heads 7–8 mm across of 15–20 fragrant, rich golden-yellow flowers produced prolifically from August to October.
Fruit. Legume linear, 10–15 cm long and 1.0–1.5 cm wide, glaucous-green at first but becoming grey-brown, twisting and distorting upon ripening.
Other distinguishing features. Upper twigs yellow-green, shiny but with a bluish-white bloom.
A suitable wattle for screening or specimen planting, even in small gardens, the fine-textured foliage and richly coloured flowers being especially attractive.
Climatic range. A, M, Mts, P, and on well-drained gravelly soils in H, and S.

Acàcia suavèolens (Latin 'sweet', referring to the perfumed flowers): Sweet-scented Wattle: widespread in a variety of habitats in all Eastern Australian states, mostly on sandy or stony soils, from the coast to the mountains.
Habit. A shrub of 1–2 m depending upon conditions of exposure and soil quality, often with thin, open growth habit but improved by regular pruning.
Leaves. Phyllodes linear to lanceolate, 10–15 cm long, 6–10 mm wide, thick and stiff, the midrib distinct, a single flat marginal gland

usually present near the base; glabrous; green or blue-green with a bluish bloom.
Flowers. Flower buds on the upper twigs stout at first, enclosed in brown, scaly bracts which soon fall to release the short axillary racemes each carrying 8–10 small to medium, pale yellow heads; flowers about 8 in each head, sweetly perfumed, flowering in winter and early spring.
Fruit. Legumes narrowly oblong, 2–4 cm long, 1.5–2.0 cm wide, flat or slightly twisted, the margins thickened, with only slight constrictions between the 3–6 transversely arranged seeds.
Other distinguishing features. Upper twigs angular and somewhat flattened, glaucous at least while young.
Climatic range. A, B, H, M, Mts, P, S.

Acàcia terminális (Latin 'terminal', referring to the apical inflorescence) (syn. *A. botrycephala*) Sunshine Wattle: found in all eastern States, usually on rocky hillsides between the coast and mountains.
Habit. A thin, open shrub of irregular shape, mostly 1–2 m tall but occasionally larger to about 3 m, then tree-like with a short trunk.
Leaves. Bipinnate, the rachis 5–12 cm long, ridged and pubescent, with a single large gland 1.5 cm or so from the base; pinnae 3–6 pairs 4–6 cm long; pinnules oblong, 8–10 mm long, 2–3 mm wide in 10–16 pairs, dark green and shiny above, pale grey-green beneath.
Flowers. In racemes 10–25 cm long, forming a loose terminal panicle; racemes with 15–30 large heads to 1.5 cm across each with 6–12 flowers, creamy-yellow to deep golden-yellow, fragrant, flowering from late May to September.
Fruit. Legume linear-oblong, 8–11 cm long, 1.5 cm wide, flat or slightly undulate, green at first with a crimson edge then dark reddish-brown when ripe, with about 8–10 seeds.
Other distinguishing features. A pretty little wattle, especially useful for underplanting tall trees on well-drained sites with coarse soils of low fertility. The flowers always look bright, even in dull weather.
Climatic range. A, H, M, Mts, P, S.

Acàcia ulicifòlia (Latin 'with leaves like *Ulex*' the Gorse) (syn. *A. juniperina*) Prickly Moses: NSW, Qld and Vic. mostly on the sandy heathlands and stony ridges of the coastal plains and Great Dividing Range.

PLATE 1

▲ Acacia cardiophylla

▲ Acacia fimbriata

▲ Acacia rotundifolia

▲ Acacia conferta

▲ Acacia rotundifolia
▶ Acacia flexifolia
▼ Acacia spectabilis

▲ Acacia elongata

PLATE 2

▲ Banksia collina

▲ Abelia x grandiflora 'Francis Mason'

▲ Breynia disticha 'Roseo-picta'

▲ Boronia mollis
◄ Acalypha wilkesiana 'Triumphans'
▼ Banksia ericifolia

▼ Berberis thunbergii 'Atropurpurea'

Habit. A stiff, spiky shrub to 1–2 m tall, of open, irregular form in the wild but denser and more floriferous when pruned annually.

Leaves. Phyllodes linear-subulate, to 1.5 cm long and 1 mm wide, standing at about 90° from the stems; base made unequal by a glandular swelling on one side; apex armed with a sharp, horny point; midrib alone prominent; glabrous and dark green.

Flowers. 25–40 in a solitary globose head about 1 cm across, on a slender peduncle 1.5 cm long, scattered along the upper twigs; creamy-yellow, flowering mainly from July to November but intermittently at other times.

Fruit. Legumes linear, 3–5 cm long, 3–4 mm wide, strongly falcate, flat but constricted between the 8–12 broadly oval seeds.

Other distinguishing features. Upper twigs finely pubescent, at least while young.

An unusual but attractive small wattle, adapting well to harsh sites and useful as a specimen plant or as a 'barrier' hedge.

Climatic range. A, H, M, Mts, P, S.

Acàcia vestìta (Latin 'a garment or clothing', referring to the pubescent foliage and branchlets): Hairy Wattle: North-eastern Victorian highlands and Central and Southern Tablelands and coastal slopes in NSW.

Habit. A shrub to 3–4 m with a short trunk, dividing early into a mass of spreading branches forming a broad, rounded bush.

Leaves. Phyllodes ovate-elliptical to 1.5 cm long and 7–8 mm wide, the sides unequal, one with a pronounced curve; apex acute with a bristle-like cusp; margin ciliate, thickened, apparently glandless; glaucous-green and densely pubescent on both sides.

Flowers. Inflorescence a terminal panicle of racemes, each 3–6 cm long, carrying 20–35 globular heads with 15–20 flowers in each head, opening to 3–5 mm balls of golden-yellow, fragrant flowers from late August to November, with a few in summer.

Fruit. Legume 5–7 cm long, 7–10 mm wide, flat, blue-grey.

Other distinguishing features. A showy wattle in foliage and flower making a useful garden subject but in need of light annual pruning to thicken the growth habit.

Climatic range. H, M, Mts, and the cooler parts of A, P, and S.

ACÁLYPHA

The latinised version of an old Greek vernacular name for a somewhat similar plant.
Chenille Plant or Red Hot Cat's Tail; or Fijian Fire-plant.
Euphorbiaceae, the Spurge family.

Generic description. A genus of tender evergreen shrubs from the tropics, mainly South-East Asia and the Pacific, with simple alternate leaves, often large and colourful, and apetalous flowers of less decorative value, in terminal tassle-like spikes. Several species are grown in Australia for their showy foliage.

Propagation. Soft-tip cuttings strike readily, preferably taken in late spring to autumn, planted in sand and peat and placed in a heated glass-house.

Cultivation. A well-drained, light soil with a high organic content is ideal, with plenty of water in spring and summer. The warmest possible position must be selected, with protection from harsh winds which seriously damage the large leaves. The plants are not frost tolerant.

Pruning. Since the foliage is the main decorative feature, plants should be grown as vigorously as possible, with moderate pruning of the annual growth in late winter, followed by additional feeding and watering.

Species and cultivars

Acálypha híspida (Latin 'with short, stiff hairs') (syn. *A. sanderi*) Chenille Plant or Red Hot Cat's Tail: Indonesia, Papua New Guinea and neighbouring islands.

Habit. An evergreen shrub to 2–3 m tall, sometimes tree-like when grown in poor light beneath taller plants, but usually kept bushy in cultivation by regular pruning.

Leaves. Ovate, 10–15 cm long and 6–9 cm wide; petiole 5–6 cm long, pubescent, often reddish; apex acuminate; margin finely serrate; midrib and main laterals reddish and prominent beneath; glabrous; bright green to reddish-bronze above, paler and dull beneath.

Flowers. Monoecious, the spectacular inflorescence a pendulous, tassel-like raceme, 25–45 cm long and 2.5 cm thick, from the upper axils; bright red to purplish-red in the species but white in the cultivar '**Alba**', flowering in summer and autumn.

Climatic range. B, P, S, T, on warm sheltered sites only.

Acálypha tòrta (Latin 'twisted', referring to the distorted leaves): Pacific region, especially the Samoan Islands.
Habit. A rounded leafy bush to 2 m or so tall and about as wide.
Leaves. Almost orbicular, to 20–25 cm long and 15–20 cm wide; petiole stout, 8–10 cm long; apex mostly extended into a fine acuminate tip to about 4 cm long, or sometimes twisted and distorted inwards; base rounded; margin prominently crenate-serrate, the teeth about 1 cm long, bluntly rounded; venation reticulate; dark reddish-maroon above and reddish-brown beneath, slightly shiny on both sides.
Flowers and fruit. Not seen.
Climatic range. B, P, S, T, on warm, frost free sites with protection from wind.

Acálypha wilkesiàna (commemorating Charles Wilkes, American explorer in Polynesia): Fijian Fire-plant or Copper Leaf: Fiji and adjacent Pacific Islands.
Habit. A shrub to 2–3 m tall with erect stems, forming an irregularly rounded bush about as broad as its height.
Leaves. Variable in shape and size but generally elliptic or narrowly to broadly ovate, from 10–30 cm long and 5–15 cm wide; petiole slender, 5–15 cm long; apex acute, acuminate or deeply emarginate; base obtuse, cuneate to deeply cordate; margin serrate, bluntly or coarsely; glabrous; colour range very wide, from mid-green to reddish-bronze and multi-coloured, some of the cultivars with a margin of contrasting colour.
Flowers. Inflorescence a tassel-like catkin 10–15 cm long, from the upper axils and often partly hidden by the leaves; mostly reddish-bronze, flowering in summer and autumn.
Fruit. Not seen.
Other distinguishing features. Upper stems pubescent, with 3 decurrent ridges below each leaf base.
'**Laciniata Variegata**' has ovate leaves, deeply cut into slender lobes and strips, irregularly marked with yellow.
'**Macafeeàna**' has ovate, acuminate, serrate leaves, coppery-green, but splashed and blotched with reddish-bronze and crimson.
'**Macrophýlla**' has ovate, acuminate, cordate, serrate leaves, reddish-brown, with pale spots and blotches.
'**Marginàta**' has large broadly ovate, acuminate, crenate-serrate leaves with prominent red veins and petiole, bronze-green, with a conspicuous 5 mm wide rosy-red margin.
'**Obovàta**' has broadly obovate or obcordate leaves, bronze-green above, reddish-brown beneath, with a rosy-red margin about 3–5 mm wide.
'**Triúmphans**' has very large leaves to 30 cm long and 20 cm wide, with a blunt-acuminate apex and crenate-serrate margin of large blunt teeth to 5 mm deep; the base colour is dark metallic-red, marked with dark pinkish-bronze and rosy-red.
Climatic range. All B, P, S, T, on warm, sheltered sites only.

ACOKANTHÈRA (syn. *Toxicophlaea)*

From the Greek, describing the mucronate anthers.
Winter-Sweet or Poison-Bush.
Apocynaceae, the Dogbane family.

Generic description. A small genus of unarmed shrubs from South Africa, with simple, opposite leaves, often colouring in winter, and fragrant flowers in axillary cymes, followed by ovoid, olive-like fruits. All parts of the plant are poisonous. The species described below is especially attractive when used in association with foliage of finer texture.

Propagation. a) Seeds sown in spring, preferably in a warm, humid atmosphere, germinate freely.
b) Soft-tip cuttings, taken in spring or summer, or firmer cuttings at other times, may be struck in a sand-peat mixture in a warm, slightly dry part of the glass-house, hormone dusts being beneficial.
c) 'Variegata' is usually apical-grafted in late winter.

Cultivation. The ideal soil is well drained, fertile and of light texture, with adequate summer water. The plant thrives in a warm, frost-free position but does not suffer seriously in temperatures of −2°.

Pruning. The plant needs an occasional trim to maintain its dense, leafy form, preferably following the spring flowers. If the poisonous fruits are a danger to children, they should be removed when first seen.

Species and cultivars

Acokanthèra oblongifòlia (Latin 'with oblong leaves') (syn. *A. spectabilis, Carissa spectabilis*) Winter-Sweet or Poison-Bush: south-eastern coast of South Africa, in warm forest areas.

Habit. An evergreen shrub to 3–4 m tall and 2–3 m wide, branching densely from near the base to form a leafy, globose bush.

Leaves. Mostly opposite, elliptic to ovate-oblong, 10–12 cm long, 3–5 cm wide; apex acute; base obtuse; margin entire; texture thick and coriaceous; dark green and shiny above, paler and dull beneath, turning reddish-purple in winter.

Flowers. Inflorescence a dense cyme in the upper axils; flowers tubulate to 2 cm long, the 5-parted limb 8–10 mm across, pure white or with a pink flush; fragrant; flowering from September to late November.

Fruit. An ovoid berry to 2 cm long, green but ripening to dark plum-red with glandular dots, exuding a poisonous white sap when the skin is broken; a single ovoid seed; fruits persist from summer to winter.

Cultivar. 'Variegàta' is slightly smaller but has handsomely coloured leaves, the dark green irregularly invaded by creamy-white with grey-green intermediate areas, the young leaves with a distinct pinkish cast, the dark green parts stained with reddish-maroon; fruits whitish with red, pink and green stains.

Climatic range. B, S, T, and warm, sheltered localities in A, M, and P.

ADENÁNDRA

Derived from the Greek words *aden* 'a gland', and *andros* 'male', referring to the glandular anthers.

Adenandra; China-flower.

Rutaceae, the Rue family.

Generic description. A small genus of evergreen shrubs from South Africa, with simple, alternate, aromatic leaves on slender branchlets, and 5-petalled rotate flowers in white and pink, flowering in late winter and early spring. Two species are often grown in Australian gardens, mainly for their attractive flowers and foliage and neat growth habit.

Propagation. Firm tip cuttings, taken in autumn, strike with some difficulty in a warm, but not over-humid atmosphere.

Cultivation. Both species perform well in a friable, sandy or gravelly soil with free drainage. The ideal climate is warm, with low atmospheric humidity, preferably where temperatures do not fall below −5°C in winter.

Pruning. Light annual pruning immediately after the flowering season is beneficial. Hard wood, older than the current 1-year-old material, should not be cut.

Species and cultivars

Adenándra fràgrans (Latin 'fragrant'): Fragrant China-flower: South Africa in the mountains east of Cape Town.

Habit. An evergreen shrub to 0.75 m tall and as wide, with dense, twiggy branchlets, kept so by regular annual pruning.

Leaves. Linear-lanceolate to oblong, to 2 cm long and 3–5 mm wide, almost sessile; apex acute with a small depressed gland; base rounded; margin entire to denticulate and slightly recurved; midrib alone prominent; glabrous and dark green above, paler and glandular beneath, aromatic when bruised.

Flowers. Rotate to 2.5 cm across, in a terminal corymbose cluster of a few to about 10 flowers carried well above the leaves, the 5 spreading, oblong-obovate petals variable in colour but mostly pale to rose-pink with a rosy-carmine central stripe, sweetly fragrant, flowering from late August to October.

Fruit. Not seen.

Other distinguishing features. Upper twigs reddish, puberulent.

Climatic range. A, H, M, Mts, P, S.

Adenándra uniflòra (Latin 'with solitary flowers'): China-flower: South Africa, mainly on sandy soils.

Habit. An evergreen shrub to 1 m tall, the dense, twiggy, growth improved by regular pruning.

Leaves. Alternate or often decussate, linear-lanceolate, 1.0–1.5 cm long and 2–3 mm wide; petiole 1 mm, pubescent; apex acute, slightly depressed; base obtuse; margin entire, recurved; venation obscure, the midrib alone evident beneath; upper surface dark green, shiny and glabrous; lower surface concave, whitish-green, glandular and aromatic when crushed.

Flowers. Solitary, terminal on short leafy twigs;

calyx funnelform, with 5 slenderly acute sepals to 1.3 cm long, green but stained red, glandular; flowers rotate to 2.5 cm across, the petals obovate to 8–10 mm wide, pure white to pale shell-pink, with a deep carmine-crimson central stripe; fragrant; stamens 10, to 3–4 mm long; flowering from September to December, then intermittently until late autumn.

Fruit. Not seen.

Other distinguishing features. Youngest twigs pubescent, becoming reddish above, the bark splitting along the internodes.

Climatic range. A, B, M, P, S, and on warm, sheltered sites on the lower Mts.

AGAPÈTES (syn. *Pentapterỳgium)*

Derived from the Greek agape 'lovely', referring to the flowers.
Agapetes.
Ericaceae, the Erica family.

Generic description. A small genus of tender, tuberous-rooted plants from South-East Asia, some epiphytic, the species described here grown for its curious flowers and habit of growth. See detailed specific description below.

Propagation. Firm-tip, leafy cuttings are easily struck in summer and autumn in a glass-house, with mist and bottom heat an advantage.

Cultivation. A warm, humid location is essential, ideally in the shelter and filtered light of taller plants, preferably in a rich leafy loam, slightly acid and with free drainage. The surface of the soil should be mulched, not cultivated.

Pruning. Young plants should be tip-pruned for the first few years to establish a dense, twiggy growth; thereafter the pendulous shoots should be allowed to flower naturally.

Species and cultivars

Agapètes sèrpens (Latin 'with a pendulous, creeping form'): lower levels of the SE Himalayas.

Habit. An evergreen, pendulous shrub to 1.5 m tall and 2.0 m wide, with many leafy, arching branches from the tuberous-rooted base.

Leaves. Simple, alternate, ovate-lanceolate, to 1 cm long and 6–7 mm wide; apex acute; base otuse; margin shallowly crenate, the notches bristly; stiff and coriaceous; glabrous; light red at

first but maturing to deep glossy green above with reddish shadings, pale green beneath.

Flowers. Solitary or in pairs in the upper axils, pendulous; pedicels about 1 cm long, crimson, bristly; calyx tubulate-campanulate to 8 mm long, with 5 sharp ridges on the body and 5 acute teeth at the apex, the whole green at first but becoming crimson; corolla tubulate, to 2 cm long and 1 cm broad with 5 sharp, longtitudinal ribs, each terminating in a reflexed acute lobe, the whole crimson with deeper herringbone markings, freely produced from early August to mid summer; stamens 10, about 1.8 cm long, yellow-brown, reaching the mouth of the corolla.

Fruit. Not seen.

Other distinguishing features. Youngest stems covered with crimson, glandular-tipped bristles, persisting for about the first year.

'Ludgvan Cross' is also available locally, with flowers in drooping clusters of 3 and 4, on crimson pedicels to 1.3 cm long and with pale-carmine corolla marked with crimson lines.

Climatic range. B, P, S, T, and in warm microclimates in A, and M.

AGÒNIS

Derived from the Greek, describing the large number of seeds in the woody capsules. Willow-Myrtle or Western Australian Peppermint Tree.
Myrtaceae, the Myrtle family.

Generic description. A small genus of Australian native trees with simple, alternate, aromatic leaves, small white flowers in sessile heads, and woody capsular fruits containing fine seeds. The principal species, *A. flexuosa* has given rise to several interesting and attractive shrub-like forms described below.

Propagation. The cultivars must be vegetatively propagated to preserve their clonal identity.
a) Soft-tip cuttings, hormone-treated and placed under mist in a controlled atmosphere are mostly used;
b) Firm-wood scions may be approach-apical-grafted on 1-year old understocks of *A. flexuosa*.

Cultivation. The cultivars perform best on a friable, well-drained soil preferably enriched with organic matter for improved moisture retention. The variegated cultivars deserve the best possible site with shelter from hot, dry or violent winds, and ideally with a background of dark green foliage for colour contrast.

Pruning. Very little pruning is necessary except to control the occasional wayward shoot. A close watch should be kept for green-reverted shoots, or in grafted plants, regrowth of the parent understock.

Species and cultivars
Agònis flexuòsa (Latin 'bent', the twigs assuming a zigzag pattern): Willow-Myrtle or WA Peppermint-Tree: SW corner of WA.
(This, the parent species of the following cultivars is fully described in the companion volume 'Ornamental Flowering Trees in Australia' — q v.)
'**Belbra Gold**' is a registered cultivar occurring in The Grampians, Vic, growing to 4–5 m tall and broad, with distinctive foliage, reddish at first, changing to pale yellow, then maturing to yellow mottled with green, giving the plant a pronounced golden colour.
'**Nana**' is a dwarf form of the parent, growing to about 1.5 m and as broad, with dense foliage, often with a reddish tinge while young, on slender twigs forming a rounded crown.
'**Variegàta**' is a well-established form now registered as a cultivar. It grows as an erect shrub to 2–3 m tall and 1.5–2.0 m wide, with drooping lateral branches, and somewhat smaller linear leaves than those of the parent, with a central stripe of pale green and a deep cream border, sometimes with a pinkish tinge while young.
Climatic range. B, M, P, S and on sheltered sites in A, H.

ALOÝSIA (syn. *Lippia*)

The latinised version of the old Teutonic name, 'Louisa', commemorating Marie Louisa, Duchess of Parma, 1791–1849.
Lemon-scented Verbena.
Verbenaceae, the Verbena family.

Generic Description. A large genus of shrubs and ground-covering perennials, mostly from temperate South America, the species described here used in warm-climate gardens for its aromatic foliage. For details, see specific notes below.

Propagation. Soft-tip cuttings taken from the new shoots in spring are easily struck in a sand/ peat mixture in a warm, humid atmosphere.

Cultivation. A well-drained, loamy or light-textured soil is ideal, with sufficient water in summer to maintain strong growth. The plant is tolerant of mild frosts but is not hardy to temperatures below −3°C, and reaches its best development in a warm, coastal environment in a sunny position.

Pruning. Flowers are borne on current season's growth which should be stimulated by good plant husbandry and late winter pruning; about half the growth made during the previous year may be removed with advantage.

Species and cultivars
Aloýsia triphýlla (Greek 'three-leafed', describing the 3-whorled leaves) (syn. *A. citriodora*, *Lippia citriodora*, *Verbena triphylla*) Lemon-scented Verbena; Argentina, Uruguay and Chile.
Habit. A partly deciduous shrub to 2–3 m tall, of loose, open growth habit but improved in density and general appearance by regular pruning.
Leaves. Simple, 3-whorled or rarely 4-whorled, lanceolate, 6–8 cm long and 1–2 cm wide; petioles 3–5 mm long; apex slenderly acuminate; base cuneate; margin minutely serrulate; midrib prominent below; finely strigillose and slightly rough to the touch and glandular-dotted on both surfaces; mid green above, slightly paler beneath; heavily lemon scented when even lightly disturbed.
Flowers. Inflorescence a terminal panicle, 10–20 cm long, with numerous small flowers in slender sprays; calyx tubulate to 3–4 mm long, with 4 small sharp teeth; corolla salverform, extending 3 mm beyond the calyx, pale lavender-purple, flowering from mid October to early autumn; flowers not spectacular but very dainty.
Fruit. Not seen.
Other distinguishing features. Upper twigs marked with fine longitudinal ridges, extending into the inflorescence.
Climatic range. A, B, M, P, S, T.

ALYÓGYNE

Derived from the Greek, referring to the connate style branches.
Lilac or Satin Hibiscus.
Malvaceae, the Mallow family.

Generic description. A small genus of Australian native shrubs from WA and SA, formerly included in Hibiscus but now separated by its distinctive 5-lobed but undivided style. The species treated here is grown mainly for its lilac-blue flowers.

Propagation. a) Seeds sown as soon as ripe; germinate readily in a warm atmosphere;
b) Soft-tip or firm-wood cuttings taken between late spring and autumn are easily struck in a sand/peat medium under glass.

Cultivation. Almost any moderately-fertile, well-drained soil is suitable, preferably sited in a sunny position sheltered from strong wind.

Pruning. Young plants should be tip-pruned frequently during the first 2 years to develop a dense, bushy habit; thereafter, regular pruning of about half the annual growth increment is desirable, immediately after the flowering period.

Species and cultivars

Alyógyne huègelii (Commemorating Baron Karl von Huegel, Austrian botanical explorer): Lilac Hibiscus: South-west WA, mainly on the coastal plains and Wheatbelts, and in SA on the Eyre and Yorke Peninsulas and Flinders and Gawler Ranges.
Habit. An open-framed shrub to 2–3 m tall and as broad in its native habitat, but made more leafy and denser in growth with annual pruning in cultivation.
Leaves. Simple, alternate, bipalmatifid, deeply-lobed into 3 or 5 divisions, the blade 4–6 cm long and as wide, the petiole 2–4 cm long; lobes of the blade oblong to obovate, irregularly sub-lobed and undulate on the margins; main veins and lower surface stellate-pubescent; dark green above paler beneath.
Flowers. Solitary in the upper axils; involucral bracteoles 10 to 13, about 6–7 mm long; calyx campanulate, 2 cm long, stellate-pubescent; petals 5, broadly obovate, the rotate flower 10 – 12 cm across; lilac-blue, with deeper veins, white toward the base; staminal column 3 cm tall, the stamens 3 mm long, the outer half of the column terminated by a 5-pronged cream style; flowering season from early spring to summer.
Fruit. A 5-valved capsule, ripening in late summer.
Other distinguishing features. Upper stems green-brown, shallowly grooved and densely stellate-pubescent.

Climatic range. A, B, I, M, P, S, and on warm sites on lower levels of Mts.

AÒTUS

Derived from the Greek 'without ears', referring to the absence of bracteoles on the calyx, which separates this genus from the closely-related *Pultenaea*.
Aotus (various) or Eggs and Bacon (one of several so named).
Fabaceae, the Pea family.

Generic description. A small Australian genus of about 15 evergreen shrubby species, the majority from WA, but several from the eastern states, one popularly used in gardens for its handsome yellow flowers. For details, see specific notes below.

Propagation. Seeds germinate readily if lightly scarified or soaked in warm water for 24 hours, then sown in a warm, moist atmosphere.

Cultivation. An open sunny position in a friable soil of moderate fertility are the basic requirements. It is sometimes found at the edges of swampy land or the margins of water-courses, but is tolerant of both moist and relatively dry soil.

Pruning. The only pruning necessary is the removal of spent flowers and a trimming of lanky shoots after they have flowered.

Species and cultivars

Aòtus ericoìdes (Latin 'with Erica-like leaves'): Common or Erica-leafed Aotus or Eggs and Bacon: all Australian states, mainly on sandy heathlands near the coast and on the slopes of neighbouring ranges.
Habit. A shrub to 1.5 m tall, with upright shoots from the base, spreading to about 1 m broad, the upper branchlets densely villous.
Leaves. Simple, alternate, scattered or sometimes whorled; linear, 12–15 mm long and 1–2 mm wide; apex acute, mucronate; petiole 1–2 mm, grey-villous; margin entire, revolute; upper surface glandular, but glabrous and dark green, heavily grey-pubescent beneath; aromatic when crushed.
Flowers. Borne in the upper axils, 1 to 3 together, in a slender, spire-like inflorescence to 20 cm long; calyx 5-lobed, campanulate to 3–4 mm long, grey-green, villous; corolla pea-shaped to 1 cm across, the erect standard petal nearly

orbicular, bilobed, rich golden-yellow, often streaked at the base with dark red lines; wing and keel petals smaller; flowering season from late August to October.

Fruit. An ovoid legume to 6–8 mm long, heavily villous, grey-green.

Climatic range. A, B, H, M, P, S, and on mild sites in Mts.

ARDÍSIA

Derived from the Greek *ardis*, describing the sharply acute anthers.

Ardisia.

Myrsinaceae, the Myrsine family.

Generic description. A large genus of mainly shrubs from the warmer parts of Asia and America, with simple leaves, small white or pink flowers and showy fruits, the species most popular in Australia described more fully below.

Propagation. Seeds germinate readily when cleaned of their fleshy covering and sown in spring in a friable material in a warm, humid atmosphere.

Cultivation. When using Ardisia as a garden shrub, choose a partly shaded, wind-sheltered position in a mild climate with only very light frosts. The ideal soil is a friable, fibrous loam or sand with free drainage. For potted plants, the soil should be similar but plants should be repotted annually, some of the outer soil ball being removed and replaced with new soil. The renovation is carried out in late winter.

Pruning. Is not usually necessary except to remove spent fruiting stems or to tip-prune a large plant to restrict its growth.

Species and cultivars

Ardísia crenàta (Latin 'with crenate leaf-margin') (syn. *A. crenulata*) main islands of Japan, neighbouring islands, Korea and China.

Habit. An evergreen shrub to 0.75 m, with many erect stems issuing from the base, forming a densely leafed crown 0.5–1.0 m across.

Leaves. Simple, alternate, oblong to lanceolate, 6–10 cm long and 2–5 cm wide; petiole 5–8 mm long, grooved above; apex bluntly acuminate; base slenderly cuneate; margin crenate, recurved, the small crimped undulations with glands between the notches; venation reticulate, midrib and main laterals raised beneath; glabrous and coriaceous; glandular-dotted; dark green and shiny above, pale-green beneath.

Flowers. In umbellate clusters at the ends of slender, speading, lateral twigs issuing from the main stem below the foliage; calyx shallow, with 5 spreading, acute, green sepals; corolla rotate, 8–10 mm across, the 5 ovate petals white, flowering from late spring to summer.

Fruit. A globose, 1-seeded drupe to 1.0 cm across, in umbellate, whorled clusters around the lateral twigs, blood-red, with whitish flesh, ripening in autumn and persisting until September or even later when sheltered; seed globose, 6 mm across, pale pinkish-brown, with fine white longitudinal veins.

Climatic range. B, M, P, S, T, and in warm, sheltered localities in A.

ARÒNIA

Derived from an ancient Greek vernacular name of a closely related plant.

Choke-berry.

Rosaceae, sub-family Pomoideae (Rose family, Pome sub-family).

Generic description. A small genus of deciduous shrubs from North America, two species grown in the cooler parts of Australia for their coloured autumn leaves and showy flowers and fruit.

Propagation. a) Seeds should be collected as soon as ripe in autumn, cleaned, and stored in just moist sphagnum moss at 4°–5°C over winter and sown in a warm place in spring.

b) Soft-tip or semi-hardwood cuttings, taken in spring to autumn, strike readily in a sand/peat mixture in a cool, humid atmosphere.

c) Suckers separated from the parent clump in winter, or mound layers, wounded and covered to 15 cm deep and lifted in the following winter, provide a few large plants reliably.

Cultivation. The species treated here are best grown in a light fertile soil, moist but not poorly drained, in a sun-exposed position, preferably in a cool, moist climate; tolerant to low temperatures to at least −8°C.

Pruning. The plants flower and fruit most prolifically on 1-to 3-year-old shoots; older stems should be removed each year to make space for new growth. No other pruning is necessary, but unwanted suckers should be removed by digging if other plants are threatened.

Species and cultivars

Arònia arbutifòlia (Latin 'with leaves like *Arbutus*'): Red Choke-berry: eastern USA.

Habit. A deciduous shrub to about 2 m tall, with a mass of erect shoots from the base, spreading slowly by suckering to at least 2 m wide.

Leaves. Simple, alternate, elliptic to obovate, to 8 cm long and 3.5 cm wide; petiole 1 cm, apex acute to shortly acuminate; base cuneate; margin finely crenulate, glandular-tipped; venation reticulate, the midrib prominent below; glabrous above except for some fine hairs on the midrib, densely tomentose beneath; dark green changing to vivid red in autumn and lasting to early winter.

Flowers. Inflorescence a broad corymb to 6 cm across, with about 12 to 18 crateriform flowers to 1.3 cm across; calyx 5-lobed, green, glandular; petals 5, oval to obovate, white but often stained or tinged pink or light red outside, flowering from late September to early November; stamens numerous, filaments creamy-white, anthers rosy-carmine.

Fruit. A fleshy pome to 6–7 mm across, globose or slightly pear-shaped, the calyx lobes persisting at the apex, bright crimson, fully coloured by late April and persisting until July.

Other distinguishing features. Young twigs pubescent, reddish-green, but becoming glabrous and grey-green when mature.

Climatic range. A, H, M, Mts, P, S.

Arònia melanocàrpa (Greek 'with black fruit'): Black Choke-berry: USA, mainly east of the Mississippi River.

A small deciduous shrub to about 1 m or less, otherwise of much the same habit of growth as *A. arbutifolia*, but with more-lustrous, glabrous leaves, and slightly larger, more-globose fruits, shiny and dark purplish-black, spectacular in autumn but not persisting beyond mid June.

Climatic range. A, H, M, Mts, P, S.

AUCÙBA

Latinised from the aboriginal Japanese name. Japanese Aucuba; Japanese Laurel; Gold-dust Tree.

Cornaceae, the Dogwood family.

Generic description. A small genus of evergreen shrubs from the Orient, with large, simple, opposite leaves, small, dioecious, purplish flowers in terminal panicles, and berry-like, drupaceous fruits. The green-leafed species is valued for the spectacular scarlet fruits of the females, the variegated cultivars for their brightly coloured leaves. For the production of fruit, a male and several female plants should be set closely together in a clump.

Propagation. Both species and cultivars may be grown by seeds, but it is better practice to propagate only from parent stock of known sex, by firm, semi-hardwood, leafy tip cuttings, taken in autumn or winter, planted in a sand/peat mixture and placed in a cool humid atmosphere, preferably under mist.

Cultivation. A light, friable soil, well drained,but not allowed to dry out in summer, is ideal, especially if dressed occasionally with coarse compost. The species is hardy in most Australian climates but may be damaged by frost in excess of −5°C. It grows best in a cool shaded place sheltered from strong sunlight, although some early morning sunlight is beneficial. Useful for interior decoration when grown in large containers.

Pruning. Is rarely necessary except to maintain the normally tidy shape and to keep the plants within their allotted space.

Species and cultivars

Aucùba japónica (Latin 'Japanese'): Japanese Aucuba: native to the main islands of Japan, mostly as an under-storey plant in mountain forests.

Habit. A shrub to about 3 m, with many erect and spreading branches from the base, forming a broad bush 3–4 m wide.

Leaves. Broad-lanceolate to elliptical, to 20 cm long and 5–10 cm wide; petiole to 2.5 cm long, channelled above; apex acuminate; base cuneate; margin coarsely and remotely serrate, mostly above the middle; venation reticulate, the midrib prominent beneath; glabrous and coriaceous; dark green and lustrous above, paler and duller beneath.

Flowers. Inflorescence a terminal panicle; flowers dioecious, the males in short erect panicles to 8 cm, the 4-petalled, purplish flowers rotate to 8 mm across, the pollen borne on 4 short stamens, female flowers in a shorter panicle, the single green stigma conspicuous; flowering period in early spring.

Fruit. A 1-seeded, fleshy drupe to 2 cm long and 1 cm wide, ovoid, singly or in clusters of 4

or 5, bright scarlet, in late autumn and winter.
'Variegàta' is a name probably once legitimately used for a clone with yellow and green coloration but has now come to apply to almost any *Aucùba* with variegated foliage. Both male and female forms are available, all handsomely marked with a more or less even distribution of yellowish spots and flecks on a dark green background. 'Crotonifòlia', 'Crotonoìdes', 'Gold Dust' and 'Maculàta' are all variations of superior quality but it seems impossible now to distinguish authentic material.

The following cultivars, however, may be identified reliably because of their distinctive colour patterns.

'Limbàta': a male clone, the dark-green leaves with a yellowish margin of irregular width.

'Picturàta' (syn. 'Aureo-maculata') the common form is a female clone, but males may also exist; leaves have a large, irregular yellow patch in middle, sometimes extending to the edge.

Climatic range. H, M, Mts, S, and in cool, moist sites in A, B, and P.

BÀECKEA

Named by Carl Linnaeus to honour his physician and botanist friend, Abraham Baeck, 1713–95, born in Soderhamn, Sweden.
Heath-myrtle (various)
Myrtaceae, the Myrtle family.

Generic description. A genus of about 70 evergreen species, dispersed in all states of Australia, growing in a variety of habitats from alpine marshes and open forest-lands to exposed sites in coastal heaths. Mostly of dense, twiggy form, several have become important components in rock gardens, especially valued for their attractive flowers in spring and summer. Leaves are simple, opposite (distinguishing Bàeckia from Leptospermum with alternate leaves); flowers are rotate, 5-petalled, mostly white but with mauve and pink in a few, borne singly or in small cymose clusters; and fruit is a small 3-celled woody capsule containing 2 seeds in each.

Propagation. Firm tip cuttings taken after the initial growth period strike readily in a sand/peat medium in a warm, moist environment.

Cultivation. See specific notes below for detailed cultural recommendations.

Pruning. A light pruning of the flowered shoots immediately after the fall of petals, is beneficial.

Species and cultivars

Bàeckia gunniàna (Commemorating Ronald Campbell Gunn, 1808–81, South African born botanical explorer in Tasmania): Mountain Heath-myrtle: SE Australian mountains, in alpine heaths and on the margins of swamps and streams.
Habit. A bushy shrub, 0.5–1.5 m tall, but occasionally reduced to prostrate form in exposed places.
Leaves. Oblong-oblanceolate, 2–6 mm long, densely crowded on the slender twigs, deeply concave, fleshy, blunt, dark green, aromatic when bruised.
Flowers. Enclosed by reddish sepals in the bud, then opening to rotate to 5–8 mm across, solitary, the 5 orbicular petals to 2 mm across, white, with a central cluster of 5–7 incurved stamens; flowering abundantly from November to March.
Fruit. Not seen.
Climatic range. H, M, Mts, and on cool sites in P and S.

Bàeckia ramosíssima (Latin 'much branched'): Rosy Heath-myrtle: SE Australia, mainly in coastal heaths and lightly-timbered forests from sea level to sub-alpine elevations, then often on rocky sites.
Habit. A variable shrub with wiry branches, sometimes prostrate to 20–30 cm tall in exposed places, or more erect to 1 m or so in sheltered heaths or among trees.
Leaves. Linear to nearly terete, 6–10 mm long, somewhat sparse but spreading widely on the twigs, entire, sharply acute, dark green.
Flowers. Solitary in the upper leaf axils, enclosed in the bud by the 5 pointed sepals of the reddish calyx; rotate, 8–12 mm across, with 5 flat, orbicular petals and a central cluster of 10 reddish stamens; pale rose-pink, varying to white or rosy-red in some forms, all flowering from late winter to summer.
Fruit. Not seen.
Other distinguishing features. In cultivation, the species performs best in a sunny location on well-drained friable soil.
Climatic range. A, H, M, P, S, and on lower slopes of Mts.

Bàeckia virgàta (Latin 'twiggy'): Twiggy Heath-myrtle: Eastern Australian heaths and elevated forests of the lower tablelands.

Habit. A bushy shrub to 2.5–3.0 m tall and nearly as broad, responding well to pruning with increased density.

Leaves. Linear-oblong to 2.5 cm long and 3 mm wide, and nearly flat; wide-spreading; glabrous; entire; glandular; dark green.

Flowers. In cymose clusters from the upper leaf axils, abundant; rotate, 5–7 mm across the 5 orbicular, spreading white petals; stamens 5 to 12, with cream anthers; flowering season from late spring to late summer.

Fruit. Not seen.

Other distinguishing features. The plant is adaptable to a wide range of climatic and soil conditions, but performs best in well-drained light soils on elevated sites away from the coast. 'Howie's Feathertips' is a well-regarded registered cultivar with shorter growth to 50 cm or so tall and about 1 m broad, its distinctive pendulous form well suited to the rock garden. The young growth is an attractive reddish-tan before assuming the normal bright green colouring of maturity. The pure white flowers, 5–6 mm across are densely clustered near the ends of the branchlets.
'Howie's Sweet Midget' is another registered cultivar with even lower growth habit to only about 30 cm tall and 60 cm broad, but otherwise similar to the parent.

Climatic range. A, B, M, P, S, and lower Mts.

BÁNKSIA

Commemorating Joseph Banks (later knighted), botanist with Captain James Cook on the voyage of 1770, when the east coast of Australia was discovered. Banksia is reputed to be the first plant collected at what is now Botany Bay.
Banksia (various).
Proteaceae, the Protea family.

Generic description. An almost wholly Australian native genus of about 50 species distributed widely but somewhat unevenly throughout the continent, with the majority occurring close to the coast, often as well as inland, on sandy or rocky land, some preferring wet sites, others dry sandy soils. All are evergreen trees or shrubs with tough, leathery, simple leaves, often with coloured tomentum and with great variety in size and shape, colourful flowers, densely arranged as an erect, cylindrical spike, and fruits of hard, woody follicles containing the winged seeds. Few plants are more closely identified with the popular image of the Australian flora than the Banksia.

The taller, tree-like species of Banksia are described in the companion volume, 'Ornamental Flowering Trees in Australia'. (q.v.)

Propagation. In most species, the fruiting 'cobs' should be cut from the plant and placed in a glass jar in a warm, dry place to shrink the woody follicles and release the seeds which germinate readily in a sand/peat mixture in a warm, humid atmosphere. Seedlings should not be allowed to become pot-bound before planting. In cool climates especially, young plants are best set out in early spring rather than autumn.

Cultivation. In general terms, the Banksias are among our hardiest plants, those described here thriving even in poor soils, although always requiring adequate water; others enjoy the free aeration and drainage of the sandy soils near the coast or the rocky or gravelly hillsides of the NSW Hawkesbury sandstones. A few tolerate exposure to sea winds, and these constitute the most important plants for seaside planting, often forming the first defensive barrier to protect gardens and dwellings against violent, salt-laden winds.

Pruning. Is neither necessary nor desirable; the development of the typically picturesque form of the Banksia is best left to natural forces.

Species and cultivars

Bánksia aspleniifòlia (Latin 'with leaves resembling *Asplenium*): NSW and Qld coastal plains and ridges, mostly on heathland and Hawkesbury sandstones.

Habit. A broad, open shrub to 1.0–2.5 m, of irregular form.

Leaves. Simple, alternate, narrow-elliptic to oblanceolate, 6–10 cm long and 1.5–2.5 cm wide; petiole 6–8 mm, rufous-pubescent at first but becoming sooty-black; apex obtuse to truncate; base cuneate; margin serrate-dentate, the edge recurved; venation reticulate with widely angled laterals; bronze and softly silky at first, becoming glabrous and dark green above, rufous-pubescent beneath, eventually whitish-green, the midrib cream.

Flowers. Inflorescence a terminal spike, 12–15 cm tall, 7–8 cm wide, borne at the junction of old and new shoots; flowers densely packed, the silky perianths pale grey-green, splitting into 4 thread-like divisions, styles projecting 1 cm or so, greenish-yellow, with a brown stigma, nearly straight when ripe, flowering from late autumn to late winter.

Fruit. A nearly cylindrical cone to 12–15 cm long, greyish and of rough texture, the apex harshly prickly, with a few fertilised follicles, grey and heavily tomentose.

Other distinguishing features. Young twigs densely rufous-pubescent, the 2-year wood becoming glabrous and dark charcoal grey, with a sooty texture.

B. aspleniifòlia is a common sight on the rocky foreshores of the Sydney coastline and in the Royal National Park, where it thrives on the poor gravel soils, but is responsive to horticultural use in native gardens and in shrub borders.

Climatic range. B, M, P, S, and on well-drained coastal sites in A and H.

Bánksia coccínea (Latin 'scarlet', referring to the colour of the flowers): Scarlet, Waratah or Albany Banksia: southern coast of Western Australia.

Habit. A shrub to 3–5 m with a stiff, erect habit on a short, woody, central trunk and sparse branches, the young stems densely tomentose.

Leaves. Broadly elliptical to nearly orbicular, 5–7 cm long, 3–5 cm wide, the petiole 3 mm, grey-floccose; apex truncate; base obtuse; margin coarsely and irregularly dentate with stiff but not sharp teeth; lateral veins widely-angled, yellowish and prominent beneath; coriaceous and stiff; mid green and dull above, whitish-green beneath.

Flowers. Terminal spike 5–6 cm long, 7–8 cm wide, at the ends of 1-year-old shoots; flowers in neat, vertical, twin rows, perianth to 2.5 cm long, white-grey at the recurved apex; style to 4 cm long, strongly hooked and bright red at first, straightening to orange-brown; flowering in September-October.

Fruit. An ovoid cone, 2–3 cm across, densely white-tomentose, ripening in summer and persisting through winter.

Other distinguishing features. The Scarlet Banksia is one of the most colourful species, its flowers held well above the foliage. Useful in eastern Australian gardens on well-drained sandy or gravelly soils, and becoming important for its durable cut flowers.

Climatic range. A, B, M, P, S.

Bánksia collìna (Latin 'from the hills', describing the plant's habitat): Hill Banksia or Golden Candlestick Banksia: southern Vic. to southern Qld, mostly on the dry gravelly ridges of the coastal plains or lower mountain slopes. Abundant in the Royal National Park, south of Sydney.

Habit. A loose, open shrub to 2–3 m when growing on its typical poor soil, but taller, more erect, and with a dense foliage when on well-drained loamy or sandy soils with adequate water.

Leaves. Linear, 7–8 cm long, 5–6 mm wide; petiole 3–4 mm, grey-tomentulose; apex obtuse or truncate, with several spiny points; margin sharply serrate; midrib yellowish and prominent beneath; glabrous, shiny and dark green above, white beneath, with a dense woolly tomentum.

Flowers. Inflorescence a dense terminal spike to 15 cm long and 7 cm broad, borne at the junctions of the lateral shoots; flowers yellow-bronze, with deep purplish-black, wiry styles, reverse-hooked 5–6 mm from the end, straightening when mature, flowering mainly from late spring to autumn but then irregularly through winter.

Fruit. A vertical cone to 15 cm, with a few woody, glabrous follicles.

Other distinguishing features. Upper young twigs crimson, densely hirsute with whitish-grey hairs but becoming glabrous in the third year.

The Hill Banksia is common around the Sydney coastline and deserves greater use by planting authorities and garden designers for its beautifully contoured form and excellent foliage.

Climatic range. B, M, P, S, the coastal areas of A and the lower levels of Mts.

Bánksia ericifólia (Latin 'with *Erica*-like leaves'): Heath-leafed Banksia: coastal NSW from the mid South Coast to the mid North Coast, mostly on the Hawkesbury sandstones and sandy heathlands, and on the lower levels of the Blue Mountains.

Habit. A shrub to 3–5 m tall, with a broad hemispherical crown densely clothed with leaves.

Leaves. Acicular to linear, 1.2–1.5 cm long, 1 mm wide; apex bifid, with 2 small, horny points; margin entire but fully revolute; glandular-dotted and dark green above, white beneath, with a green midrib.

Flowers. Inflorescence a cylindrical spike, 15–25 cm long and 8 cm wide, like a large bottle-brush, borne abundantly on the inner twigs but partly concealed by the outer foliage;

flowers numerous, arranged in 12 to 15 neat vertical rows; perianths slender, yellow-brown, forming the inner cylinder of the spike; styles long and wiry, red except for the permanently hooked, golden-yellow distal end, forming the outer cylinder; flowers rich in nectar and attractive to small birds, flowering from February to October.

Fruit. A vertical, irregularly cylindrical cone with a few fertilised, woody, greyish follicles projecting from the short wiry surface.

Other distinguishing features. Branchlets mostly whorled in clusters of 2 to 6, the youngest twigs whitish-green, the older bark becoming grey-green.

The Heath-leafed Banksia is probably the most prevalent of the genus in the eastern region, occurring in every national, state or municipal park not yet cleared for organised recreation.

Climatic range. A, B, H, Mts, P, S.

Bánksia ròbur (Latin 'the Oak', referring to the strength of the wood) (syn. *B. latifolia*) Swamp Banksia: the sandy heathlands and swampy plateaus of coastal NSW and southern QLD; abundant in the Royal National Park and Ku-ring-gai National Park, NSW.

Habit. A shrub 1.5–2.5 m tall, but usually broader to 3 m, with an irregular, open habit, the coarse tomentose branches carrying the handsome foliage and flowers.

Leaves. Narrowly elliptic to obovate, to 15–25 cm or more, 4–8 cm wide; petiole stout, 2–3 cm, brownish-tomentose; apex obtuse, shallowly retuse or emarginate; margin serrate, with irregular, sharp teeth; midrib yellowish and prominent, the main laterals widely angled; tomentose and rusty-red at first, persisting beneath, but becoming glabrous and dark green above.

Flowers. Inflorescence a dense cylindrical spike, 10–15 cm tall, 8–10 cm wide, borne at the terminals of the previous year's shoots, surrounded by a whorl of 3 or more spreading 1-year-old branchlets; yellowish- or bluish-green at first, deepening to bronze-green with black stigmas, flowering mainly from early September to early autumn while the plant is in active growth, but occasionally at other seasons.

Fruit. In a vertical cone, 10–15 cm tall, the 1–2 cm wide woody follicles partly concealed by the dry, grey residual flowers.

Other distinguishing features. Young shoots densely downy with a fine, rusty-red tomentum.

The best of the shrubby Banksias for gardens or sites with poorly drained soil; not tolerant of dry, gravelly soils but easy to cultivate on sandy soils within reach of permanent water.

Climatic range. B, M, P, S, T, and in warm seaside localities in A.

Bánksia spinulòsa (diminutive of the Latin *spinal*, 'a thorn', describing the small spines at or near the leaf apices): Hairpin Banksia: eastern Australia from Vic. to southern Qld, mostly on rocky or gravelly ridge soils. Widespread on the upper plateaus of the Royal National Park and Ku-ring-gai National Park, NSW.

Very similar in most characteristics to *B. collina* but differing in foliage, the leaves being more slender to 2 mm wide, the leaf apex is 3-pronged, the sharp teeth 0.5 mm long, and the margins are mostly entire, except for a few occasional teeth near the apex. It appears to be better adapted to dry soils, but this observation may not be conclusive.

Climatic range. A, M, P, S, and on the lower levels of Mts.

BAUÈRA

Commemorating the brothers Franz and Ferdinand Bauer, Austrian botanical illustrators, associated with Sir Joseph Banks, the author of the genus.

Dog Rose: Showy Bauera or Grampians Dog Rose.

Baueraceae, the Bauera family.

Generic description. A small genus of 3 species indigenous to eastern Australia. All are evergreen shrubs, the leaves opposite, trifoliolate, but with a 6-whorled appearance, and with small stellate flowers in the upper axils.

Propagation. Soft-tip cuttings taken between spring and early winter strike readily in a sand/peat mixture in a cool, humid atmosphere; bottom heat and mist are an advantage with winter cuttings.

Cultivation. A moist, sandy or fibrous loam is best, with water freely available in summer; the cool shade of taller plants is an advantage but they enjoy some sun; tolerant of cold to –5°C.

Pruning. The plants respond to a light annual pruning after flowering to establish a twiggy, leafy habit which flowers more abundantly.

Species and cultivars

Bauèra rubioìdes (Latin 'resembling *Rubia*', the Madder of southern Europe and Asia): Dog Rose: widespread along the eastern Australian coast from the sea to the tablelands, usually in moist, shady places on the banks of permanent streams.

Habit. An evergreen shrub to about 1 m, of broad, straggling habit, often almost prostrate, but responding well to pruning to more regular form.

Leaves. Compound, opposite, trifoliolate, the 3 leaflets lanceolate to oblanceolate, 8–15 mm long and 2–4 mm wide; apex acute; margin ciliate; glandular-dotted; dark green above, paler beneath, becoming reddish in winter.

Flowers. Solitary, on slender reddish pedicels to 1 cm near the terminals of the upper twigs; calyx stellate, to 1 cm across, with about 8 persistent, lanceolate sepals, reddish and pubescent; corolla crateriform, to 1.5 cm across, the 6 to 10 oblanceolate petals deep carmine-pink with a white midrib; stamens about 40, with yellow anthers; flowering from early September to late November, then intermittently throughout summer; flower colour variable from a deep pink to white.

Fruit. 2-celled capsule with several oval seeds, ripening in summer.

Climatic range. H, M, Mts, S and on cool, moist sites in A and P.

Bauèra sessiliflòra (Latin 'with sessile flowers'): Showy Bauera or Grampians Dog Rose: The Grampians, western Vic.

Habit. An evergreen shrub of 1 to 2 m, with a dense twiggy habit forming a broad bush of irregular shape.

Leaves. Compound, opposite, trifoliolate, the leaflets lanceolate to oblanceolate, 8–20 mm long and 2–5 mm wide; apex acute; margin entire-ciliate; glandular-dotted and with sparse shaggy hairs above, densely pubescent beneath; upper surface bright green, paler below.

Flowers. Solitary or in pairs in the axils of the upper shoots; sessile; calyx campanulate to 1.5–2.0 mm, pubescent, with 6 lobes to 2 mm long, green, tinged with red; corolla funnelform to rotate, of 5 or 6 oblanceolate petals 6–8 mm long and 3 mm wide, forming a showy flower about 1.5 m across, cyclamen-purple with slightly deeper veins; stamens 10 or 12, the filaments purple, the anthers black-purple, flowering from late August to late November.

Fruit. Not seen.

Other distinguishing features. Upper twigs reddish-brown, with fine tomentum.

Climatic range. H, M, Mts, and on cool, moist, sheltered sites in A, P, and S.

BAUHÍNIA

Commemorating the Swiss botanist/herbalist brothers Bauhin.

South African Orchid Bush.

Caesalpiniaceae, the Caesalpinia family.

Generic description. A variable genus of more than 150 species, comprising trees, shrubs and climbers, all from the warmer climates of both hemispheres and all marked by the bilobed leaves with a short awn between the lobes, the open-funnelform, 5-petalled flowers, and the long, flat legumes containing the round, disc-like seeds. The species described below is one of the most ornamental and useful in warm climates with only light or no frosts. The taller, tree-like species of Bauhinia are described in the companion volume 'Ornamental Flowering Trees in Australia'. (q.v.)

Propagation. Seeds should be sown as soon as fully ripe, preferably in a warm glass-house. Seedlings need protection from cold until all risk of frost is over.

Cultivation. The species described below is best grown in rich, friable, well-drained soil in a warm place, preferably exposed to full sun, but protected from cold or salty winds. In marginal climates it is an advantage to plant on elevated ground to allow cold air to drain away freely below.

Pruning. *B. gálpinii* may be grown as a free-standing shrub when it is improved with moderate annual shortening of the flowered shoots after each flowering period. Alternatively, it is often trained as an espalier by shortening the facial shoots appropriately and by tying the long lateral stems to a suitable support.

Species and cultivars

Bauhínia gálpinii (commemorating E. E. Galpin, South African botanical author): South African Orchid Bush: eastern Transvaal.

Habit. An evergreen shrub of sprawling, horizontally inclined habit, 2–3 m tall but often 3–4 m broad.

Leaves. Simple, alternate, bilobed and often nearly orbicular but with the typical awn between the lobes, 4–8 cm long and as broad, the petiole to 1 cm; apex of each lobe very blunt; base obtuse to cordate; margin entire; venation reticulate, with 7 main veins radiating from the base; mid green and glabrous above, paler beneath, slightly pubescent on the main veins.

Flowers. Inflorescence a short terminal or axillary raceme of 6–12 flowers; calyx spathe-like, splitting along its inner side; petals 5, with a slender claw and round limb to 3.5 cm long, radiating equally from the centre; brick-red, flowering abundantly from January to April.

Fruit. A flat, woody legume, 10–15 cm long and 2–3 cm wide, knife-like on one edge but thickened on the other, green at first, then ripening to reddish-brown in early winter; seeds 2 to 6, flat, button-like, brown.

Climatic range. B, T, and on warm sites in S.

BEGÒNIA

Commemorating Michel Begon, seventeenth-century French botanist and Governor of Santo Domingo.

Begonia (various).

Begoniaceae, the Begonia family.

Generic description. A large and varied genus of over 900 species and hybrids, some of great value as ornamental shade-loving plants and grown especially for their wealth of showy bloom and sometimes striking foliage. Leaves are simple, alternate, stipular and mostly oblique, either smooth or hairy, and most are attractively coloured. Flowers are borne in branching cymes over the crown of the plant, on laterals issuing from the erect main stems, or in the upper axils of the tall canes of the bamboo type; flowers are monoecious, the males with large showy petals, the females usually smaller but with an attractive, 3-winged ovary subtending the flowers, which may be white, pink, or red; the ovaries contain numerous fine seeds. The species treated here are permanent plants, not annuals or tuberous-rooted, but suitable for outdoor cultivation, preferably with some shelter.

Propagation. a) cuttings are the most reliable form of propagation; nodal cuttings of 5–15 cm, depending upon internodal length, are taken between early spring and autumn, planted in individual containers of sand and peat and placed in a warm, humid atmosphere, the striking medium kept a little drier than is customary. b) Well-matured plants may often be divided into several divisions, preferably in late winter, some leaves being removed to reduce the transpiration rate during the re-establishment period.

Cultivation. Begonias grow best in a friable, fertile soil, ideally somewhat sandy and well drained, but given adequate water during dry times. They enjoy winter sunshine but need protection from summer heat and violent dry winds. Warm, humid climates are best, with low temperatures not exceeding 2°C.

Pruning. A few of the oldest shoots should be pruned away at the base each year in early spring to encourage the growth of new water-shoots; spent inflorescences should be removed after flowering to keep the plant tidy.

Species and cultivars

Begònia coccínea (Latin 'scarlet'): Scarlet Tree Begonia or Bamboo Begonia: Orgaos Mountains of south-eastern Brazil.

Habit. An evergreen species, with erect bamboo-like stems to 2–3 m tall from a crowded base.

Leaves. Obliquely ovate-oblong, to 15–18 cm long and 6–8 cm wide; apex acuminate; base obliquely cordate; margin wavy, coarsely dentate; glabrous and glossy; dark green above, paler beneath, or reddish in the seedlings and cultivars.

Flowers. Inflorescence a large, pendulous cyme from the axils of the upper branches and main stems, the rachis glabrous, scarlet, swollen at the joints; flowers numerous, the staminate flowers rotate, about 1.5 cm across, the 4 petals unequal, the stamens short, with golden-yellow anthers; pistillate flowers larger, subtended by a showy ovary with 3 fin-like wings, the whole 4.5–5.0 cm long, bright coral-red and of waxy texture, flowering from October to early winter.

'**Álba**' is similar but has white flowers.

'**Càrnea**' has flesh-pink flowers.

Begonia coccinea has been hybridised with many other species, giving rise to some hybrids of exceptional merit, of which the following are representative:

'**Beatrice Roseby**' has erect growth to about 2 m tall, large green leaves margined with dull red, and large bunches of soft pink flowers.

'**Corallina de Lucerna**' grows to about 2 m tall,

the leaves 20–25 cm long, dark green with silver spots above, and deep metallic-red beneath; flowers are rosy-red, borne in large pendulous clusters 15–20 cm across.

'**Dora Gould**' is very similar to 'Beatrice Roseby' but has salmon-pink flowers in large pendulous trusses.

'**Mabel Roseby**' has large clusters of near-white flowers; leaves are metallic-green above and reddish beneath.

'**Madame de Lesseps**' is a tall strong grower to over 2 m, with leaves green above and metallic-red beneath; flowers are in heavy clusters, white, the showy stamens with golden-yellow anthers.

'**Mrs Christian Thornett**' is taller than usual to 2.5 m, with large white flowers, and green leaves heavily spotted with white.

'**President Carnot**' has erect growth habit 1–2 m tall, the white-spotted, green leaves large and very showy, metallic-red beneath; flowers are bright red.

'**Smithii**' has bronze-green leaves above with metallic-red beneath, and large clusters of rose-pink flowers.

Begònia x *credneri:* Interspecific hybrid between *B. metallica* and *B. scharffiana*.
Habit. A leafy shrub to about 1 m tall, the red stems with white pubescence.
Leaves. Obliquely-ovate, 12–18 cm long and 9–12 cm wide, the petioles 8–15 cm long; margins coarsely dentate; dark olive-green and shiny above, pubescent, crimson beneath, white-pubescent, especially on the prominent veins.
Flowers. About 2.5 cm across, borne on an erect stem to 30 cm tall, red with white hairs, the calyx with 3 red, spreading, wing-like hairy sepals, the petals white, with a beard of crimson hairs; flowering from late spring to autumn.
Fruit. None — the plant is sterile.

Begònia x *íngramii:* (Commemorating Collingwood Ingram, English botanical author): interspecific hybrid between *B. nitida* and *B. fuschioides.*
Habit. An attractive bushy shrub about 1 m tall, with stout basal shoots forming an irregularly-rounded crown.
Leaves. Slender, oblique on a red petiole; margin deeply serrated; metallic-green above, red beneath.
Flowers. Large, in sparse clusters, rose-pink, flowering in autumn and winter.
Fruit. None — the plant is sterile.

Begònia metállica: (Latin 'of metallic colour'): Brazil.
Habit. An attractive erect bush to 1.0–1.5 m.
Leaves. Obliquely-ovate to 12–15 cm long, cordate at the base; coarsely serrate; dark metallic-green and shiny above, paler beneath, with prominent red veins and white pubescence.
Flowers. Clustered on an erect peduncle, white with dense white hairs, the general colour appearing as pink.
Climatic range. All B M P S T and in sheltered warm parts of A.

BÉRBERIS

The latinised form is derived from *Berberys*, the Arabic vernacular name for the plant.
Barberry (various).
Berberidaceae, the Barberry family.

Generic description. A large genus of ornamental shrubs, mostly from the northern temperate zone, with both evergreen and deciduous species, all with simple leaves, (thus differing from the always-imparipinnate leaves of *Mahonia*), yellow flowers, solitary or in umbels, racemes, or panicles, at the terminals of the youngest shoots or in the upper axils, the flowers with 6 sepals and 6 petals in series of 3; fruit is a small globose or ellipsoidal berry, red, blue, or black, often with a blue or whitish bloom; the wood and inner bark of stems and roots is yellow; spines, actually modified leaves, are either simple or 3-parted, very sharp and dangerous to handle. The species described are amongst the hardiest ornamental and fruiting plants, especially valued in austere climates for their flowers, foliage, and/or fruits; some are useful as hedges where the sharp spines may be an advantage.

Propagation. a) Seeds germinate readily if collected as soon as ripe in autumn/winter, cleaned of the outer pulp and sown at once in a warm, moist atmosphere; alternatively, they may be sown out-of-doors in a cool, moist place to germinate in spring.
b) Clonal material, or species whose seeds are not available, must be vegetatively propagated by soft-tip cuttings taken in spring to autumn, or more mature tips in winter, planted in a sand/peat mixture in a warm, humid atmosphere.
c) Hardwood cuttings of deciduous species and cultivars strike readily in the open if planted

deeply in a moist, friable medium, in prepared beds or in separate containers.

Cultivation. Any friable, well-drained soil of reasonable fertility is suitable; a fully sun-exposed position is essential, especially for the coloured-foliaged sorts. Additional irrigation in times of drought will maintain the quality of the leaves and ensure better autumnal colour. Clean cultivation, especially of stoloniferous plants such as couch-grass, should be maintained because of the danger from the sharp spines when weeding near a Berberis. In uncut hedges, this practice is especially necessary, otherwise the hedge may become completely overgrown by an aggressive grass like kikuyu.

Pruning. *B. thunbergii* 'Atropurpurea' and *B. x ottawensis* 'Superba' are grown for the quality and colour of their purple leaves and respond well to hard pruning of at least half the annual growth in late winter. Other deciduous cultivars, grown for their foliage, may be pruned lightly, but the natural dwarfs should not be treated severely. *B. wilsoniae* should have several of the oldest basal shoots removed completely each winter, after the fruits have fallen, to make space for new young growth from the base. *B. darwinii* requires little attention apart from shortening any straggling branchlets.

Species and cultivars

Bérberis dárwinii (commemorating Charles Darwin and his scientific expedition of 1835 to the native habitat of the species in *Beagle*): Darwin Barberry: Chile and Argentina, generally in latitudes 35° to 55° S.

Habit. An evergreen shrub, 2.0–3.5 m tall, of irregular and somewhat open branching habit unless subjected to regular pruning. A very handsome plant in foliage and flower, suitable for specimen, hedging or walling.

Leaves. Alternate or in closely set fascicles, obovate, but trilobed at the apex, 2–3 cm long, 1.0–1.3 cm wide; petiole 2 mm; apex lobes each with a sharp spine 1–2 mm long; base cuneate; margin occasionally entire, but usually with 4 spiny serrations; glabrous; dark green and lustrous above, pale yellowish-green below.

Flowers. Inflorescence a drooping axillary raceme, 7–10 cm long; flowers to 20 or more, with 2 sets of yellow sepals, 3 large and 3 small, petals 6, to 8–10 mm long, 5–6 mm across, deep golden-yellow, with some scarlet markings outside; stamens 6, forming a cage-like structure around the single clavate pistil; filaments yellow, anthers cream; flowering period from early October to December.

Fruit. A raceme of 12–15 ellipsoidal to globose berries, 6–8 mm long, in summer; the capitate style 3 mm long, persisting throughout.

Other distinguishing features. Upper twigs with a dense, rufous pubescence. Spines at the nodes divided into claw-like fans of 5–7 sharp points to 4–6 mm long.

Climatic range. H, M, Mts, and in cool, elevated microclimates in A, P, and S.

Bérberis x ottawénsis 'Purpùrea' (Latin 'from Ottawa', and Greek — *porphura*;): The misnamed *B. thunbergii* 'Superba' of the trade: the interspecific hybrid of *B. thunbergii* and *B. vulgaris*, developed at the Ottawa Experimental Station.

Habit. A deciduous shrub to 2 m or so and as wide, with globose form.

Leaves. Alternate, or whorled in fascicles of 3–4 on most nodes, obovate, 3–5 cm long, 1.5–2.0 cm wide, the blade tapering finely into the short petiole; apex obtuse-mucronate; base cuneate; margin mostly entire but occasionally remotely spinose (indicative of the leaves of *B. vulgaris*); glabrous; dark maroon-purple above, greenish-purple beneath, turning to orange-scarlet and purple in autumn.

Flowers. In small umbels of about 6–12, cup-shaped, 6–8 mm across, yellow, with reddish sepals outside, flowering sparsely in October and November.

Fruit. A small ellipsoidal berry to 1 cm long and 4–5 mm wide, bright scarlet and glossy, produced sparsely in April-June, containing a single, slender, brown seed embedded in a thin, yellowish pulp.

Other distinguishing features. Twigs dark reddish-brown, with 4–8 shallow longitudinal ridges; nodal spines single or 3-fold, to 1.3 cm long, slender, very sharp, reddish-brown; inner bark and wood yellow.

Climatic range. A, H, M, Mts, P, S.

Bérberis sargentiàna (commemorating Charles S. Sargent, botanical author and Director of the Arnold Arboretum at Boston, Mass.): Sargent Barberry: western Hupeh in central China, at an elevation of 1500 m or more.

Habit. An evergreen shrub to 2–3 m tall, with an open framework of long flexible shoots, made pendulous by the weight of the fruit in season.

PLATE 3

▲ Calliandra haematocephala

▲ Boronia muelleri
▶ Berberis thunbergii 'Atropurpurea Nana'
▼ Boronia heterophylla

▲ Boronia heterophylla

▲ Bauhinia galpinii

▼ Boronia 'Telopea Valley Star'

PLATE 4

▲ Cassia eremophila

▲ Callistemon phoeniceus

▲ Callistemon 'Candy Pink'
► Cassia artemisioides
▼ Callistemon viminalis 'Captain Cook'

▼ Callistemon 'Harkness'

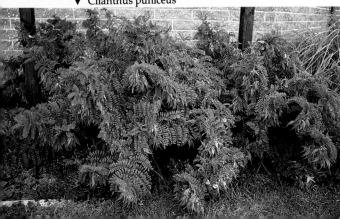

▼ Clianthus puniceus

Leaves. Alternate on young vigorous shoots but in 3- to 8-leafed fascicles at the older nodes, narrowly elliptic to oblong-lanceolate, 5–10 cm long and 1.5–2.5 cm wide; apex acute but spinose; base cuneate to the 5 mm petiole; margin serrate, the 20 or more teeth on each side spinose; midrib prominent beneath; glabrous and coriaceous; reddish when young, then dark green and lustrous above, light yellow-green beneath, some leaves turning yellow to red in autumn.

Flowers. Inflorescence a small umbel of 10–15 or more flowers, on slender 2.5 cm pedicels from the short axillary spurs; buds ellipsoidal at first but opening to narrow-campanulate, about 5 mm long and 6–8 mm wide, with pale-yellow petals, flowering from October to December.

Fruits. A small ellipsoidal, 1-seeded berry about 7 mm long and 4–5 mm wide, 10 or more toegther in the axils of the 1-year-old wood, dark bluish-black, slightly pruinose, ripening in April-May, a disc-shaped cap at the distal end of each fruit.

Other distinguishing features. Upper shoots glabrous, red at first but maturing to pale grey, with several ridges extending down from the nodes; internodes somewhat zig-zagged; spines 3-pronged, at 90° angle from the stem, at the nodes, 4–6 cm long, slender, woody, pale brown, very sharp.

Climatic range. H, M, Mts, and in cool, elevated microclimates in A, P, and S.

Bérberis x *stenophýlla* (Greek 'with narrow leaves'): interspecific hybrid between *B. darwinii* and *B. empetrifolia*): Narrow-leafed Barberry.

Habit. A mostly evergreen shrub to 2.5 m tall, with slender, arching branches from the base, carrying the abundant foliage, flowers and fruit.

Leaves. Linear to slightly oblanceolate, 1.5–2.0 cm long, 2–4 mm wide; apex spinose; base finely cuneate; margin entire but revolute; lustrous dark green above, whitish-green beneath.

Flowers. Inflorescence an axillary raceme of 4–10 flowers; flowers large, to 8–10 mm, on slender 6–7 mm pedicels, the long branchlets clothed with flowers over a length of 0.5 m or more; deep sulphur-yellow, flowering from early October to late November.

Fruit. A sub-globose berry to 8 mm across, several to about 10 together, blue-black, with a pruinose bloom, fruiting in April-May.

Other distinguishing features. Spines single or 3-parted, to 7–8 mm long, the middle spine the largest, all slender and very sharp; youngest twigs pubescent, becoming reddish-brown and glabrous.

Climatic range. A, H, M, Mts, P, S.

Bérberis thúnbergii (commemorating Dr Carl P. Thunberg, celebrated Swedish botanical explorer in the Orient and author of *Flora Japonica* and *Flora Capensis*): Japanese Barberry: central and southern islands of Japan.

Habit. A deciduous shrub to about 1 m tall and 1.5 m wide, with dense, twiggy growth forming a leafy, bun-shaped bush.

Leaves. Alternate on young shoots, but clustered in fascicles at the older nodes, obovate to spathulate, 2–3 cm long; apex obtuse or acute with a small mucro; base cuneate; margin entire; glabrous; bright green above, slightly blue-green beneath, becoming yellow, orange and scarlet in autumn.

Flowers. Solitary, or mostly in a few-flowered umbel of 3–5 together, cup-shaped to 8 mm across, with 6 petals and 6 sepals, pale sulphur-yellow, flowering from late September to November.

Fruit. An ellipsoidal fleshy berry to 8–10 mm long, lustrous scarlet, fully ripe and coloured by late April but persisting throughout winter.

Other distinguishing features. Spines at the axils simple or only very rarely 3-fold, slender, 1.5–2.0 cm long, very sharp and dangerous to handle; stems prominently grooved longitudinally; inner bark and wood of stems and roots yellow.

'Atropurpùrea': Purple Japanese Barberry: Japanese cultivar. Has taller growth to at least 2 m or more, with many upright branches from the base; leaves dark reddish-purple, changing to brilliant claret-red in autumn; flowers and fruit are produced normally if the plant is not pruned, but it is usually grown for its leaves and then pruned severely in late winter.

'Aùrea' resembles 'Atropurpurea' in growth habit but is smaller, to about 1 m tall and wide, with yellow foliage, especially bright in spring but becoming yellowish-green in summer and autumn. Needs to be grown in a sunny place to produce the best colour.

'Atropurpùrea Nàna' (syn. 'Little Favourite') of dwarf habit, seldom more than 0.5 m tall, with dense, twiggy growth, small leaves and the reddish-purple colour of 'Atropurpurea'.

'Keller's Surprise' (syn. 'Keller's Variety') similar to 'Atropurpurea Nana' in growth habit but has bright-green leaves, splashed and spotted with reddish-maroon, pink, and white at first, but gradually losing the reddish cast as the growth rate declines in autumn.

'**Superba**' is now *Berberis* x *ottawensis* 'Purpurea' (q.v.).

Climatic range. A, B, H, M, Mts, P, S.

Berberis wilsóniae (commemorating the wife of Ernest H. Wilson, botanical explorer of the Orient): Wilson's Barberry: Yunnan and Szechwan, western China.

Habit. A mostly deciduous shrub, but becoming more evergreen in warm climates, to 1.0–1.5 m tall with a hemispherical shape, somewhat irregular in outline, and fine, twiggy branchlets.

Leaves. In alternately arranged fascicles of 4–8 leaves, from 1.5 to 3.0 cm long and 6–8 mm wide, broadly oblanceolate; apex rounded or acute-mucronate; margin entire; glabrous; mid to grey-green above, glaucous beneath, dull on both surfaces, changing to yellow, orange, and red in autumn, the more vivid in cool climates.

Flowers. Inflorescence a small umbel of 6–10 flowers on 3 mm pedicels; flowers 5–8 mm across, deep golden-yellow, flowering from early October to December.

Fruit. A broadly ellipsoidal or globose berry to 7 mm long and 5–6 mm wide, with a short, peg-like apical style, in small bunches up to about 10, borne closely against the 1- and 2-year-old wood in autumn, usually lasting from April to July; fruits apricot-pink at first but ripening to deep coral-red, pruinose, but somewhat translucent.

Other distinguishing features. Upper twigs angular, with prominent ridges, mid-brown to purplish; spines 3-parted, the central spine the longest to 1 cm long, all sharp and slender.

Climatic range. A, H, M, Mts, P, S.

BORÒNIA

Commemorating the Italian botanist, Francesco Borone, 1769–1794.

Boronia (various).

Rutaceae, the Rue family.

Generic description. Evergreen, Australian native shrubs of more than 50 species, well-known for their showy, often-perfumed flowers and attractive foliage. The leaves are simple or compound, some highly aromatic, flowers are star-shaped, with 4 petals and 4 sepals, borne singly or in small clusters amongst the upper twigs, and fruit is a 4-loculed capsule, splitting when ripe to scatter the small, smooth brown or black seeds.

Propagation. a) Seeds, collected as soon as ripe, may be sown fresh in a friable material in a warm atmosphere, but germination is sometimes erratic;

b) Firm tip cuttings, taken between mid spring and late summer, strike readily in a coarse sand in a cool, humid atmosphere, and are preferred by most growers.

Cultivation. While each species has individual preferences in climate, soil, and other environmental features, most boronias enjoy certain common conditions such as well-drained sandy soil, with a low organic content and with free aeration, as well as protection from strong, direct sunlight and drying winds, and with sufficient water to maintain an even water-status in the soil, especially in spring and summer. Mulches of pebbles or large flat 'floater' stones are useful in maintaining a uniformly cool root-run and in conserving soil water in dry times. Organic mulches, especially of fine-textured material such as compost, lawn clippings and peat are often detrimental if placed close to the crown of the plant's root system, because of the possible development of collar-rot.

Pruning. Very light pruning of the recently-flowered shoots only is helpful in stimulating a more dense growth, and extends the otherwise rather short life span considerably. A moderate dressing of blood and bone fertiliser, at 50 g/m^2 at time of pruning encourages new growth.

Species and cultivars

Borònia anemonifòlia (Latin 'with Anemone-like leaves'): eastern Australia, mainly on cool, well-drained sites on the tablelands.

Habit. A shrub to about 1 m tall with a bun-shaped crown to 1.5 m broad, with arching stems from the base.

Leaves. Compound, trifoliolate, variable but commonly 3–4 cm long and about as broad; leaflets simple or branched near the apex, thick and somewhat fleshy, 5–15 mm long, furrowed and dark green above, paler below; glandular and strongly aromatic.

Flowers. In a small axillary umbel of 1 to 3 flowers on 30–40 cm long drooping sprays; calyx green, with acute sepals; corolla stellate, about 1 cm across, the 4 petals ovate, deep rose-pink in the bud, opening to blush-pink; stamens 8, in a cage-like cone 2 mm tall, the filaments white-hairy with yellow anthers; lightly fragrant; flowering from early September to December.

Fruit. Not seen.

Other distinguishing features. Upper twigs dull green, glandular, with internodal stripes of brown pubescence. **var.** *variábilis* is considered to be a superior form with broader, thicker leaves, mostly 5-foliolate, and slightly paler flowers.

Climatic range. H, M, Mts, and on cool sites in A, P, S.

Borònia crenulàta (Latin 'leaves with a finely crenate margin). Southern coast of WA, mainly on the sandy heathlands around Albany.

Habit. A small shrub to 0.5–1.0 m tall with slender shoots, rarely bushy, but of dainty form, roughly hemispherical when mature.

Leaves. Simple, opposite, obovate, to 1 cm long and 3–4 mm wide; petiole 1 mm long; apex shortly acute; margin entire, but becoming finely crenulate above the middle; glabrous; finely glandular-dotted and slightly aromatic; dull, dark green on both surfaces.

Flowers. Inflorescence a 1–3-flowered cyme in the opposite axils of the upper shoots, forming a racemose spray to 10–15 cm long just below the terminals; calyx reddish-green; petals imbricate in the bud, forming a slender cone, but spreading to stellate form to 1.3 cm across, pale carmine-pink, the outside with a deep carmine-red stripe; stamens 8, the white, densely pubescent filaments to 2 mm, with green anthers; flowers produced from late August to October.

Other distinguishing features. Upper twigs squarish, green, but stained red above, puberulent.

Climatic range. A, B, M, P, S, and in warm, sheltered microclimates in Mts.

Borònia dèanei (commemorating Henry Deane, one-time Engineer-in-Chief of the NSW Government Railways): Deane's Boronia: Central and Southern Tablelands of NSW.

Habit. An erect shrub, 1–2 m tall, the slender branches arching outwards from the base, drooping slightly at the ends.

Leaves. Simple, opposite, slenderly linear, 5–10 mm long; apex obtuse, margin entire but recurved; aromatic when bruised; dark green above, paler and warted beneath.

Flowers. In small terminal cymes, conical in the bud, opening to stellate form, 10–12 mm across, the 4 ovate petals reflexed when fully open; rosy-magenta at first, maturing to rose-pink, mauve-pink or white, flowering in October and November.

Other distinguishing features. Young twigs grey-green, often roughened by warty oil glands.

Climatic range. H, M, Mts, and on cool, moist sites in A, P, and S.

Borònia denticulàta (Latin 'with minutely dentate margin'): Mauve Boronia: southern coast of WA.

Habit. An upright shrub to 1 m or so tall, with thin, open growth unless frequently pruned, when it develops a globose form to 1 m wide.

Leaves. Simple, opposite, linear, 2.5–3.5 cm long and 3–4 mm wide, almost sessile; apex acute, with a soft bristly point; margin denticulate with marginal glands; midrib alone evident; minutely glandular, and aromatic when bruised; dark green.

Flowers. Inflorescence terminal above the upper leaves, in a mass of 3-flowered cymes, flowers conical in the bud, the 4 petals broad-ovate, forming a stellate flower 1.5–2.0 cm across, and reflexing fully when open; mauve-pink, flowering from early September to late October; stamens 8, the glandular filaments incurved and ciliate, with orange anthers.

Other distinguishing features. Upper twigs terete, but glandular-warty, dark green and shiny.

Climatic range. A, B, M, P, S, and in warm, sheltered microclimates in Mts.

Borònia floribúnda (Latin 'with abundant flowers'): Pale-pink Boronia: Central NSW, mainly on well-drained sites on the sandstone ridges between the coast and the Blue Mountains, but occasionally on loamy soils with free drainage.

Habit. A slender shrub to 1 m or more tall, somewhat sparse in growth, but flowering abundantly on slender twigs.

Leaves. Compound, opposite, imparipinnate, the winged rachis to 2.5 cm long; leaflets usually 5 to 9, in opposite pairs, lanceolate to narrowly-oblong, 1.5–2.0 cm long and 2–5 mm wide; apices acute-mucronate; bases often oblique; margins entire; finely glandular-dotted; glabrous; bright green above, paler beneath; aromatic when bruised.

Flowers. Inflorescence a series of small cymes in the axils of the upper twigs; calyx 5–6 mm across, with spreading green sepals; petals 4, opening to form a stellate flower 2 cm across, the petals broadly ovate, acuminate, pale pink to nearly white or uncommonly rose-pink, glabrous and waxy, flowering from early September to November; stamens 8, the filaments with green anthers, bearing a tuft of whitish woolly hair; flowers mildly fragrant.
Other distinguishing features. Upper twigs squarish, with distinct decurrent ridges below the nodes, green when young, becoming brown.
Climatic range. A, B, M, P, S, and on warm, sheltered sites on lower elevations of Mts.

Borònia fràseri (commemorating Charles Fraser, 1789–1831, first Superintendent of the Royal Botanic Gardens, Sydney): Fraser's Boronia: central NSW, on a variety of moist sites from the heathlands of the Royal National Park to the sheltered slopes of the Blue Mountains.
Habit. One of the taller boronias growing to 1.5 m tall, often thin and lanky in the subdued light of the gullies but denser in the open, especially when pruned annually.
Leaves. Compound, opposite, imparipinnate, the winged rachis about 3 cm long, with mostly 3 or 5 leaflets in opposite arrangement, oblanceolate-oblong to 2 cm long dark green and almost glabrous; glandular and aromatic when bruised.
Flowers. In an axillary umbel of 5 or 6 cruciate flowers to 1.5 cm across, the 4 petals broadly ovate, strongly ribbed, deep rose-pink, borne on 4-angled reddish stems; flowering season from early September to December.
Fruit. Not seen.
Climatic range. A. H, M, Mts, P, S.

Borònia heterophýlla (Greek 'with different or variable leaves'): Kalgan or Red Boronia: southern coast of WA, mainly on low-lying sites around Albany.
Habit. A dense shrub to 1.5 m or so tall, with erect twiggy growth, improved in density by regular pruning.
Leaves. Variable, some simple and linear, 2.5–3.5 cm long and 2–3 mm wide, others imparipinnate, to 3.5 cm long with 3 or 5 leaflets; apices acute; bases tapered to the narrowly winged rachis; margins entire; glabrous; glandular-dotted and aromatic when bruised; dull, dark green above, paler beneath.

Flowers. Solitary in the opposite axils of the upper leaves, forming a racemose spray 15 to 20 cm long; calyx reddish-green, the spreading, ovate sepals with acute apices; buds conical, imbricate, opening to an urceolate-campanulate flower 9–10 cm long and 8–9 cm wide, of variable colour, some fuchsia-purple, others phlox-pink, rose-pink to magenta-rose; strongly perfumed, flowering from late September to mid November; stamens 8, the longer 4 with incurved, carmine-red filaments to 2 mm long and heart-shaped, black anthers, the shorter 4 half as long, with yellow anthers.
Climatic range. A, B, M, P, S, and in warm, sheltered microclimates in Mts.

Borònia ledifòlia (Latin 'with leaves like *Ledum*', a North American shrub): Sydney Boronia: NSW, mostly on the sandy heathlands, gravel and sandstone ridges between the coast and the tablelands and in similar habitats in south-eastern Qld.
Habit. A shrub, 1–2 m tall, of sparse, erect growth in its native habitat but responsive to cultivation and pruning, becoming dense and heavily flowered.
Leaves. Variable, from simple to compound, the trifoliolate form usually separated as **var. *triphylla*:** the simple-leafed form has opposite, lanceolate to narrow-elliptic leaves, 2.5–3.5 cm ong and 5–10 mm wide; apex acute to obtuse; base cuneate to the 2 mm petiole; margin entire; recurved; heavily glandular, and aromatic when crushed; glabrous and dull green above, pale green and stellate-tomentose beneath.
Flowers. Solitary or in twos or threes in the upper leaf axils; calyx to 4 mm across, the sepals broad, brownish-red and glandular; petals valvate in the carmine-red, spherical bud, opening to a stellate flower 1.5–2.0 cm across, bright mauve-pink, flowering from early July to late October; stamens 8, forming a small dome in the centre, the filaments pink, anthers yellow.
Other distinguishing features. Upper twigs and branchlets scabrous, with a pebbly-woolly surface, brown and finely tomentose.
Climatic range. A, B, M, P, S, and in sheltered microclimates on the lower levels of Mts.

Borònia megastígma (Greek 'with large stigma'): Brown Boronia: southern coast of WA, mainly around King George Sound, along the fringes of the forest-lands, often on somewhat moist sites.
Habit. A small, thin bush to about 1 m tall with

slender twigs, forming a rounded shape to 0.75 m wide; made more durable by cultivation and regular pruning.

Leaves. Compound, opposite, mostly trifoliolate, the leaflets to 1.3 cm long and 1 mm wide; apex obtuse; margin entire; surface pebbly, with numerous pellucid oil glands; aromatic when bruised; dark green.

Flowers. Solitary or in pairs in the upper axils, forming a raceme 8–10 cm long; calyx reddish-green, 3–4 mm deep, the ovate sepals spreading to 6 mm across; petals orbicular to 7 mm wide, forming a cyathiform flower 1 cm across, dark purplish-black outside and yellowish-green inside, flowering from August to late October; stamens 8, in 2 series of 4, the longer series with large purple-black anthers, the others with creamy-yellow anthers; stigma a large, 4-lobed mound, dark velvety-brown; flowers sweetly and very heavily perfumed.

Other distinguishing features. Upper twigs nearly square, puberulent, yellow-green, becoming grey.

'**Chándleri**' (syn. 'Burgundy') a seedling variant with flowers of deep reddish-burgundy outside and yellow-green inside.

'**Lùtea**' has yellow flowers.

Climatic range. All A, B, M, P, S, and in warm, sheltered microclimates in Mts.

Borònia móllis (Latin 'softly hairy'): Soft Boronia: Central and lower North Coast of NSW between the coast and tablelands, mainly on moist, sheltered sites with better-class soils, or occasionally on the rocky ridges of the Hawkesbury sandstone areas.

Habit. A shrub to 1.5–2.0 m tall with a thin, open habit, but improved by regular pruning to become globose and densely foliaged.

Leaves. Compound, opposite, imparipinnate, the main rachis 2.5–3.0 cm long, winged laterally between the leaflets, and densely stellate-pubescent; leaflets mostly 3, 5 or 7, elliptic-ovate to obovate, 1.5–1.8 cm long, the terminal to 3.5 cm long, and all 6–8 mm wide, sessile; apices obtuse; margins entire but crimped; midrib alone distinct; mid green and dull above, sparsely stellate-pubescent, paler and densely pubescent below; aromatic when bruised.

Flowers. Inflorescence a 4–6-flowered umbel, densely stellate-pubescent; calyx crimson, the linear sepals spreading at first, then reflexed; petals 4, valvate in the conical bud, opening to a neat stellate flower 2 cm across, rosy-purple,

with a deeper purple central rib, glabrous above but pubescent along the rib beneath, flowering from August to late October; stamens 8, with crimson filaments to 1 mm long, and golden anthers, all arising from a 3 mm wide, disc-like receptable.

Other distinguishing features. Upper branchlets and twigs densely stellate-pubescent. '**Lorne Pride**' belongs here as a registered cultivar from the Camden Haven River valley, distinct from the parent species in its compact, hemispherical growth habit to 1.5 m tall and a little broader, and in its tolerance of an open sun-exposed position.

Climatic range. A, B, M, P, S, and on warm, sheltered sites in Mts.

Borònia molloÿae (commemorating Georgiana Molloy, 1805–43, distinguished amateur plant collector in south-west WA) (Syn. *B. elatior*) Tall Boronia: south-west WA on moist, sheltered sites between King George Sound and Cape Naturaliste.

Habit. One of the largest of the genus, growing to 2 m or so on favourable sites in the open, but even taller in the reduced light of the forests.

Leaves. Compound, imparipinnate with mostly 5–7 leaflets, occasionally up to 11; leaflets linear, 10–20 mm long, 2–3 mm wide; apices acute with a short sharp point; margin entire; dark green and sparsely hairy above, whitish-green and pubescent beneath.

Flowers. Solitary in the upper axils, the buds conical at first, supported by 4 broadly-ovate pink sepals; petals 4, above 6–8 mm long, overlapped in the buds, broadly ovate, with a short acute apex, opening to cup-shape, dark rose-pink to rosy-red, flowering from mid-September to November.

Fruit. Not seen.

Climatic range. A, B, M, P, S, preferably on sheltered moist sites.

Borònia muèlleri (commemorating Baron Ferdinand von Mueller): von Mueller's Boronia or Tree Boronia: eastern Vic., mainly on better-class forest-lands.

Habit. A shrub, 1.0–2.5 m tall, forming a broad, irregular bush of roughly hemispherical shape, but occasionally in its native habitat, a loose, open, straggly bush.

Leaves. Compound, opposite, imparipinnate, with mostly 7 or 9 leaflets spreading widely from the narrowly winged rachis; leaflets linear, to 1.5

cm long and 2 mm wide, glabrous and dark green, heavily glandular and aromatic when bruised.

Flowers. Inflorescence a 3–5 flowered cyme in the opposite axils of the upper shoots; calyx 4 mm across, with spreading green sepals; buds globular, deep rose-pink, opening to a stellate flower, 1.3 cm across, with 4 spreading, ovate petals, orchid-pink, fading to nearly white when fully mature, flowering abundantly from early September to early November; stamens 8, white to pale green, silky pubescent, the anthers yellow; pistil bright green.

Other distinguishing features. Upper twigs green, slender, glandular.

Climatic range. H, M, Mts, and on cool, moist, sheltered sites in A, P, and S.

Borònia pinnàta (Latin 'with pinnate leaves'): Feather-leafed or Pinnate Boronia: eastern Australia, mostly on sandy or gravelly soils between the coast and the tablelands.

Habit. A shrub to 1.5 cm tall and often wider, loose and sparsely leafed in its native habitat, but responding to cultivation and regular annual pruning with more abundant foliage and flowers.

Leaves. Compound, opposite, pinnate, the main rachis 3–4 cm long with 5 to 9 somewhat-remote leaflets; petiole flattened, slightly winged and grooved above; leaflets sessile, linear, 1.5–2.5 cm long and 2–5 mm wide; apices acute-mucronate; bases obliquely cuneate; margins entire or shallowly notched; glandular-dotted, and strongly aromatic when bruised; dark green and barely shiny above, paler beneath.

Flowers. Inflorescence a series of 3 to 6 small cymes in the upper leaf-axils; calyx claw-like, the sepals spreading, acute, green with crimson tips; flower buds squat-globose, the 4 petals imbricate, but opening to a stellate flower to 2 cm across, pale rosy-mauve to rosy-purple, occasionally nearly white; only mildly fragrant; flowering from early August to November; stamens 8, the greenish-white pubescent filaments with green anthers; pistil green.

Other distinguishing features. Upper twigs smooth, glabrous, green but red above.

'Spring White' is a registered cultivar with clear white flowers.

Climatic range. A, B, M, P, S, T, and on sheltered sites on the lower levels of Mts.

Borònia pilòsa (Latin 'having long, soft hairs'): Hairy Boronia: SE Australia, mainly on sandy heathlands but also on elevated rocky sites.

Habit. A shrub of variable character according to its environment, about 1 m tall; given a cool, undisturbed root-run and regular light pruning, the plant is densely leafy and prolific in flowers.

Leaves. Compound, imparipinnate, like a small claw with mostly linear to terete leaflets about 1 cm long; apices acute to obtuse; margins entire; dark green and softly hairy; glandular and aromatic when bruised.

Flowers. Solitary or in small cymose clusters from the upper leaf axils; calyx reddish-green with 4 acute spreading sepals; corolla stellate, about 1 cm across, the 4 ovate petals with pointed tips; variable from nearly white to deep rosy-magenta; lightly fragrant; stamens 8, forming a claw-like central mass with yellow anthers; flowering seasons early spring to summer.

Fruit. Not seen.

Other distinguishing features. Upper twigs dark reddish-green, softly pubescent.

Climatic range. A, H, M, P, S, and on lower levels of Mts.

Borònia serrulàta (Latin 'with serrulate leaf-margins'): Native Rose: sandstone ridges and heaths of the Sydney to lower Blue Mountains region.

Habit. A small bush to 0.75–1.0 m tall, sometimes loose and open when in poor native soils, but improved by cultivation and regular pruning to a rounded, densely foliaged form.

Leaves. Simple, opposite, obovate or narrowly rhomboidal, 1.5–1.8 cm long and 9–12 mm wide; petiole 1–2 mm long, whitish, flattened above; leaves arranged in a nearly-flat plane by the slight twisting of the petiole; apex acute to acuminate; base cuneate, often obliquely so; margin irregularly and shallowly serrulate, reddish on the edge; glandular; glabrous; dark green, with red shadings at the base, especially when young; aromatic when bruised.

Flowers. Inflorescence a dense terminal cyme of a few to 20 flowers, on 3–5 mm pedicels; calyx with 4 slender, acute sepals to 3–4 mm long, green, with red shadings; flower buds ovoid, cyathiform when mature, rarely opening fully; petals 4, elliptic to ovate, to 1.5 cm long, 9–10 mm wide, rosy-purple to deep rose-pink, fragrant, flowering from late August to October; stamens 8, the pink filaments 3–4 mm long, the anthers cream, hairy; style and broad stigma green.

Other distinguishing features. Upper twigs pale green but almost hidden by the single-planed leaves.

Climatic range. A, B, M, P, S, and on sheltered sites on the lower levels of Mts.

Borònia subulifòlia (Latin 'with awl-shaped leaflets'): Budawang Range and the upper slopes of the Clyde River basin in NSW, in deep sandy soils on sheltered forest land.

Habit. A shrub of 1 m or so tall, forming a dense rounded bush 1–2 m broad.

Leaves. Compound, opposite, imparipinnate, the main rachis 1 cm long, with 7 to 9 subulate leaflets to 1.5 cm long; apices acute-mucronate; base slightly tapered; finely pubescent and minutely glandular; aromatic when bruised; dark green.

Flowers. Solitary in the upper axils, forming a racemose spray 15–18 cm long; pedicels 3–4 mm long, with subulate bracts; calyx lobes green, with red margin; petals valvate at first, later spreading and recurving, 1 cm long and 5–6 mm wide, phlox-purple, paling towards the centre, flowering from late September to November; stamens 8, the white pubescent filaments 2 mm long, with yellow anthers, the floral disc purple, with green pistil.

Climatic range. H, M, Mts, and on cool, moist, sheltered woodland sites in P and S.

BÒSSIAEA

Commemorating Boissieu La Martiniere, botanist with La Perouse's 1785 voyage of exploration to the Pacific and Australia.
Bossiaea or Water Bush.
Fabaceae, the Pea family.

Generic description. An Australian genus of about 50 shrubby species occurring in all States, growing on sandy or other well-drained soils on woodland sites. Leaves are simple, alternate or opposite, almost lacking in some species, apart from minute scales borne on flattened green cladodes which provide for photosynthesis. Flowers are pea-shaped, solitary in the upper axils, mostly yellow but with either red, brown or purplish parts. They are commonly grown in native plantations for their showy flowers.

Propagation. Seeds are lightly scarified or soaked in warm water for 24 hours as a prelude to sowing in a humid atmosphere, preferably in individual containers to minimise root disturbance when planting out.

Cultivation. Almost any sandy or gravelly soil with free drainage is suitable, ideally mulched with coarse vegetative matter to maintain an even water and temperature status in the root zone.

Pruning. Young plants should be tip-pruned early and frequently until the required size and shape are attained, then lightly trimmed annually after the flowering period.

Species and cultivars

Bòssiaea heterophýlla (Greek 'with diverse leaves'): Variable Bossiaea: eastern Australia, on the sandy heathlands of the coast to the lower levels of the adjacent plateaus and tablelands.

Habit. An erect, somewhat thin shrub to 1 m tall; one of the most common plants in the heathland national parks along the NSW coast.

Leaves. Variable, those on the lower terete stems ovate to obovate, those on the upper flattened twigs linear-lanceolate, from 2 to 3.5 cm long, thick, coriaceous, dull grey-green.

Flowers. Pea-shaped, borne singly in the upper axils; calyx campanulate, 5–6 mm long with broad upper lobes, reddish-green; corolla 1.5 cm across, the bilobed standard broad, clear yellow with a small fan of brownish-crimson at the base; wings and keel petals smaller, brownish-crimson; flowering mainly in autumn.

Fruit. An oblong, flat legume to 2 cm long and 7–8 mm wide, containing about 5 rounded seeds.

Climatic range. A, B, H, M, P, S, and on the lower levels of Mts.

Bòssiaea scolopéndria (Greek 'resembling a millepede' referring to the unilateral arrangement of the flowers): Broom Bossiaea: NSW, on sandy coastal heathlands, plateaus and lower tablelands.

Habit. A thin, open shrub to about 1 m tall with erect, flattened and winged cladodal stems to 1 cm wide, the abundant flowers arranged on one side.

Leaves. Normal leaves ovate, confined to the young plants, but mostly reduced to scale leaves marking the nodes on the upper stems.

Flowers. Solitary, pea-shaped, about 1.5 cm across, set about 1.5 cm apart in 2 parallel rows on the upper cladodes; standard petal reniform, notched at the apex, clear yellow with a brownish-crimson fan and veins at the base, and a butterfly-shaped yellow patch; wing and keel petals smaller; flowering in spring.

Fruit. An oblong legume 3–4 cm long and 1 cm broad, with thickened edges, containing 5–6 ovoid seeds.

Climatic range. A, B, M, P, S, and on lower levels of Mts.

BOUVÀRDIA

Commemorating Charles Bouvard, one-time Superintendent of the Royal Gardens in Paris. Scented Bouvardia.

Rubiaceae, the Madder family.

Generic description. A small genus of soft-wooded shrubs from Mexico and Central America, with simple, opposite or whorled leaves and salverform flowers in terminal cymes, the main colour range in red, pink and white. Some are short-lived, especially in marginal climates. The single species described below is still grown in Australian gardens as a survivor of a much longer list of cultivars, once popular garden and cut-flower plants.

Propagation. a) Soft-tip cuttings are struck under mist, preferably over bottom heat;
b) Root cuttings are also used, taken from a field-grown plant in winter and potted individually.

Cultivation. A warm, sunny place is essential for best results, preferably sheltered from wind. The soil needs to be well-drained and kept fertile by regular feeding and watering during the active growing period.

Pruning. The growth of new water-shoots from the base should be encouraged by hard pruning in late winter to replace the old decrepit stems that have flowered.

Species and cultivars

Bouvàrdia longiflòra 'Humbòldtii': Scented Bouvardia: Mexico.

Habit. A tender shrub to about 1 m tall, with erect stems from a basal rootstock, brittle and easily damaged by strong wind unless supported by a cage of wire-mesh about 50–60 cm tall.

Leaves. Simple, opposite, lanceolate, 4–8 cm long, 1.5–2.5 cm wide; apex acuminate; base tapered to the 4–5 mm petiole; margin entire;

midrib prominent beneath; glabrous; dark green above, paler beneath.

Flowers. Borne in terminal cymes clear of the upper leaves; corolla salverform, the slender tube 6–8 cm long, the 4-lobed limb spreading to 3 cm, the lobes ovate-oblong; pure white, sweetly and strongly perfumed; flowering period from early December to late autumn.

Fruit. Not seen; the plant appears to be sterile.

Other distinguishing features. Upper stems shallowly channelled between the nodes, pale to dull green but reddish on the sun-exposed side.

Climatic range. B, P, S, T, and in heated conservatories in colder climates.

BRACHYSÈMA

Derived from the Greek words describing the uncommonly short standard petal.

Pea-bush.

Fabaceae, the Pea family.

Generic description. A small genus of Australian native plants, mostly from the sandy heaths of the WA coast, one of which has become a popular feature in eastern gardens on account of its silvery-green foliage and attractive red flowers. Leaf arrangement varies from opposite to alternate, sometimes with modification to mere scales; flowers are pea-shaped, the keel the largest part, the standard the smallest, all enclosed in a large campanulate calyx; and the fruit is a small inflated legume.

Propagation. a) Seeds, sown as soon as ripe, usually germinate freely if soaked in warm water for 12 hours or so, or alternatively, if lightly scarified.
b) Cuttings root with some difficulty; soft-tip shoots taken in early autumn are best, preferably hormone-dusted and planted in a sand/peat mixture in a humid atmosphere.

Cultivation. The species described below grows best in a light or sandy loam, well drained but with adequate water in summer. It usually fails on heavy, wet soils. It enjoys exposure to sun but will tolerate some shade, and cold to at least −5°C without serious injury.

Pruning. Like most native shrubs, it benefits from a moderate pruning immediately after flowering, to induce a dense, twiggy growth with better foliage.

Species and cultivars

Brachysèma lanceolàtum (Latin 'with lance-shaped leaves'): Swan River Pea-bush: SW coastal plains of WA.

Habit. An evergreen shrub to about 1 m tall, with decumbent lower branches, forming a handsome broad bush 1.5–2.0 m across.

Leaves. Simple, mostly opposite, lanceolate, 4–8 cm long and 1.5–2.0 cm wide; petiole 5–7 mm, silky pubescent; apex acuminate; base broadly cuneate; margin entire but undulate; silvery-green and pubescent when young, becoming dark green and glabrous above.

Flowers. Solitary, or in 2–3 flowered clusters, in the axils of the previous year's growth; calyx campanulate, to 1.5 cm long with prominent ribs and 5 sharp teeth, silky-pubescent; corolla pea-shaped, the short standard barely visible beyond the calyx lobes, red and white with a yellow blotch, the wings to 1.5 cm long, oblanceolate-falcate, red and white, the keel prominent, to 2.5 cm, falcate, cardinal-red, enclosing the 10 free stamens and pistil, flowering from late August to November.

Fruit. An elongate legume to 2–3 cm, ripening in October and November with or after the main flowering season.

Other distinguishing features. Upper twigs and branchlets dark metallic-green to red, with a fine silky pubescence, but becoming glabrous in maturity.

Climatic range. A, M, P, S, and on well-drained sites in B and warm, sheltered sites in H and Mts.

BRÈYNIA (syn. *Phyllanthus*)

Commemorating Johann Breyn, seventeenth-century botanical author.
Snowbush.
Euphorbiaceae, the Spurge family.

Generic description. A small genus of tender plants from South-East Asia, Indonesia and the Pacific region, one species grown in warm Australian climates for its decorative foliage. See below for specific details.

Propagation. Soft-tip cuttings taken in spring and summer, or firmer material taken in autumn or winter, strike easily in a warm, humid atmo-sphere. Careful selection of the parent stock ensures plants of good form and foliage coloration.

Cultivation. Protection from frost and harsh wind is essential. The plant is best grown in a warm, seaside environment, ideally on a coarse, well-drained soil liberally dressed with organic matter.

Pruning. Frequent tip-pruning thickens the growth. Old sparse shoots should be removed at the base to clear the way for new water-shoots.

Species and cultivars

Brèynia disticha (Latin 'two-ranked', referring to the leaf arrangement) (syn. *B. nivòsa*) Snowbush: Pacific Islands.

Habit. An evergreen shrub to 1 m tall with erect flexuose stems arising from a crowded base.

Leaves. Simple, alternate, distichous, obovate to elliptic, 2–5 cm long on a 2 mm petiole; apex obtuse; base rounded; margin entire; venation reticulate, the midrib prominent; glabrous; pink at first, becoming mid-green, variegated and mottled with white spots and splashes.

Flowers. Monoecious, solitary or in clusters from the upper axils, but of little decorative value.

'**Atropurpurea**' has deep ruby-red variegated leaves.

'**Roseo-picta**' is the form usually grown, with leaves pinkish at first, changing to white, with fine green spots and flecks, some dark plum-red, others deep green, spotted and marbled with white, red and deep pink, with paler markings.

Climatic range. B, P, S, T, on warm, sheltered sites only.

BRUNFÉLSIA (syn. *Franciscea*)

Commemorating Otto Brunfels, a sixteenth-century German monk and botanical illustrator.
Yesterday-today-tomorrow.
Solanaceae, the Nightshade family.

Generic description. A small genus of ever-green shrubs from the warmer latitudes of South America, Central America and neighbouring islands, with simple, alternate leaves, solitary or cymose flowers of funnelform or salverform shape, borne mostly in winter and spring, and with fruit a globose berry, reputedly poisonous.

B. bonodora is the most popular species in Australian gardens, deservedly so for its showy flowers produced over a long season.

Propagation. a) Seeds, sown as soon as ripe in a warm, humid atmosphere, germinate freely.

b) Soft-tip cuttings, taken between late spring and early autumn, strike readily in a sand/peat mixture in a warm, humid atmosphere.

Cultivation. *B. bonodora* is somewhat sensitive to cold and grows best in a sun-exposed position with temperatures remaining above 0°C. It prefers a light, friable soil with free drainage, but with additional water in dry times, especially in summer.

Pruning. A light pruning after the flowering season is beneficial, but the natural form of the plant should not be spoiled by over-severe clipping.

Species and cultivars

Brunfelsia bonòdora (Latin 'sweet-smelling') (syn. *B. latifolia*, *B. australis*) Yesterday-today-tomorrow: Central America to south-eastern Brazil.

Habit. An evergreen shrub to 2–3 m tall and 2 m wide, with an irregular framework of branches and a dense canopy of attractive leaves.

Leaves. Oval to ovate, 5–10 cm long, 4–5 cm wide; apex acute; base obtuse to broadly cuneate; margin entire; venation reticulate, the main laterals anastomosed near the edge; glabrous; mid green and slightly shiny on both surfaces, the young leaves often purplish in cool weather.

Flowers. 1 to several in terminal clusters; calyx urceolate to 1 cm long, with 5 pointed apical teeth; corolla salverform, the tube slender to about 2.5 cm long, the 5-parted, rotate limb 4–5 cm across, deep violet at first, then lavender-blue with a white-eyed centre, fading to nearly white over a 2 to 3 day cycle, all colours being present on the bush at once; sweetly perfumed, flowering abundantly from September to late November, with a few flowers in summer.

Fruit. A globose berry to 1.5 cm across, smooth skinned, with a small mucro at the apex, green at first but ripening to brown; supported by the 5 persistent sepals, then about half the length of the berry; fruits reputed to be poisonous.

Climatic range. B, S, T, and on warm, sheltered sites only in M and P.

BÚDDLEIA

Commemorating Adam Buddle, English cleric, botanist and plantsman.
Butterfly Bush or Summer Lilac; Orange Ball Tree; Sage-leafed Buddleia.
Loganiaceae, the Logania family.

Generic description. A widely distributed genus with representatives from South America, the Orient, India and Africa, mostly woody shrubs with evergreen or sometimes deciduous leaves, nearly always opposite, and showy flowers in spikes, panicles, or globose heads. All are useful as flowering shrubs, hardy in most Australian climates and tolerate polluted atmospheres better than most plants.

Propagation. a) Soft-tip cuttings, taken in spring or summer from non-flowered shoots, strike readily in a sand/peat mixture in a warm, humid place.

b) Semi-hardwood cuttings, taken in autumn, or hardwood cuttings of older material taken in winter, are also successful.

Cultivation. Almost any friable, fertile soil will suit the Buddleias but they respond strongly to rich, well-drained soils in a sunny position, and plenty of water in spring and summer, especially when in flower.

Pruning. *B. davidii* and its cultivars, and *B. globosa*, flower on young wood of the current year's growth, and need to be pruned in late winter by shortening the flowered shoots to within several nodes of the older wood, but preserving the natural form as much as possible. If growing vigorously in mid spring, the new shoots should be tipped when about 20 cm long to stimulate the growth of flowering laterals.

B. salviifolia is treated similarly, but pruning is deferred until after flowering in spring.

B. alternifolia flowers on the previous year's wood, as well as on the new season's wood; it is best treated in late winter to a complete removal of about half the number of older shoots, to make way for the new material from the lower branches.

Species and cultivars

Búddleia alternifòlia (Latin 'with alternately arranged leaves'): Weeping Butterfly Bush: NW China, abundant in the province of Kansu.

Habit. A partly deciduous shrub or small tree to 3–5 m tall, best grown as a single-stemmed standard tree to better display its elegant pendulous form and flowers.

Leaves. Simple, alternate, lanceolate, 6–10 cm long and 2–3 cm wide; apex acute; margin mostly entire but often irregularly and shallowly sinuate; glabrous and dark green above, but paler with a dense, whitish-grey pubescence below.

Flowers. Inflorescence an umbellate cluster to 2–3 cm across, in the leafy axils of the previous year's growth, many clusters arranged closely to form a 30–100 cm long, pendulous chain of flowers; corolla tubulate to 8–10 mm long, expanding into the 4-lobed limb; lilac-mauve, with a deeper violet throat, flowering abundantly in late spring and summer; sweetly perfumed.

Fruit. Not seen.

Other distinguishing features. Upper young stems silvery-grey, with a slightly scaly surface.

Climatic range. H, M, Mts, and on cool, elevated sites in A, P, and S.

Búddleia dàvidii (commemorating Abbé Armand David, nineteenth-century French missionary and plant collector in China): Orange-eye Butterfly Bush: China.

Habit. An evergreen shrub to 3 m tall and as wide, with the main branches radiating from the centre, and many lateral flowering branchlets, forming a handsome, hemispherical bush of strong vigour.

Leaves. Simple, opposite, narrow-elliptical to lanceolate, 15–20 cm long and 4–5 cm wide, with a 3 mm petiole; apex acuminate; margin serrate; midrib prominent beneath; dark green, glabrous but velvety above, whitish-tomentose beneath.

Flowers. Inflorescence a terminal, densely packed, spike-like panicle, 20–25 cm long; flowers salverform, about 1 cm long and 5–6 mm across the expanded limb, lilac-purple, with an orange-yellow throat, flowering mainly from December to April; flowers have a slightly unpleasant scent, but are attractive to butterflies.

Other distinguishing features. Upper stems squarish, with a fine white tomentum.

var. *veitchiana* has larger panicles of flowers than those of the species, lavender, with an orange eye.

'**Veitchiana Variegata**' is similar to the variety but has leaves with a cream margin.

Many cultivars are in general use, with large flowers and a wide colour range. The following are representative of those offered by nurseries.

'**Empire Blue**': dark violet-blue, with bright-orange eye.

'**Fascinating**': rosy-lilac, with large panicles to 45 cm long.

'**Flaming Violet**': rich magenta-violet.

'**Ile de France**': royal-purple.

'**Pink Pearl**': lilac to mauve-pink.

'**Royal Red**': royal-purple to claret-red.

'**White Bouquet**': white, with an orange eye.

'**White Profusion**': white, with an orange eye; a dwarf bush.

Climatic range. A, B, H, M, Mts, P, S.

Búddleia globòsa (Latin 'with a spherical form', referring to the rounded clusters of flowers): Orange Ball Tree: coastal Peru and Chile.

Habit. An evergreen shrub 3–4 m tall and as wide, with an arching framework of main branches carrying the pendulous branchlets and foliage.

Leaves. Simple, opposite, lanceolate-elliptic, 10–15 cm long and 2–3 cm wide; apex slenderly acuminate; margin crenulate; veins prominent beneath; glabrous and mid green above with a rough pebbly surface, densely yellowish-white and tomentose beneath.

Flowers. Inflorescence a sparse, terminal and axillary panicle, mostly clear of the upper foliage; flowers tubulate, in a globose head about 2 cm across, on 3–7 cm long peduncles; flowers honey-perfumed, bright orange-yellow, flowering from November to March.

Fruit. Not seen.

Other distinguishing features. Young branchlets and inflorescence with a yellowish-white tomentum.

Climatic range. A, B, H, M, Mts, P, S.

Búddleia salviifolia (Latin 'with leaves like a Salvia', probably *S. leucantha*): Sage-leafed Buddleia: central and southern Africa.

Habit. A vigorous, evergreen shrub to 3–4 m tall, with several main branches from the short trunk, and pendulous branchlets, at least when in flower.

Leaves. Simple, opposite, lanceolate, 5–15 cm long and 3–4 cm wide; petiole 4–5 mm long; apex finely acuminate; base truncate to cordate; margin puckered and bluntly denticulate; venation conspicuously reticulate, the midrib prominent beneath; densely rugose, and dull, dark green above, whitish-green below.

Flowers. Inflorescence a dense terminal panicle, 12–15 cm long and 7–8 cm broad, many together, crowding the ends of the upper branchlets to almost cover the plant; corolla tubulate 6–8 mm long, the 4 short lobes incurved at first but opening partly to expose the violet-blue inner surface and the orange-yellow throat, the tube silky-tomentose; flowering from late June to late September, with a sweet, spicy perfume.

Fruit. Not seen.

Other distinguishing features. Upper stems squarish, whitish-green and heavily tomentose.

Climatic range. B, M, P, S, T, and in warm microclimates in A.

BURCHÉLLIA

Commemorating William John Burchell, author and botanical explorer in South Africa.
Wild Pomegranate or Buffalo-horn.
Rubiaceae, the Madder family.

Generic description. A monotypic genus. The species is not commonly seen in gardens but deserves a more important place for its good foliage and showy flowers.

Propagation. a) Seeds, sown in late winter or spring in a warm place, germinate well.
b) Semi-hardwood cuttings, taken in late summer or autumn, strike readily in a warm, humid glass-house.

Cultivation. A light, fertile, well-drained soil with abundant summer moisture is preferred, in a warm locality not subject to heavy frosts; the plant is not seriously damaged by frost to –2°C. Suitable for either filtered shade or exposure to full sun.

Pruning. The plant may need an occasional trim to preserve the tidy, rounded shape. A light pruning after the spring flowering will prevent fruit production and improve the foliage quality.

Species and cultivars

Burchéllia bubalina (supposedly from 'bubal', the native hartebeest, the ripened calyx having antelope-like horns at the apex) (syn. *B. capensis*) Wild Pomegranate or Buffalo-horn; South Africa, from the Cape to the Tropic of Capricorn.

Habit. An evergreen shrub to about 3 m tall, of broadly globose shape with many upright leafy branches from the base.

Leaves. Simple, opposite, elliptical to ovate, 6–10 cm long and 3–5 cm wide; apex acute; base obtuse to subcordate; margin entire; stipules short, membranous; venation reticulate, the midrib and main laterals prominent beneath; glabrous, except for the slightly bristly main vein below; dark green and slightly shiny above, bright green beneath.

Flowers. Inflorescence a terminal, sessile umbel of 10–12 flowers in a whorl of 4 involucral scales; calyx urceolate, with 5 acicular sepals; corolla tubulate, to 2 cm long and 6–7 mm wide, with 5 short teeth at the apex, bright orange-red to scarlet, flowering mainly from September to November but also sparsely throughout summer.

Fruit. A fleshy, urceolate berry with 1 to several embedded seeds.

Climatic range. B, M, P, S, T, and on warm, sheltered sites in A.

BÚXUS

The classical Latin name for the European Common Box, *B. sempervirens*.
Box (various).
Buxaceae, the Box family.

Generic description. A small genus of slow-growing, evergreen shrubs and small trees from the Mediterranean region, central Asia, and the Orient, grown in all temperate countries for their showy, glossy foliage and close twiggy growth, essential qualities in plants used for topiary work. Leaves are simple, opposite, entire, in a variety of greens from pale to very dark, with some variegated forms, tough and coriaceous; flowers are monoecious, the sexes separate on the same plant, mostly in the same inflorescence, apetalous and of little decorative interest, most flowers hidden amongst the leaves; fruit is a small, fleshy, apically horned capsule with several glossy, black seeds in each.
Buxus is commonly grown as a container plant for terrace planting, clipped to a regular, mostly formal shape, and is highly regarded for this purpose because of its great hardiness and durability.

Propagation. Semi-hardwood, leafy tip cuttings, 2–5 cm long, taken between late spring and early winter, strike readily in a sand/peat mixture in a cool, humid atmosphere.

Cultivation. The species listed below thrive in almost any moderately fertile soil with free drainage; plants growing in the ground are tolerant of austere conditions, but container-grown plants must be regularly watered, especially when grown on sunny, wind-exposed terraces. All species are hardy in low temperatures to at least −10°C.

Pruning. Topiary plants are clipped to a variety of shapes as frequently as required; pruning of other plants is usually confined to control of size and to thicken the growth habit while young.

Species and cultivars

Búxus baleárica (Latin 'from the Balearic Islands', in the western Mediterranean: Balearic Islands Box: Spain and Mediterranean offshore islands.

Habit. A large shrub or small tree to 8–10 m tall, with a stout trunk and gnarled and twisted branches when old, forming an irregularly rounded crown, but normally grown in cultivation as a clipped plant of somewhat formal and regular shape.

Leaves. More or less in a single plane, broad-lanceolate to elliptic-ovate, 3–5 cm long and 1.5–2.0 cm wide; petiole about 5 mm long, pubescent; apex obtuse to slightly emarginate; base obtuse to broadly cuneate; margin entire, except for a few remote vestigial notches, and slightly recurved; venation finely reticulate, more prominent beneath; glabrous and coriaceous; bright green and slightly lustrous above, paler and dull beneath.

Flowers. Apetalous, a solitary pale-yellow pistillate flower encircled by several staminate flowers in a small axillary cluster partly concealed amongst the leaves; perfumed; flowering in October and November.

Fruit. An ovoid capsule with the short apical prongs typical of the genus; capsule green at first, ripening to brown, the 3 valves splitting to release the blackish-brown lustrous seeds in summer and autumn.

Other distinguishing features. Upper twigs, green, striate, pubescent when young but becoming glabrous and dull grey.

Climatic range. A, B, M, P, R, S, and in warm, sheltered micro-climates in Mts.

Búxus microphýlla var. *japónica* (Greek 'small-leafed', and Latin 'from Japan'): Japanese Box: Japanese islands.

Habit. A dense shrub to about 2–3 m when grown freely, but usually seen as a shaped plant, either in hedge or topiary form.

Leaves. Obovate to obcordate, 1.5 to 2.5 cm long and 1.0–1.5 cm wide; petiole 3–4 mm long, flattened, finely puberulent; apex obtuse or retuse, sometimes with a short mucro; base cuneate; margin entire; venation indistinctly penninerved, the midrib with a conspicuous white stomatic band beneath; coriaceous; bright green and lustrous above, pale yellowish-green beneath.

Flowers. Inflorescence a small, sessile, axillary or terminal cluster, the sexes separate, a single pistillate flower in the middle, encircled by several staminate flowers, all apetalous, perfumed and attractive to bees, flowering in October and November.

Fruit. An obovoid capsule to about 1 cm long and 8 mm wide, the 3 valves each bearing 2 apical prongs about 2–3 mm long; capsule green at first, ripening to brown in late summer; seeds 2 in each valve, oblong, glossy black, about 5 mm long.

Other distinguishing features. Ultimate twigs bright green, square with sharp ridges, the bark becoming cream as it matures, with some irregular longitudinal ridges of rough bark.

Climatic range. A, H, M, Mts, P, S.

Buxus sempérvirens (Latin 'evergreen'): Common Box: western Europe and UK to Asia and the Orient.

Habit. An evergreen shrub to 4 m or more in old age, with dense, twiggy growth; of indeterminate shape, but usually seen pruned or clipped into geometrical form; well known as hedging or topiary subject especially in England and Europe.

Leaves. Mostly ovate, to 2–3 cm long and 1–2 cm wide; petiole about 2 mm long, flattened, pubescent; apex obtuse or emarginate, occasionally acute; base cuneate; margin entire; venation finely penninerved at about 45° angle, the midrib alone prominent, raised and pubescent above, whitish beneath; pale green while young, becoming lustrous dark green above, paler beneath.

Flowers. In small clusters in the upper axils, but mostly obscured by the leaves, apetalous, yellowish-green, a single pistillate flower surrounded by several staminate flowers, sweetly perfumed, flowering in October and November.

Fruit. A fleshy ellipsoidal capsule, to about 1 cm long, the 3 valves each with a pair of short terminal horns, and splitting when ripe in summer to discharge the ovoid blackish seeds.

Other distinguishing features. Youngest twigs pale green, finely puberulent, becoming darker, and squared by the decurrent ridges below the leaf bases.

'Argéntea': (syn. *'Argénteo-variegáta'*) like the parent but of slower, thinner growth, the dark-green leaves with a creamy-white margin of irregular depth, the intermediate areas grey-green.

'Marginàta': (syn. *'Aùreo-marginàta'*) the leaves are glossy dark green in the middle, margined irregularly with creamy-yellow, sometimes as deep as the midrib, the intermediate areas grey-green, but pale cream and grey on the reverse side.

'Suffruticòsa': Edging Box: has a smaller, more densely compact habit, with ovate to obovate leaves 1–2 cm long with a blunt to emarginate apex, bright to dark green. This is the cultivar used to form the low edgings seen in many of the celebrated English, French and Italian formal gardens.

Climatic range. A, H, M, Mts, P, S.

CALLIÁNDRA (syn. *Inga*)

Derived from the Greek words meaning 'beautiful stamens'.

Tassel-flower; Powder-puff Flower.
Mimosaceae, the Mimosa family.

Generic description. A large genus of 150 or so shrubs and small trees, mainly from tropical America, grown for their often outstanding foliage and colourful flowers. All are evergreen, have bipinnate leaves, flowers with a very short calyx and corolla, but long, handsome stamens, mostly white, pink, red, or purple, and with leguminous fruit.

Propagation. a) Seeds sown as soon as ripe germinate readily if planted in a warm, moist environment, preferably in spring.
b) Semi-hardwood cuttings, taken in early autumn to late winter, and planted in a sand/peat mixture over bottom heat in a misted glasshouse, give satisfactory results, especially if short, stubby lateral shoots are used.

Cultivation. The species described here are best grown in a climate at least as warm as that of Sydney but all will survive an occasional very light frost if the plants are mature and well acclimatised by a cool autumn. Where doubt exists about their hardiness, plants should be covered at night when frost is expected. They should not be unduly forced, but once established, are best grown austerely to encourage a more prolific floral display.

Pruning. While not essential to flower production, some shortening of the vigorous shoots is desirable to keep the plants bushy, the better to display the flowers and foliage. Pruning is best carried out in late winter after frosts are over. *C. portoricensis* may be dealt with rather more severely and more frequently than the others, to contain its aggressive growth habit.

Species and cultivars

Calliándra haematocéphala (Greek 'with blood-red heads of flower'): Blood-red Tassel-flower: Bolivia.

Habit. An evergreen shrub with low, horizontal habit, to 3 m tall, but spreading to 4–5 m wide.

Leaves. Compound, alternate, bipinnate, the main rachis to about 3 cm long, green, glabrous and somewhat warty, the base subtended by a pair of ovate stipules 8–10 mm long; rachis divided at the apex into 2 pinnae 10–12 cm long, each with 6 to 8 pairs of ovate-oblong, obliquely falcate leaflets; apices acute; bases unequally obtuse; margins entire; veins prominent beneath; glabrous; bronze-pink when young, maturing to bright shining green; leaflets sensitive to light and cold.

Flowers. Inflorescence a globose head of about 60 flowers on a pubescent peduncle to 2 cm long, several together in the upper axils; buds clavate, 7–8 mm long; calyx 3–4 mm long, corolla 5-lobed, pale pink; stamens numerous, to 2.5 cm long, the filaments blood-red, the anthers black, the fully mature heads spherical, to 4–6 cm across, flowering in autumn and winter.

Fruit. A linear-oblanceolate, pubescent legume, about 10 cm long.

Other distinguishing features. Upper stems silvery-green, with slender pale-brown lenticels.

Climatic range. B, T, and on warm, frost-free sites in P and S.

Calliándra portoricénsis (Latin 'from Puerto Rico'): White Tassel-flower: most islands of the West Indies.

Habit. An evergreen shrub to 3–4 m tall, usually branched low, but sometimes seen as a small tree with a single trunk and loose, open crown.

Leaves. Bipinnate, stipular at the base, on a

main rachis to 4–6 cm long; with about 30 opposite pairs of linear leaflets 5–8 mm long and 1.5 mm wide; apices acute; margins entire/ciliate; all parts finely pubescent; dark green above, bright green beneath; leaves sensitive to light and cold.

Flowers. Inflorescence a globose umbellate head of 20–25 flowers, calyx 2 mm long, green, with 5 minute purplish teeth; corolla 5-lobed, green with purple apex; stamens numerous, to 2.5 cm long, with silvery-white filaments and cream anthers; flowering season mainly from October to autumn.

Fruit. A flat legume, 4–6 cm long, 6–8 mm wide, linear-oblong, one to about 6 together; brown-pubescent; explosive when ripe, discharging the several ellipsoidal, pale-brown seeds.

Other distinguishing features. Upper twigs brown-pubescent, shallowly ridged longitudinally.

Climatic range. B, S, T, and on warm, sheltered sites in M and P.

Calliándra tweèdii (commemorating James Tweedie, Scottish plant collector in South America) (syn. *Calliandra pulcherrima*) Red Tasselflower: tropical Brazil.

Habit. An evergreen shrub to 2–3 m tall and as wide, usually of spherical shape but occasionally seen as a small tree with a single trunk.

Leaves. Compound, alternate, bipinnate; leaflets linear; 5–10 mm long and 1 mm wide, in 25–30 opposite pairs; apex acute and mucronate; base unequally cordate; margin entire and finely ciliate; glabrous except for a few bristles along the rachis and pinnae; dark green above, paler beneath; leaflets sensitive to light and cold.

Flowers. Inflorescence a globose umbellate head of 10–15 flowers borne in the upper leaf axils; stamens numerous, 2.5–3.0 cm long, forming a spherical ball 6 cm across, bright scarlet, flowering prolifically from September to April.

Fruit. A flat, elongate legume to 4–6 cm long and 6–8 mm wide, linear-oblong, grooved on the flat sides and covered with brownish hair; seeds ellipsoidal to 1 cm long and 3–4 mm thick, brown; legumes explosive upon ripening in autumn and early winter.

Other distinguishing features. Upper stems bronze-green, with pale-brown lenticels, the nodes with brown, leafy stipules.

Climatic range. B, S, T, and on warm, sheltered sites in M and P.

CALLICÁRPA

Derived from the Greek *kallos* 'beauty', and *karpos* 'fruit', the most dominant feature of the genus.
Beauty-berry.
Verbenaceae, the Verbena family.

Generic description. A large genus of shrubs, or occasionally small trees, from the temperate parts of the Northern Hemisphere and northern Australia, grown mainly for their dainty flowers and colourful, clustered fruits. Leaves are simple, opposite, mostly deciduous but with a few evergreens; flowers are borne in axillary cymes, the parts usually in fours, in white, pink, blue, and purple in late spring and summer, followed by an abundant crop of small drupaceous, violet to deep-purple fruits in autumn and early winter. The fruiting stems are useful as indoor decorative material, lasting well and of striking appearance when displayed against a white or cream background with suitable lighting.

Propagation. a) Soft-tip cuttings taken in spring, or semi-hardwood cuttings taken in summer or early autumn, strike readily in a warm atmosphere.
b) Hardwood cuttings taken from the winter prunings are also used.

Cultivation. An open, sun-exposed site is best, in a mild climate with minimum temperatures remaining above –5°C. The species listed are not fussy about soil; almost any moderately well-drained, open-textured soil will do, but performance is improved on better-class loams with plentiful summer water.

Pruning. Some shortening of the fruiting branches is desirable each year to maintain a supply of vigorous, 1-year-old flowering and fruiting wood; such pruning is best done in winter, or when the fruit is at its best if required for indoor decoration, leaving several nodes on each shoot for the development of replacement growth.

Species and cultivars

Callicárpa bodinierii (commemorating Fr Emile Bodinieri, nineteenth-century French missionary in south-western China): central and western China.

var. *giráldii* (commemorating Fr Giuseppe Giraldi, nineteenth-century Italian missionary in China) is probably the most commonly grown Beauty-berry in Australian gardens.

Habit. A deciduous shrub to 2.5–3.0 m tall, with stout lower branches supporting a broad, rounded crown of slender branchlets, eventually growing to about 3 m across but usually kept smaller by annual pruning.

Leaves. Elliptic to ovate-lanceolate, 6–10 cm long and 3–5 cm wide, the pubescent petiole 8–10 mm long; apex acuminate; base cuneate; margin serrate-dentate; venation reticulate, the midrib and main laterals prominent beneath; dark green and glabrous above, paler, stellate-pubescent and glandular beneath, changing to light ruby-red and reddish-purple in autumn.

Flowers. In small axillary cymes about 3 cm across; flowers with reddish, campanulate, 4-lobed calyx, and corolla of 4 nearly orbicular petals, forming a rotate flower about 6–7 mm across, bright lilac-purple; stamens 4, about 7 mm long, the filaments whitish with golden-yellow anthers; flowers borne freely in late spring and summer on the young, current season's growth.

Fruit. A small globose drupe, 3–4 mm across, variable in colour from lavender to lilac and violet-purple, colouring in autumn and persisting into winter, even after leaf fall.

Climatic range. A, H, M, Mts, P, S.

Other species occasionally grown in Australian gardens are:

Callicárpa americàna (Latin 'from America'): American Beauty-berry: south-eastern USA: has dark green, ovate to elliptic, pubescent leaves, 5–12 cm long, pale lilac-pink to lavender-blue flowers in summer, and violet to rosy-purple fruits borne in clusters of 10 to about 20 in the upper leaf axils in autumn and early winter.

Climatic range. A, B, M, P, S.

Callicárpa dichótoma (Greek 'with bifurcated branches'): Chinese Beauty-berry (syn. *C. gracilis, C. koreana, C. purpurea*) China, Korea and Japan and neighbouring islands: a deciduous shrub to 2 m tall, and as wide, with slender, arching, purplish-pubescent branchlets bearing the dark green, oblong to obovate leaves, 7–8 cm long; flowers are pale purple in many-flowered, axillary cymes, produced in late spring and summer, followed by small, clustered, lilac-violet fruits to 3 mm across, at their best in autumn and early winter.

Climatic range. A, H, M, Mts, P, S.

Callicárpa japónica (Latin 'from Japan'): Japanese Beauty-berry: Japan, China and Manchuria: a deciduous shrub to 1.5 m tall and a little wider, with slender, erect stems, stellate-pubescent at least while young; leaves are mostly ovate to obovate, 6–10 cm long, with a finely-serrate margin, dark green but turning reddish in autumn; flowers are borne in axillary cymes to 3.5 cm across, pale rosy-purple, in late summer, followed by clusters of small globular, violet-purple fruits in autumn and early winter.

Climatic range. A, H, M, Mts, P, S.

CALLISTÈMON

Derived from the Greek *kallos* 'beauty', and *stemon* 'a stamen', describing the coloured stamens, the showy part of the flowers.
Bottlebrush (various).
Myrtaceae, the Myrtle family.

Generic description. An Australian genus of about 25 species, scattered throughout the States, all evergreen, some tree-like, others shrubby, the following species among the most popular for their colourful flowers and foliage, and ease of culture. All have simple, alternate, entire leaves, mostly green and sometimes dull and harsh, but occasionally bright green, pink, or red in spring and summer; flowers are borne on an elongated spike like a bottlebrush, the main axis extending to form the new shoot, the flowers closely sessile, the calyx squat, the 5 sepals soon falling, the 5 petals short and orbicular, the numerous stamens much longer and often spectacular in red, purplish, pink, green or cream colours; the flowers are followed by woody, capsular fruits, some persisting on the upper stems for several years.

Propagation. a) Seeds are normally sown in spring on the surface of a friable sowing medium, and barely covered with finely-sifted peat; placed in a warm, moist atmosphere, germination is quick and reliable. All species may be grown by this method.
b) Cultivars and clonal material are grown by short, leafy, tip cuttings taken in late summer and autumn, and struck in a sand/peat mixture in a cool, humid environment, preferably with mist overhead.

Cultivation. Most species are indigenous to fairly moist land, a few from the margins of swamps, but rarely in fully waterlogged soils.

PLATE 5

▲ Camellia japonica 'C.M. Hovey'

▲ Camellia japonica 'Chandleri'
▼ Camellia reticulata 'Shot Silk' *Photo by Charles Cowell*

▲ Camellia japonica 'Laurie Bray'

PLATE 6

▲ Camellia japonica 'Monjisu'

▲ Camellia sasanqua 'Setsu Gekka'

▼ Camellia japonica 'The Czar'

▲ Camellia japonica 'Shiro Chan'
◄ Camellia japonica 'Betty Sheffield
▼ Camellia hiemalis 'Kanjiro' syn. 'Hiryu'

▼ Camellia japonica 'Magnoliaeflora'

▼ Camellia sasanqua 'Plantation Pink'

The majority perform well on deep, light soils where moisture is always present in sufficient quantity to sustain normal growth. Most are hardy to light frosts, but young plants should be set out in spring and may need frost protection over the first winter.

Pruning. The tree-like species rarely need pruning except to establish a single main trunk. Those grown as shrubs are improved by a light annual pruning for the first few years until a dense, twiggy bush is established, then at 3 or 4-yearly intervals to maintain their form. All such pruning is carried out during or immediately after the main flowering period.

Species and cultivars

Callistèmon brachyándrus (Greek 'with short stamens'): Prickly Bottlebrush: western NSW, north-western Vic and eastern SA, mostly in the 300–400 mm rainfall area.
Habit. A shrub to 3–5 m tall with thin, open growth, much improved by early and regular pruning; young shoots pubescent.
Leaves. Linear-acicular, 2.5–4.0 cm long and 1 mm wide, with a needle-like, sharp apex and a grooved upper surface, the texture harsh and rigid, dark green.
Flowers. Inflorescence a sparse, loose spike to 6–8 cm long, the flowers spaced widely apart, the stamens short to 1 cm long, the colour deep scarlet-red, with bright yellow anthers, flowering mostly between November and March.
Fruit. Capsules squatly globular, 5–6 mm across, woody, grey-brown, sparsely clustered around the stems, persisting for several years; seeds numerous, slender, red-brown.
Other distinguishing features. A desert species, tolerant of dry sandy soils, but responding well to better-class loams with additional summer water and feeding.
Climatic range. A, M, P, S, and in warm microclimates in lower elevations of Mts.

Callistèmon '**Candy Pink**' is a cultivar of uncertain parentage, growing to about 2–3 m tall and about as broad, with narrow pale-green leaves and prolific crops of showy light-red flowers, occurring mostly in spring and mid-summer, the brushes 10–12 cm long and 4–5 cm broad.

Callistèmon citrìnus (Latin 'citron-like', referring to the foliage aroma) (syn. *C. lanceolatus*) Crimson or Lemon-scented Bottlebrush: eastern Australia, from Vic to central Qld, mostly on the moist coastal plains and plateaus, and lower mountain slopes.
Habit. A shrub to 3 m or more, usually on a short, single trunk with many low branches forming a globose bush, the young shoots pubescent.
Leaves. Lanceolate, 3–7 cm long and 7–12 mm wide; apex acute-mucronate; base cuneate; margin entire and thickened; coriaceous and stiff; midrib prominent; glabrous; aromatic when bruised; dark green and dull when mature, but bright green and slightly silky when young.
Flowers. Inflorescence a terminal spike, 8–10 cm long and 4–5 cm broad; calyx green; petals reddish-green; stamens numerous and closely set, to 2.5 cm long, crimson with darker anthers, flowering abundantly from early October to late November and occasionally in autumn.
Fruit. Capsules urceolate-globular, about 5 mm across, woody, grey-brown, clustered in a dense mass, some distorted or flat-sided by the close crowding; persistent; seeds narrowly linear, red-brown.
Other distinguishing features. Upper stems reddish-grey, becoming fibrous and brown-grey with age.
Climatic range. A, B, M, P, S, T, and in warm microclimates in H and Mts.

As a result of seedling variability, the species has produced a number of outstanding cultivars. Some of the most popular are listed below:
'**Austraflora Firebrand**' is a semi-prostrate form growing to about 75 cm tall with many flexible shoots from the base and central stem, spreading to 2–3 m, the terminals bearing the typical crimson brushes of the species, 8–10 cm long and 4–5 cm broad. This form is of special value as a ground-cover for embankments and steep rock gardens.
'**Burgundy**': A Victorian cultivar with the growth habit of the parent but with smaller leaves, pinkish-red at least while young, and clustered brushes to 8–10 cm long and 4–6 cm broad, beetroot-purple.
'**Clusters**' is an interesting form with flower spikes borne in a whorl-like cluster of 6 to 8, terminating the young shoots, the carmine-red brushes to 12 cm long.
'**Endeavour**' is a well-established cultivar, providing a heavy crop of bright crimson brushes to 10 cm long, the pinkish new leaves maturing to mid-green on a dense bush to about 2 m tall.

'**Lilacinus**' is a little taller than the species, often tree-like to 4–5 m tall, with small lilac brushes.
'**Lilacinus Carmineus**' is much similar but with larger brushes with carmine-red stamens and ruby-red anthers.
'**Mauve Mist**' has reddish new leaves, later turning green, and prolific crops of brushes, either singly or in small clusters, lilac-purple at first, ageing to rosy-magenta with deeper anthers.
'**Pink Clusters**' is distinct from 'Clusters' in its shorter brushes to about 8 cm and its lilac-pink stamens.
'**Reeves' Pink**' is a Victorian cultivar with reddish young leaves and phlox-pink brushes borne singly or in clusters.
'**Splendens**' is probably the best-known form of the species; it has broader leaves on a shapely bush to 3 m or so and bright crimson brushes to 12 cm long, the stamens with golden-yellow anthers, borne over an extended flowering period.
'**White Anzac**' is a low-growing bush to about 1 m tall, but spreading to 2 m or more, with large brushes to 12 cm long and 6 cm broad, white, or sometimes flushed with pink.

Callistèmon comboynénsis ('from the Comboyne Plateau'): Cliff Bottlebrush: SE Qld and North Coast of NSW, mainly on the eastern slopes of the tablelands.
Habit. A shrub to about 2 m tall and as broad, sometimes loose and open, but responding to cultivation and regular pruning.
Leaves. Young leaves and shoots reddish and softly pubescent, becoming firm and leathery; lanceolate to 6–8 cm long and 1.5 cm wide, slightly falcate; dotted with pellucid oil glands; mid-green.
Flowers. In a compact spike to 6–7 cm long, the filaments light-red but varying to carmine-pink in some forms, the anthers yellow, flowering mainly in late winter and spring.
Fruit. Capsules globular, 4–5 mm across, woody, borne in dense clusters, grey-brown; seeds numerous, reddish.
'**Prostratus**' is an unofficially-named, low-growing form with spreading growth habit to 50–60 cm tall and 1.5–2.5 m across, but otherwise similar to the parent species.
Climatic range. B, M, P, S, and on lower Mts.

Callistèmon lineàris ('line-like', from the Latin *linea* 'a flaxen thread'): Narrow-leafed Bottle-

brush: NSW, between the coast and the Blue Mountains.
Habit. A loose, open shrub of about 3 m tall with a short trunk and many ascending branches which tend to intertwine, the plant improved in density by regular pruning at least in the early years.
Leaves. Narrowly linear, 6–10 cm long and 3–4 mm wide; concave and mostly falcate; apex finely acute-mucronate; base tapered to the short, swollen petiole; margin entire but thickened; midrib alone prominent, the lower surface dotted with pellucid oil glands; stiff and coriaceous; finely pubescent when young but otherwise glabrous; dark green, with a dark red stain towards the apex, especially in cold conditions.
Flowers. Inflorescence to 15 cm long, with up to 80 flowers arranged thickly on the axis, new shoots emerging from the apex; stamens numerous to 2.5 cm long, filaments crimson, with greenish-gold anthers; style slightly longer than the stamens, crimson, the stigma green; flowers borne on long, drooping shoots in October and November and intermittently at other times, mainly in summer and autumn.
Fruit. Capsules urceolate-globular, about 6–8 mm across, with a depressed orifice, grey-green, borne in crowded clusters surrounding the stems; seeds linear, reddish.
Other distinguishing features. Upper shoots orange-brown, becoming grey in age, with conspicuous capsule-scars.
Climatic range. A, B, M, P, S, T.

Callistèmon macropunctàtus (Greek 'having large spots' referring to the oil glands) (syn. *C. regulòsus* and *C. coccíneus*) Scarlet or Vein-leafed Bottlebrush: south-east SA, western Vic. and south-west NSW.
Habit. A shrub of sparse form to 3 m or so tall and about as broad, but improved in cultivation with regular pruning, or tree-like by the removal of the lower branches.
Leaves. Linear to lanceolate, 4–7 cm long, 5–6 mm wide; apex acute, with a sharp, horny tip; margin thick; mid-rib alone prominent; glandular and aromatic when crushed; dull mid-green.
Flowers. In a cylindrical spike to 8–10 cm long and 5–6 cm broad; stamens about 2.5 cm long, varying from bright scarlet to rosy-red, all with yellow anthers.

Fruit. A squat woody capsule to 8–10 mm across, greyish, closely crowded in cylindroidal clusters; seeds reddish.

'**Violaceus**' with rosy-violet brushes probably belongs here.

Climatic range. A, H, M, P, S, and lower levels of Mts.

Callistèmon pállidus (Latin 'pale', referring to the flowers): Lemon Bottlebrush: NSW, Vic. Tas. mainly in elevated swamps and the valleys of the east-flowing rivers.

Habit. An erect shrub to about 3 m tall, branching into a loose, open crown to 2.5 m wide, from a short trunk.

Leaves. Lanceolate, 3–6 cm long, about 1 cm wide, silky-hairy while young, later glabrous; glandular and aromatic; dark to greyish-green.

Flowers. In a loose cylindrical spike, 8–9 cm long and 5–6 cm wide; stamens 2–3 cm long, whitish to pale lemon-yellow with yellow anthers.

Fruit. Capsules squat, urceolate, 6–8 mm across.

'**Austraflora Candle Glow**' is a registered cultivar of prostrate form, 10–30 cm tall, spreading to 1.5–2.5 m across, with leaves and flowers like those of the species.

'**Father Christmas**' has spikes to 10 cm long, with whitish-cream filaments and reddish anthers;

Climatic range. H, M, Mts, P, S, and on cool, moist sites in A.

Callistèmon paludòsus (Latin 'from the marshes'): Swamp or River Bottlebrush: eastern Australia, mostly on the banks of the east-flowing streams.

Habit. A shrub to 3 m or so, the short trunk dividing into an open crown 2 m or so broad, with drooping branchlets.

Leaves. Linear, 5–9 cm long, 5–8 mm wide; mucronate; midrib alone prominent; soft textured, silky and pinkish at first, becoming thick, hard, glabrous and dark green in maturity.

Flowers. A somewhat sparse spike 5–6 cm long and 2–3 cm broad, the filaments cream, anthers yellow, flowering from mid-summer to late autumn.

Fruit. Capsules squat, globular, 5 mm wide and as deep.

'**Sallyanne**' is a registered cultivar growing to about 3 m tall and 2–3 m wide with a pendulous form. The clear pink brushes, borne freely at the terminals between November and May, are distinctive.

Climatic range. H, M, P, S, and on lower Mts.

Callistèmon phoeníceus (Latin 'from Phoenicia', alluding to the country of origin, now Lebanon, of the ancient crimson-purple dyes): Fiery Bottlebrush: western coast of WA, on sandy heathlands, and margins of coastal swamps and streams.

Habit. Closely related to C. *speciosus* and perhaps merely a botanical variety of that species; of shrubby form, 2–3 m tall, the lower branches tending to remain somewhat horizontal.

Leaves. Lanceolate, 5–8 cm long and 1–2 cm wide, thick and coriaceous; midrib prominent but other veins indistinct; apex acute with a short, hard point; grey-green on both surfaces.

Flowers. Inflorescence a dense spike, 8–14 cm long and 5–7 cm broad, fiery-crimson, with yellow anthers, flowering from October to December.

Fruit. Capsules squat, globular, 5–7 mm across the sunken orifice; woody, persistent, borne in cylindroidal clusters; seeds linear, tan-brown.

Climatic range. A, B, M, P, S, T.

Callistèmon pinifòlius (Latin 'with pine-needle leaves'): Green Bottlebrush: NSW, between the coast and tablelands, in rather moist sandy soils, often near the margins of the elevated swamps of the coastal plateaus.

Habit. A shrub to 1.5–2.5 m tall, usually with a few large branches forming a thin, open bush 1–2 m wide, but improved by regular pruning.

Leaves. Narrowly linear to terete to 6–10 cm long; apex acute, sharply pointed; base tapered to the very short petiole; margin incurved, the upper surface appearing to be grooved; harsh and rigid; glabrous; dark green and rather dull.

Flowers. Inflorescence a handsome and unusual spike to 6–8 cm long and 4–5 cm broad; calyx green; petals reddish-green; stamens to 2 cm long, numerous, somewhat backward-pointing; filaments and anthers yellow-green, flowering throughout October and November.

Fruit. Capsules squat, urceolate, woody in dense clusters; seeds finely linear, reddish-brown.

Climatic range. A, B, M, P, S, T.

Callistèmon rígidus (Latin 'stiff', referring to the leaves): Stiff-leafed Bottlebrush: east coast of NSW and southern Qld, mainly in deep, moist soils in the coastal gullies.

Habit. A stiff, open shrub to 3 m or so, usually with a short trunk and low branches, forming a roughly globose bush.

Leaves. Linear, 8–10 cm long, 3–5 mm wide, falcate, pubescent when young, but becoming glabrous; apex acuminate-mucronate; margin thickened; texture harsh; dark green and somewhat dull on both sides.

Flowers. Inflorescence a terminal spike, 7–8 cm long and 5 cm wide, the new shoots appearing at the apex; stamens numerous, filaments bright red, anthers yellow when ripe, flowering mainly from October to December but intermittently throughout summer and autumn.

Fruit. Capsules globular, woody, about 4 mm across, greyish, persistent; seeds slender, numerous, reddish.

'Crimson Spokes' has radiate clusters of about 6 sessile brushes at the terminals of the outer shoots, the spikes 10–12 cm long and 4–5 cm broad, dark crimson.

Climatic range. A, B, H, M, P, S, and on warm sites in Mts.

Callistèmon speciòsus (Latin 'beautiful'): Albany or Showy Bottlebrush: south-west coast of WA; very common around King George Sound.

Habit. A shrub or small tree to about 3 m, of sparse growth in its native state but considerably improved by regular annual pruning.

Leaves. Linear-lanceolate to 8–12 cm long and 1.0–1.3 cm wide, silky-pubescent at first but becoming glabrous, dark green and dull.

Flowers. Inflorescence a large and very handsome spike 8–15 cm long and 5–6 cm wide, the filaments bright crimson, the anthers yellow, flowering throughout October and November, and sparsely through summer and autumn when grown in favourable conditions. One of the largest flowered and strongest coloured of the genus.

Fruit. Capsules squat, globular, 6–7 mm across the flattened apex; woody; greyish; persistent, borne in crowded clusters; seeds finely linear, brown.

Climatic range. A, B, M, P, S, T.

Callistèmon viminális For descriptive details of the normal, tree-like forms of the species, see 'Ornamental Flowering Trees in Australia' but the following shrubby forms are more appropriately discussed here.

'Captain Cook' is a seedling variation with small tree-like growth habit to about 2.5 m, the leaves smaller to 4–6 cm long and 5–6 mm wide, pinkish while young but becoming dark green like the parent species, the young leaves pubescent, with reddish petioles, and carried on reddish-brown twigs, the crimson brushes borne abundantly in spring, often with an additional flush in autumn.

'Dawson River' is named for the south branch of the Fitzroy River in Qld. It has a distinctly weeping form growing to 4–5 m tall and as broad across the shapely pendulous crown; leaves are greyish-green; flowers are unusually abundant, the brushes about 12 cm long with bright crimson stamens and yellow anthers, flowering mainly throughout spring.

'Harkness' is a South Australian cultivar of somewhat uncertain origin but is thought to derive from this species as one of its parents. It grows as a tall shrub to 3–5 m, usually seen on a short trunk with a dense crown of slightly pendulous branches carrying the dark green foliage; the brushes are blood-red, borne singly or more often in terminal bunches of 9 or 10 spikes, each measuring 15 cm long or more and 5–7 cm broad, produced abundantly throughout spring and early summer.

'Little John' is a dense, rounded shrub to about 1.5 m with linear-lanceolate leaves 3–4 cm long and 5–9 mm wide, grey-green, crowded on the outer twigs; flowers are deep crimson in a stout 5–6 cm spike, the new growth emerging from the apex, flowering mainly in spring but sporadically at other times.

'Rose Opal' is a registered cultivar from SE Qld, of distinctly dwarf form to about 2 m tall and 1.5 m broad, with rosy-red brushes 7–8 cm long, flowering freely in spring.

'Wilderness White' is a registered cultivar from North Qld growing to 2–3 m tall and 2 m broad with a dense pendulous form and clear white brushes about 10 cm long, flowering mainly in spring and with a few flowers at odd times in summer and autumn.

Climatic range. All A, B, M, P, S, T, and on warm sites in H, Mts.

CALLÙNA

Derived from the Greek *kallunein* 'to sweep clean', alluding to the use of Heather twigs in the manufacture of the besom, a rough broom.
Scotch Heather or Ling.
Ericaceae, the Erica family.

Generic description. A monotypic genus comprising the low evergreen shrub described in detail below. The species is abundant throughout the northern parts of the British Isles and Europe and is perhaps the best known of the Scottish flora.

Propagation. Firm tip cuttings, 3–5 cm long, taken from the 1-year-old shoots, strike readily in a coarse sand between autumn and early spring, preferably in a cool, humid atmosphere.

Cultivation. Heather thrives in a mildly acid, well-drained coarse soil, with organic matter such as granulated peat mixed throughout the root zone and mulched with rough litter, or ideally, flat 'floater' stones, to maintain a constantly cool, moist condition and to preclude root disturbance by cultivation. Soils of low fertility are best, to develop the slow-growing, dense habit of the typical wild plant. Good results are seen in a cool, elevated climate with protection from direct sun and excessive heat in summer.

Pruning. The flowered shoots of the previous year should be shortened in late winter to encourage a twiggy regrowth and to maintain a low, compact stature.

Species and cultivars

Callùna vulgàris (Latin 'common') (syn. *Erica vulgaris*) Scotch Heather or Ling: British Isles, northern Europe and the mountains of Turkey.
Habit. A low, evergreen shrub 0.5–1.0 m tall, densely branched and twiggy, forming a broad, rounded or flat-topped bush 1–2 m wide.
Leaves. Simple, decussately opposite in 4 equal ranks, forming a squarish twig pattern, oblong to narrowly ovate, 2–4 mm long; apex obtuse; base sagittate; margin revolute, entire; midrib keeled beneath; pale green or bronze when young, maturing to mid or deep green, with many variations in foliage colour in the numerous cultivars.
Flowers. Inflorescence a terminal raceme, 20–30 cm long; calyx to 8–9 mm across with 4 spreading sepals, mostly rosy-purple but variable; corolla campanulate, the 4 petals about half as long as and arranged between the sepals, rosy-purple, white, red, pink, mauve, or cyclamen; flowers borne abundantly between the late spring and autumn; stamens 8, with white flattened filaments and purplish anthers.
Fruit. A small, brown, 4-celled capsule to 2 mm diameter with minute seeds.
Other distinguishing features. Flowers are rich in nectar; there are many cultivars, mostly varying in growth habit, colour of foliage or flowers and in doubleness of flowers.
Climatic range. H, M, Mts, and on cool, elevated sites in A, P, and S.

CALÝTRIX (syn. *Calythrix*)

Derived from the Greek words meaning 'hairy calyx', referring to the long awns projecting from the calyx lobes.
Fringe Myrtle; Snow Myrtle.
Myrtaceae, the Myrtle family.

Generic description. A large genus of Australian native evergreen shrubs, most species occurring in Western Australia but several others abundant in the southern and eastern States. All are grown for their neat, bushy form and attractive, spring and summer flowers. Leaves are simple, alternate or irregularly scattered; flowers are solitary but clustered together at or near the ends of the upper shoots, the floral parts 5-merous, the persistent sepals extended at the apices into a long slender awn, the petals falling early; stamens are of indefinite number, adding considerably to the beauty of the variously coloured flowers.

Propagation. a) Seeds should be harvested carefully just before dispersal and sown at once in a friable mixture; germination is often erratic.
b) Semi-hardwood, leafy tip cuttings are mostly used, taken after the young shoots have lost their early succulence and struck in coarse sand in a cool, humid atmosphere.

Cultivation. An open, sun-exposed or lightly-shaded position in a well-drained, sandy or gravelly soil is usually required. *C. sullivanii* and *C. alpestris* are hardy to −10°C, but the others listed are best grown in milder climates with minimum temperatures remaining above −5°C.

Pruning. Regular annual pruning of the flowered shoots during or immediately after the flowering period is beneficial in thickening the growth habit and prolonging the life span.

Species and cultivars

Calýtrix tetragòna (Greek 'four-angled', referring to the 3- or 4-angled leaves): Common Fringe Myrtle: near-coastal regions of WA and SA, but also in more inland parts of the other south-eastern States.

Habit. A shrub to 1.0–1.5 m tall, of loose, open form in the wild but responding favourably to cultivation and regular pruning with more compact growth and abundant foliage and flowers.

Leaves. Alternate, crowded on the slender, reddish stems, linear, 8–10 mm long, angular; apex obtuse to abruptly acute; margin entire; glandular, and aromatic when crushed; pale yellowish-green when young, then pointing forward, dark green and spreading when mature.

Flowers. Solitary in the axils of the upper leafy twigs, forming densely clustered heads of a few to 20 or more; calyx tube with 5 triangular sepals, the apices with a long, bristle-like awn; calyx reddish-green at first, tubulate, but persisting after the petals, then dark reddish-brown; petals 5, lanceolate, to 6–8 mm long, slenderly pointed to form a dainty, stellate flower 1.5–2.0 cm across, deep pink in the bud but opening to white or pale pink; stamens numerous, usually about 20–25, the filaments white with yellow anthers, flowers from early September to early summer.

Fruit. A capsule, the calyx lobes persisting at the apex, enclosing the solitary seed, ripening in summer.

Climatic range. A, H, M, Mts, P, and in elevated parts of S.

Other species occasionally grown in eastern gardens are:

Calýtrix alpéstris (Latin 'from the lower Alps') (syn. *Lhotzkya genetylloides*) Snow Myrtle: tablelands of the south-eastern States, especially in the Grampians.

A dense, twiggy shrub to 1–2 m, with dark-green, linear leaves to 7–8 mm long; flowers rosy-carmine in the slender, spear-shaped buds but opening to stellate form to 1.5–2.0 cm across, then white inside but stained with pink outside; stamens numerous, with white filaments and yellow anthers; flowering season spring and early summer.

Climatic range. H, M, Mts, and on elevated sites in A, P, and S.

Calýtrix angulàta (Latin 'angular' referring to the 3-angled leaves): Yellow Fringe Myrtle: Swan River region of WA.

A shrub of about 1 m tall, with linear leaves 6–8 mm long; flowers are stellate to 1.6–2.0 cm across, with bright yellow petals, dull yellow calyces with a long slender tube and spreading awned sepals, and attractive creamy-yellow stamens; flowering season in early summer.

Climatic range. A, M, P, S, and on the lower levels of Mts.

Calýtrix fràseri (commemorating Charles Fraser, first Colonial Botanist of NSW): Fraser's Fringe Myrtle: WA coastal heathland between the Swan and Murchison rivers.

A loose, open shrub to 1 m tall with linear leaves to 4–6 mm long, glandular and aromatic; flowers borne singly in the upper leaf axils; calyx tube 1.3–1.7 cm long, very slender, the sepals extended into long, bristly awns; petals 5, lanceolate, to about 1.2 cm long, forming a large, stellate, rosy-carmine flower to 2.5 cm across; stamens numerous, with pinkish filaments and yellow anthers; flowering season mainly in summer but sporadically at other times.

Climatic range. A, M, P, S, and on the lower levels of Mts.

Calýtrix súllivanii (commemorating Daniel Sullivan, Victorian botanist): Grampians Fringe Myrtle: Victorian highlands, especially abundant in the Grampians.

A dense, bun-shaped shrub, usually to 1 m or less on rocky sites in the Grampians, but responding to cultivation on better soils with taller and broader growth; leaves are linear to 6–8 mm long, angular, glandular, and slightly aromatic, yellowish-green when young, maturing to deep green; flowers in dense clusters of up to 15–20, at the ends of the outer twigs of the previous year's growth; calyx 5-lobed, reddish, the sepals extended into bristly awns at the apex; petals 5, lanceolate, forming a stellate flower about 1.3 cm across, deep carmine in the closely-folded, spear-shaped bud, but opening to white inside, rosy-pink outside; stamens numerous, with white filaments and yellow anthers; flowering season October and November on the harsh, upper levels of the Grampians, but earlier on lower sites.

Climatic range. H, M, Mts, and on elevated parts of A, P, and S.

CAMÉLLIA

Commemorating Georg Josef Kamel, Moravian Jesuit missionary in the Philippines.
Camellia.
Theaceae, the Tea family.

Generic description. A genus of more than 80 species of evergreen trees and shrubs, mostly from Japan and its neighbouring islands, Korea, China and South-East Asian countries. Leaves are simple, alternate, with usually a serrate margin, often dark green and lustrous, and worth planting for this feature alone. Flowers are either solitary or in few-flowered, axillary clusters near the ends of the 1-year-old shoots, the colour range restricted at present to red, pink, and white or combinations of these colours in striped, blotched, speckled or shaded arrangement, some with a violet-purple stain when exposed to cold conditions or perhaps when grown on heavy, cold, clay soils with poor aeration; in some, the stamens and/or petaloids enhance the beauty of the flowers. The flowers of species prolific in clonal variations, such as *C. japonica*, are classified into distinct floral groups according to the number and arrangements of the petals. Fruit is a woody capsule, splitting when ripe to release the several large, angular, brownish seeds. Relatively few species have, as yet, been widely used for decorative purposes. *C. japonica* has thousands of cultivars, mostly emanating from intra-specific hybridisation amongst its own cultivars, or as bud sports. Other important species are *C. sasanqua* and *C. reticulata*, with *C. saluenensis* and several other minor species, all now providing the genetic material for the development of new interspecific hybrids such as *C. x williamsii* (*C. saluenensis* x *C. japonica*). It is reasonable to foreshadow an ever greater future for the Camellia now that ample hybridising stocks are available to those who choose to use them.

Propagation. a) Seeds sown in spring into a light, friable material in a warm, moderately moist environment, germinate readily; this method is used for (i) species whose seedling progeny show little or unimportant variability, (ii) understocks for later grafting or budding, where clonal variation in vigour is unimportant, or where non-conforming individuals may be rogued out in advance, or (iii) the seeds resulting from planned hybridisation.

b) Semi-hardwood, leafy, tip cuttings strike well if taken in the early December to late January period, preferably as the colour of the bark changes from green to nut-brown; the nature of the basal cut is not crucial, and varies with the preference of the propagator; light wounding of the base for a distance of 2–3 cm is helpful in promoting a good and extensive root system. Some propagators use hormone, root-promoting substances, others attain almost 100 per cent strikes without. Careful control of heat, atmospheric humidity and water is needed, together with a suitable mixture of about 4 parts coarse sand to 1 part of peat (by volume), all sterilised against soil and water-borne diseases. A moderately high level of humidity is desirable, but since this is the hottest season of the year, air temperatures should be kept in check by prudent use of ventilation, especially in the ridge of a glass-house. If automatic misting devices are not in use, frequent spraying of the cuttings with a fine sprinkler will help to reduce their transpiration rate. Most cultivars of *C. japonica*, *C. sasanqua* and *C. x williamsii* are commonly grown by this method.

c) Hardwood, leafy cuttings may also be taken in winter, preferably from mature stock plants exposed to low outdoor temperatures to fully ripen the wood. The cuttings are treated similarly to the summer stock but are placed on a bottom-heated bench, preferably with overhead mist, or at least frequent manual spraying as above.

d) Some cultivars are difficult to strike by cuttings, or when struck, form weak roots and consequently poor growth, e.g. *C. japonica* 'Alba Plena'. Such cultivars are often apical-grafted, by the top-cleft or whip-and-tongue methods, on understocks of appropriate size, grown either as seedlings or as cuttings. *C. sasanqua* understocks are strongly preferred to other species for their vigour and adaptability to a wider range of soil conditions. Two-to four-year-old understocks are ideal. Grafting is also practised when propagating material is in short supply, as with new or rare cultivars, or when a large plant is required in the least time. The method is equally effective with *C. japonica*, *C. sasanqua*, *C. x williamsii* and *C. reticulata*.

Cultivation. Camellias prefer slightly-acid soil, growing well within a pH range of 5.0 to 6.5, *C. japonica* performing best within the narrower range of 5.5 to 6.0 pH. All the species are more tolerant of lime than is generally recognised, and in some cases, a dying back of the terminal shoots can be checked by light applications of calcium carbonate or dolomite. Most garden soils are generally suitable, although deep, coarse, well-aerated soils, rich in organic matter give the best results. Drainage must be good, as plants grown in poorly-drained soils often suffer from Phytophthora root rot after a wet season. Some cultivars of C. *japonica* are more susceptible to root trouble than others, e.g. 'Magnoliaeflora' and 'Usu-Otome', but the species C. *sasanqua* is somewhat less troubled by poor drainage. All species resent being planted deeply, although the roots of old plants will penetrate to considerable depths.

Camellias thrive best in the Central Coastal parts of NSW, especially on the Sydney hills, and also in climates of fairly similar thermal range, conditions of light and atmospheric humidity. The amount and season of annual rainfall is not of great importance where well-drained soils discharge the surplus water quickly, and are supplied with adequate irrigation facilities and suitable water to cope with dry times. The degree of shade available during the flowering season however, is critical in the proper opening of flower buds and prevention of scorching of the petals. Flowers of some sorts are less harmed by direct sunlight than others, but all tend to brown when the opened flowers, still wet with dew or frost, are exposed to early-morning sunlight. Protection from strong winds is desirable, to prevent browning or the physical destruction of the flowers. Camellias can be grown satisfactorily near the sea, provided they are not exposed directly to salt-laden winds or strong winds from the south.

Hot, dry conditions with high evaporation levels are not suitable for good summer growth of camellias. There are many hardy native plants better adapted to the dry inland. However, if growers are prepared to provide special environmental conditions such as shade-houses and humidity control, camellias may be grown very well.

In all climates, watering is important in camellia culture. The root-zone must be kept just moist at all times; indifferent results may be expected where roots are allowed to dry out from neglect, or where soils are saturated for long periods through inadequate soil drainage. It should be noted that new growth is made in spring and early summer, with the flower buds commencing to form in mid summer and continuing to expand until flowering time in autumn and winter.

For the best results, a well-balanced feeding regime should be adopted and maintained. Mulches of fairly fresh animal manure, compost or other organic matter, or even light dressings of poultry manure, may be used. All mulching material should be thoroughly disturbed every year, preferably in early spring, before applying new material; failure to do so, and to destroy the surface feeding roots that have come up into the material, results in a building-up of the level of the root-zone; the main roots are then too deeply buried and the plants do not thrive.

Regular applications of water-soluble fertilisers are beneficial during the growing season; those with 'complete' analysis are ideal, but as an alternative, light applications of sulphate of ammonia, watered in well, give good results.

Artificial ferilisers may be used to supplement mulches of organic matter, and together, the materials should provide all the plant's non-gaseous nutritional requirements. Complete fertilisers of about 10:8:6 or 10:9:8 analysis are suitable, applied to the surface in a ring covering the outer drip area of the leaves, ideally in September to coincide with the period of greatest growth activity, and in February to sustain the plant when the flower buds are beginning to swell. The quantity of fertiliser varies with the size of the plant. Young plants of up to 4–5 years need about 100 g per square metre, scattered over the root-zone, but as the plant ages and the feeding roots extend further out, the fertiliser placement should follow, with the same ration-formula, applied to the outer drip area only. It is wasteful to place fertiliser outside or inside this band.

Pruning. Pruning is not necessary for production of flowers; plants that are growing under satisfactory soil, moisture, and climatic conditions may not need pruning for many years. Plants that have degenerated due to insufficient food or water may be rejuvenated by a moderate to severe pruning, followed by appropriate feeding and watering. Pruning should be carried out before the new growth commences in spring.

Cutting of flowers in autumn and winter will not prejudice the following season's crop of blooms, and if done with the additional aim of lightly pruning the plant, does no harm whatever.

When pruning more heavily than mere flower picking, cuts must be made to a growth bud (in the leaf axils); otherwise, particularly in the lower parts of the plant, new growth may not re-shoot and the base may become bare. Particular attention should be paid to mulching after severe pruning, as sudden exposure to the hot sun may kill the more shallow roots.

The species listed below are arranged in the order of their present popular appeal.

Species and cultivars

Caméllia japónica (Latin 'from Japan', but known also in several neighbouring islands, in Korea and western China).

Habit. An evergreen small tree to 8–10 m or more in its native habitat, with a single, short trunk and ascending branches, forming a densely-leafed cone 5–6 m or so across, but of a variety of shapes and sizes in the many cultivars, and rarely seen more than 5 m tall and 4 m wide.

Leaves. Simple, alternate, elliptical to ovate, 8–15 cm long and 3–6 cm wide, the petiole 0.5–1.5 cm long, stout; apex acute to acuminate; base acute to obtuse; margin serrate or serrulate, the teeth glandular-tipped; venation reticulate, the midrib prominent, the laterals anastomosed near the margin; glabrous and coriaceous; dark green and lustrous above, paler and shiny beneath.

Flowers. Solitary or in few-flowered clusters in the axils near the end of the 1-year-old shoots, originally single, with 5 red petals and a central cylinder of stamens but now developed into a variety of floral forms with many minor variations, flowering from early May to late September in the Sydney region. (See *Classification of floral types*.)

Fruit. An irregularly globose, woody capsule, 3–5 cm or more across, the seeds to 1 cm, angularly rounded, dark brown.

Other distinguishing features. Growth buds linear-lanceolate in outline to 1–2 cm long; upper twigs bright green at first, becoming nut-brown when mature, then aging to grey.

Climatic range. M, P, S, and in microclimates in A, sheltered from hot, dry winds and direct sun-exposure in summer and autumn; in B, with shelter from direct sun-exposure at all times and only on well-drained, coarse soils able to discharge the heavy rains quickly; and in Mts on the warmer slopes with free air drainage and with light overhead shade.

Classification of floral types

Various classification systems are in use, most designed as a basis for cataloguing or for judging blooms at competitive exhibitions. The Australian Camellia Research Society's classification is in agreement with that of other important camellia-growing countries and is used here to list examples of the floral types.

The cultivars cited represent a good sample of colour and form, and are selected for reliability of performance under good conditions in the Sydney hills district and in comparable climates. Nursery catalogues should be consulted for description of the many hundreds of cultivars available which obviously cannot be listed here.

Single. One row of not more than 8 regular, irregular or loose petals and conspicuous stamens. Examples: 'Daitairin', 'Helen Calcutt'*, 'Kamo-hon-ami', 'Midnight Serenade', 'Spencer's Pink'*.

Semi-double. Two or more rows of regular, irregular or loose petals and conspicuous stamens. Examples: 'Bob Hope', 'Drama Girl', 'Dr Tinsley', 'Emmett Pfingstl', 'Geisha Girl', 'Guilio Nuccio', 'Hana-Fuki', 'Jeanette Cousin'*, 'Jessie Burgess', 'Laurie Bray'*, 'Lovelight', 'Mrs D. W. Davis', 'Pink Gold', 'Spring Sonnet', 'The Czar'*.

Anemone form (syn. Double Centre and Incomplete Double). One or more rows of large outer petals lying flat or undulating; the centre, a convex mass of intermingled petaloids and stamens. Examples: 'Chandleri', 'C. M. Wilson', 'Elegans (Chandler)', 'Grand Slam', 'R. L.Wheeler Variegated', 'Shiro Chan'.

Paeony form (syn. Informal Double). A deep rounded flower of the following forms:

Loose paeony form. Loose petals which may be irregular, and intermingled stamens, and sometimes intermingled petals, petaloids and stamens in the centre. Examples: 'Dixie Knight', 'Dr John D. Bell', 'Erin Farmer', 'R. L. Wheeler', 'Swan Lake', 'Tiffany'.

Full paeony form. Convex mass of mixed irregular petals, petaloids, and stamens, or irregular petals and petaloids, never showing stamens. Examples: 'Carter's Sunburst', 'Easter Morn', 'Hawaii', 'Lady Loch'*, 'Margaret Davis'*, 'Marie Mackall'*, 'Mrs D. W. Davis Descanso', 'Tomorrow Park Hill', 'Tomorrow's Dawn'.

Formal Double. Fully imbricated, many rows of petals, never showing stamens. Examples: 'Betty

* Cultivars of Australian origin

Ridley', 'C. M. Hovey', 'Desire', 'Fimbriata', 'Margarete Hertrich', 'Nuccio's Gem', 'Philippa Ifould', 'Roma Risorta'.

Camellia japonica 'families' of sports
Probably more than any other popular garden plant, *Camellia japonica* has a strong tendency amongst many of its cultivars to 'sport', that is, to produce flowers of a different colour on a branch at random.

When propagated, the cuttings from this branch generally reproduce reliably. If the same sport has not already occurred elsewhere and been given a name, it may be regarded as a new cultivar and be accorded the usual procedure for establishment of a valid name.

Should other different variations occur, either directly or indirectly, a 'family' of sports is founded. Throughout the family group, the original habit of growth, nature of foliage and the floral form may remain unchanged, and only the colour of the flowers will change. The following is a well-known family group: Original cultivar, 'Aspasia Macarthur', known to be one of the original Camellias grown at 'Camden Park', NSW, owned by the Macarthur family since the early days of the colony. Its known sports are 'Lady Loch' (also occurring elsewhere, and called independently 'Edward Billing', 'Duchess of York' and at least 2 other names), 'Camden Park', 'Otahuhu Beauty', 'Margaret Davis', 'Strawberry Blonde' and 'Can Can'.

Caméllia sasánqua (latinised from the Japanese vernacular name *Sazanka*): Japan, on the island of Kyushu, and the offshore islands of Ryukyu to the south.

Habit. A small tree to 6–8 m tall in its native state, with a single trunk and elevated, conical head 4–5 m across, but much modified in the modern cultivars to be tree-like, shrubby, drooping or pendulous.

Leaves. Simple, alternate, variable in shape, but mostly elliptic to ovate or obovate, 4–8 cm long and 2–5 cm wide; petiole stout, 5–6 mm long pubescent above; apex acute to acuminate; base obtuse; margin serrulate but with rounded, gland-tipped teeth; glabrous, except for a row of erect hairs along the midrib; coriaceous; dark green and lustrous above, paler and shiny beneath.

Flowers. Originally solitary or in few-flowered clusters in the upper axils, single, with about 5 white petals and numerous stamens, and woody capsular fruits, but now developed in the cultivars to larger and more varied flowers in single, semi-double, and double form, the showy stamens with cream filaments and large yellow anthers, the flowers ranging in colour from white to the full pink range and a few rosy-reds, with several attractive bi-colours. The flowers are not as durable as those of the japonicas, but when well-grown, the plants replace their flowers quickly. They flower abundantly from late January to late June in the Sydney climate.

Climatic range. B, P, S, T, and in A, in the warmer, moister microclimates, and in M, and Mts, on warm north- or east-sloping land with good air drainage, mild temperatures, and protection from violent winds.

Classification of floral types (Sasanqua Camellias and near relatives)
The following are examples of the floral types, representing a good sample of colour and floral form:

Single. 'Exquisite', 'Fukuzutsumi', 'Narumi-Gata', 'Plantation Pink', 'Wahroonga', 'Yuletide'.

Semi-double. 'Bert Jones', 'Bonanza', 'Cotton Candy', 'Edna Butler', 'Kanjiro' (syn. 'Hiryu'), 'Little Pearl', 'Lucinda', 'Red Willow', 'Setsugekka', 'Shishi-Gashira', 'Schichi-Fukujin', 'Star Above Star'.

Double. 'Betsy Baker', 'Chansonette', 'Jean May', 'Jennifer Susan', 'Mine-no-Yuki', 'Miss Ed', 'Showa Supreme'.

Caméllia x williamsii (commemorating the late J. C. Williams of Cornwall, the breeder of the first and many subsequent cultivars): the interspecific hybrid group resulting from the crossing of *C. saluenensis*, usually as the female seed parent, with any cultivar of *C. japonica* as the male pollen parent, but on some occasions, the relationship of the sexes has been reversed: *saluenensis* is the latinised specific name referring to the Salween River, forming part of the Yunnan-Burma border.

Habit. An evergreen shrub to 2–4 m or more tall, with an upright but shrubby habit with dense foliage in many of the early cultivars, but certain to be extended into other growth forms in the future.

Leaves. Simple, alternate, mostly elliptic to narrow-ovate, 5–10 cm long and 2.5–4.0 cm wide; petiole 5–7 mm, pubescent above; apex acute to acuminate; base cuneate; margin sharply serrulate, less so near the base, the points gland-tipped; venation finely reticulate, the midrib prominent; glabrous and coriaceous; dark green and lustrous above, bright green and shiny beneath.

Flowers. Variable in colour and form but generally following the classification of *C. japonica*, with semi-doubles predominating. The flowers are borne singly or in small sessile clusters in the upper axils, a few red or white but mainly restricted so far to the pink range, all flowering over the mid season to late periods from early June to late July.

Climatic range. B, M, P, S, T, and in A with regular irrigation and shelter from hot, dry winds, and in Mts on warm, sloping sites with good air drainage, mild temperatures, and protection from violent winds.

Classification of floral types (Camellia x williamsii cultivars resulting from crosses between the parent species, C. saluenensis and C. japonica)

Already over 200 cultivars of this hybrid group have been named, some early second-generation material now beginning to appear in increasing numbers. The following cultivars represent a good sampling of the colours and forms available.

Semi-double. 'Bowen Bryant'*, 'Citation', 'Crinkles'*, 'Donation', 'Galaxie', 'Glad Rags'*, 'Jamie'*, 'Kia-Ora', 'Lady Cutler', 'Lady Gowrie'*, 'Lady's Maid'*, 'Margaret Waterhouse'*, 'Shocking Pink'*, 'Tiptoe'*,

Anemone form. 'Elegant Beauty', 'Senorita'.

Paeony form. 'Anticipation', 'Debbie', 'Elsie Jury', 'South Seas', 'Tatters'*.

Formal double. 'E. G. Waterhouse'*, 'E. G. Waterhouse Variegated'*, 'Sally J. Savage'*, 'Water Lily', 'Winter Gem'*.

Caméllia reticulàta (Latin 'netted', referring to the venation of the leaves): Yunnan, western China, at an elevation of 2000 to 3000 m.

Habit. An evergreen tree, reputed to grow to 15 m or more in its native habitat. Local plants, as yet only young, are much smaller and have an open angular framework of branches and a sparse canopy of leaves.

Leaves. Simple, alternate, broadly elliptic to narrow-ovate, 8–12 cm long and 4–5 cm wide; petiole 1–2 cm; apex acuminate; base cuneate; margin finely serrate; venation reticulate, the midrib prominent; dark green and somewhat dull at times, paler beneath.

Flowers. In the wild form are solitary, small, to about 8 cm across, cupped and mostly single, with 7–8 broad petals and a central cylindrical cluster of stamens, pink or with pink variations, and very free-flowering. In cultivation, the flower shapes have been developed into semi-double to double flowers, often 20 cm across, some with loose-paeony or anemone form, in a colour range of red, pink, and white with many bi-colours, flowering mainly in July and August. Despite difficulties in propagation and their present high cost, the Reticulata Hybrids are sure to become increasingly popular. Of the over 200 cultivars listed, only 24 or so are original Yunnan importations, about half the remainder being progeny of crosses with *C. japonica*, *C. sasanqua*, *C. x williamsii*, *C. saluenensis*, *C. granthamiana*, *C. pitardii* and possibly other species or hybrids, the rest seedlings of the originals. Several local specialist nurserymen and a few other enthusiasts have imported many of the best Reticulatas from a number of sources, chiefly the USA and New Zealand, and these are appearing on the market in an ever-increasing variety. Nursery catalogues should be consulted for descriptions of the many fine cultivars available.

Climatic range. M, P, S, and in microclimates in A, sheltered from hot, dry winds and direct sun-exposure in summer and autumn; in B, with shelter from direct sun-exposure at all times and only on well-drained, coarse soils able to discharge the heavy rains quickly; and in Mts, on the warmer slopes with free air drainage and with light overhead shade.

Camellia reticulata and hybrids

The following cultivars represent a good sampling of the colours available.

Red range. 'Captain Rawes', 'Crimson Robe' (Dataohong), 'Dr Clifford Parks', 'Otto Hopfer', 'Red Crystal', 'San Marino', 'Tom Durrant', 'William Hertrich'.

Pink range. 'Buddha', 'Butterfly Wings', 'Chrysanthemum Petal', 'Howard Asper', 'Lasca Beauty', 'Lois Shinault', 'Milo Rowell', 'Shanghai Lady', 'Shot Silk', 'Valentine Day', 'Valley Knudsen', 'Willow Wand', 'Winner's Circle'.

Bicolor range. 'Cornelian', 'Moutancha', 'Purple Gown'.

White. 'White Retic'.

* Cultivars of Australian origin

CÁNTUA

Derived from the Peruvian for the local species. Sacred Flower of the Incas.

Polemoniaceae, the Phlox family.

Generic description. A small genus of tender, evergreen plants from the warmer parts of South America. The species described below is attractive if grown well in a warm climate.

Propagation. Firm tip cuttings, taken in autumn-winter, strike readily in a warm humid atmosphere in a sand/peat mixture.

Cultivation. A sheltered, sun-exposed position in a warm, humid climate is best but the plant is hardy along the northern coast of Tasmania. The soil should be light, friable and freely drained. Some support is necessary to raise the plant above ground to display the flowers fully; a cylinder of welded-mesh 2 m tall is ideal if held secure against wind with 3 or 4 stout stakes driven firmly near the circumference.

Pruning. Young plants should be tip-pruned occasionally, and tied or intertwined in the mesh of the support; thereafter, a shortening of the flowered shoots by half their annual growth, is beneficial.

Species and cultivars

Cántua buxifòlia (Latin 'with leaves like *Buxus*') (syn. *C. dependens*) Sacred Flower of the Incas.
Habit. An evergreen shrub of about 2 m tall, of lax habit unless supported, inclined to cascade somewhat untidily upon its own stems.
Leaves. Simple, alternate, linear to lanceolate, the short petioles flattened and pubescent; apex acute-mucronate; base cuneate; margin entire; venation indistinct; dark green and barely shiny above, slightly paler beneath, and pubescent on both surfaces.
Flowers. Pendulous, solitary in the upper axils of the past season's drooping twigs, on short leafy spurs 1 cm or so long; calyx tubulate, 1.5 cm long, 7 mm wide, ribbed with 10–12 prominent, green, longitudinal ridges, pubescent and 5-lobed at the apex; corolla tubulate, 6–8 cm long and 8 mm wide, twisted and folded into a narrow spiral cone at first, but flared at the mouth when open, with 5 obovate lobes to 2 cm long, the tube ribbed and orange-scarlet, the limb rosy-magenta; stamens 5, the filaments apricot-yellow; flowers are borne in racemose

clusters of 6 to 10, flowering in October and November.
Other distinguishing features. Upper twigs yellowish-green, pubescent at first, but soon glabrous, buff-white, and marked with prominent leaf-bases.
Climatic range. A, B, M, P, S, T.

CARÍSSA

Probably a latinised translation of the aboriginal name of one of the species.

Natal Plum.

Apocynaceae, the Dogbane family.

Generic description. A small genus of about 20 species from Africa, Asia and Indonesia, evergreen and spiny, with simple, opposite leaves; mostly white, perfumed, salverform flowers; and fleshy, edible fruits. A useful and attractive plant for the shrub garden in warm localities.

Propagation. a) Seeds are sown as soon as ripe in autumn, preferably under glass.
b) Short, semi-hardwood cuttings, taken in autumn or winter, and planted in a peat/sand mixture on bottom heat, strike satisfactorily.

Cultivation. A sunny position in a warm, sheltered garden is desirable, preferably close to the coast, with protection from salty wind; the plant is safe to 0°C but is seriously damaged by heavy frosts. It responds favourably to a well-drained, light loam or sandy soil, adequately supplied with water in summer.

Pruning. Light pruning to control wayward growth may be necessary occasionally; an old, neglected plant may be reconditioned by more severe pruning in late winter, when recovery is rapid during the following spring.

Species and cultivars

Caríssa macrocàrpa (Latin 'having large fruit') (syn. *Arduina grandiflora*) Natal Plum: South Africa.
Habit. An evergreen, globose shrub, 3–4 m tall, with several basal stems supporting the twiggy, leafy branchlets.
Leaves. Ovate to oval, 7–8 cm long and 4–5 cm wide; petiole to 5 mm; apex obtuse, but with a short thorn-like mucro; base obtuse; margin entire; glabrous; dark green and lustrous above, paler beneath.
Flowers. Inflorescence a terminal cyme of 2–4

large to 1 cm long and 2 small to 6 mm long, oblong to oval, pale yellow with greenish veins; petals 5, obovate to 2 cm long and nearly as broad, the flower rotate-crateriform to 3.5–4.0 cm across, buttercup-yellow; stamens 7, with yellow filaments and brown anthers; style 1, green; flowers borne freely from early March to May.

Fruit. A cylindrical pod 10–12 cm long and 7–9 mm thick, green at first, ripening to brown; seeds numerous in 2 rows, ovoid, to 5 mm, lustrous dark brown.

Climatic range. A, B, M, P, S, T.

Cássia corymbòsa (Latin 'with corymbose inflorescence') (syn *C. floribunda*) Argentina.

Habit. An evergreen shrub to 2–3 m tall, often seen on a single stem when crowded among other plants, but of broad bun-shape when grown naturally in good light.

Leaves. Paripinnate to 4–5 cm long, with 3 pairs of leaflets, with a small, ovoid gland between the lowest pair; leaflets variable in shape and size; apices bluntly pointed or rounded; margins entire, green and translucent but not yellow; midrib prominent beneath; dark green and only slightly shiny above, paler beneath and glabrous, apart from a small tuft of hair on the lower midrib, but not as pronounced as in *C. coluteoides*.

Flowers. Inflorescence composed of many axillary, corymbose racemes, 4–6 cm long, each carrying 6 to 10 flowers; flowers similar to those of *C. coluteoides* but slightly smaller to 3.5 cm across, flowering from early March to May.

Fruit. As in *C. coluteoides*.

Climatic range. A, B, M, P, S, T.

Cássia didymobótrya (from the Greek words meaning a double bunch of grapes, the application somewhat obscure): Abyssinia, Kenya and neighbouring countries, mostly at an elevation of 1000 to 2000 m.

Habit. A broad, evergreen shrub to 3–4 m tall and 4.5 m wide, forming a bun-shaped bush with a short main trunk and many radiating branches.

Leaves. Paripinnate, the main rachis 20–45 cm long, subtended by a pair of broad-ovate, green, leafy stipules about 1.0 to 1.5 cm wide; leaflets 14–20, in opposite pairs, oblong, 2.5–5.5 cm long and 1–2 cm wide, sensitive to cold and when exposed, folding neatly along the rachis;

apices obtuse-mucronate; margin ciliate; midrib prominent beneath; dark green and dull above, paler beneath; of unpleasant odour when bruised.

Flowers. Inflorescence an erect raceme, 15–35 cm long, several together in the upper leaf axils, the unopened flowers enclosed by 5 dark brown, rhombic, deciduous sepals; corolla crateriform to 3 cm across, the 5 yellow petals broad-obovate to 2 cm long; stamens 10, 7 fully developed, 2 of which are very large, the others abortive; flowers borne freely between December and winter.

Fruit A flat, elongate pod to 10 cm long and 1.5 cm wide, green at first, ripening to brown, the 16–20 seeds arranged transversely and ripening in late autumn.

Climatic range. A, B, I, M, P, S, T.

Cássia eremóphila (Greek 'of the deserts', referring to its habitat) (syn. *C. nemophila*) Desert Cassia: found in all states except Tas, mainly in the drier parts with annual rainfall as low as 100 mm, especially abundant between the western slopes of the Great Dividing Range and the Flinders Ranges.

Habit. An evergreen shrub to 2–3 m, with nearly equal branches from the base, forming a globose bush of somewhat irregular shape.

Leaves. Paripinnate, the rachis to 2.5 cm long, with 1 or 2 opposite pairs of leaflets, almost sessile; leaflets linear to 2–3 cm long and 2 mm wide; apices acute with a short recurved point; margins entire but incurved; midribs prominently keeled below; brittle; dark green to slightly grey-green; a small gland appears between the lower pair of leaflets.

Flowers. Inflorescence a 1–5 flowered raceme in the upper axils; flowers on slender yellow-green pedicels to 7–8 mm long; calyx with 2 broadly ovate sepals and 3 small sepals, all persisting after the petals; petals 5, nearly orbicular, forming a cup-shaped flower to 1 cm across, primrose-yellow, flowering profusely over the crown of the plant from early September to late November; stamens 9, with chocolate-brown anthers, incurving towards the centre; pistil falcate, green, curved over the stamens.

Fruit. A flat legume 4–6 cm long and 5–8 mm wide, grey-green at first, ripening to brown.

Climatic range. A, B, I, M, P, S, on well-drained soils only.

CEANÒTHUS

An ancient Greek vernacular name for a native plant of little consequence, but later awarded to this genus by Linnaeus because of its strong similarity.

Ceanothus; Californian Lilac.

Rhamnaceae, the Buckthorn family.

Generic description. An important genus of showy flowering shrubs or small trees from western USA and Mexico, with simple, alternate or opposite, evergreen or deciduous leaves, mostly conspicuously trinerved, and often stipular at the base. The flowers are blue, violet, white, or pink in terminal racemes, panicles or umbels, the floral parts mostly 5-merous, the petals and sepals placed alternately around the cup-shaped receptacle; the 5 stamens are opposite the petals, coloured and a showy feature of the flower. Fruit is drupaceous, drying and splitting into 3 cells, each with a single seed. Popularly used in south-eastern Australia, the following species and hybrids are well regarded for their showy flowers and ease of cultivation.

Propagation. a) Seeds of pure species are used whenever available, but some variability of type may be anticipated in the seedlings.

b) Soft-tip or firm semi-hardwood leafy cuttings, taken between spring and early autumn, strike readily in a warm, humid environment.

Cultivation. Ceanothus grows well in light, friable, freely-drained soils, even coarse sands and gravels, provided its water requirements are met in dry times. An open, sun-exposed position is best, ideally with shelter from boisterous winds, in a mild climate with a regularly distributed rainfall. There are probably more Ceanothus plants in Victoria than in all the other States together.

Pruning. Tip-pruning during the first several years is beneficial in building up a dense, leafy growth habit, but thereafter, the plants should be pruned annually, only after the flowers have faded, to remove the spent inflorescences and to control rampant shoots.

Species and cultivars

Ceanòthus x *édwardsii* a hybrid between *C. divaricatus* and *C. veitchianus*, raised in a Victorian nursery and commemorating the propagator, the late Edward Edwards: the most commonly planted Ceanothus in Australian gardens.

Habit. An evergreen shrub to 1.5–2.5 m tall, of dense globose shape to 2.5–3.0 m broad, with fine twiggy branchlets, handsome leaves and abundant flowers.

Leaves. Simple, alternate, ovate to oval, to 3.5–5.5 cm long and 1.5–2.5 cm wide; petiole to 6 mm long, pubescent; apex acute to obtuse; base rounded; margin finely dentate, each notch tipped with a small gland, the edge recurved between the glands; venation reticulate, the 3 main veins depressed above, prominent beneath, and confluent at the petiole; dark green and glossy above, paler beneath; glabrous except for the pubescent veins below.

Flowers. Inflorescence a dense spike-like panicle, 4–5 cm long, composed of many individual corymbose clusters of about 5 to 10 flowers, the main rachis somewhat stout, green and leafy at the base, and 6–8 cm long; flowers on slender pedicels about 4 mm long; calyx lobes 5, ribbed before opening, then incurved; petals 5, cup-shaped, on slender spreading claws; stamens 5, with pale-blue filaments and yellow anthers; flowers bright blue, about 4–5 mm across, borne abundantly in the upper axils of the leafy 1-year-old shoots in late spring.

Fruit. None produced.

Other distinguishing features. Upper stems channelled longitudinally by the 3 clear ridges decurrent from the axils of the short axillary twigs.

Climatic range. A, H, M, Mts, and in cool microclimates in P and S.

Ceanòthus thyrsiflòrus (Latin 'with flowers in a thyrse'): Californian Lilac: western USA between the Sierra Nevada and the Pacific Ocean.

Habit. An evergreen shrub to 4–5 m, or sometimes grown as a small tree.

Leaves. Simple, alternate, ovate to elliptic, 2–5 cm long and 1.5–2.5 cm wide, the stipules subulate; petiole 5–10 mm, pale green; apex obtuse; base rounded; margin crenate, recurved, glandular-tipped; 3 main veins converging at the base, whitish and finely puberulent beneath; glabrous; dark green and lustrous above, paler below.

Flowers. Inflorescence a thyrse or narrow panicle to 5–7 cm tall, on 6–12 cm leafy lateral shoots, the rachis pale green and slightly downy; pedicels slender 8–10 mm long; flowers pale blue, flowering from early October to mid November.

PLATE 7

▲ Camellia reticulata 'Purple Gown'

▲ Camellia japonica 'Pink Gold'
◄ Camellia reticulata 'Dr Clifford Parks'   *Photo by Charles Cowell*
▼ Camellia 'Spring Sonnet'

▼ Camellia reticulata 'Cornelian' *Photo by Charles Cowell*

▼ Camellia japonica 'Lady Loch'

▼ Camellia japonica 'Carter's Sunburst'

▼ Camellia reticulata 'Valentine Day'   *Photo by Charles Cowell*

PLATE 8

▲ Cassia coluteoides

▲ Cassia coluteoides

▲ Ceanothus x edwardsii

▲ Ceanothus 'Mountain Haze'
► Chamelaucium uncinatum
▼ Chamelaucium uncinatum

▼ Coleonema pulchrum 'Sunset Gold'

Fruit. A 3-celled capsule, splitting at the apex to release the seeds.

Other distinguishing features. Upper stems angular by the 3 decurrent, finely pubescent ridges below each leaf.

Other species and hybrids occasionally grown are:

Ceanòthus x *bùrkwoodii:* an English hybrid of somewhat uncertain parentage named for the raiser, Albert Burkwood, principal of a UK nursery firm. An evergreen shrub to about 2.5 m tall, dense and bushy when well managed, with broadly elliptic, serrate leaves to 3.5 cm long, lustrous green above and whitish-grey tomentulose beneath, the main veins prominent; flowers in axillary and terminal panicles 5–8 cm tall, numerous, each about 5 mm across, vivid bright blue, with darker stamens; flowering from late October to late summer.

Ceanòthus coerùleus (Latin 'sky-blue') (syn *C. azureus*) Azure Ceanothus: Mexico. A deciduous or partly evergreen shrub, 3–5 m tall, with upper stems, inflorescences, petioles and lower leaf surfaces densely grey-tomentose; leaves alternate, ovate to oblong-elliptic, 3–6 cm long, serrate, dark shining green above; flowers deep blue in an erect panicle to 10–12 cm tall, mostly from the upper leaf axils in summer and early autumn: an important parent of many of the modern hybrids.

Ceanòthus x *delilìànus:* here belong the so-called French hybrids, the result of complicated crosses of several species and their cultivars, mainly by French growers.

'Gloire de Versailles', one of the early introductions into Australian gardens, is a strong-growing deciduous shrub to about 2.5–3.0 m tall, with heavy, erect panicles of pale-blue flowers from early summer to autumn.

'Marie Simon' is much the same but has pale rose-pink flowers.

Ceanòthus x *veitchìànus* (commemorating the English nurseryman, James Veitch): reputedly a natural interspecific hybrid of *C. thyrsiflorus* and *C. rigidus*, originating in California.

A large evergreen shrub to 3 m or more with alternate, oval to obovate, shining dark green leaves with a glandular, serrate margin, and grey-green reverse; the vividly deep-blue flowers are borne prolifically in 5–7 cm tall panicles over the crown of the plant, in October and November.

Climatic range. All A, H, M, Mts, and in cool microclimates in P and S.

CERATOSTÍGMA

Derived from the Greek, describing the horn-like shape of the stigmas.
Ceratostigma.
Plumbaginaceae, the Leadwort family.

Generic description. A small group of about 8 species of low shrubs or perennial herbs, with alternate leaves often colouring to yellow and crimson in autumn; intensely blue, salverform flowers in summer and autumn; and oat-like, capsular fruits. Two shrubby species are grown extensively for their showy flowers and foliage and easy culture.

Propagation. a) Soft-tip cuttings root easily in a sand/peat mixture from spring to autumn.
b) Semi-hardwood cuttings are also used in autumn and winter, with benefit from mild bottom heat.

Cultivation. Ceratostigma grows well on a variey of well-drained soils, the more luxuriantly on a friable, fertile soil, but is also useful on poor gravels and in sand. An open sunny position, with shelter from harsh or salty wind is ideal. Tolerant of cold to −5°C without great harm.

Pruning. After the last of the autumn foliage colour in winter, the plants should be cut severely to about half their size to remove the seed capsules which otherwise give rise to numerous volunteer seedlings, and to encourage new, vigorous growth in spring.

Species and cultivars

Ceratostígma gríffithii (commemorating William Griffith, early nineteenth-century British botanist and collector in India): slopes of the Himalayas in western China.

Habit. A small evergreen shrub to about 50 cm tall, with a dense mass of erect and spreading stems from the crowded base.

Leaves. Simple, alternate, obovate to lyrate, 3–4 cm long and 1–2 cm wide; apex obtuse; base tapered to a 2 mm wide, stem-clasping, hairy petiole; margin bristly with red hairs; main veins hairy; dark green above, paler beneath.

Flowers. Borne in a terminal and axillary umbellate cluster, the flowers opening in succession; corolla salverform, the ribbed tube about

1 cm long, cyclamen to rosy-mauve, the 5-lobed limb 1.5 cm across, the segments broadly obovate, cornflower blue; flowers sheathed at the base in reddish bracts; stamens 5; flowering period from December to autumn.

Fruit. A slender lanceolate capsule about 1 cm long, pale reddish-brown.

Other distinguishing features. Leaf bases extended into a pair of auricles, resembling stipules, at the nodes.

Climatic range. A, B, M, P, S, T, and on warm sites in H and Mts.

Ceratostígma willmottiànum (commemorating Ellen A. Willmott, English botanical author): central and western China.

Habit. A deciduous shrub, usually 0.5–1.0 m tall and 1.5 m broad, forming a dense, bun-shaped bush.

Leaves. Simple, alternate, narrowly-rhombic, 3–7 cm long and 1–3 cm wide; apex acute, with a terminal bristle; base cuneate; margin ciliate; bristly on both surfaces; bright green above, paler beneath, turning red, orange, or yellow in autumn.

Flowers. Inflorescence a dense, terminal umbellate cluster, the 30–50 flowers opening in succession, a few together; flowers salverform, with a long, slender, rose-pink tube to 2 cm long, expanding to a 2 cm limb of 5 obovate segments, deep blue, paler towards the centre and with some coral-red shadings, flowering from January to early May.

Fruit. A slender, lanceolate capsule to 1.5 cm long, borne in clusters after the flowers, green at first but becoming pale brown.

Other distinguishing features. Stems angled, changing direction at each node, shallowly grooved, green but with reddish stripes, running longitudinally, about 1 mm apart.

Climatic range. A, B, H, M, Mts, P and S.

CÉSTRUM (syn. *Habrothamnus*)

A name of Greek origin but of uncertain application.

Cestrum; Jessamine.

Solanaceae, the Potato family.

Generic description. A genus of tender plants, mostly shrubs, from tropical America, with simple, alternate, entire leaves on often soft, succulent stems; tubulate flowers in terminal or axillary inflorescences, mostly cymes or panicles, with red, yellow, greenish, or white flowers; followed by small round, fleshy berries. All parts should be regarded as poisonous. The species in common cultivation in eastern Australia are mainly grown for their perfume or long flowering qualities.

Propagation. Soft-tip cuttings taken in spring and summer, or semi-hardwood cuttings taken in autumn and winter, strike readily in a sand/peat mixture in a warm, moist atmosphere; bottom heat is beneficial in winter.

Cultivation. The Cestrums are easy to cultivate in a moderately fertile, friable soil of free drainage, in a warm, sunny position, preferably sheltered from strong or salt-laden winds.

Pruning. Some of the oldest stems should be entirely removed in late winter each year, to make way for the growth of new basal watershoots which carry more abundant and better flowers; otherwise, only the spent inflorescences need be removed at the end of the flowering season.

Species and cultivars

Céstrum aurantìacum (Latin *aurum* 'gold', referring to the colour of the flowers): Orange Cestrum: Guatemala.

Habit. An evergreen shrub to about 3 m tall, of loose, open habit, the outer stems tending to droop from the weight of the flowers.

Leaves. Lanceolate to narrow-elliptic, to 12–15 cm long, 3–4 cm wide; petiole about 1 cm long; apex acute to acuminate; margin entire; midrib and main veins prominent beneath; glabrous; leaves thin with a soft texture; dark green and dull above, paler and slightly shiny beneath; unpleasant smelling when crushed.

Flowers. Inflorescence a mass of panicles at the end of the youngest stems; flowers tubulate; calyx green, with 4–5 mm acute teeth; corolla tube to 2 cm long, of slender taper to the expanded limb, the 5 acute lobes reflexed, the tube orange-yellow, the limb greenish-yellow; flowers sweetly perfumed, especially at night, flowering abundantly in summer, mainly in February and March.

Fruit. A greenish-white berry to about 8 mm, ripening in late autumn and early winter.

Climatic range. A, B, M, P, S, T.

Céstrum 'Newellii' (commemorating the raiser): of garden origin but parent(s) uncertain.

Habit. An evergreen shrub, 2.5 m tall and 1.5 m

wide, with many erect shoots arising from the base, arching gracefully outwards near the top.

Leaves. Ovate to elliptical, 10–12 cm long and 5–6 cm wide; petiole about 1.3 cm long; apex acuminate; base obtuse; margin finely ciliate; midrib and 8 to 10 pairs of main lateral veins prominent beneath and crimson pubescent; dark green above, paler beneath, densely tomentose on both surfaces; of unpleasant odour when bruised.

Flowers. Inflorescence a cluster of terminal and axillary cymes of up to 80 or so flowers; calyx slender-campanulate to 1 cm long, crimson, with 5 subulate teeth; corolla tubulate, expanded above the middle and terminating in an open, 5–lobed mouth, the whole 1.5 to 2.5 cm long, the 5 stamens inserted in the tube; flowers rosy-crimson, flowering abundantly from September to March but extending into winter in mild climates.

Fruit. A small, round berry, 8–10 mm across, green at first, but ripening to dark red in winter.

Other distinguishing features. Upper twigs and petioles green but covered with a thick, reddish-purple pubescence.

Climatic range. B, P, S, T, and in warm microclimates in A and M.

Céstrum noctùrnum (Latin *nocturnus*, 'of the night', referring to the strong perfume at night): Night-scented Jessamine: West Indies.

Habit. An evergreen shrub to 3–4 m tall and about as wide with slender, arching branches from the base.

Leaves. Elliptic-ovate to broadly lanceolate, to 8–10 cm long and 3.5–4.0 cm wide; petiole 8–10 mm long; apex acuminate; base acute; margin entire; midrib and 6–10 main laterals prominent; texture soft and somewhat succulent; thin and glabrous; bright green and shining above, paler and duller beneath.

Flowers. Inflorescence a short panicle of 5–10 cm long, borne terminally on short leafy laterals from the new wood; calyx tubulate to 3 mm long, with 5 short teeth, pale green; corolla slenderly tubulate to 2 cm long, broadening to 3 mm at the apex, the limb opening slightly, with 5 narrowly acute lobes, greenish-yellow; stamens 5, pistil 1; flowers strongly and sweetly perfumed at night, flowering abundantly from late January to May.

Fruit. A thin-walled, ovoid berry 5–7 mm long, green at first, but whitish when ripe in early

winter, the 1–3 black, flattened seeds 3–4 mm long.

Other distinguishing features. Upper twigs bright green, glabrous, with slender longitudinal lenticels.

Climatic range. A, B, M, P, S, T.

Céstrum purpùreum (Greek 'purple') (syn. *C. elegans*, frequently confused with *C. fasciculatum*) Purple Cestrum: Mexico.

Habit. An evergreen shrub to 3–4 m tall, with many long, flexible stems arching gracefully outwards to form a vase-shaped bush to 3m wide.

Leaves. Lanceolate, to 6–10 cm long, 2.0–3.5 cm wide; petiole 7–8 mm long, channelled above; apex acuminate; margin entire; midrib and main laterals prominent beneath; texture soft and velvety, but of unpleasant odour when bruised; dark green and barely shiny above, bright green and dull beneath.

Flowers. Inflorescence a pendulous panicle of smaller cymes, borne at the terminals of the youngest shoots, drooping with the weight of flowers; individual cymes with 12–15 flowers, on a plum-purple peduncle 1–4 cm long, densely tomentose, subtended at the base by a small leaf; flowers numerous, 2.0–2.5 cm long; calyx tubulate to 5 mm long, with 5 sharp 1 mm teeth, blackish-purple; corolla tubulate, to 2.0 cm long, 2 mm wide at the base, broadening to 4 mm at the top, the mouth expanded into 5 acute teeth to 8–9 mm across, but later reflexing fully; faintly perfumed; plum-purple, the lobes with greyish segments between the teeth; stamens 5; filaments white, anthers yellow; pistil 1 as long as the tube, with large green stigma; flowering from late summer to winter.

Fruit: A succulent, round berry to 1.2 cm or so, light purplish-red, borne in drooping clusters in late winter.

Climatic range. A, B, M, P, S, T.

CHAENOMÈLES

Derived from the Greek words describing the gaping of the 5-celled ovary when ripe.
Flowering Quince; Japonica.
Rosaceae, the Rose family; sub-family Pomoideae.

Generic description. A small but important genus of deciduous shrubs from the Orient, valued especially for the showy flowers which adorn the bare branches in winter and early spring, as well as for their ability to thrive in almost any soil or position, in a wide range of climates. Leaves are simple, alternate, stipulate, the twigs often spiny; flowers are single or double, in clusters of 1 to several, before or with the early leaves, the floral parts in fives, the colours white, pink, red, or orange, followed by a hard, quince-like pome, ripening to yellow and then fragrant, containing many shiny seeds.

Propagation. a) Semi-hardwood leafy cuttings taken in summer to early autumn, or hardwood cuttings in winter, strike readily in a sand/peat mixture in a warm, humid atmosphere, the hardwoods often planted outdoors.
b) Root cuttings about 5 cm long also root satisfactorily.
c) Mound layers may be used to produce a limited number of relatively large plants; the mound is prepared in winter-early spring, the layer stems being wounded as deeply as the cambium tissue, and mounded to a depth of 20–30 cm; following development of new roots, the layers are lifted in early winter for potting or planting out.

Cultivation. The Flowering Quinces are not particular in their cultural requirements, provided the drainage is free and the position is at least partly exposed to the sun. When properly established, they tolerate drought conditions, and cold to at least −10°C, but should not be neglected during hot, dry summers. They are commonly seen in many inland districts, some with a low annual rainfall.

Pruning. Flowers are borne on fully matured 1- to 3-year-old stems and these may be cut freely for decoration. Retention of all growth soon congests the interior of the plant to the detriment of the flowering stems. About one-third of the oldest shoots should be removed completely each year, to provide more space for the development of the remainder; such pruning is best carried out immediately after the flowering season, unless flowers are cut earlier.

Species and cultivars

Chaenomèles japónica (Latin 'from Japan') (syn. *Cydonia japonica, Cydonia maulei, Chaenomeles japonica* var. *alpina, Chaenomeles alpina* and others) Japanese Flowering Quince: main islands of Japan.
Habit. A small deciduous shrub to less than 1 m tall, with a sprawling habit to 1.5–2.0 m wide, twiggy but somewhat thin and open in charac-

ter, the branchlets armed with short, slender woody spines.
Leaves. Broad-obovate, 3.0–5.5 cm long and 2.5–4.0 cm wide; apex obtuse to rounded; margin crenulate and reddish; venation reticulate, midrib and main veins prominent beneath; glabrous and shining dark green above, paler and glossy beneath.
Flowers. Solitary or in few-flowered umbellate clusters in the axils of the 1-year-old shoots, extending for 15 to 25 cm from the terminal; calyx urceolate, green, the 5 blunt lobes crimson; corolla rotate to 2.5 cm across, with 5 broad-obovate petals to 9–10 mm across, clawed at the base, bright flame-scarlet, flowering in late August and September; stamens 20–25, the whitish filaments in a cylindrical column, the anthers cream.
Fruit. A globose pome to 3–4 cm across, flattened at the poles like a small apple, green at first, ripening to dull yellow, of fragment aroma; used extensively in Japan for making jelly; seeds numerous, pale brown.
Other distinguishing features. Upper twigs slender, flexuous, grey-green, but reddish and pubescent while young; thorns at most nodes on short spine-like twigs, the points to 4 mm long, hard and sharp.
'Sàrgentii' (commemorating Charles S. Sargent, Director of the Arnold Arboretum, Mass. USA): has a shorter growth habit than the species, with bright-orange, single flowers.
Climatic range. A, H, M, Mts, P, S.

Chaenomèles spèciosa (Latin 'showy') (syn. *C. lagenaria*) Chinese Flowering Quince: much planted in Japan and often thought to be indigenous, many of the cultivars developed in Japan having the common name, Japonica, but actually the plant is native to China.
Habit. A deciduous shrub to 2–3 m tall, with sucker-like growths from the base and many erect branches, forming a bush of stark beauty in winter and early spring when the bare stems produce their showy flowers.
Leaves. Tending to be whorled at the older nodes; variable from lanceolate-elliptic to oblong or obovate, 5–10 cm long, 2.5–4.0 cm wide petiole 1.0–1.5 cm long, slightly pubescent and deeply channelled above, subtended by a pair of serrate stipules to 2.5 cm across; apex acute to rounded; base cuneate; margin finely serrate; midrib and main veins pubescent and prominent

beneath; glabrous otherwise; reddish when young, maturing to bright green, somewhat dull above, shiny beneath.

Flowers. Borne singly or in umbellate clusters of up to 6; calyx campanulate, glabrous, 5-lobed, to 1.5–2.0 cm long and 1.5 cm across, pale green with reddish shadings; corolla rotate to 3–5 cm across, the 5 petals broadly obovate, red, pink, white, or bi-coloured in the many cultivars, the 20 or so stamens and 5 styles in a vertical column, filaments whitish, anthers yellow; flowers borne on the bare branches before or with the early leaves in June to October.

Fruit. A hard, sessile, ovoid pome about 5–6 cm long, green at first but ripening to yellow in summer and autumn, then with a pleasant quince-like fragrance.

Other distinguishing features. Branches spiny, the short laterals armed at the terminals and sometimes at the nodes with a hard, sharp, woody thorn, the black tip about 5 mm long. The following cultivars are representative of the many available:

'**Falconnet Charlet**': flowers semi-double, salmon-pink, with rose-pink shadings.
'**Moerlòosei**': flowers single, white, with rose-pink blotches and shadings.
'**Nivàlis**': flowers single, pure white.
'**Ormond Crimson**': a locally raised seedling with larger than usual flowers, double, crimson.
'**Ormond Scarlet**': of similar origin, with large flowers, double, scarlet.
'**Ròsea Grandiflòra**': flowers single, white blotched with pink, some fully rose-pink.
'**Ròsea Plèna**': flowers semi-double, pale rose-pink.
'**Rùbra Grandiflòra**': flowers single, large, deep crimson.
'**Sangúinea Plèna**': flowers large, semi-double, bright red.
'**Sìmonii**': flowers semi-double, small to medium, flattish, dark blood red; low spreading habit.
Climatic range. A, H, M, Mts, P, S.

Chaenomèles x *supèrba*: interspecific hybrid between *C. japonica* and *C. speciosa*. The cultivars presently available are mostly of smaller growth habit than *C. speciosa*, few exceeding 2 m tall, with other characteristics such as stems, shape of leaf, and leaf-margin generally following one parent or the other, the colour range similar to that of *C. speciosa*.
'**Cameo**': flowers double, salmon to apricot-pink.

'**Crimson and Gold**': flowers large, single, dark blood-red with golden-yellow anthers; dwarf, spreading habit.
'**Knap Hill Scarlet**': flowers large, single, orange-scarlet; dwarf, compact habit.
'**Mandarin**': flowers single, glowing mandarin-red.
'**Pink Lady**': flowers large, single bright rose-pink.
'**Rowallane**': flowers large, single, crimson; broad low growth.
'**Vermilion**': flowers single, bright orange-vermilion.
'**Winter Cheer**': locally raised cultivar of long standing; flowers single, orange-scarlet; dwarf, compact habit; flowers earlier than most.
Climatic range. A, H, M, Mts, P, S.

CHAMELAÙCIUM
(often spelt *Chamaelaucium*)

The derivation is somewhat uncertain, some authorities favouring reference to 'Chamaileuke', a kind of Poplar with pale stems, others to 'Chamelaia', a small Daphne-like shrub, neither reference appearing to be particularly relevant.
Geraldton Wax-plant; Common Wax-flower.
Myrtaceae, the Myrtle family.

Generic description. A small genus of indigenous Australian plants with simple acicular leaves, mostly oppositely arranged and bearing translucent oil glands, exuding a citron-like perfume when crushed; flowers are 5-petalled, rotate, pink, red, or white, flowering in winter and spring, bearing a coronet of 10 stamens attached to the rim of the receptacle; seeds are produced in a small, woody capsule, ripening in summer. Wax-plant is one of the best known natives, grown in all States, and extremely handsome when well managed, both as a garden plant or as a cut flower for indoor use.

Propagation. The mature, hardened-off, tip growths with pale-brown bark, carried over the crown of the plant in late summer, make the best cuttings; shoots of 3–5 cm long are planted singly in small tubes in a 3:1 sand/peat mixture, and kept in a warm, humid atmosphere until rooted. The roots are very brittle and will not survive root disturbance when transplanting.

Cultivation. A well-drained sandy or gravelly soil, preferably on a warm, sunny hillside, usually provides the best conditions. The plant is extremely sensitive to poor water and air drainage in the soil, and in some cases it is beneficial to build up the level of the garden bed an additional 20–30 cm or so to allow surplus water to drain away freely in wet periods. Tolerant of only light frosts to −2° or −3°, it particularly enjoys the shelter provided by a warm north- or east-facing wall or fence.

Pruning. Young plants should be tip-pruned frequently during the first few years to thicken the growth; mature plants should be pruned annually in December, or as soon as the flowers are fully spent, cutting lightly only into the current year's flowered shoots. Cutting flowers carefully for decoration may suffice, but old wood should not be pruned.

Species and cultivars

Chamelaùcium uncinàtum (Latin 'hooked', referring to the recurved apex of the leaf): Geraldton Wax-plant: western coast of WA.

Habit. An evergreen shrub or small tree to about 3 m, of sparse growth in its native habitat, but improved by annual pruning to form a rounded bush with more abundant foliage and flowers.

Leaves. Opposite, acicular, 2.0–2.5 cm long, nearly terete but slightly angular; apex with a short, hooked point; base tapered to a flattened, very short petiole; surface glandular and somewhat warty, aromatic when crushed, with a citron-like fragrance; young leaves pale green, maturing to dark green, and only slightly shiny; red-flowered forms have reddish upper stems.

Flowers. Borne mostly in pairs, on slender 1 cm pedicels, in the upper axils or terminally, occasionally in threes or fours; calyx broadly campanulate to 5–7 mm across, green glandular; corolla of 5 orbicular or broad-ovate petals in crateriform-rotate shape, 2.0–2.5 cm across; stamens 10, attached to the rim of the receptable, forming a coronet with a deep-crimson centre; flowers abundant from July to November, in a variety of colours from white, through the typical lilac-pinks to deep rose-pink and red, the coloured variants often bearing cultivarietal names describing their colour; all such material should be vegetatively worked to preserve its clonal purity.

Fruit. A small, woody capsule containing 1 to several fine seeds.

Other distinguishing features. Upper twigs pale green near the terminals, becoming straw-yellow, then greyish with somewhat stringy bark.

'**Album**' resembles the parent species, but has white flowers.

'**Bundara Excelsior**' has heavy crops of pale mauve flowers.

'**Bundara Mystic Pearl**' has pink-mauve flowers fading to pale-pink.

'**Bundara Supreme White**' has pure white flowers.

'**Dowell**' has large light-purple flowers with recurved petals.

'**Munns**' is late-flowering, of upright growth habit with pink flowers, deeper in the centre and on the edges.

'**Newmanii**' has reddish flowers and reddish twigs.

'**Pink Pearl**' has large deep rose-pink flowers.

'**University**' has large flowers, maturing to deep purple.

Climatic range. All A, B, H, I, M, P, S, and on the warmer, lower elevations of Mts.

CHIMONÁNTHUS

Derived from the Greek words for 'winter-flowering'.

Winter Sweet.

Calycanthaceae, the Calycanthus family.

Generic description. A small Oriental genus of shrubs with simple, opposite leaves, enclosed in stiff scales during winter, solitary flowers borne at the nodes in advance of the leaves, the sepals and petals of similar form and termed 'tepals', yellowish and very fragrant, the stamens 5 or 6, and fruit an urceolate or ellipsoidal receptacle with several large seeds. (The genus is not synonymous with *Calycanthus*, the American Allspice, from which it differs in provenance, and the smaller number of stamens.)

Propagation. a) Seeds germinate well if sown in spring in a warm humid atmosphere.

b) 'Simple' layers are also commonly used, laid down in early winter, maintained carefully until the following winter, then severed and lifted for potting or planting out.

Cultivation. An open, sun-exposed position on a well-aerated, friable, fertile soil is ideal, preferably in a mild climate with minimum temperatures above −8°C.

Pruning. One-year-old flowering laterals

should be shortened to several buds to stimulate strong regrowth; the cutting of long basal stems for indoor decoration during the flowering season is beneficial in thinning out the often-congested base of a mature plant to allow new water-shoots to develop strongly

Species and cultivars

Chimonánthus praècox (Latin 'appearing early'): Winter Sweet (syn. C. *fragrans*) China, but introduced to Japan.

Habit. A deciduous shrub to 2.5–3.0 m tall, with many erect shoots from a crowded base.

Leaves. Lanceolate-elliptic to ovate, 8–12 cm long and 3–5 cm wide; petiole 4–5 mm long, bright green; apex acute to acuminate; base cuneate, often unevenly so; margin entire, slightly recurved and minutely ciliate; both surfaces rough to the touch; bright green and lustrous above, paler beneath, changing to soft yellow in autumn.

Flowers. At the nodes, on 2–5 mm pedicels, deeply vase-shaped to funnelform, to 2.5 cm wide, the outer larger tepals translucent and dull yellowish, the inner smaller series chocolate to purplish-brown; flowers heavily perfumed, flowering from early July to September.

Fruit. An ellipsoidal receptacle to 3–4 cm long, ripening in winter.

C. grandiflòrus is a form with strong growth and deep-yellow flowers.

'Lùteus' has large deep-yellow, translucent flowers.

Climatic range. All A, H, M, Mts, P, S.

CHOÍSYA

Commemorating Prof. Jacques D. Choisy, nineteenth-century Swiss botanist and author. Mexican Orange Blossom.
Rutaceae, the Rue family.

Generic description. A monotypic genus from Mexico, the single, evergreen species described below. It is popular in the warm-temperate climates for its glossy foliage and white, perfumed flowers, used mainly in the shrub border or as a foundation plant.

Propagation. Firm tip cuttings taken between May and July strike readily in a sand/peat mixture in a heated, misted glass-house.

Cultivation. A fertile, light soil with free drainage, and full exposure to sunlight are the best conditions for healthy growth. Good plants are often seen growing against the north wall of a building under fairly dry soil conditions. Tolerant of light frosts to –3°C, it will survive in colder districts such as Canberra (ACT) and Orange (NSW) if planted in a warm, sheltered place.

Pruning. A light pruning after flowering helps to keep the plant dense and its foliage close to the ground.

Species and cultivars

Choísya ternàta (Latin 'in groups of three', referring to the trifoliolate leaves): Mexican Orange Blossom: temperate Mexico.

Habit. An evergreen shrub to about 2 m tall and as wide, of mostly globular form when grown in the open.

Leaves. Compound, opposite, trifoliolate, the grooved petiole and leaflets of about equal length; the 3 sessile leaflets oblanceolate, to 5–6 cm long and 2–3 cm wide; apex obtuse; base cuneate; margin entire; thin but coriaceous; glabrous, with numerous pellucid oil glands, and aromatic when bruised; lustrous green above, paler beneath.

Flowers. Inflorescence a cluster of corymbose cymes, each with 2–5 flowers on slender pedicels and standing clear of the upper leaves; calyx 1 cm wide, of 5 spreading, greenish sepals; flowers rotate, to 2.5 cm across, of 5 obovate, concave, white petals; stamens 10, the filaments white, 4–5 mm long, the anthers golden-yellow; flowers sweetly fragrant, flowering from early September to November.

Climatic range. A, B, M, P, S, T, and on warm, sheltered sites only in H and Mts.

CHORIZÈMA

Derived from the Greek words describing the separate free filaments.
Flame Pea.
Fabaceae, the Pea family.

Generic description. An Australian native genus, mostly from WA, with evergreen, simple leaves often with spinose margins, pea-shaped flowers in terminal racemes, and leguminous fruits, splitting at the apex to release the small, shiny, brown seeds. The species described below is a popular dwarf plant valued for its brilliant flowers over a long season.

Propagation. a) Seeds should be soaked for 24 hours in warm water to soften the seed-coat, then sown in a friable mixture in a warm place. b) Firm-tip cuttings, taken in late summer to mid winter, strike readily in a sand/peat mixture in a humid glass-house with mist irrigation.

Cultivation. A sandy loam with free drainage is the best soil; the position should be in full sun or dappled shade, in a climate with minimum temperatures above −3°C.

Pruning. A light pruning of the spent flower stems immediately after flowering helps to thicken the growth and to maintain the tidy shape.

Species and cultivars

Chorizèma cordàtum (Latin 'with cordate leaf base'): Heart-leafed Flame Pea: SW coast of WA, mainly around the Swan River district.

Habit. An evergreen shrub to less than 1 m, with numerous, thin, twiggy branchlets forming a rounded, globose bush.

Leaves. Alternate, ovate, 3–5 cm long and 1.5 –2.5 cm wide; petiole 2–3 mm long, green; stipules to 2 mm, bristle-like, dark brown; apex acute-mucronate; base cordate; margin dentate-spinulose and undulate; midrib depressed above, prominent beneath; glabrous; bright green above, paler beneath.

Flowers. Inflorescence a cluster of main terminal, and subordinate axillary, racemes to 12–15 cm long, each with 12 to 15 widely spaced flowers to 1 cm apart; flowers pea-shaped, on slender pedicels 3 mm long; calyx tubulate, with 5 acute teeth; standard orbicular to reniform, to 2 cm across, with a central rib and emarginate apex, bright orange-red, veined crimson, with a broad yellow patch at the base; wings broadly ovate-oblong, deep carmine-crimson; keel folded, not opening widely, pale green with deep-purple tip, enclosing the 10 free stamens; flowering from early August to November.

Fruit. A small legume, splitting at the apex and 2 sides into 2 boat-shaped halves, persisting with the dried calyx after dispersal of the seeds.

Climatic range. A, B, M, P, S, and in warm, sheltered microclimates on the lower levels of Mts.

CÍSTUS

Latinised from Greek vernacular name.
Rock Rose (various).
Cistaceae, the Cistus family.

Generic description. An important genus of shrubs from the Mediterranean countries, often growing on exposed, inhospitable sites near the sea, almost always on well-drained, gravelly or stony soils. Leaves are simple, opposite, often villous or stellate-pubescent, mostly dark green or whitish, several exuding the sticky, fragrant resin called ladanum; flowers, of very short duration, are rotate or crateriform, of 5 broad petals, borne on viscid pedicels in few-flowered terminal or axillary cymes in late spring and summer; sepals, numbering 3 or 5 according to species, are often broad, concave, hirsute and coloured; the numerous stamens, mostly about 1 cm long, are golden-yellow, forming an attractive colour contrast with the white, pink, mauve, or reddish-purple petals.

Propagation. a) Seeds sown in spring germinate readily in an open, friable mixture in a warm place with carefully regulated moisture supply. b) Soft- and firm-tip cuttings, taken in late summer and autumn, are also used, essentially so for clonal material, the preferred medium being coarse and well aerated, ideally placed in a cool, humid atmosphere.
Germinated seedlings or rooted cuttings should be potted as soon as practicable to minimise root disturbance.

Cultivation. An open, sun-exposed position is a necessity for normal flower production. Drainage must be very free, preferably in a coarse, sandy or gravelly soil. Plants thrive best in Mediterranean type of climates, but are rarely successful in warm, humid climates. Fine specimens are to be seen in and around Adelaide.

Pruning. Young plants should be tip-pruned frequently during the first year or two to build up a dense mass of twiggy flowering shoots, then shortened moderately, immediately after the last of the flowers, to reduce the flowered shoots by about half length of annual growth.

Species and cultivars

Cístus álbidus (Latin 'whitish', referring to the colour of leaves): western Mediterranean.
A dense shrub to 1.5–2.0 m, usually broader than tall, the sessile leaves ovate-oblong to 5 cm, white-tomentose, on white downy twigs; flowers

shallowly crateriform to 6 cm across, in terminal cymes of about 5 or 6, the 5 broad-obovate petals lilac-pink with yellow basal blotches and a central cluster of yellow stamens.

Cístus crèticus (Latin 'from Crete' but found also in most eastern Mediterranean countries) (syn. *C. villosus*) Hairy Rock Rose.
A broad shrub to 1 m tall, of widely variable habit, the young twigs villous, heavily viscid, green, but reddish above; leaves lanceolate to oblong or ovate, 5–6 cm long and 1–3 cm wide, dark green and barely shiny above, whitish-green beneath, stellate-pubescent on both surfaces; petioles stem-clasping, densely pubescent, whitish-green; flowers rotate to 8 cm across, in a terminal cyme of 5 or 6 flowers on 1.5 cm pubescent pedicels, the 5 petals broadly obovate, bright fuchsia-purple to rosy-mauve, with a deep crimson patch, and flushed with yellow at the base of each; stamens golden-yellow, 6–7 mm long; style whitish, cushion-shaped.

Cístus críspus (Latin 'curly', referring to the leaf margins) (syn. *C. pulverulentus*) Curly-leafed Rock Rose: western Mediterranean countries.
A dense, low shrub to about 0.75 m, with a broad base and decumbent lower branches, the young stems densely white-villous; leaves sessile, ovate-lanceolate, 3–5 cm long and 1.5 cm wide, roughly wrinkled above, the margin finely undulate, grey-green and densely stellate-tomentose; flowers rotate to shallowly crateriform to 4–5 cm across, in close terminal clusters of about 4, deep reddish-cerise to cyclamen; stamens golden-yellow.

Cístus x cýprius (Latin 'from Cyprus'): a hybrid of garden origin, reputedly between *C. ladanifer* and *C. laurifolius*.
A strong-growing, erect shrub to 1.5–2.0 m, with the glutinous, sweet-smelling gum of the female parent covering its branchlets, leaves and flowering twigs; leaves narrowly elliptic-ovate, 5–6 cm long and 2 cm wide, narrowed at both ends, with finely undulate margins, mid green above, grey-tomentose beneath; flowers shallowly crateriform, 6–8 cm across, in terminal cymes of 3 to 5, covering the crown of the plant, the broad-obovate petals white, with a deep-carmine, feathered blotch at the base, the flowers supported by yellow, scaly, pubescent sepals; stamens golden-yellow.
'**Albiflòrus**' is similar but has pure-white petals.

Cístus ladánifer (Latin 'yielding ladanum', a fragrant, resinous gum used in perfumes and medicines): Gum Cistus: western Mediterranean countries.
An upright shrub 1.0–1.5 m tall, with a clear, viscid exudation covering the upper stems, upper surfaces of leaves and the inflorescence; leaves lanceolate to 8–9 cm long and 2 cm wide, the petiole about 7–9 mm long, splayed at the base, channelled above; leaves dark green above, whitish-tomentose beneath; flowers solitary on short axillary spurs, saucer-shaped to 8–9 cm across, the broad, obovate, frilled petals to 4 cm wide, thin and fragile, white, with a 1 cm brownish-crimson blotch at the base marked with deep crimson on the edges; stamens 8–10 mm long, bright yellow.

Cístus laurifòlius (Latin 'with leaves like *Laurus*'): Laurel-leafed Rock Rose: western Mediterranean countries.
A large, open shrub to 2 m or more, of irregular globular shape; leaves lanceolate to narrow-ovate, 6–7 cm long and 3–4 cm wide, petiolate, channelled above, tapered narrowly to both ends, slightly undulate on the edge, dark green and viscid above, grey- to brown-tomentose beneath; flowers rotate to 6–7 cm across, the 5 obovate petals overlapped to form an almost circular flower, borne in a terminal cyme of 5 or 6, the buds very large, enclosed in yellowish, pubescent sepals; flowers white, suffused with yellow at the base, the stamens also yellow, but deeper in colour.

Cístus x purpùreus (Latin 'purple'): an interspecific hybrid, reputedly between *C. ladanifer* and *C. creticus*.
A broad-based bush to 1.0–1.25 m tall and a little wider, the lower branches decumbent, the crown bun-shaped; leaves lanceolate, 4–5 cm long and 1.5 cm wide, on slender, reddish, viscid stems, nearly sessile, concave and rugose above, the ends equally tapered, the margin wrinkly-undulate, slightly grey-green above, white stellate-tomentose below; flowers rotate-crateriform, 7–8 cm across, in small, terminal clusters of mostly 3 or 4, the 5 broad-obovate petals with crepe-like texture and ruffled margin, purplish-carmine, with a basal blotch of chocolate-maroon; stamens golden-yellow.
'**Brilliancy**'. Orchid Rock Rose: rosy-carmine, with a small deep-maroon blotch at the base of the petals; stamens golden-yellow.

Cístus salvifòlius (Latin 'with *Salvia*-like leaves'): Sage-leafed Rock Rose: Mediterranean and southern European countries.

A low procumbent shrub to 0.75 m tall and 1.5 m wide, with slender, spreading, stellate-pubescent branches, viscid and slightly aromatic; leaves elliptic to slightly ovate, 2–4 cm long and 1–2 cm wide, wrinkled and rough, and dark grey-green above, whitish-grey below, stellate-pubescent on both surfaces; flowers rotate, 4–5 cm wide, solitary or in small cymes of up to 3, the 5 obovate petals crepe-like at the edge, white, suffused with yellow at the base, with showy golden-yellow stamens.

The following cultivars do well in Australian gardens:

'Silver Pink'. An early and now well established plant in Australian gardens, of hybrid origin, thought to be a cross between *C. creticus* and *C. laurifolius*.

An attractive plant, growing to a broad, bun-shaped bush to 0.75 m tall and often twice as wide; leaves lanceolate to 5–6 cm long, resembling those of *C. laurifolius*, but dark green and slightly viscid above, grey-green below; flowers shallowly cup-shaped to 6–7 cm wide, the obovate petals somewhat angular at the apex, silvery-pink, paler towards the centre, and without blotches at the base, but with showy golden-yellow stamens.

'Sunset' is an old and well-regarded cultivar of *C.* x *pulverulentus*, the interspecific hybrid between *C. albidus* and *C. crispus*.

A spreading shrub to 0.75 m tall but usually much wider, with decumbent lower branches; leaves ovate-lanceolate to 5–7 cm long, with a finely undulate margin, dark sage-green above, whitish-grey and villous beneath; flowers rotate to 5–6 cm across, rosy-cerise, with golden-yellow stamens.

Climatic range. All species perform well in A, H, I, M, Mts, P, and on selected elevated sites, preferably on the Hawkesbury sandstone areas of S.

CLERODÉNDRUM (syn. *Clerodendron*)

Derivation obscure but thought to be from the Greek words referring to its disputed medicinal qualities.

Blue Butterfly Bush; Glory Bower (various).
Verbenaceae, the Verbena family.

Generic description. A large genus of tender plants, mostly from the tropical parts of Africa and South-East Asia, only a few used in Australian gardens. The species are mostly evergreen but some lose their leaves when exposed to cold temperatures. Leaves are mainly opposite, flowers are terminal, or in the upper axils, of various shapes and colours and produced mostly in summer.

Propagation. a) Seeds are sown as soon as ripe, in a friable mixture in a warm glass-house.
b) Soft-tip cuttings, taken in spring or summer, or semi-hardwood cuttings taken in autumn, strike readily in a sand/peat mixture in a heated and misted part of a glass-house.

Cultivation. All species are sensitive to cold and give their best performance in a sunny or lightly shaded situation, sheltered from cold and violent winds, in a fertile, freely drained soil. *C. ugandense* is a strong-growing species tolerant of light frosts to 0°C without serious injury, but all should be grown in the warmest possible exposure.

Pruning. After all risk of frost has passed, *C. ugandense* should be pruned in early spring reducing the length of last season's growth by at least half, and shaping the bush into its natural obovoid form.

Species and cultivars

Clerodéndrum ugandense (Latin 'from Uganda'): Blue Butterfly Bush: western Kenya, around Nairobi and Mount Kenya, to Lake Victoria and Uganda, often at elevations of 1000 m or more; although astride the Equator, from 2°S to 4°N, the climate is cool and temperate in winter, with light frosts.

Habit. An evergreen shrub to 3 m or so, with an upright, branching habit.

Leaves. Simple, opposite or 3 whorled, narrow-elliptic to oblanceolate, 8–10 cm long and 2–3 cm broad; apex acute to acuminate; base cuneate; margin ciliate, with coarse serrations near the apex; midrib prominent beneath, the surface glandular dotted; glabrous; dark green above, paler beneath.

Flowers. Inflorescence a loose, terminal panicle to 12–15 cm tall, of many flowers opening in succession; calyx campanulate to 3 mm long; corolla of 4 obovate, wing-like pale-blue petals and 1 deeply concave, dark violet-blue petal twice as long as the others, the whole to 3 cm long and 2 cm wide; stamens 4, long exserted, curving over the top of the flower, pale blue; flowering period from November to April, or even later in warm microclimates.

Fruit. A berry-like drupe, green at first but ripening to black; seeds ovoid to 6 mm, creamy-white, ripening in autumn-winter.

Other distinguishing features. Stems roughly hexagonal or square, olive- to bright-green.

Climatic range. B, P, S, T, and in warm microclimates in A and M.

Other species occasionally grown in Australian gardens are:

Clerodéndrum búngei (commemorating Prof. Alexander von Bunge, nineteenth-century Ukranian botanist) (syn. *C. foetidum*) China.

Habit. An evergreen shrub to 1.5–2.0 m tall with many erect shoots from the base, branching towards the terminals.

Leaves. Ovate-cordate, 10–18 cm long and only slightly narrower, the petiole 8–12 cm long, puberulent; dull dark green above, paler and densely reddish-pubescent beneath, at least on the prominent veins.

Flowers. Inflorescence a terminal corymbose cluster 10–12 cm across, the flowers tubulate, opening to 2 cm across the spreading, 5-petalled limb, magenta-red, fragrant, flowering in late summer and autumn.

Climatic range. A, B, M, P, S, T.

Clerodéndrum philippinum (Latin 'from the Philippines') (syn. *C. fragrans*) Fragrant Glory Bower: China and offshore islands.

Habit. A deciduous shrub to 1.5–2.0 m tall, with slightly ridged tomentose stems spreading upwards and outwards from the base.

Leaves. Broadly ovate, 10–20 cm long and 10–12 cm across; apex acute to shortly acuminate; base cordate; margin shallowly dentate; dark green and puberulent, at least while young; unpleasantly aromatic when bruised.

Flowers. Inflorescence a broad, terminal corymb of about 50 flowers, carried clear of the upper leaves; flowers singly, shortly funnelform to 3 cm across, the 5 rounded petals pale pink, heavily fragrant, flowering in summer and autumn; sepals crimson.

'Pleniflòrum' (Latin 'with double flowers'): has fully double flowers to 3.5 cm across, soft shell-pink with deeper rose-pink shadings.

Climatic range. B, P, S, T, and in warm sheltered microclimates in A and M.

Clerodéndrum speciosíssimum (Latin 'very showy') (syn. *C. fallax*) Red Glory Bower: Java and neighbouring islands.

Habit. A tender evergreen shrub to about 2 m tall with erect, squarish shoots forming a globose bush to 1.5 m wide.

Leaves. Broadly ovate, 15–20 cm long and 10–12 cm wide on a stout, pubescent petiole 15–20 cm long; apex acute to shortly acuminate; base cordate; margin mostly entire or shallowly sinuate; pubescent on both surfaces; dark green above, paler beneath; of unpleasant odour when crushed.

Flowers. Inflorescence an erect, terminal panicle, 25 to 35 cm tall and 12–15 cm broad, composed of many flowers arranged in small clusters of 6 to 10; flowers club-shaped at first, with a long slender tube, the limb of 5 narrow oblanceolate petals spreading to 4–5 cm across, and reflexing fully when mature; stamens 4, long exserted, the filaments red; flowering season through summer to autumn.

Climatic range. B, P, S, T.

Clerodéndrum trichótomum (Latin 'with branchlets ternately divided'): Harlequin Glory Bower: the Orient, mainly China, Korea, Japan and neighbouring islands.

Habit. A large deciduous shrub to 3 to 5 m tall, usually with a broadly rounded form, but occasionally tree-like when grown on a single stem.

Leaves. Ovate, 15–20 cm long and 6–12 cm wide; petiole 4–8 cm long, pubescent; apex acuminate; base cordate to obtuse; margin entire or coarsely crenate or sinuate; venation tri-nerved at the base, with 2–3 pairs of other prominent veins; puberulent and dark green above, paler beneath.

Flowers. Inflorescence a terminal, corymbose cluster, 10–15 cm across, consisting of numerous 3-pronged cymes, all clear of the upper leaves; calyx funnelform, with 5 lanceolate-ovate, acuminate sepals to 1.5 cm long, red and succulent, spreading to stellate form and reflexing when mature; corolla slenderly tubulate below, to 2.5 cm long, the 5-lobed limb expanding to 2.5 cm across, fragrant, white; stamens 4, with reddish-purple anthers; flowers abundant in summer and early autumn.

Fruit. A globose, fleshy drupe to 5–7 mm across, deep turquoise-blue, lustrous, the stellate calyx then crimson, providing a striking colour contrast in autumn and early winter.

var. *fargesii* (commemorating Fr Paul Farges, nineteenth-century French missionary in China): central and western China: is somewhat similar but the young leaves are coppery-red, becoming bright green at maturity, the calyx being green at first, maturing to pink, with pale turquoise-blue fruits.
Climatic range. A, B, M, P, S, T.

CLIÁNTHUS

Derived from the Greek words meaning 'glory' and 'flower', describing the showy pea-shaped flowers.
Glory Pea or Sturt's Desert Pea; New Zealand Kaka Beak.
Fabaceae, the Pea family.

Generic description. A small genus of two species, one from Australia, the other from New Zealand, with evergreen, alternate, imparipinnate leaves, large pea-shaped flowers in short, axillary, racemose clusters, and inflated, 2-celled, leguminous fruits containing many small seeds.

Propagation. C. *formosus* is best grown by seeds planted directly into their permanent positions in early spring, or in large individual containers so as to minimise root disturbance at planting time. The seed coat is extremely hard and needs to be scarified, or filed carefully in one small spot, so that water may penetrate; the seeds are then sown at once in a coarse well-drained material kept just-moist until germination is complete. C. *puniceus* is treated similarly or may be propagated by semi-hardwood leafy tip cuttings taken after the young growth hardens slightly in summer and autumn, or in winter if a heated glass-house is available.

Cultivation. C. *formosus* is a natural xerophyte, thriving in hot, dry, desert conditions, or elsewhere in coarse, gravelly or sandy soil with perfect drainage, sheltered from excessive rain. C. *puniceus* is less sensitive to its environment but best results are obtained in similar soil conditions, in a mild climate with only light frosts.

Pruning. C. *formosus* is short-lived and is often treated as an annual, with fresh sowings of seeds each year in early spring; plants in a healthy state growing in a suitable environment may be kept for an additional year or two, however, by light pruning of the flowered stems only, immediately after the flowers fade. C. *puniceus* too, is the better for moderate pruning of the youngest shoots after flowering.

Both species may be made to climb or scramble over wire-covered supports or tree stumps to a height of 1 or 2 m, or made to cascade over an embankment or low wall. C. *puniceus*, being the more permanent in growth, makes a fine espalier plant against a sunny wall.

Species and cultivars

Cliánthus formòsus (Latin 'beautiful') (syn. C. *dampieri*, C. *speciosus*) Desert Pea, Glory Pea or Sturt's Desert Pea; native of dry regions of the Australian interior: the official floral emblem of SA.

Habit. An evergreen, procumbent plant spreading to about 1.0–1.5 m across, becoming erect only when supported.

Leaves. Compound, alternate, imparipinnate to 10–15 cm long, with the 11 to about 21 nearly sessile leaflets in opposite pairs; leaflets elliptic to slightly obovate, 2.0–3.5 cm long and 1–2 cm wide; apices obtuse to acute; margin entire but often softly ciliate; stipules broad and foliaceous, partly stem-clasping; midrib prominent beneath; finely puberulent above but densely villous beneath; soft silvery-grey.

Flowers. Inflorescence a dense, axillary raceme of up to 10–12 flowers on an erect, angular peduncle of 10–15 cm, standing clear of the upper leaves; calyx to 2 cm long, with 5 slender, acuminate, pubescent lobes; corolla pea-shaped to about 6–8 cm long, held perpendicularly on drooping, reddish pedicels to 1.3 cm long, standard petal uppermost, with acute apex and swollen, glossy blue-black base; wing petals much smaller, linear; keel petals folded closely together, drooping downward to form a long sharp tail; all parts intensely scarlet-red, flowering abundantly in late winter to mid spring; stamens 10, 1 free, the others in a sheathed bundle.

Fruit. An inflated, oblong-acuminate legume to about 5 cm long, containing many small, kidney-shaped seeds, ripening and dehiscing in early summer.

Other distinguishing features. Stems procumbent, striate and shallowly ridged, green, with purplish-red stripes; pubescent, at least while young.

Climatic range. A, I, M, P, on dry or well-drained sites only.

Cliánthus puníceus (Latin 'reddish-purple'): NZ Kaka Beak: North Island of NZ.

Habit. An evergreen shrub or weak-stemmed climber to 2 m or so tall, of irregular, somewhat lax habit of growth, usually in need of support.

Leaves. 10–15 cm long, with 15–25 leaflets, not always in opposite arrangement; leaflets linear-lanceolate to 2–3 cm long and 5–6 mm wide; apices obtuse; bases rounded, on petiolules of 1 mm; margins entire but recurved; midrib prominent beneath; dark green and glabrous above, whitish-green and puberulent beneath.

Flowers. Inflorescence a drooping raceme carrying about 10 to 20 flowers, on slender 1–2 cm pedicels; calyx campanulate to 1 cm long, mid green, with 5 slender, claw-like teeth; corolla pea-shaped to about 7 cm long; standard erect, folded dorsally, with an acuminate apex; wings much shorter to about 2.5 cm, lanceolate-falcate; keel petals drooping, as long as the standard, folded closely together, forming a slender acuminate point; all parts variable in colour from pale to deep blood-red, flowering during November and December.

Fruit. An inflated, 2-celled, pale-green legume to 7–8 cm long and 1.3 cm broad, the numerous seeds yellow and brown.

Other distinguishing features. Youngest shoots finely pubescent.

'**Albus**' has ivory-white flowers; '**Ròseus**' has pink flowers, but both are otherwise similar to the parent species.

Climatic range. A, H, I, M, Mts, P, S, on well-drained sites only.

CODIAÈUM

Probably derived from the Indonesian vernacular name.

Croton or Variegated Laurel.

Euphorbiaceae, the Spurge family.

Generic description. A small but important ornamental genus from South-East Asia and the South Pacific Islands with simple, alternate leaves, extremely variable in shape and colour, the feature for which the plant is grown extensively in warm coastal and tropical gardens. The flowers are monoecious in axillary racemes but of little decorative importance.

Propagation. a) Seeds sown as soon as ripe in a friable mixture in a warm, humid glass-house, germinate readily, but cannot be depended upon to reproduce the parent reliably.

b) Clonal material is grown from firm tip cuttings taken in late summer to late autumn, planted in a sand/peat mixture in individual containers in a heated and misted glass-house.

c) Aerial layers are sometimes used when only a few plants are wanted.

Cultivation. The species is grown out-of-doors in sunny, warm sheltered microclimates in northern coastal regions, but defoliates quickly and is liable to serious injury from even light frosts; a friable soil with a high organic content and very free drainage is the most suitable.

Pruning. Plants are usually shaped by pruning to fit their allotted space, and are more attractive when tip-pruned occasionally to develop lateral branching and more abundant foliage.

Species and cultivars

Codiaèum variegàtum var. *píctum* (Latin 'bi- or multi-coloured'; 'brightly coloured in blotches, splashes, spots, etc.'): Melanesian Pacific Islands, and Indonesia, especially the Celebes, Moluccas and Halmahera.

Habit. An evergreen shrub, 1.5–2.5 m tall, with a short trunk soon dividing into ascending branches forming an erect, ovoid bush.

Leaves. Simple, alternate, petiolate, the shape variable from slender-linear to broad-elliptic, with or without lobes or marginal irregularities; apices acute, acuminate or attenuate; base finely or broadly tapered; glabrous and coriaceous, the midrib and main veins prominent beneath; sap milky-white; colours vary from green to yellow, orange, light to deep red, pink, and white, in an infinitely wide range, in a state of constant change with the continual introduction of new seedling forms. The variations are classified into groups according to shape and colour, with hundreds bearing individual cultivarietal names.

Nursery or conservatory collections should be inspected for a sampling of the extremely large range available.

Climatic range. B and T in the open; other climates only in heated glass-houses.

COLEONÈMA

From the Greek describing the base of the petals.
Breath of Heaven or Confetti Bush.
Rutaceae, the Rue family.

Generic description. A small genus of shrubs from South Africa with mostly acicular, aromatic foliage, and small, rotate flowers in white, pink, or red, flowering abundantly in winter and spring.

Propagation. a) Seeds germinate easily but give rise to plants of uncertain flowering quality, of dubious value as nursery stock.
b) Clonal material is propagated by soft-tip cuttings, taken in late summer and autumn, and struck in a sand/peat mixture in a humid atmosphere, preferably over bottom heat.

Cultivation. The ideal conditions for growth are full exposure to sunlight, a fertile soil, preferably sandy, with free drainage, and an occasional application of organic material as a mulch to conserve soil water during hot, dry times. Neither species enjoys exposure to strong wind which tends to dislodge the surface collar roots and blow the plant over. They are not safe in temperatures below −5°C and are not recommended for cold climates because of the risk of damage by late frosts during the spring flowering season. They make good hedges if cut regularly when young, and brought slowly to the required height, but are seldom successful if allowed to attain their full height before shaping is commenced.

Pruning. Young plants should be pruned moderately, on young wood only, to shape them at the end of the flowering season in October. With the recommencement of growth, the growing tips should be pinched out 3 or 4 times to develop dense, twiggy growth.

Species and cultivars

Coleonèma álbum: (erroneously, the *Diosma ericoides* of gardens and the nursery trade). White Breath of Heaven: Cape Province of South Africa, mostly on heath-like scrub in the south-western region.
Habit. A densely leafed, evergreen shrub to 1.5 m tall and 1.8 m wide, erect while young, becoming bun-shaped in maturity, but inclined to be loose and open in character unless pruned regularly as above.
Leaves. Simple, alternate, acicular, 5–7 mm long and 1 mm wide; apex acute-acuminate with a

short bristle; margin finely ciliate; bright green when young, but dark green in summer; strongly aromatic when bruised.
Flowers. Solitary or in few-flowered axillary and terminal clusters; calyx broadly campanulate to 3 mm long, with 5 linear, green lobes; corolla shortly salverform, with a rotate limb to 5 mm across, of 5 obovate petals, white, flowering from late July to October.
Fruit. A ribbed, campanulate capsule to 5 mm long, with 5 distinct, short horns at the apex, green at first, ripening to brown, and splitting at the apex to discharge the small seeds.
Climatic range. A, B, M, P, S, T, and in warm, sheltered sites only in H and Mts.

Coleonèma púlchrum (from the Latin *pulcher,* 'beautiful') (syn. *Diosma pulchra*) Breath of Heaven or Confetti Bush: South Africa, mainly the south-western coast of the Cape Province.
Habit. An evergreen, globose shrub to 2 m, of loose, open character if unattended, but improved by regular pruning as set out above; dwarf-growing forms are available.
Leaves. Simple, alternate, acicular, 5–7 mm long and 1 mm wide; apex acute-acuminate, with a short bristle; margin finely ciliate; dotted with translucent oil glands; bright green when young but dark green in summer; mildly aromatic when bruised.
Flowers. Solitary or in few-flowered clusters, mainly at the terminals of short, reddish twigs near the ends of the branchlets; calyx campanulate to 3 mm long, with 5 linear, green lobes; corolla shortly salverform, with a rotate limb to 8–10 mm across, of 5 obovate petals, rosy-mauve to rosy-red, often with a deeper stripe in the middle of each petal; faintly perfumed, flowering from June to October; wide variation is seen in flower colour in seedlings, many being quite inferior to the vegetatively grown stock offered by reputable nurserymen.
Fruit. A ribbed, campanulate capsule to 5 mm long, with 5 distinct horns at the apex, green at first, ripening to brown, and splitting at the apex to discharge the small seeds.
'Sunset Gold' is a compact dwarf form, to about 0.75 m tall, with the pink stellate flowers of the parent species, but with pale-yellow foliage intensifying to deep golden-yellow in late summer and autumn, when grown in a sun-exposed position.
Nurserymen and gardeners have isolated a number of other seedling forms displaying char-

acteristics of growth habit and flower colour sufficiently distinct from the parent species to rate cultivarietal status and be offered accordingly. Such names as 'Nànum', 'Compáctum', 'Rùbrum' and 'Red Form', while not always nomenclaturally legitimate, describe and identify such material.

Climatic range. A, B, M, P, S, T, and in warm, sheltered sites only in H and Mts.

COPRÓSMA

Latinised from the Greek *kopros* 'dung', and *osme* 'a smell', referring to the unpleasant odour of the bruised foliage of *C. foetidissima*.
Coprosma; Looking-glass Plant or Taupata.
Rubiaceae, the Madder family.

Generic description. A genus of evergreen shrubs and sometimes trees, mostly native of New Zealand, with opposite, simple leaves, often lustrous; dioecious flowers of little decorative interest; and small drupaceous white, yellow, orange, red, or purplish fruits. The plants are mostly grown for their tolerance of salty winds along the coast where they are often seen as hedges and shelter planting in gardens, parks, and golf-courses, generally succeeding where other hardy material fails.

Propagation. Soft-tip or semi-hardwood cuttings, taken at almost any time of the year, strike readily in a sand/peat mixture, preferably in an atmosphere of warmth and high humidity.

Cultivation. The ideal conditions for optimal growth are a friable soil, not over-rich, but with free drainage and plentiful summer water. Any open, sunny aspect suits them, even along the most exposed parts of the coast within the influence of the sometimes boisterous, salt-laden winds. They are also suitable for inland planting in places with low temperatures remaining above −5°C; in cold conditions, superficial damage to the upper twigs and leaves may occur but the plants soon regenerate from the basal stems.

Pruning. Regular pruning, at least annually, is desirable to maintain the dense leafy character for which the plants are grown. Unless hedged, the plants should be allowed to retain their natural shape as much as possible.

Species and cultivars
Coprósma x *kiřkii*: the interspecific hybrid resulting from the natural crossing of *C. acerosa*

and *C. repens*, whose habitats adjoin in the North Island of New Zealand.
Habit. A low-growing, evergreen shrub of sprawling habit, to 1 m or more tall when not restrained, but often pruned to spread widely to 3 m or more, forming an attractive ground or embankment cover of dense, small-scale foliage.
Leaves. Linear-oblong to narrowly oblanceolate, 2–3 cm long and 4–7 mm wide; petiole 1–2 mm, pubescent, whitish-green; apex acute or obtuse; base slenderly cuneate; margin entire; venation somewhat obscure above, but slightly translucent and anastomosed near the margin; glabrous and bright glossy green above, paler, glossy but finely puberulent below, especially on the veins.
Flowers. Not seen.
Fruit. A pale-blue, fleshy, ellipsoidal drupe 7–8 mm long, produced in autumn but often partly obscured by the foliage.
Other distinguishing features. Youngest twigs pale brown, puberulent, becoming grey in maturity.
'Kiřkii Variegàta' is similar, but has green and ivory-white variegated foliage.
Climatic range. A, B, M, P, S, T, and in warm microclimates in the lower Mts.

Coprósma rèpens (Latin *repere*, 'to creep along the ground', referring to the decumbent lower stems) (syn. *C. baueri*, *C. retusa*) Looking-glass Plant or Taupata: New Zealand, native to the rocky foreshores and sandy heaths of the North Island and the warmer parts of the South Island.
Habit. An evergreen shrub, usually 2–3 m tall and often shaped by pruning, but in age and when unrestrained, developing tree-like form to 8 m with a broad, flat-topped crown, especially when not exposed to strong wind.
Leaves. Broad-ovate to oval, 5–10 cm long and 5–6 cm wide; petiole 1–2 cm long, fleshy, grooved above; apex variable, mostly rounded or shallowly retuse, with a small, broadly acute projection at the tip; base broadly cuneate; margin entire; glabrous, thick and fleshy; venation reticulate with conspicuous, glandular, emerald-green depressions at the junction of the veins; midrib and main laterals translucent; lustrous-green above, paler and dull beneath.
Flowers. Dioecious, the staminate flowers in a tight umbellate cluster on 1–2 cm long peduncles; pistillate flowers in smaller clusters of 4 to 6, all greenish-white, among the upper leafy shoots and often almost wholly hidden.

Fruit. A fleshy, obovoid drupe 6–8 mm long, several together in a cluster, orange-yellow, usually ripening between January and March.

Other distinguishing features. Upper stems pale green and fleshy, squarish, with small green stipules at the nodes between the opposite leaf bases.

'**Marble Queen**' is a cultivar with attractive cream and green variegated leaves, the ground colour cream, with irregular patches and splashes of dark glossy green, mostly in the middle; in some plants a solid green blotch of irregular size and shape dominates the centre. Upper twigs are whitish but eventually become green.

'**Marble Chips**' is probably a bud-sport from the above, with green and cream stippled and spotted variegation, in about equal parts of each.

'**Picturàta**' has a central, creamy-yellow blotch, surrounded by the dark glossy green of the parent species, and an intermediate zone of pale lettuce-green caused by the mixture of the two solid colours.

'**Variegàta**' has the parent's glossy green leaves, with a creamy-yellow margin of irregular width, and pale grey-green beneath.

Climatic range. All A, B, M, P, S, T.

CORÒKIA

The latinised version of the native Maori name, Korokio.

Wire-netting Bush.

Cornaceae, the Dogwood family.

Generic description. A small genus of evergreen shrubs from New Zealand with simple, alternate leaves, small axillary, yellow flowers, and drupaceous fruits. Two species are grown in Australian gardens for their unusual and interesting branch pattern.

Propagation. Firm-tip cuttings, 6–8 cm long, strike readily in a sand/peat mixture in a cool, humid atmosphere, preferably between late spring and autumn.

Cultivation. Any moderately fertile, freely drained soil is suitable, ideally in a sun-exposed position, in a climate with warm summers and cool winters, the lowest temperatures remaining above –5°C. The species described below are also suitable for seaside gardens, preferably with some shelter.

Pruning. An annual trim after the summer flowering season is beneficial to maintain control of the angular, irregular growth habit.

Species and cultivars

Coròkia cotoneáster (Latin 'resembling the small-leafed Cotoneasters'): Wire-netting Bush: both islands of NZ.

Habit. An evergreen shrub to 3 m tall and as wide, of twiggy growth and with thin, much-angled branchlets, giving rise to its apt common name.

Leaves. Simple, alternate, but confined to short axillary spurs, broadly spathulate, 8–10 mm long and 5 mm wide; petiole 2 mm, flattened, cream; apex rounded-emarginate; base tapered abruptly below the middle; margin entire; glabrous; dull green above, whitish-grey and finely tomentose beneath.

Flowers. Solitary or in twos or threes from the upper twigs, on grey-green pedicels 2–3 mm long; calyx stellate to 3 mm across with 5 acute teeth; corolla stellate to 1.3 cm across, of 5–7 primrose-yellow petals; lightly perfumed; flowers from early October to January.

Fruit. A fleshy, globose drupe, 7–8 mm long, orange to bright red in March-May.

Other distinguishing features. Upper twigs thin, wiry, flexuose, changing direction markedly at the nodes, the bark reddish-grey; often grown as a potted plant on terraces, balconies or occasionally indoors.

Climatic range. A, H, M, Mts, P, S.

Also grown occasionally is:

Coròkia x *virgàta* '*Cheesemanii*': (commemorating T. F. Cheeseman, New Zealand botanical author) is the best-known of the interspecific hybrid progeny of *C. cotoneaster* and *C. buddleioides* whose habitats intermingle in the North Island.

The hybrid has more erect growth to about 2.5-3.5 m, larger leaves to 3.5 cm long, and bright yellow flowers and reddish fruits similar to those of *C. cotoneaster*.

Climatic range. A, H, M, Mts, P, S.

CÓRREA

Commemorating José Correa da Serra, 1751–1823, Portuguese botanist.

Native Fuchsia; White Correa.

Rutaceae, the Rue family.

PLATE 9

▲ Clianthus formosus

▲ Cotinus coggygria
► Crowea saligna *Photo by Bro P. Stanley*
▼ Correa reflexa *Photo by P.M. Althofer*

▲ Cytisus scoparius var. prostratus

▲ Crotalaria semperflorens

▼ Cytisus x praecox

PLATE 10

▲ Cotoneaster conspicuus

▲ Cytisus multiflorus

▲ Catharanthus roseus
▶ Cotoneaster pannosus
▼ Coleonema pulchrum (Red form)

▼ Cotoneaster glaucophyllus f. serotinus

▼ Coleonema pulchrum

▼ Cotoneaster lacteus

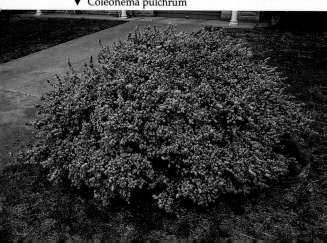

Generic description. A small Australian genus with species occurring in all States; leaves are simple, evergreen and opposite, flowers are either solitary or in small terminal clusters, the floral parts in fours, and fruit is a 4-loculed capsule. Found often in cool, shaded places beneath taller trees or near the margins of permanent streams, *C. pulchella* and *C. reflexa* are especially useful in woodland gardens; *C. alba* is tolerant of the sandy soils and salty atmosphere of the coast.

Propagation. a) All species will germinate from seeds, but are often slow and unreliable.
b) Most growers use soft-tip or slightly older leafy cuttings, taken between spring and autumn, struck in a sand/peat mixture in a cool, humid atmosphere. Hormone cutting powders are beneficial.

Cultivation. Each species has its own peculiar requirements for best performance, but all may be grown in a friable, moderately fertile soil with free drainage.

Pruning. Tip-pruning of young plants for the first several years is desirable to build up a densely leafed bush; thereafter, reduction of the flowered shoots by about one-quarter of their length, immediately after the flowering season, maintains a leafy and orderly form.

Species and cultivars

Córrea alba (Latin 'white', referring to the flowers): White Correa: exposed places near the coasts of SE Australia, from SA to the NSW Central Coast.
Habit. An evergreen, leafy bush to 1.5 m tall, of dense, somewhat irregular form, often shaped by the violent salt-laden winds of the coast.
Leaves. Broadly obovate to orbicular, to 2.0–3.5 cm long and nearly as wide; petiole 3–5 mm, densely stellate-pubescent; apex rounded; base broadly rounded; margin entire and slightly undulate; venation indistinct, apart from the prominent midrib beneath; coriaceous; dark grey-green, slightly shiny and sparsely pubescent above, whitish-glaucescent and densely stellate-pubescent beneath.
Flowers. Solitary or in clusters of 2 to 4, at the terminals of the youngest twigs, on pubescent pedicels 3–4 mm long; calyx cyathiform to 4 mm deep and wide, the mouth with 4 shallow teeth; corolla tubulate-funnelform at first, but soon splitting into 4 slender, white or pale-pink segments and spreading to 2.5 cm wide in rotate

form, flowering abundantly from late autumn to late winter or early spring.
Fruit. Not seen.
Other distinguishing features. Youngest twigs beset with bright-orange, stellate pubescence, becoming greyish, the hairs then black.
Climatic range. A, H, M, P, S.

Córrea pulchélla (Latin 'beautiful or pretty'): SE Australia, mainly on better-class soils in sheltered places along creek margins.
Habit. An evergreen shrub of less than 1 m tall, spreading to 1.5 m or so, forming an attractive leafy bush, ideal for foreground planting.
Leaves. Variable, but most forms have linear to lanceolate shape, 2–3 cm long and 3–6 mm wide; petiole pale green, 2–4 mm long; apex obtuse, shallowly notched; margin entire but sometimes irregularly notched; glandular-dotted and slightly aromatic when bruised; dark green and shiny above, paler beneath.
Flowers. Solitary, terminally or in the upper axils, on slender red pedicels 1 cm long; calyx cyathiform, about 4 mm across the truncate mouth; corolla opening to a 2 cm tube, 7–8 mm at the widest part, with 4 reflexed lobes at the mouth, variable but mostly salmon-scarlet, orange-vermilion or coral-red, flowering from late winter to mid October; stamens 8, with white filaments and brown anthers.
Other distinguishing features. Upper twigs slender, finely pubescent, green, but reddish above.
Climatic range. A, H, M, P, S, and in the warmer microclimates of Mts.

Córrea refléxa (Latin 'bent back', referring to the corolla lobes) (syn. *C. speciosa*) one of the several Native Fuchsias: SE Australia, commonly in sheltered gullies, sometimes at elevations of 1000 m.
Habit. A shrub to about 1–2 m tall, of irregular globose form.
Leaves. Variable, but mostly ovate, 2.0–3.5 cm long and 1.5 cm wide; petiole 3–4 mm long; apex rounded; base obtuse to cordate; margin entire but recurved; dark green and shiny, but glandular-roughened, pale green and stellate-pubescent beneath.
Flowers. Mostly solitary at the terminals of the upper twigs on short, pubescent, red pedicels; calyx cyathiform, 8–9 mm across, brown-green, roughly stellate-pubescent; corolla tubulate to 3.5 cm long, 1.3 cm wide, narrowing slightly

near the 4-lobed recurved mouth; mostly bright red, merging to pale green near the mouth, flowering from early September to late November; stamens 8, the filaments creamy-green, the anthers yellow, exserted beyond the tube.

Other distinguishing features. Upper twigs rough with coarse, stellate pubescence, reddish-green.

'**Dusky Bells**' is a registered cultivar from Victoria with a more compact and leafy growth habit to 60–75 cm tall and about 3 m broad, smaller leaves only slightly recurved at the margin, and smaller but more numerous flowers, dusky-crimson outside, paler within the tube, the lobes with a deeper stripe, flowering at the same time as the species.

'**Fat Fred**' is also a Victorian-raised cultivar, distinct from the species in its larger flowers, the corolla crimson-red with greenish-yellow tips.

Climatic range. A, H, M, Mts, P, S.

CÓTINUS

An ancient Greek name of obscure derivation. Smoke-bush.

Anacardiaceae, the Cashew family.

Generic description. A genus of two species recently separated from *Rhus* because of their simple, not compound, leaves. Both species are deciduous, with broadly oval to nearly orbicular leaves which colour vividly in autumn; flowers are dioecious or polygamous in loose, terminal panicles, at length resembling a puff of smoke, developing fruit as a small drupelet, dotted randomly throughout the panicle. The species described is highly regarded as one of the best autumn-colouring shrubs, and its cultivars for their purple leaves and flowers.

Propagation. a) The species, *C. coggygria*, may be grown from seeds collected before dispersal in autumn and sown in spring.

b) Simple layers are mostly used for the cultivars, laid down in autumn into shallow containers of well-prepared fibrous soil, buried slightly below the level of the surrounding soil and detached and lifted the following winter.

c) Hardwood cuttings, taken from the pruned stems in winter, are sometimes used, the more successfully if treated with a root-promoting powder.

Cultivation. An open, sun-exposed position is essential for the best foliage colour; the soil should be freely drained, not necessarily highly fertile, but should not lack water in dry times.

Pruning. Moderately heavy pruning in late winter is usually practised to reduce the number of growth buds on each shoot by about two-third, with consequent increase in vigour and larger leaves.

Species and cultivars

Cótinus coggygria (derived from the Greek vernacular name for the species): Smoke-bush: southern Europe, Middle Eastern countries and central China.

Habit. A deciduous shrub to 3–4 m tall and as broad, with a generally rounded outline, but when pruned severely, with many erect shoots from the lower stems.

Leaves. Simple, alternate, oval or obovate to nearly orbicular, the blade 5–10 cm long and 4–8 cm wide; petiole slender, 3–5 cm long; apex round or slightly notched; base obtuse; margin entire; both surfaces glabrous but not glossy; mid to dark green above, paler beneath, changing to a brilliant display of yellow, orange, and scarlet in autumn, the colour more intense in an austere climate.

Flowers. Inflorescence a terminal, plumose panicle to 30 cm tall and 15 cm wide; flowers polygamous, stellate, to 4 mm across, with 5 elliptical, yellow petals, giving rise to the long, hairy pedicels which constitute the main feature of the plant; panicle smoky-grey, flowering from late October to December, but persisting until autumn with a pale, almost-white colour.

Fruit. A flattened drupelet to 3 mm or so, carried obliquely on the peduncle; dark brown.

Other distinguishing features. Young stems bronze-green, with conspicuous pale-brown lenticels.

'**Purpùreus**': Purple-flowered Smoke-bush: similar to the parent but the young leaves are reddish-green, becoming dark green in late spring and summer, and changing to the colours of the species in autumn; the inflorescence is reddish-grey at first, deepening to dark purplish-red in autumn and fading slightly in early winter.

'**Fòliis Purpùreis**': Purple-leafed Smoke-bush: similar to the parent in habit, but more frequently seen as a severely pruned plant with larger leaves and less twiggy branchlets; leaves are deep purplish-red in spring, paling slightly in summer, but changing to bright ruby-red in autumn; the inflorescence is a spectacular purplish-red, the small yellow flowers providing an attractive colour contrast during the main flowering season from late October until December, the inflorescences persisting until autumn.

Climatic range. All A, H, M, Mts, and on cool, elevated sites in P and S.

COTONEÁSTER

Derived from the Greek, describing the similarity of the flowers to those of the Quince, a genus of the same family.

Cotoneaster.

Rosaceae, sub-family Pomoideae (the Rose family, Pome-fruit sub-family).

Generic description. A large and important genus of more than 50 species, mostly from southern Asia and especially China, with both evergreen and deciduous kinds as small trees, shrubs, and low, spreading ground-covers. All have simple, alternate, entire leaves, some with spectacular autumnal colouring; small white or pinkish flowers, solitary or in corymbs; followed by showy fruits, mostly red but occasionally black or yellow, making a colourful contribution to the autumn-winter garden display. Some are useful specimen plants, some are best used for screening or hedging, others for rock gardens and as ground-covers, while a few of the moderate growers are ideal as walling plants.

Propagation. a) The species are grown by seeds, collected as soon as fully ripe, cleaned by maceration and flotation, and sown immediately before the testa dries and hardens, in a friable medium in a warm, humid atmosphere; germination is usually complete in several weeks.
b) Cultivars, varieties and hybrids are best grown by semi-hardwood, tip cuttings taken from late autumn to mid winter, preferably cambium-sliced at the base for 2–3 cm and treated with root-promoting dust, then planted in a sand/peat mixture in a heated and misted glass-house.
c) Grafted plants, except for the propagation of standard plants, are not a good proposition, since the development of adventitious basal shoots below the graft union is almost inevitable and likely to overgrow the scion. Dwarf-growing prostrate or drooping varieties or cultivars may be grafted on more erect-growing species to accelerate their development, but should be checked frequently for regrowth of the understock.

Cultivation. An open, sunny position with shelter from salty sea winds is ideal, although most species will perform reasonably well in partial shade. They are tolerant of poor soils and even erratic water supply, but respond to better treatment with larger and more abundant fruit crops. All are hardy to at least −10° C in the more severe Australian climates but are seen at their best in the cool, moist tablelands regions on good soils and with only mild frosts.

Pruning. Single specimens, grown in shrub borders or on lawns, should be allowed to retain their natural form as much as possible, but to improve their density of growth should be tip-pruned lightly and frequently during their early development. To restrict their sometimes aggressive growth, major pruning may be carried out at 3- or 4-yearly intervals; the flowering and fruiting display is likely to be reduced for the following year because of the removal of much of the 1-year-old flowering wood. It is important to select carefully from the wide range of species to ensure that the planting site allows for the full development of growth. A large grower should never be pruned severely to fit a small space.
Hedges. The development of a dense, leafy hedge, rather than berry production, should be the aim during the first few years. Later, the shortly clipped fruiting wood may produce a diminished crop of berries. Species with small leaves and naturally twiggy growth like C. *conspicuus*, are ideal as hedges.
Walling. Plants should be trained against the wall or fence, by use of dowels or wire supports, to the shape required. Surplus growth should be pruned away from the face, without removing an excessive amount of fruiting wood. It is very poor practise to plant a large, aggressive grower on a small wall or fence merely to ensure quick coverage — it soon outgrows its allotted space and becomes an endless pruning problem. The species best suited to walling are C. *conspicuus*, C. *dammeri*, C. *franchetii*, C. *horizontalis* and its forms, C. *microphyllus* and C. *salicifolius* var. *floccosus*.

Species and cultivars

Cotoneáster adpréssus **var. praècox** Latin; describing the closely pressed branches and the early spring flowers) (syn. C. *nanshan*) western China.

Habit. A mostly deciduous shrub of horizontal habit, the stems building on each other to form a broad mound to 0.5 m tall, but usually much wider; well adapted to the rock garden or as a walling plant.

Leaves. Broadly ovate to obovate or nearly orbicular, to 2.5 cm long and 2 cm wide, stipulate; petioles 2 mm long, crimson; apex acute-mucronate; base cuneate; margin entire but coarsely undulate; main veins prominent and pubescent beneath; dark green above, bright green beneath, changing to orange and scarlet in autumn.

Flowers. Solitary or in 2–3 flowered corymbs, 6–7 mm across, the petals pink outside but white inside, flowering in October and November.

Fruit. Borne on short twiggy laterals in ones to threes, sub-globose, 1.0–1.5 cm across, bright red; March to June; seeds 2.

Other distinguishing features. Twigs dark crimson, with dull rufous pubescence and brown lenticels.

Climatic range. A, H, M, Mts, P, S.

Cotoneáster apiculàtus (Latin 'ending with a short point', referring to the leaves): Cranberry Cotoneaster: foothills of the western Himalayas.

Habit. A low shrub of procumbent form while young, later increasing to 1 m or so tall but somewhat broader; mostly evergreen in warm climates but becoming deciduous in harsher conditions.

Leaves. Orbicular to obovate, about 8–10 mm across; apex apiculate, the tip declined; base rounded; margin entire; glabrous and shining green above, paler and puberulent beneath, a few leaves colouring red before falling in autumn.

Flowers. Borne in clusters of 1 to 3 in the upper axils, crateriform, 6–7 mm across, whitish with pink shadings, flowering in October-November.

Fruit. Globose to slightly obovoid, 6–7 mm across, borne on the upper side of the prostrate stems in autumn; glossy scarlet.

Other distinguishing features. Young shoots downy, becoming reddish above where exposed to the sun; prostrate stems in contact with the soil may self-layer.

Climatic range. A, H, M, Mts, P, S.

Cotoneáster bullàtus (Latin *bulla*, 'a bubble', referring to the puckered, irregular surface of the leaves): western China.

Habit. A deciduous shrub to 3 m or more, the open, vase-shaped branch pattern with several main stems. One of the best of the deciduous kinds for its showy fruit and large leaves which colour well in autumn; best used in the shrub border in the rear rows.

Leaves. Broad-elliptic to ovate, 5–10 cm long and 4–6 cm wide; petiole 3–5 mm long; midrib and main laterals deeply impressed above, prominent beneath, finely pubescent; bright green but scarcely shiny above, pale grey-green beneath, changing to orange-yellow and red in autumn; surface of leaves bullate.

Flowers. Inflorescence a small corymb of 3–8 flowers, the corolla to 1 cm across, the broad petals pinkish outside, white inside, the stamens with pink anthers, flowering in October and November.

Fruit. Obovoid to 8–9 mm, in corymbose clusters of 3–8, bright red, ripe in early April, lasting until late May; seeds 5.

Other distinguishing features. Upper twigs reddish-brown, with fine brown pubescence.

Climatic range. A, H, M, Mts, P, S.

Cotoneáster buxifòlius (Latin 'with leaves like *Buxus*'): Nilgiri Hills in southern India.

Habit. An evergreen shrub 0.5–1.8 m tall with dense, twiggy growth to 1.5 m wide, of spreading form, carrying an abundance of foliage and fruits.

Leaves. Elliptic to obovate to 1.0–1.5 cm long and 8–10 mm wide; petiole pubescent to 3 mm; apex mucronate; margin recurved; dark green above, paler and densely pubescent beneath.

Flowers. Several to about 6 in a small corymb; crateriform to 7–8 mm across, pink outside, white inside; stamens with pinkish anthers; flowering in October and November.

Fruit. Globose-obovoid to 7–8 mm long, bright crimson, April-June.

Other distinguishing features. Youngest twigs brown-tomentose, becoming glabrous and reddish.

Climatic range. A, B, M, P, S, T.

Cotoneáster conspícuus (Latin *conspicere*, 'to catch sight of', referring to the brightness of the fruit): western China, eastern Himalayas and Tibet.

Habit. An evergreen shrub to about 2 m, usually broader than tall, of loose, spiky habit, branching in irregular pattern. A fine species for walling or hedging because of the dense, twiggy growth.

Leaves. Elliptical to 1.5 cm long and 7 mm wide, tapering equally to base and mucronate apex; petiole 2–3 mm; dark green, glabrous and shiny above, heavily pubescent and whitish beneath.

Flowers. Mostly solitary, on short lateral spurs dotted along the older shoots; flowers to 1 cm across, pinkish outside, white inside; stamen filaments whitish, anthers rosy-purple; flowering in October-December.

Fruit. A pome to 7–8 mm, the sepals persisting at the apex; bright crimson; 2 seeded; ripe by early April and lasting until August.

Other distinguishing features. Upper twigs pubescent, but soon glabrous, purplish-green and rough.

'Decòrus' has a flat prostrate form, useful for ground-covering.

Climatic range. A, H, M, Mts, P, S.

Cotoneáster 'Cornubia': a hybrid of somewhat uncertain parentage but with *C frigidus* predominating, possibly with *C. salicifolius* as the other parent.

Habit. A large, rounded shrub or small tree to 4–6 m tall, with a single, short trunk branching early into several heavy, arching limbs with pendulous branchlets, but often and readily trained to tree-like form by pruning in the first 2 or 3 years; almost evergreen in mild climates, but partly deciduous where cold is more severe. An outstanding Cotoneaster for its bountiful crops of large scarlet berries which last well into late winter.

Leaves. Narrow-elliptic to lanceolate, 6–10 cm long and 2.5–3.5 cm wide; petiole reddish, to 1 cm long; the midrib and 9–14 pairs of lateral veins depressed above, pink and prominent beneath; leaves dark green and shiny above, glaucous and heavily tomentose below, some changing to orange or scarlet before falling.

Flowers. Inflorescence a large corymb of 50–60 flowers, on short lateral spurs about 5–6 cm long; flowers white, but stained carmine outside, flowering in late October and November.

Fruit. Globose, larger than most to 9–10 mm across, lustrous scarlet-red, ripening in April, persisting and deepening in colour until August.

Other distinguishing features. Youngest twigs deep red, densely pubescent, but becoming glabrous and dull mahogany when more mature.

Climatic range. A, H, M, Mts, P, S.

Cotoneáster dámmeri (commemorating Carl Udo Dammer, nineteenth-century German botanical author) (syn. *C. humifusus*) central China.

Habit. An evergreen, prostrate shrub rarely more than 30–40 cm tall but spreading and layering freely to 2 m or more wide, generally following the shape of the ground or trailing over walls or embankments. Probably the most prostrate species, ideal for the rock garden or for decorating retaining walls.

Leaves. Variable from elliptic to narrow-obovate, 1.5–4.0 cm long and 1–2 cm wide, the petiole 4–8 mm long, channelled, bright red; apex obtuse to emarginate; midrib and 5–6 pairs of laterals depressed above, slightly prominent beneath; glabrous and dark glossy green above, pale glaucous-green beneath, a few leaves changing to red before falling in autumn-winter.

Flowers. Mostly solitary on short lateral spurs scattered along the prostrate stems; flowers crateriform, 1 cm across, white; stamens with reddish-purple anthers; flowering from October to December.

Fruit. Obovoid, to 8–9 mm deep and 7–8 mm across near the black-tipped apex, but narrower towards the base, borne singly on the upper side of the prostrate stems; bright coral-red; April to June; seeds 5, acutely angular, 4 mm long, reddish.

Other distinguishing features. Young twigs bright red and slightly pubescent at first, but maturing to dark chocolate-red with numerous brown lenticels.

Climatic range. A, H, M, Mts, P, S.

Cotoneáster franchétii (commemorating Adrien R. Franchet, nineteenth-century French botanist and author of a number of important Cotoneaster species from western China): Yunnan and western China to Tibet.

Habit. An evergreen shrub to 3 m tall and 2–3 m wide, with many erect stems arising from the base, arching gracefully outwards; of dense, leafy habit, ideal for walling or hedging.

Leaves. 2.5–4.0 cm long and 1.0–1.8 cm broad, broadly elliptic to obovate, the petiole to 3 mm long; dark green and shiny above, sparsely pubescent while young, silvery-white and heavily pubescent below; some leaves turn orange and scarlet before falling in autumn.

Flowers. Inflorescence a small corymb to 2 cm across, the flowers about 6 to 15, each 8–9 mm across, white, with crimson stains and blotches, especially on the outside, flowering on short, leafy, axillary spurs, in November and December. One of the most handsome in flower.

Fruit. Obovoid, to 9–10 mm long, slightly less in diameter, depressed at the apex, borne in small groups of 1 to about 6 at the ends of short lateral spurs, salmon-pink at first, with a yellowish cheek, deepening to dark salmon-orange and finally scarlet, March to June; seeds 3.

Other distinguishing features. Youngest twigs green, with woolly tomentum, becoming reddish-brown and glabrous, with prominent brown prominent lenticels.

Climatic range. A, H, M, Mts, P, S.

Cotoneáster frígidus (Latin 'from a cold region'): lower levels of the Himalayas.

Habit. A partly deciduous shrub or small tree to 5 m or so, with several large spreading branches carrying the drooping branchlets. One of the best of the larger species for foliage and fruit.

Leaves. Elliptic-oblong, 6–10 cm long and 2.5–3.5 cm wide; petiole to 1 cm long, pubescent; glabrous slightly shiny and dark green above, but paler and densely pubescent beneath, some changing to orange and red before falling in autumn-winter.

Flowers. Inflorescence a pubescent corymb, 6–8 cm across, with 30–50 flowers on short lateral shoots near the ends of the branchlets; flowers 9–10 mm across, white, flowering in October and November; stamens about 20, filaments white, anthers purple.

Fruit. In a large corymbose cluster of up to 40 or more; sub-globose to slightly obovoid, to 7–8 mm long; bright red, ripening in April and lasting to July; seeds 2, cream, angular.

Other distinguishing features. Upper shoots reddish, pubescent, becoming mahogany-red when mature.

Climatic range. A, B, H, M, Mts, P, S.

Cotoneáster glaucophýllus f. *serotínus* (Greek 'with blue-grey leaves'; Latin 'late', referring to the persistence of the fruit): western China.

Habit. An evergreen shrub to 4 m tall and as wide, with several stout branches near the base of the short trunk forming a broad hemisphere with pendulous branchlets; with early training and pruning, may be grown as a small tree to 5–6 m tall with a short trunk.

Leaves. Elliptical or slightly obovate, 5–7 cm long and 3–4 cm wide; petiole to 1 cm, finely pubescent; apex obtuse and mucronate; midrib

reddish and 7–8 pairs of main veins prominent beneath; glabrous, dark green and shiny above, slightly glaucous and downy below at first, becoming glabrous, some leaves turning scarlet in autumn-winter before falling.

Flowers. Inflorescence a terminal corymb, 4–5 cm across, of 20 to 50 rotate flowers to 8 mm across, white, with about 20 stamens with crimson anthers; flowers borne abundantly on 4–10 cm long leafy shoots in November.

Fruit. A fleshy, 2-seeded pome, to 7–8 mm across, slightly obovoid, with a flattened apex, borne in umbellate clusters of 25–45 at the ends of short spurs along the pendulous branches; fruit scarlet-red, the persistent calyx with dark-grey, shaggy hairs; fruit fully coloured by late March, persisting until July.

Other distinguishing features. Upper twigs pubescent while young, becoming glaucous and reddish; veins on the upper surface of leaves not deeply impressed as those of *C. lacteus*.

Climatic range. A, H, M, Mts, P, S.

Cotoneáster henryànus (commemorating Dr Augustine Henry, English plant collector in China and botanical author): central China.

Habit. A large, partly deciduous shrub to 3–4 m tall, of open, branching habit with several main trunks and a vase-shaped outline with pendulous ends, but sometimes trained as a single-trunked tree, then reaching 5–6 m tall.

Leaves. Narrowly elliptic to 6–12 cm long and 2–3 cm wide, one of the largest of the genus; petiole 6–10 mm, reddish beneath, grooved above; the red midrib and 9–12 pairs of main veins depressed on the upper, bullate surface, prominent beneath; woolly-pubescent when young, becoming glabrous, except on the midrib beneath; bright to mid green above, pale green to glaucous beneath, some changing to yellow or red before falling in autumn-winter.

Flowers. Inflorescence a small corymb to 5–6 cm across, with up to 20 flowers to 9–10 mm across, white, the 20 or so stamens with purplish anthers; flowering abundantly in October-November.

Fruit. In small bunches of a few to about 15–20; obovoid, to 7 mm long, with 5 persistent, greenish-grey calyx lobes; fruit bright crimson, coloured fully in April and lasting to July; seeds 2 or 3, to 3 mm long, flattened on the inner side.

Other distinguishing features. Youngest shoots bright reddish-green, pubescent at first

but maturing to reddish-chocolate with brown lenticels.
Climatic range. A, H, M, Mts, P, S.

Cotoneáster horizontális (Greek 'level, like the horizon'): western China.
Habit. A partly deciduous shrub, rarely above 0.5 m tall but often 2 m broad, the main and lateral branches radiating horizontally to form a bun-shaped mound. A fine rock-garden, walling or embankment plant with tractable habit, readily adapted to horizontal or vertical training.
Leaves. Broadly oval to obovate, 5–15 mm long and nearly as wide; petiole 2–3 mm, pubescent; apex mucronate; dark green, glabrous and shiny above, paler and pubescent beneath, some changing to orange and red in autumn-winter before falling.
Flowers. Inflorescence a small corymb of 1–3 flowers, carried close to the 1-year-old twigs, regularly spaced on both sides of the shoots; flowers 4–5 mm across, white inside, pink outside, flowering in October-November.
Fruit. A fleshy, 3-seeded pome to 5–6 mm, subglobose to obovoid, borne singly or in twos or threes on the fan-like twigs; bright scarlet-red, from late March until July, especially prolific in cool climates.
var. *perpusíllus* has very small leaves to 6 mm long, and the fan-like growths on which the flowers and fruits are borne are much finer.
'Variegátus' has generally smaller and more elliptical leaves with acuminate apex, and a distinct but narrow, creamy-white margin on the dark-green leaves; fruit is borne very sparsely.
Climatic range. All A, H, M, Mts, P, S.

Cotoneáster lácteus (Latin 'milky', referring to the white flowers) (syn. *C. parneyi* of the nursery trade) western China.
Habit. A large, evergreen shrub to 3–4 m tall and a little broader, with a number of heavy branches forking away from the main trunk near the base to form a hemispherical mound, the branchlets pendulous with the weight of fruit. Sometimes trained by pruning to tree-like form.
Leaves. Simple, narrow-elliptic to oblanceolate, 6–8 cm long and 3.0–3.5 cm wide, the reddish petiole 1.0–1.5 cm long; apex obtuse but with a small mucro; margin entire but slightly recurved; venation reticulate, the midrib and about 8 pairs of laterals deeply impressed on the upper surface, prominently raised beneath; glabrous and dark green above, pale grey-green and heavily

tomentose beneath, some leaves turning orange or red before falling in autumn-winter, most becoming dark metallic-green when exposed to hard frost.
Flowers. Inflorescence a dense corymb, 6–8 cm across, of up to 60 or more flowers, on short lateral shoots; flowers crateriform, to 5 mm across, white, the 20 or so stamens with rosy-red anthers, flowering during November-December.
Fruit. A 2-seeded pome 6–8 mm across, globose but slightly obovoid, borne in bunches of 35–65 fruits on lateral and terminal spurs scattered along the upper branches for about 1 m or so; fruits red, fully coloured by early April and lasting until late August.
Other distinguishing features. Youngest twigs whitish-pubescent, but soon smooth and reddish-green. Probably the most abundant-fruiting Cotoneaster commonly grown in Australia.
Climatic ranges. A, B, H, M, Mts, P, S.

Cotoneáster microphýllus (Greek 'small-leafed'): Himalayas and south-western China.
Habit. A small evergreen shrub to 1 m tall, of open, irregular, somewhat spiky habit to 1 m or so broad, but of more compact growth when pruned occasionally.
Leaves. Spathulate to obovate, 8–10 mm long and 3–4 mm wide; apex acute-mucronate; base cuneate to the 3–5 mm petiole; margin entire but abruptly recurved; midrib prominent and reddish beneath; glabrous lustrous and dark green above, glaucous and densely pilose beneath.
Flowers. Mostly solitary, on short lateral spurs, sometimes in twos or threes, flowers crateriform, 8–9 mm across, white; stamens with purplish anthers; flowering from late October to December.
Fruit. 3-seeded pome, 7–8 mm across, slightly obovoid, borne singly but abundantly on short lateral spurs, bright red; April to July.
Other distinguishing features. Upper twigs reddish-brown, glossy, but covered with fine whitish hair.
var. *cochleàtus* (Latin 'formed like a spiral', application obscure): lower Himalayan region to Yunnan: a fine low-growing variety to 30–45 cm tall and 1–2 m wide, with small evergreen, obovate to nearly orbicular leaves 8–12 mm long, the upper surface dark lustrous green, the lower surface glaucous, with a whitish pubescence; flowers are white, solitary at the terminals of the short lateral spurs; fruit is ellipsoidal,

9–10 mm long and 8 mm wide, carmine-crimson, slightly dull, making a spectacular display from April to June. Ideal for the rock garden or for training on a wall or embankment. (Treated as a species by some authors.)

var. thymifòlius (Latin 'with leaves resembling Thyme'): Himalayas: like its parent species but has a finer, more twiggy habit, better suited to walling or for the rock garden; leaves are rarely more than 7 mm long, oblanceolate with emarginate apex and recurved margin, lustrous and dark green above but white-pubescent beneath; fruits are obovoid, 6–8 mm deep, bright red from April to June.

Climatic range. All A, H, M, Mts, P, S.

Cotoneáster pannòsus (Latin 'ragged', referring to the heavy tomentum on the reverse side of the leaves): SE slopes of the Himalayas to Yunnan.

Habit. An evergreen shrub to 4–6 m tall, with many long, slender shoots arching outwards to form a vase-shaped bush about 4 m wide. The species is a fine screening plant and is used also for walling.

Leaves. Elliptical, 2.5–4.0 cm long and 1.5 cm wide; petiole slender to 4–6 mm long, pubescent; midrib and 6–7 pairs of laterals prominent beneath; leaves dark green and glabrous above, white-tomentose beneath, often soiled to blackish in a polluted atmosphere.

Flowers. Inflorescence a 5–15 flowered corymb, whitish-pubescent throughout; flowers rotate, white but often reddish on the outside, 8 mm across; stamens with purplish anthers; flowers borne on 2–3 cm long lateral spurs, from October to December.

Fruit. A 2-seeded pome to 9–10 mm across, slightly flattened at the poles, in small, tight bunches of a few to about 10, evenly scattered along the long, arching branches; fruits pale red at first, with some darker streaks, but maturing to crimson from April until July. Fruits among the largest and most handsome of the genus.

Other distinguishing features. Fruiting stems pendulous, with glossy, chocolate-brown bark.

Climatic range. A, B, H, M, Mts, P, S.

Cotoneáster salicifòlius **var. floccòsus** (Latin 'Willow-leafed' and 'woolly-leafed') Willow-leafed Cotoneaster: western China.

Habit. An evergreen shrub to about 4 m tall and as wide, with long, slender arching branches forming a broad, hemispherical bush, well suited to specimen or walling use.

Leaves. Lanceolate to narrow-elliptic, 6–8 cm long and 1.5–2.0 cm wide; petiole 5–7 mm long, reddish and pubescent; midrib and 9 to 14 pairs of laterals prominent beneath, the midrib distinctly red; bright to dark green above and lustrous, but glaucous and woolly-tomentose beneath, some leaves changing to orange and red before falling in autumn-winter. One of the most attractive Cotoneasters in foliage.

Flowers. Inflorescence a pubescent corymb of 15–20 flowers on leafy, axillary shoots 3–4 cm long; flowers crateriform to 7 mm across, white, the stamens with reddish-purple anthers, flowering during October-November.

Fruit. A fleshy, 2–3 seeded pome to 8–9 mm across, slightly obovoid, in loose corymbs of 15–20 fruits, salmon-red at first but deepening to coral-red when ripe in April, lasting well until August.

Other distinguishing features. Fruiting stems red at first, becoming dark metallic-green on the exposed side, with pale-brown lenticels.

Climatic range. A, H, M, Mts, P, S.

Cotoneáster simonsii (commemorating Dr J. C. Simons, plant collector in South-East Asia): Simons' Cotoneaster: Khasi Hills in Assam to eastern Himalayas.

Habit. A partly deciduous shrub of upright habit to 2–3 m tall, the many erect shoots arching outwards at the crown. An important walling or hedging species, especially in mild climates where it tends to remain evergreen.

Leaves. Broad-elliptic to broad-ovate, 2.0–2.5 cm long and 1.5 cm wide; petiole to 3 mm; slightly pubescent on both surfaces, more so on the veins; texture somewhat thin and soft; dark green above, paler beneath, the deciduous leaves colouring to yellow and red in autumn-winter.

Flowers. Inflorescence a few-flowered corymb, the flowers to 8 mm across, white with a little pink on the outside, flowering during October-November.

Fruit. An obovoid pome to 9–10 mm long, in clusters of 2–4 on short lateral spurs, scarlet-red when fully developed in early May and lasting until July; seeds 3 or 4.

Other distinguishing features. Youngest twigs reddish with a dense rufous-brown tomentum.

Climatic range. A, B, M, P, S, T, and on warm, sheltered sites in H and Mts.

Cotoneáster tomentòsus (Latin 'with a woolly mat of fine hairs'): central and southern Europe to western Asia.

Habit. A mostly evergreen shrub to about 3 m tall, of graceful arching form, but losing some leaves in the cooler climates.

Leaves. Ovate to broadly oval, 4–5 cm long and 2.0–2.5 cm wide; petiole reddish, 2–3 mm long; midrib and main veins conspicuous below; sparsely pubescent, but dark green and glossy above, densely tomentose and silvery-white beneath.

Flowers. Inflorescence a small drooping corymb of a few to about 10 densely tomentose flowers to 8 mm across, white inside, pink outside, flowering in October and November.

Fruit. A 3–5-seeded pome to about 8 mm long, slightly obovoid, borne in clusters of 5–10, mostly at the ends of short, lateral shoots, brick-red to scarlet, and lustrous except for a tuft of tomentum at the apex; fruiting from April to late June.

Other distinguishing features. Upper twigs dark reddish-brown, smooth and lustrous beneath the woolly tomentum.

Climatic range. A, H, M, Mts, P, S.

Cotoneáster x *wàtereri* (commemorating the noted English nurseryman, John Waterer): the collective name for the hybrid progeny of the cross between *C. frigidus* and *C. henryanus*: most of the progeny display somewhat similar growth characteristics, but with an interesting variation in fruit colour which, besides the usual scarlet and crimson range, includes yellow and cream, with pink shadings, in several of the named cultivars.

Habit. A mostly evergreen shrub to 5 m or more, usually with several large branches from the base, forming an open-crowned bush with somewhat pendulous branchlets, especially so when in fruit, becoming tree-like when trained by early pruning, then a fine small shade tree, well suited to parks or streets.

Leaves. Narrowly elliptic to ovate-lanceolate, 5–10 cm long and 3–6 cm wide; petiole red, 1.5 cm long, slightly pubescent; venation depressed above, the midrib and 10–14 pairs of laterals pinkish and prominent beneath; dark green above, somewhat glaucous below and densely tomentose, at least while young.

Flowers. In corymbose clusters of about 40–50, borne on short lateral twigs to 4–8 cm long; flowers 8–10 mm across, mostly white but with pinkish reverse on the obovate petals; anthers purplish; flowering from late September to November.

Fruit. In a cluster of 40–50, globose, 9–10 mm across, mostly scarlet to crimson, but varying to yellowish in some cultivars, ripening in April and lasting to late winter.

Other distinguishing features. Young twigs pubescent, later glabrous and bright chocolate-red.

Climatic range. A, H, M, Mts, P, S.

CROTALÀRIA

Derived from the Greek *crotalum* 'a rattle', referring to the free movement of the seeds in the dried, inflated pods.

Bird Flower; Rattle-box.

Fabaceae, the Pea family.

Generic description. A large and varied genus scattered through the warmer latitudes of Central America, and from India to northern Australia, with a few in tropical Africa. Both simple and compound leaves are common, the flowers mostly in terminal racemes standing well clear of the leaves. The two species described below are popular in eastern Australia, usually occupying a place at the rear of the shrub border where their rather unattractive, bare stems may be concealed by other low plants.

Propagation. a) Seeds germinate readily if collected as soon as ripe and soaked in warm water for 24 hours prior to sowing in spring.

b) Soft-tip cuttings taken in spring strike satisfactorily in a sand/peat mixture in a warm, moist atmosphere.

c) Root cuttings, treated as above, are also used successfully.

Cultivation. The species treated here are easily grown in a well-drained, friable soil of moderate fertility in a wind-sheltered but sunny position, but must not be exposed to severe cold although they are not seriously damaged by temperatures of –1° C.

Pruning. Both species should be pruned lightly to a rounded shape immediately after flowering, to remove the spent inflorescences and to encourage new growth and a fresh crop of flowers.

Species and cultivars

Crotalària agatiflòra (Latin 'with flowers like *Agati'*, another member of the Pea family): Bird Flower: northern Australia to eastern India, mostly on coastal heathland.

Habit. An evergreen shrub to 2–3 m tall, of loose, open habit in the wild but improved by pruning and cultivation.

Leaves. Compound, alternate, trifoliolate, the 3 leaflets elliptic to ovate, 4–5 cm long, 3.0–3.5 cm wide, on petiolules to 3 mm long; petiole slender, 5–10 cm long; apices acute, mucronate; bases obtuse; margins entire; glabrous; glaucous-green above, paler and pruinose beneath.

Flowers. Inflorescence a terminal raceme, 15–25 cm long, of 25–30 flowers, on pedicels about 1 cm long; flowers pea-shaped; the calyx to 1 cm long, with 3 acuminate pale-green lobes; corolla with erect, broad-ovate standard petal to 4 cm long and 3 cm wide, yellow-green; oblong wings to 2 cm long, coloured as the standard; keel pale yellow, ovate, 4–5 cm long, with a purple-tipped, acuminate tail; the flowers bear a striking resemblance to a small bird attached to the stem by a long beak; flowers are abundant October to July, but also during winter in warm localities.

Fruit. An inflated, oblong pod, 4–5 cm long, on a slender 1–2 cm stalk.

Climatic range. B, S, T, and on warm sheltered sites in A, M, and P.

Crotalària semperflòrens (Latin 'always flowering'): Indian Rattle-box: India.

Habit. An evergreen shrub of open character to 3–4 m tall and nearly as wide, with a short trunk and ascending branches.

Leaves. Simple, alternate, ovate to slightly obovate, 10–15 cm long and 8–10 cm broad; petiole to 2 cm long, pubescent, with a pair of green, scale-like rudimentary leaflets at the base; apex acute, mucronate; base obtuse; margin entire but slightly undulate; midrib and 8–10 pairs of laterals prominent beneath; glabrous and bright green above, grey-green and pubescent on the lower surface.

Flowers. Inflorescence a terminal raceme 20–25 cm long, often branched into paniculate form; flowers pea-shaped; calyx crateriform to 1 cm long, greenish, with 5 acute sepals; corolla with a nearly orbicular standard to 3 cm wide, clear yellow but with fine purplish lines on the back; oblong wings to 2 cm long, of similar coloration, both parts ageing to tan-brown on

the outside; keel to 2 cm long, yellow-green with a blackish-streaked beak; flowers borne mainly in June and July, but intermittently throughout summer and autumn in warmer climates.

Fruit. An inflated legume to 5 cm long when fully developed, the persistent style forming a long, slender beak.

Other distinguishing features. Upper twigs and branchlets pubescent and prominently grooved.

Climatic range. B, S, T, and on warm sheltered sites in A, M, and P.

CRÒWEA

Commemorating James Crowe, English physician and amateur botanist.
Crowea.
Rutaceae, the Rue family.

Generic description. A small genus of Australian shrubby plants, formerly combined with *Eriostemon*, commonly seen in the bush and in native gardens, grown for their long winter and spring flowering season and easy culture.

Propagation. a) Seeds, sown in spring in a warm, moist atmosphere, germinate freely.
b) Semi-hardwood cuttings, taken in late summer to late autumn, are planted in a sand/peat mixture and struck in a humid environment, preferably on a warm, misted propagating bench under glass.

Cultivation. Best grown in sandy bush soil with a high leaf-mould content, ideally with a light overhead shade in a climate similar to that of the Sydney hills, with little or no frost.

Prunings. A more densely foliaged plant may be developed by regular light pruning in late spring after the flowering period; only the youngest flowering wood should be cut, just severely enough to remove the remains of the inflorescences.

Cròwea exalàta (Latin 'wingless' referring to the terete twigs): Small Crowea: SE tablelands of NSW and Central Coast plateaus, and on the mountain slopes of eastern Vic, found on harsh sandstone areas as well as better class loamy soils.

Habit. An evergreen shrub to 0.75 m tall, with erect and spreading slender shoots forming an open, hemispherical bush to 1.5 m wide.

Leaves. Simple, alternate, linear to narrowly

oblanceolate to 2.0–3.5 cm long and 5–7 mm wide; petiole channelled, scarcely distinguishable from the blade; apex shortly acute-mucronate; margin entire; glabrous, but heavily glandular with translucent oil glands, and aromatic when bruised; bright green at first, becoming darker above, paler beneath.

Flowers. Solitary towards the end of the upper leafy twigs, on 5 mm pedicels, the pointed buds ovoid to 1.5 cm long, coral-red at first, opening to stellate form 2 cm across; petals broadly lanceolate, reflexing slightly at the tips, pale pink to bright rosy-purple, flowering from late autumn to November, then intermittently during summer, especially in cool sheltered places.

Fruit. A schizocarp, with small brown seeds.

Other distinguishing features. An attractive small plant, thriving in a cool, well-mulched root-run and so ideal in the rock garden or where sheltered by tall neighbouring plants or non-invasive ground-covers.

'Austraflora Green Cape' is a registered cultivar occurring naturally in the Ben Boyd National Park on the South Coast of NSW. The plant is prostrate in habit, growing to about 15 cm tall and spreading to nearly 1 m broad, with mauve flowers, the petals later changing colour first to white, then green.

'Bindelong Compact' is another registered cultivar from eastern Vic. occurring naturally as a low, bun-shaped mound 50 cm tall and about 1 m broad, with abundant deep pink flowers over the crown of the bush, maturing to deep purple at length. The main flowering period is summer to autumn.

Climatic range. H, M, Mts, and on cool, sheltered sites in P and S.

Cròwea salígna (Latin 'Willow-like', referring to the leaves): Willow-leafed Crowea: NSW, between the coast and the lower tablelands, mainly on sandy heathland and the rocky sandstones of the plateaus.

Habit. An evergreen shrub to 1 m or so tall, with an erect, somewhat sparse growth habit, but responsive to cultivation and regular pruning.

Leaves. Simple, alternate, linear to lanceolate, 3–5 cm long and 4–13 mm wide; apex acute; base tapered finely to the indistinct petiole; margin entire but thickened; midrib alone prominent; glabrous, but dotted with pellucid oil glands, and aromatic when crushed; green and slightly shiny, sometimes slightly glaucous-green.

Flowers. Solitary in the upper axils of the 1-year-old shoots; pedicels 6–7 mm long, thick, pale green, scaly at the base; calyx short, with 5 oblong-ovate, membranous sepals to 2 mm long; petals 5, lanceolate, 1–2 cm long, 7–8 mm wide, forming a stellate flower 3 cm across; petals mauve-pink, with deeper central veins and a waxy texture; stamens 10, the translucent, white, pubescent filaments forming an ovoid cone, the reddish-brown anthers joined at the apex; flowering from early autumn to mid spring.

Fruit. A small schizocarp, splitting at the apex when ripe to release the small, ovoid, brown seeds, 2 to each cell.

Other distinguishing features. Upper twigs grey-green, made angular by the prominent ridge decurrent beneath each leaf base.

Climatic range. A, B, M, P, S, T.

CÙPHEA

Derived from the Greek, describing the curved, hump-backed shape of the tubular calyx.
Cigar Flower or Cuphea.
Lythraceae, the Loosestrife family.

Generic description. Mostly low, evergreen shrubs from Mexico or neighbouring countries, grown throughout the world for their abundant flowers of curious form. Leaves are simple, opposite, rarely whorled or alternate, the flowers tubulate, lacking or with very short petals, but with a well-developed calyx, often with a sac-like swelling at the base.

Propagation. Soft-tip cuttings, taken from spring to autumn, root easily in a sand/peat mixture in a warm, humid atmosphere; winter cuttings are sometimes used, bottom heat then being an advantage.

Cultivation. Cupheas grow well as outdoor garden plants in climates with minimum temperatures above –1°C, especially on light soils in a sunny exposure. If damaged by heavy frosts, the injured parts should be retained to serve as protection to the basal stems until spring, then pruned away.

Pruning. Young plants should be tip-pruned frequently in the first year or so to promote dense, twiggy growth, thereafter reduced by about a quarter of the total height in late winter to remove the spent flowering wood.

Cùphea hyssopifòlia (Latin, referring to the leaves, which resemble those of the medicinal and culinary herb, *Hyssopus officinalis*): Mexico and Guatemala.

Habit. An evergreen, bun-shaped shrub to 0.6 m tall with a dense leafy crown.

Leaves. Simple, opposite, linear-lanceolate to 1.5 cm long and 2–3 mm wide, almost sessile; apex acute; base rounded; margin entire; slightly hairy on the lower midrib; dark green above, paler beneath, a few turning yellow in autumn and early winter.

Flowers. Solitary or in pairs in the axils of the young shoots; calyx curved, tubulate to 6–7 mm, purplish at the apex, with 6 minute sharp teeth; corolla stellate to 7–8 mm across, with 6 obovate petals, crepe-like, violet-red to reddish-purple; flowers borne abundantly from late spring to winter.

Fruit. A disc-like, compressed capsule about 1 mm across, green but ripening to brown and dispersing its seeds widely.

Other distinguishing features. A plant not to be encouraged because of its extreme fecundity; already a serious pest in several warm-temperate countries.

Climatic range. A, B, M, P, S, T.

Cùphea ígnea (Latin 'fiery red') (syn. *C. platycentra*) Cigar Flower: Mexico.

Habit. A small, evergreen shrub to 1 m tall and 1.5 m wide, the thin, soft, twiggy stems with abundant leaves and flowers.

Leaves. Simple, opposite, broadly lanceolate to 5–7 cm; apex acuminate; base tapering to the short petiole; margin entire; glabrous; mid green above, paler beneath.

Flowers. Solitary in the upper axils or in a few-flowered clusters; apetalous; calyx tubulate to 2.5 cm long and 4 mm wide, with swollen base and slender 5–7 mm pedicel, most of the tube scarlet, but ending with a 6-pronged, slightly-flared mouth, green at first, later ash-white with a dark red ring; stamens slightly exserted; flowers abundant from early December to May.

Fruit. Not seen.

Climatic range. B, P, S, T, and on warm, sheltered sites in A and M.

Cùphea micropétala (Greek 'with small petals'): sometimes confused with *C. jorullensis*: Mexico.

Habit. An evergreen shrub to 1.5 m tall and 2.0 m wide, with many woody stems from the base.

Leaves. Simple, opposite or irregularly alternate; linear-lanceolate 6–10 cm long, 1.0–1.5 cm wide; apex acuminate; base acuminate; margin entire; venation reticulate, the pale-green midrib and main laterals nearly transparent; slightly scabrous on both surfaces; dark green above, paler beneath, often stained purple-red in winter.

Flowers. Borne singly in a loose racemose pattern towards the terminals of the current growth; calyx tubulate to 2.5–3.0 cm long and 6–7 mm wide, obliquely rounded at the base, one side with a sac-like swelling, longitudinally grooved, ending in pronged, glandular teeth; petals 6, minute, red-tipped, within the tube; stamens 11, within the tube; tube pubescent, greenish at first, becoming lemon-yellow, heavily suffused with scarlet at the base and extending to the apex on top of the tube, flowering period from December to July.

Fruit. To 1.5 cm long and 5–7 mm wide, at the base of the pistil and totally enclosed by the tube until it withers and is split asunder by the ripened fruit; seeds disc-like to 1 mm broad, green at first, but ripening to brown in late autumn and winter.

Climatic range. B, P, S, T, and warm, sheltered sites in A and M.

CYPÈRUS

The classical Greek name for the plant.
Egyptian Paper Plant; Papyrus; Umbrella Plant.
Cyperaceae, the Cyperus family.

Generic description. A large genus of over 500 species of perennial plants from Middle Eastern and other neighbouring countries, mostly tropical or warm-temperate. One species, Papyrus, has a unique place in horticultural history as the plant used by the ancient Egyptians for the manufacture of paper. Several species appear commonly in ornamental plantings.

Growth develops from shallow rootstocks protected by a few short basal leaves, sometimes reduced to scaly sheaths, and a mass of slender erect stems crowned by an umbrella-like cluster of involucral leaves surrounding the flower spikes.

Propagation. a) Seeds sown as ripe, barely covered, on a bed of moist potting mix;
b) Cuttings of flower-heads planted with a short length of stem in a constantly-moist medium of sand/peat or in shredded sphagnum moss;

c) Division of an established clump during early spring.

Cultivation. Most species are found on the margins of permanent water. In cultivation, a large container of fertile potting soil, standing in shallow water, provides ideal conditions. They tolerate the sun but should be protected from strong winds. Repotting into fresh soil every second year or so keeps the plants healthy and in strong growth.

Pruning. Removal of spent or damaged stems is the only treatment necessary.

Species and cultivars

Cypèrus alternifòlius (Latin 'with alternate leaves'): Umbrella Plant or Umbrella Palm: islands of the western Indian Ocean, in particular Madagascar and the Mascarenes.
Habit. A perennial with a crowded clump of rush-like stems to about 1 m tall, the green stems shallowly-ribbed.
Leaves. Basal leaves reduced to short, inconspicuous scales; involucral leaves linear, 15 to about 20, 10–20 cm long, 2 cm wide, spreading horizontally from the crown, then drooping at the ends; shallowly striate, bright green and strikingly handsome when well grown.
Flowers. Borne in a compound umbel of many small brown spikelets on long peduncles, above and among the involucral leaves, but of little decorative value.
Fruit. A chaffy achene with blackish seeds.
'**Grácilis**' is a dwarf form, smaller in all its parts.
Climatic range. B, P, S, T and on warm, sheltered sites in A and M, and indoors elsewhere.

Cypèrus papyrus (taken from the former generic name Papyrus): Egyptian Paper Plant; Papyrus: tropical Africa, especially abundant in the Nile Valley.
Habit. A perennial plant of vigorous growth to 2–3 m tall, spreading by thick underground rhizomes, the erect stems bluntly 3-angled, 2–4 cm thick, dark green.
Leaves. Basal leaves reduced to scales, sheathing the erect stems; involucral leaves a few to about 10, 8–15 cm long, 2 cm wide, linear-lanceolate, striate, greenish-brown.
Flowers. Borne in a drooping, mop-like compound, inflorescence up to 30 cm or so long, carrying the pale brown flowering spikelets.
Fruit. A chaffy achene, with blackish seeds.

Other distinguishing features. *C. papyrus* will survive deeper water than most other species, up to 30–40 cm deep, but in cultivation performs best at the shallow margin of permanent water.
Climatic range. B, P, S, T and on warm sheltered sites in A and M and indoors elsewhere.

CÝTISUS

Derived from the Greek *kytisos*, the ancient vernacular name for a closely related plant.
Broom (various).
Fabaceae, the Pea family.

Generic description. A European genus of mostly evergreen shrubs with simple or compound, trifoliolate leaves, the broom-like, twiggy growths sometimes almost leafless; flowers are typically pea-shaped, the standard, wings and keel petals often of different colours, some with bright colour contrasts in the cultivars; fruit is a flattened, elongate legume with small, rounded, hard-coated seeds. Most species flower in spring and are useful garden plants because of their extreme hardiness and showy flowers.

Propagation. The species described here are grown from short tip cuttings, 5–6 cm long, of ripened current year's wood taken in late autumn or early winter, and struck in a sand/peat mixture, preferably in individual containers placed in a warm, humid atmosphere.

Cultivation. A freely drained, slightly-acid, friable soil is suitable, preferably of rather low fertility to preclude over-vigorous growth. A fully sun-exposed position in the cooler climates produces the best floral display.

Pruning. Removal of spent flowered shoots immediately after the flowering season is the main operation. Several of the oldest stems may also be removed entirely each year to open up the centre of the plant and to encourage the development of new material from the base. The typical arching character of the plant should be preserved, not destroyed by trimming into geometrical shapes.

Species and cultivars

Cýtisus x *kewénsis* (Latin 'from Kew'): a hybrid developed at the Royal Botanic Gardens, Kew, UK between *Cytisus ardoinii*, a low, ground-covering broom from alpine regions in Southern France, and *Cytisus multiflorus*, the white-flowered Portugal Broom.

Habit. A deciduous shrub of prostrate form to 50–75 cm tall but with trailing stems, the plant spreading to 2 m or so broad.

Leaves. Mostly compound, trifoliolate, the leaflets linear-oblong to 10–15 mm long, but occasionally simple; apices acute; silky-pubescent, especially while young; mid-green above, paler beneath.

Flowers. Scattered abundantly in the axils of the slender outer shoots in clusters of 1 to several, pea-shaped, 1.5 cm across, the erect standard petal much the largest; lightly fragrant; pale creamy-yellow; flowering from late September to November.

Fruit. Not seen: the plant is probably sterile.

Climatic range. A, H, M, Mts, P, S.

Cýtisus x *pràecox* (Latin 'appearing early in spring'): hybrid between *Cytisus multiflorus*, the white-flowered Portugal Broom, and *Cytisus purgans* from which it derives its yellow flowers; Warminster Broom, referring to the district of origin in Wiltshire, UK.

Habit. A deciduous shrub to about 2 m tall, with a loose, open habit, the slender twigs arching outwards and drooping at the ends.

Leaves. Simple, oblanceolate, 1.5–2.0 cm long, but occasionally trifoliolate, borne alternately on the channelled twigs; silky-pubescent, especially while young; silvery-green.

Flowers. Solitary or in pairs in the leafless axils, pea-shaped to 1.5 cm across, borne in long sprays on the outer shoots; creamy-yellow, with a heavy perfume; flowering period from mid-September to late October.

Fruit. A flattened legume about 3 cm long, with 1–3 seeds.

'**Álbus**' is shorter, to 1 m, with more pendulous habit and white flowers.

'**Lùteùs**' has deeper yellow flowers than the parent; several other similar forms bear colour-identifying names, e.g. '**Allgold**'.

Climatic range. A, H, M, Mts, P, S.

Cýtisus purpùreus (Greek 'purple'): Purple Broom: Southern Europe, mostly at sub-alpine levels.

Habit. A deciduous shrub of roughly mound shape, about 75 cm tall and to 2 m broad, the crown irregular, with a few nearly erect but arching stems.

Leaves. Compound, trifoliolate, on a 2 cm petiole, the leaflets elliptic to obovate, 1.5–2.5 cm

long; glabrous and dark green above, paler beneath.

Flowers. Borne in 1–3-flowered clusters in the upper axils, the sprays extending for 30 cm or more; flowers pea-shaped to 2 cm long, the erect standard semi-circular, slightly emarginate at the apex, the other petals smaller, all lilac-purple, flowering in spring.

Fruit. A legume about 3 cm long, with several rounded seeds.

Other distinguishing features. Several cultivars are listed in nurseries, with colour variations from pure white and mauve-pink to purple, all much like the parent species otherwise.

Climatic range. H, M, Mts and on cool, elevated sites in A, P, S.

Cýtisus scopàrius (Latin 'broom-like', referring to the numerous, nearly-leafless, erect twigs): Scotch Broom or Common Broom (syn. *Sarothamnus scoparius*) British Isles and western Europe, but naturalised in many temperate countries.

Habit. An evergreen, sparsely foliaged shrub to 2 m or so, with a mass of erect shoots from the base, forming an open bush to 1.5–2.0 m wide.

Leaves. Of both kinds, trifoliolate near the base of the plant, but mostly reduced to a solitary leaflet in the upper twigs, alternate, the trifoliolate leaves to 2.5 cm long, the petiole conspicuously flattened and laterally winged; leaflets oblanceolate, to about 1.5 cm long and 6 mm wide; apices acute; margins entire; mid green above, paler beneath; simple leaves similar but confined to the upper part of the plant.

Flowers. Mostly solitary in the upper axils; calyx campanulate to 5 mm long, with 2 shallowly toothed lobes; corolla pea-shaped, the standard orbicular to 2 cm across, bright yellow with a few faint, brownish streaks near the base; wings narrowly elliptical to 2 cm long, deep golden-yellow; keel 2 cm long, yellow; stamens 10, the filaments cream, the anthers orange-red; style 1, strongly incurved to form a nearly circular ring; flowering season, October and November, then sparsely throughout summer and early autumn.

Fruit. A slender, pubescent, green legume to about 4 cm long, ripening to black.

Other distinguishing features. Branchlets and twigs pubescent, at least while young, winged with 5 to 7 pronounced, longitudinal ridges.

Climatic range. A, B, H, M, Mts, P, S.

The following list represents a sample of the cultivars deriving from *C. scoparius* and *C.* x *dallimorei* (the hybrid of *C. scoparius* 'Andreanus' and *C. multiflora*) commonly grown in Australia.

'**Andreànus**': rich lemon-yellow standard, reddish-tan wings, and yellow keel with a fine red edge.

'**Andreànus Aùreus**': lemon-yellow standard, veined crimson at the base, deep-yellow wings, and lemon keel. (Both the above cultivars are common garden escapes on the Central and Southern Tablelands of NSW.)

'**Bùrkwoodii**': mahogany-red standard and wings, with a keel of dark crimson, with a yellow edge.

'**C. E. Pearson**': mahogany-red and yellow standard, with scarlet wings and keel.

'**Cornish Cream**': pale-cream standard and keel, the wings deep lemon-yellow.

'**Crimson King**': deep-crimson standard, and slightly paler wings and keel.

'**Daisy Hill**': cream standard, suffused with rosy-pink, and maroon wings.

'**Dorothy Walpole**': rosy-cerise standard, with crimson wings.

'**Firefly**': yellow standard, with bronze-crimson wings.

'**Lord Lambourne**': creamy-yellow standard, and crimson wings.

'**Maria Burkwood**': apricot-yellow standard, suffused with pink, and crimson and yellow wings and keel.

'**Sulphùreus**': almost wholly pale sulphur-yellow, with deeper edges.

Cýtisus x *spachiànus* (commemorating Edouard Spach, nineteenth-century French botanical author) (syn. *C. racemosus*, also *Genista* and *Cytisus fragrans*) interspecific hybrid between *C. canariensis* and *C. stenopetalus*.

Habit. An evergreen shrub to 3 m or more, usually with a short trunk, soon branching to form a broad, globose, densely twiggy bush.

Leaves. Compound, alternate, trifoliolate, the leaflets oblanceolate to obovate to 2 cm long, nearly sessile on a common petiole 6–7 mm long; apices obtuse-mucronate; base cuneate; margin entire; venation somewhat indistinct under the silky pubescence below; dark green, glabrous and slightly shiny above.

Flowers. Inflorescence a terminal raceme, 8–10 cm long, in abundance over the crown of the plant; flowers pea-shaped, about 1.5 cm long, deep golden-yellow, flowering from mid September to late October.

Fruit. A slender legume, pale green and silky-pubescent at first, ripening to tan-brown, the halves twisting and recurving slightly to expel the several seeds.

Other distinguishing features. Upper branchlets greyish, silky-pubescent, becoming glabrous and somewhat striate.

Climatic range. A, H, M, Mts, P, S.

DÁPHNE

The Greek word meaning 'Laurel,' from an ancient association with the Sweet Bay, *Laurus nobilis*, the plant used by the Greeks for laurel wreaths and garlands.

Daphne; Garland Flower, etc.
Thymelaeaceae, the Mezereum family.

Generic description. A large genus of evergreen and deciduous shrubs from Europe, Asia, and the Orient, with simple, alternate, entire leaves; flowers are in umbels or dense racemes in the upper axils, or terminally, the flowers without petals but with sepals developed into petal-like form, coloured in white, yellow, lilac, pink, red, and purple. Several species are used in Australian gardens, *D. odora* and its cultivars being the most popular, especially in cool climates.

Propagation. a) Soft or firm, leafy tip cuttings, taken in December-January from virus-free stock, and struck in a sand/peat mixture in a cool, moist atmosphere are usually successful.

b) Simple layers, laid down in winter and severed and lifted the following winter, provide a limited number of larger plants reliably.

Cultivation. A well-drained, slightly acid soil of a coarse, freely aerated texture in a cool part of the garden, preferably on a southerly slope, is ideal. In heavy soils, the planting position must either be artificially drained or raised above the surrounding level. The soil should be kept cool with a thick, fibrous mulch and protected from hot overhead or westerly sun. The species treated come from austere climates and will tolerate low temperatures to −5° or −6°C without serious harm.

Pruning. Flowers may be cut for indoor decoration, and if done in moderation, this probably helps to keep a normal, healthy plant compact.

Species and cultivars

Dáphne x *bùrkwoodii* (commemorating the English nurseryman, A. Burkwood): interspecific hybrid of *C. cneorum* and *C. caucasica*.

Habit. A partly deciduous shrub to about 1 m tall and wide, the crown rounded into a semi-globose form.

Leaves. Simple, alternate, oblanceolate, 2–3 cm long, 4–6 mm wide; apex acute; base slenderly cuneate; margin entire; bright green and shiny above, paler and dull beneath.

Flowers. Inflorescence a mass of small terminal umbels, each with 5–8 flowers, forming into an elongate panicle 10–12 cm long; flowers apetalous, the calyx salverform, with a slender tube opening to a stellate limb about 1 cm across, pale pink, sweetly perfumed; flowering in September and October and intermittently at other times during summer.

Climatic range. H, M, Mts, and the cooler, elevated hills of S.

Dáphne cneòrum (derivation uncertain): Garland Flower: sub-alpine levels of central Europe.

Habit. An evergreen, low bun-shaped shrub to about 0.5 m tall, but often twice as wide, with pubescent branchlets.

Leaves. Simple, alternate, but clustered densely near the growth terminals, oblanceolate, 2.0–2.5 cm long, 3–5 mm wide; apex obtuse; base cuneate; margin entire; puberulent at first but becoming glabrous; dark green and shiny above, glaucous beneath.

Flowers. Inflorescence a dense terminal umbel of 10–20 sessile flowers; apetalous; tubulate calyx slender to 1.3 cm, expanding to a broad, 4-lobed, stellate limb 8–10 mm across, deep rose-pink, flowering abundantly over the crown of the plant in September and October; flowers sweetly perfumed.

Climatic range. H, M, Mts, and the cooler, elevated hills of S.

Dáphne génkwa (derivation obscure): Western China.

Habit. A deciduous shrub to about 75 cm tall and as broad, with many slender stems arising from the centre, arching outwards to form a hemispherical bush.

Leaves. Usually opposite, but not always; lanceolate-elliptic, 3–6 cm long, 1.5 cm wide; apex acute; margin entire; reddish green at first, then bright green and glabrous above, paler and pubescent beneath.

Flowers. Apetalous, the calyx salverform, 1.5 cm long and 1 cm across the limb, borne in axillary clusters of about 5 to 7, forming long sprays on the leafless stems in early spring; calyx lobes lilac-blue; faintly perfumed.

Fruit. Not seen.

Climatic range. H, M, Mts and on cool, elevated sites in P, S, preferably on soils of limestone origin.

Dáphne mezèreum (Latinised from the Arabic name for the plant): Mezereum: Europe, Asia Minor, Caucasus.

Habit. A deciduous shrub to 1 m or so, the many erect stems forming a loose, open bush.

Leaves. Alternate, oblanceolate, 5–7 cm long and 2 cm wide; narrowed at the base and apex; margin entire; glabrous and mid-green above, grey-green beneath.

Flowers. Borne in small clusters of 2 to 4 in the upper axils of the previous year's growth; apetalous; calyx 4-lobed, about 1 cm across, silky-pubescent outside; rosy-purple, sweetly fragrant; flowering in late winter before the new leaves.

Fruit. A globose berry about 8 mm across, many together clustered close to the upper stems in autumn; poisonous; bright red.

Climatic range. H, M, Mts and on cool, elevated sites in P, S.

Dáphne odòra (Latin 'sweet smelling'): Winter Daphne: China but introduced and common in Japan.

Habit. An evergreen shrub of usually less than 1 m tall and 1.5 m wide, with a low, sprawling habit of well-leafed, woody branches.

Leaves. Simple, alternate, lanceolate-elliptic, 8–9 cm long and 2–3 cm wide; apex acute; base acute-cuneate to the 2 mm petiole; margin entire; dark green and glossy above, paler and dull beneath.

Flowers. Inflorescence a dense, terminal umbel of up to 30 flowers at the ends of the short, leafy, 1-year-old shoots, subtended by several leafy scales; flowers apetalous; calyx tube to 1 cm long, expanding to a 2 cm limb of 4 regular lobes, spreading at right angles; stamens 8, in 2 series of 4, as long as the tube; anthers yellow; flowers variable in colour from white to purple, very fragrant, flowering abundantly from May to October.

'Alba' has white flowers, pale ivory-cream at the base.

PLATE 11

▲ Cytisus x spachianus

▲ Euphorbia pulcherrima 'Annette Hegg'
◄ Daphne cneorum
▼ Euphorbia veneta

▼ Duranta erecta 'Variegata'

▼ Eatsia japonica

▼ Epacris purpurascens

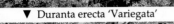

▼ Felicia fruticosa

PLATE 12

▲ Elaeagnus pungens 'Maculata'
▶ Felicia amelloides
▼ Eupatorium megalophyllum

▲ Eriostemon australasius

▼ Euphorbia pulcherrima 'Henrietta Ecke'

▼ Euonymus europaeus

▼ Erica vestita

▼ Erica peziza

'**Aureo-margináta**' has flowers like those of 'Rubra' but with leaves margined with creamy-yellow.
'**Rúbra**' has flowers deep wine-red outside and pale rosy-purple to white inside.
Climatic range. H, M, Mts, P, S, and on the cooler, more elevated parts of A.

DARWÍNIA

Commemorating Dr Erasmus Darwin, British botanical author; grandfather of Charles Darwin of the 'Beagle' voyages.
Darwinia; Scented Myrtle; and a variety of other names of regional significance.
Myrtaceae, the Myrtle family.

Generic description. An Australian genus of about 35 shrubby species, all evergreen, mostly from WA where the 'Bell' species in particular are held in high regard for their unusual flowers, some growing in very restricted habitats, and have proved to be difficult to maintain in cultivation.
The species listed here however are more adaptable in the climates nominated.
Leaves are simple, alternate or scattered on slender heath-like twigs; flowers vary widely, from those with small tubulate form in dense terminal heads with long-exserted styles, representative of most of the eastern species, to the group with heads surrounded by spectacular floral bracts, known as the 'Bells' of their western habitats.

Propagation. Generally, seeds have a low fertility rate and are difficult to raise. Leafy cuttings are more reliable, preferably those from ripened shoots in autumn and early winter, planted in individual containers of sharp sand/peat and placed in a humid environment. Hormone rooting treatments are worthwhile.

Cultivation. The following species are best grown in well-drained sandy or light gravelly loams, preferably in a sunny but wind-sheltered place where frosts are not severe. All enjoy the light shade of taller trees.

Pruning. Early tip-pruning to thicken the growth is beneficial, together with removal of old straggly stems from time to time.

Species and cultivars
Darwínia citriodòra (Latin 'lemon-scented'): Lemon-scented Myrtle: south-west WA, mainly on the granite soils of the Darling Range, often on partly-shaded sites.
Habit. A shrub to 1 m or so, often thin and open in its native habitat but responding well to pruning in cultivation, then dense, with abundant foliage.
Leaves. Opposite-decussate, ovate-oblong to 10–12 mm long and 6–8 mm wide; apex obtuse; base rounded; margin entire, recurved; midrib prominent beneath; glandular and aromatic when crushed; grey-green, sometimes stained ruby-red in cold weather.
Flowers. In small terminal heads of 4–6, sheathed at the base by a leafy involucre, the inner 4 segments green, stained with yellow and red; corolla tubulate, the 5 yellowish petals almost closed over the 10 stamens; styles 4 to 6, red, long-exserted; flowering from mid-winter to early summer.
Fruit. A fleshy nut developing from the matured calyx, containing a single seed.
Climatic range. A, H, M, Mts, P, S.

Darwínia fasciculàris (Latin 'clustered together in a bundle'): Tufted Darwinia, Meat Plant or Clustered Scented Myrtle: southern Qld, and Central Coast and Blue Mts of NSW, mainly on sandstone ridges and heathlands.
Habit. A dense shrub to about 1 m, erect and leafy, but further improved by regular pruning after flowering.
Leaves. Linear to terete, 10–15 mm long and 1–2 mm wide crowded into dense fascicles; apex acute with a short hard point; margin entire; bright to deep green.
Flowers. In terminal clusters of up to 20 set in a rosette of leaves; corolla tubulate, 6–7 mm long, often closed at the mouth concealing the 10 stamens; pale cream at first, becoming pink then dull-red, the bright red style projecting to 2 cm, resembling a pin-cushion; flowering period from July to December.
Fruit. A fleshy, 1-celled nut containing a single seed.
Climatic range. A, B, H, M, Mts, P, S.

Darwínia òldfieldii (commemorating Augustus Oldfield, botanical collector in WA): West Coast sandplains of WA.
Habit. A shrub to about 75 cm tall and a little broader, thin and open in the wild but improved in cultivation with regular light pruning.
Leaves. Spirally-arranged to almost cover the branchlets, ovate-oblong, 5–6 mm long and 2–3

mm wide; apex obtuse; base almost decurrent with the twigs; margin entire, finely hairy and slightly recurved; glabrous and grey-green above, paler beneath.

Flowers. In erect terminal heads of 10–15, scattered over the crown of the plant supported by a series of greenish-red involucral bracts; corolla tubulate, deep red, enclosing the 10 stamens but with a prominent greenish-red style; flowering period from late winter to early summer.

Fruit. Not seen.

Climatic range. A, B, M, P, S, preferably on sandy soils with light overhead cover.

DEÙTZIA

Commemorating Johann van der Deutz, patron of the Swedish botanist Carl Pehr Thunberg, author of the genus.

Deutzia or Wedding Bells.

Philadelphaceae, the Philadelphus family (formerly included in Saxifragaceae, the Saxifrage family).

Generic description. A large genus of deciduous shrubs mostly from the Orient, with hollow stems, simple, opposite leaves, and white or pinkish flowers commonly in terminal panicles on the upper lateral shoots, flowering in spring; fruit is a brownish, 3–5-valved capsule with numerous small seeds. The Deutzias are a familiar sight in cool-climate gardens, valued especially for their attractive flowers and ease of culture.

Propagation. Soft-tip or semi-hardwood leafy cuttings, taken from the current year's shoots between late spring and autumn, strike readily in a cool, humid atmosphere; hardwood cuttings are also used in winter.

Cultivation. The ideal climate is cool and humid, with clean atmosphere and with winter temperatures not lower than −10°C. They are best grown in a sunny position, on a fertile soil that drains well, and respond to liberal feeding in early spring and regular watering.

Pruning. Deutzias flower in spring on short leafy shoots arising from the previous year's growth and should be pruned only after the flowering period, never during winter or early spring. The hollow stems are short-lived and need to be replaced by new water-shoots from the base every few years, the best treatment being to remove about one-third of the total number of old shoots at ground level each year, immediately after flowering, and to reduce the flowered laterals slightly to remove the spent flowers and to encourage strong replacement growth.

Species and cultivars

Deùtzia grácilis (Latin 'slender', referring to the leaves and twigs): native to the highlands and slopes of the main islands of Japan.

Habit. A deciduous shrub to about 1.5 m tall, with a mass of slender, erect shoots from a central clump, arching outwards at the ends.

Leaves. Simple, opposite, (but not decussate on the ultimate twigs) ovate-lanceolate, to 7–8 cm long and 2.5–3.0 cm wide; apex acuminate; base obtuse; margin somewhat distantly serrulate, the small teeth set above the plane of the blade; main veins prominent beneath; bright green and stellate-pubescent above, slightly paler and glabrous beneath.

Flowers. Inflorescence an erect panicle to 8–10 cm tall, borne on the 15–18 cm long, current-season's leafy shoots; calyx to 4 mm long, campanulate, green, with 5 triangular short teeth; petals 5, oblong-obovate, 9–10 mm long and 4 mm wide, reflexed when open, pure white; stamens in 2 series, 5 short to 4 mm, and 5 long to 8 mm, all winged and with 2 short teeth at the apex, filaments white, anthers yellow; styles 3, longer than the stamens; flowers borne abundantly from mid October to November.

Other distinguishing features. Ultimate twigs copper-brown, terete, smooth but becoming pale grey, streaked with tan and developing a hollow centre.

'**Albo-marmoràta**' has its green leaves irregularly spotted and splashed with creamy-white.

Climatic range. A, H, M, Mts, P, S.

Deùtzia x lemóinei (commemorating the raiser, Victor Lemoine of Nancy, France): interspecific hybrid between *D. gracilis* and *D. parviflora*.

Habit. A deciduous shrub to 1.5–2.5 m tall, with well-branched, erect form.

Leaves. Lanceolate, 6–8 cm long and 1.5–2.5 cm wide; apex acuminate; base obtuse to broadly cuneate; margin serrulate; main veins prominent beneath; nearly glabrous; bright green above, paler beneath.

Flowers. Inflorescence a terminal panicle 8–10 cm long; flowers 2 cm across on slender, pale-green pedicels 5–7 mm long; calyx urceolate

2–3 mm long, with 5 acute sepals; corolla funnelform to 1 cm long, with 5 elliptic-ovate, white petals 5 mm wide, shallowly ribbed outside; stamens 10, in 2 series, the filaments white, winged and serrately notched near the apex, the anthers cream; styles 2 to 4, white, 8–9 mm long; flowers prolific in October.
Other distinguishing features. Upper twigs pale green, shallowly grooved, clustered in a whorl of 6 or 8; older bark grey; stems hollow.
Climatic range. A, H, M, Mts, P, S.

Deùtzia longifòlia (Latin 'with long leaves'): western China.
Habit. A deciduous shrub to 2 m or so, with erect stems arising from a crowded base, forming a rounded crown.
Leaves. Lanceolate to oblong, 5–12 cm long, on 3–6 mm petioles; apex acuminate; base cuneate; margin serrulate; densely stellate-pubescent and rough above; dark greyish-green on the upper surface, whitish-green below.
Flowers. Inflorescence a corymbose panicle, 7–8 cm across, the numerous single flowers to 2.5 cm across, white or with pinkish-purple shadings outside, flowering in October and early November.
'Veìtchii' (commemorating James Veitch, English nurseryman): one of the best of the genus, with large, deep lilac-pink flowers, becoming somewhat paler when open.
Climatic range. A, H, M, Mts, P, S.

Deùtzia x ròsea (Latin 'rose-pink'): interspecific hybrid between *D. gracilis* and *D. purpurascens*.
Habit. A deciduous shrub to 1.2 m tall, the many slender branches forming a vase-shaped crown.
Leaves. Ovate to oblong-lanceolate to 6 cm long and 3–4 cm wide; apex acuminate; base cuneate; margin serrulate; sparsely stellate-pubescent; bright green at first, becoming darker in maturity.
Flowers. In a short terminal panicle, campanulate to 2 cm across, pale blush-pink inside, carmine-pink outside, flowering in October and early November.
'Campanulàta' has larger white flowers with a reddish-purple calyx.
'Carmínea' has large frilled-edged flowers, rosy-carmine in the bud, opening to pale pink, with a reddish-purple calyx.
'Grandiflòra' has larger flowers of the same colour as the species.

Climatic range. All A, H, M, Mts, P, S.

Deùtzia scàbra (Latin 'rough', referring to the leaf surfaces): Rough-leafed Deutzia; main islands of Japan.
Habit. A deciduous shrub to 2.5–3.0 m tall, with erect, cane-like stems from the base, the upper parts crowded with leafy twigs.
Leaves. Broadly lanceolate to ovate, 5–10 cm long and 2.5–3.5 cm wide; petiole 2–3 mm long, grooved above, stem-clasping at the base; apex acuminate; base rounded; margin serrulate, the small teeth raised above the plane of the blade; veins depressed above, raised beneath; scabrous and stellate-pubescent on both surfaces; dull dark green above, paler beneath.
Flowers. Inflorescence an erect, stellate-pubescent panicle 8–12 cm long; pedicels 5–7 mm long; calyx campanulate to 4 mm long and broad, green with 5 acute sepals to 3 mm long; petals 5, lanceolate-oblong, 1.8 cm long, mostly pure white but occasionally with a faint pink flush outside; stamens 10, the white filaments dentately-lobed near the apex, anthers cream; flowers produced abundantly from mid October to late November.
Other distinguishing features. Upper twigs terete, copper-green and finely pubescent; older bark peeling.
'Candidíssima' has double, pure white flowers, the stamens modified to additional petaloids in the centre.
'Marmoràta' Variegated Rough-leafed Deutzia, the leaves being spotted with creamy-white.
'Pride of Rochester' has very large double flowers, white but faintly tinted rosy-carmine outside; probably the best Deutzia grown in Australia.
'Punctàta' has dark green leaves, with whitish spots, and white flowers.
Climatic range. All A, H, M, Mts, P, S.

DILLWÝNIA

Commemorating the nineteenth-century British botanist, Lewis W. Dillwyn.
Parrot-pea: Eggs and Bacon (one of several so called).
Fabaceae, the Pea family.

Generic description. An indigenous genus of heath-like evergreen shrubs with about 20 species scattered mostly in eastern Australia. Leaves are simple, slender, sometimes almost cylindrical or needle-like, and the small pea-shaped flowers are mostly yellow/brown, borne in terminal racemose clusters in the upper leaf axils.

Propagation. Seeds should be scarified prior to sowing in sterilised sandy soil with a little peat added. Cuttings of ripened tip shoots are also used, best treated with a hormone rooting material in a sand/peat mixture, placed in a humid atmosphere.

Cultivation. Simulated heathland conditions on light soils with free drainage and adequate summer water are the main requirements for good results.

Pruning. Regular shortening of the flowered shoots promotes a dense, leafy growth and an abundance of flowers.

Species and cultivars

Dillwýnia retòrta (Latin 'twisted back', referring to the leaf margins) (syn. *D. ericifòlia*) Twisted Parrot-pea: eastern Australia, on heathlands, sandstone plateaus and lower tablelands.

Habit. A loose, open shrub to 1–2 m with spreading branches.

Leaves. Alternate or scattered, spread at 90° angle on the slender twigs, spirally-twisted, narrow to nearly cylindrical, 6–12 mm long and 0.5 mm wide; apex pointed; margin finely ciliate, fully revolute; glabrous; dark green.

Flowers. Solitary or in small corymbose clusters in the upper axils; calyx campanulate to 4 mm; corolla pea-shaped, the standard broadly bilobed, yellow with a small red basal fan, the wings and keel erect and much shorter; flowering from early July to late October.

Fruit. An ellipsoidal legume 5–6 mm long, green at first, becoming dark brown before splitting to release the 2 seeds.

Climatic range. A, B, M, P, S and on sheltered sites in Mts.

DODONÀEA

Commemorating Dr Rembert Dodoens, sixteenth-century physician.
Sticky Hop-bush: Large-leafed Hop-bush.
Sapindaceae, the Soapberry family.

Generic description. A widespread genus, mostly in the Southern Hemisphere, principally Australia, but with one important ornamental cultivar from New Zealand. The genus has

simple or compound, alternate leaves, sometimes resinuous and viscid, small apetalous flowers in terminal or axillary panicles or racemes, and winged capsular hop-like fruits.

Propagation. Both species treated here reproduce fairly reliably from seeds sown in late winter in a warm, humid place.

Cultivation. A moderately fertile soil is required, preferably light, open and freely drained; plants need to be grown in a sunny position to produce the best colour in leaves and capsules. Tolerant of coastal salty winds, but when so exposed, best grown as an annually pruned shrub.

Pruning. Light pruning of the 1-year-old wood in early spring improves the foliage, and helps to restrict the growth to suit the small garden.

Species and cultivars

Dodonàea triquetra (Latin 'three-cornered', referring to the fruits): Large-leafed Hop-bush: eastern Australia, from Vic. to Central Qld, mostly on the coastal heathlands and adjacent plateaus.

Habit. An evergreen bushy shrub to about 3 m tall, sometimes developing small tree-form when crowded.

Leaves. Simple, alternate, lanceolate to narrowly elliptic, 5–10 cm long; apex acute to acuminate; base slenderly cuneate; margin entire; glabrous; dark green above, paler beneath.

Flowers. In small clusters among the upper leaves; mostly dioecious, lacking petals, the 5 sepals and 8 stamens not conspicuous.

Fruit. A papery, 3-angled capsule about 1 cm long and as broad, 10 to 20 in each cluster on thread-like peduncles, green at first, becoming brown or purplish-red, the 3 vertical greenish wings projecting laterally; fruits ripen in late spring.

Other distinguishing features. Upper twigs and branchlets angular, reddish-brown.

Climatic range. B, M, P, S, T and on sheltered sites in A and Mts.

Dodonàea viscòsa 'Purpùrea' (Latin *viscidus* 'sticky'; and Greek *porphura* 'purple'): Purple-leafed Sticky Hop-bush: the species is indigenous to Australia and both islands of NZ but the cultivar was discovered in the South Island.

Habit. A fast-growing, evergreen shrub or small tree to 3–5 m tall, denser and more attractive in foliage when pruned to shrub form.

Leaves. Simple, alternate, oblanceolate, 10–12 cm long and 1.5–2.5 cm wide; apex obtuse or emarginate, with a small mucro; base narrowly cuneate; margin entire, but slightly undulate and recurved; venation reticulate, the midrib prominent beneath; venation reticulate, the midrib prominent beneath; coriaceous; glabrous but viscid, and rough with resin glands on both surfaces; mid green, stained with dark chocolate-purple, especially above and on the midrib beneath.

Flowers. In a terminal panicle, small, yellowish-green, but not showy and of little ornamental value.

Fruit. A 3–winged membraneous capsule to about 2 cm across, colouring handsomely to dull purplish-red in summer, and lasting into winter as a decorative feature.

Other distinguishing features. Upper twigs angular, with prominent longitudinal ridges.

Climatic range. A, B, H, M, Mts, P, S.

DREJERÉLLA (syn. *Beloperone*)

Commemorating Solomon Thomas Nicolai Drejer, 1813–1842, lecturer in Botany at the Veterinary School of the University of Copenhagen, and author of *Flora Danica*.

Shrimp-plant; Beloperone.

Acanthaceae, the Acanthus family.

Generic description. A small genus of tender shrubs from tropical America, one species grown in Australia for its rapid growth and unusual but handsome flowers. See specific notes below for details.

Propagation. Soft-tip or semi-hardwood cuttings taken in summer or autumn, or from the winter prunings, strike readily in a warm, moist environment.

Cultivation. A rich, friable soil with free drainage is best, preferably in a partly shaded position in a warm coastal climate with little or no frost, and with protection from strong wind.

Pruning. The plant should be pruned moderately in late winter to remove spindly growths and to encourage new flowering shoots from the base.

Drejerélla guttàta (Latin *gutta* 'a drop', referring to the abundance of cell-water released by guttation) (syn. *Beloperone guttata*) Shrimp-plant: tropical Mexico.

Habit. A soft-wooded, evergreen shrub to about 1 m tall, the swollen-jointed stems forming a rounded bush, almost always in flower.

Leaves. Simple, opposite, elliptic-ovate, 8–10 cm long and 3–4 cm wide; apex acute; margin entire but ciliate; texture soft and somewhat succulent; mid green and dull above, bright green and slightly shiny beneath.

Flowers. Inflorescence a dense terminal or axillary spike, 8–10 cm long and 2.5–3.0 cm thick; flowers tubulate, 3.0–3.5 cm long, pubescent, 2–lipped, the lower lobe trifid at the apex, the upper lobe emarginate; pure white, but with 2 purple-carmine stripes on the inside of the lower lobe; stamens 2, with white filaments; flowers carried in imbricated, brick-red to greenish, floral bracts (modified sepals) of broadly ovate shape to 2 cm long and 1.5 cm wide, borne in groups of 3, the outer bract forming the leafy sheath of the spike; flowering season from early December to late March, and intermittently throughout winter.

'**Lutea**' and '**Chartreuse**' appear to be identical, with lime-yellow bracts, but otherwise are of similar habit to the parent species.

Climatic range. B, M, P, S, T and on warm, sheltered sites in A, H, and lower Mts.

DURÁNTA

Commemorating the sixteenth-century Italian botanist, Dr Castore Durante, 1529–1590.

Golden Dewdrop, Pigeon-berry, or Sky-flowers.

Verbenaceae, the Verbena family.

Generic description. A small genus of hardwood shrubs from Central and South America with simple, opposite leaves, evergreen except in cold climates, blue, violet, or white flowers in terminal or axillary racemes or panicles, flowering during summer, followed by decorative drupaceous fruits in autumn and winter. The species treated here is well regarded because of its handsome foliage, flowers and fruit and its adaptability to a wide range of growing conditions. It is equally well suited to culture as a large shrub or small specimen tree. The fruits are poisonous and adequate precautions should be taken to prevent their ingestion, especially by small children.

Propagation. Soft-tip cuttings taken in spring, or firm-wood, leafy cuttings in autumn or winter, root satisfactorily in a warm, humid environment; a bottom-heated bench with mist overhead is advantageous.

Cultivation. The plant thrives in coastal climates or mild inland parts with only light frosts, preferably in a sun-exposed position on a well-drained, moderately fertile soil. Temperatures below −2° or −3°C cause defoliation and possible injury to the flowering and fruiting wood.

Pruning. Ideally grown as a small tree on a single trunk with a rounded crown, kept so by suppression of the water-shoot growths from the base; a periodic pruning of the crown to control its shape and size is sometimes necessary. While the fruiting branches are within easy reach of the ground, the spent fruiting twigs should be removed, but this eventually becomes impracticable in larger specimens.

Species and cultivars

Duránta erécta (Latin 'upright', but not necessarily of narrow growth habit) (syn. *D. plumieri*, *D. ellisia*, *D. repens*) Golden Dewdrop, Pigeonberry or Sky-flower: Central America, West Indies and tropical South America.

Habit. An evergreen tree to 4–5 m tall, with a single trunk or several trunks with squarish drooping branches; normally with slender, very sharp spines, but not always so, some clonal forms being almost or quite spineless. Sometimes modified by pruning to shrub form with many erect stems from the base.

Leaves. Opposite, but occasionally 3-whorled, ovate, obovate or rhombic, 3–8 cm long and 2–4 cm wide; apex acute to acuminate; margin variable, from entire to remotely crenate or sharply and coarsely serrate; midrib and main veins prominent beneath; dark green and slightly shiny above; glabrous on both surfaces.

Flowers. Inflorescence a loose panicle, comprising 5 to 10 slender racemes 8–12 cm long, each carrying up to 25–30 flowers; calyx tubulate to 5 mm long, purplish-green; corolla salverform, lavender-blue, the slender tube 5 mm long, opening to a 5-lobed limb to 1.0–1.5 cm across, the lobes broadly obovate, with a conspicuous dark-violet stripe down the middle, the throat of the tube white; flowers are borne profusely from November to early April.

Fruit. A 2-nutlet, fleshy drupe to 1.5 cm long and 1.0 cm across, lemon-shaped, enclosed in the enlarged persistent calyx, borne in pendulous, terminal and axillary racemes, 5 to about 30 fruits in each raceme; green at first but ripening to yellow, glossy and very showy from February to April. The fruits are poisonous.

Other distinguishing features. Young shoots squarish, some armed with slender, sharp spines to 2.5 cm long.

'Álba' is somewhat similar but has white flowers with a greenish throat, mostly entire-margined leaves, and slightly stronger growth.

'Variegàta' is like the parent species but the leaves are 3-toned, bright green and grey-green, irregularly margined with a creamy-yellow edge and tending towards purplish in cold weather; the cultivar is very spiny, deriving as a bud-sport from an unusually spiny form of the parent.

Another variegated-foliated form of *D. erecta*, as yet apparently without a legitimate name, and like 'Variegata' deriving as a bud-sport, has leaves splashed and speckled with creamy-white and turning purplish in late autumn and winter, especially in cold climates.

Climatic range. B, M, P, S, T, and in warm microclimates in A.

ÉCHIUM

Derived from the ancient Greek name for the plant.

Pride of Madeira; Viper's Bugloss.

Boraginaceae, the Borage family.

Generic description. A genus of subshrubs and trailing herbs from the Mediterranean countries and offshore islands, one grown in Australia for its interesting and showy flowers. See specific notes below for details.

Propagation. a) Seeds sown as soon as ripe germinate readily in a warm but not over-humid atmosphere.

b) Short side-shoots, removed from the older stems and treated as cuttings in individual containers, root easily in a warm glass-house.

Cultivation. The species listed is native to well-drained soils on mountainsides and is accustomed to austere conditions. Under cultivation, a coarse, gravelly soil, and frugal treatment with water and plant food, produces the best results with better and more abundant flowers. The plant is tolerant of only light frosts to −1° to −2°C.

Pruning. Spent inflorescences should be pruned away after flowering; trailing shoots that exceed their space allocation should also be removed.

Species and cultivars

Echium fastuòsum (Latin 'proud', alluding to the commanding appearance of the flower spikes): Pride of Madeira: Canary and Madeira Islands.

Habit. An evergreen, many-headed plant, of shrubby form to 1.5 m or more tall when pruned occasionally, but of nondescript shape when grown naturally, the long snake-like stems sprawling over the ground and ascending at the ends.

Leaves. Simple, alternate, lanceolate to narrow-elliptic, 15–25 cm long and 4–8 cm wide, but decreasing in size near the terminals; petiole to 2 cm long, splayed to 1 cm wide, flattened, densely pubescent; apex attenuate; base cuneate; margin entire, but densely ciliate; venation depressed above, prominent beneath; all parts densely white-pubescent; dark green above, paler beneath.

Flowers. Inflorescence a terminal, spike-like panicle, 30–50 cm long and 10 cm wide at the base, tapering to the pointed apex; flowers numerous, in small clusters of about 8, on 1 cm peduncles; calyx tubulate-campanulate, 6–7 mm long, with 5 slender green sepals, all parts densely pubescent; corolla lilac-purple at first, opening to salverform to 1 cm across, pale gentian-blue; stamens 5, to 1.3 cm long, the filaments pale lilac-purple, with violet-blue anthers; flowering season from late September to early December.

Fruit. A berry of 4 small nutlets, dispersing freely when ripe.

Other distinguishing features. Upper stems thick, pale green, with dense white pubescence.

Climatic range. A, B, H, M, P, S, T, and in warm, sheltered microclimates in Mts.

ELAEÁGNUS

Derived from the Greek, describing the olive-like appearance of the fruit.
Japanese Oleaster.
Elaeagnaceae, the Oleaster family.

Generic description. A genus of useful shrubs and small trees, evergreen or deciduous, some with spiny branches, grown mainly for their attractive foliage. Leaves are simple, alternate, green or variegated, often covered on the lower side with silvery-brown scales; flowers are campanulate or tubulate, richly fragrant, but inconspicuous on the lower side of the upper twigs; the drupaceous fruits are red, brown, or yellowish.

Propagation. a) Seeds of the parent species germinate readily if sown immediately.
b) The cultivars are grown by soft-tip or semi-hardwood cuttings, taken in late spring or summer and struck in a sand/peat mixture in a warm, humid atmosphere.

Cultivation. The Japanese Oleaster is tolerant of a wide range of soils but thrives in a well-drained, light soil with adequate summer water, in an open sunny position.

Pruning. The plants described are self-shaping but often benefit from an annual shortening of the long branches to induce a dense, leafy habit; they may be pruned more severely for hedging, but should not be closely clipped.

Species and cultivars

Elaeágnus púngens (Latin 'sharp-pointed', referring to the spines): Japanese Oleaster: main islands of Japan, often in wind-exposed places.

Habit. An evergreen shrub to 3–4 m tall and 4–6 m wide, the main branches horizontal or drooping to ground level, forming a broad bun-shaped bush.

Leaves. Lanceolate to narrow-elliptic, 8–12 cm long and 3–4 cm wide, the petiole to 1 cm; apex acute; base cuneate or obtuse; margin crinkled with irregular notches, somewhat revolute; dark green and lustrous above, silvery-white beneath, with scaly main vein and scattered brown, glandular dots.

Flowers. In 1- to 3-flowered clusters, pendulous at the nodes of the young shoots; apetalous, the 1 cm calyx squarish with 4 longitudinal ridges, 4-parted at the apex; sweetly perfumed; creamy-white but with brown dots, flowering between February and April.

Fruit. A single-stoned, ellipsoidal drupe to 1.5 cm long, with persistent, club-like calyx extending beyond the distal end; peduncle slender to 5 mm; fruit reddish-brown, with silvery-brown spots and scales, borne in groups of 1 to about 3 in autumn and winter.

Other distinguishing features. Some short lateral branchlets have blunt spines.

'Aurea' is like the species but has leaves with a bright-yellow margin of irregular width, from 1 mm to about 6 mm wide.

'Maculàta' (syn. 'Aureo-variegata') is a more spectacular form, with a large, yellow central patch and dark-green margin, with occasional pale-green and dark-green splashes superimposed on the yellow.

Climatic range. A, H, M, Mts, P, S.

ENKIÁNTHUS

Derived from the Greek, referring to the swollen involucre of one of the species.
Enkianthus or Bell-flower.
Ericaceae, the Erica family.

Generic description. A genus of Oriental shrubs, mainly deciduous, with simple, alternate leaves but often appearing to be whorled; pendulous, campanulate flowers at the terminals of the 1–year-old shoots, usually in racemes or umbels; and fruit a 5-celled capsule, containing several winged seeds.

Propagation. a) Seeds are sown in a mildly-acid, peaty sowing-medium in a warm, humid atmosphere.
b) Leafy tip-cuttings about 4–5 cm long taken in late spring to autumn, or more mature material taken in late autumn and winter, root somewhat erratically, preferably in a warm controlled-environment glass-house; root-promoting dusts are beneficial.

Cultivation. The Bell-flowers are best grown in a cool, moist climate with clean air, and low temperatures not exceeding −8°C, on a mildly-acid, well-aerated light soil with a high organic content, but which drains freely. The soil surface should be mulched with coarse compost, organic litter, or with flat 'floater' stones to maintain an even temperature and water-status in the soil and to preclude root disturbance by unnecessary surface cultivation. They grow well in filtered shade but colour better in an open, sunny aspect.

Pruning. Apart from shortening or removal of the occasional wayward shoot, the plants seldom need pruning and develop their flowering potential better without interference.

Enkiánthus campanulátus (Latin 'with bell-shaped flowers'): mountains of the main islands of Japan.
Habit. An erect, deciduous shrub 2.5–3.5 m tall, with leaves mainly confined to the upper twiggy branchlets; very old plants often reach 7–8 m tall.
Leaves. Simple, alternate, but appearing to be whorled at the ends of the slender twigs, elliptic to obovate, 3–6 cm long and 1.5–3.0 cm wide; apex acute; margin finely serrulate, the small teeth bristly; midrib and main veins raised and with dense, axillary tufts of brownish hair beneath; bright green but not glossy above, lustrous green beneath, changing to orange, scarlet, and crimson, in autumn.
Flowers. Inflorescence a terminal, corymb-like raceme of about 8–10 flowers, the brown-pubescent main rachis to 5 cm long; calyx about 4 mm across, with 5 linear-lanceolate sepals 3–4 mm long; corolla campanulate to 1 cm long and 8 mm wide, not gibbous at the base, the 5 short lobes only slightly reflexed at the apex; variable in colour, but mostly pale creamy-green with deep-carmine veins and shadings at the apex, flowering in October and November; stamens 10, in 2 series, the filaments creamy-green, the anthers cream, pistil 7–8 mm long, green.
Fruit. An ellipsoidal brown capsule 6–8 mm long, containing the several winged seeds.
Other distinguishing features. Upper twigs reddish-grey, smooth, the ultimate twigs roughened by the numerous leaf-scars.
Climatic range. H, M, Mts, and on cool, elevated sites in A, P, and S.

Enkiánthus cèrnuus (Latin 'bending downwards'): main islands of Japan.
Habit. A deciduous shrub to 2.5–3.0 m tall, erect, with a dense mass of twiggy branchlets forming the crown.
Leaves. Elliptic-ovate, 3–5 cm long, 1–2 cm wide, borne on pubescent petioles 4–6 mm long; apex acute; base cuneate; margin crenulate; glabrous and mid-green above, paler and pubescent on the midrib beneath, changing to a vivid display of yellow and crimson in autumn.
Flowers. In a short terminal raceme of up to 12–15 broadly-campanulate pendulous flowers 6–9 mm long; white, with laciniate lobes at the mouth; flowering in late spring.
Fruit. An ellipsoidal capsule about 6–7 mm long, with winged seeds.
f. *rùbens* (Latin 'red'): is the very fine clonal form usually available in nurseries; the flowers are creamy white at the base but deep rose-red on the lobes and upper half of the corolla.
Climatic range. H, M, Mts and on cool, elevated sites in A, P, S.

Enkiánthus perulàtus (Latin 'with conspicuous perules', the chaffy, protective scales around some overwintering buds) (syn. *E. japonicus*) Japanese Bell-flower: main islands of Japan, mostly in the mountains.

Habit. An erect, deciduous shrub, 1.5–2.0 m tall, often shaped like a miniature tree with a distinct lower trunk and dense, twiggy crown of irregularly globose form; a popular Bonsai subject because of its naturally slow growth, twiggy habit and small leaves.

Leaves. Simple, alternate, nearly opposite but clustered in whorl-like groups at the terminals, rhombic-ovate to obovate, 2–4 cm long and 1.0–1.5 cm wide; apex acute to acuminate; margin finely serrulate, mostly above the middle, the fine bristly serrations incurved; midrib prominent below; glabrous except for a fine line of hair on the upper midrib and a tuft of white hair at the base of the lower midrib; pale green when young, deepening when mature, slightly paler beneath, changing to orange, scarlet, and crimson in autumn, some leaves only partly colouring.

Flowers. Inflorescence a terminal umbel of 6–8 pendulous flowers on slender, 2 cm, recurved, whitish-green pedicels; calyx with a green base and 5 slender, white, claw-like sepals to 2–3 mm long; corolla urceolate, to 8–9 mm long and 6 mm broad, the base gibbous with 5 narrow sac-like ridges extending half-way to the narrowed 5-lobed apex, pure waxy-white, flowering from late September to November, lightly fragrant; stamens 10, the filaments white-pubescent, anthers cream, awned at the apex.

Fruit. An ovoid to ellipsoidal capsule, 8–9 mm long, on straightened pedicels, the winged seeds dark brown.

Climatic range. H, M, Mts, and on cool, elevated sites in A, P, and S.

EPÁCRIS

Derived from the Greek, referring to the hilltop habitat of several of the common species.
Heath; Native Fuchsia; Fuchsia Heath; etc.
Epacridaceae, the Epacris family.

Generic description. A genus of Australian and New Zealand evergreen shrubs with small scattered leaves, mostly sharply acuminate and often sessile, and solitary axillary flowers on the young shoots, the mostly bi-coloured corolla tubulate or campanulate with a spreading limb

of 5 lobes. Flowers are produced mainly in winter and spring, but intermittently at other times in various habitats.

Propagation. a) Seeds, collected before natural dispersal, germinate erratically even when sown in ideal conditions of heat and moisture control. b) Soft-tip cuttings, taken between late spring and early autumn, root well in a coarse sand in a humid atmosphere, preferably under mist.

Cultivation. The species described below perform satisfactorily on a light sandy or medium loam with free drainage, ideally in a moist, humid climate with minimum temperatures remaining above –5°C.

Pruning. A moderate pruning of the flowered shoots helps to develop a dense bush with more abundant foliage and flowers.

Species and cultivars

Epácris impréssa (Latin 'sunken below the general level' referring to the dimples at the base of the corolla): Common or Victorian Heath, the official floral emblem of that State: Vic, Tas, SA, and NSW, mainly on sandy heathlands and slopes of the tablelands.

Habit. A erect shrub to about 1 m tall but occasionally larger in the subdued light of the forests.

Leaves. Scattered, sessile, linear to ovate-lanceolate, 10–15 mm long, often recurved; apex acute; margin entire; midrib prominent beneath; glabrous; mid-green.

Flowers. Solitary on recurved pedicels in the upper axils, forming a long racemose spray to partly or fully conceal the erect stems; calyx with 5 ovate sepals, 2–3 mm long, whitish-green; corolla tubulate, pendulous, 1.5–2.5 cm long, the 5 apical lobes flared outwards, the base with 5 shallow dimples near the apex of the sepals, white, through the pink range to red and crimson; stamens 5, with yellow anthers, the single red style exserted; flowering period from winter to late spring.

Fruit. A dehiscent, 5-celled capsule with numerous seeds.

var. *grandiflòra* (Latin 'with large flowers'): is the Grampians Heath, where it grows on the rocky upper levels under harsh conditions of temperature and water; it is distinct from the species in its broader, double, rosy-carmine flowers, and shorter but broader grey-green, heavily-pubescent leaves.

'Cranbourne Bells' is a registered cultivar from the eastern sand-belt of Victoria, with large, double flowers, opening from pale pink to white.

Climatic range. A, H, M, P, S and on lower levels of Mts.

Epácris longiflòra (Latin 'with long flowers'): Native Fuchsia or Fuchsia Heath: NSW coastal heathlands, plateaus and lower tablelands, usually on moist, sandy or rocky sites.

Habit. A shrub to 1 m or so tall, of very irregular, sparse growth in its native habitat, but responding to cultivation and pruning to form a roughly globose bush of dense, leafy habit.

Leaves. Simple, alternate but occasionally scattered in irregular pattern, spreading at right angle from the stems, ovate to ovate-lanceolate to about 1 cm long and 5–7 mm wide, sessile; apex acuminate with a fine sharp point; base sub-cordate, partly clasping the stem; margin entire; glabrous and coriaceous; reddish when young, maturing to dark shining green above, paler beneath.

Flowers. Solitary, drooping from the upper axils, but crowded together to form a racemose spray 15 cm or more long; pedicels 4–5 mm long, reddish and puberulent; calyx tubulate, with 5 acute sepals, green; corolla tubulate, 2.0–2.5 cm long and 3.5 mm broad in the tube, often curved, the 5–lobed limb expanded to about 1.3 cm across, the tube bright crimson, gradating to white towards the limb; stamens 5, attached within the tube; style white, exserted shortly beyond the limb; flowering season mainly in late winter and spring, but intermittently throughout summer in cool microclimates.

Fruit. A dehiscent, 5–celled capsule with small seeds.

Climatic range. A, M, Mts, P, S.

Epácris microphýlla (Greek 'with small leaves'): Coral Heath: eastern Australia, on a variety of sites from dry sandy heaths near the sea to the rocky ridges of the plateaus and tablelands, occasionally on wet, swampy land.

Habit. An evergreen shrub of indeterminate shape in its natural habitat, usually open and thin to 1 m or so tall but denser and of more regular shape when grown well under cultivation.

Leaves. Simple, alternate or scattered, ovate to 2–4 mm long; apex acute to acuminate; base cordate, sessile; margin entire; glabrous and coriaceous; reddish-green when young, maturing to dark green.

Flowers. Solitary in the upper axils in a spike-like or racemose form, extending to 15 cm or more down the 1-year-old stems; corolla clavate and rosy-red in the bud, opening to funnelform, expanding to a broad, stellate limb to 5–6 mm across, of 5 acute lobes, white or with pinkish stains on the outer surfaces; flowering season from late winter to early summer.

Fruit. Not seen.

Climatic range. A, B, H, M, Mts, P, S.

Epácris purpuráscens (Greek 'becoming purple'): Port Jackson Heath: NSW, usually on moist loam or sandy soils on the ridges and gullies between the coast and lower tablelands.

Habit. An erect shrub to 1.5 m or so, somewhat sparse and irregular in the wild but improved by regular pruning.

Leaves. Alternate, sessile, ovate, 1.0–1.5 cm long, 5–7 mm wide, set closely together to almost conceal the stems; apex acuminate; base rounded with a pair of blunt auricles which partly enfold the stem; margin entire; venation inconspicuous; glabrous; bright green.

Flowers. Almost sessile, solitary in the axils of the upper twigs in a spike-like inflorescence 20–25 cm long; involucral bracts and sepals creamy-white; corolla tubulate, the 5 spreading lobes forming a radiate flower 8–10 mm across, pale pink to nearly white, with a reddish-purple flush; flowering period from late winter to October.

Fruit. A small round, 5–celled capsule, splitting from the apex to release the numerous seeds.

Climatic range. B, M, P, S and on sheltered sites on lower Mts.

ERÌCA

Derived from the ancient Greek vernacular name of the plant, *Ereike*.

Erica; Heath (various); Heather (now properly applied to *Calluna*).

Ericaceae, the Erica family.

Generic description. A large genus of evergreen shrubs or small trees from Europe and South Africa, widely grown for their attractive flowers and neat foliage. Leaves are simple, whorled, mostly linear and recurved; flowers are borne at the terminals and in the axils of the 1-year-old shoots, forming spike-like racemes or dense panicles; flower shapes are tubulate, campanulate, or inflated about the middle of the tube, the mouth with 4 short lobes, in a wide variety of colour from white to pink, red, crimson, mauve, purple, and yellow; the calyx has 4 short, free sepals; and fruit is a small, 4–celled capsule enclosed by the persistent corolla, the seeds minute and numerous.

Only a small percentage, probably less than 20 per cent, of the 600 or more species of Erica have been introduced into Australia, and some of these appear now to have been lost to cultivation. However, several nurserymen and botanic gardens in the southern States have assembled and preserved good collections, despite diminished popularity of the genus in recent years. An outstanding collection is to be seen at Wittunga Botanic Garden, Blackwood, South Australia, administered by the South Australian Botanic Garden Board. A great number of Erica species, mainly from South Africa were collected and planted at Wittunga by the late Messrs Edwin Ashby (father) and A. Keith Ashby (son), to form the largest assemblage of the genus in Australasia. A visit to the garden in the Mount Lofty Range during the main flowering season between mid winter and late spring is well worth while.

Propagation. Firm-tip cuttings, 1–2 cm long, are taken in autumn and early winter and struck in a coarse river-sand with a little peat added; a cool, humid part of the glass-house is preferred.

Cultivation. Ericas are not the easiest exotic plants to grow but, where climatic and soil conditions are favourable, are worth a special effort to satisfy their requirements. The ideal soil is mildly acid, of coarse granular texture, with a peat content sufficient to retain moisture moderately well, especially during the heat of summer, but to release the surplus soil-water freely during prolonged wet weather. For lasting satisfactory results, a flourishing symbiotic relationship between the plant species and its mycorrhizal fungus must first be established. In soils not previously used to grow Ericas, it is customary to introduce the fungus by means of a small quantity of soil known to carry it. The soil in the pots of nursery-grown Ericas is usually sufficient. Otherwise, for cuttings or seedlings struck or germinated in a sterile material, an importation of 'Erica' soil should be made. A mulch of gravel or of large 'floater' stones should be used to avoid root disturbance. Ericas are not comfortable in a climate with high atmospheric humidity — the drier atmosphere of the

Adelaide and Melbourne climates is more to their liking, but where summer temperatures are excessively high, they are best grown on elevated sites. Many fine specimens are seen in the Mount Lofty Range in South Australia, the Dandenongs region in Victoria and along the coast of northern Tasmania. There are few successful plantings along the eastern Australian coastal strip, but on the adjacent tablelands, occasional well-grown plants are found.

Pruning. Regular annual pruning of the flowered shoots, immediately after the flowers fade, maintains a compact, leafy growth habit, but pruning should be confined to the young 1-year-old wood only.

Species and cultivars

The following list of species, with brief descriptions, is a fair representative sampling of those believed to be presently available from Australian nurserymen.

Erica arbòrea (Latin 'tree-like'): Mediterranean region. A shrub or small tree to 2–3 m tall in cultivation, but much larger in its native habitat; leaves 3-whorled, linear, 4–7 mm long, glabrous, bright green; flowers in a dense terminal panicle 25–30 cm tall, the nearly globular corolla 4 mm long, white, fragrant; flowering season, late winter to early spring.

Erìca baccans (Latin 'shaped like a berry'): Berry Heath: SW Cape of Good Hope, South Africa.
A dense, upright shrub to 1.5 m tall with pale grey-green, 4-ranked, linear-falcate leaves, 6–7 mm long, pointing forward to nearly obscure the stems; flowers in terminal clusters of about 4, the corolla globose-urceolate, 5–7 mm long, rosy-salmon, persisting for several months in a dry, scarious state, finally turning pale brown; flowering season, late winter to early spring.

Erìca baùera (commemorating the Austrian botanist brothers, Franz and Ferdinand Bauer) (syn. *E. bowiana*) Bridal Heath: SW Cape of Good Hope, South Africa.
An erect shrub to 1.5 m or so, with a somewhat open growth habit, improved in density by regular pruning; leaves linear-oblong, 3–5 mm long, held horizontally or slightly reflexed, dark grey-green; flowers tubulate-urceolate, 2–3 cm long, inflated in the middle, borne in pendulous

clusters of 10–20, waxy-white, blush-pink, rose-pink, to rosy-carmine; flowering season, spring to autumn.

Erìca canaliculàta (Latin 'channelled longitudinally'): Purple Heath, Tree or Christmas Heather: sometimes offered as *E. melanthera*, a distinct, comparatively rare species: SW Cape of Good Hope, South Africa.
An irregularly globose shrub to 2–3 m tall, but often much larger in old native specimens; leaves 3–whorled, linear, 4–6 mm long and 1 mm wide, the margin revolute, dark green and finely granular above, with some fine pubescence, whitish-green beneath, with a green strip along the midrib; flowers in a large terminal panicle, the corolla campanulate, 3 mm long, with 4 fluted lobes, mauve-pink but deeper at the edges; stamens 8, with white filaments and black anthers; flowering season, April to July. The most widely planted Erica in Australian gardens.

Erìca càrnea (Latin 'flesh-pink'): Spring Heath or Snow Heather: mountains of central and southern Europe (syn. *E. herbacea*).
A prostrate shrub to 0.5 m tall, with spreading, decumbent stems forming a broad mat to about 2 m across; leaves 4-whorled, linear, 3–7 mm long, dark green; flowers in small axillary racemes of up to 4, the corolla tubulate-urceolate, 5 mm long, dark rosy-red, with exserted crimson anthers; flowering season, late winter and early spring; many clonal selections exist, with floral colour varying from white through the pink range to rosy-purple and deep ruby-red.

Erìca x cavendishiàna (commemorating William George Spencer Cavendish, sixth Duke of Devonshire, one-time President of the Royal Horticultural Society): Cavendish Heath.
A low shrub to 0.5 m tall with dark-green, linear-revolute leaves 6–7 mm long, almost covering the twigs; flowers are borne in a dense, spike-like panicle to 15–20 cm tall, the lemon-yellow corolla tubulate to 2 cm or so long, with 4 reflexed terminal lobes; flowering season, late winter to early summer.

Erìca cerinthòides (Latin 'like a *Cerinthe*', the Honey-wort): Red Hairy Heath: widespread in South Africa.
An erect, open bush to 1 m or so tall, made more compact by regular pruning; leaves 4 to 6 whorled, linear to 7 mm long, forward-pointing, puberulent, dark green; flowers in terminal clusters of a few to 20 or more, tubulate-urceolate to 3–4 cm long, closely narrowed at the mouth, densely pubescent, variable in colour from white and deep pink to crimson; flowering season, winter and spring.

Erìca cinerea (Latin 'ash-grey'): Bell Heather: British Isles and western Europe.
A dense, twiggy and often twisted shrub to 0.5 m tall, but spreading with age to 2 m across; leaves 3-whorled, linear, 5–7 mm long, glabrous and dark green; flowers in small, terminal, umbellate clusters of up to 10, sometimes extending to racemose form to 10 cm long; corolla ovoid-urceolate, 6–7 mm long, the mouth closely narrowed, rosy-purple in the species but white, pink, lilac, and red in the many clonal variations; flowering season, early summer to autumn.

Erìca x darleyénsis (Latin 'from Darley Dale', the locality of a large English nursery): hybrid between *E. carnea* and *E. mediterranea*: Darley Heath.
A low shrub 0.5 to 1.0 m tall, of somewhat loose, open growth but improved by regular pruning; leaves 4-whorled, linear to 1.3 cm long, dark glossy green; flowers in few-flowered clusters forming a leafy raceme 8–15 cm long, the corolla tubulate-urceolate, 7–8 mm long with a constricted throat, pale rose-pink in the type with deep crimson anthers, varying to white, blush-pink, deep rose-red, and magenta in the cultivars; flowering season late autumn and winter.

Erìca holoserícea (Greek 'wholly covered with silky hairs'): Cape of Good Hope, South Africa.
A small, compact shrub to 0.75–1.0 m tall; leaves cylindrical-falcate, 10–12 mm long, the apex with a soft spine, the margin fully recurved, dark green; flowers drooping, borne singly but forming a dense, terminal raceme; calyx campanulate, about 5 mm long, pale pink, persistent; corolla broadly tubulate to 8 mm long, shortly exserted beyond the sepals, deep cyclamen pink; flowering season, late winter and early spring.

Erìca lusitánica (Latin 'from Lusitania', now Portugal): Portuguese or Spanish Heath: Iberian Peninsula.
An upright shrub to 2–3 m tall and 1.5–2.0 m

wide, with dense foliage massed in slender vertical spires; leaves 3-whorled or scattered irregularly, linear-acicular, 6–7 mm long, fully revolute, bright green; flowers in few-flowered clusters forming a fastigiate panicle 20–25 cm long, borne abundantly over the crown of the plant; calyx stellate, white to pale pink; corolla tubulate, 5 mm long, dull rosy-crimson in the bud but maturing to white, with a faint rosy flush; stamens with white filaments and black anthers; flowering season June to August.

Erìca mammòsa (Latin 'nippled'): Red Signal Heath: SW Cape of Good Hope, South Africa. A loose, open shrub of 1 m or so, made more dense and floriferous by regular pruning,; leaves 4-whorled, linear, 9–12 mm long, dark green, contrasting sharply with the pale yellowish-green twigs; flowers in dense, pendulous clusters to 8–10 cm long, near the terminals; corolla tubulate, 3 cm long, constricted at the mouth, variable in colour, mainly in the red and crimson hues, the cultivar '**Coccinea**' a striking signal-red, and perhaps the most popular of the species.

Erìca pezìza (derivation obscure): Velvet Bell Heath: Cape of Good Hope, South Africa. A dense, leafy shrub to 1 m or so; leaves 3-whorled, linear, 5–6 mm long, carried on slender, reddish-brown branchlets; flowers borne singly in great abundance on the upper twigs, forming a dense paniculate mass, almost concealing the foliage; corolla cup-shaped, nearly globular, 4–5 mm long, finely pubescent, sweetly perfumed, pure white; flowering season, spring.

Erìca règia (Latin 'royal'): Royal Heath: southern Cape of Good Hope, South Africa.
A shrub of 0.6–0.8 m tall, of somewhat open growth unless pruned regularly; leaves 4- to 6-whorled, linear, 8–10 mm long, pointing forward to almost conceal the yellowish twigs, soft-textured, bright to dark green; flowers in whorled clusters of about 12 to 20 or so, drooping from the upper twigs; corolla tubulate to 2 cm long, inflated in the middle, slightly constricted near the reflexed lobes of the mouth; glistening crimson, slightly paler towards the green stellate calyx, but variable amongst the seedlings; flowering season, late winter to early spring.
'**Variegàta**' is one of the most spectacular of the

Ericas, with a bi-coloured corolla, the proximal half pure white, the distal half bright scarlet, the throat whitish with an exserted, blackish stigma; the corolla is carried in a bright-green stellate calyx with reddish shadings.

Erìca sessiliflòra (Latin 'with stalkless flowers'): Green Heath: SW Cape of Good Hope, South Africa.
A shrub to 1 m or so tall, somewhat irregular and sparse in growth unless regularly pruned; leaves linear to 10 mm or more, crowded and pointing forward in a graceful curve to partly conceal the stem, mid green; flowers in a densely arranged, terminal spike of close whorls; corolla a slender, falcate tube to 3 cm long, pale green, all arching outwards and downwards; flowering season winter and early spring.

Erìca tétralix (Greek 'with 4-ranked leaves'): Cross-leafed Heath or Bog Heather: British Isles and western Europe.
A dwarf shrub to 0.5 m with low, dense habit of growth to 1–2 m wide in old age; leaves decussately 4–whorled, linear to 4 mm long, with revolute margin, dark green above, densely white-tomentose beneath; flowers in terminal umbellate clusters of up to 10–12 flowers, covering the crown of the plant; corolla tubulate-campanulate, 6 mm long, narrowed at the mouth, glistening rose-pink, but many clonal forms are offered with white, pale-pink, or crimson flowers; flowering season, early summer to late autumn.

Erìca vàgans (Latin 'wandering' hence, widely dispersed): Cornish Heath: southern Britain and south-western Europe.
A dense, twiggy shrub of 0.5 mm with a broad, flat-topped crown 1–2 m wide; leaves mostly 4- to 5-whorled, linear, 4–8 mm long, dark green; flowers in a spike-like raceme to 12–15 cm long at the terminals of the pale-brown shoots; corolla elongate-campanulate, 3–4 mm long, slightly contracted at the mouth, rosy-carmine in the species but with white, pale pink, and rosy-red in the cultivars; flowering season, late summer to early winter.

Erìca ventricòsa (Latin 'inflated in the middle'): Wax-flowered Heath: SW Cape of Good Hope, South Africa, at elevations of up to 1200 m.
A stiff bush to 1 m tall, usually kept lower in cultivation by regular pruning; leaves

4–whorled, linear to 1.5 cm long, spreading, mid green with bronze-green tips, ciliate along the margins; flowers in dense, terminal clusters over the crown of the plant; calyx of 4 slenderly stellate, green lobes; corolla urceolate to 2.5 cm long, broad at the base, contracted near the spreading, 4–lobed mouth, blush-pink but usually deeper in the throat, of waxy texture; flowering season, late spring and summer.

Erìca vestìta (Latin 'clothed with hairs'): Wide-mouthed or Trumpet Heath: SW Cape of Good Hope, South Africa.
A densely leafed shrub to 1 m or so tall; leaves acicular, 10–12 mm long, soft textured, bright green; flowers in a dense cluster of 20 or more, at or just beneath the terminals; flowers tubulate to 3 cm long, the 4 lobes of the mouth flared slightly, with stamens as long as the tube, and whitish pistil slightly exserted; colour is variable from white to red, the best crimson and blood-red forms offered as named cultivars; flowering season, spring and early summer.

Erìca x *wìlmorei* (commemorative name of unknown derivation): Wilmore Heath.
A dense bush of 0.6 m tall; leaves 3- or 4-whorled, linear, 6–7 mm long, greyish-green; flowers in a crowded spike-like raceme just beneath the terminals; corolla tubulate to 2.5 cm long, the 4 apical lobes slightly reflexed, bright rose-pink with a white tip; several cultivars are offered with crimson or double flowers; flowering season, winter and early spring.
Climatic range. All H, M, Mts, and in cool elevated parts of A, P and S.

ERIOSTÈMON

Derived from the Greek, *erion* 'wool' and *stemon* 'a stamen', referring to the ciliate filaments.
Eriostemon or Wax-flower.
Rutaceae, the Rue family.

Generic description. A genus of Australian native shrubs with simple, alternate leaves, more or less prominently glandular, the tubercles appearing on both leaves and twigs; the white, pink, or red stellate flowers have 10 stamens with flattened ciliate filaments and glabrous anthers, a pistil of 5 green carpels and green, globular stigma; and fruit is a dry schizocarp, each cell containing a single, shiny, brownish seed. The following species are grown exten-

sively for their attractive floral display over a long season.
Propagation. a) Seeds, collected when fully ripe are immersed in warm water and allowed to soak for 24 hours, then sown in a friable medium in a warm, moist environment, preferably in early spring.
b) Soft-tip cuttings taken in late spring to late summer, or semi-hardwood cuttings taken in autumn and winter, strike readily in a sand/peat mixture in a warm, misted glass-house; the use of root-promoting dust is beneficial.
Cultivation. Eriostemons are at their best in a light loam soil, or a sandy soil improved with organic matter, in a wind-sheltered position, preferably in the dappled shade of fine-textured, overhead trees. They must have adequate water, especially in spring and summer but the surplus must drain away freely. A generous pebble mulch, or a few flat 'floater' stones help to maintain a cool root-run and conserve moisture in dry times.
Pruning. Young plants should be tip-pruned frequently in the first year or two to build up a dense, leafy growth but thereafter a healthy plant may have at least one-third of the annual growth removed immediately after flowering; flowers may be cut for indoor decoration as well as to prune the plant.

Species and cultivars
Eriostèmon australàsius (Latin 'Australian') (syn. *E. lanceolatus, E. salicifolius*) Pink Wax-flower: Central Coast of NSW, mainly on the deep sandy soils of the heathlands and gravelly ridges of the sandstone plateaus.
Habit. An evergreen shrub, 1.5–2.0 m tall, with slender, ascending branches forming an open, sparse plant, narrow at the base but well leafed and with abundant flowers above.
Leaves. Linear, 3–6 cm long and 5 mm wide; apex acute; margin entire, slightly thickened; venation obscure; dotted with pellucid oil glands and aromatic when bruised; glabrous, dull grey-green, upper surface concave.
Flowers. Solitary in the upper axils in sprays to 15–30 cm long, on grey-green pedicels; calyx with 5 rounded, green, ciliate sepals; corolla opening to stellate form 3 cm across, of 5 lanceolate petals, 7 mm wide, roseine-purple, flowering from early winter to late spring or to early summer when grown in a sheltered place; stamens 10, forming a broad cone, the filaments

white, pubescent, ribbon-like, with orange-red anthers.

Other distinguishing features. Upper twigs angular, with decurrent ridges below the leaf-bases.

Climatic range. A, B, M, P, S, T.

Eriostèmon buxifòlius (Latin 'with leaves like *Buxus*', the Box): Box-leafed Wax-flower: Central and mid North Coast of NSW, mainly on sandy heathlands.

Habit. A spreading shrub to 1.5 m tall, with arching stems arising from the base, forming a roughly hemispherical outline.

Leaves. Alternate, but often opposite or 3-whorled, obovate, ovate or oblong, to 1.5 cm long and 6–8 mm wide; apex acute-mucronate, recurved; base obtuse; margin entire but made irregular by the warty tubercles; venation obscure; slightly rough, shiny and mid-green above, heavily warted, paler and dull beneath.

Flowers. Solitary in the upper axils, forming a racemose spray to 8–10 cm long; pedicels reddish, 5–6 mm long; calyx a shallow cup, green, with 5 claw-like sepals; corolla conical and imbricate in the bud, carmine-red, opening to a stellate flower to 1.5 cm across; petals lanceolate-oblong, 3–4 mm wide, white but stained carmine-red outside, usually on the overlapped half of each petal; stamens 10, the flat, whitish filaments 3 mm long, with orange-red anthers; flowers produced from early September to December.

Other distinguishing features. Upper stems terete, but warty and pubescent.

Climatic range. A, B, M, P, S, and on sheltered, warm sites on the lower Mts.

Eriostèmon myoporoìdes (Latin 'like a *Myoporum*', another native shrub with glandular leaves): Long-leafed Wax-flower or Native Daphne: southern Qld and NSW, especially between the coast and Blue Mountains, and in north-eastern Vic, mainly along the margins of the east-flowing streams.

Habit. A shrub to 1 m tall, with a rounded bun-shaped outline and many spreading branches radiating from the crowded base.

Leaves. Linear to linear-lanceolate, 6–9 cm long and 7–12 mm wide; apex acute-mucronate; base sessile, tapered; margin entire; thick and slightly fleshy; venation indistinct but midrib raised beneath; surface warty with translucent tuber-

cles, aromatic when crushed; dark green above, sometimes reddish in winter, paler and dull beneath.

Flowers. In an axillary umbellate cluster of mostly 5, borne on a warty peduncle 1 cm long; calyx green with 5 shallow teeth; flower buds clavate, the 5 oblanceolate, spreading petals stellate when open; flowers to 1.8 cm across, pure white with an occasional streak of magenta-rose on the reverse side, flowering from early August to November, stamens 10, the white filaments flattened and ciliate, forming an urceolate cone 3–4 mm deep, the anthers reddish-orange; pistil green, exserted from the 5 supporting carpels.

Other distinguishing features. Upper stems dark green, conspicuously warty, the leaf-scars with 3 clear resin canals.

Several selections of *E. myoporoides* are available, all regarded as improvements on the type usually offered by nurserymen.

'Clearview' series from Mr Bill Cane of Maffra, Victoria are all outstanding in colour, form and abundance of flowers.

'Mountain Giant' is a larger grower than the 'Clearview' Eriostemons, with bigger leaves, and flowers spread thickly along the erect, spreading branchlets.

'Stardust' is an interspecific hybrid between *E. myoporoides* and *E. buxifolius*, raised in Victoria and promoted by the Selection Committee of the Australian Federation of Nurserymen's Associations as the Shrub of the Year for 1975.

Climatic range. A, B, H, M, P, S and on warm sites in Mts.

Eriostèmon verrucòsus (Latin 'covered with warts') (syn. *E. obovalis*) Fairy Wax-flower: sheltered gullies of SE Australia.

Habit. A shrub to about 1 m tall, with slender, arching branchlets forming an open bush, sometimes of sprawling habit, to 1.5 m.

Leaves. Obovate, to 1 cm long and 6–8 mm wide, nearly sessile; apex obtuse or obcordate; margin entire, slightly incurved; glabrous, thick and somewhat succulent; dark green above, coarsely warted beneath.

Flowers. Solitary on 1 cm pedicels in the upper class axils; pedicels verrucose and thickened towards the small-cupped calyx; flower buds imbricate, ovoid, slightly pinkish, but opening to stellate form to 2 cm across, the 5 petals lanceolate, 5 mm wide, glistening waxy white, the reverse shaded pale pink, flowering from late August to early December, stamens 10, forming a broad cone, the flattened white filaments 3–4 mm long, slightly pubescent, the anthers orange-red at first, paling to white; pistil green, slightly shorter than the stamens.

Other distinguishing features. Upper stems roughened by coarse warty tubercles, darkgreen. 'J. Semmens', a double-flowered form, is available with slender pendulous stems, thickly covered with fully-double, white stellate flowers.

Climatic range. A, H, M, Mts, P, S.

ESCALLÒNIA

Commemorating Antonio Escallon, a seventeenth-century botanist and plant explorer in South America, and associate of Mutis, the author of the genus *Escallonia*.

Escallonia.

Escalloniaceae, the Escallonia family.

Generic description. A genus of ornamental, mostly evergreen shrubs and trees from the temperate parts of South America, with alternate, simple leaves, often glandular and aromatic, and flowers in terminal panicles or racemes, in pink, red, or white, some mildly fragrant. The species described here are easy to cultivate, giving a generous return in showy flowers over a long season; with their tough, wind-tolerant foliage, they are well able to thrive in harsh seaside conditions.

Propagation. Soft-tip cuttings taken in spring, or semi-hardwood tips taken in autumn, root readily in a humid, but not necessarily heated environment, the cool side of a glass-house being ideal; a mixture of coarse sand and peat is a suitable rooting medium.

Cultivation. Escallonias are among the most versatile plants, flourishing in a moderately fertile soil with free drainage, but managing quite well on poor soils, provided adequate summer water is available. They are best suited by full exposure to the sun, in a mild climate with temperatures not falling below –5°C. If foliage is damaged by the occasional severe frost, it should be retained until spring to protect the more permanent parts of the plant from further injury.

Pruning. Pruning should be carried out immediately after flowering has finished, or, in cool climates, delayed until early spring; up to half or more of the previous season's growth should be removed and the plant shaped as required.

Regularly pruned and cultivated plants respond with improved flowers and foliage.

Species and cultivars

Escallònia bifida (Latin 'forked or divided into two', probably referring to the notched leaf apices) (syn. *E. montevidensis*) Montevideo region of Uruguay, and in southern Brazil.

Habit. A large evergreen bush to 4–5 m tall, of loose, open habit, sometimes attaining tree-like form.

Leaves. Lanceolate to oblanceolate, 5–8 cm long and 1.5–2.0 cm wide, the flattened petiole to 3 mm; apex variable, acute, obtuse or slightly emarginate; margin serrulate; midrib whitish, prominent beneath; glabrous; slightly shiny and dark green above, pale and glandular beneath.

Flowers. In a broad terminal panicle, 10–15 cm tall, the lower half arising from the upper leaf-axils; flowers clavate in the bud, opening to a 5-petalled, stellate flower to 1.5 cm across, the white petals obovate, with a slender claw at the base; calyx campanulate to 5 mm long, with 5 claw-like sepals; flowers sweetly honey-scented, flowering from late October to mid autumn.

Fruit. A soft-wooded capsule containing numerous blackish seeds.

Other distinguishing features. Upper stems striate, slightly angular, mid brown above, pale green beneath, viscid while young.

Climatic range. A, B, M, P, S, T.

Escallònia x exoniensis (Latin 'from Exeter'): interspecific hybrid between *E. rosea* and *E. rubra*.

Habit. A large, vigorous shrub to 4–5 m tall, with strong erect shoots from the crowded base, the angular young stems pubescent and glandular.

Leaves. Elliptic-ovate, to 4 cm long and 2 cm wide, dark lustrous green above, paler beneath.

Flowers. In glandular, terminal panicles about 9–10 cm tall, pale rosy-carmine in the clavate bud, opening to blush-pink or white, flowering from mid spring to late autumn.

Climatic range. A, B, M, P, S, T.

Escallònia x iveyi (commemorating the raiser, an English horticulturist): interspecific hybrid between *E. bifida* and *E. x exoniensis*.

Habit. An upright shrub, 3.0–3.5 m tall and 2.5 m wide, of dense growth with abundant foliage, the twigs ridged and often pubescent.

PLATE 13

▲ Fuchsia 'Mission Bells'

▲ Euphorbia milii
◄ Fuchsia 'Gartenmeister Bonstedt'
▼ Hovea acutifolia

▼ Hibbertia astrotricha (syn. H. empetrifolia)

▼ Forsythia x intermedia

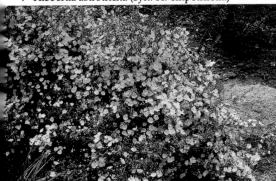

▼ Greyia sutherlandii

▼ Hebe hulkeana

PLATE 14

▲ Isopogon dubius *Photo by Bro. P. Stanley*

▲ Halimium (Cistus) lasianthum ssp. formosum

▲ Hydrangea macrophylla

▲ Indigofera australis
▶ Hebe x franciscana 'Blue Gem'
▼ Iboza riparia

▼ Hypocalymma robustum

Leaves. Elliptic to obovate, to 6 cm long and 2.5–3.0 cm wide, on a flattened 3 mm petiole, the margin finely crenulate-serrulate, glabrous and lustrous dark green above, paler beneath, with shiny veins.
Flowers. Prolific, in a cone-shaped, terminal panicle 12–15 cm tall, the corolla large, spreading to slightly recurved, white with a faint pink flush before opening, flowering from late spring to autumn.
Climatic range. A, B, M, P, S, T.

Escallònia laèvis (Latin 'with smooth stems') (syr. *E. organensis*) Orgaos Mountains of southern Brazil.
Habit. A dense, evergreen shrub to about 2 m, of globose form, with many branches from the base, the outer twigs angular, glabrous, glandular and slightly viscid.
Leaves. Elliptic to obovate, 7–8 cm long and 2–3 cm wide, on a 2–3 mm reddish petiole; apex obtuse; margin serrate-dentate, the lower half less so, or quite entire; dark green and shiny above, paler beneath; glandular and aromatic when crushed.
Flowers. Inflorescence a cone-shaped terminal panicle, 7–10 cm tall, the 5-petalled, funnelform flowers to 1.3 cm across, waxy in texture, rosy-red in the clavate bud, opening to phlox-pink; calyx green, glandular; flowering season from summer to early autumn.
Fruit. A soft-wooded, mid-brown capsule, ripening in autumn.
Climatic range. A, M, P, S, and on warm sites in H and Mts.

Escallònia rùbra **var.** *macrántha* (Latin 'red' and 'large-flowered'): southern Chile, mainly on exposed foreshores and coastal hillsides.
Habit. A large, evergreen bush to 3 m or more, sometimes tree-like when in sheltered places, but mostly seen as a pruned shrub of globular shape, then dense and thickly foliaged.
Leaves. Narrow- to broad-elliptic or obovate, 4–8 cm long and 2.5–4.0 cm wide; petiole 3 mm long, flattened and broad; apex broadly acute or shortly acuminate; margin bluntly crenate-serrate, mostly towards the apex, glandular; glabrous, dark green and lustrous above, paler, glandular and sticky beneath and slightly aromatic.
Flowers. Inflorescence a 2–4 flowered cyme in the upper axils, many together forming a ter-

minal panicle 8–10 cm tall; pedicels 7–8 mm long, reddish, pubescent and glandular; calyx campanulate to 5–6 mm long, spreading to stellate form when mature, pubescent and glandular; corolla blood-red, the petals separated to the base and spreading; stamens to 6–7 mm long, the filaments carmine-red, the anthers yellow; flowering season from October to early autumn.
Fruit. A terminal cluster of soft-wooded capsules.
Other distinguishing features. Upper stems terete, pale green, pubescent, glandular and viscid.
Climatic range. A, M, P, S, and in the milder parts of H and Mts.
Escallonia cultivars derived from various species and hybrids
The 'Donard Escallonias' derive from cross-pollinations between various parent species, made by the Slieve Donard Nursery Company of Newcastle, Northern Ireland. The following cultivars are known to have been imported into Australia and are probably still available in nurseries.
'Apple Blossom' has a dwarf, compact habit to 2 m tall, with flowers of rosy-carmine buds, opening to shell-pink and fading to nearly white.
'Donard Beauty' has large rosy-red flowers in small terminal racemes; of moderate growth to 2 m tall, with somewhat drooping branchlets carrying 3 cm long, broad-elliptic, aromatic leaves of lustrous deep green.
'Donard Brilliance' has large bright rosy-crimson flowers in erect terminal panicles; growth is vigorous, upright but somewhat open, with sharply serrated, medium sized, shining green leaves.
'Donard Gem' is a dwarf grower to about 1 m or so, with an attractive twiggy growth habit, and small, glandular, mid green leaves; flowers are large, shell-pink and fragrant.
'Donard Seedling' is a very early introduction, with strong leafy growth to 2–3 m tall, the outer smaller branches pendulous; leaves are mid green, obovate to 3 cm long; flowers are borne in small racemes, pale pink, fading to blush-pink.
'Slieve Donard' has slender, arching branches forming a globose bush to 2 m or so tall, the leaves obovate to spathulate to about 2.5 cm long, sharply serrate, at least above the middle, glandular, shining dark green; flowers large, in

terminal and axillary racemes of about 7–8 flowers in each, flesh-pink, with rosy-carmine streaks and splashes.

Cultivars from other sources
'**C. F. Ball**' (commemorating the raiser, an Irish horticulturist) has large, rosy-crimson flowers in erect, terminal racemes; of vigorous growth to 2–3 m tall with glossy, bright-green leaves of medium size.
'**Edinénsis**' (Latin 'from Edinburgh', specifically in this case, the Edinburgh Botanic Gardens) has a globose form to about 2.5 m tall, the outer branches drooping, glossy bright green, elliptic-ovate leaves to 2.5 cm long, and large, rosy-carmine flowers opening to clear phlox-pink.
'**Frétheyi**' is a large, erect bush to 3 m or so tall, with ovate, glossy green leaves to 4–6 cm long and 2–3 cm wide, paler and glandular beneath; flowers are borne in a dense, terminal, cone-like panicle to 10–12 cm or more, the large, open flowers pale shell-pink.
'**Gwendolyn Anley**' is deciduous or nearly so, with a broad, spreading habit 1 m or less tall, but usually 2–3 m wide, well suited to ground- or bank-covering roles; leaves are small, obovate, serrulate and dark green; flowers are almost rotate, on short lateral spurs, soft carmine in the bud, opening to blush-pink or nearly white.
'**Ingramii**' (commemorating Collingwood Ingram, English botanical author) is a shrub to 3 m tall and about as wide, with dense, twiggy growth and lustrous, dark-green, elliptic leaves to 4–5 cm long and 2–3 cm wide, glandular and aromatic; flowers are large, deep rosy-carmine in the bud but opening to rose-pink.
'**Róckii**' (commemorating Joseph F. C. Rock, Austrian botanical explorer) is an upright, vigorous shrub to 3 m or more tall and 2–3 m wide, with undulate, elliptic-ovate, glossy green leaves to 4–6 cm long; flowers are in large erect panicles, pale shell-pink.
'**William Watson**' (commemorating a one-time Curator at Kew Gardens, London): is a strong-growing, upright shrub to 2.5 m tall and 1.5 m wide, with elliptic to ovate leaves almost covering the stems, the margins sharply serrate, dark shining green, flowers are in short terminal racemes of 10–12 flowers, deep pink to rosy-red, the petals fully reflexed when mature.
Climatic range. All A, B, M, P, S, and in mild parts of H and Mts.

EUÓNYMUS

The ancient Greek name for one of the local species, probably *E. europaeus.*
Spindle-tree.
Celastraceae, the Staff-tree family.

Generic description. A large genus of evergreen and deciduous shrubs, ground-covering climbers and a few small trees from the temperate parts of Europe, Asia and especially the Orient and North America. Leaves are simple and opposite, some colouring well in autumn; flowers, with parts in fours and fives, are either solitary or in small simple or compound cymes, mostly inconspicuous or hidden by the leaves; and fruit is a somewhat fleshy, 3- to 5-celled capsule, with the seeds enclosed in an orange- or red-coloured aril. The following species are popular in Australian gardens for their attractive foliage, the deciduous kinds especially in autumn, and the often colourful fruit.

Propagation. a) The species may be raised by seeds collected as soon as ripe, cleaned and kept in moist sphagnum moss at $4°–5°C$ until spring, then sown in a friable mixture.
b) Clonal material is grown by firm-tip cuttings, taken between early summer and winter, planted in a sand/peat mixture, preferably in a warm, humid environment.

Cultivation. Euonymus grows satisfactorily in a well-drained, moderately fertile soil, preferably in a cool-temperate, moist climate. All are best placed with full exposure to sun.

Pruning. A moderate shortening of the more vigorous leading shoots in late winter is beneficial, but pruning is otherwise unnecessary, except to confine a plant to a restricted space.

Species and cultivars
Euónymus alàtus (Latin 'winged', referring to the corky, wing-like outgrowths on the branchlets): Winged Spindle-tree: China, Korea, Manchuria and Japan.
Habit. A deciduous shrub to 3 m or so, of somewhat irregular open form, usually founded on a short main trunk, with horizontally inclined branchlets.
Leaves. Rhombic-elliptic, oblanceolate or slightly obovate, 2–6 cm long and 1.5–3.0 cm wide; petiole to 2 mm, flattened and channelled above; apex shortly acuminate, with a short awn-like mucro; margin sharply serrulate;

midrib prominent above; glabrous; bright to dark green above, paler beneath, changing to a brilliant display of coral-red, crimson, orange, and scarlet in autumn.

Flowers. In cymes of 3, the peduncle flattened, 7–15 mm long; calyx a flattened disc 3 mm wide, with 4 or 5 green sepals; petals 4 or 5, broadly ovate to 2 mm, yellowish-green, the flower rotate to 5–6 mm across, flowering in October and early November; stamens 4 or 5, with green filaments and golden-yellow anthers.

Fruit. A 3-celled, purplish capsule, somewhat globose but depressed at the poles, with rounded lobes containing the ellipsoidal, brown-black seeds embedded in a bright-orange to coral-red aril, in autumn.

Other distinguishing features. Young twigs squarish, with rectangular, knife-like, grey wings, 4–6 mm deep, projecting at right angles, especially conspicuous and interesting in winter; autumn foliage colour is outstanding.

'**Compáctus**' has a low, densely leafed habit to 2 m tall but is otherwise similar to the parent.

Climatic range. A, H, M, Mts, and on cool, elevated sites in P and S.

Euónymus europaèus (Latin 'European'): European Common Spindle-tree: British Isles, Europe and Asia.

Habit. A densely branched, erect, deciduous shrub to 3–4 m tall and as wide, but sometimes trained, or occurring naturally in old age, as a small tree to 5–6 m tall founded on a single erect trunk.

Leaves. Elliptic-ovate, 4–8 cm long and 1.5–2.5 cm wide, the petiole 5–10 mm long; apex acute to slightly acuminate; margin finely crenate-serrate; venation reticulate, somewhat translucent; glabrous; dark green and barely shiny above, paler and dull beneath, colouring to orange and scarlet in autumn.

Flowers. Inflorescence a small cyme of mostly 3 or 5 flowers the peduncle to 2.5 cm long; flowers rotate to 8–9 mm across, the parts 4-merous, yellowish-green, flowering in October and November.

Fruit. A cymose cluster of 4-celled capsules to about 1.0–1.5 cm across and 6–7 mm deep, pumpkin-shaped, with 4 conspicuous, rounded lobes, ripening in late autumn and winter to coral-red, the aril bright orange; seeds ovoid, white.

Other distinguishing features. Upper twigs smooth, green, the overwintering buds prominent.

Climatic range. A, H, M, Mts, P, S.

Euónymus japónicus (Latin 'from Japan'): Japanese Spindle-tree: coastal plains and hills of China, Korea and Japan, often on wind-exposed sites.

Habit. An evergreen shrub to 3–4 m tall and often as wide, or more so in old age, with an upright leafy habit well adapted to screening or hedging. Some variations in growth habit occur, from low-growing, globose bushes of 1–2 m, to erect, almost fastigiate forms.

Leaves. Obovate to oval, to about 6 cm long and 3–5 cm wide; apex obtuse or barely acute; base slightly tapered to the 1 cm petiole; margin crenate; glabrous; glossy dark green above, paler and dull beneath, but variously coloured and patterned in the cultivars.

Flowers. In several- to many-flowered, axillary cymes, mostly hidden among the upper leaves; greenish-cream, the floral parts in fours; flowering season from late spring to summer.

Fruit. A slightly pumpkin-shaped, 3–4 celled capsule, about 1 cm across, borne on slender pedicels 5–7 mm long, in a cymose cluster amongst the outer leaves, green at first, but ripening in autumn to pink or coral-red, with orange seeds.

Other distinguishing features. Stems slightly 4-angled.

Euonymus japonicus is an extremely variable species, especially in the colour patterns of the leaves. Mainly through bud-mutations or perhaps as seedlings, scores of variegated-leafed forms have developed, the best given valid, mostly descriptive names, and distributed widely through normal nursery channels. The cultivars listed below, some seen only rarely in Australian gardens or even in botanical collections, appear to be correctly named and described, and to have maintained in cultivation the character of the originally imported stock.

'**Albo-marginàtus**': leaves green, with a narrow 1–4 mm wide creamy-white margin.

'**Macrophýllus Albus**': leaves large, pale green, with a broad, irregular whitish margin; syn. 'Latifolius Albus', 'Latifolius Variegatus', 'Latifolius Albo-marginatus'.

'**Aùreo-marginàtus**': leaves green and grey-green in the irregular central patch, with a bright-yellow margin.

'Aùreo-pictus': leaves dark green, with an irregular patch of creamy-yellow in the middle, the petioles and twigs also coloured, often streaked or suffused with green; syn. 'Medio-pictus'.

'Aùreo-variegàtus': leaves bright green with a bright-yellow central blotch.

'Aùreus': leaves predominantly yellow, especially on the upper young shoots, with a bright-green margin; habit narrow and erect, to 2 m or so tall.

'Ovàtus-aùreus': leaves margined with a broad irregular edge of bright golden-yellow, suffused throughout into the central green blotch; sometimes wholly yellow on the upper young twigs; of low, globose form, to 1.5–2.0 m tall.

'Viridi-variegàtus': leaves bright green, streaked and marked with pale green and yellow in the middle; syn. 'Duc d'Anjou'.

Climatic range. All A, B, H, M, Mts, P, S.

EUPATÒRIUM

Commemorating King Eupator of the ancient kingdom of Pontus (now part of northern Turkey, bordering the Black Sea), reported on by Pliny in his *Natural History*, for his contribution to primitive medicine.

Shrub Ageratum; Mist-flower; Thoroughwort.

Asteraceae, the Aster family (formerly Compositae, the Composite family)

Generic description. A large and varied genus, with many annuals and herbs, and some useful but tender shrubs. The species described below are soft-wooded, with very large, opposite leaves, and handsome flowers borne in terminal panicles, the prominent styles giving the flowers their characteristic fluffy appearance. They are particularly useful in mild climates for providing a foil in form and colour to other spring-flowering plants.

Propagation. Thin, twiggy, semi-hardwood cuttings with short internodes, taken in autumn and winter, strike readily in a warm environment; larger stems, cut when pruning in late spring, are also used, mostly struck in individual containers of a sand/peat mixture.

Cultivation. A friable, fertile soil with free drainage is best, with adequate water in dry times. Sensitive to even light frosts, they should be grown in a warm situation, not necessarily in full sun, but ideally, with some dappled overhead shade and protection from strong winds.

Pruning. The flowered branches are shortened to several nodes from the older wood, immediately after the flowering period, to preclude the development and dispersal of the nearly buoyant pappuses. New shoots arising from the pruning should be tip-pruned once in summer, when about 20–30 cm long, to increase branching and the number of flower-heads.

Species and cultivars

Eupatòrium megalophýllum (from the Greek, describing the large leaves): southern Mexico and neighbouring tropical countries.

Habit. An evergreen shrub to about 2 m tall and as wide, with many strong shoots radiating from the centre to form a leafy, globose bush.

Leaves. Simple, opposite, broad-ovate, 15–25 cm long, 15–20 cm wide, the petiole 8–10 cm long; margin serrate-dentate; venation prominent beneath, with a thick, purple tomentum when young; upper surface pubescent and rugose, dark green and dull, paler and pubescent below.

Flowers. Inflorescence a terminal corymbose panicle, 20–30 cm across, the involucre urceolate to 8 mm long, with numerous purple scales, the styles 5 mm long and thread-like, issuing from the outer flowers, each head 1.5 cm across, flowers mildly perfumed; violet-blue, flowering from late September to November.

Eupatòrium sòrdidum (syn. *E. ianthinum*) southern Mexico: is somewhat similar, but smaller in all parts; young stems are covered with a dense, beetroot-purple tomentum; flowers are fragrant, violet-blue in spring.

Climatic range. Both species B, S, T, and in warm, sheltered microclimates in A and M.

EUPHÒRBIA

The origin of the name is uncertain but is thought by some authorities to have derived from Euphorbus, a Greek physician attending the court of King Juba of Mauritania, West Africa.

Poinsettia; Scarlet Plume; Crown of Thorns; Venetian Spurge; etc.

Euphorbiaceae, the Spurge family.

Generic description. A large, variable genus of over 1000 species from tropical or subtropical climates, mostly shrubby and with a milky-white sap, often toxic or at least irritating to sensitive skins. Leaves are simple, alternate, but the inflorescence leaves may show some variation in arrangement and often constitute the main decorative feature, as in *E. pulcherrima*. The true flowers are unisexual, several together in a cyathium, to the wall of which is adjoined a labiate nectar gland, often colourful. Both evergreen and deciduous species are present. *E. pulcherrima*, especially, is grown in almost every country for its brilliant display of floral bracts, a popular glass-house plant in climates too cold for its outdoor use.

Propagation. *E. pulcherrima* is grown from soft-tip cuttings taken during summer and early autumn from mature stock plants brought into the glass-house for the purpose, and forced with very rich soil, adequate water, high temperatures (25°–30°C) and bright light. The cuttings are individually potted in small pots or tubes in a sand/peat mixture and subjected to bottom heat and high atmospheric humidity until well rooted. Alternatively, hardwood cuttings may be taken in late winter-early spring from the pruned stems, and struck as above in individual containers. Other species may be treated in much the same manner but usually with lower levels of atmospheric humidity. Rooted cuttings of *E. fulgens* and *E. pulcherrima* should be tip-pruned as soon as new shoot growth commences, to encourage the development of laterals, and be continued until a dense, rounded bush is formed.

Cultivation. *E. pulcherrima* as an outdoor plant must not be exposed to cold or windy conditions and is better when grown in the warmest part of the garden, preferably in full sun, with a rich, well-drained soil, It is also light-sensitive, growing vigorously but not forming flower buds or floral bracts when exposed to daylight of more than 12 hours per day; in the shorter days of autumn and winter, flower and bract development is initiated and proceeds while day-length is 10 hours or less. Commercial growers regulate the production of plants for the floral trade by controlling day-length with light-proof shade cloth, and the thermal range by various heating devices to maintain a proportionate temperature.

Pruning. After the stems of *E. pulcherrima* have flowered, they should be reduced by most of their length into the general shape of plant required. New shoots will appear in spring and these should be tip-pruned at least once before February to induce a dense, leafy habit with more numerous flowering stems. *E. fulgens* is treated similarly but the other species listed are best not pruned unless to control their size.

Species and cultivars

Euphòrbia fúlgens (Latin 'shining' or 'glittering') (syn. *E. jacquiniaeflora*) Scarlet Plume: tropical Mexico.

Habit. A tender, evergreen shrub to 1.0–1.5 m tall, with a short trunk soon dividing into many slender branches, forming a loose, open bush.

Leaves. Lanceolate, 4–8 cm long and 2–3 cm wide; petiole 2–3 cm; apex acuminate; base slenderly cuneate; margin entire; venation penninerved, the midrib prominent and reddish; bright green and glabrous above, paler beneath.

Flowers. Inflorescence a number of few-flowered cymes in the upper axils, spreading over 25–30 cm or more of the drooping shoots; cyathium glands orange, the 5 floral bracts spreading widely, broadly obovate or orbicular, bright scarlet, the flower on a pedicel of 1–2 cm, flowering from May to late September, or later in warm climates.

Other distinguishing features. Upper stems smooth, glabrous, bright green, with white sap exuding when the bark is broken.

Climatic range. B, S, and T, in sheltered, frost-free microclimates only.

Euphòrbia mīlii (syn. *E. splendens*) Crown of Thorns; Madagascar.

Habit. A low, sprawling shrub of usually less than 1 m tall, but often 2 m broad, the soft, succulent stems armed with sharp, but flexible spines.

Leaves. Randomly scattered, mostly towards the end of the shoots, singly or in whorls of up to 4, oval to obovate, 3–4 cm long and 1.5 cm wide; apex acute-mucronate; margin entire; midrib tomentose beneath, prominent and translucent; mid to pale green on both surfaces, sometimes with a fine crimson margin.

Flowers. Inflorescence a dichotomous cyme, the reddish peduncle 3–7 cm long, coated with an adhesive exudation and normally carrying 8 or 16 flowers (cyathia); involucre short and green, expanded laterally into a pair of petal-like, broad-ovate, scarlet bracts, each about 1 cm across, the apex finely mucronate; calyx with 5 scarlet sepals; flowers borne abundantly from September to February but intermittently throughout the year, especially in warm places.

Other distinguishing features. Stems armed with black-tipped, greyish spines to 2 cm long, widely angled on the grey-brown stems, sharp and tapering from the expanded base but relatively soft and easily bent sideways; bark leathery and tough-skinned, but exuding a milky-white sap when broken.

Climatic range. A, B, I, M, P, S, T.

Euphòrbia pulchérrima (Latin 'most beautiful') (syn. *Poinsettia pulcherrima*) Poinsettia: native to the warm, humid, lower slopes of the mountains of southern Mexico within 100 km of Mexico City.

Habit. A large, rounded shrub to 4 m tall and as wide, based on a short trunk and many erect, succulent branches, variable in foliar persistence, being evergreen on the warm Queensland coastal strip but more or less deciduous in higher latitudes; young stems are hollow and somewhat fragile, easily damaged by strong winds.

Leaves. Broadly lanceolate to broadly ovate-elliptic, 10–25 cm long and 5–15 cm wide, the petiole 5–12 cm long, terete but grooved above, usually reddish; apex acute to acuminate; base broadly cuneate; margin entire or dentately lobed, the lobes broadly triangular, with wide, shallow sinuses between; glabrous above but finely pubescent beneath; midrib prominent and whitish-green; leaves bright to dark green above, paler beneath; often glandular at the junction of petiole and blade.

Flowers. Inflorescence a broad, flattish cyme at the terminals of the current year's shoots, subtended at the base by floral bracts, usually lanceolate to oblanceolate, arranged in flat, radiate form 25–35 cm across, glowing scarlet-crimson, lasting from May to October; true flowers in a green, fleshy, glabrous cyathium of campanulate-urceolate form, to 8 mm long and 6–7 mm broad, the anthers of the several stamens reddish, with bifid stigmas; an orange-yellow, mouth-like nectar gland about 5 mm across adjoins one side of the cyathium.

Other distinguishing features. The thin bark exudes a milky-white sap when broken; the sap is toxic, and contact with the eyes or with sensitive skins should be avoided.

Several cultivars are presently in Australia, some probably developed as sports from the parent species, with white, cream, or pink floral bracts. Some cultivars have been introduced from California and may well be followed by many others.

'Henriette Ecke' is a fine double, with about twice the normal number of bracts, of intense red, on a somewhat more open-growing plant to 2–3 m tall, with relatively fewer flowering stems than the parent, but probably more floriferous if pruned appropriately.

'Annette Hegg' is the multi-headed, dwarf clone growing to about 2.5 m tall, featured locally as a potted plant. It originated in the indoor plant nursery of Thormod Hegg and Son of Lierbyen, Norway, in 1964 and has since been distributed throughout the world to accredited growers. It has produced a number of sports, identified by cultivarietal names, many featuring the name 'Hegg'.

Both of these cultivars have come from the specialist Poinsettia nursery founded by Albert Ecke, who migrated from Germany to California in 1902. Many new forms have been isolated in commercial cultivation, named commemoratively for various members of the Ecke family.

Climatic range. All B, S, T, and in warm microclimates in A, M, and P.

Euphòrbia venèta (Latin 'Venetian', referring to its southern European habitat, especially around the Adriatic Sea) (syn. *E. wulfenii*) Venetian Spurge.

Habit. A small evergreen shrub to 1 m tall, usually with a short central trunk and many nearly equal stems, forming a broad, rounded crown to 1.5 m across, the terminal of each stem dividing into 4 or 5 shorter, subordinate growths resembling an umbel.

Leaves. Crowded spirally, drooping downwards to cover the upper stems; linear to 3–4 cm long, 5 mm wide, but becoming shorter and broader, and yellowish just beneath the inflorescence; petiole 1 mm, flattened; apex acute; base tapered slightly; margin entire; glabrous; glaucous-green and dull above, paler beneath.

Flowers. Inflorescence a terminal umbel of 6–10 or more flowers on slender, yellow-green pedicels about 3 cm long, issuing from a rosette of yellow-green floral leaves; flowers subtended by 2 or 3 broad-ovate bracts about 1 cm long and 1.5 cm broad, bright yellow-green, spreading widely and concave above; cyathium urceolate to 5 mm deep, 2- or 3-glandular at the base, the involucre with 4 yellowish sepals and stamens at the apex, and a bulbous green pistil with bifurcate stigmas; flowering from early August to November.

Other distinguishing features. Lower stems

terete, coppery-brown, glabrous, roughened by the many small, crescent shaped leaf-scars; upper twigs pale green, red on the sunny side; all stems exude a milky-white sap when the bark is broken.

Climatic range. A, B, I, M, P, S, T.

EURÝOPS

Derived from the Greek words meaning 'having broad eyes', alluding to the large round flowers. Euryops.

Asteraceae, the Aster family (formerly Compositae, the Composite family).

Generic description. A genus of evergreen shrubs from South and Central Africa, with simple, alternate leaves, some deeply pinnatisect, the inflorescence a solitary capitulum, the flowers with yellow ray- and disc-florets, the fruit a bristly pappus.

Propagation. Short, leafy, semi-hardwood cuttings taken in autumn or winter are best, preferably struck in a sand/peat mixture in a warm atmosphere.

Cultivation. The species treated here is hardy to at least −2°C, but thrives in the warmer climates. The best soil is freely drained, sandy or gravelly, not neglected for water in dry times.

Pruning. A light annual pruning over the crown of the plant is beneficial, immediately after the main flowering season in late spring.

Species and cultivars

Euryops pectinàtus (Latin 'comb-like', referring to the leaf-margin): South Africa.

Habit. An evergreen shrub to 1 m or so tall, with many spreading branches from the short-stemmed base, forming a rounded, bun-shaped crown.

Leaves. Pinnatisect, 6–9 cm long and 2.0–2.5 cm wide, with about 10 opposite pairs of deep lobes 5–15 mm long and 2–3 mm wide, linear; apices acute; bases blunt, sessile; margins entire; deep green but densely white-woolly tomentose throughout.

Flowers. Inflorescence a single capitulum to 4–5 cm across on a slender 15–18 cm, tomentose peduncle, several to about 5 together from near the terminals; involucre urn-shaped, 1 cm across, 7–8 mm deep, the base flattened, the rim divided into about 14 acute, linear lobes, divided

to half the depth of the receptacle, reflexing when the flower opens; ray-florets, usually 13 or 14, oblanceolate, with an emarginate apex, 2 cm long, 6–7 mm wide, bright yellow; disc-florets numerous, in a mounded mass 1.3 cm across, orange-yellow; flowering season from mid August to late spring.

Fruit. A slender achene with a whitish, bristly pappus attached.

Other distinguishing features. Upper stems densely white woolly-tomentose.

Climatic range. A, B, I, M, P, S, T, and on warm sites in lower parts of Mts.

EXOCHÒRDA

Derived from the Greek words describing the fibrous placenta.

Pearl Bush.

Rosaceae, the Rose family.

Generic description. A small genus of deciduous shrubs from the Orient with simple, alternate leaves, white flowers in axillary or terminal racemes, and woody capsular fruits, the species described below grown for its showy flowers.

Propagation. a) Seeds, sown in spring in a warm, humid atmosphere germinate readily.
b) Soft-tip or semi-hardwood leafy cuttings taken in summer or autumn root satisfactorily in a misted glass-house; hardwood cuttings taken from the prunings in late winter are also used.

Cultivation. The plant is easy to cultivate and responds well to the better class soils, preferably in a tablelands climate, with a moist summer and where minimum temperatures do not exceed −8°C.

Pruning. The complete removal of about one-third of the basal shoots each year in late winter to make way for new water-shoot growth is beneficial; spent inflorescences should be shortened back immediately after flowering.

Species and cultivars

Exochòrda racemòsa (Latin 'with flowers in a raceme') (syn. *E. grandiflora*) Pearl Bush: eastern China.

Habit. A deciduous shrub to 3 m tall, developing a spherical form when mature, with many erect shoots arising from the base.

Leaves. Elliptic to obovate, 6–8 cm long and 3–4 cm broad; petiole 1.0–1.5 cm long, channelled above; apex rounded-mucronate; base cuneate; margin entire, but irregularly serrate near the apex on strong shoots; the whitish-green midrib and main laterals prominent beneath; texture thin; glabrous; dark to bright green above, glaucous beneath, changing to yellow in autumn but not usually spectacular.

Flowers. Inflorescence a short terminal raceme, 6–7 cm long, of about 8 shallow, crateriform flowers each 3.5–4.0 cm across; calyx short, green, with 5 broad fringed sepals; petals 5, pure waxy-white, broad-obovate, with a narrow base, attached to the rim of the receptacle with clear spaces between; lightly fragrant; stamens 15 to about 25 spread around the rim; filaments white, anthers cream, flowers borne abundantly from early September to late October.

Fruit. A woody capsule to 1 cm long, with 5 semicircular, wing-like valves held at the inner edge by the central septum, but separating when ripe to release the 2 winged, disc-like, brown seeds 8 mm long, the fruits maturing in late summer.

Other distinguishing features. Young shoots green, smooth at first but becoming furrowed and mid-brown, with small circular lenticels.

Climatic range. A, H, M, Mts, P, S.

FÁTSIA

The latinised form of the aboriginal Japanese name for the plant.
Fatsia.
Araliaceae, the Ginseng family.

Generic description. A small genus of several species from the Orient, grown for their bold foliage, the white flowers in large, terminal panicles, and the small, black fruits. The species treated here is a popular display plant, especially impressive when used in contrast with fine-textured foliage.

Propagation. a) Seeds are sown as soon as ripe in autumn-winter, in a light fibrous material, preferably in the warmth of a glass-house or heated frame.
b) Short, stocky lateral shoots taken when 8–10 cm long root easily as leafy cuttings.

Cultivation. Any light, fibrous, well-drained soil suits the plant, the better the soil and general treatment, the larger and better the foliage. Plants grown in part shade with protection from strong wind give the best results. Often grown as a tubbed plant for well-lit interiors, or for outdoor use, preferably not in full sun, but ideal on shady terraces or porches or under the filtered shade of taller plants. Safe to −2°C.

Pruning. The plant is better if old, lanky shoots are removed to provide space for the new leafy growths from the base.

Species and cultivars
Fatsia japónica (Latin 'from Japan'): once combined with but now separated from *Aralia*, which has pinnately compound leaves: native to the coastal forests of Japan and the islands to the south, and to South Korea.

Habit. An evergreen shrub to about 3 m tall, with a few thick branches from the base carrying the large, showy foliage.

Leaves. Simple, alternate, palmately-lobed, the blade 15–30 cm long, the petiole 15–50 cm long; lobes 7 or 9, the sinuses about half the depth of the blade; apices acute to acuminate; base subcordate; lobes serrately margined; main veins prominent beneath; coriaceous and glabrous except for the woolly tomentum in the lower axils; dark green and lustrous above, paler beneath.

Flowers. Inflorescence a large terminal panicle with thick, fleshy stems; flowers in umbels of 20–35, on pedicels to 1.5 cm; calyx a green cup 2–3 mm across; petals 5, triangular, reflexed, greenish-white; stamens 5, to 5 mm long, standing clear of the cream disc; flowers to 5 mm across, flowering from April to June.

Fruit. A small, fleshy drupe to 7 mm, globular, green at first, with 5 persistent sepals, ripening to black in May to July, in large terminal umbels of up to 35 fruits.

Climatic range. A, B, H, M, P, S, and T.

FEIJÒA

Commemorating the Brazilian botanist, de Silva Feijo.
Fruit Salad Plant.
Myrtaceae, the Myrtle family.

Generic description. A South American genus of evergreen, edible-fruited plants of two species, the one described below popular in Australia as a flowering/fruiting shrub; as yet not important commercially, although in other parts of the world, notably in southern Europe, New Zealand and California, it is grown extensively for its fruit.

Propagation. a) Seeds germinate readily when sown in a friable mixture in autumn or winter, preferably in the controlled environment of a glass-house; many seedlings appear to be self-sterile and do not pollinate their flowers effectively. This problem is not apparent under orchard conditions, especially where there are bees and other pollen-carrying insects. In isolated specimens, the problem may be overcome by grafting in a few scions from other plants to the upper branches.

b) Cultivars, selected for improved quality of fruit or other desirable features, may be struck as semi-hardwood, leafy tip cuttings in autumn in a heated and misted glass-house, or are apical-grafted by whip-and-tongue or top-cleft methods in late winter on seedling understocks brought into active growth for several weeks before grafting.

Cultivation. A friable soil with free drainage is ideal, preferably enriched with organic matter and not neglected for water in dry times, especially in summer. The plant is tolerant of low temperatures to −2°C but should be allowed to acclimatise to cold conditions gradually and not be unduly forced into young soft growth.

Pruning. The plant is self-shaping but may be made to grow more densely if pruned lightly every few years in late winter.

Species and cultivars

Feijòa sellowiàna (commemorating the German botanical explorer and collector, Friedrich Sellow, who discovered the species in southern Brazil): Fruit Salad Plant: South America, around the latitude of the Tropic of Capricorn, chiefly in the valleys of the Parana and Paraguay rivers.

Habit. An evergreen shrub to about 4 m tall, mostly of globose form of the same width, but occasionally seen as a small tree as the result of early pruning and training.

Leaves. Simple, opposite or 3-whorled, elliptical to oblong to 5–8 cm long and 2.5–4.0 cm wide; petiole terete to 1 cm long; apex variable, from obtuse to emarginate; base acute, margin entire but slightly recurved; midrib and main laterals prominent beneath; coriaceous; dark green, glabrous and lustrous above, silvery-white and tomentose beneath.

Flowers. Solitary or in opposite pairs in the leaf-axils of the new season's growth, all major parts covered with a fine brown or whitish tomentum; calyx tubulate to 6–7 mm long and 4 mm wide, expanding into a broad globose head 8 mm across, the 4 cup-shaped sepals greenish-tomentose outside, crimson within; petals 4, to 1.5 cm long, orbicular or reniform, drooping between the sepals and folded inwards somewhat like a cowrie shell, fleshy and waxy, white outside, lilac-purple inside; stamens about 60, in an erect cluster, filaments currant-red, anthers pale yellow; pistil 1, currant-red; flowering freely mainly during November but occasionally extending into summer.

Fruit. An edible berry to 8 cm long and 4 cm broad, but larger in the cultivars, with a leathery, dull-green skin and a whitish-green, pulpy interior with the many small, dark-brown seeds embedded, ripening in autumn and early winter. The flavour is peculiarly its own, but suggestive of various other tropical fruit flavours, hence the common name.

Other distinguishing features. Youngest twigs grey-green, whitish tomentose, somewhat angular, but maturing to brown with a scaly peeling bark.

'**Choiceàna**','**Gigántea**' and '**Supèrba**' are improved cultivars with larger fruits and, reputedly, superior flavour.

'**Variegàta**' has dark-green leaves, heavily margined with cream.

Climatic range. A, B, M, P, S, T.

FELÍCIA

Commemorating George Felix 1773–1846, of Regensburg, Bavaria.
Felicia; Blue Daisy.
Asteraceae, the Aster family (formerly Compositae, the Composite family).

Generic description. African evergreen shrubs with simple leaves, arranged alternately or rarely oppositely, showy, daisy-like flowers with mostly mauve to lilac-blue colours with a yellow central disc, and fruit an achene with a whitish, bristly pappus. They are grown for their prolific spring flowers and tidy low habit, making them useful as front-row material in the shrub border.

Propagation. a) Seeds, of *F. amelloides* especially, germinate easily at any time of the year in a friable mixture, and frequently naturalise in a garden.

b) Soft-tip cuttings, taken from younger succulent shoots during the growth season, strike satisfactorily in a well-aerated medium, with mist and humidity control beneficial.

Cultivation. Both species enjoy a sun-exposed position in a warm climate but will tolerate cold to at least −3°C. The soil need not be over-rich but must be well drained; the plants respond to additional water in prolonged dry times.

Pruning. Removal of the spent inflorescences after flowering is desirable. The long trailing shoots of *F. fruticosa* should then be shortened to encourage the development of heavy-flowering laterals.

Species and cultivars

Felícia amelloides (Latin 'like *Amellus*', another genus of the same family) (syn. *Agathaea coelestis*) Blue Daisy: native to wind-exposed, sandy sites along the Eastern Cape coast of South Africa.

Habit. An evergreen subshrub to 0.5 m tall, spreading to 0.75 m wide, bushy, but seldom woody at the base.

Leaves. Simple, opposite, slenderly oval to obovate, 2–6 cm long and 1.5–2.5 cm wide; petiole to 1 cm, grooved above, apex obtuse-mucronate; margin ciliate; venation indistinct apart from the translucent midrib, prominent beneath; bright green on both surfaces, but more shiny above.

Flowers. Flower-heads solitary, on 12–18 cm long, hispid terminal peduncles issuing from the ends of the leafy new shoots; inflorescence a capitulum; ray florets 12 or 13, forming a rotate flower about 3 cm across, of various colours in the violet-blue range, disc 8–10 mm across with numerous, buttercup yellow, tubulate flowers; the plant flowers abundantly over the crown from early September to late November, then more sparsely throughout summer and autumn.

Fruit. An ovoid achene of 3 mm, dark brown, with a 5 mm, white, bristly pappus at the apex, ripening 1 to 2 months after the flowers fade.

Other distinguishing features. Young stems cylindrical, pale green, sparsely hispid.

Climatic range. A, B, H, M, P, S, and in warm, sheltered microclimates in Mts.

Felícia fruticòsa (Latin 'of shrubby habit') (syn. *F. angustifolia*) Trailing Felicia: widespread in coastal and inland parts of South Africa.

Habit. An evergreen shrub to 0.5 m tall, but spreading in a broad bun-shape, the main branches horizontally inclined.

Leaves. Simple, alternate, linear to oblanceolate, 1.5 cm long and 2 mm wide; petiole 1 mm,

broadly triangular; apex acute, base long cuneate; margin entire; venation inconspicuous apart from the translucent midrib; surface granulose-glandular, aromatic when bruised; glabrous; bright green on both surfaces.

Flowers. Flower-heads solitary at the terminals of short leafy shoots; pedicels slender, 2.5 cm long, green but often stained with purple, inflorescence a capitulum; ray florets 16 to 20, forming a flat, rotate flower, 2.5–3.0 cm across, violet-blue, with a paler reverse; disc florets yellow, numerous, forming a 5 mm mound in the centre; flowers abundant from mid September to late November.

Fruit. An achene with a bristly pappus attached, ripening in summer.

Other distinguishing features. Upper twigs with pale-brown bark.

Climatic range. A, B, H, M, P, S, T, and in the warm parts of Mts.

FORSÝTHIA

Commemorating William Forsyth, Scottish horticulturist.

Golden Bells.

Oleaceae, the Olive family.

Generic description. A small genus of showy deciduous shrubs with simple, opposite leaves which often colour in autumn, yellow flowers appearing before the leaves in early spring, and capsular fruits. Some are of semi-pendulous habit, responding well to training over lattice or other support as walling plants. All are prized in the spring landscape for their bright colour.

Propagation. a) Soft-tip cuttings in spring, or semi-hardwood tip cuttings in summer, root satisfactorily in a sand/peat mixture in a cool but humid place.

b) Hardwood cuttings in June or July are also used.

c) Self-layering species like *F. suspensa* may be increased in late winter by severing and lifting the trailing shoots that have rooted at the nodes.

Cultivation. The Forsythias are easy to cultivate and deserve a well-drained, fertile soil and an assured summer water supply. They are at their best in a sun-exposed position and especially spectacular in spring if grown against a dark-green background. All are safe in low temperatures to at least −8°C.

Pruning. Flowers are borne on the overwintered, 1-year-old shoots which must *not* be pruned in winter, but may be cut when in flower for indoor decoration without harming the plant. When flowering has finished, several of the oldest shoots should be removed entirely at the base to make space for new vigorous shoots which will flower abundantly the following spring.

Species and cultivars

Forsýthia x *intermèdia:* an interspecific hybrid between *F. suspensa* 'Sieboldii' and *F. viridíssima.*
Habit. A deciduous shrub to 3–4 m tall, with upright growth based on a single basal trunk, and many ascending, arching branches of about equal size.
Leaves. Ovate or broadly elliptical to 6–9 cm long and 3.5–4.0 cm wide, the petiole reddish; sharply serrate on the upper half of the leaf; venation reticulate, translucent; bright green but not shiny above, paler and dull beneath; glabrous.
Flowers. Solitary, or in 2- to 6-flowered racemes, on short peduncles arising from the 1- and 2-year-old branches; calyx green, with 4 obovate sepals; corolla to about 2 cm long, the lobes lanceolate-oblong, pale lemon-yellow, with a few streaks of orange in the throat, flowering from early September to mid October; stamens 2, anthers arrow-shaped, deep orange; style exserted beyond the tube, the stigma bifurcate.
Other distinguishing features. Branchlets with imperfectly lamellate pith, more or less solid at the nodes.
One of the most handsome early-flowering shrubs; several outstanding cultivars are available:
'Spectábilis', perhaps the best-known clone of the group, is fully deciduous on the tablelands, forming an upright but outward-arching bush to 2.5 m or so tall, the stems clustered with small bunches of larger-than-usual flowers of clear bright yellow.
'Lynwood' is a more recent introduction, resembling 'Spectabilis' in the main features, but the flowers are larger with broader petals, and even more prolific in flower.
'Karl Sax' is newer still, as an introduction by the Arnold Arboretum in Massachusetts. It has large flowers, freely produced on upright, spreading branches, the flowers deep rich yellow, with the characteristic orange lines in the throat.

Climatic range. All A, H, M, Mts, P, S.

Forsýthia suspénsa (Latin 'hanging down', referring to the drooping branches): Golden Bells: China.
Habit. A deciduous shrub to 2.5–3.5 m tall, with slender, flexible branches, ascending at first, but then arching outwards and drooping to form a broadly hemispherical mound, but well adapted to wall culture.
Leaves. Simple or rarely trifoliolate, opposite, broadly ovate, 3–8 cm long and 2.5–4.5 cm wide; petiole to 1.8 cm long, slenderly channelled above; apex mostly acute, occasionally obtuse; base obtuse; margin sharply serrate, but entire near the base; venation finely reticulate; glabrous; bright green above, paler beneath, changing to dull yellow in autumn.
Flowers. Solitary, or in few-flowered clusters in the axils along the drooping branches; pedicels about 1.5 cm long; calyx lobes 4, linear, 5–7 mm long; corolla 2.5 cm across, of 4 oblong-obovate lobes, deep golden-yellow, flowering abundantly from early September to November.
Other distinguishing features. Stems slender, with 4 shallow, surface ridges and a hollow centre.
var. *fòrtunei* (commemorating Robert Fortune, botanical explorer) is more vigorous, with a somewhat stiffer habit, but otherwise similar.
var. *sièboldii* (commemorating Dr Philipp F. von Siebold, German botanist) has an almost prostrate habit, rarely taller than 1 m, but usually spreading by self-layering to 3 m or more wide, well suited to large-scale ground-covering; flowers and foliage are similar to those of the parent.
Climatic range. A, H, M, Mts, P, S.

Forsýthia viridíssima (Latin *viridus*, 'green', referring to the bright-green leaves): China.
Habit. A deciduous shrub to 2–3 m tall, with many cane-like branches arising from the crowded base and arching outwards to form a hemispherical bush about 2–3 m wide.
Leaves. Lanceolate to narrow-elliptic to about 8 cm long and 1.5–3.0 cm wide; petiole to 1.5 cm, channelled above; apex finely acute; base cuneate; margin mostly entire near the base, but sharply serrate towards the apex; midrib and main lateral veins prominent beneath; glabrous; dark green and slightly shiny above, becoming rich claret-red in autumn.

Flowers. In axillary clusters of one to about four, appearing before the leaves; pedicels 5 mm long, scaly; calyx lobes 5, elliptic-ovate to 5 mm long, green, shaded purple; corolla stellate, the 4 lobes 7–8 mm wide and slightly reflexed at the edges, but sometimes 5- or rarely 6-lobed, butter-yellow, in advance of the leaves in late September to mid October; stamens 2, the yellow anthers barely clear of the corolla tube; faintly perfumed.

Other distinguishing features. Upper branches squarish, yellowish-green, with a silvery cuticle and sparse brown lenticels, the core lamellate.

Climatic range. A, H, M, Mts, P, S.

FREMONTODÉNDRON (syn. *Fremontia*)

Commemorating its discoverer, John C. Fremont of the US Army.
Flannel-bush.
Bombacaceae, the Bombax family (formerly included in Sterculiaceae, the Sterculia family).

Generic description. A small genus of tender, evergreen shrubs from SW USA and Mexico, with alternate, palmately-lobed, partly deciduous leaves, and flowers lacking in petals, but with a large, yellow-orange, 5-cleft calyx. An attractive group of plants for warm, preferably rather dry, climates.

Propagation. a) Seeds sown as soon as ripe germinate readily in a warm environment.
b) Firm-tip cuttings are sometimes used, taken in late summer and struck in coarse sand in a warm glass-house.

Cultivation. The species described below is tender and young plants are best planted out in late spring in a loose, friable soil with free drainage, in a warm, sunny locality. It is safe to about –3°C but is likely to defoliate when exposed to more severe conditions.

Pruning. Mature plants should have their long, erect branches shortened in late winter, and the plants fed liberally to increase the number and quality of flowers.

Species and cultivars

Fremontodéndron califòrnicum (Latin 'from California'): Flannel-bush: California.
Habit. A mainly evergreen shrub to 3–4 m tall, of globose form, about as wide as its height.

Leaves. Simple, broadly ovate and mostly palmately-lobed, but sometimes nearly entire, about 4–8 cm long and as broad, the middle lobe the largest, the 2 lateral lobes often with smaller lobes near the base; petiole about 1.5–2.0 cm long, densely rufous-pubescent; apex obtuse, sometimes mucronate; base cordate; margin mostly lobed, the sinuses about 5 mm deep, the margin otherwise irregular; venation palmate, the 3–5 main veins prominent beneath; upper surface sparsely stellate-pubescent, the lower surface densely so, especially on the main veins; blade brownish-green above, grey-brown beneath.

Flowers. Apetalous, solitary, on short shoots from the upper axils; flower buds ovoid, rufous-pubescent, opening to a cyathiform flower 6–8 cm across, with 5 broadly ovate to orbicular sepals, each with a short mucronate apex and a hirsute nectar gland at the base, stellate-pubescent on the outside, glabrous on the inner surface; canary-yellow, deepening to saffron-yellow, with reddish shadings in the centre and outer edges; flowers from early October to late summer.

Fruit. An ovoid hairy capsule, with ellipsoidal, blackish seeds.

Climatic range. A, B, M, P, S, T.

Other distinguishing features. Upper twigs heavily pubescent.

FÙCHSIA

Commemorating Prof. Leonard Fuchs, sixteenth-century German physician and botanical author.
Fuchsia.
Onagraceae, the Evening-primrose family.

Generic description. A large genus of over 100 species of mostly tender shrubs and trailing plants, the majority from South and Central America. The genus is distinguished by its simple, evergreen, opposite or 3-whorled leaves; showy, solitary, pendulous flowers on long, slender pedicels, in a wide colour range covering white, pink, red, mauve, and violet, the sepals and corolla usually of contrasting colours, the stamens and pistil exserted; and fruit a fleshy, ellipsoidal, plum-coloured berry. Adaptable to a wide range of uses and planting situations, fuchsias are considered among the finest of spring- and summer-flowering shrubs for warm climate gardens.

Propagation. Soft-tip cuttings of 2 to 4 nodes strike readily in a sand/peat mixture, if taken between late spring and autumn, and placed in a warm humid atmosphere; firmer material may also be used during autumn and winter. Hormone dusting powders and humidity control are beneficial.

Cultivation. Fuchsias are at their best in a mild climate with little or no frost, and with sufficient rainfall or irrigation to sustain growth during hot weather. The stems are brittle and easily broken by violent wind; stakes, or preferably wire mesh cylinders, are useful to reduce wind damage in exposed places. The ideal soil is slightly acid, friable and fertile, well aerated, and with a high organic content, but draining freely after rain. While most cultivars and species are tolerant of sun-exposure in moist climates, when grown in hot, dry, inland places, all are better for a light, overhead shading; shade-houses are often used for this purpose. In cold climates, fuchsias may be grown effectively in pots or tubs and overwintered indoors. Such plants need annual repotting, with some of the outer soil and roots removed and replaced by fresh compost/soil material.

Pruning. Young plants should be pinch-pruned frequently during the first year or two to develop a compact, leafy growth habit. Thereafter the annual growth may be reduced by at least half in late winter to keep the plant in good shape for further flower production. Additional feeding with a complete fertiliser at monthly intervals during the period of active growth helps the plant to maintain its full floral display.

Species and cultivars

Fùchsia x hybrida. The modern fuchsias are a result of repeated hybridisation with a number parent species, mainly *F. magellanica, F. coccinea, F. fulgens, F. arborescens* and several other minor species, all contributing various important features such as growth habit, hardiness, floral form, and colour.

In the main fuchsia-growing countries, hundreds of cultivars are available, in a wide range of growth habit, from low prostrate sorts and the pendulous 'spillers' or 'cascades', ideal for hanging baskets, to the taller, shrubby kinds which may reach 2 m or more tall.

Nursery catalogues should be consulted for details of the currently popular cultivars.

All flower from late October to early June.

Other Fuchsia species/cultivars grown occasionally are:

Fùchsia arboréscens (Latin 'becoming tree-like') (syn. *F. syringaeflora*) Mexico.

A large, evergreen shrub to 3–5 m tall, or small tree when so trained by pruning, with dark-green, shiny, broad-lanceolate to elliptic leaves 6–12 cm long, and large, terminal, corymbose panicles of showy flowers from late autumn until spring, and sparsely at other seasons; flowers rosy-magenta, with a short, ovoid ovary and slender, tubulate calyx with 4 spreading, narrow sepals and 4 pointed, slender petals, all of about equal length.

Fùchsia corymbiflòra (Latin 'with flowers in a corymb'): lower levels of Ecuador and Peru.

An evergreen shrub to 2 m or so tall, with loose, pendulous growth from a sparse, woody framework; the large leaves are elliptic-ovate, dark green and somewhat pubescent; the flowers are borne in drooping, corymbose clusters, the tubulate calyx to 7–8 cm long, tapered slenderly to the ovoid ovary at the base, expanded into a 4-lobed limb, the 4 acute petals a little shorter and located between the sepals, all light crimson in the species, but in **'Alba'**, the calyx tube and sepals are white, the corolla crimson.

Fùchsia magellánica (Latin 'from Magellanes', South America) is represented in Australian gardens by its variety **macrostèma** (Greek 'with long stamens') (syn. *'Grácilis'*) of the nursery trade.

This old and still popular fuchsia has a slender, arching habit of growth to 2.5 m or so tall and as wide, often trained in espalier style on lattice or wire-mesh supports.

Leaves are lanceolate-ovate to 3–4 cm long and 1.5–2.0 cm wide, on 1 cm reddish petioles, pubescent at least while young; the showy flowers, to 3–4 cm long, are borne on slender, drooping pedicels 4–5 cm long, singly or in pairs from the upper axils, the bright-crimson calyx with 4 long, slender sepals at least twice the length of the shortly campanulate violet-purple corolla.

'Variegàta' is similar but has leaves bordered with a cream margin.

Fùchsia triphýlla (Latin 'with leaves in threes'): West Indies. This is the principal parent species of the group called Triphylla Hybrids, several of which are well regarded in Australian gardens for their dwarf, compact habit of growth, showy foliage and long flowering season. Leaves are opposite, or mostly 3- or 4-whorled, elliptic to ovate, 6–10 cm long and 3–5 cm wide, on a red, pubescent petiole to 2 cm long, bronze-green to dark green above, reddish beneath, with prominent red veins. Flowers are borne in a panicle or short, terminal racemes, the calyx tube to 2–4 cm or more long, slender but expanded into a 4-lobed limb; the 4 short petals set between the calyx lobes.

'Gartenmeister Bonstedt' is the most commonly planted cultivar, justifiably popular for its abundant, bright-scarlet flowers and velvety, reddish-green leaves.

'Coralle' has coral-red flowers, and greener foliage than that of the other cultivars.

'Souvenir de Heinrich Heinkel' has coral-pink flowers, with deep reddish-purple foliage.

Climatic range. All B, M, P, S, T, or with winter protection in A, H, and Mts.

GARDÈNIA

Named by Linnaeus to honour Alexander Garden, 1730–1791, Scottish physician and amateur plant collector in southern USA.
Gardenia.
Rubiaceae, the Madder family.

Generic description. A large and varied genus of evergreen shrubs mainly from South-East Asia and South Africa, with glossy, green, simple leaves, arranged oppositely or in whorls of 3, and sweetly scented, white flowers produced in late spring and summer, forming an important florists' crop. Fruit is a ribbed, green berry, ripening to orange, containing numerous small seeds. Gardenias are among the most popular plants in Australian gardens, grown especially for their perfumed flowers and attractive foliage.

Propagation. Semi-hardwood, leafy tip cuttings, 5–8 cm long, taken with a heel of older wood in autumn and winter, strike satisfactorily in a sand/peat mixture in a warm, humid atmosphere; hormone dusts are beneficial.

Cultivation. A rich, cool, well drained soil, in part- or dappled shade, in a warm-temperate to subtropical climate, usually produces the best results. The soil should be slightly acid, to 5.5–6.0 pH, and should be dressed regularly with well prepared compost to which a complete fertiliser is added. Adequate water must be maintained from late spring to autumn.

Pruning. Little pruning is necessary, apart from a general light shaping of the plant after the summer flowering period.

Species and cultivars
Gardènia augústa (Latin 'notable, grand or majestic') (syn. *G. jasminoides, G. florida*) south-eastern China and Japan.

Habit. An evergreen shrub to 1.0–1.5 m tall, with a broad hemispherical habit to 2 m or more wide, very twiggy and producing an abundance of handsome leaves and flowers over a long season.

Leaves. Simple, opposite, only rarely 3-whorled, elliptic to obovate, 5–10 cm long and 2–4 cm wide; apex short acuminate; margin entire; venation reticulate, with 6–8 pairs of prominent laterals; glabrous; dark green and lustrous above, paler and duller beneath.

Flowers. Solitary in the upper axils, standing clear of the topmost leaves; calyx tubulate to 2 cm long, with 5–6 well developed, sharp ribs, and free, linear teeth about 2 cm long, bright-green; flower buds clavate at first, with spirally twisted, greenish outer petals, opening to a 5–6 petalled, rotate flower about 6–7 cm across, the petals broadly ovate to oblanceolate, white, but inclined to brown slightly in age; sweetly and heavily perfumed, flowering in the main flush during November and December, then sparsely until May.

Fruit. An obovoid, ribbed berry about 2 cm long, with numerous seeds embedded in a yellowish pulp.

Other distinguishing features. Branchlets becoming very twiggy towards the outer surface of the plant.

'Grandiflora' (Latin 'with large flowers') is similar but of taller form to 2 m or more, with larger, opposite or 3-whorled, elliptic leaves to 10–12 cm long and 4–5 cm wide, of a somewhat more lustrous, brighter green; flowers are much larger, to 10–12 cm across, the 20 or so obovate petals pure white, spreading on the outer perimeter but erect in the centre, resembling a semi-double rose.

'Fortuneàna', 'Magnìfica', 'Professor Pucci' and other large-flowered cultivars are not significantly different.

'Ràdicans' (Latin 'with rooting stems') has a low, broad, almost prostrate habit of growth, rarely more than 0.5 m tall, but usually 1.5–2.0 m wide, the lowest branches often self-layering; leaves are smaller, lanceolate to narrow-elliptic, to 4 cm long and 1 cm wide, and bright glossy

green; flowers are semi-double and loosely and irregularly arranged, 4–5 cm across, with 15 – 25 twisted and often distorted petals, pure white, flowering very profusely, especially during late November and December.
Climatic range. A, B, M, P, S, T.

Gardènia thunbèrgia (commemorating the Swedish botanist Carl Pehr Thunberg, who worked extensively in South Africa in the 1770s): Star Gardenia: South Africa, between Eastern Cape and Natal and in the warmer parts of Transvaal, mostly in humid forest-lands with high rainfall.
Habit. An evergreen, erect shrub to about 3 m tall and 2.5 m wide, usually with a single trunk and horizontally inclined, stiff, 3-whorled branches.
Leaves. Simple, mostly 3-whorled, elliptic to ovate or obovate, 6–12 cm long and 2–4 cm wide; petiole 5 mm long; apex finely acuminate; margin entire, undulate; glabrous and somewaht coriaceous; main vein and 7–10 large laterals creamy-green, with a blister-like gland at the axils; dark green and glossy above, pale green beneath.
Flowers. Solitary at the terminals and in the upper axils; flowers salverform with a 7–9 cm, slender tube and spreading 6–8 cm wide limb, spirally folded at first, divided into 8 to 10 obovate lobes; pure milky-white and sweetly perfumed, flowering from late November to late February and intermittently until late autumn.
Fruit. A fleshy berry, 5–8 cm long and 4 cm wide, grey-green, and heavily scaled and speckled with fine brown lenticels; calyx lobes persistent; seeds numerous, embedded in the firm whitish pulp; fruits ripening in autumn and persisting for 1–2 years.
Other distinguishing features. Nodes slightly swollen; stems partly enclosed by a pair of papery scales; youngest twigs dark green, aging to grey-green; lateral branches developing between the nodes.
Climatic range. A, B, M, P, S, T.

GÁRRYA

Commemorating Nicholas Garry, nineteenth-century Secretary of the Hudson Bay Company. Garrya or Silk-tassel Bush.
Garryaceae, the Garrya family.
Generic description. A small genus of ever-

green shrubs and trees indigenous to North America, with simple, opposite leaves; apetalous, dioecious flowers, borne in long pendulous racemes, the flower parts in fours; and fruit a globular berry containing 1 or 2 seeds. One species, described below, is grown occasionally in Australian gardens for the attractive staminate catkins.

Propagation. Semi-hardwood leafy cuttings, taken in late spring to autumn, strike readily in a sand/peat mixture, in a warm humid atmosphere. Male plants are most commonly offered by nurserymen but females may be propagated in the same way.

Cultivation. Garryas thrive in an open, sun-exposed position in freely drained, coarse-textured soil, preferably in a cool, humid climate with low temperatures remaining above –5°C.

Pruning. The spent inflorescences should be pruned away after flowering, together with shoots failing to conform to the general growth habit.

Species and cultivars
Gárrya ellíptica (Latin 'with leaves like an ellipse'): western USA, mainly on the slopes of the coastal ranges of California.
Habit. An evergreen shrub to 3 m or so tall, of loose, irregular shape, often trained in espalier form to fully display the showy flowers.
Leaves. Elliptic or broadly oval, 6–8 cm long and 3–4 cm wide, petiole to 1 cm, flattened above; apex obtuse, mucronate; base broadly cuneate or acute; margin entire but undulate; thick and coriaceous; bright green, glabrous and slightly shiny above, grey and tomentose beneath, becoming smoother when mature.
Flowers. Dioecious, in terminal and axillary racemes, the pistillate inflorescence 5–7 cm long, grey-woolly, enclosed by 2 sharply horned, acute, brown bracts to 5 mm long; staminate flowers, the more decorative, silvery-grey, the catkins 20–25 cm long, hanging vertically, in profusion, during July and August.
Fruit. A globose berry, with grey-silky exterior, borne on fertilised female plants only, in summer.
Other distinguishing features. Upper stems finely pubescent, becoming glabrous in the second year.
Climatic range. A, B, M, P, S, and in mild microclimates on the lower levels of Mts.

GOMPHOLÒBIUM

Derived from the Greek, referring to the inflated, club-shaped fruits.
Wedge Pea.
Fabaceae, the Pea family.

Generic description. A small genus of Australian native evergreen shrubs, a few grown in gardens for their showy spring flowers and attractive foliage. The species described in detail below are the most commonly seen, and in their main features are representative of the genus.

Propagation. The hard-coated seeds should be warm-water treated for 24 hours, then sown at once in a friable medium in a warm, humid atmosphere.

Cultivation. A freely drained, light soil in a sun-exposed position is ideal, preferably in a mild climate with low temperatures remaining above −5°C.

Pruning. Moderate pruning of the newly flowered shoots helps to develop and maintain a dense, twiggy growth habit with abundant foliage and flowers.

Species and cultivars

Gompholòbium grandiflòrum (Latin 'large-flowered': in this case the flowers are somewhat smaller than those of *G. latifolium*, but clearly larger than those of the remainder of the genus): Large Wedge Pea: NSW Central Coast heathlands and stony ridges, between the sea and the lower tablelands.
Habit. An evergreen shrub 1–2 m tall, with a loose, open character in its native habitat, but responding to cultivation and regular pruning to form a compact, globose bush to 2 m wide.
Leaves. Compound, alternate, mostly trifoliolate, digitately arranged, the leaflets joining closely together at the common 1 mm petiole; leaflets acicular, 1.5–2.5 cm long and 1–2 mm wide; apices acute-mucronate; bases attenuate; margins entire, thickened and revolute; glabrous; dark green.
Flowers. Solitary or in pairs from the upper axils on 6–10 mm pedicels; calyx splitting into 5 lanceolate sepals about 1 cm long, dark blackish-green and glabrous outside, paler and finely downy inside; corolla papilionaceous, the standard orbicular, 2.0–2.5 cm across, obcordate, with slightly incurved edges, butter-yellow; wings obovate to 1.5 cm long, erect, butter-yellow; keel boat-shaped, of 2 concave lobes, yellow-green with blackish-green shadings, ciliate, enclosing the 10 stamens with curved, white filaments and yellow anthers; flowers abundant from early September to late October.
Fruit. An ovoid legume to about 2 cm long, containing 15–20 seeds, ripening in early summer.
Climatic range. A, B, M, P, S and on warm sites on lower Mts.

Gompholòbium latifòlium (Latin 'broad-leafed'): Golden Glory Wedge Pea: Qld, NSW and Vic. mostly on sandy or rocky sites between the coast and tablelands.
Habit. An upright shrub to about 2 m, the upper branches twiggy and flexible.
Leaves. Alternate, trifoliolate, the leaflets linear, 3.5–5.0 cm long, 4–6 mm wide; apex obtuse; base cuneate; margin entire; bright green above, grey-green beneath.
Flowers. Pea-shaped, the largest of the genus, even those of *G. grandiflòrum;* standard petal broadly ovate, about 3 cm across; wing and fringed keel petals smaller; all clear yellow, the standard with a greenish fan at the base; calyx 5-lobed, the sepals yellowish-green, with a pubescent margin; flowering period from August to late October.
Fruit. An ovoid, inflated legume, 1–2 cm long, developing between the wing petals before they fall, and ripening quickly afterwards, pale green, containing about 10–12 seeds.
Climatic range. A, B, M, P, S, and on warm sites on lower Mts.

GREVÍLLEA

Commemorating Charles F. Greville, an early President of the Royal Horticultural Society.
Grevillea; Spider-flower etc.
Proteaceae, the Protea family.

Generic description. A very large and diverse genus of Australian native evergreen trees and shrubs, some low enough to qualify as groundcover, others tall and woody enough to be valuable timber trees. The main features of foliage and flower show extremely wide variations in general character. Leaves are simple, but may be linear, lanceolate, to broadly ovate, or divided pinnately, bipinnately or palmately into fine lobes or divisions. Flowers have several common features such as the tubulate perianth of 4 segments, variously coloured, splitting down the

PLATE 15

▲ Lagerstroemia indica 'Rubra'

▲ Pimelia ferruginea 'Magenta Mist'

▲ Grevillea longifolia

▲ Grevillea 'Robyn Gordon'
◄ Grevillea hookerana
▼ Ixora chinensis 'Prince of Orange'

▼ Fremontodendron californicum

▼ Gardenia augusta

PLATE 16

▲ Hibiscus 'Golden Bell'
▼ Hibiscus 'Crown of Warringah'

▲ Hibiscus 'Celia'
▼ Hibiscus 'Fire Engine'   *Photo by Les Beers*

▲ Hibiscus 'Catavki
▼ Hibiscus mutabilis 'Plena'

Photo by Les Beers

▼ Hibiscus 'Dawn'

▼ Hibiscus 'Crown of Bohemia'

Photo by Les Beers

▼ Hibiscus mutabilis

Photo by Les Beers

side to release the style, held by its stigma until the pollen ripens, then released to more or less straighten. Inflorescences vary widely from small umbellate, spidery, or wheel-like clusters, to long slender racemes, sometimes one-sided large brushes, the main colours being red, orange, apricot, yellow, cerise, mauve, pink, and white, in a variety of colour combinations. Fruit is a woody follicle with a persistent style, drying and splitting to release the 1 or 2 winged seeds for dispersal by wind. The shrubby species are popularly used in small and large gardens, especially in native gardens where they often predominate. A few, of low spreading habit, are useful for covering steep embankments or for providing a ground-cover between other taller plants.

Propagation. a) Seeds must be collected from the green follicles before they ripen fully and discharge their seeds; they are sown at once, or in spring, in a light, friable mixture in a warm but relatively dry atmosphere.

b) Most species and cultivars with short, twiggy growths may be struck by firm-tip cuttings taken in late summer, autumn or winter, planted in a sand/peat mixture in a warm, humid atmosphere; wounding the base to the depth of the cambium and applying a hormone type, root-promoting dust is beneficial.

Cultivation. The species and cultivars described below come from a wide variety of climates and environments, requiring almost individual soil and cultivation methods for the best result. See specific notes below for details.

Pruning. The shrubby kinds almost all benefit from a light pruning of the outer shoots after the flowering season.

Species and cultivars

Grevíllea acanthifòlia (Latin 'with leaves like Acanthus'): Acanthus-leafed Grevillea: Blue Mountains and lower Northern Tablelands of NSW, mainly on the margins of elevated swamps and streams.

Habit. A shrub of 2 m or so tall, with horizontally inclined growth to 3 m wide.

Leaves. Pinnatisect, to 6 cm long and 3 cm wide, deeply 9- to 11-lobed, the lobes further tri-lobed; apices acute, bristle tipped; glabrous, dark green above, pale green beneath.

Flowers. Inflorescence a 1-sided raceme, 6–7 cm long, in the upper axils, tapering to a slender apex, with about 100 flowers opening progressively from the base; flowers in pairs; perianth purple-green and silky-tomentose outside, violet-purple inside; limb silky-pubescent, splitting to release the hooked, lilac-purple style; style nearly straight, 2.5 cm long, the stigma bright green; flowers produced freely from mid-September to late summer.

Other distinguishing features. Leaf-bases partly clasping the stem, the twigs ridged by the decurrent bases. Grows best in partial shade, in moist soils within reach of permanent water.

Climatic range. A, H, M, Mts, P, S.

Grevíllea alpìna (Latin 'from the mountains'): Mountain Grevillea: tablelands of southern NSW and Vic.

Habit. A low shrub, 0.5–2.5 m tall, with a broad, twiggy habit, often wider than the height, but variable according to soil and degree of exposure; many forms are offered in nurseries, some useful as ground covers.

Leaves. Of variable shape from broadly elliptic to linear, mostly less than 1 cm long; margin entire; dark green and white pubescent above, densely villous beneath.

Flowers. Inflorescence a clustered raceme of 6–12 flowers at the ends of short lateral twigs, perianth of ram's-horn shape to 1 cm long, stout, swollen at the base, splitting over the outer arc, the limb globular but 4-crowned, the whole finely pubescent; style to 1.5 cm, the stigma bright green; flowers of various colour combinations, red, orange, cream or yellow on the limb, the style red or pinkish; flowers from June to November.

Other distinguishing features. Upper twigs green, white-pubescent. Best at higher elevations, on freely drained, gravelly or sandy soils with full exposure to sun.

'Dallachiana' is an old and popular cultivar with red/cream flowers.

Climatic range. A, H, M, Mts, and on cool, elevated sites in P and S.

Grevíllea bánksii (commemorating Joseph Banks, botanist with Captain James Cook's expedition to eastern Australia in 1770; later knighted): SE Qld, in the open forest-lands between the coast and the Great Dividing Range.

Habit. A small shrubby tree to 3–4 m tall, usually with a single main trunk and a densely branched, rounded crown, but often seen as a large hemispherical shrub to 2–3 m tall and as wide.

Leaves. Simple, pinnatisect, 20–25 cm long, with 9–11 linear segments separated deeply to near the midrib; midrib prominent beneath; upper surface dark green, with a fine silky pubescence, the lower surface silver-silky, densely pubescent.

Flowers. Inflorescence an erect terminal raceme, 8–12 cm long, the flowers 40 to 80; perianth tube 1.2 cm long, pubescent and reddish outside, glabrous and deep crimson inside; style crimson, looped at first, but straightening to 3 cm long, the stigma yellow; flowers borne freely from August to December, but intermittently throughout the year.

Other distinguishing features. Young twigs somewhat angular by the decurrent ridges below the leaf bases; grey-tomentose. An attractive species if grown well on freely drained, light loamy soils in an open, sunny position, with regular pruning to remove spent inflorescences.

'**Alba**' has white flowers, but is otherwise very similar.

'**Kingaroy Slippers**' as a registered cultivar belongs here as a probable mutation from *G. banksii*, growing to 2–3 m tall, with the same shrubby, tree-like form and pinnatisect leaves. The purplish-red flowers differ from those of the parent in that the stigma, upon release from the ovary, carries the slipper-like perianth tube with it on the end of the nearly-straight style. Flowering season and other features are as for the species.

Climatic range. A, B, M, P, S, T.

Grevíllea bipinnatífida (Latin 'with leaves bipinnately lobed', but not divided into individual leaflets): WA, mainly in the Swan River valley and the slopes of the Darling Range.

Habit. A mostly prostrate to low-growing shrub to less than 1 m, with lax pubescent stems, but usually taller to 2 m or so in cultivation.

Leaves. Bipinnately lobed, the main rachis 8–10 cm long; primary segments 11 to about 15, further cleft into 1 to several sharp-pointed lobes; apices spinose, base of leaf winged, merging into the petiole; glabrous; dark grey-green.

Flowers. Inflorescence a drooping raceme to 10 cm long on a rust-red, pubescent rachis from the axils of the upper twigs; perianths dull-red and deep rose-pink, about 1.5 cm long, strongly recurved into the ram's-horn shape at the limb; silky-pubescent; style crimson, 3 cm long with a yellowish stigma; flowers abundant from early spring to late summer.

Other distinguishing features. An attractive species for coarse, well-drained soils in hot climates, with low atmospheric humidity.

Climatic range. A, I, M, P, S, and lower Mts.

Grevíllea biternàta (Latin 'with leaves twice divided into 3 divisions'): southern coast of WA.

Habit. A shrub of variable form, mostly a cascading ground-cover, forming a dense mat to 0.5 m tall and 2–3 m wide, commonly producing a few erect stems to 1.5–2.0 m tall, but which in cultivation are mostly pruned away to preserve the low prostrate form.

Leaves. Biternate, divided into 2 or commonly 3 branches, each about 1 cm long, these further divided into 3 linear divisions; apices spinose; midribs raised prominently beneath; yellowish-green.

Flowers. Inflorescence a raceme 2.5–3.0 cm long in the upper axils; flowers about 50, borne in pairs along the whitish rachis; perianth white, with four segments forming the creamy-yellow, globose limb; style white; sweetly honey-perfumed, flowering from late August to November.

Other distinguishing features. A fine prostrate plant, ideal as a ground-cover in large-scale landscapes. Hardy to several degrees of frost, but liable to damage in more severe conditions; thrives on a variety of freely drained soils.

Climatic range. A, B, M, P, S, T.

Grevíllea '**Boongala Spinebill**': a hybrid with a fine record in cultivation, produced by Sid Cadwell of 'Boongala', Annangrove, NSW.

Habit. A shrub to 1.5–2.0 cm tall with an open spreading form to about 3 m broad.

Leaves. Simple, deeply pinnatisect, 15–18 cm long and 3.5–4.5 cm broad; segments 15 to 25 on each side of the rachis, slightly falcate, a few with a small secondary lobe towards the apex, the tips sharp but not stiff; bright green and glabrous above, paler and pubescent beneath.

Flowers. Inflorescence a one-sided raceme 8–10 cm long from the upper leaf axils; perianths dark crimson; styles bright crimson, heavily hooked at first but nearly straight at release; stigma large and flat; flowering from early spring to late autumn.

Other distinguishing features. Upper stems reddish, angular and pubescent, at least while young.

Climatic range. A, H, M, Mts, P, S.

Grevíllea càleyi (commemorating George Caley, botanical collector for Sir Joseph Banks): Caley's Grevillea: rocky sandstone plateaus of the NSW Central Coast strip.

Habit. A slender shrub to 3 m or so tall and 3–4 m wide, with horizontally inclined main branches.

Leaves. Deeply pinnatisect, 20–25 cm long, the 15–16 pairs of lobes cut to within 1 mm of the midrib, the lobes 2 cm long; apices acute, with a sharp mucro; margins entire but recurved; minutely pubescent and dark green above, white-tomentose beneath.

Flowers. Inflorescence a 1-sided raceme 5–6 cm long, from the upper axils; flowers 50–60, in pairs; perianth tubulate, deep crimson but with white tomentum, the limb reflexed; style nearly straight when released, 2.5 cm long, deep rosy-purple, with a broad green stigma; flowering from September to December.

Other distinguishing features. Young leaves and twigs silky-crimson, older shoots whitish, marked between the nodes by 3 decurrent ridges from the leaf-bases. An attractive plant with especially handsome foliage, but needs to be pruned occasionally to develop its best performance.

Climatic range. A, B, M, P, S.

Grevíllea 'Canberra Gem': a hybrid of *G. juniperina* x *G. rosmarinifolia* from the Department of Interior's Yarralumla Nursery at Canberra.

Habit. A shrub of 1.5–2.5 m tall, resembling *G. rosmarinifolia*, the habit stiff, open and of erect form.

Leaves. Linear-acicular, to about 2 cm long; apex acute; margin entire, but finely ciliate and fully recurved; dark green and glabrous above, pubescent beneath but hidden by the recurved margin.

Flowers. In an umbellate raceme of 15–20 flowers of bright coral-red, the globular limb green, the coral-red style straightening to 2.5 cm long, the perianth slightly pubescent, flowering from August to October.

Other distinguishing features. Upper twigs pale brown, with a dense mat of whitish hairs. An attractive and hardy grevillea, surviving low temperatures of at least −8°C, preferring an open, sunny aspect and sandy or loamy soil with free drainage.

Climatic range. A, H, M, Mts, P, S.

Grevíllea 'Clearview David': a hybrid between *G. rosmarinifolia* and 'Crosbie Morrison'.

Habit. A leafy shrub to 2.5 m tall, forming a dense, twiggy bush to 3 m across.

Leaves. Linear-acicular to 3 cm long; apex acute; margin entire, recurved; rugose, with a few soft white hairs above, silky white-pubescent beneath.

Flowers. Inflorescence a terminal raceme of 10–15 flowers; perianth 1 cm long, rosy-crimson of ram's-horn shape; style straightening to 1.3 cm, deep crimson with large, oblique stigma; flowers from June to November.

Grevíllea 'Crimson Glory' is a registered cultivar of hybrid origin from a possible crossing of *G. acanthifolia* and *G. willisii*.

Habit. Of low mound shape to 30 cm tall and about 1.5 m broad.

Leaves. Simple, deep green, 8 cm long and 4 cm broad, the margins deeply lobed, sharply tipped, glabrous and lustrous above, paler and pubescent beneath, the midrib prominent.

Flowers. Toothbrush type, on the terminals of short branchlets, about 5 cm long, crimson, flowering between September and May.

Grevíllea 'Evelyn's Coronet': a registered cultivar developed as a hybrid between *G. buxifolia* and *G. lavandulacea*.

Habit. A shrub to 1.5 to 2.0 m tall and about as broad, with dense, twiggy growth, enhanced by moderate annual pruning; upper young stems pubescent, pale green.

Leaves. Acicular, 2–3 cm long, 2–3 mm wide; apex acute, with a fine bristle at the tip; margin slightly recurved; dark green above, paler beneath, pubescent on both surfaces.

Flowers. Flowers in ovoid, spidery heads of 20–30 at the terminals of the upper shoots; perianth 7–8 mm long, strongly recurved, dusky-pink with a greenish limb; style reddish-purple, straightening at length of nearly 2 cm long; all parts silky-pubescent; flowering sporadically throughout the year but most abundantly in spring.

Climatic range. A, H, M, Mts, P, S.

Grevíllea hookeràna (commemorating Sir Joseph Dalton Hooker, British botanist): Hooker Grevillea: southern coast of WA.

Habit. A large shrub to 3–4 m tall with horizontally inclined branches, forming a wide bush 4–5 m across.

Leaves. Deeply pinnatisect, 12–15 cm long and 6–7 cm wide; pinnate segments 11–21, mostly in opposite pairs, 3 mm wide; margins entire; bronze-red at first, maturing to dark green and glabrous above, whitish-green and silky-pubescent beneath, with a prominent midrib.

Flowers. Inflorescence a 1-sided 'toothbrush' type, 6–9 cm long, with up to 60 or more backward pointing flowers, arranged in pairs on a stout pubescent rachis; perianth curved to 1 cm long, silky-pubescent, greyish outside, crimson inside, the limb globular, fully recurved; style nearly straight to 3 cm after release, deep crimson, the stigma slightly paler; flowers borne from August to December.

Other distinguishing features. Branches and outer twigs silky pubescent. Several forms are recognised. All are handsome, spreading shrubs with attractive leaves and flowers produced over a long season. They are best grown in the open on light soils with free drainage.

Climatic range. A, M, P, S, and on the lower, warmer levels of Mts.

Grevíllea 'Ivanhoe': an interspecific hybrid between *G. asplenifolia* and *G. caleyi*.

Habit. A shrub to 1.5–2.5 m tall, spreading to about 3 m wide.

Leaves. Pinnatisect, 10–12 cm long and 2–3 cm wide; margin with 10–12 narrow lobes to 1.5 cm long, the sinuses to within 1 mm of the midrib, the lobes about 1 cm apart, angled at about 70° from the midrib; midrib and main lobal-veins prominent beneath; bright coppery-red and slightly pubescent at first, becoming dark green and glabrous above, paler and silky beneath.

Flowers. Inflorescence a 1-sided toothbrush type, the flowers numerous, greyish-pink in the bud, the perianth 8–9 cm long, dusky-red with white pubescence, carmine inside the tube, the limb globose and recurved; style straightening to 2.5 cm after release, coral-red with a large yellow stigma; flowers are abundant from July to November.

Other distinguishing features. Upper twigs coppery-red, covered with a fine coat of rufous to grey tomentum. A well-established early hybrid, respected for its unusual but handsome foliage and ease of culture in a wide range of soils and climates.

Climatic range. A, B, M, P, S, and on the lower, warmer levels of Mts.

Grevíllea juniperina (Latin 'with leaves like a Juniper'): Juniper-leafed Spider-flower; the local form from the coastal plateaus and lower tablelands; other forms from parts of SE Australia.

Habit. A dense shrub to 2 m or more, with a twiggy habit to about 3 m wide.

Leaves. Linear, 1.5–2.0 cm long and 2 mm wide; apex acute, spinose; margin entire, recurved; bright shining green above, grey-silky beneath.

Flowers. Infloresence a terminal, umbellate raceme of 20–30 flowers; perianth slender, nearly straight, to 1.5 cm long, mostly bright red, but varying to pink, greenish-red, or yellow, silky-pubescent, the limb globose, rufous, reflexed fully, the segments twisting and spiralling when mature, after release of the style; style nearly straight to 2.8 cm long, crimson with large yellow stigma; flowering season August to November.

'Molonglo' is a registered cultivar developed in Canberra, useful as a low spreading plant on steep planting sites, especially in cool climates. It grows to about 1 m tall and a little broader with sharp-pointed linear leaves to 2 cm long with recurved margins, and apricot perianths and bright red styles.

Other distinguishing features. Hardy in all but the coldest parts of the tablelands and performing well in an open, sunny aspect on reasonably fertile, sandy or gravelly soils.

Climatic range. A, H, M, Mts, P, S.

Grevíllea lanígera (Latin 'woolly', referring to the hairy lower surface of the leaves): Woolly Grevillea: SE Australia, mainly on rocky sites, often elevated.

Habit. Variable in habit from the taller forms of about 1.5 m or so, to the rounded shrubby forms of 50–75 cm and a few genuine ground covers, several identified by geographical names.

Leaves. Sessile, linear to narrowly oblong, 10–20 mm long and 2–3 mm wide, pointed forward to partly cover the stems; apex obtuse; margin recurved; texture thick; pubescent and grey-green above, silky-hairy and whitish green beneath.

Flowers. In a dense terminal raceme of about 8–10 ram's-horn type flowers, the curved perianth deep pink to red, with a cream or yellow tip, the pubescent style deep red with a large yellowish-red stigma, flowering in late winter and spring.

Other distinguishing features. Upper twigs green, pubescent. Hardy and tolerant of a wide range of soils and severe climates.
Climatic range. A, H, M, Mts, P, S.

Grevíllea lavandulàcea (Latin 'with leaves like Lavender'): Lavender Grevillea: western Vic., and SA, mainly around the Gulfs.
Habit. A low shrub of 0.5 m to 2.0 m tall, with dense twiggy growth, forming a broad, bun-shaped bush 1.5 m or so wide, but very variable.
Leaves. Linear, 1.5–2.0 cm long and 2–3 mm wide; apex acute-mucronate; base tapered to the squarish petiole; margin entire, recurved; puberulent and dark green, heavily pubescent and whitish-green beneath.
Flowers. Inflorescence a short terminal raceme of 8–12 flowers; perianth about 1 cm long, broadly curved at the base with a fully recurved limb, red, but paling to cream above; style crimson-red, the oblique stigma darker, flowering season, August to December.
Other distinguishing features. One of the best of the smaller growing grevilleas, the fine-textured, grey foliage a pleasant background to the showy abundant flowers. All enjoy a well-drained, light or sandy soil in a sunny exposure. Several good forms have been isolated, their trade names indicative of their habitat.
'Penola' form has heavily white-pubescent foliage and twigs, with red and white perianth and a crimson style.
'Tanunda' form has grey-green, heavily-pubescent leaves, the perianth rose-pink, paler near the whitish limb, the style rose-pink with a crimson stigma.
'Victor Harbour' form has smaller green leaves, flowers 6–10 in a dense umbellate cluster, the perianth large, coral-red, the limb pale buff, the style crimson.
Climatic range. A, M, P, S, and in lower, warmer parts of Mts.

Grevíllea **'Mason's Hybrid'** (commemorating the raiser, Joe Mason, of Kentlyn Nursery, Campbelltown, NSW): a registered cultivar originating as a hybrid between *G. banksii* and *G. bipinnatifida*.
Habit. An erect bush to 2–3 m tall, dense and leafy, somewhat horizontally inclined, at least while young, eventually growing to 2 m or so broad.
Leaves. Simple, deeply pinnatisect, 15–18 cm long, 10–12 cm wide, the linear segments bearing slender secondary lobes; dark green and slightly shiny above, paler and pubescent beneath.
Flowers. Inflorescence a terminal raceme to 12–15 cm long, with 60–80 flowers on one side of the pubescent, greenish rachis; perianth yellowish-orange, maturing to deeper orange-scarlet; style fully hooked at first, nearly straight after release, to 4 cm long, crimson; flowering throughout the year with peak in spring.
Climatic range. A, B, M, P, S, T, and lower levels of Mts.

Grevíllea **'Misty Pink'** is a registered cultivar occurring as a hybrid between *Grevillea banksii* and *G. sessilis.*
Habit. Erect plant with an open, tree-like habit to 2–3 m or so, vigorous while young but then becoming denser in growth, especially with regular pruning.
Leaves. Simple, pinnatisect to 15–25 cm long, divided nearly to the midrib into 9–15 linear segments, dark green above, white-pubescent beneath.
Flowers. In an erect, terminal raceme to about 15 cm long; flowers numerous, the perianths pale dusky-pink outside, crimson inside, the cream style looped at first but straightening to 3 cm; flowering season mainly in spring and early autumn but extended by frequent removal of spent flowers.
Other distinguishing features. Upper twigs grey-green, angular and finely pubescent. An attractive plant useful for its taller growth habit and ideal as a background subject where its sometimes sparse lower stems may be concealed by smaller plants.
Climatic range. A, B, M, P, S, T.

Grevíllea **'Pink Parfait'** is a seedling from the above cultivar, similar in most respects but has rosy-crimson flowers borne in a slightly larger raceme 18–20 cm long, mainly in spring and autumn.

Grevíllea **'Pink Surprise'**: a hybrid between *G. banksii* and *G.* 'Mundubbera': a tall, open plant to 5 m or more and about 3 m wide, with 'banksii' type, grey-green leaves to 20–25 cm long, and terminal, pubescent racemes up to 20 cm long, the perianths pale-pink with creamy-yellow hooked styles, flowering prolifically in spring and autumn.

Climatic range. Both above cultivars A, B, M, P, S, T.

Grevíllea 'Olympic Flame': a hybrid between *G. alpina* 'Dallachiana' and *G. rosmarinifolia*.
Habit. A dense shrub, 1.0–1.5 m tall, with a fine, twiggy growth to 2 m wide.
Leaves. Alternate, but appearing to be whorled in threes, linear-lanceolate to 2 cm long and 4 mm wide; margin entire but recurved; dark geen and glossy above, silvery-green and pubescent beneath.
Flowers. Inflorescence a terminal raceme, densely crowded with 20–30 flowers; perianth tubulate rosy-red; style crimson, straightening to 3 cm long; flowers from mid-winter to late September.
Other distinguishing features. A fine grevillea, revelling in an open, sunny position on light soil and responding to annual tip-pruning to thicken the growth.
Climatic range. A, B, H, M, Mts, P, S.

Grevíllea 'Pink Pearl': an outstanding cultivar of hybrid parentage.
Habit. A shrub to 2–3 m tall and 3–4 m across, with horizontally inclined branches carrying an abundance of leaves and showy flowers.
Leaves. Resemble those of *G. rosmarinifolia*.
Flowers. Inflorescence an umbellate 'spidery' raceme of up to 25 flowers, borne at the end of leafy shoots from the upper branchlets; perianth 1.5 cm long, 4 mm wide, squarish in the tube, nearly straight, deep coral-pink, the limb recurved, globular, green before splitting into its 4 segments, then whitish; style bright coral-pink, straightening to 2.5 cm long, the stigma oblique, 2.5 mm across; flowers profuse from August to November.
Other distinguishing features. A well-known grevillea, giving a good performance on freely drained, light soils in a wide range of climates.
Climatic range. A, B, H, M, Mts, P, S.

The 'Poorinda' grevilleas were produced by Leo Hodge of Ellaswood, eastern Victoria, who was invited to nominate his 'best dozen' for inclusion here. His choice is:
Grevíllea 'Poorinda Beauty' is a hybrid of *G. alpina* and *G. juniperina*, growing to 2 m tall and 2–3 m wide, with pubescent, linear-lanceolate, grey-green leaves 1.5 cm long and 3 mm wide, and orange-red flowers in a tight, pendulous

wheel-like cluster, with a red style, flowering from August to November.

Grevíllea 'Poorinda Blondie' is a seedling selection from *G. hookerana*, with the vigorous growth habit of the parent, growing to 3.5 m tall and at least as broad, the serrated pinnatisect leaves to 15 cm long, dark green above, silvery-pubescent beneath, the 1-sided 'toothbrush'-type, racemose flowers golden-yellow, flowering freely from late August to November.

Grevíllea 'Poorinda Golden Lyre' is a hybrid of *G. alpina* and *G. victoriae* with a spreading growth habit to 1 m tall and somewhat wider, with elliptic-ovate, green leaves 2.5–3.5 cm long and 1.2 cm wide, the flowers large, in a 'claw'- to 'wheel'-type cluster, the perianth yellow, the style pink, with a green stigma, flowering in late winter and spring.

Grevíllea 'Poorinda Illumina' is a hybrid of *G. lanigera* and *G. lavendulacea*, growing to 1 m tall and 1 m wide, with slender, linear leaves 1.6 cm long and 3 mm wide, grey-green above, silvery pubescent beneath, the flowers in a claw-like 'wheel' form, the perianth deep maroon-pink, paling to ivory, with a deep-maroon style, flowering from late winter to mid spring.

Grevíllea 'Poorinda Jennifer Joy' is a hybrid of *G. linearis* and *G. punicea*, growing to 1.5 m tall and as wide, with linear leaves to 3.5 cm long and 5 mm wide, green above, silvery-pubescent beneath, the flowers in a loose, 'spidery' cluster, the perianth mauve, the style reddish, flowering in late winter and spring.

Grevíllea 'Poorinda Leane' is a hybrid of the NSW form of *G. juniperina* and *G. victoriae*, growing to a large, open bush 2.5 m tall and as wide, the linear leaves 4 cm long and 6 mm wide, shiny green above, silvery-pubescent beneath, the 1-sided claw-type flowers with buff-yellow perianth, tinged with apricot, the style salmon-red, occasional flowers with the 'wheel'-type flowers of *G. victoriae*; flowers winter and spring.

Grevíllea 'Poorinda Peter' is an early hybrid between *G. acanthifolia* and *G. asplenifolia*, the shrub to 2.5 m tall and as wide, of somewhat horizontally inclined form, the dark-green, shiny leaves linear-pinnatisect, to 15 cm long and 4 cm wide, with 8 to 12 lanceolate lobes; flowers are in a 1-sided 'toothbrush'-type raceme to 5–6 cm long, the perianth greyed-pink, with a whitish-green base, silky-pubescent, the style rosy-carmine, with bright green stigma; flowers abundant from early September to late November.

Grevíllea '**Poorinda Rondeau**', a hybrid between *G. baueri* and *G. lavandulacea*, is a spreading bush 1 m tall and 1.5 m wide, with linear-lanceolate, recurved leaves 1.5 cm long and 3–4 mm wide, the upper surface rough and dark green, the lower paler and pubescent; flowers are prolific in a small, cluster-type raceme of 10–12 flowers, the ram's-horn perianth deep rosy-crimson, and the 1.5 m style pubescent and deep crimson, flowering from August to December; upper twigs reddish, heavily silky-pubescent.

Grevíllea '**Poorinda Rosy Morn**' is a hybrid of *G. baueri* and *G. lavandulacea*, making a spreading shrub 1 m tall and 1.5 m wide, the bright-green linear leaves 2.5 cm long and 6 mm wide, the large flowers in a claw-like cluster, the perianth and style bright coral-red, flowering from late winter to mid spring.

Grevíllea '**Poorinda Royal Mantle**' is a hybrid of *G. laurifolia* and *G. willisii*, with broad, prostrate growth 0.25 m tall but eventually 6–7 m across, forming a dense, leafy carpet ideal as a large-scale ground-cover; leaves are variable, some large and broad like *G. laurifolia*, others pinnatifid 13–15 cm long and 2.5 cm wide; flowers are in a 1-sided 'toothbrush'-type raceme, the perianth and style light red, flowering from September to November.

Grevíllea '**Poorinda Ruby**', a hybrid of *G. alpina* '**Dallachiana**' and *G. lavandulacea*, has a procumbent form 0.5 m tall but 1–2 m wide, attractive and very useful as a ground cover; leaves are green, linear, 1.2–1.5 cm long, the flowers bright ruby-red in claw-like clusters at the end of short, lateral twigs, from late winter to November.

Grevíllea '**Poorinda Vivacity**' is a hybrid between *G. oleoides* and *G. punicea*, forming a compact, globose shrub about 1 m tall, the lanceolate-elliptic leaves 4 cm long and 10–11 mm wide, green above but silvery-pubescent beneath; flowers are produced in a fan-shaped cluster like those of *G. punicea*, the perianth bright orange-red, the style scarlet-red, flowering from late winter to mid spring.

Climatic range. All A, B, H, M, Mts, P, S.

Grevíllea speciòsa (Latin 'showy') (syn. *G. punicea*) Red Spider-flower: the sandy and stony land of the plateaus and heaths between the coast and tablelands of NSW.

Habit. A thin, open shrub to 3 m tall, with slender branches but responding to pruning and cultivation with improved density and better foliage and flowers.

Leaves. Simple, often 3 together at each node, lanceolate to elliptic, 2–3 cm long and 7–12 mm wide; apex acute-mucronate; margin entire but recurved; glabrous, slightly shiny and dark green above, pale green and silky-pubescent beneath.

Flowers. Inflorescence a fan shaped, clustered raceme of 15–25 flowers on a 1 cm peduncle; perianth to 1.3 cm, straight but with recurved limb, crimson, silky-pubescent; style to 3.5 cm long, dark crimson with large pink stigma, flowering from July to December.

Other distinguishing features. Upper twigs angular by the decurrent ridges below the leaf-bases.

Climatic range. A, H, M, Mts, P, S.

Grevíllea rivulàris (Latin 'from the margin of a rivulet'): Carrington Falls Grevillea: Upper Kangaroo River valley, near Robertson, NSW.

Habit. A shrub to 1.5–2.0 m tall, spreading to 3–4 m wide, the main branches horizontally inclined.

Leaves. Leaves bipinnatisect, 4–6 cm long and 5–7 cm wide, the main rachis 1–2 mm wide, slightly winged at the edges; primary divisions to 3.5 cm long, about 6 in number, resembling the main rachis, 1.0–1.5 cm apart, mostly opposite, each subdivided into 5 or less segments to 1.5 cm long and 2 mm wide; apices finely acute, spinose; glabrous and dull dark green above, paler beneath.

Flowers. Inflorescence an axillary or terminal 1-sided raceme to 5–6 cm long, with about 25 flowers in pairs along the smooth, green axis; perianth to 1.3 cm long, squarish, pale rosy-violet, the limb fully recurved; style rosy-violet with bright green upper end, and large stigma; flowers abundant from early September to November.

Other distinguishing features. Upper twigs angular by the decurrent internodal ridges, dark purplish-red above, green beneath, pubescent; leaf-bases broad, clasping the stem. A fine grevillea of comparatively recent introduction, but assured of success in gardens because of its showy flowers and unusual and attractive foliage.

Climatic range. A, H, M, Mts, P, S, preferably on cool, moist sites with dappled shade.

Grevíllea 'Robyn Gordon': a hybrid between *G. banksii* and *G. bipinnatifida*.

Habit. A low, horizontally inclined bush to 1.0–1.5 m tall and somewhat wider, in form approximately intermediate between the parents.

Leaves. Simple, deeply bipinnatisect, to 12 cm long and as wide, with 11–15 linear prongs; upper surface dark green, the lower side bright green and finely silky-pubescent, midribs prominent; apices of segments acute-bristly; margins entire but recurved.

Flowers. Inflorescence a dense, terminal raceme, 10–15 cm long, of 90–100 flowers, borne in pairs, rachis with black-tipped red hairs; pedicels 1.2 cm long; perianth dusky-crimson, pubescent, strongly ribbed, recurved sharply at the globose, orange-red limb; style straightening to 4.5 cm long, deep crimson, pubescent, the stigma large, oblique, crimson; flowers abundant from early August to November, then intermittent through summer and autumn.

Other distinguishing features. Upper stems grey-pubescent, ribbed decurrently below the leaf-bases. A strikingly handsome grevillea, thriving in well-drained, loamy and sandy soils, in fully sun-exposed sites.

Climatic range. A, B, M, P, S, T, and on the lower warmer levels of Mts.

Grevíllea rosmarinifòlia (Latin 'with leaves like rosemary'). Rosemary Spider-flower: eastern coastal strip of NSW and Vic. to Wilson's Promontory.

Habit. A shrub to 2.5 m tall, with a dense, spreading habit to 3 m wide.

Leaves. Linear, 2.5–3.5 cm long and 1–2 mm wide; apex acute with a short point; margin entire, recurved; translucent midrib alone distinct; dark green and glabrous above, paler and pubescent beneath.

Flowers. Inflorescence an umbellate raceme of 6–15 flowers on slender, crimson pedicels; perianth of ram's-horn shape, crimson on the outer edge, pink and cream on the inner; style straightening to 2 cm long, crimson, with large oblique stigma; flowering season from early August to November.

Other distinguishing features. Upper twigs finely pubescent. Very variable when grown by seeds, producing a wide range of forms:

'**Desert Flame**' belongs here, similar to the parent in most respects, but with bright orange-scarlet flowers from May to August; the Nurserymen's Association 'Shrub of the Year' for 1973.

'**Jenkinsii**' has deeper-coloured flowers and slightly larger leaves.

'**Lutea**' is cream, with about 6 blackish stripes on the outer curve of the perianth, the style cream with green base and stigma.

Climatic range. All A, B, M, P, S, and in the lower, warmer levels of Mts.

Grevíllea '**Sandra Gordon**': a hybrid between *G. sessilis* and *G. pteridifolia*.

Habit. A plant of tall, open growth habit to 3.5–4.0 m, tree-like in vigorous youth but becoming denser and shrubby if pruned moderately after or during the flowering period.

Leaves. Simple, pinnatisect, 15–25 cm long, with about 11–15 linear segments, separated deeply to near the midrib; segments 10–15 cm long, 2–4 mm wide, midribs depressed above, prominent beneath; upper surface dark green with a fine silky pubescence, at least while young, the lower surface silvery-white and densely pubescent.

Flowers. In an erect terminal raceme 12–20 cm long and 5–7 cm wide on a stout pubescent rachis, the 100–150 flowers arranged closely in neat spiral rows; perianths 'ram's-horn' type, densely pubescent and white outside, yellowish-green inside; style butter-yellow, looped at first but straight when mature to 3.5 cm long; flowering from March to late October.

Other distinguishing features. Young shoots silvery-tan, pubescent, with shallow longitudinal ridges decurrent from the leaf bases.

Climatic range. A, B, M, P, S, T.

Grevíllea victòriae (commemorating Queen Victoria, 1819–1901): Royal Grevillea: tablelands of Southern NSW, ACT and Vic.

Habit. A densely-leafed shrub of broad bun shape to about 1.5–2.0 m tall and as broad, some forms taller and more open in habit, producing also variations in flower colour.

Leaves. Variable, but mostly lanceolate to elliptic-obovate, 4–6 cm (or rarely 10 cm) long and 1–2 cm wide; apex acute with a short, recurved point; margin entire, dark green and glabrous above, paler and densely pubescent beneath.

Flowers. Variable, in most forms numbering 15–25 in a 'spider' type raceme, 4–6 cm long, from the upper and lateral shoots; perianth tubulate, 1 cm long, nearly straight, silky-pubescent, dusky-red, deciduous, the reddish style persisting; main flowering season in summer, with occasional flowers through autumn and winter.

Other distinguishing features. Young twigs densely tomentose, reddish above, grey-green beneath. A reliable grevillea for cold climates.

Climatic range. A, H, M, Mts, P, S.

HALÍMIUM (formerly included with *Helianthemum*)

Derived from the Greek *halimos* 'maritime'.
Portuguese Rock Rose.
Cistaceae, the Cistus family.

Generic description. A small genus strongly resembling *Cistus*, but distinct on account of its 3-valved capsules. The single species described is seen occasionally in local gardens especially near the coast where it often forms an attractive component in rock garden plantings.

Propagation. a) Seeds sown in spring germinate readily in an open friable mixture kept somewhat drier than usual.
b) Soft- and firm-tip cuttings, taken in late summer and autumn, are commonly used, planted in a coarse, well-aerated medium.

Cultivation. An open sunny position is best, preferably in a Mediterranean-type climate. The ideal soil is coarse in texture, freely drained and of low to moderate fertility. The plant is hardy to at least −5°C.

Pruning. Young plants need to be tip-pruned frequently during the first several years to build up a dense mass of short, twiggy growths for improved flower production, thence lightly pruned annually, immediately after the flowering period.

Species and cultivars

Halimium lasiánthum subsp. *formòsum* (Greek: 'with woolly flowers'; Latin: beautiful): (syn. *Cistus formosus, Helianthemum formosum*) coastal regions of Portugal.

Habit. An evergreen shrub to about 1 m tall but of broad, low profile to 2 m or more wide.

Leaves. Simple, opposite, oblong or obovate to 3.5 cm long and 1.5 cm broad; apex acute; base cuneate; margin entire; closely pubescent, grey-green above, whitish beneath.

Flowers. Shallowly crateriform or rotate, about 4 cm across, of 5 obovate petals, borne in clusters at the ends of short, lateral shoots; flower buds coarsely hirsute and slightly sticky, the 3 sepals acute to acuminate; petals buttercup-yellow, each with a small purplish-brown spot near the base; flowering season from early October to late November.

Fruit. A 3-valved capsule splitting when ripe to release the fine seeds.

Climatic range. A, H, I, M, Mts, P, and on dry sites only in S.

HAMAMÈLIS

Derived from the Greek words referring to the concurrence of the fruit and flowers.
Witch-Hazel.
Hamamelidaceae, the Witch-Hazel family.

Generic description. A small genus from the Orient and North America, with simple, alternate, deciduous leaves usually with an oblique base; the perfumed flowers are borne in terminal and axillary clusters, the 4 narrow, yellow petals twisted and curled, the calyx of 4 recurved sepals, brownish-yellow or red, the 8 stamens in 2 dissimilar series of 4; and the fruit is a 2-celled, horned capsule containing 2 lustrous, black seeds. The species described below are grown occasionally in cool-climate gardens for their curious flowers and/or colourful autumnal foliage.

Propagation. a) Seeds should be collected before discharge from the somewhat explosive capsules and sown at once in a cool, humid place; germination is slow, often taking at least a full year or more.

b) 'Simple' layers are usually laid down in winter, maintained carefully until the following winter, then severed and lifted for potting or planting out into permanent positions.

Cultivation. An open, sun-exposed position is best, preferably in a cool, moist climate on fertile, loamy soil. Both species listed are hardy to cold to at least −8°C.

Pruning. The cutting of long basal shoots at flowering time for indoor decoration is generally beneficial in plants not trained as trees; whether needed for this purpose or not, some of the oldest shoots should be thinned out each year to clear the way for new water-shoots. The best flowers and leaves are borne on strong young basal shoots of 1 to 3 years grown to their full length, not shortened or 'trimmed'.

Species and cultivars

Hamamèlis móllis (Latin 'softly hairy'): Chinese Witch-Hazel: central and western China.
Habit. A deciduous plant to 4–5 m tall, often trained in the early years to a single trunk, but sometimes modified by pruning or by adverse conditions to shrub-like form, then with a spreading, somewhat horizontal shape.
Leaves. Broadly obovate, 8–12 cm long and 5–10 cm wide, on 1 cm petioles; apex acute to shortly acuminate; base obtuse to cordate, mostly oblique; margin coarsely sinuate-dentate, the teeth terminating the main lateral veins; venation reticulate between the midrib and 6 or 7 pairs of laterals; texture soft while young, becoming coriaceous when mature; mid green and pubescent above, grey-green and densely stellate-pubescent beneath; autumn colour deep golden-yellow.
Flowers. In axillary clusters on the 1- and 2-year-old wood, the globular buds densely rufous-pubescent; calyx yellow-brown, the 4 spreading sepals chocolate-brown inside; petals linear, 2 cm long, curling irregularly, golden-yellow; flowers sweetly fragrant, flowering in winter, mainly July and August, but often later in severe climates.
Fruit. An ovoid capsule, 1.5 cm or so long, the 2 cells horned at the apex; seeds 2, lustrous black, expelled forcibly at the ripening of the capsule.
Other distinguishing features. Young twigs densely stellate-pubescent, becoming smoother and glabrous by the second year.

Climatic range. H, M, Mts, and on cool, elevated sites in A and S.

Hamamèlis virginiàna (Latin 'from Virginia'), but also extending into north-eastern USA and the St Lawrence valley.
Habit. A shrub to 4 m or so tall when grown naturally, but readily adapted to tree-like form by selecting the dominant leading shoot and suppressing competitors; the crown has a somewhat horizontally inclined form.
Leaves. Obovate, 6–12 cm long and 4–8 cm wide; petiole slender, to 2 cm long; apex shortly acuminate; base asymmetrical, the longer lobe cordate, the shorter obtuse; margin coarsely sinuate-dentate, less so near the base; venation reticulate between the midrib and 5 or 6 main lateral veins on each side, all prominent below; glabrous; dark green and shining above, paler beneath, changing to bright buttercup-yellow in autumn; leaves strongly resemble those of *Parrotia persica*.
Flowers. In clusters of 3 in the upper axils, the petals linear, curled and twisted, yellow, flowering in autumn among the leaves.
Fruit. A cluster of 3 ovoid, woody capsules supported by persistent calyx lobes beneath, the surface pubescent, the apex with 2 blunt horns, splitting when ripe in winter to release the lustrous black seeds.
Other distinguishing features. Young twigs flexuose, covered with yellowish-brown tomentum.
Climatic range. H, M, Mts, and on cool, elevated sites in A and S.

HÈBE (formerly combined with *Veronica* as a section or subgenus)

Commemorating Hebe, the Goddess of Youth in Greek mythology.
Shrub Speedwell.
Scrophulariaceae, the Figwort family.

Generic description. A large genus of shrubs and small trees from the Southern Hemisphere, principally New Zealand, with simple, opposite, evergreen leaves, occasionally reduced to scale-like form, the terminal pair with or without a small opening at the base termed a 'leaf-bud sinus', the presence and shape of which assists in identification; flowers are broadly funnelform or salverform, with 4-merous parts, borne mainly in dense racemes in the upper axils, but rarely in terminal panicles, e.g. *H. hulkeana*; the two stamens are attached to the interior of the corolla which has a single exserted pistil; seeds are produced in soft-wooded capsules. Most species flower abundantly between late spring and autumn, with a few lasting into winter. They are popular in Australian gardens for their handsome flowers and foliage, long flowering season and neat growth habit.

Propagation. Soft-tip cuttings taken in early spring, or firmer wood taken between summer and winter, strike readily in a sand/peat mixture in a warm, humid environment, bottom-heat and mist being beneficial.

Cultivation. All the species listed here thrive in an open, sunny position and tolerate the salty winds of the seashore better than most other introduced species. They are best grown in a mild climate with only light frosts, but when well acclimatised are not seriously damaged by low temperatures to −5°C. Well-drained garden soils are generally suitable, but *H. albicans*, *H. cupressoides* and *H. hulkeana* enjoy a coarse sandy or gravelly soil with very free drainage.

Pruning. An annual light to moderate pruning to remove spent inflorescences and capsules is necessary to help keep the plants neat, with a dense, leafy habit.

Species and cultivars

Hèbe álbicans (Latin 'becoming white): South Island of NZ, on the lower levels of the mountains.

Habit. A small evergreen shrub about 1 m tall or often less, but spreading to a broad bun shape to 1.5 m, the lower branches decumbent.

Leaves. Oblong-obovate, 2–3 cm long and 1.8 cm wide; sessile; apex acute; base broadly obtuse to truncate or sub-cordate; margin entire; glabrous; terminal leaf-bud with little or no sinus; glaucous-grey.

Flowers. Inflorescence a dense raceme to about 3 cm long, in opposite pairs in the axils of the upper leaves; calyx tubulate, with 4 ovate, green lobes; corolla tubulate with 4 spreading lobes, white; stamens 2, the filaments white, anthers blackish-purple; flowering season from late November to March.

Fruit. A brownish ovoid capsule, ripening in late autumn.

Other distinguishing features. Upper twigs almost concealed by the overlapping leaves.

Climatic range. H, M, Mts, and on cool, elevated sites in A, P, and S.

Hèbe x andersonii (commemorating the raiser, Isaac Anderson-Henry, Scottish horticulturist): inter-specific hybrid between *H. salicifolia* and *H. speciosa*, both parents from NZ.

Habit. An evergreen shrub to 1.5 m tall and 1.5–2.0 m wide, with many erect and spreading stems from the base, forming a dense, leafy bush of hemispherical outline.

Leaves. Lanceolate-elliptic or oblanceolate, 7–10 cm long and 2.0–2.5 cm wide; petiole about 3 mm long, broadly splayed and slightly stem-clasping; apex acute; margin finely ciliate, almost entire, recurved; glabrous; thick and slightly leathery; leaf-bud sinus broadly elliptical to 2 mm long, ciliate within; leaves bright to mid green above, paler beneath.

Flowers. Inflorescence a cluster of up to 6 to 10 racemes in the upper axils; racemes 10–15 cm long and 2.5 cm wide; calyx to 3 mm, with 4 acute, green sepals; corolla tubulate-funnelform to 8 mm long, the 4-lobed limb spreading to 6 mm wide; aster-violet at first, fading to white, the mature raceme bi-coloured; stamens 2, the filaments violet, fading to white, anthers deep violet, aging to brown; style violet, persistent; flowers abundant in summer, then less so and smaller throughout autumn and early winter.

Fruit. Capsules flattened, green and lustrous at first, ripening to dark chocolate-brown, the persistent style exserted to 1 cm.

Other distinguishing features. Upper stems green, made somewhat oval in section by the internodal ridge below the leaf-bases.

'Andersonii Variegàta' is similar, but with leaves margined with creamy-white, the central green panel invaded with irregular, grey-green patches and streaks, the edges suffused with rosy-carmine, at least during cooler weather.

Climatic range. A, B, H, M, Mts, P, S.

Hèbe 'Autumn Glory': an English cultivar of uncertain origin, long established in Australian gardens.

Habit. A small, evergreen shrub to about 0.75 m tall, but usually slightly broader, the lower branches decumbent.

Leaves. Obovate to about 2 cm long and 1 cm wide; apex acute; tapered to the narrowly truncate base with little or no leaf-bud sinus; margin entire; venation obscure, except for the midrib and 2 laterals running parallel with the margin; glabrous; dark green above, slightly paler beneath; young leaves bright green, with a reddish-violet edge.

Flowers. Abundant in axillary racemes to 4 cm long, usually about 6 racemes together; flowers deep violet-purple, the tube paler to almost white, with stamens and style of similar colour; flowering season from early summer to late autumn.

Fruit. A papery-woody capsule about 3 mm long, nearly round, but local plants lacking in seeds.

Other distinguishing features. Upper stems terete, deep chocolate-purple, the lateral twigs slightly flattened.

Climatic range. A, B, M, P, S, T, and in warm, sheltered microclimates in H and Mts.

Hèbe 'Carnea' (Latin 'flesh pink'): a NZ plant of uncertain hybrid status.

Habit. An evergreen, leafy shrub to 1.0–1.5 m tall, with a loose, open habit, unless thickened by pruning, often 2 m wide, the lower branches decumbent.

Leaves. Linear-lanceolate to slightly oblanceolate and falcate, 8–9 cm long and 1.0–1.4 cm wide; apex acute; petiole 1–2 mm, partly stem-clasping; margin entire; midrib prominent beneath and slightly translucent; glabrous, dark shining green above, paler and duller beneath; terminal leaf-bud with a very short, narrow sinus.

Flowers. Inflorescence a showy raceme, 5–8 cm long and 2–3 cm wide, usually 4 together in opposite pairs from the upper axils; calyx 2 mm long, 4–lobed, green; corolla tubulate-funnelform to 7 mm long and as wide, rosy-purple, aging to white progressively, producing a distinctly bi-coloured raceme; stamens 2, the filaments white, with blackish-purple anthers, the single style deep rosy-purple; flowers abundant from early autumn to late winter.

Fruit. Capsules green at first, ripening to chocolate-brown, ovoid, to 3 mm long, the blackish style persisting.

Other distinguishing features. Upper twigs dark reddish-bronze, smooth and glabrous.

Hèbe 'Carnea Variegata' is slightly smaller in growth habit, otherwise resembling the parent, but has leaves with a broad, creamy-white edge, partly invading the normal green ground-colour

to produce an intermediate zone of greyish-cream.

Climatic range. A, B, M, P, S, T.

Hèbe cupressoìdes (Latin 'resembling *Cupressus*', referring to the closely-set, scale-like leaves): South Island of NZ, mainly on the foothills and lower slopes of the Alps.

Habit. An evergreen shrub to about 1.5 m tall, with many erect, finely divided, twiggy branchlets arising from the base, forming a broad, conical bush to 1 m wide.

Leaves. Scale-like, ovate-triangular, the base closely pressed and clasping the stem in a whip-like formation, the tip standing free, bearing a strong resemblance to *Cupressus* leaves; dark glaucous-green and handsome enough to warrant planting for its decorative foliage alone.

Flowers. In small clusters at the ends of the youngest twigs; corolla tubulate with 4 spreading lobes, pale violet-blue at first, but fading to nearly white when mature, flowering from early December to early autumn.

Fruit. A brownish capsule, ovoid to obovoid to 2 mm long, ripening in late summer and autumn.

Other distinguishing features. The plant is of somewhat temperamental character in the Sydney climate, occasionally dying without apparent cause; possibly sensitive to the often saturated, heavy loamy soils of the Cumberland plain.

Climatic range. A, B, M, P, S, preferably on well-drained, open sites.

Hèbe diosmifòlia (Latin 'with *Diosma*-like leaves'): frequently confused with and wrongly called *H. buxifolia*: North Island of NZ,

Habit. An evergreen shrub to 1–2 m tall and about as wide, bun-shaped, with a dense mass of twiggy growths.

Leaves. Opposite but mostly angled in a common upward direction; lanceolate to oblanceolate, 1.5–2.0 cm long and 4–5 mm wide; apex acute, to very shortly and abruptly acuminate; margin slightly translucent, with 3 to 5 incised serrations on each side; venation indistinct, apart from the cream, translucent midrib and 2 faint, almost-parallel, lateral veins; glabrous; leaf-bud sinus to 3 mm long, narrowly elliptical; dark green and shiny above, paler and duller beneath.

Flowers. Borne in an axillary (but apparently terminal), hemispherical corymbose cluster of

short-stemmed racemes, each about 2 cm long; calyx campanulate; corolla salverform-funnelform, 6–7 mm across, of 4 nearly equal, broadly ovate lobes, pale violet at first but soon fading to white; filaments white, anthers pale violet; flowers borne abundantly over the crown of the plant from late August to summer.
Fruit. An ovoid capsule, green and fleshy at first, ripening to mid brown.
Climatic range. A, B, H, M, Mts, P, S.

Hèbe x *franciscàna* (Latin 'from San Francisco', the locality of the plant first validly named): interspecific hybrid between *H. elliptica* and *H. speciosa* (syn. *H. decussata, H. lobelioides*).
'Blue Gem': an old cultivar from Great Britain, long established and much planted in Australian gardens.
Habit. An evergreen shrub to 1.0–1.5 m tall, with a dense mass of branches from the base, forming a broad bun-shaped bush as wide, to twice as wide, as its height.
Leaves. Opposite in neat decussate rows, spreading at a wide angle with the stem, narrowly elliptical to oblanceolate or obovate, 2.5–3.5 cm long and 1.5–2.0 cm wide, apex acute to obtuse, base rounded; margin entire; midrib yellowish, translucent; glabrous except for a little pubescence on the main nerve, and somewhat fleshy; terminal-bud of young leaves with an oval sinus 3 mm long; dark green and shiny above, paler and dull beneath.
Flowers. In a dense raceme 2.5–4.5 cm long and 2.0–2.5 cm across, on a stout green peduncle; calyx campanulate to 3 mm long, with 4 green acute sepals; corolla broad-funnelform, 8–9 mm long and 1.0–1.3 cm across the spreading lobes; violet, but nearly white in the throat, the colour deepening to dark violet in the winter; filaments violet, anthers darker; style reddish-violet; flowers abundant over the crown of the plant from November to late March, then sparsely throughout autumn to early winter.
Fruit. A capsule to 5 mm long but seeds apparently abortive.
Other distinguishing features. Upper twigs with decussately-opposite, internodal stripes of fine puberulent down; twigs terete and otherwise smooth and green, aging to dark purplish-brown and woody. One of the best seaside shrubs, with pronounced tolerance of salty winds.
'Variegàta' is similar but has leaves with a broad, irregular, creamy-yellow margin, and

intermediate areas of pale grey-green.
Climatic range. A, B, M, P, S, T, and in warm, sheltered microclimates in H and Mts.

Hèbe hulkeàna (commemorating T. H. Hulke, New Zealand botanical collector): New Zealand Lilac: north-eastern coastal districts of South Island of NZ, sometimes exposed to harsh sea winds.
Habit. An evergreen shrub to 1 m tall, with many erect stems from the base, forming an open-framed bush to 1 m wide, made denser and more prolific in flower if pruned annually.
Leaves. Broadly elliptic-ovate or sub-orbicular, 2–5 cm long and 1.5–3.0 cm wide; petiole 5–8 mm long; apex obtuse; base broadly cuneate to rounded; margin bluntly serrate, the points glandular; glabrous; lustrous dark green, with a distinctly red edge, paler beneath.
Flowers. In a terminal panicle 25–50 cm tall; calyx campanulate, the green sepals slightly pubescent; corolla salverform-funnelform to 1 cm across, with 4 spreading, ovate to obovate, pale lilac or lavender-blue petals; stamens 2; pistil 1, exserted; flowers appear from early October, and persist until late November.
Fruit. A soft-wooded, brown capsule, splitting at the apex when ripe in late summer.
Other distinguishing features. Upper twigs reddish, slender, becoming grey and more or less leafless in the second year.
Climatic range. A, H, M, Mts, P, and on dry or well-drained sites in B and S.

Hèbe 'Inspiration': interspecific hybrid between *H. diosmifolia* and *H. speciosa*, from NZ.
Habit. An evergreen shrub to 1 m or less tall, but spreading to a compact bun-shaped bush to 1.5 m wide.
Leaves. Oblanceolate to narrowly obovate to 2.5–3.0 cm long and 1 cm wide, on dark plum-red twigs; apex obtuse; margin entire but sparsely and shallowly serrulate towards the apex, as in the parent, *H. diosmifolia*; venation obscure, apart from the purplish-red puberulent midrib; upper surface somewhat pebbly, but dark lustrous green, paler and smoother beneath, the extreme edge purplish-red; terminal bud with an ovate sinus of 2 mm at the base.
Flowers. In a 4–5 cm long racemose cluster, on a purplish-red peduncle from the upper axils, the individual, broad-funnelform flowers large and densely arranged, violet-purple at first, fading to pale lilac and eventually nearly white,

giving a distincly bi-coloured effect; stamens long exserted, the filaments deep lilac, aging to white, anthers deep purple; flowering season late spring and summer, with a few occasional flowers at other times.

Fruit. A soft-wooded capsule to 5–6 mm long, but fertility of seeds not tested.

Other distinguishing features. Upper twigs with decussately-opposite, internodal stripes of fine pubescence.

Climatic range. A, B, M, P, S, T.

Hèbe parviflòra (Latin 'with small flowers'): Love-bush: NZ, in both North and South Islands.

Habit. An evergreen shrub to 2–3 m tall with a short main trunk carrying the abundant foliage on a broadly rounded crown.

Leaves. Linear to 3–4 cm long and 4–5 mm wide; apex finely acute to acuminate; margin entire; venation indistinct except for the yellowish translucent midrib; glabrous but only barely shiny; leaf-buds with little or no sinus; bright green above, only slightly paler beneath.

Flowers. Inflorescence an erect raceme to 5–8 cm long and 1.5 cm across, borne in pairs in the upper axils, carrying up to 80–100 flowers, on 2–3 mm pedicels; calyx to 2 mm long, green; corolla funnelform to campanulate, 4–lobed, white or faintly tinged with lilac; filaments white, anthers lilac at first, becoming blackish-violet; flowering season from November to March, and intermittent at other times.

Fruit. Small, dark brown capsules follow the flowers, ripening in late summer and autumn, the styles persisting.

Other distinguishing features. Youngest twigs yellowish-green, becoming brown, the stems encircled by the clearly defined, but shallow nodal ridges.

Climatic range. A. B. M, P, S, T.

Hèbe speciòsa (Latin 'showy'): NZ, in both North and South Islands.

Habit. An evergreen shrub to 1 m or so tall, maturing to 1.5 m wide in a broad, bun-shaped bush with many erect stems from the base.

Leaves. Narrowly obovate, 7–8 cm long and 3 cm broad; petiole 2–3 mm long, flattened and pubescent above; apex obtuse; base broadly cuneate; margin entire; midrib prominent beneath; glabrous; leaf-bud sinus broadly elliptical, ciliate within; shining dark green above, paler beneath.

Flowers. Inflorescence an axillary raceme about 7 cm long and 3 cm broad, the numerous flowers on slender 3–4 mm pedicels; calyx narrowly campanulate to 3 mm long, with 4 boat-shaped sepals; corolla tubulate to 7–8 mm long, expanding at the limb to 5–6 mm across the 4 lobes; reddish-purple, paler at the base and edges; stamens to 1 cm long, the filaments purplish with darker anthers; style pale reddish-purplish, to 1.5 cm long; flowering season November to late autumn.

Fruit. A compressed, ovoid capsule to 7–8 mm long, green and fleshy at first, ripening and drying to mid brown, with the style persisting.

Other distinguishing features. Upper twigs somewhat square, ridged below the leaves, swollen at the nodes, green and glabrous.

'**Imperialis**' appears to be a trade name of no validity, the plant so represented being identical with the species.

'**La Seduisante**' resembles the parent in most respects but has purplish-red leaves while young, retaining the red midrib to maturity, then dark green and glossy above, paler beneath; the flowers are bright violet-purple in colour of corolla, filaments and anthers; twigs are purplish-red at first, becoming olive-green.

'**Variegàta**' resembles the parent species but the leaves have a broad margin of creamy-white, a large intermediate area of grey-green, the deep green of the species being confined to the middle; young leaves are often stained with rosy-carmine, especially in winter.

Climatic range. A, B, M, P, S, T, and in warm, sheltered microclimates on the lower elevations of Mts.

HELIOTRÒPIUM

Derived from the Greek, *helios* and *tropos*, referring to a similarity to certain plants whose flowers turn with the sun.

Heliotrope or Cherry-pie.

Boraginaceae, the Borage family.

Generic description. A large genus mainly from Central and temperate South America, the species treated here popularly used in Australian warm-climate gardens for its attractive foliage and perfumed flowers.

Propagation. Soft-tip cuttings taken in spring and summer, or semi-hardwood tips taken in autumn and winter, strike well in a warm, humid atmosphere.

Cultivation. A well-drained, fertile soil with adequate summer water, and protection from cold are the main requirements. The species is at its best in the warmer part of the garden, used either as a foreground low shrub or lattice-supported wall specimen.

Pruning. Moderate pruning of the old shoots is desirable in early spring to develop new flowering shoots.

Species and cultivars

Heliotròpium arborescens (Latin *arbor*, 'a tree', referring to the woody lower stems of the species as distinct from those of the soft-wooded annuals) (syn. *H. peruvianum*) Common Heliotrope: tropical parts of Peru.

Habit. An evergreen shrub to less than 1 m tall but often 1.5 m wide, the lower stems decumbent, but with upright flowering twigs.

Leaves. Simple, alternate, oval or elliptic, 6–8 cm long and 3–4cm wide; apex acute or shortly acuminate; base acute; margin entire, ciliate; midrib and about 8 pairs of laterals prominent; pubescent on both surfaces; see cultivar details for colours.

Flowers. Inflorescence a terminal cyme 5–10 cm across; flowers numerous; calyx 2–3 mm long, with 5 acute, pubescent lobes; corolla funnelform to salverform, 5–7 mm long and 5 mm wide at the 5-lobed, flared limb; sweetly perfumed; flowers abundant, in the violet to mauve colour range, from early spring to late summer.

'**Aùreum**' has showy golden-yellow foliage, especially bright when grown in a sunny place, and lavender-blue flowers.

'**Lord Roberts**' has dark-green leaves, heavily shaded greenish-purple, and deep violet-blue flowers.

'**President Garfield**' has mid green leaves and mauve-blue flowers.

Climatic range. All B, P, S, T.

HETEROCÉNTRON (syn. *Heeria*)

Derived from the Greek, referring to the dissimilar anthers.
Pink Heterocentron or Heeria.
Melastomataceae, the Melastoma family.

Generic description. A small genus of tender, evergreen shrubs and perennials from tropical America, one grown in local gardens for its showy flowers and foliage. See specific notes below for details.

Propagation. Nodal cuttings taken from the young succulent shoots during the growing period, or firmer wood during the autumn-winter months, strike readily in a coarse sandy material in a warm, humid atmosphere.

Cultivation. A warm, sheltered site, free from cold or violent winds, is essential, preferably in a mild, frost-free climate. Any moderately fertile soil with good drainage is suitable.

Pruning. The plant should be induced to produce new watershoot growth by complete removal of some of the oldest stems at the base each year, ideally in early spring.

Heterocéntron macrostáchyum (Greek 'with large spikes' (syn. *H. roseum*) Mexico.

Habit. An evergreen shrub to 1 m or less, with many soft-wooded, erect stems arising from the crowded base.

Leaves. Simple, opposite, narrowly elliptical, 4–8 cm long and 2–4 cm wide; apex acute; margin ciliate-bristly; venation reticulate, the midrib and main laterals deeply impressed above, prominently raised beneath; strigose on both surfaces; bright green and shiny above, paler beneath, changing to dull reddish-brown in autumn and winter.

Flowers. In terminal panicles, 10–15 cm tall, on red, square, strigose stems; rachis, peduncles and 5 mm long pedicels bright red; calyx urceolate to 5 mm long, tuberculate, with 4 spreading sepals, bright cardinal-red; corolla rotate to 1.5 cm across, of 4 obovate petals, pale cyclamen-purple; stamens in 2 series, each of 4, long-exserted beyond the petals; flowering season autumn and winter.

Fruit. A small urceolate capsule, with numerous fine seeds.

Other distinguishing features. Stems conspicuously square, reddish, strigose at least while young.

'**Album**' has white flowers but is otherwise similar to the parent.

Climatic range. B, P, S, T, and in warm, frost-free microclimates in A and M.

HIBBÉRTIA

After George Hibbert, British plant collector.
Guinea-flower.
Dilleniaceae, the Dillenia family.

Generic description. A large, mostly Australian genus of about 100 species, several used in native gardens for their attractive yellow flowers, the plants described below considered to be the best of the genus. Leaves are simple, alternate, some entire but others with deeply broken margins; flowers are rotate, with 5 broad-spreading petals of short duration; seeds are borne in a globose follicle.

Propagation. Soft-tip cuttings are taken in late spring, and planted in a sand/peat mixture in a warm, humid atmosphere.

Cultivation. A free-draining, coarse sandy soil with leaf-mould or peat added is suitable, preferably in a sun-exposed position in a mild climate.

Pruning. A moderate shortening of the flowered shoots immediately after the last flowers helps to develop and maintain a compact leafy habit.

Species and cultivars

Hibbértia astrótricha (derived from the Greek, referring to the stellate pubescence) (syn. *H. empetrifòlia*) Trailing Guinea-flower; Eastern Australia, mostly on well-drained sandy or gravelly soils in open forest.

Habit. A low scrambling shrub to 30–60 cm tall, spreading to 1 m or more; compact and leafy in cultivation.

Leaves. Lanceolate-oblong, 5–8 mm long, 2–4 mm wide; apex obtuse, mucronate; base rounded; margin entire, recurved; tuberculate, stellate-pubescent and bright green above, paler beneath.

Flowers. Solitary on 2–3 cm pedicels in the outer axils; calyx of 5 reddish-green sepals to 3 mm long; petals 5, bilobed-obovate, forming a rotate flower about 1.5 cm across, deep yellow; stamens about 10, with conspicuous, oblong, yellow anthers; flowering in late September and October.

Fruit. Not seen.

Other distinguishing features. Upper twigs dark red-tan.

Climatic range. A, B, H, M, P, S and on lower levels of Mts.

Hibbértia bracteàta (Latin 'bearing bracts'): Stiff Guinea-flower: Central NSW, mostly on gravelly ridges, between the coast and lower tablelands.

Habit. A small evergreen shrub, 0.5–1.0 m tall, normally sparse but responding to pruning and cultivation to become dense and abundant in flower.

Leaves. Linear-oblong, 1–2 cm long and 3–5 mm wide; apex acute; base cuneate; margin entire, recurved; midrib prominent beneath; slightly scabrous, but shiny and dark green above, paler and tomentulose beneath.

Flowers. Terminal or axillary, 1 to about 6 together, each flower borne in a rosette of hairy involucral scales; calyx to 1 cm long, densely silky-hirsute outside, mid brown; petals 5, broad-ovate, emarginate, spreading to form a rotate flower 2.0–2.5 cm across, clear yellow; stamens mostly 16, eccentric with large linear anthers to 3 mm long, yellow; flowering season from September to early November.

Fruit. Carpels normally 5, globose, dehiscing at the apex to release the several seeds in each.

Other distinguishing features. Youngest twigs mid brown, tomentulose, older shoots with darker chocolate-brown shredding bark.

Climatic range. A, B, M, P, S, and on sheltered microclimates on the lower Mts.

Hibbértia obtusifòlia (Latin 'with blunt leaves'): Grey Guinea-flower: SE Australia, in coastal heathlands and open forests of the lower tablelands.

Habit. A shrub to 50–75 cm tall, spreading to 1 m or so, with almost prostrate main branches and many erect slender, stellate-hairy branchlets bearing the leaves and flowers.

Leaves. Oblanceolate, 2–4 cm long and 1 cm wide; apex rounded or obtuse; base tapered narrowly; margin entire; grey-green and minutely pubescent.

Flowers. Solitary in the upper axils from stout, ovoid buds, with 5 red-tipped, ovate sepals; corolla rotate, 2.5–3.0 cm wide, with 5 broad, obcordate petals, clear yellow; stamens about 30, prominent; flowering from late winter to early summer.

Fruit. A 3-celled follicle.

Climatic range. A, B, H, M, P, S and on lower Mts.

PLATE 17

▲ Hibiscus 'Madonna'

▲ Hibiscus 'Surfrider'

▲ Hibiscus 'Mary Wallace'

▲ Hibiscus 'Freddie Brubaker'
▼ Hibiscus syriacus 'Hino-maru'

▲ Hibiscus syriacus 'Ardens'
▼ Hibiscus mutabilis

▲ Hibiscus 'Boondah'
▼ Hibiscus 'Norman Stevens'

Photo by Les Beers

PLATE 18

▲ Leptospermum nitidum

▲ Isopogon anethifolius

▲ Lambertia formosa

▲ Hypocalymma angustifolium

▼ Leptospermum squarrosum

▲ Kerria japonica 'Plena'
◀ Kunzea capitata
▼ Prostanthera rotundifolia

Hibbértia serícea (Latin 'silky'): Silky Guinea-flower: SE Australia, on coastal sandy heath-lands and stony hillsides of the lower tablelands.
Habit. A shrub to 50–75 cm tall, with a mass of silky-hairy twigs forming a dense bush to about 1 m broad.
Leaves. Crowded, linear to narrow-oblong, 1–2 cm long and 4–5 mm wide; apex and base obtuse; margin entire; stellate-hairy and silky; grey-green.
Flowers. Solitary or in small clusters at the terminals of the leafy upper twigs; rotate to 2 cm wide, the 5 spreading obovate petals deeply-notched at the apex; yellow, softly villous; stamens about 15, eccentric, conspicuous, yellow; flowering from spring to mid-summer.
Fruit. Not seen.
Climatic range. A, B, H, M, P, S and on lower Mts.

HIBÍSCUS

An ancient Greek name for one of the species. Hibiscus (various), Confederate Rose, Shrub Althea, etc.
Malvaceae, the Mallow family.

Generic description. A large and varied genus comprising evergreen and deciduous trees, shrubs, and herbaceous perennials and annuals, widely dispersed through the warm climates, but with a few deciduous species from temperate zones, mostly with palmately-lobed or -veined leaves, a showy corolla of funnelform or campanulate shape with stamens united into a handsome column, the calyx gamosepalous with 5 lobes, supported by an involucre of slender bracteoles.

Propagation. *H. mutabilis, H. syriacus.* Hardwood cuttings to about 10 cm long, taken in the June-August period strike readily in a sand/peat mixture in individual containers in a warm glass-house.
H. rosa-sinensis, H. schizopetalus. Soft-tip or semi-hardwood cutings, 5–6 cm long taken in summer to autumn; or hardwood cuttings, 8–10 cm long, taken in September from the prunings, are also used; planted in a sand/peat mixture as above.
The tender Hawaiian cultivars may be top-cleft grafted on hardy, vigorous understocks such as 'Rose Scott', 'Wilder's White', 'Apple Blossom', 'Dawn' or 'Agnes Galt'. Plants so worked develop more rapidly, with strong growth and have greater resistance to collar-rot, especially when planted on cold, wet soils. Understock cuttings, 18–20 cm long, are planted in individual containers in summer or early autumn and struck in the ordinary way, then brought into a heated glass-house in early September to fully activate their cambium cells. Outdoor-grown dormant scions, 5–10 cm long, of the Hawaiian cultivars are partly defoliated and worked on the understocks in late September and October.

Cultivation. *H. mutabilis, H. rosa-sinensis, H. schizopetalus.* These species are suitable only for mild climates, in a sunny, wind-protected locality, although a few cultivars show greater resistance to cold, surviving the Melbourne climate without serious injury from frost. They are best grown in a fertile, well-drained soil with plenty of summer water. They rarely thrive in the raw sands of the coastal areas but respond readily to improved soils and attention.

H. syriacus. This is the hardiest species treated here, tolerating the cold of the tablelands to −10°C without injury, but like the others, is best grown in good, well-drained soil in full sun.

All species are heavy feeders and need to be supplied at frequent, regular periods, especially in spring and summer, with a generous ration of balanced plant food, supplemented with adequate water.

Pruning. *H. mutabilis.* An annual pruning removes the spent inflorescences and unsightly fruiting capsules. The naturally globose shape should be maintained but all branches reduced in length by half or more of the annual growth, cutting always to healthy buds, in late winter or early spring, just before the onset of new growth.

H. rosa-sinensis. Most cultivars benefit from an annual pruning to establish and maintain a dense growth habit for the development of better flowers and foliage. The cultivars need almost individual attention, some requiring only light pruning, while others are treated more severely. The pruning is confined mainly to the 1-year-old growth, cutting to a healthy bud in the desired direction, preferably in late September when all risk of frost is over. As the new shoots sprout strongly in October and November, they should be tip-pruned once or twice to encourage lateral growth with more abundant flowers.

H. schizopetalus. As above but with light pruning only.

H. syriacus. This species should be pruned fairly severely, to about two-thirds the annual growth in the first 2 or 3 years to establish a dense bush, but thenceforth, only light pruning, of about a quarter of the annual growth, is necessary to maintain the quality of flowers and foliage.

Species and cultivars

Hibíscus mutábilis (Latin *mutare* 'to change', referring to the changeable colour of the flowers): Confederate Rose: SE China.

Habit. An almost deciduous shrub, sometimes tree-like but mostly of hemispherical shape to 3–4 m, with many straight stems arising from the base, densely leafed and attractive in foliage and flowers.

Leaves. Simple, alternate, broad-ovate, palmately-lobed, 12–15 cm long and 15–18 cm across; petiole about as long as the blade; apices of the lobes long-acute; base deeply cordate; margin coarsely dentate; venation palmately reticulate, the prominent main veins pubescent; mid green above, paler beneath, both surfaces finely tomentose.

Flowers. Solitary in the upper axils, on 13–15 cm long pedicels, the 9–11 bracteoles linear, green; the 5-cleft calyx at first forming a ribbed, ovoid bud, the sepals expanding to 2.5 cm, pale green and tomentose; petals 5, obovate, mostly white with pale pink shading on the right margin, the colour changing to red as the flower ages, the whole to 15 cm across; staminal column to 2 cm tall, ending in the 5–pronged style; flowering season March to May.

Fruit. A globose capsule about 3 cm across, with 5 segments each supporting the many 2 mm, hairy, dark-brown seeds, ripening in summer unless removed in the spring pruning.

Other distinguishing features. Upper stems tomentose, green, becoming brown-grey, heavily marked with pale-brown lenticels; leaf-scars cordate, 4 mm across.

'Plènus' has double flowers, hemispherical in shape to 9–10 cm across with many petals, all except the outer ring twisted and curled to form a flower somewhat like a paeony, the petals heavily veined; white at first, with the outer 5 petals stained red, but changing to pink, then rosy-red as the day advances, white, red, and all intermediate stages being present at once.

Climatic range. A, B, M, P, S, T.

Hibíscus ròsa-sinénsis (Latin 'Rose of China'): Chinese Hibiscus: South-East Asia, mainly southern China and Vietnam but now naturalised in many tropical Pacific islands.

Habit. An evergreen shrub, or small tree when so trained, 2.0–3.5 m tall, mostly subject to regular pruning which modifies its natural shape; the many cultivars have individual growth habits, some dwarf to less than 1.5 m, others exceeding 3 m when well grown.

Leaves. Simple, alternate, variable in shape, but mainly ovate, the blade 8–15 cm long and 6–12 cm across; petiole 2.5–5.0 cm long; apex acute to slightly acuminate; base obtuse, truncate or sub-cordate; margin crenate to dentate, the teeth large; venation reticulate, the midrib and main laterals prominent and thinly stellate-pubescent; otherwise mostly glabrous, but some cultivars slightly pubescent; shining dark green above, paler and dull beneath.

Flowers. Solitary in the leaf-axils of the young, current year's growth, on 5 to 8 cm long pedicels, subtended at the base by a pair of subulate stipules to 1.5 cm long; calyx 2–3 cm long, the 5 lanceolate sepals joined at the middle, with an involucre of 6 to 8 linear bracteoles about as long as the calyx; corolla campanulate-funnelform, of 5 broadly obovate petals opening widely at the mouth to 10–12 cm across, or as much as 20 cm across in the modern Hawaiian cultivars; originally small, single and crimson-red, but through hybridisation with other closely related species, now available in almost every variation of the main colours of red, pink, orange, yellow, and white; staminal column 6–10 cm long, usually spirally twisted, the numerous stamens branching upward from the top half, the 5-pronged style with velvety stigma-pads emerging from the apex, all parts variously coloured, often making a showy contrast with the corolla; most flowers last for one day only, closing at night and soon falling, but many of the newer sorts are 2–day flowered; flowers borne from early December to winter, terminating earlier in frosty places, lasting throughout winter in milder climates. Some cultivars have double flowers with several corollas and an inner series of narrower petals, the staminal column petaloid and often grotesquely distorted.

The various Hibiscus societies have classified the cultivars into floral shape and colour groups with appropriate and self-explanatory names such as Fully Double, Semi-double, Overlapped

Single, Windmill Single, Recurved Single, Rosette Double, Cup and Saucer Double, Miniature and Tricolour.

Growth habit is classified as:
Low or dwarf — less than 1.5m tall
Average or medium — 2–3 m tall
Tall or very tall — above 3 m tall

Flower size is classified as:
Small — flowers measuring 10–15 cm across
Medium — flowers measuring 15–20 cm across
Large — flowers measuring 20–26 cm across
Nursery catalogues should be consulted for descriptions of the many hundreds of cultivars available in eastern Australia.

One of Australia's leading hibiscus growers, Les Beers, of Hibiscus Park Nursery Pty Ltd, Warriewood, NSW, was invited to nominate his best selection for inclusion here. To satisfy a wide range of preferences for size of plant, floral shape and colour, his selection is as follows:

Cultivar name	Height	Details of flowers
'Agnes Galt'	tall	Medium, single, rose-pink with deeper centre
'Apple Blossom'	v. tall	Medium, singe, pale pink with red centre
'Big Tango'	low	Large, single, tomato red with white centre
'Boondah'	average	Medium, single, bright rose-pink
'Brucei'	average	Medium, single, golden yellow with cream centre
'Camdenii' (syn. 'Sinensis')	average	Small, single, bright scarlet
'Cameo Queen'	low	Large, single, lemon-yellow with pink centre
'Catavki'	average	Large, single, velvety claret red
'Celia'	average	Medium, single, pastel apricot with pink centre
'Crown of Bohemia'	low	Medium, double, golden yellow to orange
'Crown of Warringah'	low	Medium, double, soft pastel apricot
'Dawn'	tall	Medium, single, flesh pink with red centre
'Delight'	average	Small, single, bright lemon yellow
'D.J. O'Brien'	average	Medium, double, apricot-orange with carmine centre
'Edith Parsons'	low	Medium, double, chrome yellow with red centre
'El Capitolio'	average	Small, semi-double, unusual form, bright scarlet
'El Capitolio Sport'	average	Small, semi-double, unusual form, soft apricot with red centre
'Elegans' (syn. 'Aloha')	low	Medium, single, cerise-pink with lemon edge
'Fire Engine'	low	Large, single, brilliant scarlet
'Florida Sunset'	low	Small, single, orange-red with yellow edge
'Freddie Brubaker'**	average	Large, single, rich gold with red eye
'Full Moon'**	average	Medium, double, lemon yellow with white centre, perfumed
'General Corteges'	average	Medium, single, bright scarlet
'Golden Belle'**	low	Large, single, bright golden-yellow
'Isobel Beard'	low	Medium, double, soft lavender with red centre
'Johnsonii'	low	Medium, single, apricot gold with red centre
'Kinchen's Yellow'	average	Large, single, lemon yellow with white centre
'Island Empress'	average	Medium, double, cerise-red with claret centre
'Lady Cilento'**	average	Large, single, bright orange with yellow streaks and splashes
'Lambertii'	low	Medium, double, rich scarlet
'Madonna'	low	Large, single, white with deep cerise centre
'Marjorie Coral'	low	Large, single, rose-pink with red eye
'Mary Wallace'	average	Large, single, orange-red with gold edge
'Mini Skirt'**	low	Medium, single, cerise-red with white spots and splashes
'Mollie Cummings'	average	Medium, single, rich velvety-red

Cultivar name	Height	Details of flowers
'Mrs George Davis'	tall	Medium, double rich rose-pink
'Nathan Charles'**	low	Medium, single, velvety-cerise with paler edge
'Norma'	average	Medium, single, rich gold with red centre
'Norman Stevens'	low	Medium, single, bright apricot with large white centre
'Peachblow'	average	Medium, double, soft rose with carmine centre
'Ross Estey'**	average	Medium, single, apricot-pink to orange-rose
'Ruth Wilcox' (syn. *'Albo laciniatus'*)	tall	Small, single, satin-pink
'Sabrina'	tall	Medium, double, rich cerise-red
'Scarlet Giant'	average	Large, single, vivid scarlet
'Surfrider'	low	Large, single, golden-orange with red centre
'The Path'**	average	Large, single, orange with gold edge and lemon splashes
'Thelma Bennell'	average	Medium, single, glowing cerise red
'Vasco'	low	Medium, single, bright lemon with white centre
'White Kalakaua'	average	Medium, double, creamy-white with light pink blush
'Wilder's White'** (syn. *H. arnottianus*)	v. tall	Medium, single, pure white with red style; perfumed.

** = 2-day flowers

Climatic range. B, T, and in warm, sheltered microclimates in P and S, with a few of the older, more hardy cultivars suitable for the warmer parts of A and M.

Hibíscus schizopétalus (Latin 'having split petals'): Kenya, Tanzania and Malagasy.
Habit. An evergreen shrub to 2–3 m tall, with growth habit resembling that of *H. rosa-sinensis*, but usually more open, with drooping branchlets and smaller leaves.
Leaves. Simple, alternate, ovate-elliptical to 5–6 cm long, the petioles to 2.5 cm; apex acute-acuminate; base cuneate to obtuse; margin serrate, less so near the base, venation indistinct apart from the midrib and the few main laterals; glabrous; shining dark green above, paler and dull beneath.
Flowers. Solitary in the leaf-axils of the new shoots, on slender pedicels to 10–15 cm long; calyx tubulate, 1.5–2.5 cm long, the 5–8 bracteoles subulate and very short to 2 mm; petals strongly recurved, about 3–5 cm long, finely segmented into many linear-lanceolate lobes; scarlet to crimson, with pinkish streaks; staminal column pinkish-red, very slender, to 10 cm long, drooping, the red stamens on the outer third, the style with 5 velvety pads; flowering season from early December to late autumn.
Fruit. A woody capsule to 3 cm long, cylindroidal with 5 segments, ripening in autumn to release the smooth ovoid-reniform seeds.
Climatic range. A, B, M, P, S, T.

Hibíscus syriàcus (Latin 'of Syria'): the species is not indigenous to Syria, but, like many others, was introduced from the Far East via the ancient route of the early silk traders, to become closely identified with its adopted country and named accordingly by Linnaeus: Shrub Althea: eastern Asia, from India to the Orient.
Habit. A hardy, deciduous shrub to 2.5–3.5 m, mostly of erect growth with many ascending stems forming a narrow-domed leafy bush, but occasionally grown as a small tree on a single short trunk.
Leaves. Simple, alternate, rhombic-ovate to 8–10 cm long, often with 3 conspicuous lobes; petiole to 1.5 cm; apex acute to acuminate; base cuneate; margin lobes, coarsely serrated; 3 main veins prominent, converging at the base; dark green and dull above, paler beneath; glabrous on both surfaces except for a few remote stellate hairs on the veins of the lower side.
Flowers. Solitary in the axils of the current year's growth; unopened buds ovoid-globose to 2 cm long; bracteoles 6 or 7, acicular to 1.5 cm long, green, sparsely stellate, calyx campanulate-funnelform, 1.8–2.0 cm long with mostly 5 irregular, triangular sepals, green; corolla funnelform, with 5 broad obovate petals 6–7 cm

long, mostly overlapping each other, with prominent veins converging at the base; flowers 9–10 cm across when mature, in white, pink, red, magenta, violet, and blue, mostly with a contrasting-coloured centre of red, crimson, or maroon; staminal column erect to 5 cm tall, with numerous cream or yellow stamens below the 5-pronged white, cream, or yellow style; flowering from December to April.

Fruit. A dry, ovoid capsule, splitting vertically into 5 valves to release the kidney-shaped seeds in late autumn and winter.

Other distinguishing features. Upper twigs grey-green, with pale-brown lenticels.

Hibiscus syriacus cultivars The following cultivars represent a good sampling of the colours and forms available in nurseries:

'Admiral Dewey': double, pure white.

'Ardens': s/d, rosy violet with maroon centre.

'Blue Bird': single, violet-blue, streaked maroon in the centre, with cream-yellow stamens.

'Boule de Feu': double, bright purplish-red.

'Carnation Boy': double, lavender fading to silvery-grey.

'Coelestis': single, violet-blue, with maroon centre and cream-yellow stamens.

'Diana': single to 12 cm, pure white with some petaloids.

'Duc de Brabant': double, deep reddish-violet.

'Flying Flag': s/d, white with carmine centre radiating through the petals.

'Hamabo': single, pale pink, with streaked carmine centre.

'Hino Maru': single to 12 cm, white with red centre.

'Lady Stanley': s/d, pale blush pink, with maroon centre.

'Monstrosus': single, white with purplish-maroon centre.

'Rosalinda': double, rich wine-red with carmine centre.

'Totus Albus: (syn. **'Snowdrift'**) single, pure white.

'White Supreme': double, creamy-white with deep maroon centre radiating through the petals.

'Woodbridge': single to 12 cm, light rosy-red, with carmine centre.

'W.R. Smith': single, pure white, with pale yellow centre.

Climatic range. All A, H, M, Mts, P, S.

HOLMSKÌOLDIA

Commemorating Theodor Holmskiold (born Theodor Holm, 1731), Professor of Medicine and Natural History at the University of Soro, Denmark.
Chinese Hat Plant; Cup and Saucer Plant.
Verbenaceae, the Verbena family.

Generic description. A small genus of evergreen shrubs from India, Africa and South-East Asia, one grown in warm climates for its curious flowers. Leaves are simple, opposite, and evergreen except in marginal climates, the flowers with tubulate corolla and expanded, saucer-shaped calyx. The plant is of adaptable habit, suitable for a specimen or for training on a warm wall.

Propagation. Soft-tip cuttings taken in spring or summer strike readily in a sand/peat mixture in a warm, humid environment; firm-tip, leafless cuttings taken in winter are also successful.

Cultivation. The ideal is a warm, sunny position with protection from cold wind, in a coastal climate with only light or no frosts; vigorous growth is made on fertile soils but plants often flower better on poorer soils. In either case, free drainage is essential.

Pruning. When used as a wall plant, only the spent flowering shoots are pruned lightly; otherwise, several of the oldest basal shoots should be removed completely each year to make way for new water-shoots.

Species and cultivars

Holmskioldia sanguínea (Latin *sanguis*, 'blood', referring to the colour of the flowers): Chinese Hat Plant: India and Nepal, on the lower mountain slopes.
Habit. An erect, evergreen, open-branched shrub to 3.5 m tall, with many long stems from the base, arching gracefully outwards at the ends.
Leaves. Ovate, to 10 cm long and 5 cm wide; petiole 1.5–2.5 cm long; apex acute; base cuneate to truncate; margin coarsely crenate; venation reticulate; dark green above, paler beneath.
Flowers. Inflorescence a terminal raceme, many together at the ends of the upper branches; calyx shallow-crateriform 2.5 cm across, bright brick-red; corolla tubulate to 2.5 cm long, curved, clavate at first, but opening and reflexing at the

apex to expose the 4 stamens, scarlet-red; flowering abundantly from April to late May, extending into winter in warm localities and occasionally into early spring.

Fruit. An obovoid drupe to 1 cm long, 4–lobed, but rarely seen.

Other distinguishing features. Stems squarish, grooved on the 4 sides, green, with brown lenticels.

Climatic range. B, P, S, T, and in warm, sheltered microclimates in A and M.

HÒVEA

Commemorating Anthony P. Hove, Polish botanical collector.
Purple Pea Bush; Holly-leafed Hovea; Common Hovea.
Fabaceae, the Pea family.

Generic description. A small genus of Australian native plants, with about 12 species well dispersed over the continent, all shrubby and evergreen, with alternate, simple leaves, and blue or violet pea-shaped flowers freely produced in late winter and spring, the species described below all colourful and worthy representatives of the genus.

Propagation. Seeds collected as soon as ripe and treated in warm water for 24 hours to soften the hard seed-coat, germinate readily if sown in a warm, moist atmosphere.

Cultivation. Normally found in the shelter of other plants at the edge of the coastal wet sclerophyll forest-land, *H. acutifolia* responds well to a wind protected site in part shade, in a fertile, loamy soil well supplied with water in dry times; suited best to warm localities with little frost. The Western Australian species prefer sandy or granitic soils with free drainage.

Pruning. The flowered twigs should be pruned moderately immediately after the main flowering season to induce a dense, twiggy growth.

Species and cultivars

Hòvea acutifòlia (Latin 'with acute apex'): Purple Pea Bush: southern Qld and northern NSW, between the coast and the tablelands.

Habit. An evergreen, erect shrub to about 2 m, somewhat loose and open in character in its native habitat, but responding to garden cultivation and annual pruning with a more densely leafed habit.

Leaves. Lanceolate, 6–8 cm long and 1.0–1.5 cm wide, the petiole to 5–6 mm long; apex acute to acuminate; base obtuse to cuneate; margin entire but recurved; midrib prominent beneath; glabrous and glossy dark green above, but densely rufous-tomentose beneath, extending to the petiole.

Flowers. Inflorescence a 2–3 flowered, racemose cluster in the upper axils, the flowers pea-shaped; calyx about 5 mm long, the lower half of 3 subulate lobes, the upper half united into a broad emarginate hood; corolla 1.3–1.5 cm across, the standard nearly orbicular, pale violet-purple, with a feather of green at the base; wings deep violet; keel deep royal-purple above, shading to white beneath, flowering freely in August and September.

Fruit. An oval, swollen legume 1.5–2.0 cm long, green at first, ripening to black; seeds kidney-shaped, dark brown, ripe in mid spring and dispersed by explosive force.

Other distinguishing features. Upper twigs and branchlets densely rufous-tomentose.

Climatic range. B, T, and in warm, sheltered coastal microclimates only in P and S.

Hòvea chorizemifòlia (Latin 'with leaves resembling *Chorizema*'): Holly-leafed Hovea: mainly in the hills and slopes of the Darling Range.

Habit. An upright shrub to 1 m or less, with many slender shoots from a crowded base, denser in cultivation.

Leaves. Lanceolate to narrowly ovate-lanceolate, 4–8 cm long and 1.5–2.5 cm wide; petiole 8–10 mm long, brown-tomentose; apex acuminate, spine-tipped; margin coarsely dentate-spinose; midrib and main veins prominent; glabrous; dark green or slightly glaucous-green, only slightly paler beneath.

Flowers. In few-flowered clusters from the upper axils; standard petal nearly orbicular, largest, to 1.5 cm across, strongly bi-lobed; wing petals smaller, obovate; keel petals folded together, enclosing the 10 sheathed stamens; corolla parts deep violet, the standard with a small white fan at the base; flowers borne from mid winter to early October.

Fuit. Not seen

Other distinguishing features. Youngest stems with thick brownish tomentum.

Climatic range. A, B, M, P, S and on lower elevations of Mts, preferably in an open, sun-exposed site with coarse sandy soil.

Hòvea longifòlia (Latin 'with long leaves'): Long-leafed Hovea: eastern Australia, on sandy heathlands and the margins of open forests.

Habit. A shrub to about 2 m tall and about as broad when mature, but erect and slender in youth.

Leaves. Linear-oblong, 5–10 cm long, 5–8 mm wide; petiole with a short mucro; margin entire, revolute at the edge; lower midrib prominent; dark green, glabrous and of pebbly texture above, paler green to brownish and densely tomentose beneath.

Flowers. Solitary or in small clusters from the upper leaf axils; corolla pea-shaped to 1.3 cm across, variable in colour in the blue-violet range; calyx and bracteoles densely woolly-tomentose; flowers abundant during September and October.

Fruit. An oblique legume, broadly ovoid to 1 cm long, with a woolly surface, ripening in early summer; seeds reniform, dark brown.

Climatic range. B, M, P, S and on the warmer lower slopes of Mts in northern NSW and Qld.

Hòvea trispèrma (Greek 'three-seeded'): Common Hovea: WA, mainly on the coastal sandy heathland and lower foothills of the Darling Range.

Habit. A small shrub of 1.0–1.5 m with a loose, open shape in the wild but responding to cultivation and regular pruning with denser growth of slender, erect shoots from the base.

Leaves. Variable from narrowly elliptic to linear-lanceolate, 4–6 cm long and 1.0–2.5 cm wide, carried on slender, brown-tomentose upper stems; petiole 1–2 mm; apex acute-mucronate; margin entire, slightly thickened; midrib alone prominent beneath; glabrous and dark green above, brown-tomentose beneath, especially on the midrib.

Flowers. Solitary or in twos and threes from the upper axils, on pedicels to 5–6 mm long; calyx funnelform, the upper lobe strongly hooded over the remainder, all densely tomentose; corolla pea-shaped; the reniform standard petal emarginate, violet; wings and keel petals deep violet, much smaller, the keel folded closely to partly enclose the 10 stamens; flowering season from early August to late September.

Fruit. A broad, glabrous legume, with three or more seeds.

Climatic range. A, B, M, P, S, on warm, sunny sites with sandy, well-drained soils.

HYDRÁNGEA

Derived from the Greek, describing the shape of the seed capsules.
Hydrangea.
Hydrangeaceae, the Hydrangea family (formerly included in Saxifragaceae).

Generic description. A genus of 25 to 35 species from the Americas and the Orient, three of them among the most widely planted ornamental shrubs. All are more or less deciduous with handsome toothed, opposite leaves, and with flowers of two kinds, the inner ones small and fertile, the outer series large and sterile (although some have wholly sterile flowers), and capsular fruits with very fine seeds. In several species, e.g. *H. macrophylla*, the plants are sensitive to the pH value of the soil, the flowers being blue in acid soils and pink or red in alkaline soils.

Propagation. a) Soft-tip cuttings 5–8 cm long, taken in October or November, or single-bud cuttings with a base of the old stem attached, strike readily in a sand/peat mixture, especially if kept warm and moist in a heated glass-house. b) Mature wood, taken in winter and cut to any reasonable length, also strikes readily in a glass-house or warm bush-house.

Cultivation. The species listed below thrive in a well-drained and well-aerated, friable soil, preferably sandy or of light loam, to which is added copious quantities of organic matter to provide improved water-holding capacity, as well as a reserve of plant food. They give their best performance in a cool, moist climate with mild summers and a well-distributed rainfall. They are tolerant of cold to −5°C without permanent frost injury but in more severe conditions young soft shoots may be seriously damaged, although such plants will shoot again in spring from adventitious buds at the base. Hydrangeas enjoy the sun for limited periods, especially in the early morning, but are comfortable also in the light shade of tall trees. Some protection from strong, dry, summer wind is desirable and at such times, a fine spray of water played on the flowers and leaves will prevent windburn and sunburn.

Being soft-wooded and very leafy, they are strong feeders, making heavy demands on the soil, especially in spring and early summer. Their requirements may be met by an annual mulch of well-prepared compost or clean animal manure to help maintain a friable, crumbly structure in

the soil, and an application of a complete fertiliser at the rate of 250 g per m^2, applied in early
spring and lightly forked in to the root zone.

Colour

Both forms of the species *H. macrophylla* are
variable in flower colour according to the pH
value of the soil and the consequent availability
of aluminium and iron, as well as the individual
ability of each cultivar to assimilate the
materials. At any given pH level, some cultivars,
the whites excepted, will produce colours of
stronger value than others, although all will
follow the general rule of 'acid for blue, alkaline
for pink'. At the lower acid levels, around pH
4.5–5.0, flower colour, at least in those cultivars
with a potential for deep colours, will be in the
violet and deep-blue range, paling through the
deep mauves at pH 5.0–6.0, then through the
mauve-pinks at pH 6.0–6.5 to the clear pinks at
pH 6.5–7.0 and the rosy-reds and light crimsons
above pH 7.0.

The main bluing elements, aluminium and iron,
are unavailable to the plant in limed soils of the
neutral and alkaline range and such soils produce pink to red flowers. Nearly neutral soils,
producing indefinite colours, may be made more
alkaline with the prospect of more positive
colours, by the addition of calcium carbonate at
the rate of 250 g per m^2 once per year.

In unlimed soils, colours may be changed to the
blue range by use of 4 parts of sulphate of aluminium and 1 part of sulphate of iron, used at
the rate of 30 g of the mixture dissolved in 20
litres of water and applied evenly over the root
zone. The treatment is given once per month in
March and April, then in August, September
and October.

It is more difficult to maintain colour control in
ground-grown plants than those in containers.
The danger of applying excessive quantities of
chemical materials to ensure or hasten the colour
change must be avoided. Hydrangeas make their
best growth at pH 5.5–6.5 and their performance
deteriorates very markedly in soils much beyond
an additional unit at either end of the scale, that
is pH 4.5 on the acid end and 7.5 on the alkaline
end.

Pruning. *H. macrophylla* flowers in early
summer, on young stems arising from the previous year's growth which has survived the winter
in good condition. When grown with adequate
light, food and water, most plants will flower
abundantly, although some of the newer sorts

often give only mediocre flowering results and
are rarely if ever improved by heavy pruning.

The heavy winter pruning of the older, more
robust Hydrangeas is now rarely practised, but
some light pruning is desirable to maintain a
supply of healthy, young flowering wood by the
removal of worn-out or crowded material that
may congest the centre of the plant.

During the spring growing period, some of the
weaker shoots may be thinned out to provide
better spacing for the stronger ones. After flowering, the spent shoots should be reduced to a
pair of good, plump buds and the young,
unflowered shoots left untouched.

Renovation pruning, such as removal of worn-
out branches or dead wood, is best carried out in
late winter after most of the leaves have fallen.
In severe climates, winter pruning is detrimental,
since the removal of the foliage canopy exposes
the inner wood and growth buds to freezing
temperatures. If the upper shoots are damaged
by cold they are best left intact until all risk of
frost is over, then reduced to the uppermost
pairs of sound buds and the resultant growth
thinned out appropriately.

It is not good practice to prune a tall-growing
cultivar to fit a small space; far better to trans-
plant to a more suitable place and replace with a
dwarf-growing sort.

Hydrángea macrophýlla (from the Greek
macros 'long', and *phullon* 'a leaf', describing the
large leaves): Japan, Korea and China to India,
often near the coast, but sheltered from harsh
wind by taller shrubs and trees.

Habit. A deciduous shrub, variable in size but
mostly within the 0.5–2.0 m range of height and
width, the central trunk thick and woody, giving
rise to many erect and spreading stems producing the showy terminal flowers and forming a
broad, hemispherical shrub.

Leaves. Simple, opposite, of variable shape, but
mostly broadly ovate, 10–20 cm long and 8–12
cm wide; petiole stout, 2–4 cm long; apex acute
to shortly acuminate; base obtuse or broadly
cuneate; margin coarsely serrate; venation reticulate, the main veins prominent beneath;
glabrous; dark to bright green and lustrous
above, paler beneath.

Flowers. Inflorescence a broad corymb at the
terminals of young current season's and previous year's growth, in summer from mid
November to early February. Two forms are
recognised: Hortensias and *Lacecaps*.

Hortensias (f. *macrophylla*): inflorescence large and round-headed, 15–25 cm across, all flowers sterile, with 4 broad-ovate or orbicular petal-like sepals, overlapped at the edges, from entire to heavily serrated on the margins, the florets 2.0 to 5.0 cm across, the 4 small ovate petals falling early and of no consequence. This group is numerically superior to all other sections of the genus, now numbering hundreds of cultivars, most deriving from hybridists in Germany, France and the Netherlands. (See separate list of cultivars.)

Lacecaps (f. *normalis*): inflorescence somewhat smaller and flatter, 12–20 cm across, with the outer ring of flowers large and sterile like the Hortensias, the inner flowers small and fertile. (See separate list of cultivars.)

Climatic range. A, B, M, P, S, T, and in warm, sheltered micro-climates in H and Mts.

Table. A selection of well-performed Cultivars of Hortensias (f. *macrophylla*)

Cultivar name	Height	Details of flowers
'Altona'	Tall	Serrated sepals; holds colour into autumn; retain spent flowers until brown'
'Ami Pasquier'*	Dwarf	Plain sepals; bright red or dark violet-blue
'Benelux'	Medium	Plain sepals
'Caroline'	Tall	Serrated sepals; large florets
'Deutschland'*	Medium	Plain sepals; deep carmine-rose or violet-blue; holds colour into autumn; retain spent flowers until brown
'Europa'	Tall	Plain sepals;
'Fruhlingserwachen'	Medium	Serrated sepals; very large florets; holds colour into autumn; retain spent flowers until brown
'Gertrude Glahn'	Tall	Plain sepals, abundant flowers
'Hamburg'	Tall	Serrated sepals; large florets; holds colour into autumn; retain spent flowers until brown
'Heinrich Seidel'*	Tall	Serrated sepals; deep carmine-pink or violet-purple
'Kluis Superba'	Medium	Plain sepals
'La Marne'	Tall	Serrated sepals; large florets
'Le Cygne'	Tall	Plain sepals; pure white — colour does not change with pH of soil.
'Mme E. Mouillere'	Tall	Serrated sepals; white florets with small blue eye
'Nixe'*	Dwarf	Plain sepals; deep carmine-red or violet-blue
'Odin'	Medium	Plain sepals
'Parsifal'*	Medium	Serrated sepals; deep ruby-red or violet-blue
'Princess Beatrix'*	Medium	Plain sepals; rosy-crimson or rosy-violet
'Red Cap'*	Dwarf	Plain sepals; carmine-red or violet-blue
'Rubis'*	Medium	Plain sepals; large florets; ruby-red or violet-blue
'Sensation'	Tall	Plain circular sepals
'Souvenir du President Doumer*	Dwarf	Plain sepals; dark maroon or violet-blue
'Venus'	Medium	Plain sepals; large florets
'Westfalen'*	Medium	Plain sepals; carmine-red or violet-blue

Key to symbols: Tall 1.25–2.0 m,   Medium 0.75–1.25 m,   Dwarf 0.45–0.75 m.

*Cultivars capable of producing flowers of deeper than usual colour.

Lacecaps (f. *normalis*)

'Blue Wave' is a shrub of medium to tall height, and more across, the flowers are both fertile in the centre and sterile around the perimeter, in a flattish corymb to 15 cm across. The plant will tolerate an open, sunny position but is better in light shade with adequate water in spring and summer. Is best grown as a blue colour.

'Maculata' is a variegated-foliaged cultivar, seen occasionally in Australian gardens, with flattish heads of fertile flowers in the centre and a thin ring of sterile flowers outside, the dark-green leaves margined with a creamy-white edge.

'**Mariesii**' is a shrub of medium height and width, the flowers borne in a broad, flattish corymb with a mixture of small, fertile flowers mostly in the centre of the head, but with a majority of large sterile flowers around the perimeter and scattered sparsely over the crown of the head. Is best grown as a pink colour.

Hydrángea paniculàta (Latin 'with flowers in a panicle'): eastern China, Japan and neighbouring islands.

A large, deciduous shrub to 5 m or more tall with a broad, bun-shaped crown to 6 m or so wide, sometimes tree-like in its native habitat. The parent species of the widely planted cultivar:

'*Grandiflòra*' (Latin 'with large flowers'): Pee Gee Hydrangea

Habit. A broad, hemispherical shrub growing to 3 m tall and about as wide.

Leaves. Simple, opposite, ovate to elliptic, 8–12 cm long, 5–7 cm wide; petiole 1.5–3.0 cm long; apex acuminate; base broadly cuneate; margin serrate; pubescent at first, then persisting on the lower veins; dark green above, paler beneath, yellowish in autumn.

Flowers. Inflorescence a terminal panicle of conical form, 25–30 cm tall when well grown, 15–18 cm wide; flowers all sterile, of 4 broadly elliptic to ovate sepals, creamy-white at first but turning to rosy-purple in age, flowering from late December to late February.

Fruit. Not produced, flowers sterile.

Other distinguishing features. For larger flower heads, the plant should be pruned in late winter by reducing the flowered shoots of the previous season's growth to 1 or 2 pairs of healthy buds; otherwise, mere removal of the inflorescence will result in a greater number of small heads of flower.

Climatic range. A, H, M, Mts, P, S.

Hydrángea quercifòlia (Latin 'with leaves like an Oak'): Oak-leafed Hydrangea: USA, mostly to the south-east of the Mississippi River valley.

Habit. A deciduous shrub to 2 m tall, spreading to 3–4 m in favourable conditions, the branchlets densely rufous-pubescent.

Leaves. Simple, opposite, broadly ovate, 15–20 cm long and 10–15 cm wide; petiole variable to 10 cm or more long; apex acuminate; base cuneate to truncate; margin pinnately-lobed, with 2 or 3 coarse lobes on each side, serrately edged; midrib and main lateral veins prominent beneath; pubescent at first but becoming smooth and dark green above, whitish-tomentose beneath, changing to orange-scarlet in a spectacular display in autumn.

Flowers. Inflorescence a terminal, conical panicle, 15–20 cm tall and 10–12 cm wide, with a mixture of small fertile, and large, flat, sterile flowers, creamy-white at first but maturing to rosy-purple, flowering from January to May, the best flowering results being attained when planted in rich soil with full sun exposure.

Fruit. Not seen.

Other distinguishing features. Pruning treatment as for *H. paniculata* 'Grandiflora'.

Climatic range. A, B, M, P, S, and in warm, sheltered microclimates in H and Mts.

HYPÉRICUM

The name used by the ancient Greeks for a Mediterranean species, but of uncertain application. Hypericum; St John's Wort; Rose of Sharon; Gold-flower.

Hypericaceae, the St John's Wort family (or by some early authors, Guttiferae).

Generic description. A large and varied genus of shrubs, some evergreen, but mostly deciduous, with simple, opposite leaves; the yellow crateriform flowers, either solitary or in few-flowered cymes, have prominent golden stamens, free or sometimes fascicled; followed by ovoid, dry capsular fruits. Several are grown extensively in Australia for their bright, showy flowers and colourful foliage.

Propagation. a) Soft-tip or semi-hardwood leafy cuttings taken in late spring, summer or autumn, strike easily under normal propagating conditions.

b) Leafless hardwood cuttings taken at pruning time in late winter are also satisfactory.

Cultivation. The plants are usually grown in full sun but will tolerate some shade. Soils of average quality are suitable but free drainage is essential. Watering should not be neglected in dry times, especially during the late spring and summer flowering seasons. The species listed are hardy in low temperatures of –5°C but become fully deciduous at –3°C.

Pruning. Apart from the removal of unsightly seed capsules after flowering time, major pruning is best deferred until winter to take advantage of the persistent, coloured leaves. The normal rounded shape should be the aim, the severity of the treatment depending upon the subsequent maintenance; a well cared for plant may be reduced by half if additional feeding and watering are assured to restore the growth quickly.

Species and cultivars

Hypéricum x *moserànum* 'Tricolor': the variegated-leafed form of the interspecific hybrid between *H. patulum* and *H. calycinum*: Variegated Gold-flower.

Habit. A nearly evergreen subshrub about 0.5–0.75 m tall, of broad bun-shape to 1 m wide, more sensitive to cold than others and best grown in a warm, sheltered place.

Leaves. Like those of *H. pseudohenryi*, but smaller, softer and mid green, with a creamy-white variegation and a reddish edge, the intermediate areas grey-green; stems are reddish.

Flowers. Either solitary or in 2- or 3-flowered cymes at the terminals of the new season's shoots; flowers smaller than other kinds, with a shading of brown at the base of the yellow petals; stamens in 5 fascicles, shorter than the petals; flowering from late spring to late summer; styles 5, green, slightly shorter than the stamens.

Fruit. A 5-celled capsule, green at first, ripening to pale brown.

Climatic range. A, B, M, P, S, T.

Hypéricum pseudohénryi (commemorating Dr Augustine Henry, Irish consular official, and plant collector in China) (syn. *H. patulum* 'Henryi') Yunnan and Szechwan, near the eastern foothills of the Himalayas at elevations up to 3000 m.

Habit. A shrub of 0.75–1.5 m tall with slender, arching branches forming a hemispherical bush to 1.5 m wide, loose and open but improved with additional sustenance and regular annual pruning. Normally almost fully deciduous but becoming more evergreen in warm climates.

Leaves. Elliptic-ovate, 3.0–6.5 cm long and 1.5–3.0 cm wide, petiole 1–2 mm long, deeply channelled above; apex acute-mucronate; base obtuse; margin entire; midrib prominent beneath; surface dotted with pellucid glands and somewhat unpleasant when bruised; glabrous and dark green above, paler and slightly glaucous beneath, becoming yellow, orange, and scarlet before falling in late winter.

Flowers. Solitary, or in cymes of up to 7 flowers, at the terminals of the new season's growth; calyx of 5 ovate, acute, green sepals often stained crimson; corolla imbricate and twisted spirally in the ovoid bud, opening to a rotate flower 3–6 cm across, the 5 obovate petals yellow; stamens in 5 fascicles, each of about 50 stamens, the filaments 1.5–2.0 cm long, slightly shorter than the petals, yellow; anthers deep yellow; styles 5, slightly recurved at the greenish stigmas; flowers borne freely from late November to early January, less abundantly throughout summer and early autumn.

Fruit. A woody capsule, 1.5–2.0 cm long, ovoid-conical, green at first, ripening by late summer to dark grey, and persisting into winter; seeds numerous, dark chocolate-brown.

Other distinguishing features. Young branchlets angular, nearly square at first but less so at maturity; winter buds prominent.

Climatic range. A, B, H, M, Mts, P, S.

Other Hypericums offered by nurserymen are:
Hypéricum fórrestii (commemorating George Forrest, Scottish plant explorer and collector in China) (syn. *H. patulum* 'Forrestii') western China.

A low, broad growth habit with round, not angular, stems, large, pale golden-yellow flowers in a prolific display, and much broader sepals, but otherwise similar to *H. pseudohenryi*.

Hypéricum 'Hidcote' (commemorating Hidcote Manor, the English garden to which the origin of the plant is ascribed, although its parentage is obscure) (syn. *H. patulum* 'Hidcote', *H. patulum* 'Hidcote Gold').

Spreading growth to 1.5 m tall but usually much wider, the large, shallow-cupped flowers with broadly overlapped, deep golden-yellow petals, slightly incurved at the edges, and a neat ring of shorter than usual, golden-yellow stamens and a tall central column of 5 separate styles, each recurved at the apex; flowers are borne freely over an extended season from early summer to late autumn.

Hypéricum kouytchense (the latinised version of the central China province, Kweichow) (syn. *H. patulum* 'Grandiflorum', *H. patulum* 'Sungold')

A broad, hemispherical form to 1.5 m tall and 2 m wide, with drooping branchlets carrying the many golden-yellow, 6 cm wide, nearly flat flowers with showy long styles and stamens, reddish-orange anthers, and reddish capsules; flowers prolific between late November and February.
Climatic range. All A, B, H, M, Mts, P, S.

Hypéricum leschenaùltii (commemorating the French botanical collector Louis Theodor Leschenault de la Tour, 1773–1826): native of the highlands of Indonesia.
A somewhat tender, evergreen species to 1.5 m tall and 2 m wide, with large, cup-shaped flowers to 8 cm across, of unusual depth, the very broad petals overlapping by at least one-third at their edges, deep golden-yellow, flowering from late spring until late autumn, longer than other Hypericums; stamens are shorter than usual, arranged in 5 bundles, each of more than 50.
Climatic range. A, B, M, P, S.

Hypéricum x *'Rowallane'* (commemorating Rowallane, the Northern Ireland garden when it appeared as an interspecific hybrid between *H. hookeranum* 'Rogersii' and *H. leschenaultii*.
Somewhat similar to *H. leschenaultii* in its cupped form and large golden-yellow flowers but is more hardy to cold and grows well in the lower mountains as well as other temperate climates.
Climatic range. A, B, H, M, P, S and lower Mts.

HYPOCALÝMMA

Derived from the Greek, alluding to the translucent, veil-like appearance of the calyx lobes.
Narrow-leafed Myrtle, Swan River Myrtle or Pink Myrtle.
Myrtaceae, the Myrtle family.

Generic description. A small genus of about 12 species from Western Australia, mainly from the sandy coastal plains, all evergreen, with simple, opposite leaves, small axillary flowers in pairs, or often whorled as in the species described, the parts 5-merous, and with capsular fruits.

Propagation. Soft-tip leafy cuttings taken at any time from spring to autumn are struck readily in a sand/peat mixture in a warm environment.

Cultivation. While indigenous to poor soils, both species grow well in a light sandy loam,

improved by the addition of leaf-mould or other organic matter, and light dressings of organic fertiliser, with adequate water in spring and summer. The species listed tolerate low temperatures to at least −3°C but are risky in more severe climates.

Pruning. The cutting of flowers is beneficial since it is done at the best possible time and involves mainly the youngest twigs; the graceful, pendulous character of the plants should not be spoiled by severe pruning.

Species and cultivars
Hypocalýmma angustifòlium (Latin 'with narrow leaves'): Narrow-leafed or Pink-flowered Myrtle; SW coastal region of WA, mainly in the shelter of other taller plants in the sandy heathlands.
Habit. An evergreen shrub to 1 m, with a thin, twiggy character to 1.5 m wide, becoming denser in cultivation and with pruning.
Leaves. Narrowly linear to 2.5 cm long and 1– 2 mm wide; sessile; apex acute-mucronate; margin entire; midrib alone distinct; dark green and glandular, the young leaves paler.
Flowers. Sessile, in pairs in the upper axils, often 4 flowers at each node forming a close whorl; calyx shallow crateriform to 3–4 mm across, with 5 broad-ovate sepals; petals 5, broad-ovate, erect, 3–4 mm across, both parts pinkish-white and translucent; stamens numerous, as long as the petals, filaments whitish, anthers cream; flowering daintily, but not spectacularly, from early September to November.
Fruit. A fleshy capsule with 5 cells opening at the apex to release the small seeds.
Other distinguishing features. Young shoots square, with 4 distinct sharp ridges, pale buff aging to mid brown.
Climatic range. A, H, M, Mts, P, S.

Hypocalýmma robústum (Latin 'strong-growing'): Swan River Myrtle or Pink Myrtle; sandy heathlands of the western coast of WA, especially in the Swan River region.
Habit. A shrub of about 1 m, of loose, erect growth in the wild but responding favourably to cultivation and regular pruning.
Leaves. Linear to narrowly lanceolate, 2.0–2.5 cm long and usually 2–3 mm wide; apex finely tapered and often slightly reflexed at the tip; margin entire; midrib prominent; glabrous; dark green above, slightly paler beneath.

Flowers. In twos to fours in sessile clusters at the nodes of the upper twigs of the previous year's growth; calyx shallowly crateriform to 4 mm across, with 5 broad green lobes; corolla rotate to 1.0–1.3 cm, the 5 petals nearly orbicular, bright pink; stamens numerous in a whorl on the rim of the receptacle, the filaments white, the anthers yellow; flowering season extends from early August to late October.

Fruit. A fleshy capsule, the 2 cells opening when ripe to release the several seeds in each.

Other distinguishing features. An extremely attractive small shrub with abundant flowers which last well when picked.

Climatic range. A, B, M, P, S, on open sunny sites, with well-drained sandy soil.

IBÒZA (syn. *Moschosma*)

The native vernacular name of the species.
Misty Plume Bush.
Lamiaceae, the Mint family (formerly Labiatae).

Generic description. A small genus of African plants with soft, often herbaceous stems, simple, opposite, toothed leaves, aromatic when bruised, and erect panicles of pale-coloured flowers, appearing mostly in winter.

Propagation. Soft-tip cuttings, taken in spring from the rapidly growing shoots resulting from the winter pruning, are easily struck in a sand/peat mixture in a warm, moist atmosphere.

Cultivation. The plant needs protection from strong wind, mixing well with other plants which afford it additional support and warmth. It is best grown in a fully sunny position, in a light, friable soil that drains well after heavy rain. Sensitive to cold but not seriously damaged by temperatures down to 2°C.

Pruning. Plants should be pruned annually by removal of about three-quarters of the previous year's growth as soon as flowers have finished in July, to shape the plant into semi-globular form.

Species and cultivars

Ibòza ripària (Latin *ripa*, 'a river bank', referring to the habitat of the first plants discovered): Misty Plume Bush: SE South Africa.

Habit. A soft-wooded, more or less deciduous shrub to about 2 m, with an open, somewhat irregular habit.

Leaves. Ovate, 5–8 cm long and 3–4 cm wide; petiole to 1.5 cm, white-pubescent, fleshy; apex acute; base obtuse; margin coarsely or doubly crenate; main veins prominent beneath; pubescent on both surfaces; aromatic when crushed; soft-textured; mid green and dull above, paler beneath.

Flowers. Inflorescence a terminal panicle 15–35 cm long, standing clear of the upper leaves; individual flowers in whorls of 6, campanulate-labiate, 3–4 mm long, with 5 nearly equal lobes at the open mouth; calyx very short, with acute teeth; stamens 4, with pale-mauve filaments and purple-black anthers, exserted just clear of the pale mauve-pink corolla; flowers in June and July.

Fruit. Not seen.

Other distinguishing features. Stems very brittle and easily broken in wind, slightly 4-angled, brown-green, with some longitudinal green streaks.

Climatic range. B, P, S, T, and in warm, sheltered microclimates in A and M.

ÌLEX

The ancient Latin name of the Holly Oak, the leaves of which resemble those of the Holly.
Holly (various).
Aquifoliaceae, the Holly family.

Generic description. A large and important group of evergreen and deciduous trees and shrubs mainly from the northern temperate zone, grown extensively in the cooler parts of Australia for their handsome, often variegated foliage, and showy, mostly red, winter fruits. Leaves are simple, alternate, entire or spinose-dentate or serrate, flowers are dioecious and borne singly or in small axillary clusters, yellowish-white and of little decorative interest but when fertilised, providing the globose drupaceous fruits, usually containing up to about 8 seeds.

Propagation. a) Seeds are used to raise large quantities of plants where clonal purity is of little consequence, such as for understocks for grafting or for hedge-row plants; seeds are collected when fully ripe, cleaned of the fleshy pulp by maceration and flotation, then sown at once in a friable mixture placed in a cool, sheltered shade-house.

b) Semi-hardwood tip cuttings, 5–6 cm long, taken in early autumn from sturdy ripened shoots, are the usual choice; the cuttings are stripped of the basal leaves, are slice-wounded at the base, treated with root-promoting dust and planted to about half their length in a coarse sand/peat mixture placed in a warm, humid atmosphere.

c) Alternatively, clonal material is often grafted by any of several common methods, top-cleft and whip-and-tongue being most favoured among the apical forms, and side-cleft and side-veneer among the lateral forms; the ideal time is late winter, using outdoor-grown, fully dormant scions and potted, pre-activated, 1-year-old seedling understocks.

Cultivation. Hollies grow to perfection in deep, friable soils with a high organic content, either naturally retentive of moisture or with added irrigation in hot dry summers. An open sunny position is best, in a cool, temperate climate, the listed species being hardy to low temperatures of at least −8°C.

Pruning. While usually dense and leafy in growth habit, hollies undoubtedly benefit from careful early pruning to establish the natural form of the species or to check over-vigorous or wayward shoots. Pruning is best done in late winter.

Species and cultivars

Ìlex aquifòlium (the ancient Latin classical name for the Holly, now used both as a subgeneric and specific name): English Holly: Great Britain, Europe, North Africa and Asia, to the Orient.

Habit. An evergreen, erect bush, 5–10 m tall, with slender, upright form in youth but broadening to a medium dome in age or occasionally tree-like on a single trunk. Old trees are much larger.

Leaves. Extremely variable in cultivation, mostly elliptical to ovate, 4–8 cm long and 3–4 cm wide; petiole stout, 6–10 mm long; apex mostly a sharp spine, but acute when non-spinose; base obtuse to cuneate; margin thickened, undulate, with 5 to 9 sharp spines, old plants and some cultivars often bearing leaves with few or no spines; texture stiff and coriaceous; glabrous; dark green and lustrous above, paler beneath, some forms with silver-white or yellow variegations.

Flowers. Are borne in a 1- to 8-flowered, umbellate inflorescence in the upper axils on 6–8 mm pedicels; flowers are dioecious, the staminate flowers the more numerous; calyx 3–4 mm wide, the 4 sepals green with reddish edges; petals 4, obovate to orbicular, in a rotate flower to 1 cm wide, yellowish-white, perfumed, flowering in late spring and early summer; stamens 4, the males with conspicuous yellow anthers on the white filaments, the females with an enlarged green pistil.

Fruit. A fleshy, globose drupe to about 8–10 mm wide in clusters of several to about 8, the flesh soft, pulpy and yellowish, with an unpleasant odour, the outer skin glossy, crimson with a few pale glandular dots; seeds mostly 4, yellowish; fruits ripen between May and August.

Other distinguishing features. Upper twigs green or purplish-red while young, somewhat angular or grooved.

I. aquifolium is the parent of many cultivars highly valued as ornamental plants. The following are among the most popular seen in Australian gardens.

'**Argéntea Marginàta**' (Latin 'with silver-white margin'): a name loosely used to cover many green/white forms, but originally applied to a female clone with green young branchlets, ovate leaves 5–6 cm long, variably spinose, dark lustrous green, with a narrow (3–5 mm) margin of creamy-white.

'**Argéntea Marginàta Elegantíssima**' (Latin 'very elegant or graceful'): a male clone with bright-green branchlets, smaller ovate-elliptic leaves 4–5 cm long, with smaller, more numerous spines, the leaves dark shining green in the middle, creamy-white at the broad (5–7 mm) edge, the intermediate areas grey-green.

'**Argéntea Marginàta Péndula**' (Latin 'pendulous'): Perry's Weeping Holly: a female clone with attractive pendulous habit, purplish-green branchlets, the leaves oblong-ovate to 7–8 cm, the margins regularly spinose, the upper surface lustrous dark green, and grey-green in the adjacent middle areas, with a broad but irregular creamy-white margin.

'**Argéntea Mèdio-pícta**' (Latin 'with a silvery-white painted middle'): Silver Milkmaid Holly (syn. 'Albo-picta') both male and female forms are available with bright-green branchlets, small leaves to 3–5 cm long, markedly undulate and coarsely spinose, with a large, irregular, creamy-white patch in the middle, sometimes reaching the edge, and a broad, irregular, dark-green margin, the intermediate areas pale grey-green.

'**Argéntea Regìna**' (Latin 'queenly or regal'): Silver Queen Holly: a male clone with reddish-purple branchlets, large broad-elliptic to ovate leaves 6–7 cm long and 3–5 cm wide, somewhat undulate and coarsely spinose, dark shining green in the middle and margined with a broad, irregular, creamy-white edge, the intermediate areas grey-green.

'Aùrea Mèdio-pìcta' (Latin 'with golden-yellow painted middle'): Golden Milkmaid Holly: has both male and female clones in the same colour pattern, the branchlets green or slightly reddish, with small, very undulate and coarsely spined leaves to 3–4 cm long, with a large, irregular blotch of yellow in the middle and a broad green margin, often invading to the midrib; mostly represented in local gardens by the broad-leafed form 'Aùrea Mèdio-pìcta Latifòlia', with larger leaves to 8 cm long, with a few coarse spines mainly in the upper half or else almost spineless, the middle with a large, irregularly branched patch of yellow, the edge dark lustrous green, the pale-green intermediate areas sometimes invading to the midrib.

'Aùrea Regìna' (Latin 'queenly or regal'): Golden Queen Holly: a male clone with green branchlets, broad-elliptic leaves to 6–8 cm long, coarsely spined and undulate near the apex, dark glossy green in an irregularly branched central patch and a broad, irregular, golden-yellow margin often invading the green to the midrib.

'Fèrox' (Latin 'fiercely armed, thorny'): Hedgehog Holly: a male clone with purplish-red branchlets and small, narrowly ovate, dark-green leaves to 5 cm or so long, with a many-spined margin, and numerous additional small, erect spinules on the upper surface.

'Fèrox Argéntea' has a narrow margin and spines of silvery-white.

'Fèrox Aùrea' has a golden-yellow central blotch and green spines.

'J. C. van Tol' (commemorating the noted Dutch nurseryman) (syn. Polycarpa) an erect bush or tree to 5 m tall with dark, lustrous-green, elliptic-ovate leaves to 7–8 cm long, the margins either entire or with a few forward-pointing short spines mostly near the apex, the upper surface of the blade slightly convex; fruits abundant, large to more than 1 cm across, glossy crimson, fully coloured in May and persisting until spring.

Climatic range. All A, H, M, Mts, P, S.

Ilex cornùta (Latin 'horned', referring to the marginal spines): Chinese Holly: eastern China, mainly along the valley of the Yangtze Kiang River.

Habit. An evergreen shrub, 3–5 m tall and about 3 m wide, with dense dark-green foliage concealing the inner framework of trunk and branches; usually globose-conical but occasionally seen as a small single-trunked tree.

Leaves. Variable in shape but mostly oblong to 5–7 cm long and 2.0–3.5 cm wide across the middle; petiole to 4–5 mm long; apex with 3 sharp and stiff spines spreading at about 45°, the middle spine depressed below the others; base mostly squarely truncate with 2 smaller spines at 90° to the midrib, or rounded without spines; margin entire between spines or with several minor spines, or almost spineless in some forms, the edge somewhat translucent; glabrous; lustrous and dark green above, duller and pale green beneath.

Flowers. Inflorescence an axillary, umbellate fascicle of 2 to about 7 flowers; dioecious; floral parts in fours, the calyx green with red tips; flowers rotate to 1 cm across, creamy-white, flowering abundantly in late spring.

Fruit. In small umbellate clusters, the berries squarish-globose to about 1 cm across and 7–8 mm deep between the somewhat flattened poles, scarlet but not especially glossy, with minute, glandular dots on the surface; seeds mostly 4, ellipsoidal with shallow ridges, ripening in May and persisting until December, the best period about early October; fruits with an unpleasant odour when crushed.

Other distinguishing features. Upper twigs bright green, with clear longitudinal ridges.

Climatic range. A, B, H, M, Mts, P, S.

INDIGÓFERA

Derived from the Latin, meaning 'bearing indigo', a blue dye.
Indigo-plant.
Fabaceae, the Pea family.

Generic description. A large genus of mostly evergreen shrubs or herbaceous perennials from the near-tropical countries, some of commercial value in the production of indigo, several others important decorative plants. Leaves are mostly imparipinnate with subulate stipules, flowers are pea-shaped in racemes in white, pink, or light purple, flowering mainly in spring, and the fruits are leguminous.

Propagation. Propagated by seeds sown as soon as ripe, or by semi-hardwood cuttings struck in a sand/peat mixture, placed in a warm, humid environment.

Cultivation. The species described are easy to cultivate, requiring only a moderately fertile soil with free drainage and exposure to full sun. They are tolerant of light frosts to −4°C but are damaged by more severe conditions.

Pruning. The removal of spent inflorescences, unless wanted for seed production, maintains a neat appearance; no other pruning is necessary. Surplus suckers may be removed with a sharp spade.

Indigófera austràlis (Latin 'southern'): Austral Indigo-plant: widespread throughout the continent but more abundant on the heavier soils of the dry sclerophyll forests of eastern Australia.

Habit. A plant of thin, shrubby form to 1 m or so, with a few flexible stems from the base, or in shady places somewhat taller, but in all cases responsive to regular pruning in cultivation without sacrificing its graceful form

Leaves. Imparipinnate, 6–8 cm long, with 9 to about 15 elliptic-oblong leaflets, each 1.0–1.5 cm long and varying in width; leaflets in opposite pairs on slender petiolules 1–3 mm long, the channelled rachis stipulate at the base; apices obtuse or slightly notched, glabrous above but finely bristly below, especially on the prominent midrib; dull blue-green.

Flowers. In an axillary raceme 5–8 cm long, with 25–30 pea-shaped flowers each about 6–8 mm across; calyx cup-shaped, 2 mm across, reddish, finely pubescent; corolla variable from nearly white to claret-red, most commonly rosy-magenta with a small white fan at the base of the standard and along the base of the keel; flowering period extends from early September to December and sporadically at other times.

Fruit. A slender cylindrical legume, 3–6 cm long, glabrous, green at first, ripening to brown, then splitting to release the hard-coated seeds in summer.

Other distinguishing features. Upper stems purplish-red, flexuose between the nodes.

Climatic range. A, B, H, M, Mts, P, S.

Indigófera decòra (Latin 'ornamental' or 'attractive') (syn. *I. incarnata*) Chinese Indigo Plant: main islands of Japan and in central China.

Habit. A small shrub to about 0.75–1.0 m tall, with slender, ascending shoots, spreading slowly by suckers to form a many-stemmed clump.

Leaves. Compound, alternate, imparipinnate, the main rachis 7–12 cm long, with swollen base, glabrous, crimson with whitish bloom; leaflets mostly 9 or 11, narrowly elliptic to ovate-lanceolate, 3.5–5.0 cm long and 1.5–2.0 m wide; apices acute-mucronate; bases cuneate; margins entire; texture thin and soft; midrib prominent beneath; bright green above, glaucous-green beneath.

Flowers. Inflorescence a raceme, 12–15 cm long, from the upper axils; flowers pea-shaped on slender red pedicels 3 mm long; calyx a shallow cup with short, claw-like sepals; flowers 1.5–2.0 cm long, the standard oblong, whitish with pale lilac-purple veins at the base; wing petals rosy-purple; keel folded, enclosing the stamens, phlox-purple; stamens 10, united into a slender cylinder 1.3 cm long; flowers from late October to mid December.

Fruit. A slender legume to 4 cm long.

'Alba' has white flowers but is otherwise similar.

Climatic range. A, B, M, P, S, and in warm microclimates in Mts.

IOCHRÒMA

Derived from the Greek words, describing the violet-blue colour of several of the species.
Iochroma.
Solanaceae, the Nightshade family.

Generic description. A small genus of tender shrubs from South America with evergreen, simple, alternate leaves and blue, violet, red, yellow, or white tubulate flowers in umbellate clusters, grown in warm climates for their good foliage and attractive flowers borne over a long summer and autumn flowering season.

Propagation. Soft-tip cuttings in early spring, or semi-hardwood cuttings in autumn-winter, strike readily in a sand/peat mixture in a warm, humid atmosphere.

Cultivation. The species listed are tender and liable to damage by heavy frost but may be regarded as safe to about −1°C without serious injury. They are best grown in a warm, sunny corner or in the protection of other evergreens, in a light loamy or sandy soil with plentiful summer water.

Pruning. Most plants need a little pruning in late winter to restrict the often over-vigorous growth; such plants produce better flowers more

PLATE 19

▲ Murraya paniculata
► Nandina domestica
▼ Melaleuca lateritia *Photo by Bro P. Stanley*

▲ Mahonia bealei

▼ Pieris formosa var. forrestii 'Wakehurst'

▼ Leptospermum scoparium var. rotundifolium

▼ Melaleuca steedmanii *Photo by Bro P. Stanley*

▼ Kolkwitzia amabilis

PLATE 20

▲ Mussaenda erythrophylla

▲ Mussaenda frondosa

▲ Leptospermum squarrosum

▲ Leptospermum scoparium var. scoparium 'Martinii'

◄ Pimelia ferruginea
▼ Pieris formosa var. forrestii

▼ Heliotropium arborescens 'Aureum'

▼ Pieris 'Bert Chandler'

attractively displayed over the surface of the bush.

Species and cultivars

Iochròma cyàneum (Greek *kuanos*, 'blue', referring to the colour of flowers) (syn. *I. tubulosum*) Ecuador, Colombia and Peru.
Habit. An evergreen, tender shrub, 3–4 m tall, of loose, open character naturally but improving in growth habit when regularly pruned.
Leaves. Broadly elliptic to ovate, 10–12 cm long and 5–6 cm wide; apex acute or shortly acuminate; base attenuate to the 2–3 cm long, grooved petiole; margin entire but coarsely undulate; venation reticulate, prominent beneath; soft to the touch and pubescent, especially beneath; bright green above, paler and somewhat dull below.
Flowers. Inflorescence a drooping terminal or axillary umbel of about 15–25 flowers, on slender 1.0–2.5 cm pedicels; calyx green, campanulate to 1 cm long, with 4 or 5 lobes; corolla tubulate about 3.5 cm long, the cylindrical tube about 5 mm wide but expanding to 1 cm wide across the 5-lobed limb, deep indigo-blue, the limb fringed with white pubescence; stamens 5, inserted; flowering from December to February, then sparsely until winter.
Fruit. Not seen.
Other distinguishing features. Upper twigs green and pubescent, with conspicuous elongate pale-brown lenticels.
Climatic range. B, M, P, S, T.

Iochròma fuchsioìdes (Latin 'like a Fuchsia', referring probably to *Fuchsia boliviana*, which it resembles mostly in floral form and colour): tropical Peru.
Somewhat similar to the preceding species in growth habit, developing into a loose open shrub 2.5 to 3.5 m tall, with nearly glabrous, evergreen, elliptic-ovate, green leaves, flowers in a drooping umbel from the upper leaf-axils, tubulate to about 5 cm long, slightly flared at the mouth to an expanded limb with 5 shallow lobes, the flowers orange-red, at their best from November to February.
Climatic range. B, M, P, S, T.

Iochròma coccìneum (Latin 'scarlet'): tropical Central America and Mexico.
Resembles *I. fuchsioides* in the main characters but is generally regarded as inferior to that species; the undulate leaves are about as large but have a long-acuminate apex and are more densely pubescent, especially on the midrib and main laterals; flowers are borne in few-flowered, drooping umbels from November to February, the flowers narrowly tubulate to 5 cm long, slightly flared at the 5-lobed mouth, dull scarlet.
Climatic range. B, M, P, S, T.

Iochròma grandiflòrum (Latin 'with large flowers'): Ecuador and neighbouring tropical countries.
Resembles *I. cyaneum* in the main characters but the leaves are more broadly ovate and shorter, with a denser covering of pubescence; flowers are in small pendulous umbels of 3 to about 6, the calyces more broadly urceolate, the 5 short lobes closing to a smaller mouth, the corolla with a more widely flared, 5-lobed limb, the lobes recurving slightly; flowers are deep violet-purple, flowering from November to February.
Climatic range. B, M, P, S, T.

IRESÌNE

Derived from the Greek, alluding to the woolly stems of some species.
Blood-leaf.
Amaranthaceae, the Amaranthus family.

Generic description. A small genus of tender, succulent-stemmed plants from South America, several grown for their showy coloured foliage, the species described below, often seen in local gardens, used mainly for its bright leaves which help to relieve a preponderance of green in a landscape.

Propagation. Soft-tip cuttings taken between spring and autumn root readily in a sand/peat mixture in a warm, humid atmosphere.

Cultivation. Any freely drained soil of moderate fertility meets the plant's requirements. It grows well in either sunny or part-shaded positions but must be protected from frost and violent winds.

Pruning. The current year's shoots should be shortened slightly during late winter, after all risk of frosts is over.

Species and cultivars

Iresìne hèrbstii (commemorating a Kew horticulturist named Herbst): Uruguay, southern Brazil and northern Argentina.
Habit. An evergreen, soft-wooded shrub to

about 1 m tall, naturally of loose, open growth but usually modified by annual pruning.

Leaves. Simple, opposite, ovate to sub-orbicular, 8–12 cm long and 6–10 cm wide; petiole 2–5 cm long, terete but broadly channelled above; apex shortly acuminate; base rounded to broadly cuneate; margin rough, finely ciliate; venation depressed above, prominently raised and pubescent beneath; texture soft and somewhat succulent; finely pubescent on both surfaces; bright magenta around the main veins, deep ruby-red between the veins.

Flowers. In a short terminal panicle, on a reddish pubescent rachis from the upper young shoots, the many small flowers enclosed in chaffy bracts; silvery-cream but of little decorative value; flowering season summer and autumn.

Fruit. Not seen; local plants probably sterile.

Other distinguishing features. Upper stems soft, succulent and brittle.

'**Aùreo-reticulàta**' has creamy-white main veins stained with pale ruby-red, the interveinal spaces bright green, occasionally marked with red; upper stems ruby-red; otherwise similar to the parent species.

Climatic range. B, M, P, S, T, on sheltered, frost-free sites only.

ISOPÒGON

From the Greek, describing the woolly appendages of the cone-scales.

Drumsticks or Cone-bush.

Proteaceae, the Protea family.

Generic description. A genus of Australian native shrubs, grown in gardens for their curious and interesting character and easy culture. Leaves are much divided in the species described below, or plainer in others of lesser importance; the flowers are mostly yellow but sometimes pinkish, many flowers forming a regular spiral in a cone-like inflorescence, each subtended by an acicular floral bract; the cones retain their viability for several years allowing the seeds to be collected whenever required.

Propagation. Seeds are collected from fully mature cones, preferably from the previous year, and sown in individual containers to minimise root disturbance when transplanting. A friable mixture is best, in a somewhat dry atmosphere but not allowed to dry out fully at any stage.

Cultivation. The species described are indigenous to well-drained, rocky, gravelly or coarse sandy soils of low fertility, and perform well in gardens when grown on this kind of material; heavier soils should be artificially drained or beds raised to discharge surplus soil water. An open sunny aspect is ideal in a climate with minimum temperatures not below −4° or −5°C.

Pruning. All species are of attractive form unlikely to be improved by pruning excepting to restrain an occasional wayward shoot.

Species and cultivars

Isopògon anemonifòlius (Latin 'with Anemone-like leaves'): Drumsticks or Erect Cone-bush: coastal plain and lower Blue Mountains of NSW mostly on the poorer soils of the Hawkesbury plateaus.

Habit. An erect, evergreen shrub, 1.5 to 2.5 m tall, with ascending branches.

Leaves. Simple, alternate, tripinnatisect, 6–10 cm long, with 2 or 3 pairs of lobes of decreasing size towards the apex; apices acuminate; margins entire; glabrous; dark green and slightly shiny on both sides, becoming reddish-purple in winter.

Flowers. Inflorescence a cone-like spike to 2 cm diameter, at the terminals of the young shoots; perianths slender to 1.5 cm long, splitting when ripe into 4 segments at the apex and reflexing fully; all parts lemon-yellow, flowering from mid September to late October.

Fruit. A globular grey cone to 2 cm across, the many scale-like seeds with white-woolly appendages.

Other distinguishing features. Upper twigs dark purple, with white silky pubescence.

Climatic range. A, M, Mts, P, S.

Isopògon anethifòlius (Latin 'with leaves like *Anethum*', the spicy herb, Dill): Narrow-leafed Cone-bush: coastal plain and lower Blue Mountains, mostly on poor soils derived from the Hawkesbury sandstones.

Habit. A shrub of similar form to the preceding species but generally of shorter, broader growth habit.

Leaves. Simple, alternate, tripinnatisect, to 9–10 cm long, the rachis and branches of the leaves fully recurved, brownish-red when young, becoming green when mature; otherwise similar to the leaves of *I. anemonifolius*.

Flowers. Inflorescence a round to ovoid, cone-like spike to 3.5 cm long, the flowers arranged in a regular spiral fashion around the pale-green cone; perianths pale yellow, to 1 cm long; segments 4, recurving fully when ripe, flowering from mid September to late October.

Fruit. A woody cone of ovoid shape to 4 cm long and 1.5 cm wide, with numerous grey-black, imbricated scales supporting the small seeds.

Other distinguishing features. Upper twigs bright green at first, becoming deep red, contrasting sharply with the pale-green petioles.

Climatic range. A, M, Mts, P, S.

Isopògon dùbius (Latin 'doubtful', perhaps because of early uncertainty about its generic identity) (syn. *I. roseus*) Rose Cone-bush: WA, mainly along the Darling Range and Swan River districts.

Habit. A small evergreen shrub to 1 m or less, with ascending leafy stems.

Leaves. Simple, bi- or tripinnatisect to 5–7 cm long, flat and rigid, the ultimate segments slenderly linear and sharply acute, with a generally fine texture; bright green to glaucous-green.

Flowers. Inflorescence a solitary cone-like, globular spike to 4.5 cm across, borne at the terminals of the previous year's shoots; perianths to 3 cm long, club-shaped at first on slender stems, rose- to mauve-pink; segments 4, reflexing and curling fully when ripe to release the yellow style; flowers profuse in late winter and early spring.

Fruit. A woody, globose cone with closely imbricated, grey scales.

Other distinguishing features. Young stems densely pubescent, purplish, but becoming glabrous and reddish-green when mature.

Climatic range. A, M, P, S, and lower Mts on sandy or coarse soils with free drainage.

IXÒRA

Derived from the native name of a local Indian god.
Ixora.
Rubiaceae, the Madder family.

Generic description. A large genus of tender evergreen shrubs and trees from the tropics, often grown in the warmer parts of Australia for their handsome flowers. Leaves are mostly opposite or occasionally whorled, the flowers in large terminal or axillary corymbs in a variety of attractive colours, mainly white, yellow, orange, pink, or red, and fruit a black, 2-celled berry. The plants are often grown in large pots placed indoors.

Propagation. Soft-tip cuttings taken in spring strike readily in a sand/peat mixture in a warm, humid glass-house; bottom heat and mist are beneficial.

Cultivation. A freely drained, friable soil with a high organic content is most suitable in a partly shaded position protected from strong sunlight and drying winds, ideally in a mild climate without frosts.

Pruning. When mature and in good health, an Ixora may be pruned of at least half the annual growth, either immediately after the autumn flowers or in late winter, to keep the plant in its neat globose form and to remove the spent inflorescences.

Species and cultivars

Ixòra chinénsis (Latin 'from China'), but actually indigenous to most South-East Asian countries, especially Indo-China, southern China and Taiwan.

Habit. An evergreen shrub to 1–2 m tall, usually based on a short trunk, branching repeatedly into a twiggy globose bush to about 2 m wide.

Leaves. Simple, opposite, elliptic to oblong, 8–14 cm long, 4–6 cm wide; apex shortly and abruptly acuminate; base tapered to the 2–3 mm broad petiole; margin entire but coarsely undulate; venation reticulate, the whitish midrib and main veins prominent beneath; glabrous; bright green above, paler beneath.

Flowers. Inflorescence a dense, terminal corymb to 10 cm across, the numerous flowers salverform to 2.5–3.0 cm long, with a slender tube and broad-rotate, 4-lobed limb, deep buff, changing to orange and scarlet; stamens 4, the yellow anthers lying horizontally and radially along the junctions of the corolla lobes; style slightly exserted, red; flowers borne profusely over the crown of the plant from summer to late autumn.

Fruit. A fleshy, 2-seeded, black berry, ripening in early winter.

Other distinguishing features. Upper stems terete, but slightly grooved between the nodes;

stipules between the opposite leaf-bases acicular, to 4–5 mm long.

'**Prince of Orange**' is probably the most common cultivar in Australian gardens; flowers are bright orange-scarlet, produced in abundance in late summer and autumn, usually at its best in March and April.

Climatic range. B, P, S, T, in warm, sheltered microclimates only.

JASMÌNUM

The latinised form of the Arabic native name, *Ysmyn*.

Jasmine or Jessamine.

Oleaceae, the Olive family.

Generic description. A widely varied genus of shrubs and climbers, evergreen or deciduous, with compound or simple leaves arranged oppositely or alternately, the stems either solid, or hollow with lamellate partitions. Several species are adaptable to shrub form but are more appropriately classified as climbers and are not treated here. See specific notes below for details of the two most commonly used shrubs.

Propagation. The main method of propagation is by firm, leafy tip cuttings, 5–8 cm long, taken between late spring and autumn, preferably struck in a sand/peat mixture in a warm, moist environment.

Cultivation. The species treated here are easy to cultivate, requiring only a moderately fertile, well-drained soil and a sunny position in a mild climate with temperatures not below –3°C.

Pruning. For the best flowering performance the plants should be pruned as little as possible, but may occasionally need to be checked in growth to confine them to their allotted place.

Species and cultivars

Jasminum hùmile '**Revolùtum**' (Latin 'low', referring to the habit of growth and 'to turn around', referring to the edges of the leaflets): lower Himalayas and central China.

Habit. An evergreen shrub to 3 m tall, of loose, irregular growth but more or less hemispherical in outline.

Leaves. Compound, alternate, imparipinnate to 10–12 cm long, with 5 or 7 leaflets, the largest at the terminal; leaflets elliptical to ovate, to 4 cm long and 2.5 cm wide; apex acute; base cuneate, often unequal; margin entire; venation reticulate, the main laterals somewhat translucent; glabrous, soft and slightly fleshy; bright green above, paler beneath.

Flowers. Inflorescence a terminal cyme of 10–20 flowers on leafy, spur-like lateral growths; calyx campanulate to 3 mm long, green, with 5 subulate teeth; pedicels about 1 cm long; corolla salverform, about 2 cm long, the tube slender, the limb expanded to 2.5 cm wide into 5 broadly obovate lobes, bright yellow, flowering in September and October; perfumed; stamens 2, within the tube, with large sagittate anthers.

Other distinguishing features. Upper stems dark green, warty and somewhat angular.

Climatic range. A, B, M, P, S, T.

Jasminum mésnyi (syn. *J. primulinum*) Primrose Jasmine: Yunnan, south-western China.

Habit. An evergreen shrub or scrambler with long weak stems issuing from a common base and arching outwards to form a large bun-shaped bush, adaptable to training as either a shrub or semi-climber.

Leaves. Compound, opposite but occasionally alternate, trifoliolate, but rarely simple, of variable shape and size but mostly 8–10 cm long, the terminal leaflet largest to 6–9 cm long, lanceolate, the others 5–7 cm long, broadly lanceolate to elliptical; petiole to 1 cm long, deeply grooved above; apex acute and mucronate; base cuneate; margin entire to finely ciliate; glabrous; bright green and somewhat shiny above, dull green beneath.

Flowers. Solitary, on short axillary shoots about 2 cm long, usually borne on the 1- and 2-year-old outer stems for a length of 1 m or more; calyx of 6 linear-lanceolate, green sepals 5–6 mm long; corolla rotate to 4–5 cm across, the slender tube about 1 cm long, the lobes 6 in the simple flower but often 'doubled' to 9 or 11, obovate to 1.5 cm wide, deep yellow, with fine orange lines radiating from the centre; stamens 2, within the corolla tube; pistil 1, slightly exserted; flowering abundantly from early August to November, the peak period in early September.

Other distinguishing features. Upper twigs bright green, conspicuously 4-angled by the pronounced longitudinal ridges extending between the nodes.

Climatic range. A, B, M, P, S, T.

JUSTÍCIA (syn. *Cyrtanthera, Jacobinia, Libonia*)

After James Justice, Scottish horticultural author. Justicia (various).

Acanthaceae, the Acanthus family.

Generic description. A genus of evergreen shrubs from Mexico, Central America and the warmer parts of South America, with opposite, simple leaves, and flowers of various colours and forms of inflorescence, but mainly tubulate, distinctly 2-lipped, with 2 stamens and a single pistil. Several are seen in Australian gardens, the two species listed being the most common.

(The taxonomy of the family Acanthaceae is presently under review. Pending an authoritative decision to the contrary, the 'collective' system is preferred here for simplicity and conciseness.)

Propagation. Soft-tip cuttings taken in spring and summer, or firmer material taken in autumn or from the winter prunings, strike readily in a sand/peat mixture placed in a warm, humid atmosphere.

Cultivation. All species are sensitive to violent winds and low temperatures below 0°C, but, grown in a sun-exposed or lightly shaded position, in a warm climate with a rich soil and regular attention to watering and feeding, give a good return in handsome and abundant foliage and flowers.

Pruning. Regular annual winter pruning of the flowered wood is beneficial to encourage the development of new flowering shoots from the base.

Species and cultivars

Justicia carnea (Latin 'flesh-pink') (syn. *Jacobinia carnea, Jacobinia magnifica, Cyrtanthera magnifica, Cyrtanthera pohliana* var. *obtusior*) Brazil.

Habit. An evergreen, erect shrub to 1.5 m tall, with soft, brittle, squarish stems arising from a central clump.

Leaves. Blades ovate-lanceolate to ovate-elliptic, 10–15 cm long; apex acuminate; base cuneate-decurrent to the 3–4 cm petiole; margin entire but undulate; main veins prominent and

downy beneath; otherwise glabrous; dark green and shiny above, dull purple beneath.

Flowers. Inflorescence a terminal thyrse to 10–12 cm tall, the flowers numerous, subtended at the base by a cluster of purplish floral leaves to 1.5–2.0 cm long; calyx tubulate to 1 cm long, with 5 narrow lobes; corolla tubulate to 5–6 cm long, split to about the middle into 2 halves, both prominently ribbed and slightly pubescent, variable in colour from pale pink to rosy-purple, but mostly flesh-pink; stamens 2, the filaments white, anthers dark purple with a white face; style 1, pale pink, very slender; flowering season extends from early summer to late autumn.

Fruit. Not seen.

Other distinguishing features. Upper stems often trichotomous, finely pubescent, ridged, swollen above the nodes, green to purplish.

Climatic range. B, M, P, S, T.

Justicia rizzinii (commemorating Carlos Toledo Rizzini, Brazilian botanist) (syn. *Libonia* and *Jacobinia floribunda*) Yellow Justicia: eastern Brazil.

Habit. An evergreen shrub to about 1 m tall with many ascending and spreading stems of about equal size radiating from the base to form a dense bush about 1.5 m wide.

Leaves. Alternate or opposite, broadly elliptic to oval, 2–3 cm long and 1.0–2.5 cm wide; petiole 3–5 mm long, pubescent; apex acute, base obtuse; margin entire; main veins prominent beneath; dark green and glabrous above except for the pubescent midrib, whitish-green beneath.

Flowers. Inflorescence a few-flowered raceme, several together forming a loose panicle at the end of the young shoots; calyx tubulate, 4–5 mm long, with 5 acute teeth at the apex, dark reddish-purple; corolla tubulate to 3 cm long, ribbed, pubescent, divided at the apex into 2 lips about 5 mm long, the lower one trifid; tube scarlet at the base, yellow at the apex; flowering season extends over most of the year with the peak period in winter and spring; stamens 2, the filaments whitish, the anthers cream; pistil 1, whitish.

Fruit. Not seen.

Other distinguishing features. Young twigs softly pubescent, with swollen nodes.

Climatic range. A, B, M, P, S, T.

KÁLMIA

After Dr Pehr Kalm, botanist and explorer of eastcoast USA in mid 1700s.
Mountain-Laurel; Calico-Bush.
Ericaceae, the Erica family.

Generic description. North American plants indigenous mainly to the eastern half of USA, widely grown for their attractive evergreen, simple, alternate leaves, showy flowers in terminal corymbs standing above the foliage, and small capsular fruit with minute seeds. Few more attractive shrubs exist and where favourable conditions prevail it is well worth growing. The delicate shell-pink flowers are remarkably beautiful and the foliage also is attractive.

Propagation. a) The simplest method of propagation is by seeds, collected as soon as ripe and sown in spring in a mildly acid germinating medium; finely ground sphagnum moss worked through a sand/peat mixture is ideal, preferably placed in a cool, moist atmosphere.
b) Firm tip cuttings taken in late summer to winter are struck with some difficulty in a cool, misted atmosphere.
c) Simple layers, set down in late autumn-early winter and severed the following autumn, give reliable results and well-advanced plants.

Cultivation. The plants are closely related to the Rhododendrons and require substantially the same treatment for their best growth. They are at home on sandy/peat soils of pH 5.0–6.0, but dislike clay or lime in any form. The soil should be kept moderately moist during hot summers and a thick, fibrous mulch helps in this. They thrive in the dappled shade of tall overhead foliage, the colour of the flowers more attractive in the somewhat subdued light. Ideally grown in a cool, humid climate and safe in temperatures as low as −10°C; good specimens are seen in all the best horticultural districts along the tablelands.

Pruning. Removal of spent flower clusters, if not required for seed production, is the only pruning necessary, but an occasional wayward shoot may also need to be removed and is best done immediately after the spring flowering.

Species and cultivars

Kálmia latifòlia (Latin *latus*, 'broad', and *folium*, 'a leaf', referring to the broad leaves): Mountain-Laurel: USA, from Canada to the Gulf of Mexico, on the elevated land between the Atlantic Coast and the Appalachian Mountains.

Habit. An evergreen shrub, usually seen at 2–3 m tall but likely to be twice as large or even tree-like in old age; of dense, leafy habit in youth, with a medium-domed shape.

Leaves. Alternate or sometimes appearing to be whorled near the growth junctions, broadly lanceolate to elliptical, 8–12 cm long and 4–5 cm wide; petiole to 2 cm long, reddish above, extending into the conspicuous main vein; apex shortly acuminate; base cuneate; margin entire; dark green and glabrous above, paler beneath.

Flowers. Inflorescence a terminal, many-flowered corymb, the flowers standing clear of the leaves on slender, glabrous pedicels 3–5 cm long; calyx cup-shaped, with 5 spreading, acute lobes; corolla shallowly crateriform, somewhat pentagonal, 2.0–2.5 cm across, shell-pink with some purplish markings on the inside; stamens 10, the filaments slender, whitish-pink, curved and held captive in small sacs in the corolla but straightening later when touched by insects, or by the expansion of the corolla, to release the pollen and fertilise the receptive stigma; flowering period early October to late December.

Fruit. A small globular, bristly, 5-valved capsule about 5–6 mm wide, the spreading, persistent calyx with 5 narrow, triangular teeth, brownish-green but ripening to brown-grey in early winter.

Other distinguishing features. Upper twigs pubescent, bright green, becoming reddish-brown, with large, projecting leaf-scars.

Mountain-Laurel is somewhat variable in flower colour when grown from seeds; in cultivation it has produced a number of clonal variations from white to deep purplish-pink, all otherwise similar to the parent.

f. *rùbra* 'Clementine Churchill' has rosy-red buds opening to bright pink.

Climatic range. H, M, Mts, and on cool, moist, hilly sites in A, P, and S.

KÉRRIA

Commemorating William Kerr, plant collector from Kew Gardens, who introduced the plant into England from China in 1804.
Kerria; Japanese Rose; Globe-flower.
Rosaceae, the Rose family.

Generic description. A genus of a single species of shrub from China and Japan, grown for its bright-yellow, single or double flowers in spring and graceful, cane-like stems with pleasant foliage.

Propagation. a) Soft-tip or semi-hardwood cuttings taken in spring or summer strike readily in a sand/peat mixture in a cool, humid atmosphere.

b) Stems brought down to ground level and covered layer themselves and may be detached and lifted after about a year.

c) An old established clump may be divided into several new plants.

Cultivation. An easy to cultivate plant, Kerria grows well in any moderately fertile soil with free drainage, in a sunny or lightly shaded position, preferably in a cool, moist climate with temperatures not below −6°C.

Pruning. Several of the older flowering shoots should be removed entirely at the base each year to make way for the growth of new watershoots. No other pruning is necessary.

Species and cultivars

Kérria japónica (Latin 'from Japan'): mountains of the main islands of Japan and also in southwestern China.

Habit. A deciduous shrub to 2 m tall and 1.5 m or more wide when mature, with long, slender, cane-like shoots arising from a suckering clump.

Leaves. Simple, alternate, ovate to ovate-lanceolate, 10–12 cm long and 4–5 cm wide; petiole 1 cm long; apex long and finely acuminate; base obtuse; margin biserrate; midrib and main veins prominent, pubescent beneath; bright green and glabrous above, paler and dull beneath, colouring to yellow in autumn before falling.

Flowers. On short terminal and axillary spurs, the pedicels to 6 mm; calyx green, cup-shaped, with 5 broadly ovate, reflexing sepals; corolla rotate, 3.5–4.5 cm across, with 5 petals and numerous stamens; deep yellow, flowering from September to November.

Other distinguishing features. The smooth, bright-green shoots are ornamental in winter, especially when displayed on a white wall.

'Plena' (syn. *'Pleniflòra'*) the more common plant, with large, double flowers of deep golden-yellow.

Climatic range. A, H, M, Mts, P, S.

KOLKWÍTZIA

After Prof. R. Kolkwitz, a German botanist.
Beauty Bush.
Caprifoliaceae, the Honeysuckle family.

Generic description. A monotypic genus from China, the single species one of the most beautiful of all deciduous shrubs grown in Australia.

Propagation. Soft-tip cuttings taken in spring or early summer, or semi-hardwood cuttings taken in late summer, root easily in a warm, moist atmosphere; hardwood cuttings taken when dormant in winter are also used.

Cultivation. A well-drained, medium-textured soil, with full exposure to the sun is ideal. The addition of extra food and water during the main growing period ensures better flowers in the following year. The plant is hardy in the coldest Australian climates to at least −10°C.

Pruning. The spent flowers and several of the oldest basal stems should be pruned away immediately after the flowering season each year, to make way for younger, more-productive shoots from the base. The plant should never be shorn to a uniform surface since this destroys the natural arching form of the branches.

Species and cultivars

Kolkwítzia amábilis (Latin 'lovely', referring to the floral display): central China.

Habit. A deciduous shrub to 2–3 m tall and as wide, with many erect arching branches arising from the common base.

Leaves. Simple, opposite, narrow-ovate, 6–9 cm long, 2.0–3.5 cm wide; petiole pilose to 4–5 mm long; apex long-acuminate; base obtuse; margin finely ciliate, with remote, gland-tipped, serrate teeth; midrib and main laterals prominent beneath; dark green and slightly shiny above, paler beneath, but red and yellow in autumn.

Flowers. Inflorescence a corymb of 10–20 paired flowers, borne terminally on the upper lateral twigs; peduncles slender to 1 cm; calyx crimson, 5-lobed, 5 mm long and spreading widely; corolla campanulate to 2.5 cm long, 5-lobed, the upper 2 slightly reflexed at the mouth, finely pubescent; white to blush-pink, with rosy-carmine veins on the outside and a net of bright-orange veins inside; faintly perfumed; stamens 4; flowering from October to mid November.

Fruit. A small corymbose-cluster of dry achenes with brown bristles, ripening in summer and persisting until dispersed by wind in autumn.

Other distinguishing features. Upper twigs puberulent, pale brown, with swollen nodes; older bark grey and rough, and becoming deeply furrowed vertically.

Climatic range. A, H, M, Mts, P, S.

KÚNZEA

Commemorating the German botanist, Prof. Gustav Kunze of the University of Leipzig.
Kunzea; Tick-bush; Pink-buttons; etc.
Myrtaceae, the Myrtle family.

Generic description. A small genus of Australian native evergreen shrubs, several used popularly in gardens for their neat foliage, shrubby habit and showy flowers. Leaves are simple, alternate and mostly small; flowers have a fleshy, urn-shaped calyx, minute sepals and petals, but numerous free stamens in white, pink, violet, or red, the flowers borne in terminal globular heads or elongate spikes, mainly in spring and early summer; fruit is a 3–5 celled, rounded fleshy capsule, the seeds small and numerous.

Propagation. a) Seeds collected and sown as soon as ripe germinate readily in a warm moist environment.
b) Soft-tip cuttings taken between late spring and autumn, or firmer material taken in winter, root well in a sand-peat mixture, under mist in a warm glass-house.

Cultivation. The Kunzeas described below are hardy plants, easy to cultivate, provided the soil is of moderate fertility and drains freely. They are seen at their best on deep sandy or gravelly soils improved with organic matter, in a sunny position. All are tolerant of mild frosts to −3°C without distress.

Pruning. While of naturally attractive habit, all are better for a light pruning, into the young growth only, immediately after flowering.

Species and cultivars

Kúnzea ambígua (Latin *ambigere*, 'to be uncertain', referring to some initial doubt about its true identity): Tick-bush: widely distributed along the sandy heathlands, gravelly ridges and rocky gullies of eastern Australia.
Habit. An evergreen shrub to 2–3 m tall, with an open branching habit, responding well to regular pruning and additional cultivation.
Leaves. Simple, alternate or in small clusters,

linear-lanceolate to oblanceolate, 5–10 mm long; petiole 1 mm long, flattened, whitish-green; apex acute to acuminate; margin entire but finely ciliate; venation indistinct but with pellucid oil glands; bright green when young, aging to dark green on reddish-brown, pubescent twigs.
Flowers. In umbellate heads of 10–20 or more, sessile or nearly so, on axillary spurs among the upper twigs; calyx campanulate to 4 mm long, with 5 short acute lobes; petals 5, broadly ovate to orbicular, 2–3 mm across, spreading, white, forming a rotate flower 1 cm across; stamens 20 to 30, about 7–8 mm long, with slender white filaments and cream anthers; flowers produced from late October to mid December.
Fruit. A woody, campanulate capsule to 4–5 mm across, with persistent lobes, opening into 5 valves in mid summer to release the seeds.
Other distinguishing features. Youngest twigs whitish, silky-pubescent, becoming light brown, with stringy bark, shredding in long strips.
Climatic range. A, B, H, M, Mts, P, S.

Kúnzea báxteri (commemorating William Baxter, British botanist): Baxter's Kunzea: southern coast of WA, often on exposed heathlands.
Habit. An evergreen shrub to 2–3 m tall, with a stiff upright habit, somewhat sparsely leafed, unless under cultivation with regular pruning.
Leaves. Linear-oblong to 1.2–1.5 cm long and 2–4 mm wide, slightly overlapping to partly conceal the shoots; petiole 1 mm or less; apex acute, slightly thickened; margin entire-ciliate; glabrous; pale-green when young, becoming dark green and slightly shiny on both surfaces.
Flowers. Inflorescence a cylindrical spike to 6 cm long and 6 cm broad, at the terminals of the new shoots; flowers 20–30, sessile; calyx campanulate-urceolate to 8 mm long and across the open-rimmed mouth, dull crimson, the lobes to 5 mm long, green, acute; petals 5, orbicular, 5 mm wide, deep crimson; stamens numerous, attached to the rim of the receptacle, filaments bright crimson, 2 cm long, anthers yellowish; style crimson, 3 cm long; flowers borne freely from September to November.
Fruit. A fleshy, sessile capsule, red at first, ripening to brown-grey, the 5 valves recessed deeply within the rim; seeds small, numerous.
Climatic range. A, M, P, S, and on the warmer, lower slopes of Mts.

Kúnzea capitàta (Latin *caput*, 'the head', describing the inflorescence): Pink Buttons: NSW and Vic., mainly on sandy heathlands and rocky ridges between coast and the tablelands.

Habit. An evergreen shrub to 1.0–1.5 m, with erect branches forming an open bush 1 m or so wide, thickened and improved by cultivation and pruning.

Leaves. Oblanceolate, 5–10 mm long and 2–5 mm wide, pointing upwards to partly cover the twigs; petiole 1 mm, cream; apex acute-mucronate; margin entire, irregularly ciliate; pubescent; dark green and dull; aromatic.

Flowers. Inflorescence a terminal globose head of several to about 12 flowers, the new growth appearing at the apex; calyx tubulate-urceolate 5 mm long and 3 mm wide, green and densely villous outside, red inside, with 5 acute spreading sepals; petals 5, orbicular to 1 mm, arranged between the sepals, amethyst-violet; stamens 5–6 mm long, slender, very numerous, free, around the rim of the receptacle, filaments amethyst-violet, anthers cream; style 1, to 5 mm long, deep violet-crimson; flowering during September and October.

Fruit. A campanulate-urceolate capsule 5 mm long, not woody; seeds small, numerous.

'Badja Carpet' is named for its native habitat, the Big Badja Mountain, near Cooma, NSW: the recently discovered form, now a registered cultivar, has a prostrate habit of growth to 0.5 m or so tall, spreading to 3 m wide, forming a densely-leafed mat suitable for use as a ground-cover. Its white flowers are produced in small clusters of up to 6 or 8, at the ends of short lateral shoots, flowering in spring. It is more tolerant of cold than its parent species.

Climatic range. A, B, M, P, S, and in warm microclimates in the lower Mts.

Kúnzea parvifòlia (Latin 'with small leaves'): Violet Kunzea: NSW and Vic., mostly on moist sandy sites on coastal plateaus and lower slopes of the Snowy Mts.

Habit. A small shrub of about 1 m tall, with a slightly pendulous, spreading form, often to 2.5 m wide, the youngest shoots reddish.

Leaves. Linear-oblong, 2–4 mm long, 1–2 mm wide, pubescent at first, finally glabrous, dark grey-green.

Flowers. In a semi-spherical head about 10 mm across at the terminals of the upper twigs, the new shoots emerging from the apex; flowers like fluffy pompons, with prominent stamens 2–4 mm long, rosy-violet, the stamens with cream anthers; flowering period from September to early summer.

Fruit. A rounded, 3-celled capsule, 2–3 mm across, fleshy, containing numerous small seeds.

Climatic range. H, M, Mts, P, S, and on cool, elevated sites in A.

Kúnzea pulchélla (Latin 'pretty or handsome') (syn. *K. sericea*) Granite Kunzea: south-west WA, mainly on granite soils 200–400 km from the West Coast.

Habit. A somewhat stiff, sparse shrub 2–3 m tall but becoming dense and more heavily foliaged if pruned periodically.

Leaves. Obovate, to 1.5 cm long with a short pointed apex; silky while young, later glabrous and leathery, silvery-grey.

Flowers. In a globose cluster of up to 10 at the ends of short laterals; calyx tube campanulate, 1 cm across, with 5 prominent lobes; petals small, rounded; stamens to 2.5 cm long, bright crimson with cream anthers; flowering mainly from spring to early summer.

Fruit. A non-woody capsule with numerous small seeds.

Climatic range. A, I, M, P, S, and on lower slopes of Mts.

LAMBÈRTIA

Commemorating Aylmer B. Lambert, British botanical author.

Mountain Devil or Honey-flower.

Proteaceae, the Protea family.

Generic description. A small genus of Australian native shrubs, the majority from Western Australia, the best-known species described below from NSW. Leaves are simple, 3- or 4-whorled, often with a spiny apex, flowers are sessile, solitary or in clusters of 7, subtended by involucral bracts, flowering mainly in spring and summer; fruit is a woody follicle, with 2 long and 1 short sharp horns enclosing the flat, winged seeds.

Propagation. a) Seeds are extracted by exposing the woody follicles to warm, dry conditions, as on a sunny window-ledge; sown in spring in a friable material, they germinate readily.

b) Semi-hardwood leafy cuttings, taken between late summer and late winter, strike easily in a sand/peat mixture in a warm, humid atmosphere.

Cultivation. *L. formosa* thrives when grown in well-drained, fertile soils of a loose, open texture, but with adequate water in summer.

Pruning. Young plants benefit from an occasional tip-pruning in the early years to restrict lanky growth and to develop a dense, twiggy habit.

Species and cultivars

Lambèrtia formòsa (Latin 'beautiful'): Mountain Devil: NSW, mainly on the sandy heathlands and rocky hillsides of the Hawkesbury sandstone areas.

Habit. An evergreen shrub of 2 m or so tall, of open, indefinite shape in its native habitat but improved by occasional pruning.

Leaves. 3-whorled, linear, 3.5–8.5 cm long and 2–5 mm wide, broadest above the middle; petiole 2–3 mm, pubescent; apex obtuse, with a fine sharp spine; margin entire, thickened, recurved; midrib prominent beneath; texture stiff and coriaceous; dark green, glabrous, rugose and shiny above, whitish-tomentose beneath.

Flowers. Inflorescence a terminal cluster of 7 tubulate flowers subtended by several whorls of spreading, silky reddish bracts forming an involucre, the inner series of 6, to 4–6 cm long, the outer series 1.0–1.5 cm long; perianths in vertical clusters of 7, tubulate to 3–4 cm long, white-hirsute inside, currant-red, paling to white at the base; styles exserted to 2.0 cm beyond the perianth, scarlet; flowers produced from early November to late autumn.

Fruit. A 2-valved, woody follicle about 1 cm long in the body, with 2 long horns above and 1 short, thick horn below; green and of rough texture; seeds 2, flat, winged.

Climatic range. A, H, M, Mts, P, S.

LANTÀNA

Derived from the plant's resemblance to *Viburnum lantana*, the Wayfaring Tree of Europe and western Asia.
Lantana.
Verbenaceae, the Verbena family.

Generic description. A genus of somewhat tender, erect or trailing shrubs, mostly from Central America, with simple, opposite or whorled leaves, rough on both surfaces, salverform flowers in umbellate or corymbose heads in a variety of colours, and small drupaceous fruits. The parent of the modern dwarf-growing cultivars, *L. camara*, has escaped from cultivation in some warm-climate countries, including Australia, where it is proclaimed a noxious weed by many municipal and shire authorities. Most cultivars are either sterile or produce so few seeds that they are easily dealt with as potential weeds.

Propagation. Soft-tip cuttings taken at any time of the year strike readily in a sand/peat mixture in a warm, humid atmosphere.

Cultivation. Although the lantanas will tolerate austere conditions of soil and water supply, they are seen at their best in fertile, light soils with free drainage, but well supplied with water during dry times. They flower more freely in a fully sunny position in a frost-free climate, preferably coastal but with protection from salty winds.

Pruning. Regular tip-pruning every few months while the plants are young is essential to form compact growth, but when the desired shape is established, the plants require only annual pruning and shaping, usually in late winter.

Species and cultivars

Lantàna camàra (the West Indian native name): West Indies and Central America.

Habit. An evergreen shrub to 4 m or so tall with a broad crown, but more usually seen in its dwarf garden forms pruned to rounded or other shape up to 2 m tall or as a hedge in a variety of shapes.

Leaves. Simple, opposite, broadly ovate, 7–8 cm long and 3–4 cm wide; petiole 8–10 mm long; apex acute; base obtuse; margin crenate-serrate; venation reticulate, the midrib and main veins prominent beneath; aromatic when crushed; scabrous, especially above; hispid on both surfaces, prominently on the veins; dark green and slightly shiny above, paler and dull beneath.

Flowers. Inflorescence a condensed, umbellate spike of 20–30 flowers on a 3–5 cm peduncle, 6 to 10 spikes together in the upper axils of the new shoots; calyx tubulate to 2–3 mm, greenish; corolla salverform, about 1 cm long, the tube very slender and incurved near the top, the limb 4- or 5-parted; stamens 4, attached to the middle of the tube; flowering abundantly from October to May and intermittently through winter, in a variety of colours such as mauve, pink, creamy-yellow, orange, and red, some with white or orange throats.

See list of cultivars for colour range of the cultivated sorts.

Fruit. The cultivars are mostly sterile but occasionally produce seeds like the parent's in the form of a cluster of small black, fleshy drupes in autumn and winter.

Other distinguishing features. Upper stems squarish, with swollen nodes, densely coated with short, stiff, erect hairs and occasionally a few prickles, becoming brown, hard and brittle.
'Chelsea Gem': scarlet flowers, with a few orange flowers in the centre, the former colour predominating in autumn and winter.
'Christine': larger flowers than most, scarlet in the centre and orange at the outer edges, with a low, prostrate habit of growth.
'Diadem': cream and pink flowers.
'Drap d'Or': deep golden-yellow flowers.
'Gol Gol': coppery-yellow flowers maturing to copper-red.
'Minnie Basle': white and mauve-pink flowers.
'Snowflake': white flowers with a yellow-centre.
Climatic range. All B, M, P, S, T, and in A where frosts are only very light.

Lantàna montevidénsis (Latin 'from Montevideo', Uruguay) (syn. *L. sellowiana*) Trailing Lantana: central-eastern South America.
Habit. An evergreen, trailing shrub, broadly prostrate to 3 m wide, but rarely more than 1 m tall unless supported.
Leaves. Simple, opposite, ovate, 4–5 cm long, 2–3 cm wide; petiole 5–6 mm, grooved above; apex acute; base cuneate; margin denticulate-crenulate; veins depressed above, prominent beneath; finely pubescent; aromatic when bruised; mid green above, often with a purplish stain in winter, pale green beneath.
Flowers. Inflorescence an axillary, umbellate spike of about 20 flowers, subtended by green, leafy bracts forming a loose involucre, the many flowers issuing from the upper tiers; peduncles slender, 5–6 cm long, green pubescent; flowers salverform, the tube to 1 cm long, the limb irregularly 4-lobed and 7–8 mm across, rosy-lilac, some of the innermost flowers with a white eye and a bright golden-yellow flush in the throat of the tube; lightly perfumed; flowering throughout the year while in strong growth, but especially handsome in winter in warm, frost-free localities.
Fruit. Absent; local plants are probably sterile.
Other distinguishing features. Youngest stems green or purplish, becoming metallic-bronze and somewhat square in cross section.
Climatic range. A, B, M, P, S, T.

LAVÁNDULA

Derived from the Latin *lavare* 'to wash', referring to the use of lavender in toiletry.
Lavender (various).
Lamiaceae, the Mint family (formerly Labiatae).

Generic description. A small genus of about 25 species of low, evergreen shrubs with aromatic leaves, simple but sometimes bipinnatifid, and flowers borne in terminal, spike-like racemes with lavender-blue flowers. The species are native to the countries around the Mediterranean where they have been used in toiletry for centuries, two of the species treated below presently responsible for the bulk of the oil used in modern perfumery and soap manufacture. These and others are used as decorative plants in hedges, herbaceous borders, or as specimens in mixed plantings, mainly for their low, compact habit with attractive grey foliage and their blue, lavender, or sometimes white flowers.

Propagation. Leafy tip cuttings 3–4 cm long, with a small heel of older wood, are taken from stock-plants grown under somewhat severe conditions; between late autumn and late winter is the best time in the Sydney climate. The cuttings are planted in coarse sand with a little peat added and kept rather drier and cooler than other cuttings, without bottom heat or mist.

Cultivation. The aim should be to simulate the climate of southern Europe, with full exposure to sun, wind and moderately low temperatures. The ideal soil is light and friable, of limestone or granite origin, or otherwise of coarse texture, well drained and not over irrigated. They are safe to low temperatures of at least −5°C but are not usually satisfactory in climates warmer than that of Sydney.

Pruning. Some light shaping may be necessary occasionally to restrain untidy growth, but the main pruning task is to remove the spent flower stems as they die.

Species and cultivars
Lavándula angustifòlia (Latin 'with narrow leaves') (syn. *L. officinalis, L. vera*) native only to a restricted area of the Basses Alpes and Hautes Alpes in the south-east of France, at elevations between 500 m and 1200 m or more.

Habit. A small, evergreen subshrub to 1 m tall or less, usually of dense globose habit with an abundance of twiggy shoots carrying the soft grey foliage.

Leaves. Simple, opposite, linear to narrow-lanceolate, 3–4 cm long, 4–6 mm wide; apex acute; base obtuse; margin entire but revolute; dove-grey on both surfaces with a silky-white tomentum; aromatic.

Flowers. Inflorescence a loose, cylindrical spike to 4–5 cm long on an erect peduncle 5–8 cm long, unbranched, from the terminals of the young shoots, never from the leaf-axils below; flowers in whorled clusters of up to 7, subtended at the base of each whorl by a pubescent, floral bract with only very short points; calyx tubulate to 5 mm long, 12- to 14-ribbed, pubescent, shallowly toothed at the apex, one larger than the others; corolla tubulate, longer than the calyx, 5-lobed, bilabiate; lavender-blue, but variable in its seedlings; flowering from early October to late January.

Other distinguishing features. *L. angustifolia* is the source of the best quality oils, entirely free of camphor, and is so highly valued that it is seen only rarely in the open market. All the lavenders grown by the Bridestowe Estate at Nabowla, Tasmania, are this species and the plantings are considered to be the only successful attempt to grow the species commercially outside its native alpine habitat in France.

Climatic range. A, H, M, Mts, P.

Lavándula latifòlia (Latin 'with broad leaves') (syn. *L. spica*) Spike Lavender: Mediterranean coastal regions from Spain to Yugoslavia, at altitudes below 700 m.

The more common species, with taller, more vigorous growth, larger and broader, oblanceolate leaves to 5 cm or more and with longer, linear floral bracts with long points; the peduncles produce branching laterals upon which smaller inflorescences appear; it is otherwise somewhat similar to *L. angustifolia*.

The oil, known as Oil of Spike, is inferior, being crude in odour and harsh. Importantly, it is highly camphoraceous and therefore unfit for high quality perfumery, but is a valuable ingredient in the manufacture of some soaps.

Climatic range. A, H, M, Mts, P, S.

Lavándula x *intermèdia* (Latin 'in between'): the so-called Old English Lavender: natural hybrids have occurred between the two above species which intermingle at intermediate elevations in the French Alps. The many named cultivars listed in nursery catalogues are mostly products of this interspecific cross. 'Alba', 'Hidcote', 'Munstead', etc., all belong here and are broadly but inexactly referred to as Old English Lavenders.

Both parent species are either French Alpine or Mediterranean maritime plants and were brought to England by the Huguenots, the French Protestants driven into exile after the revocation of the Edict of Nantes in 1685; the two species have had ample time to acclimatise and naturalise in their adopted country and are thought of as natives.

Plants of this hybrid group provide most of the lavender oils used in perfumery. They lack the finer qualities of both parent species but are highly productive, and the oil can be produced economically.

Climatic range. A, H, M, Mts, P, S.

Lavándula dentàta (Latin *dens*, 'a tooth', referring to the leaf-margin): Toothed Lavender: Spain and near-neighbouring Mediterranean countries.

Habit. An evergreen shrub to 1.5 m with a dense, leafy habit, forming a slightly irregular, globular bush, the largest of the lavenders.

Leaves. Simple, opposite, linear, 2.5–3.0 cm long and 7–9 mm wide; apex acute; base obtuse and sessile; margin recurved and dentately notched with blunt teeth; both surfaces heavily pubescent; mildly aromatic when crushed; soft grey-green.

Flowers. Inflorescence a tightly-packed, cylindrical, spike-like raceme to 5 cm long and 1.0–1.5 cm wide, borne terminally on 12–15 cm peduncles, square and densely pubescent; flowers 5 to 7 in a whorled cluster, subtended by a broad, leaf-like bract at the base; calyx tubulate to 4–5 mm toothed; corolla tubulate to 3–4 mm beyond the calyx, with 5 nearly equal lobes; lavender-blue, several of the uppermost bracts similarly coloured; flowers lightly perfumed, flowering most abundantly in winter and early spring but sparsely at other times.

Other distinguishing features. The species has little value for its oil but is a popular ornamental plant because of its pleasant foliage and long flowering season.

Climatic range. A. H, M, Mts, P, S.

Lavándula stoèchas (Latin 'from the Stoechades Islands'), off the southern coast of France, but in fact, common throughout southern Europe, especially maritime Spain, France and other countries to Turkey and North Africa: French Lavender.

Habit. A dense, low shrub to 1 m tall, with many low branches soon dividing and forming a broadly spherical bush with abundant foliage.

Leaves. Simple, opposite, linear, to 2.5 cm long and 2–3 mm wide; apex acute with a short mucro; base obtuse, sessile; margin entire but recurved; midrib prominent beneath; fine tomentose; soft and flaccid; aromatic when bruised; grey-green.

Flowers. Inflorescence a deep, cylindrical, spike-like raceme to 2.5 cm long and 1 cm wide on a stout peduncle of 1 to 5 cm at the terminals of the young shoots, the flowers subtended and partly concealed by green, leafy bracts; calyx green, saccate, to 5 mm long; corolla tubulate, to 4–5 mm with 5 nearly equal lobes, lavender-blue on the tube, blackish-purple on the limb; flowers in neat, 4-ranked rows with the 4 uppermost floral bracts projecting from the apex in opposite, dissimilar pairs, deep purple; flowering from late August to December, then intermittently throughout summer.

Other distinguishing features. The plant is of little value for its low-grade oil but is an attractive and hardy, decorative species.

Climatic range. A, H, M, Mts, P, S.

LEONÒTIS

Derived from the Greek for 'lion's ear', which the flowers are supposed to resemble.

Lion's Ear.

Lamiaceae, the Mint family (formerly Labiatae).

Generic description. A genus of mostly evergreen shrubs, but with a few short-lived perennials, from South and Central Africa, represented mainly in Australian gardens by the species described in detail below.

Propagation. Soft-tip cuttings taken in spring or early summer, or semi-hardwood tips taken in winter, strike readily in a warm, moist environment.

Cultivation. The plant performs well in almost any moderately fertile, friable soil with free drainage. Kept bushy by regular pruning. Lion's Ear is tolerant of the salt-laden winds of the coast but is sensitive to low temperatures below about −2°C.

Pruning. Newly flowered stems should be shortened just below the inflorescence immediately after flowering, to keep the plant neat and compact.

Species and cultivars

Leonòtis leonùrus (from its resemblance to *Leonurus*, another genus of the same family): Lion's Ear: SE South Africa.

Habit. An evergreen shrub to 2 m tall and as wide, with many erect stems arising from the crowded base.

Leaves. Simple, opposite, linear-lanceolate, about 10 cm long and 1.0–1.5 cm wide, tapering narrowly to base and apex; margin coarsely serrate mostly above the middle; both surfaces strigose and rough in texture; veins prominent below; dark green above, paler beneath.

Flowers. In dense, axillary whorls at the upper nodes, 25–35 flowers in each whorl; calyx tubulate, 1.5 cm long, with 10 ribs and short teeth at the apex; corolla labiate-tubulate, about 4 cm long, the tube slender and split at the apex, enclosing the 4 stamens, the drooping lip near the middle of the tube; corolla covered with bright-orange hairs; flowers abundant between November and April.

Fruit. Seeds numerous, borne in the persistent, slender, tubulate calyces forming hemispherical heads at the upper nodes.

Other distinguishing features. Upper stems hairy, square in cross-section and shallowly channelled on the 4 sides.

Climatic range. A, B, H, M, P, S, T, and on warm sites in lower Mts.

LEPTOSPÉRMUM

Derived from the Greek *leptos* 'slender', and *sperma* 'a seed', describing the fine brownish seeds.

Tea-tree (the leaves of *Leptospermum scoparium* are supposed to have been used by the early Australian settlers to make a crude tea).

Myrtaceae, the Myrtle family.

Generic description. A mostly Australian genus of some 30 local species, all evergreen, with simple, alternate leaves; rotate flowers, borne singly or in a few-flowered clusters in the upper leaf-axils or on short axillary spur-like out-growths; and woody capsular fruits containing the slender seeds. The local and New Zealand species, *L. scoparium*, has produced a number of cultivars which constitute most of the plantings in Australia. Several of the other species are worth far greater use in gardens as ornamental flowering shrubs or for their good foliage or tolerance of salt-laden sea winds.

Propagation. a) All species may be grown by seeds but do not always reproduce the parent plant reliably; sown in spring in a friable medium in a warm, sheltered place, germination is normally rapid and prolific.
b) Semi-hardwood or soft-tip cuttings, taken at almost any season, strike readily in a warm, humid environment, preferably treated with hormone powder and planted in individual containers to minimise root disturbance when planting out.

Cultivation. The cultivars of *L. scoparium* are more at home on improved and well-drained garden soils, with regular attention to watering in dry times, frequent tip-pruning, and spraying for disease and pest control. The other species are more hardy, most thriving on any freely drained light soil in the temperature range of their native habitat.

Pruning. *L. scoparium* and its cultivars especially, but other species as well, are improved in density and flowering quality by a moderate annual pruning of the youngest shoots only, immediately after the flowering period.

Species and cultivars

Leptospèrmum flavéscens (Latin 'yellowish' referring to the cream petals): Yellow Tea-tree; Tantoon: coastal plains and adjacent slopes of the Great Dividing Range in Qld and NSW, usually on creek banks.
Habit. Variable, mostly a thin, rangy shrub of 2–4 m, the short trunk and main branches with rough stringy bark; some dwarf forms grow to only 1 m or so tall, with arching, almost pendulous branches and angular twigs.
Leaves. Oblanceolate, 10–15 mm long and 2–4 mm wide; apex obtuse to acute; margin entire; glabrous; mid-green.
Flowers. Solitary but in a racemose chain along the new shoots, globular in the bud, the pinkish sepals enclosing the petals, opening to rotate or slightly cupped, 10–15 mm across the 5 orbicular, cream or white petals on the rim of the green

calyx tube; stamens numerous, slightly incurved, the filaments white, with brown anthers; flowering period from late winter to early summer.
Fruit. A globose, 5-valved woody capsule about 8 mm wide; grey-brown; seeds slender, numerous.
'**Cardwell**' is an extremely floriferous cultivar from North Qld, growing to about 2 m, with pendulous branches and white flowers.
'**Pacific Beauty**' is much planted in Qld for its heavy crop of white flowers on a pendulous habit of growth.
Climatic range. A, B, M, P, S, T.

Leptospèrmum lanígerum (Latin 'woolly', referring to the heavily pubescent flower buds): Woolly Tea-tree: widespread in SE Australia, often seen on low-lying sites with indifferent drainage.
Habit. A small tree to 5 m or so, mostly with a short trunk soon dividing into many erect branches, forming a vase-shaped crown to 3–4 m wide.
Leaves. Oblanceolate, 8–15 mm long and 2 mm wide; petiole 0.5 mm long, flattened, whitish and finely pubescent; apex acute to shortly acuminate; base cuneate; margin entire; slightly silky-pubescent and grey-green above, densely pubescent and silvery-grey beneath.
Flowers. Solitary at the end of leafy twigs 1.0–1.5 cm long, many issuing from the upper branchlets, forming a racemose inflorescence 12–15 cm long; calyx urceolate to 4–5 mm across, dark green but covered with deciduous, brownish-pubescent scales, sepals 5, pale brown; corolla to 1.4 cm wide, wide, the 5 orbicular petals slenderly clawed at the base, pure white; stamens about 25–30, 2–3 mm long, the filaments white, anthers nut-brown; flowers abundant from early October to mid November.
Fruit. A rounded capsule of 6–8 mm across with a flat apex, green at first, ripening to brown-grey.
Other distinguishing features. Upper twigs slender, buff-yellow, older branchlets with ridged bark.

var. macrocàrpum (Greek 'with large fruit'): Large-fruited Woolly Tea-tree: sheltered sites on the Blue Mts of NSW.
Habit. Somewhat smaller than the parent species, mostly about 1.5 m tall and a little broader, usually of irregular but dense growth, its vigour reflecting the quality of the site.
Leaves. Oblanceolate to oblong to 1.8 cm long and 1 cm broad, shiny and dark green.

Flowers. Rotate to 2.5 cm across, the 5 orbicular petals bright pink, but varying in seedlings to white, lime-yellow or rosy-crimson, with a coronet-like ring of cream stamens around the large central green disc, and a single greenish style; flowering is somewhat intermittent between late spring and autumn.

Fruit. A large domed capsule about 1 cm or more across the apex; nut-brown.

Climatic range. A, H, M, Mts, P, S.

Leptospèrmum laevigàtum (Latin 'smooth', describing the glabrous leaves): Coast Tea-tree: southern and eastern Australian coast, from SW WA to the Qld border, mostly on heathlands and sandhills close to the sea-shore.

Habit. A small tree to 6 m or so, or a many stemmed shrub to 3–4 m tall, usually forming a dense thicket with abundant foliage, tolerant of the salty, boisterous winds of the coast.

Leaves. Obovate to 2.5 cm long and 6–8 mm wide; petiole 1–2 mm long, slightly flattened; apex obtuse or shortly acute-mucronate; margin entire; venation indistinct, apart from the 3 main veins converging at the base; glabrous and coriaceous; somewhat glaucous-green on both surfaces.

Flowers. Solitary in the upper leaf-axils, sessile, 5–petalled, rotate to 1.5 cm across, the petals not overlapping, obovate to orbicular, white; calyx tube glabrous, green, hemispherical to 7 mm across the flat top, the calyx lobes to 1 mm long, spreading, triangular; stamens numerous, attached to the rim of the greenish disc; flowers borne freely from August to late December.

Fruit. A hemispherical, woody capsule, ripening to dark brown-grey, the 8–10 loculed ovary splitting to release the small linear-triangular seeds.

Other distinguishing features. Upper twigs angular, and bi-coloured by the decurrent whitish strips of bark overlying the brown-grey bark beneath.

One of the most useful plants for seaside planting; young plantings should be closely spaced and pruned lightly in the early years to encourage the development of a thick, twiggy growth. Old plants resent severe pruning.

Climatic range. A, B, M, P, S, T.

Leptospèrmum nìtidum (Latin 'lustrous' or 'shiny', referring to the glabrous leaves): Glossy Tea-tree or Grampians Tea-tree: SW Vic. highlands and NW Tas: sometimes classified as a variety of *L. lanigerum*.

Habit. A shrub to 3 m or so with somewhat open character and indefinite shape in its native habitat on rocky or poor scree soils, but modified by cultivation and pruning to become dense and compact.

Leaves. Oblanceolate to obovate, to 2 cm long and 8–10 mm wide; petiole 2–4 mm long, cream; apex acute-mucronate; margin ciliate or entire; venation indistinct apart from the midrib and 2 nearly parallel laterals; pale green and silky-pubescent when young, becoming dark green, glabrous and shiny in maturity.

Flowers. Solitary at the end of short, leafy lateral twigs; calyx shallowly crateriform to 3–4 mm deep but 8–9 mm across the cup, the 5 cream sepals narrowly triangular; flowers rotate to 3 cm wide, perhaps the largest of the genus, the 5 white, orbicular petals to 1.2 cm wide, slenderly clawed at the base, arranged between the sepals; stamens about 35–40, on the edge of the green receptacle, filaments white, anthers creamy-brown; pistil large, green; flowers produced during October and early November.

Fruit. A crateriform, woody capsule, 1 cm across, with 5 raised cells and a prominent rim.

Other distinguishing features. Youngest twigs squarish, whitish-green and finely pubescent, becoming buff-yellow, then dark brown in age. 'Copper Sheen' is a smaller, more compact bush to about 2 m tall, with reddish stems and dark coppery-red leaves, giving it its appropriate name, and large greenish-yellow flowers with a dark-green disc.

Climatic range. A, H, M, Mts, P, S.

Leptospèrmum pètersonii (commemorating W. J. Peterson, the collector of the first recorded specimens from Wilson's Peak on the Qld–NSW border, near the junction of the Great Divide and the McPherson Range) (syn. *L. citratum*) Lemon-scented Tea-tree: northern NSW and southern Qld.

Habit. A small evergreen tree to 3–5 m tall, with a short trunk and slender, pendulous outer branchlets, often used as a pruned shrub, then dense and heavily foliaged.

Leaves. Linear-lanceolate to 3.5 cm long and 4–5 mm wide; apex obtuse, often shallowly emarginate; margin entire; midrib and 2 parallel laterals only visible; heavily glandular and strongly aromatic when bruised; pale reddish-green at first, especially in cool climates, becoming dark and shiny above, paler beneath; the strong citron foliar fragrance is especially pleasant.

Flowers. 1.5–2.0 cm across, solitary on short axillary twigs; calyx shallowly crateriform to 6 mm across, green, glabrous, with 5 orbicular sepals 2 mm long, reddish-green; petals 5, broadly obovate, to 5–6 mm long, with a narrow claw at the base, between the sepals, pure white; stamens about 40, around the rim of the receptacle, filaments white, anthers brown; style 3–4 mm tall, green; flowers abundant in December and January.

Fruit. A 5-celled woody capsule, opening at the apex when dry to release the numerous, finely linear brownish seeds.

Other distinguishing features. Youngest twigs angular, with knife-like, decurrent ridges below the leaf-bases; young bark reddish-green, becoming grey in age.

Climatic range. A, B, M, P, S, T, and in warm microclimates on the lower levels of Mts.

Leptospèrmum scopàrium **var.** *rotundifòlium* (Latin 'with rounded leaves'): Round-leafed Teatree: NSW, mainly between the coast and the lower levels of the tablelands, often on poor sandy or gravelly heathland soils.

Habit. An evergreen shrub to 1.5–2.5 m tall, with twiggy growth on a rounded bush, often somewhat wider than its height.

Leaves. Broadly ovate to orbicular, 7 mm long and 6 mm wide; apex acute, the mucronate point recurved; base obtuse; margin entire; densely glandular dotted and aromatic when bruised; dark green and slightly shiny.

Flowers. Mostly solitary on short axillary twigs arising from the 1-year-old wood; calyx campanulate with 5 acute lobes, green; petals 5, orbicular, concave, not overlapped, forming a rotate flower 2.5 cm across, white to pale pink but occasionally deep rose-pink to mauve-pink; stamens 20–25, in a single series on the rim of the green receptacle; flowers produced from late September to December.

Fruit. A woody, shallowly campanulate capsule, with numerous acicular brown seeds, ripening in summer to autumn.

Other distinguishing features. Youngest twigs reddish-tan, pubescent, becoming grey-brown with ridges of stringy, loose bark.

'Julie Ann' is a registered cultivar from the NSW South Coast with prostrate habit, 25–30 cm tall and 1 m or so broad, slightly smaller leaves and flowers than those of the parent, but otherwise much the same. Its tolerance of frost and salty winds is reported.

Climatic range. A, M, P, S, and in warm microclimates in Mts.

Leptospèrmum scopàrium **var.** *scopàrium* (Latin 'broom-like', referring to the twigs): Broom Teatree (in Australia), Manuka (in New Zealand): NSW, mainly on moist land between the coast and lower tablelands, and in both islands of NZ in the same type of habitat.

Habit. A shrub to about 3 m, of erect form at first, eventually broadening to almost spherical shape, with many slender upright shoots from the crowded base and mallee-like rootstock.

Leaves. Linear to ovate-lanceolate, 1.5–2.0 cm long and 2–3 mnm wide with a very short, flat petiole; apex acute with a sharp mucro; margin entire, but with fine, translucent glandular dots towards the edge; midrib and 3 to 5 main longitudinal veins prominent; glabrous, except for some occasional long silky hairs along the lower edge of the petiole and main vein; slightly reddish when young in spring, becoming dark green on both surfaces.

Flowers. Solitary on short shoots in the upper axils, but borne so densely as to resemble a raceme; flower buds globose at first, enclosed within 5 deciduous, brown papery scales; calyx broadly campanulate with 5 triangular sepals, the whole to 1 cm across; petals 5, orbicular, meeting but not overlapped at the edges, the flower rotate to 2 cm across; predominantly white in the species, but occasionally pinkish, the cultivars extended in colour from white to deep pink and crimson, in single and double form; flowers are borne prolifically from late winter to summer.

Fruit. Capsule urn-shaped, to 6–8 mm across the 5-celled apex, green at first but persisting and becoming brown when picked, and then soon dispersing the numerous slender brown seeds.

Other distinguishing features. Upper twigs pubescent and angular, the bark stringy and pale grey.

Climatic range. A, B, H, M, Mts, P, S.

The developed cultivars are too numerous to be listed fully here but the following represent the colours and forms available from nurseries, whose catalogues should be consulted for further details.

'Álbum Flòre-plèno' is a strong-growing erect bush to 2.5–3.0 m, with green foliage and fully-double white flowers to 1.5 cm across, flowering from late August to mid October.

PLATE 21

▲ Prostanthera ovalifolia

▲ Pyracantha angustifolia

▼ Photinia x fraseri 'Robusta'

▲ Prunus glandulosa 'Alba Plena'
◄ Podalyria calyptrata
▼ Ribes sanguineum 'King Edward VII'

▼ Photinia glabra 'Rubens'

▼ Prunus glandulosa 'Rosea Plena'

PLATE 22

▲ Pyracantha atalantioides

▲ Punica granatum

▲ Retama monosperma

▲ Pukeiti Rhododendron Trust Garden, New Plymouth,

▲ Pyracantha angustifolia
◄ Potentilla fruticosa 'Klondyke'
▼ National Rhododendron Garden, Olinda, Victoria

▼ Rhododendron Azalea Kurume 'Hinode-giri'

'**Fairy Rose**' is a compact, medium-sized grower to 1.5 m tall and as wide, with dark reddish-green foliage and fully-double rose-pink flowers, deepening with age, in September and October.
'**Kéatleyi**' is an erect bush of strong growth to 2.5–3.0 m tall, with pubescent, dull grey-green foliage and twigs, and fluted single flowers to 2.5 cm across, white with red markings, from late August to late October.
'**Lámbethii**' has tall, upright growth to 3 m, with green foliage often tinged with red, and very large single flowers to 3 cm across when well grown, in pale to deep pink and crimson, the colours often appearing on the same flower, flowering heavily from May to October. Probably the best cultivar presently grown in Australia.
'**Nànum**' is a low-growing plant mostly less than 0.75 m tall and of broad globular form, with small reddish-green leaves and twigs, and single pale rose-pink flowers with a red centre, the colour deepening to light crimson, from September to November.
'**Nìchollsii**' is an erect grower to 2.5 m, with dark reddish-green foliage and twigs, and single dark-crimson flowers 1.5 cm across. The first of the dark-red cultivars and now largely superseded by its improved forms, '**Nìchollsii Improved**' and '**Nìchollsii Magnìficum**'; flowers from mid September to late November.
'**Red Damask**' is a strong-growing compact bush to 2.5–3.0 m tall, with dark reddish-green leaves and twigs, and large double, bright blood-red flowers, at their best from late August to mid October.
'**Robert Tarrant**' is a medium-sized plant of compact, bushy form to 2 m tall, with green foliage and large double, rose-pink flowers in September and October.
'**Ròseum Flòre-plèno**' has erect but densely compact growth to 2.0–2.5 m tall, with green foliage and large 2 cm wide, fully-double shell-pink flowers, from early September until early December.
'**Ruby Glow**' is an upright, somewhat-open bush to 3 m tall, with reddish-green foliage and dark red pubescent twigs, and large, fully-double, deep-crimson flowers, in September and October.
'**Scarlet Carnival**' has an upright growth habit to 2 m or so, with reddish-green foliage, and fully-double scarlet to blood-red flowers, somewhat later flowering from late October to early December.

'**Sunraysia**' is the double-flowered form of 'Lambethii' with white, pink, and crimson on the same flower, borne prolifically like the parent from May to October.

Leptospèrmum squarròsum (Latin 'with overlapping parts', referring to the imbricated bud-scales) (syn. *L. persiciflorum*) Peach-flowered Tea-tree: found in all eastern States; in NSW, mainly on the Hawkesbury sandstone country between the coast and the tablelands.
Habit. A shrub of loose, open character to 2–3 m tall, but rather more slender.
Leaves. Variable in shape, mainly linear-lanceolate to ovate to 1 cm long, the short petiole flattened; apex acuminate, prickly; base obtuse; margin entire; glabrous; glandular dotted and slightly aromatic when crushed; dull dark green.
Flowers. Solitary in the upper axils, or on short spurs with a fascicle of leaves at the base; calyx campanulate to 3–4 mm long, the 5 triangular, broad lobes 3 mm long, membranous and nearly transparent; petals 5, between the calyx lobes, broadly obovate to orbicular, spreading to rotate form 1.5–2.0 cm across, white or pinkish, flowering from late spring to summer, sometimes until early winter.
Fruit. Capsule 8–9 mm deep and 1.3 cm across, the base crateriform, brown-grey with a crazed surface, the rim projecting prominently, the 5 valves hemispherically domed, the style sometimes persistent; seeds red-tan, acicular to 3 mm long, very numerous.
Other distinguishing features. Upper twigs terete, yellowish at first, becoming greyish, and angular by the decurrent bark shreds.
Climatic range. A, B, M, Mts, P, S.

LEUCOPÒGON

Derived from the Greek *leucos* 'white', and *pogon* 'a beard', referring to the white-woolly corolla lobes. Beard-heath, various.
Epacridaceae, the Epacris family.

Generic description. A genus of more than 100 species of evergreen shrubs mainly from Australia but a few from the western Pacific region. All are evergreen, most of thin, twiggy growth habit; the small flowers are tubulate or campanulate, pink or red in the bud, opening to white, the inner surface of the petals with a dense white-woolly beard.

Propagation. Tip cuttings taken in late summer

and treated with root-promoting material are probably the best method of propagation.

Cultivation. The commonly-cultivated species usually perform best on well-drained coarse soils with additional watering in dry times, well mulched with vegetative litter or gravel, in the dappled shade of taller plants.

Pruning. Tip-pruning after the flowering period stimulates the growth of lateral twigs with increased flower production.

Species and cultivars

Leucopògon ericòides (Greek 'like *Erica*', referring to the growth habit: Pink Beard-heath: SE Australia, mostly on sandy or stony soils in the coastal heaths, forested plateaus and lower tablelands.
Habit. A thin, open shrub of 1–2 m tall on poor soils but responding to cultivation and regular pruning with more compact habit and denser foliage.
Leaves. Simple, alternate, spreading widely, linear-oblong, 6–10 mm long, 1 mm wide, sessile; apex acute with a sharp, bristly point; margin entire, recurved; silky-tomentose and dark green above, paler beneath.
Flowers. Sessile, solitary or in small spikes of 2–5 in the leaf axils along 20–30 cm of the upper twigs; sepals 5; corolla to 5 mm long, spear-shaped in the bud, opening with 5 spreading linear-lanceolate lobes, pink outside, densely white-woolly inside; flowering from late July to October.
Fruit. A small ovoid drupe ripening in early summer.
Climatic range. A, H, M, Mts, P, S.

Leucopògon virgàtus (Latin 'having long straight twigs') Common Beard-heath: widespread on sandy heaths in SE Australia and Qld.
Habit. A thin, open shrub with wiry stems growing to 1 m at best, but often smaller on poor soils.
Leaves. Alternate, linear-lanceolate, 8–12 mm long; apex acuminate; margin incurved but entire, some partly clasping the stems; glabrous; dark green.
Flowers. Inflorescence a short spike at the terminals and upper axils; flowers several, reddish and slenderly conical in the bud; calyx with 5 ovate sepals; corolla tubulate, 6–10 mm long, the 5 obovate lobes reflexed, spreading, densely white-woolly inside, sweetly perfumed; flow-

ering from September to mid-summer.
Fruit. A rounded 3–5 celled drupe, ripening in summer.
Climatic range. A, B, H, M, Mts, P, S.

LEUCÓTHOË (syn. *Andromeda*)

Commemorating Leucothoë, daughter of Orchamus, King of Babylonia in Greek mythology. Leucothoe.
Ericaceae, the Erica family

Generic description. A small genus of mostly evergreen shrubs with simple, alternate leaves on slender, arching branches; the flowers in axillary or terminal racemes, mostly urceolate with a 5-lobed calyx, mainly white but occasionally pinkish, with 10 enclosed stamens and a single stout pistil; and globose, capsular fruits. The plants are grown for their showy foliage and flowers.

Propagation. a) Seeds sown in spring germinate readily, the best medium being grated sphagnum moss kept barely moist, in a warm, humid atmosphere.
b) Semi-hardwood tip cuttings are also used, taken in late spring and struck in a sand/peat mixture in a misted, heated glass-house.

Cultivation. A cool, moist, partly shaded position is best, in a mild climate with temperatures not lower than −8°C, the most suitable soil slightly acid and peaty, or heavily dressed with organic matter.

Pruning. Young plants should be tip-pruned during their first few years, then the long drooping flowering shoots should be encouraged; a few of the oldest shoots may be removed at the base each year to make way for new growth.

Species and cultivars

Leucóthoë fontanesiàna (commemorating Prof. René Desfontaines, French botanical author) (syn. *L. catesbaei*) eastern USA between the coast and the Appalachian Mountains.
Habit. An evergreen shrub to 2 m tall, with arching pendulous stems arising from the base to form a rounded bush about 2.5 m across.
Leaves. Lanceolate to narrowly ovate-lanceolate, 6–18 cm long and 2–4 cm wide, arranged in a single plane, the twigs in a zig-zag pattern; petiole 5–12 mm long, rounded, purple; apex finely long-acuminate; base acute; margin finely and sharply serrate, more evident above the middle;

venation reticulate, the midrib prominent below; glabrous; dark green and glossy above, paler beneath, changing to deep purplish-red in autumn and persisting until spring.

Flowers. Inflorescence an axillary raceme, many together borne on the underside of the outermost twigs, the racemes 4–6 cm long, with up to 40 or more flowers on slender 3–4 mm pedicels, subtended at the base by small brown bracts; calyx with 5 acute, spreading sepals corolla urceolate, 6–8 mm long and 5 mm wide, the 5 apical lobes recurved, pink in the bud but opening to waxy-white, flowering in October and November.

Fruit. A globose capsule to 4 mm across, splitting into 5 apical valves to release the fine seeds. Young stems dark red, puberulent.

'**Rainbow**' has green leaves, variegated with creamy-white, yellow and pink, contrasting well with the reddish petioles.

Climatic range. H, M, Mts, and in cool, moist, partly shaded sites in A, P, and S.

LIGÚSTRUM

The ancient Latin name.
Privet.
Oleaceae, the Olive family.

Generic description. a genus of well-known, hardy shrubs and small trees mainly from the Orient and Europe, with evergreen or deciduous, simple, opposite leaves with entire margins; the inflorescence is paniculate, mostly terminal, the white, heavily scented flowers with 4-merous parts, the calyx campanulate, the corolla salverform with 4 reflexed lobes and 2 stamens; fruit is a small ellipsoidal or globose drupe, green at first but ripening in summer and autumn to blue or black. Several species have been used extensively in Australian gardens for hedging and screening, but their escape from cultivation to become one of the most serious threats to the NSW coastal bushland is the cause of great concern to municipal and conservation authorities.

Propagation. a) Seeds, cleaned and sown as soon as ripe or held until spring, germinate readily in any reasonably well-aerated sowing material.
b) *L. ovalifolium* 'Aureum' is grown by firmwood tip cuttings in late spring and summer, or by mature hardwood cuttings in winter.

Cultivation. Privets are not particular about soil and exposure but the coloured foliaged forms should be grown in an open, sunny aspect to develop the best foliage colour.

Pruning. As hedges, privets require frequent clipping because of their normally rapid growth. Specimen plants of the coloured-foliaged kinds may be grown more freely but should be checked regularly for reverted green branchlets, which should be removed.

Species and cultivars

Ligústrum ovalifòlium '**Aùreum**' (syn. 'Aureo-variegatum', Aureo-marginatum') Golden Privet: the parent species is indigenous to Japan, but has become so identified with western USA that it is commonly known in that country as Californian Privet.

Habit. A partly deciduous shrub to about 4 m tall when unrestricted and of erect, dense growth, but more usually seen as a pruned plant, often in geometrical form as a hedge or specimen.

Leaves. Elliptical to ovate to 5–6 cm long and 2–3 cm wide (but much smaller when restricted by pruning): petiole 3–5 mm: apex acute; margin entire; venation reticulate, the veins slightly depressed above, prominent beneath; glabrous; leaves variegated with a dark-green blotch in the centre, an intermediate margin of pale grey-green, and a broad irregular margin of yellow, some leaves being almost wholly yellow; when grown in shade, the bright yellow is reduced to pale green.

Flowers. Inflorescence an erect terminal panicle 6–9 cm long and as broad; calyx campanulate 2 mm long, green; corolla tubulate to 7–8 mm long, the limb rotate to fully reflexed, pure white; heavily and somewhat unpleasantly perfumed; flowers abundant from November to January.

Fruit. A blue-black drupe to 5 mm across, with whitish bloom.

Climatic range. A, B, M, P, S, T, and in warm microclimates in Mts.

LONÍCERA

Commemorating Dr Adam Lonitzer, sixteenth-century German botanical author.
Honeysuckle (various).
Caprifoliaceae, the Honeysuckle family.

Generic description. A large genus of shrubs

and climbing plants from the northern temperate zone, mainly Europe, the Orient, and North America, several used widely in Australian gardens for their sweetly perfumed and sometimes showy flowers. Leaves are evergreen or deciduous, always opposite, the climbers with twining stems; flowers are in pairs or in sessile whorled clusters, the corolla a long slender tube, flaring to a 5-lobed limb; fruit is a fleshy berry, often attractively coloured.

Propagation. The species treated here are normally propagated by firmwood cuttings, tips in the shrubby kinds but semi-hardwood nodal lengths in the twiners, struck in a sand/peat mixture in summer and autumn.

Cultivation. Honeysuckles are easy to cultivate, preferably grown in an open sunny position on a freely drained soil of moderate fertility. *L. nitida* is a favourite species for dwarf hedging.

Pruning. *L. fragrantissima* and *L. x heckrottii* are best pruned moderately, immediately after flowering, shortening the flowered shoots by about half their annual growth to induce a dense, leafy habit; a few of the older basal shoots of *L. fragrantissima* should be removed entirely at the base each year to encourage and make way for new water-shoot growth. *L. nitida* is usually hedged by early and persistent trimming to the low, dense form required.

Species and cultivars

Lonícera fragrantíssima (Latin 'very fragrant'): eastern China.
Habit. An almost deciduous shrub to about 2.5 m tall, with loose open growth to 2.0–2.5 m wide, many stiff, erect shoots arising from the base; in warm climates, it becomes almost evergreen.
Leaves. Broadly elliptic to obovate, 3–6 cm long and 2.0–3.5 cm wide; apex broadly acute and mucronate; base rounded, the petiole 2–3 mm long; margin coarsely ciliate; venation reticulate, the midrib and main veins white and prominent beneath, the midrib with a few fine bristles below; otherwise glabrous; dull mid green above, paler and blue-green beneath.
Flowers. Inflorescence a cluster of 2 to 4 pairs of decussately-opposite flowers at the nodes of the upper branchlets, each with a pair of leafy bracts; corolla 2-lobed, the upper lobe broad and subdivided into 4 overlapping segments, the lower lobe undivided, the open limb 1.5–2.0 cm across, waxy-white, deepening to cream in age, the tube stained with rosy-carmine; stamens 5,

with white filaments and large golden-yellow anthers; flowering period July to September; heavily and sweetly fragrant.
Fruit. A small usually solitary berry of irregular obovoid shape, about 1 cm long and 7–8 mm wide, coral-red, soft and fleshy.
Other distinguishing features. Twigs smooth, nut-brown with a solid white pith.
Climatic range. A, B, H, M, Mts, P, S.

Lonícera x héckrottii: interspecific hybrid between *L. americana* and *L. sempervirens.* 'Shrub of the Year' for 1976.
Habit. A plant of indeterminate growth habit between a shrub and a scrambling or twining climber; by pruning or training over a support it may be made to adopt either form of growth but for best results, neither treatment, once started, should be relaxed.
Leaves. Deciduous in cool climates but retaining more leaves in warm zones, broadly elliptic to 5–6 cm long, sessile, those immediately below the inflorescence joined at the base to enclose the stem; apex acute; margin entire; midrib prominent beneath; glabrous; dark green above, glaucous green below.
Flowers. In a dense, terminal, whorled spike at the end of the 1-year-old shoots, slenderly tubulate to about 5 cm long, flared into an expanded 2-lobed limb, the tube purplish-red at first, merging to coral-red towards the limb, white inside the limb, aging to yellow; pubescent; heavily perfumed; stamens exserted, with white filaments and yellow anthers, the long white pistil with a large green stigma; flowers abundant from late October to late summer.
Fruit. Not seen; plant probably sterile.
Climatic range. A, B, H, M, Mts, P, S.

Lonícera nítida (Latin 'shining', referring to the leaves): Box-leafed Honesuckle: western China.
Habit. An evergreen shrub to about 2 m tall and broad when grown naturally, but more commonly hedged or pruned to geometrical shape.
Leaves. Ovate, 7–12 mm long and 5–8 mm wide in closely adjacent pairs in a neat single plane, the nodes 4–8 mm apart; petiole 1 mm, pubescent, channelled above; apex obtuse or broadly acute; base rounded; margin entire; venation obscure above, the finely puberulent midrib and several main veins on each side more evident; bright green above but somewhat paler beneath.
Flowers. Funnelform to 7–9 mm long, 5-lobed, paired at the upper opposite axils on very short

pedicels; whitish with sweet perfume; stamens exserted, the filaments pale creamy-white, the anthers yellow; flowering season late spring.

Fruit. An ovoid to nearly globose berry to 6–7 mm across, translucent, violet-purple, fruiting in late summer and autumn but rarely seen on hedged or trimmed plants.

'**Aùrea**' (Latin 'golden-yellow'): has yellowish leaves, bright in spring but becoming dull as the growth rate declines in summer.

Climatic range. A, B, H, M, Mts, P, S.

LOPHOMÝRTUS (formerly included in *Myrtus*)

Derived from the Greek *lophos* a 'crest' or 'crown', and *Myrtus*, but of obscure application here.

New Zealand Myrtle.

Myrtaceae, the Myrtle family.

Generic description. A genus of New Zealand evergreen shrubs and small trees with simple, opposite, entire, glandular leaves, the axillary white flowers with 4 sepals and petals and numerous white stamens, and small, berry-like, blackish fruits. The two native species are uncommon in Australia, but their hybrid, described below, is a popular foliage plant deserving wider use for its pleasant foliage in a variety of colours.

Propagation. Firm-tip cuttings taken between late summer and winter strike readily in a sand/ peat mixture, preferably in a warm, humid atmosphere.

Cultivation. A well-drained, sandy or light loamy soil with a high organic content is most suitable, preferably in a mild climate with minimum temperatures above –3°C and where seasonal droughts may be countered by additional water, especially in spring and summer.

Pruning. Frequent tip-pruning of the young shoots is beneficial during the early years to build up a dense, leafy growth habit; thereafter, light annual pruning to maintain the desired shape may be necessary.

Species and cultivars

Lophomýrtus x *rálphii*: the interspecific hybrid between *L. bullata* and *L. obcordata*.

Habit. An evergreen shrub to 2–3 m or so with closely set twigs forming an upright, slender bush, but often pruned into geometrical shapes.

Leaves. Broadly ovate, obovate to orbicular, 2 cm long and 1.5 cm wide, but variable in the cultivars; apex obtuse; base rounded to the 3 mm pubescent petiole; margin entire; midrib and main laterals prominent, the interveinal spaces wrinkled and bullate; nearly glabrous; pale green above, with a pink edge and midrib, becoming deeper with maturity, and purplish-bronze beneath.

Flowers. Solitary in the upper axils, rotate, 1 cm across, the 4 petals nearly orbicular, ivory-white, the showy stamens with white filaments and golden-yellow anthers; flowering season November-December.

Fruit. A reddish-black, globose berry, 6–8 mm across.

Other distinguishing features. Youngest twigs pinkish, pubescent, becoming chocolate-brown.

'**Trícolor**' (syn. 'Variegata' and 'Gloriosa' has orbicular leaves to 1.5 cm long and as wide, with red petioles, the blades pale to mid green, margined with creamy-white, the edge often showing a fine carmine-red line, the reverse paler, suffused with bronze-pink.

'**Purpùrea**': similar in shape and size but leaves are bronze-purple above and reddish-purple beneath, the twigs also bronze.

Climatic range. A, B, M, P, S, T, and in warm, elevated parts of lower Mts.

LOROPÉTALUM

Derived from the Greek describing the slender, strap-shaped petals.

Strap-flower or Fringe-flower.

Hamamelidaceae, the Witch-Hazel family.

Generic description. A genus of a single species from eastern Asia, popular in Australian gardens for its striking spring flowers, the horizontal growth pattern being adaptable to walling or use in Japanese or Chinese style gardens. See specific notes below for details.

Propagation. a) Seeds sown as soon as ripe in a light, friable material, germinate readily.
b) Soft-tip cuttings, taken in late spring and planted in a sand/peat mixture with bottom heat and high humidity, are most commonly used.
c) Semi-hardwood cuttings are also used, taken in summer to winter, and struck as above.

Cultivation. The main requirements for normal growth are an open, sunny position sheltered from cold, boisterous winds, in a well-drained soil of moderate fertility with adequate water in dry times. Safe to –3°C but needs protection in colder winters, especially against late frosts.

Pruning. Light to moderate pruning, immediately after the spring flowers, is beneficial to remove the spent flowers and to promote a twiggy, dense growth.

Species and cultivars

Loropétalum chinénse (Latin 'from China'): Strap-flower or Fringe-flower: temperate northern India, south-eastern China and central Japan.

Habit. An evergreen shrub to 2.0–2.5 m tall, with a somewhat wider, horizontally-inclined form and abundant foliage.

Leaves. Simple, alternate, broadly elliptic, narrowly ovate to obovate 2–5 cm long, 2–3 cm wide; petiole 3–5 mm long with brown stellate pubescence; apex acute or obtuse with a small mucro; base unequally rounded; margin entire but stellate-ciliate; main veins prominent beneath; dark green and rough above, glaucous-green and stellate-pubescent beneath, especially on the veins.

Flowers. Inflorescence an umbellate cluster of 6–9 flowers on short pubescent shoots from the upper axils; shoots stipulate; calyx pubescent, with 4 spreading ovate lobes; petals 4, linear, to 2 cm long and 2 mm wide, rolled in the bud but opening to a soft, pendulous strap, crepe-like, yellowish-white, flowering from late August to late October.

Fruit. A small cyathiform receptacle 1 cm long, pubescent and grey-green, partly enclosing the 2-locular ovary, with a single, rounded, whitish seed to 5–6 mm in each compartment.

Other distinguishing features. Upper twigs greyish, but covered with brown stellate pubescence.

Climatic range. A, B, M, P, S, T, and in warm, sheltered microclimates in Mts.

LUCÙLIA

Latinised from the native name in Nepal.
Luculia.
Rubiaceae, the Madder family.

Generic description. A small genus of evergreen shrubs from the lower Himalayas, one a popular flowering plant in the warmer coastal parts of Australia. See specific notes below for details.

Propagation. a) Seeds collected as soon as ripe, just before the woody capsules split to disperse the seeds, are sown in a sterilised mixture of finely ground sphagnum moss and coarse sand, in a warm place with only moderate humidity.
b) Soft-tip cuttings, taken in spring and summer, root satisfactorily in a sand/peat mixture in a warm, humid atmosphere, preferably in individual containers to minimise root disturbance when planting.

Cultivation. The plant is somewhat capricious in growth, often dying for no apparent reason. It appears to prefer a freely drained, coarse, fibrous soil with good aeration, and with a cool root-zone, attained by use of a thick pebble or gravel mulch. Organic fertilisers and compost seem to be the best form of plant food. Thorough watering in summer is essential. A well-established plant will tolerate light frosts but young plants need protection for the first year or two.

Pruning. Pruning is often considered to be a risky practice, but in fact a well-grown plant benefits from an annual light pruning of the spent flower stems just before new growth starts in early spring.

Species and cultivars

Lucùlia gratíssima (the superlative of the Latin *gratus* 'pleasing'): lower Himalayas to Yunnan, at 1000–2000 m elevation, on lightly wooded hills.

Habit. An evergreen shrub to 3–4 m tall, of open, irregular form.

Leaves. Simple, opposite, elliptical to 20 cm long and 5–10 cm wide; petiole 1–2 cm, channelled above, densely pubescent; apex acuminate; base cuneate; margin entire; midrib and 8–10 pairs of main laterals pubescent and prominent beneath; dark green and glossy above, paler and dull below.

Flowers. Inflorescence a terminal corymb, 15–20 cm across, of 20 to 80 flowers; calyx tubulate to 5 mm, with 5 linear 1 cm sepals; corolla salverform to 3–4 cm long, the 5-lobed limb 2.5–3.5 cm across, the lobes creped at the edges; soft rose-pink, but somewhat variable; stamens 5, connate to the inside of the tube, anthers to 4 mm, yellowish-brown; style bifid, as long as the tube; flowering from April to July.

Fruit. A club-shaped woody capsule, splitting longitudinally.

Other distinguishing features. Flowers highly perfumed; upper stems squarish, olive-green.

Climatic range. B, M, P, S, T, and in sheltered, warm microclimates in A.

MACKAYA (formerly included in *Asystasia*)

Commemorating James Townsend Mackay, Scottish botanical author.
Mackaya.
Acanthaceae, the Acanthus family.

Generic description. A small genus of evergreen shrubs mainly from Africa and southern Asia, one grown occasionally in Australia for its handsome foliage and flowers. See specific notes below for details.

Propagation. Soft-tip or semi-hardwood leafy cuttings taken between mid spring and late summer strike readily in a sand/peat mixture in a warm glass-house.

Cultivation. When not pampered, Mackaya is more hardy than is generally supposed, and will tolerate light frosts to at least −2°C. The plant grows well in either filtered or full sunlight, but is prone to damage by violent winds. A friable soil of moderate fertility is ideal.

Pruning. A young plant should be tip-pruned frequently in the first 2–3 years to establish a dense, globose bush; thereafter, flowered shoots should be reduced by two-thirds or so of their length immediately after the flowering season or in late winter-early spring.

Mackaya bélla (Latin 'fair' and 'beautiful'): South Africa, mainly in the warm coastal forests of Natal.
Habit. An evergreen shrub to 2–3 m, with many erect branches forming a narrow-globose bush 1.5–2.5 m across.
Leaves. Simple, opposite in pairs of dissimilar size, narrowly elliptic to oblong, 8–12 cm long and 3–4 cm wide; petiole 5–15 mm long, flattened above, slightly pinkish; apex abruptly acuminate; base cuneate; margin irregularly dentate-crenate and undulate; midrib prominent below; glabrous but with a tuft of mauve tomentum in the axils of the 4–6 main veins beneath; texture soft dark green and shiny above, paler beneath.
Flowers. Inflorescence a short, erect terminal raceme of 5–10 funnelform flowers on the current year's shoots; calyx tubulate to 1 cm long, spindle-shaped to 3 mm wide at the middle, green with coppery-red shadings, and tapering to the 5 subulate sepals at the apex; corolla 5–6 cm long, slenderly tubulate at the 1.5 cm long base, opening to funnelform at the middle, with 5 unequal, reflexed, broad-ovate lobes at the 4 cm wide mouth, the texture finely creped, lilac, with deeper shadings and violet-purple veins in the throat; stamens 4, the fertile pair with purplish filaments and cream anthers; flowers are prolific from early November to mid summer.
Fruit. Youngest stems green, softly pubescent and succulent, with swollen nodes and channelled internodes, becoming woody and pale brown when mature.
Climatic range. B, S, T, and in warm microclimates in M, and P.

MAHÒNIA

Commemorating Bernard M'Mahon, 1775–1816, Philadelphian seedsman of Irish birth.
Mahonia; Holly Grape; Oregon Grape; etc.
Berberidaceae, the Barberry family.

Generic description. A genus of more than 100 species, once united with *Berberis* but now separated because of several major differences:
a) *Mahonia* has compound, imparipinnate, always evergreen leaves; never simple or sometimes deciduous as in *Berberis*.
b) *Mahonia* stems are never spiny; those of *Berberis* are almost always so.
c) *Mahonia* often has a fascicled racemose inflorescence; *Berberis* never has.
d) *Mahonia* has sepals in 3 series of 3, totalling 9; *Berberis* has 2 series of 3, totalling 6.
e) *Mahonia* fruits are predominantly blue-black and pruinose; *Berberis* fruits are rarely so, but mostly red. The species listed below are worth growing as landscape material for the beauty of their foliage alone. Grown well in a satisfactory environment, high-quality flowers and abundant, colourful fruits will naturally follow.

Propagation. a) Seeds should be collected as soon as fully ripe but before being taken by birds, cleaned and sown in cool, outdoor conditions in a fibrous material, or held in just-damp sphagnum moss at 4°–5°C for sowing in spring.
b) Firm stem cuttings, with most of the large leaves reduced or removed, are also used, struck in a sand/peat mixture in a cool, but humid atmosphere in autumn or winter.
c) The suckering species may be increased by lifting rooted suckers, or by inducing roots by

mound-layering the low stems, and lifting and separating the results in winter.

Cultivation. The Mahonias are best suited to cool, tablelands conditions of mild summers and cool winters, preferably in well-drained but fertile, fibrous loams. *M. aquifolium*, *M. pinnata* and *M. repens* particularly are best used in the dappled shade of light-foliaged trees such as Birches, but must not be allowed to suffer from water starvation. All the species treated here are hardy in low temperatures of at least –10°C.

Pruning. When well-grown, Mahonias need little or no pruning, but when neglected some shoots become lanky and thinly-foliaged; such material is best cut down to ground level and the plant rejuvenated with additional food and water. Subsequent growths that exceed the general height of the foliage mass may be shortened in winter.

Species and cultivars

Mahònia aquifòlium (Latin 'with leaves like Holly', the main genus of the family Aquifoliaceae): Oregon Grape: western USA and Canada from northern California to Oregon, Washington and British Columbia.

Habit. A suckering shrub to 1.0–1.5 m tall, the stems erect and bamboo-like, carrying handsome glossy foliage towards the top.

Leaves. With main rachis 12–18 cm long, smooth, wiry, and reddish, the petiole 4–6 cm long between the lowest leaflets and the clasping base; leaflets 5 to 9, elliptic to ovate, 5–8 cm long and 2.0–3.5 cm wide, in opposite pairs, with very short petiolules to less than 1 mm; apices acute; bases obtuse to truncate, mostly oblique; margins spinose, serrate-dentate and somewhat undulate; glabrous and coriaceous; midrib prominent beneath; lustrous dark green above, paler and dull beneath, the new leaves often bronze-red, a few of the older leaves changing to purple-red in autumn and winter.

Flowers. Inflorescence a dense terminal raceme, 5–8 cm long, about 5 or 6 together in a fascicle at the end of shoots and sometimes in the adjacent axils; pedicels 7–8 mm, bright green; flowers globular in the bud, opening to funnelform 5–6 mm with 6 yellow petals; fragrant; flowers abundant from late August to November.

Fruit. A showy, dark-blue berry, 7–8 mm across, with a conspicuous whitish bloom, from early autumn persisting well into winter.

Other distinguishing features. Upper shoots pale buff, the bark shallowly ridged; leaf-scars large, triangular; inner bark yellow.

Climatic range. H, M, Mts, and in cool, partly shaded positions in A, P, and S.

Mahònia beàlei (commemorating T. C. Beale; named in his honour by the noted British botanical collector in the Orient, Robert Fortune): Beale's Mahonia: eastern Himalayas to Hupeh and eastern China.

Habit. A shrub of 2–3 m, of erect habit with bamboo-like stems arising from a central clump, forming a slender, vase-shaped mass, terminated by a canopy of handsome leaves.

Leaves. With a main rachis to 35 cm long, swollen at the nodes and clasping the stem at the base; leaflets 9 to about 17, overlapping at the bases and partly concealing the rachis; the lowest pair the smallest, broadly ovate to 3 cm across, increasing through the middle pairs of 5 cm, to the largest at the apex 9–10 cm long and 7–8 cm wide; apices and margins with 5–9 spiny, serrate-dentate lobes; bases truncate to sub-cordate; glabrous and coriaceous; dark greyish-green above, yellowish-green beneath.

Flowers. In an erect fascicle of about 10–15 racemes at the top of the main stems, the racemes 10–15 cm long and carrying about 75 flowers each; sepals in 3 series of 3, the outer series reddish-purple, the others yellow; petals 6, narrow-elliptical, pale yellow, the buds ovoid at first but opening to funnelform, flowering from early June to late September; flowers mildly fragrant.

Fruit. A 1-seeded berry, 1 cm long and 6–7 mm wide, borne in erect racemes, blue-green with a whitish bloom at first, ripening to purple-green.

Climatic range. A, H, M, Mts, P, S.

Mahònia fòrtunei (commemorating Robert Fortune, nineteenth century botanical collector in China): Fortune's Mahonia: central China, mainly Hupeh and Szechwan, at elevations of 1000 m or more.

Habit. An evergreen shrub to 1.5m tall, with erect, cane-like shoots from the base.

Leaves. With rachis from 10 to 18 cm long, the ridges sharp, nodes swollen, glabrous and bright green; leaflets mostly 5 to 9, in opposite pairs, lanceolate, 8–10 cm long and 2 cm wide; apices acuminate; bases cuneate and oblique; margins spinose with 8–12 sharp-tipped serrations on each side; midrib prominent beneath, all veins yellowish and translucent; dark green and dull above, bright green below.

Flowers. Inflorescence a terminal fascicle of 6–8 racemes, each 8–12 cm long, flowers numerous, yellow, flowering from June to September.

Climatic range. A, H, M, Mts, P, S.

Mahònia frèmontii (commemorating its discoverer, John C. Fremont, US Army explorer of the Pacific Coast region): Desert Mahonia: SW USA and Mexico.

Habit. An evergreen shrub, 2–4 m tall, of open branching growth unless made more compact by pruning, then leafy and handsome.

Leaves. With rachis 3–4 cm long; leaflets 1 to 3 sessile pairs, the smallest pair 2 cm long and 1 cm wide, the other lateral leaflets larger to 4–5 cm long, linear-lanceolate to oblong, the largest leaflet the terminal to 6 cm long; apices acuminate, spinose; margin spinose-dentate, with 2–5 sharp spines on each side; midrib prominent beneath; texture harsh and coriaceous; glaucous-green above, yellowish-green beneath.

Flowers. Inflorescence a raceme, 4–5 cm long, from the upper axils, not fascicled, carrying about 5–6 flowers; sepals yellowish-green in 3 dissimilar series, the 6 petals larger, forming a campanulate flower 5 mm deep, opening to 1 cm across, buttercup-yellow, flowering from June to September.

Fruit. Ovoid, larger than most, to 1.5 cm long and 1.2 cm wide, blue-black, with a heavily pruinose skin.

Other distinguishing features. An attractive foliage plant deserving greater use, especially in dry-climate gardens where it may be valuable as a specimen or barrier hedge.

Climatic range. A, H, I, M, Mts, P, S, on well-drained sites only.

Mahònia lomariifòlia (Latin 'with leaves like those of *Lomaria*'): central and western China in Szechwan and western Yunnan at elevations to 3000 m.

Habit. An evergreen shrub to 3–4 m tall, with many erect, bamboo-like shoots arching outwards at the top, the leaves mainly confined to the ends of the shoots.

Leaves. With a rachis to 25–55 cm long, swollen at the nodes of the leaflets and expanded at the base to clasp the stem; leaflets 10 to 20 opposite pairs, variable in shape from ovate near the base and about 2 cm long, to lanceolate-falcate to 10 cm from the middle upwards, all sessile; apices long-acuminate; margins and apices armed with 5 to 7 extremely sharp, serrate-dentate spines; bases truncate; venation 3-nerved, reticulate; glabrous; bright green and somewhat shiny above, paler and dull beneath.

Flowers. Inflorescence a terminal fascicle of erect racemes each to about 15–20 cm long; flowers numerous on 5–7 mm pedicels, ovoid in the bud, enclosed by the 9 ovate sepals in 3 dissimilar series; petals 6, slender to 6 mm long, yellow; flowering from May to August, the raceme progressively deciduous from the base, about half the raceme in flower at a time.

Fruit. An ellipsoidal berry about 6 mm long and slightly narrower, blue-black with a whitish bloom, ripening between April and May.

Other distinguishing features. As yet, an uncommon plant in Australian gardens, but one which is likely to become popular as an accent feature because of its very handsome foliage and unusual habit of growth.

Climatic range. A, H, M, Mts, P, S.

Mahònia pinnàta (Latin 'with pinnate leaves'): western USA, mainly between the Rocky Mountains and the coast.

Habit. An evergreen shrub to about 2.0–2.5 m tall, with erect, cane-like shoots carrying the attractive leaves which resemble those of *M. aquifolium* but are less lustrous and have a much shorter petiole.

Leaves. With main rachis to 8–10 cm long; leaflets mostly 7 or 9 but occasionally up to 11 or 13, sessile, narrowly ovate to 5–6 cm long and 2–3 cm wide; apices acute; bases broadly cuneate; margins undulate and spinose with 8–10 sharp-tipped, serrate teeth on each side; midrib prominent beneath; bright green and only slightly shiny above, paler beneath with a bluish bloom.

Flowers. Inflorescence a fascicle of about 5 racemes from the axils of the upper leaves, the racemes 5–8 cm long, similar to those of *M. aquifolium* in detail, bright yellow, fragrant, flowering from late August to October.

Fruit. As for *M. aquifolium*.

Other distinguishing features. The more numerous foliar-spines and leaflets help to separate this species from *M. aquifolium*.

Climatic range. A, H, M, Mts, P, S.

Mahònia rèpens (Latin 'creeping', describing the low, stoloniferous habit): Californian Holly Grape: western USA, between the Rocky Mountains and the coast.

Habit. A low, evergreen shrub to 0.5 m or less, of creeping, stoloniferous growth, increasing the width of the clump each year; useful as a ground cover, especially in uneven, rocky ground where mowing is precluded.

Leaves. With main rachis to 10–12 cm long, with 3–4 cm between the lowest leaflets and the base; leaflets 3, 5 or mostly 7, sessile, ovate to 5–7 cm long and 2.5–3.5 cm wide; apices acute; bases rounded or truncate, often obliquely so; margins spinulose-serrate, the 8–13 spines on each side about 1–2 mm long; dull glaucous-green above, paler beneath, often turning reddish in autumn-winter in cool climates.

Flowers and Fruits. As for *M. aquifolium*.

Climatic range. A, H, M, Mts, P, S.

MALVAVÍSCUS

Derived from *Malva*, the ancient Latin name for the Mallow, and *viscidus*, 'sticky', referring to the glutinous sap of some of the species.
Cardinal's Hat Plant.
Malvaceae, the Mallow family.

Generic description. Tender plants from Central America with colourful foliage and flowers, becoming popular as garden plants along the warm coastal districts of eastern Australia. See specific notes below for details.

Propagation. Semi-hardwood tip cuttings, taken in winter or early spring, strike readily in a sand/peat mixture in a warm, moist atmosphere.

Cultivation. A sheltered, sunny position in the warmest part of the garden is the ideal location, the best soil being a light sandy-loam with free drainage and adequate summer water. The plant is easily damaged by even light frost and may need protection for the first year or two.

Pruning. Pruning should be delayed until spring when all risk of frost is over, then applied as for Hibiscus, by removal of half or more of the annual growth, the plant's natural shape being preserved as far as possible.

Species and cultivars

Malvavíscus arbòreus var. *mexicànus* (Latin *arbor*, 'a tree'; 'from Mexico' (syn. *M. arboreus* var. *penduliflorus*) Cardinal's Hat Plant: Mexico, Central America and neighbouring islands.

Habit. An evergreen shrub to 2–3 m tall, with a broad, bun-shaped outline to 3 m wide, occasionally seen as a small, round-headed tree.

Leaves. Simple, alternate, ovate, 15–20 cm long and 8–10 cm wide, the petiole about one third the length of the blade; apex acuminate; base obtuse; margin crenate-serrate, sometimes with 2 shallow lobes towards the apex; venation based on the 5 main veins meeting at the base; mostly glabrous; dark green and slightly shiny above, paler and dull beneath.

Flowers. Pendulous, borne singly, or 2 to 4 in the upper axils, on pubescent pedicels 3–5 cm long; bracteoles linear, 5 to 7, green, 1.0–1.5 cm long; calyx tubular, with 3 prominent acute teeth slightly longer than the bracteoles, green; petals 5, oblanceolate to obovate, 6–8 cm long and 3.5 cm wide, spirally arranged, longitudinally ridged with 6 to 8 prominent veins, closely furled at first but loosening to form an irregular funnel, about 6 cm long and 3–4 cm wide; scarlet, prolific; December to winter; staminal column spirally twisted and terminating just clear of the petals, with a 10-branched, red style and about 30 filaments.

Other distinguishing features. Upper twigs bright green, slightly pubescent.

Climatic range. B, S, T, and in warm, frost-free microclimates in A, M, and P.

MELALEÙCA

Derived from the Greek *melas* 'black', and *leukos* 'white', describing the fire-blackened trunk and white bark of the upper trunk and larger branches of *M. quinquenervia*.
Paper-bark (various), mainly applied to the tree-like species; Honey Myrtle (various), mainly applied to the shrubby species. (The name 'Tea-tree' correctly belongs to *Leptospermum*.)
Myrtaceae, the Myrtle family

Generic description. An Australian native genus of evergreens, comprising a few large trees and many shrubs, all with simple, alternate or opposite leaves, some with oil glands; flowers are solitary, or in more or less elongate spikes or tufted heads, the new shoots often extended beyond the upper flowers; calyx and corolla are present but inconspicuous, the stamens being the showy feature, in white, cream, yellow, pink, mauve, red, or purplish, united in 5 claw-like bundles, often resembling a small tree, the coloured filaments free above the short trunk, with mostly contrasting-coloured anthers; fruit is a sessile, woody, 3-celled capsule containing many fine, acicular seeds, carried on the stems for several years in a viable condition, but when removed or subjected to abnormal heat as from a bushfire, the capsule dries and shrinks to release the seeds quickly.

Propagation. a) Twigs bearing mature capsules are cut from the plant and placed in a glass jar in a warm, dry place to shrink the capsules and release the seeds, which are sown in spring in a friable material, barely covered with finely sifted peat.
b) Semi-hardwood tip cuttings 3–5 cm long, are taken between summer and mid winter, and planted in a sand/peat mixture in a warm, humid atmosphere; used for clonal material as well as for many species.

Cultivation. The genus is represented by several species in almost every type of climate and environment, from the edges of tropical forests to sandy heathlands, swamps, or from poorly-drained clays, and dry inland areas with sandy or gravelly soils. Most species are versatile however, and will perform satisfactorily in a variety of conditions. See specific notes below for individual cultural requirements.

Pruning. The shrubby kinds benefit from an annual light pruning to maintain their density of growth, quality of foliage and abundance of flowers. All such pruning is carried out immediately after the main flowering period.

Species and cultivars

Melaleùca decussàta (Latin 'with leaves in opposite pairs', the pairs at right angles to each other): Totem-pole Honey Myrtle: south-eastern SA, and the Grampians region of western Vic.
Habit. An evergreen shrub 2.5–3.0 m tall, usually of open character but denser when grown well and pruned annually, then a globose bush about 2.0–2.5 m wide.
Leaves. Simple, opposite, linear, 8–10 mm long and 1.0–1.5 mm wide; petiole 1 mm long, swollen, whitish; apex acute; base cuneate; margin entire; venation obscure; concave and smooth above, roughened beneath by the numerous glandular dots; aromatic when bruised; dark glaucous-green.
Flowers. Inflorescence a squat cylindrical spike to 2.5 cm long, new growth often extending from the apex; stamens numerous, mauve-lilac, with cream anthers, flowering from mid October to late summer.

Fruit. A squat, woody capsule, usually about 12 together in a dense cylindrical cluster, partly enveloped by the swollen stem and forming the totem-pole character of the common name.
Other distinguishing features. Upper twigs buff coloured, striped by decurrent ridges beneath the leaf bases.
Climatic range. A, H, M, Mts, P, S, preferably on moist sites.

Melaleùca diosmaefòlia (Latin 'with foliage like *Diosma*'): Diosma-leafed Honey Myrtle; southern coast of south-western WA.
Habit. An evergreen shrub to 2–3 m tall, of irregular globose form with an angular, twiggy habit and attractive, fine-textured foliage.
Leaves. Simple, alternate but neatly spiralled, narrowly ovate, 8–10 mm long and 3–5 mm wide; petiole whitish, 1 mm long; apex acute; base rounded; margin entire; venation obscure, the midrib slightly raised beneath; heavily glandular-dotted and aromatic when bruised; dark to bright green.
Flowers. Inflorescence a short dense spike to 4–5 cm long, borne on the 1-year-old shoots, the new growth extending from the apex; stamens 1.5–2.0 cm long, with yellowish-green filaments and cream anthers; flowers partly hidden among the twigs, from early spring to early summer.
Fruit. A cluster of thick, greyish woody capsules to 1 cm across, slightly depressed into the twigs and persisting for several years.
Other distinguishing features. Upper twigs whitish-green, soon becoming brown, marked longitudinally by the decurrent ridges below the leaf bases, but almost concealed beneath the abundant, closely set leaves.
Climatic range. A, B, M, P, S.

Melaleùca ellíptica (Latin 'shaped like an ellipse', referring to the leaves): Granite Honey Myrtle: south-west WA, mainly between the Goldfields and the South Coast.
Habit. A woody shrub to 2 m tall, often dwarfed by harsh conditions in its native habitat, but improved in cultivation.
Leaves. Opposite, ovate to elliptic-oblong, 10–15 mm long; apex recurved; texture leathery; dull grey-green, but briefly bright green in spring.
Flowers. In a cylindrical spike, 6–8 cm long among the upper branchlets; stamens bright

crimson, with yellow anthers; flowering period in spring and early summer.

Fruit. A congested aggregate of woody capsules, held on the upper twigs for several years.

Climatic range. A, M, P, S, and on warm sites in H, Mts.

Melaleùca fúlgens (Latin 'shining' or 'glittering'): Scarlet Honey Myrtle: southern coast of WA, mostly on well-drained rocky heathland.

Habit. An evergreen shrub, 2.5–3.0 m tall, of loose, open habit unless subjected to regular pruning to develop a denser habit of growth.

Leaves. Simple, opposite, linear, 1.5–2.5 cm long and 2–4 mm wide; petiole 1 mm; apex acute, often with a reflexed tip; base cuneate to attenuate; upper side concave; midrib only distinct; surface with black glandular dots; glaucous-green on both surfaces.

Flowers. Inflorescence a short spike, 6–7 cm long, on short lateral shoots among the upper branchlets, the new season's shoots emerging from the apex; claws to 2.5 cm long, the filaments purplish-carmine with golden-yellow anthers, flowering from early September to mid December.

An attractive species suitable mainly for the shrub border or native garden on light soils, preferably enriched sands with free drainage, and kept moderately dry in the eastern high-rainfall areas.

Climatic range. A, B, M, P, S.

Melaleùca huègelii (commemorating Baron Karl von Huegel, Austrian botanical explorer): Chenille Honey Myrtle: south-western WA, mainly on sandy heathlands near the coast.

Habit. An evergreen shrub to 2–3 m tall, with a single short trunk soon dividing into a mass of erect branches, forming a slender, upright bush to 1.5 m wide.

Leaves. Simple, alternate or scattered, imbricated closely against the twigs, ovate-lanceolate, 5–8 mm long and 1–2 mm wide; sessile; apex acuminate; base broadly truncate; margin entire; glabrous; dark green and shiny, contrasting well against the pale twigs.

Flowers. Inflorescence a slender cylindrical spike to 8–10 cm long, comprising up to 100 or more sessile flowers, opening from the base; buds globose, whitish-mauve, opening to creamy-white; staminal bundles to 1 cm long, finely divided into 8 to 10 filaments with pale-cream anthers; flowering abundantly in handsome, vertical brushes from early November to January.

A species with spectacular spikes and good-looking foliage, best suited to the rear of a shrub border, on well-drained, fertile soils but tolerant also of wetter soils on the margins of permanent streams.

Climatic range. A, B, M, P, S.

Melaleùca hypericifòlia (Latin 'with leaves like *Hypericum*'): Red-flowered Honey Myrtle or Hillock Bush: Central Coast of NSW, mainly on the elevated swampy plateaus and the edges of watercourses draining the Hawkesbury sandstone areas.

Habit. An evergreen shrub, loose and open, and of indefinite form in its native habitat, but responding to cultivation with dense foliage and an attractive, semi-pendulous habit; usually seen as a shrub about 2–3 cm tall, pruned to a variety of shapes.

Leaves. Simple, opposite, mostly arranged in neat decussate rows, broadly lanceolate to elliptical, 2.5–3.0 cm long and 1 cm wide; apex acute, sometimes shortly mucronate; base obtuse, merging with the 2 mm concave petiole; margin entire but slightly recurved; midrib and 2 main laterals prominent; heavily dotted with translucent oil glands; glabrous; dark green above but becoming purplish-red toward the apex, especially in winter, paler green beneath; strongly aromatic when crushed.

Flowers. Inflorescence a dense spike like a bottlebrush, 6–7 cm long, the new growth emerging from the apex; stamens red, conspicuous, in 5 bundles of about 20 filaments in each; flowering abundantly in September to November but then intermittently throughout summer.

A useful and decorative species well adapted to a variety of sites, both moist and somewhat dry, or even sandy soils, combining good foliage quality with a long flowering season; sometimes used as a walling plant with good effect if well trained.

'Ulladulla Beacon' is a registered cultivar with almost prostrate form 30–60 cm tall, spreading to 1–2 m, useful as a ground-cover or rock garden plant, especially near the sea where its tolerance of salt-laden wind is clearly evident.

Climatic range. A, B, M, P, S, T.

Melaleùca incàna (Latin 'hoary' or 'greyish', referring to the colour of the foliage): Grey-leafed Honey Myrtle: south-western coast of WA.

Habit. An evergreen shrub, 2–3 m tall, usually growing on a low-branched main trunk, forming a spreading bush with branches drooping at the ends.

Leaves. Simple, of various arrangements from alternately-scattered to opposite or sometimes 3-whorled, all on the same branchlet; leaves spreading but curving forwards, linear to lanceolate, to 1 cm long and 2 mm wide; apex acute; base tapered to the 1 mm, tomentose, red petiole; margin entire but ciliate; venation indistinct apart from the midrib; tomentose, with soft, white hairs on leaves and twigs; leaves reddish-green at first, becoming grey-green with a red edge, changing to greyish-purple in winter.

Flowers. Inflorescence a dense, cylindrical spike, 1–3 cm long and 2 cm wide, borne at the terminals of short lateral growths, with 25–40 spirally arranged, greenish-yellow flowers, the new shoots not appearing at the apex until the flowers fade; stamens in 5 claws, each 5 mm long, with 8–9 pale greenish-yellow filaments and yellow anthers, flowering from late August to October, but later in cold climates.

Other distinguishing features. Youngest twigs straw coloured, with a dense white pubescence. An extremely showy species in both foliage and flower, the pendulous character making it a useful plant for specimen, hedge or screening. 'Nana' is a compact, dwarf form with a mass of tightly-clustered leaves.

Climatic range. A, B, M, P, S, and in warm microclimates in H and Mts.

Melaleùca laterítia (Latin *later*, 'a brick', describing the bright brick-red colour of the flowers): Robin Red-breast Bush: south-western WA.

Habit. An evergreen shrub to 3 m or so, usually with a short main trunk and ascending branches, forming a slender open bush 2–3 m wide.

Leaves. Simple, alternate, linear, to 2 cm long and 1 mm wide; petiole 1–2 mm long, flattened above, pale yellow; apex acute; base attenuate; margin entire; midrib barely visible; finely dotted with pellucid oil glands; yellow-green at first but maturing to dark green on both surfaces.

Flowers. Inflorescence a dense cylindrical spike, 5–7 cm long and 4–5 cm wide, borne on short laterals among the youngest shoots; flowers 50–70 in spirally arranged rows; stamens in 5 bundles of 7 to 9 in each, filaments 2 cm long,

bright orange-scarlet or brick-red, contrasting vividly with the green foliage which extends from the apex of the inflorescence during the flowering season from spring to early autumn.

A species noted for its pleasant, fine-textured foliage and spectacular flowers, and a useful constituent of the shrub border, preferably in the rear where its base may be concealed by low-growing planting.

Climatic range. A, B, M, P, S.

Melaleùca nesóphila (from the Greek *nesos* 'an island', and *philos* 'loving'; referring to its luxuriant growth on Doubtful Island, WA, where it was first recorded — it grows also on the adjacent mainland): Showy Honey Myrtle: southern coast of WA and neighbouring islands.

Habit. An evergreen shrub to 2–3 m tall, with a short main trunk and low branches forming a dense, erect bush, but taller and more vigorous to at least 4 m tall and 3 m wide in cultivation.

Leaves. Simple, alternate, narrowly obovate to 2 cm or so long and 5–8 mm wide; apex acute, often mucronate; margin entire; glabrous; venation indistinctly 3-nerved; coriaceous but brittle; aromatic when crushed; glandular; dark green but only slightly shiny.

Flowers. Inflorescence a terminal globose head to 2.5 cm across, of 20–30 flowers, the early buds green with a purplish apex, tightly compacted in a 7–10 mm head; stamens in 5 clawed bundles, each with about 10–12 filaments to 1 cm long, pale violet at first, aging to nearly white, with creamy-white anthers, the head showing several colours together, flowering abundantly throughout summer from early December.

Other distinguishing features. A handsome species well suited to tall screening or as a specimen in the rear of the native garden; hardy and tough, with a preference for well-drained gravelly or sandy soils, and responding to light annual pruning.

Climatic range. A, B, M, P, S.

Melaleùca nodòsa (Latin 'knotted' referring to the clustered seed capsules): Central coastal NSW to Qld, mainly on clayey soils with indifferent drainage.

Habit. A bushy shrub to 2–3 m tall, the short trunk soon dividing into twiggy branches with dense foliage.

Leaves. Alternate or scattered, linear 1–2 cm long and 2 mm wide; apex acute with a sharp

horny point; margin entire; glandular and aromatic; dark green and glabrous on both surfaces.
Flowers. In a terminal globose spike, 1.0–1.5 cm across with 10–15 flowers; calyx campanulate, pale green; staminal bundles about 2–3 mm long, the green filaments 5–6 mm long, with yellow anthers; flowering period in spring.
Fruit. A spherical cluster of 15–25 woody capsules, the aggregate 6–8 mm across encircling the twigs; capsules pale brown, 2–3 mm wide, with fine seeds.
Other distinguishing features. Upper branchlets with smooth, pale-grey, shiny bark.
Climatic range. A, B, M, P, S.

Melaleùca pulchélla (Latin 'beautiful'): Clawed Honey Myrtle: SW coastal districts of WA.
Habit. A small evergreen shrub to 1 m tall, usually slightly wider, with a loose, open habit; pruned annually, it becomes dense with more abundant flowers.
Leaves. Simple, scattered, often alternate, elliptic to broad-obovate, to 4–5 mm long and 5 mm wide; apex obtuse to sub-acute; base broad, sessile; margin entire; bright green when young, mid green when mature.
Flowers. Solitary or in few-flowered clusters, sessile, near the terminals of the young shoots; stamens in 5 clawed bundles to 1.3 cm long, curving inwards to the centre, the 5 expanded petals forming a flat, rotate base; mauve, flowering from November to January.
Other distinguishing features. A beautiful small shrub when grown well on a sandy or gravelly soil with free drainage, but for best results must be tip-pruned annually to thicken the growth habit.
Climatic range. A, B, M, P, S.

Melaleùca rádula (Latin *radere*, 'to scrape', referring to the rough bark of the lower stems): Graceful Honey Myrtle: western coast of WA, mainly between the Murchison and Swan rivers, on sandy heathlands.
Habit. An evergreen shrub to 2–3 m tall, with loose, open habit in the wild but improved by pruning and cultivation to become a compact, leafy bush with attractive foliage.
Leaves. Simple, opposite, narrow-linear, to 3 cm long and 2 mm wide; apex finely acute; base sessile, swollen; margin entire; heavily glandular-dotted, especially on the lower surface, and aromatic when bruised; mid green but slightly glaucous.

Flowers. Inflorescence a spike of 6–8 flowers; stamens in 5 clawed bundles to 1 cm long, filaments bright mauve, anthers cream; pistil clavate, exserted, green; flowering September–November.
Other distinguishing features. Twigs have a rough, stringy bark, pale brown at first, becoming reddish-brown.
An attractive species with bright, showy flowers, mainly used in native gardens on well-drained sandy or light loamy soils.
Climatic range. A, B, M, P, S, T.

Melaleùca scabra (Latin 'rough'): Rough Honey Myrtle: south-west WA, mainly on coastal sandy heathlands between the Swan River and Esperance Bay.
Habit. A variable shrub, some forms almost prostrate to 30–50 cm tall and useful as groundcovers, but mostly taller to 1 m or so with erect arching branches.
Leaves. Linear, 2–3 cm long, nearly terete, scattered thickly and overlapping on the upper twigs; apex acute with a short hard point; thick and fleshy; texture rough; dark- to grey-green.
Flowers. In a dense terminal head, hemispherical, the flowers densely packed together; staminal bundles 1 cm long, the filaments variable in colour but mostly rosy-mauve with bright yellow anthers; flowering period from late August to November.
Fruit. A mass of tightly-congested capsules surrounding the twigs and persisting for several years.
Climatic range. A, B, H, M, P, S and on lower Mts.

Melaleùca squamea (Latin 'scaly'): Swamp Honey Myrtle: eastern Australia, on elevated heathlands usually near permanent water.
Habit. A shrub to 2 m tall and about as broad, somewhat sparse, with stiff branches but responding well to cultivation and regular pruning.
Leaves. Densely scattered on the young shoots, linear-lanceolate to narrowly ovate, 6–12 mm long; spreading; apex acute, the tip incurved; base splayed; midrib and 2 other veins prominent; bright green when young, becoming darker in age, then often reddish, especially in winter.
Flowers. In a terminal globose head about 15–20 mm across, the growth axis not extending through the heads; stamens about 8 mm long, in

flat-clawed bundles of up to 10, varying in colour from white and cream to mauve or pale pink, with creamy-white anthers, flowering prolifically from early spring to summer.
Fruit. A squat woody capsule, many crowded together into a globose cluster, persisting for several years.
Other distinguishing features. Upper shoots softly pubescent and whitish-grey while young, the older bark grey and somewhat spongy.
Climatic range. H, M, Mts, P, S and on cool, moist sites in A.

Melaleùca squarròsa (Latin 'scaly' or 'rough'): Scented Honey Myrtle: SE Australia, mainly on damp, low-lying sites near the coast, especially abundant on the coastal plain traversed by the Prince's Highway in southern NSW and eastern Vic.
Habit. An evergreen shrub to 3–4 m, but sometimes taller when on fertile soils with improved drainage, then tree-like with a single trunk and a slender conical crown.
Leaves. Simple, opposite, in 4 neat rows arranged decussately, ovate to broad-lanceolate, 8–15 mm long and 4–5 mm wide; apex acuminate; base obtuse to sub-cordate; margin entire; venation with 5–7 main veins and numerous pellucid oil glands; young leaves pale green, older foliage dull mid green.
Flowers. Inflorescence a cylindrical terminal spike to 4 cm long on the upper 1-year-old twigs, new growth emerging from the apex; stamens in 5 clawed bundles to 6–8 mm long, about 10 creamy-white filaments on each claw, with yellow anthers; flowers sweetly perfumed, flowering from mid October to December.
Other distinguishing features. Upper twigs almost squared by the loose decurrent strip of pale-grey bark below each node; stems maturing to olive-green.
A showy, tall species with dark-green leaves, providing a good background to the abundant cream flowers. Hardy in most soils but at its best on deep, fertile loams and sands, with medium to high rainfall.
Climatic range. A, H, M, Mts, P, S.

Melaleùca steedmanii (commemorating H. Steedman, a WA botanical collector): Steedman's Honey Myrtle: south-west WA, mainly in the northern wheatbelt region.
Habit. A thin shrub to 1.5 m tall, improved in cultivation by regular pruning after the flowering period.
Leaves. Decussately-opposite on thin woody twigs; linear-lanceolate to 3–4 cm long; apex acute; glabrous; pale grey-green.
Flowers. in a dense spike, the new growth emerging from the apex; buds globular, opening to large bright crimson flowers, the filaments tipped with yellow anthers; flowering period from September to early summer.
Fruit. A woody capsule, many clustered on the older wood.
Climatic range. A, M, P, S and on sheltered sites in Mts.

MELÁSTOMA

Derived from the Greek words describing the staining qualities of the fruit.
Pink Lasiandra.
Melastomataceae, the Melastoma family.

Generic description. An important genus in the tropics but apart from the species described below, contributing little to Australian horticulture. Most species are shrubs with large, simple leaves, and showy flowers borne singly or in small clusters; the stamens have the characteristic sickle shape of the *Tibouchinas*, hence the common name.

Propagation. Soft-tip cuttings taken in spring, or semi-hardwood cuttings in late winter, root readily in a sand/peat mixture in a warm, humid atmosphere.

Cultivation. The species is suitable only for warm, frost-free gardens as far south as Sydney; it is easily damaged by frost and should be covered at night in marginal areas. A sunny position with shelter from cold wind is best, on a friable soil with free drainage, preferably sandy.

Pruning. A well-managed plant should be pruned lightly to hemispherical shape in early spring after all risk of frost is over.

Species and cultivars

Melástoma malabáthricum (Latin 'from the Malabar Coast, India') (syn. *Lasiandra rosea, Tibouchina rosea*) India to northern Australia, mainly Qld.
Habit. An evergreen shrub to 2 m tall and wide, with many stems from the base.
Leaves. Simple, opposite, elliptic-ovate, 8–12 cm long, 5–7 cm wide; petiole rufous-bristly, 2 cm long; apex acute to acuminate; base obtuse;

margin finely strigose, the bristles set close to the margin; main veins 5, nearly parallel, decreasing in size from the centre, prominent beneath; upper surface dark green and shiny, but finely strigose, the lower surface pale yellow-green and strongly bristled on the veins.

Flowers. Inflorescence a terminal cyme of 1 to 10 flowers; calyx tube campanulate-urceolate 1.5 cm long and 1 cm wide, with whitish silky hairs, subtended by a pair of leafy involucral scales; calyx lobes 5 or 6, lanceolate-elliptic to 1 cm long, green with a red stain; corolla crateriform, 8 cm across, of 5 or 6 obovate petals, mostly rosy-mauve, flowering intermittently but mainly from January to May; stamens 10, in 2 series, all strongly falcate and jointed at the middle.

Fruit. A fleshy capsule to 1.5 cm, the apex truncate, with 5 or 6 locules containing the numerous fine granular seeds.

Other distinguishing features. Upper twigs angular, amost square, reddish-brown with stiff hairs.

Climatic range. B, T, and on sheltered sites in warm localities in S.

MICHÈLIA

Commemorating Pietro Antonio Micheli, 1679–1737, Italian botanist.
Port-wine Magnolia.
Magnoliaceae, the Magnolia family.

Generic description. A small genus of mostly-evergreen trees and shrubs scattered throughout southern Asia and the warmer parts of the Orient, some formerly included in *Magnolia* but now separated mainly on account of their smaller, highly-perfumed, axillary flowers. All have simple leaves, solitary axillary flowers, the sepals and petals very similar, and pronounced floral perfume, especially noticeable at night.

Propagation. Semi-hardwood cuttings, preferably taken in late summer or autumn when the plants are not in vigorous growth, root satisfactorily in a sand/peat mixture in a humid glasshouse provided with mist and bottom-heating facilities; a small heel of older wood at the base of the cuttings is often preferred.

Cultivation. The *Michelias* perform satisfactorily in a well-drained, moderately fertile soil, in a sunny position with shelter from violent winds, especially those from the sea which may cause salt injury. All are safe in temperatures above 0°C but are risky in more severe climates.

Pruning. *M. annonifolia* and *M. figo* are largely self-shaping but respond favourably to a moderate trim after the spring flowering season to stimulate the growth of flowering twigs.

Species and Cultivars

Michèlia annonifòlia (Latin 'with leaves like *Annona*', the Custard-apple): habitat uncertain, believed to be Indo-China.

Habit. An evergreen shrub to about 3 m tall, with a short trunk and several low branches forming a loose, open shrub of roughly globose shape.

Leaves. Simple, alternate, obovate, 8–10 cm long and 4–5 cm across; apex acuminate with a blunt tip; base cuneate to the stout, pubescent, 5 mm petiole; margin entire, undulate; midrib prominent beneath, whitish-green, with stiff black bristles; bright green and glabrous above, paler beneath.

Flowers. Solitary in the upper axils on stout woolly pedicels; buds to 3 cm long, enclosed in a hairy floral envelope; tepals 6, elliptic-obovate, 3 cm long and 2 cm wide, concave, fleshy, creamy-yellow, margined with reddish-purple; sweetly-perfumed; stamens about 30, to 1.2 cm long, purple at the base and along the spine of the anthers; carpels clustered on an erect cone-like receptacle to 2 cm long; flowering period from late September to early summer.

Other distinguishing features. Young twigs brown-pubescent.

Climatic range. A, B, M, P, S, T.

Michèlia figo (the native vernacular name for the plant in Cochin-China, South Vietnam) (syn. *M. fuscata*) Port-wine Magnolia: warm-temperate SW China.

Habit. An evergreen shrub to about 3 m tall, broadly conical to 3 m wide, the main trunk eventually stout, the many branches curving outwards and upwards and dividing repeatedly to carry the abundant foliage.

Leaves. Simple, alternate, narrowly elliptic or broadly lanceolate, 5–10 cm long and 2.0–3.5 cm wide; petiole 3–4 mm long, pubescent; apex acuminate to a narrowly rounded point; base cuneate; margin entire; midrib slightly prominent below; glabrous and coriaceous; bright lustrous green above, paler and dull beneath.

Flowers. Solitary in the upper axils, on stout 7–8 mm pedicels covered with a thick, reddish-brown tomentum; flower buds enclosed in a brownish-tomentose envelope, splitting and

PLATE 23

▲ Rhododendron Azalea 'Splendens'

▲ Prostanthera rotundifolia
► Rhododendron Azalea Kurume 'Yaye-hiryu'
▼ Rhododendron Azalea Kurume 'Kirin'

▼ Pyracantha fortuneana

▼ Raphiolepis delacourii

▼ Pyracantha fortuneana

PLATE 24

▲ Rhododendron Azalea Kurume cvs

▲ Rhododendron Azalea 'Lady Poltimore'
◄ Rhododendron Azalea Kurume 'Omoine'
▼ Rhododendron Azalea Mollis 'Hugo Koster'

▼ Rhododendron Azalea 'Agnes Neale'

▼ Rhododendron Azalea Mollis 'Hortulanus H. Witte'

▼ Rhododendron Azalea 'Exquisite'

▼ Rhododendron Azalea Mollis 'Directeur Moerlands'

soon deciduous; tepals usually 6, in 2 series, all concave-elliptical, thick and fleshy, yellowish-purple outside, deepening towards the base, deep vinous-purple inside; stamens about 35, purplish, 6–8 mm long, surrounding the erect, green conical receptacle to 1.3 cm; flowers are produced from early September to late November; sweetly and heavily perfumed.

Fruit. Upper twigs green, covered at first with a dense mat of dark red-brown tomentum; older bark grey, with whitish streaks.

Climatic range. A, B, M, P, S, T.

MURRAÝA (incorrectly *Murraea*; syn. *Chalcas*)

Commemorating Dr Johann Murray, eighteenth-century Swedish botanist.
Orange-Jessamine or Satin-Wood.
Rutaceae, the Rue family.

Generic description. A small genus from South-East Asia with dark-green, pinnate leaves and white, perfumed flowers followed by red, berry-like fruits.

Propagation. Semi-hardwood cuttings, preferably with a heel of older wood, taken in autumn-winter, strike somewhat erratically; a sand/peat mixture should be used, with bottom heat and mist an advantage.

Cultivation. The best soil is friable, well drained and enriched with organic matter. In the warm climates, almost any position will do but in the Sydney or cooler climates, a sun-exposed, sheltered aspect is desirable. It is not considered to be safe in temperatures less than −1°C.

Pruning. A light annual pruning after the autumn flowering is an advantage in maintaining the dense twiggy habit, with improved flower production.

Species and cultivars

Murraỳa paniculàta (Latin 'with flowers in a panicle'): Orange-Jessamine or Satin-Wood: eastern India to the Malay Peninsula (syn. *M. exotica*).

Habit. An evergreen shrub to 3 m tall and wide, densely branched from the base, forming a globose bush of neat and attractive appearance.

Leaves. Compound, alternate, imparipinnate, the rachis 7–8 cm long, glandular beneath, the base decurrent; leaflets 5 to 9, oblanceolate to obovate, 2–4 cm long, 1.0–1.5 cm wide; apices obtuse or emarginate; bases cuneate; margins entire; glabrous but thickly dotted with pellucid oil glands; young leaves pale green, maturing to glossy dark green above, paler beneath.

Flowers. Inflorescence a corymbose panicle of 10–20 flowers, borne among or clear of the upper leaves; calyx campanulate to 2 mm, with 5 short apical teeth, green; corolla clavate at first, opening to funnelform, 2.0–2.5 cm across, the 5 oblong-lanceolate petals recurving; stamens 10, of unequal length, the filaments white, the anthers green-cream, exserted beyond the petals; style 1, stout, with green stigma; flowers strongly and sweetly perfumed, borne in abundance in spring, usually October and November and again in late summer or early autumn, but intermittently at other times, usually after good rains.

Fruit. An ovoid berry to 1.5–2.0 cm long, green at first but ripening in winter to spring to glossy crimson, fleshy, with one round seed; fruit not abundant in the Sydney climate.

Other distinguishing features. Upper stems bi-coloured, the yellow-brown bark marked by the dark-green decurrent leaf-bases; lower stems roughened by vertical fissures.

Climatic range. B, S, T, and in warm, sheltered microclimates in M and P.

MUSSAÉNDA

The Latin version of the native vernacular name.
Flag-bush; Ashanti Blood; etc.
Rubiaceae, the Madder family.

Generic description. A genus of tropical plants, mostly shrubs or part-climbers, with evergreen, opposite leaves; red, orange, or cream salverform flowers in terminal cymes, a calyx of sometimes-coloured sepals and with an occasional sepal modified to become leaf-like, either whitish or red, to considerably enhance the beauty of the plant; and fruit is a small, ovoid berry. The species described below are colourful and highly decorative in a suitably warm, humid climate.

Propagation. a) Soft-tip cuttings are taken in spring, planted in sand/peat in a warm, humid atmosphere, desirably in a misted, heated glasshouse.
b) Thin, spindly hardwood cuttings, taken in July-August are treated as above, all preferably treated with root-promoting powder.

Cultivation. *Mussaendas* need the warmest and

most protected part of the garden, ideally in a completely frost-free locality, on a light, fibrous or sandy soil with free drainage; adequate summer water should be made available. Both species are sensitive to even light frosts; should injury occur, the damaged leaves and upper twigs should be retained as protection for the basal parts, but be pruned away in spring.

Pruning. A light annual pruning of the previous year's growth is beneficial but should be deferred until October before the start of new growth.

Species and cultivars

Mussaénda erythrophýlla (from the Greek, meaning 'red-leafed'): Ashanti Blood: Equatorial Africa, mainly in the upper basin of the Congo River.

Habit. An evergreen shrub to 2–3 m tall, with a horizontally inclined habit, densely covered with showy leaves and flowers.

Leaves. Simple, opposite, broadly ovate, 8–12 cm long, 6–10 cm wide, the petiole 3–4 cm, red-pubescent; apex acute; base obtuse, often oblique; margin ciliate; midrib and main lateral veins heavily pubescent and prominent beneath; surface soft and velvet-like; dark green above, pinkish-green beneath; stipules bi-lobed, 7–8 mm long, brown-pubescent.

Flowers. Inflorescence a terminal cyme of 12 to 20 flowers; calyx campanulate, 4–5 mm long, with 5 slender, linear sepals all with a dense crimson pubescence, one sepal sometimes modified to leaf-like form to 7–8 cm long and 5–6 cm wide, broadly ovate, bright blood-crimson above, paler beneath; corolla tubulate to 2 cm long and 3 mm wide, the limb 2.0–2.5 cm across, cream but with a densely crimson-hairy centre, faintly perfumed, flowering from late December to March, and occasionally throughout winter, especially in warm climates.

Fruit. A fleshy, ellipsoidal berry to 2 cm long, green but with a dense coat of crimson hairs; 4-celled, containing numerous fine black seeds.

Other distinguishing features. Upper twigs bright green, with short reddish-brown pubescence.

Climatic range. B, T, and warm microclimates along the coastal fringe of S.

Mussaénda frondòsa (Latin 'having many leaves'): White Flag-bush; southern India, Sri Lanka and the Malay Peninsula.

Habit. An evergreen shrub to 2–3 m tall, with a densely foliaged crown and a broad, horizontally inclined branch pattern to 2–4 m wide.

Leaves. Simple, opposite, ovate-elliptic, 10–15 cm long and 5–9 cm wide, the petiole to 2 cm, channelled and shallowly winged on the upper side; apex abruptly acuminate; base cuneate, sometimes obliquely so; margin entire; midrib and main lateral veins pubescent and prominent below, otherwise glabrous; bright green and slightly shiny above, paler beneath; stipules to 1 cm long, green, with rufous hairs, bi-lobed.

Flowers. Inflorescence a trichotomous terminal cyme; calyx tubulate-campanulate to 4–5 mm, with 5 slender, linear sepals to 1 cm long, beset with red strigose hairs, one of the sepals sometimes modified to leaf form to 10 cm long and 6–7 cm wide, broadly ovate, creamy-white, with pale-green veins beneath; corolla salverform, the strigose tube slender to 2.5–3.0 cm long and 3 mm wide, the 5 ovate lobes opening to a rotate limb 2.5 cm across, deep orange above, pale cream-yellow beneath, flowering from late December to March and intermittently throughout winter.

Fruit. A fleshy, 4-celled, ellipsoidal berry to 1 cm long and 6 mm wide, green, with a small brown areole at the apex, containing many fine seeds.

Other distinguishing features. Upper stems green, with reddish, strigose hairs, becoming glabrous in the second year.

Climatic range. B, T, and warm microclimates along the coastal fringe of S.

MYÓPORUM

Derived from the Greek, alluding to the pellucid oil glands on the leaves and their role in controlling loss of water by transpiration.
Boobialla; Water Bush.
Myoporaceae, the Myoporum family.

Generic description. A widely-scattered genus of about 35 species, the majority from Australia and New Zealand, the others from the Western Pacific and South-East Asia. Several are grown as landscape material in Australian gardens, especially valued for their tolerance of arid conditions in the Interior, or resistance to salt-laden winds on the coastal fringe. See specific notes below for details.

Propagation. Seeds, sown as soon as fully ripe, or by leafy cuttings of the firm shoots taken in autumn or winter, placed in a sheltered, warm environment.

Cultivation. See individual recommendations below.

Pruning. All species benefit from tip-pruning during the early years to thicken the growth, preferably performed after the spring flowers.

Species and cultivars

Myóporum acuminàtum (Latin 'leaves tapering to a long slender point') (syn. *M. montànum*) Western Boobialla or Water Bush: found in all mainland states, usually in low-rainfall zones, but also abundant along the east coast, often in exposed places near the sea or in the shelter of deep bays or on river banks.

Habit. An evergreen plant varying considerably in size and shape from an almost prostrate shrub of 1 to 3 m, to small tree-like form with an elevated crown. Either shape is easily contrived by judicious pruning.

Leaves. Simple, alternate, lanceolate to elliptic, 6–12 cm long and 1–2 cm wide, on a 1–2 cm petiole; apex acuminate; base narrowly cuneate; margin entire; glabrous; mid-green; somewhat fleshy, with translucent glandular oil-dots.

Flowers. Solitary, or in axillary clusters of 1 to 6, broadly funnelform to 6 mm long, the 5 broad lobes reflexed, white with reddish-purple spots; stamens 4, exserted beyond the corolla; flowering period from spring to mid-summer.

Fruit. A globose, succulent drupe about 8 mm across, greenish at first, becoming bluish-purple when ripe.

Other distinguishing features. Western Boobialla occurs in a wide variety of habitats, mainly on well-drained sandy or stony land, often on creek-banks. It is drought tolerant and is often used as a screen plant or wind-break around homesteads in dry regions.

'**Monaro Marvel**' is a registered cultivar with a low, mound-like habit of growth to 30 cm tall, spreading to 2–3 m. It is mainly used as a ground-cover, especially in rock gardens and embankments.

Climatic range. A, I, M, P, S, and on lower Mts.

Myóporum floribúndum (Latin 'with abundant flowers'): Slender Myoporum: SE Australia, mainly on the rocky slopes and sheltered, cool gullies of the mountain ranges.

Habit. A slender shrub to about 3 m tall, mostly with a short trunk and low, spreading horizontal branches.

Leaves. Simple, alternate, narrowly linear to 7–9 cm long and 2–4 mm wide, hanging vertically from the outer twigs; apex acute, with a recurved tip; margin revolute; midrib deeply depressed above; glandular and slightly sticky; dark green.

Flowers. Solitary or clustered thickly in the axils on the upper side of the outer twigs for up to 20 cm or more; open funnelform, with 5 equal lobes, white; stamens long exserted; flowering period spring.

Fruit. Not seen.

Other distinguishing features. Best suited to a partly shaded environment on well-drained soils.

Climatic range. H, M, Mts, P, S.

Myóporum parvifòlium (Latin 'with small leaves'): Creeping Boobialla: southern states of Australia, mostly on sandy or gravelly-clay soils in low rainfall areas.

Habit. A densely-leafed prostrate bush, usually less than 0–25 m tall, spreading to 2–3 m broad.

Leaves. Linear-oblong, 2–3 cm long and 5–6 mm wide; erect on the trailing stems; slightly concave; apex acute; margin glandular-serrate in the upper half; somewhat fleshy; mid-green, with reddish shadings.

Flowers. Open funnelform 12–15 mm across, singly or in small clusters of 2–4 in the upper leaf axils; lobes oblong, spreading; stamens 4, long-exserted; corolla white, with purplish spots in the throat; flowering abundantly from late spring into summer.

Fruit. A fleshy drupe, globose, 2–4 mm across, green at first, ripening to rosy-purple.

Other distinguishing features. A hardy and attractive plant for use as a ground-cover or embankment plant especially for dry conditions.

Climatic range. A, I, M, P, S, and on lower Mts.

MYRTUS

The ancient Greek name for *M. communis*. Myrtle.
Myrtaceae, the Myrtle family.

Generic description. A once-large genus, but now reduced by the separation of many of the Southern Hemisphere species to other genera, notably *Lophomyrtus* and *Ugni*. The remaining species, is described in detail below. It is a useful plant in temperate climates, being seen mainly as a garden shrub, or topiary or terrace plant, where its dark-green foliage and dainty summer flowers are always attractive.

Propagation. Semi-hardwood tip cuttings, taken between late spring and early winter, strike readily in a warm, humid atmosphere.

Cultivation. The Myrtle grows satisfactorily in a moderately fertile, friable soil with free drainage, in a wide range of mild climates, but not in severely cold conditions with low temperatures below −8°C.

Pruning. The plant is self-shaping into an attractive, somewhat open bush when not pruned, but responds favourably to a light tip-pruning in late winter with denser foliage and more compact growth habit.

Species and cultivars

Myrtus communis (Latin 'common'): Common Myrtle: Mediterranean region, from Spain to India.

Habit. An evergreen shrub or small tree to 3–4 m tall, often pruned to spherical or other geometrical shape in hedging or topiary.

Leaves. Simple, opposite, broadly lanceolate to narrowly ovate, 3–5 cm long and 1.0–1.5 cm across; apex sharply acute; base cuneate, often obliquely to the 1 mm petiole; margin entire; venation reticulate, with the midrib raised beneath and intramarginal vein distinct; glabrous and coriaceous, but with numerous translucent oil glands; aromatic when crushed; dark green above, paler green beneath.

Flowers. Solitary in the upper axils, on slender pedicels to 1.5 cm long; calyx campanulate with 5 purplish sepals; corolla rotate, 1.5–2.0 cm across, of 5 concave, broadly oval white petals, often with reddish-pink shadings on the reverse; stamens conspicuous and very numerous, 5–6 mm long, the filaments white, anthers creamy-yellow, the single pistil slightly longer than the stamens; sweetly perfumed; flowering period from summer to early winter.

Fruit. A fleshy, ellipsoidal berry to about 1.4 cm with slightly flattened poles, the 5 calyx lobes persisting at the apex, pruinose, purple-black; seeds about 10–12, whitish, kidney-shaped.

'**Variegata**' has leaves with a conspicuous, showy, cream margin.

Climatic range. A, B, M, P, S, and on warm sites at lower elevations of Mts.

NANDINA

The latinised form of the ancient Japanese vernacular name, 'Nanten'.
Sacred-bamboo or Heavenly-bamboo.
Berberidaceae, the Barberry family.

Generic description. A genus of a single species growing in the Japanese Islands, China, and eastern India, said to be the most commonly used plant in Japan. Of shrubby habit with many erect, cane-like stems from the basal clump, the plant has alternate, bi- or tri-pinnate leaves with small ovate leaflets, white flowers in erect, terminal panicles, and scarlet berries.

Propagation. a) Seeds are sown as soon as harvested in winter or spring; each berry contains 2 seeds closely pressed together — for more uniform germination the seeds should be separated before sowing.
b) Old plants may be divided into a number of new divisions in winter.

Cultivation. The plant thrives in well-drained, rich loam or sandy soils in an open sunny position, responding with rapid growth and handsome foliage which may colour well in autumn and winter. When grown in shade, the leaves are inclined to be pale green without the attractive red colours seen in the open. The plant is hardy and tolerant of harsh climatic conditions with minimum temperatures of −10°C.

Pruning. Some of the oldest canes should be removed at ground level each winter to clear the way for new suckering shoots from the base. The spent fruiting stems should also be removed, but no other pruning is necessary.

Species and cultivars

Nandina doméstica (Latin *domus*, 'a house'): Sacred-bamboo; Japan, China, and South-East Asia to eastern India.

Habit. An evergreen shrub with a bamboo-like habit to 2 m tall, the clump spreading slowly at the base through the growth of suckers.

Leaves. Compound, alternate, bi- or tri-pinnate to 45 cm long, the rachis sheathed at the base, green or dark red, swollen at the joints; leaflets in threes or fives, the terminal leaflet largest to 5–6 cm long, broad-lanceolate to ovate; apices acuminate; margins entire; glabrous; dark to bright green above, turning to crimson in autumn-winter.

Flowers. Inflorescence an erect, terminal panicle to 30–35 cm, with many small, white flowers; calyx of about 4 whorls of 3 white sepals; petals in 1 whorl of 3, obovate 9–10 mm long, reflexing fully; stamens 6, anthers linear to 5 mm, yellowish; flowers mainly in summer and autumn.

Fruit. A round, 2-seeded berry to 8–9 mm, scarlet in April and lasting well until August, even when cut for indoor decoration.

'**Nana Purpurea**' has broader leaflets, and reddish colour throughout the year, on a dwarf, rounded bush to 0.45 m tall and wide.

'**Pygmaea**' has a compact, globose form to 0.5 m tall and broad, with dense foliage turning to crimson, ruby-red and scarlet in autumn and winter.

Climatic range. A, B, H, M, Mts, P, S.

NÈRIUM

The latinised version of 'Nerion', the ancient Greek name for the plant, drawn from *neros* 'moist', because of its affinity for moist soils. Oleander.

Apocynaceae, the Dogbane family.

Generic description. A small genus of long-flowering, evergreen shrubs and small trees with 3-whorled, simple, entire leaves, showy funnelform-salverform flowers in terminal cymes, some cultivars with semi- or fully-double flowers, and fruit of two long, slender follicles. They are especially valued for their tolerance of salt-laden winds and dry, sandy soils. Their long flowering season and wide range of coloured cultivars make them additionally attractive to planters. All parts of the plants should be regarded as poisonous when eaten, although many of the claims made on this point cannot be substantiated.

Propagation. a) Seeds collected from cultivars should not be used since they are unlikely to reproduce the quality of the parent.

b) Semi-hardwood cuttings reproduce the parents reliably and should always be preferred; cuttings of about 8–10 cm, taken in autumn, are suitable, striking easily in a sand/peat mixture kept uniformly moist in a warm, humid atmosphere.

Cultivation. Almost any type of soil will suit Oleanders, but they respond best to a friable, well-drained soil, fully exposed to sun for most of the day. They will tolerate dry soils but perform poorly in wet soils as do most other terrestrial plants, although they relish additional water during their main growing and flowering seasons. They are safe to low temperatures of at least −5°C, but need protection from heavier frosts by being grown in the warmest part of the garden, with good air-drainage below their planting position.

Pruning. Well-grown plants may be pruned fairly severely in winter to preserve their dense, shrubby habit, but one such pruning every 3 years is usually sufficient; in the intermediate years the pruning is confined to removal of the flowered shoots with their developing seed follicles.

Species and cultivars

Nèrium oleánder (derivation obscure, but probably from the local vernacular name for the species): Mediterranean and Middle Eastern countries.

Habit. An evergreen shrub varying from 2 to 4 m tall in the cultivars, with many erect, spreading shoots from the base, forming a broad hemispherical shape when untrained, but easily made into 'standard' form.

Leaves. Simple, 3-whorled, lanceolate, 15–20 cm long, 2–4 cm wide; apex acute; margin entire; petiole to 1 cm long; midrib pale cream, prominent; glabrous and coriaceous; shiny dark green above, paler beneath; colour variations among the cultivars.

Flowers. Inflorescence a terminal cyme on the new season's growth; calyx to 1 cm long, reddish, with 5 subulate teeth about 5 mm long; flower buds slenderly ovoid, the lobes folded and overlapped in a clockwise direction; flowers funnelform-salverform, or doubled in some cultivars, the limb 5–6 cm across, with 5 broad, obliquely obovate lobes 2 cm wide, crimped and waved on the outer edge, the throat with petal-like appendages with laciniate ends; stamens 5, terminating in a spiral of woolly anthers enclosing the central style; some cultivars have a light, sweet perfume; flowers are borne abundantly from early November to March, then sporadically until early winter.

Fruit. A slenderly tapered follicle, 12–15 cm long and 1.0–1.5 cm wide, usually in pairs, green at first, but ripening to brown and splitting open in autumn; seeds numerous, slender, covered thickly with brown, shaggy hairs and bearing a fine pappus which aids dispersal.

The following cultivars are popular.

'**Album**': 2–3 m, single, white with faint cream base.

'**Delphine**': 2–3 m, single, dark crimson.

'**Dr Golfin**': 2–3 m, single, glowing cerise-pink.

'**Luteum Plenum**': 2 m, double, pale yellow, cream base.

'**Mme Charles Baltet**': 2–3 m, double, soft rose-pink.

'**Madonna Grandiflorum**': 3–4 m, double, white with cream base.

'**M. Belaguier**': 2–3 m, single, rose pink.

'**Mrs Fred Roeding**': 2 m, double, azalea-pink and salmon.

'**Professor Martin**': 2–3 m, single, bright rosy-carmine.

'**Souvenir d'August Roger**': 2–3 m, single, blush-pink fading to white.

'**Splendens**': 3–4 m, double, deep rose pink.

'**Splendens Variegatum**': 2–3 m, double, deep rose pink flowers, but is grown mostly for its handsome dark-green leaves with a margin of creamy-yellow.

Climatic range. A, B, M, P, S, T, and in inland towns and centres with irrigation.

ÓCHNA

The ancient Greek vernacular name for a form of the European Wild Pear, the flowers and leaves of which are supposed to be similar.
Ochna.
Ochnaceae, the Ochna family.

Generic description. A genus of mostly evergreen shrubs and small trees from the warmer parts of Asia and Africa, the commonly grown species from South Africa described here deservedly popular for its attractive foliage, flowers, and especially the showy crimson sepals.

Propagation. Freshly collected seeds are sown at once in early autumn. The volunteer plants that appear in every garden as the result of dispersal by birds are sometimes difficult to eradicate when well established. The seedlings should therefore be dealt with as early as possible.

Cultivation. An open, sunny position on well-drained friable soil, in a moderately warm climate is the ideal environment. It makes a good hedge if planted 0.5 m apart and shaped early into a dense, leafy barrier of the required form.

Pruning. The plant is most attractive when naturally grown, but may need a little pruning to contain it to reasonable bounds and to maintain the dense twiggy growth. Such pruning is done in late summer after the fruit has fallen.

Species and cultivars

Óchna serrulàta (Latin 'with serrulate margins', of leaves) (syn. *O. multiflora*) southern coast of South Africa to Natal and the warmer parts of Transvaal, mostly on the fringes of the warm, coastal forests.

Habit. An evergreen shrub to 2 m or so tall, upright at first but becoming globular in maturity.

Leaves. Simple, alternate, lanceolate to oblong, 5–7 cm long and 1.0–1.5 cm wide; apex acute; base rounded; margin sharply serrulate; midrib prominent; glabrous; reddish at first, becoming dark glossy green above but paler beneath; coriaceous when fully mature.

Flowers. In 1- to 3-flowered umbels on the upper twigs, on 1.5 cm pedicels; calyx crateriform at first but later reflexed, of 5 ovate sepals, green while young but persistent and ripening to crimson in late spring, lasting to mid-January; petals 5, orbicular, with a narrow claw, buttercup-yellow, soon deciduous in late August and September; stamens 30–40, filaments pale green, anthers saffron-yellow; style green, prominent; flowers to 3 cm across.

Fruit. A fleshy, ovoid drupe to 6 mm, seen at first as a radial cluster of 5 or 6 green berries, becoming reddish, then ripening to black to contrast with the crimson sepals and the mound-like receptacle.

Other distinguishing features. Upper stems chocolate-brown, with prominent pale-brown lenticels.

Climatic range. A, B, M, P, S, T.

OSBÉCKIA (syn. *Melastoma, Tibouchina, Lasiandra*)

Commemorating Pehr O. Osbeck, eighteenth-century Swedish botanist.
Rough-leafed Osbeckia; Small-leafed Lasiandra.
Melastomataceae, the Melastoma family.

Generic description. A genus of soft-wooded, tender plants resembling *Tibouchina* and often named so by many writers, but with much smaller leaves and flowers, fully described below in relation to the only species used to any extent in Australian gardens.

Propagation. Soft-tip cuttings taken in spring strike satisfactorily in a sand/peat mixture in the warm, humid atmosphere of a heated glass-house.

Cultivation. The species listed is suitable only for warm coastal climates with little or no frost; in marginal climates, the plants should be covered at night during the coldest month or so. A sunny position is best, preferably on a light, friable soil with free drainage.

Pruning. A moderate annual pruning in late winter after the flowering season is beneficial in maintaining the dense, leafy growth habit.

Species and cultivars

Osbéckia kewénsis (not indigenous to Kew, England, but long used there as a conservatory plant and so named, following rejection of its older invalid name, *aspera*) (syn. *O. aspera*, *O. microphylla*, and others) Rough-leafed Osbeckia: India and Sri Lanka.

Habit. An evergreen shrub to 1.0–1.5 m tall, loose and somewhat thin unless pruned regularly, then dense and globose, handsome in foliage and flower.

Leaves. Simple, opposite, broadly oval to slightly ovate, 2–4 cm long and 1.5–2.0 cm wide; apex mostly short-acute; base rounded; margin finely serrulate-ciliate; venation with 3 prominent veins and 2 lesser outer veins, all converging at base and apex; strigose on all parts; dark green and scabrous above with minute swollen dots, paler beneath, some leaves colouring to orange or scarlet before falling.

Flowers. Inflorescence an umbellate cluster of 3 to 6 flowers borne at the terminals of the upper twigs; receptacle campanulate, the 5 spreading sepals covered with red bristles; petals 5, opening to obovate-obcordate, the rotate flower to 4–5 cm across, deep royal-purple, flowering from May to September; stamens 10, the filaments green, anthers yellow; pistil 1, curved, cream-green, ripening to red.

Other distinguishing features. Upper branchlets square in cross-section, strigose.

Climatic range. B, P, S, T, and in mild, frost-free parts of A and M.

ODONTONÈMA (formerly included with *Justicia* and *Jacobinia*)

Derived from the Greek words describing the tooth-like, sterile staminodes in the throat of the corolla.

Crimson Justicia.

Acanthaceae, the Acanthus family.

Generic description. A small genus of soft-wooded plants from tropical America and West Indies, widely grown in warm climates for their handsome simple, opposite leaves, and showy red or pink flowers borne in terminal racemes.

Propagation. Soft-tip cuttings taken between spring and autumn, or firm-wood lengths taken in winter, all root easily in a sand/peat mixture in a warm, humid atmosphere.

Cultivation. A plant of easy cultivation, *Odontonema's* needs are met adequately by a mild climate, a well-drained soil of moderate fertility, and a planting position fully exposed to sun but preferably protected from violent winds which damage the brittle stems.

Pruning. Young plants should be tip-pruned during the first year or two to develop a dense mass of short flowering stems; thereafter, removal of spent inflorescences is desirable, followed in winter by a reduction of about half the growth of the previous year.

Species and cultivars

Odontonèma strictum (Latin 'upright and narrow', describing the inflorescence) (syn. *Justicia coccinea*, *Jacobinia coccinea*) Crimson Justicia: Brazil.

Habit. An evergreen shrub to 1.5 m, usually more erect than broad.

Leaves. Elliptic to ovate, 12–15 cm long and 6–8 cm wide; petiole 1–2 cm long; apex acuminate; base narrowly cuneate and narrowly winged down the petiole; margin entire; main veins depressed above, prominent beneath; glabrous, but finely pubescent on the midrib; texture soft and fleshy; dark green above, paler beneath.

Flowers. Inflorescence a terminal panicle comprising a purplish-red stalk carrying several spike-like racemes, each 5–10 cm long and 2.5–3.5 cm broad; flowers in 1- to 10-flowered fascicles, calyx crimson to 5 mm long, with 5 short triangular teeth; corolla crimson, 1.5–2.5 cm long, slender-tubulate, the 5-lobed limb spreading to 1 cm wide; stamens 2; flowering season February to May.

Fruit. Not seen.

Other distinguishing features. Upper stems soft, squarish and fleshy, dark green to purplish-red.

Climatic range. B, P, S, T.

OSMÁNTHUS

Derived from the Greek *osme* 'odour', and *anthos* 'a flower', describing the highly perfumed flowers.
Osmanthus (various).
Oleaceae, the Olive family.

Generic description. A small genus of evergreens, mainly from the Orient, with simple, opposite leaves, several with spiny margins, small white or yellow flowers, some sweetly perfumed, and small, drupaceous, purplish or black fruit.

Propagation. Semi-hardwood, leafy tip cuttings, taken in autumn or winter, root satisfactorily in a sand/peat mixture in a warm, humid atmosphere; mist is an advantage, with mild bottom heat beneficial for winter cuttings.

Cultivation. Osmanthus is easy to cultivate. The soil should be well drained and moderately fertile; full exposure to the sun is desirable, preferably in a cool, moist climate with low temperatures not exceeding −8°C.

Pruning. Little pruning is necessary except to maintain the normally tidy shape by suppressing wayward shoots.

Species and cultivars

Osmánthus delaváyi (after Abbé Jean Marie Delavay, 19th century French priest and botanical collector in the Orient) (syn. *Siphonosmanthus delavayi*) Delavay Osmanthus: western China.
Habit. An evergreen shrub to 2.5 m tall and about as wide, with stout branches, forming an irregularly globose bush.
Leaves. Ovate to elliptic, 2–3 cm long and 1.5 cm wide, nearly sessile; apex acute; margin sharply but shallowly serrate-dentate; midrib and main veins prominent beneath; glabrous and coriaceous; dark lustrous green above, paler beneath, with numerous black glandular dots.
Flowers. Inflorescence a terminal, and occasionally axillary, corymbose cyme of about 5 or 6 salverform flowers, the slender tube about 1.3 cm long, the 4-lobed limb spreading to rotate form 1.3 cm across and reflexing almost fully; white, sweetly perfumed; flowering in late winter and spring.
Fruit. In pendent clusters of about 5, on short pedicels, ovoid, purplish-black with a bluish bloom, ripening in autumn.
Climatic range. A, H, M, Mts, P, S.

Osmánthus fràgrans (Latin 'fragrant'): Sweet-scented Osmanthus: China and Japan.
Habit. An evergreen shrub or small tree, usually kept to 2.5–3.0 m when shrubby, or pruned to the single trunk of a tree, then to 6 m or more.
Leaves. Oblong to ovate-elliptic, 6–12 cm long and 3–6 cm wide; apex shortly acuminate; margin serrulate or often entire; midrib and main veins prominent beneath; glabrous and coriaceous; dark lustrous green but paler below.
Flowers. Inflorescence a short, axillary raceme from the upper young shoots; flowers funnelform, 3–6 mm across with a short tube, 4-lobed at the spreading limb; pure white; very fragrant; flowering from late winter to early December.
Fruit. Not seen.
Other distinguishing features. An old favourite in gardens for its strongly perfumed flowers, used since ancient times by the Chinese as a house decoration and to make scented tea.
Climatic range. A, B, H, M, Mts, P, S.

Osmánthus heterophýllus (Greek 'with leaves of various kinds') (syn. *O. aquifolius* and *O. ilicifolius*) main islands of Japan, and Taiwan.
Habit. An evergreen shrub or small tree to 3–4 m tall, mostly seen as an erect shrub.
Leaves. Holly-like but in opposite arrangement, variable from elliptic to obovate to 5–7 cm long and 2–3 cm wide; apex acuminate; margin either entire in mature plants or spinose in younger plants; glabrous and coriaceous; dark glossy green.
Flowers. In a short, axillary, racemose cluster of up to about 6; corolla funnelform to 5–6 mm with reflexed lobes; pure white; fragrant; flowering in autumn and early winter.
Fruit. An ellipsoidal, fleshy drupe to 1.5 cm long and 8–10 mm wide, the skin dark-purplish with a bluish bloom, ripening in winter.
'Aùreo-marginàtus' (syn. 'Aureus') has leaves margined and splashed with broad patches of pale yellow, often invading the normally green centre; intermediate areas are pale creamy-green.
'Purpùreus' has leaves deep purple-green at first, becoming slightly less purplish at maturity.
'Variegàtus' (syn. 'Argenteo-marginatus') has leaves irregularly margined and marked with creamy-white, the green centre often invaded by the lighter colour, then pale creamy-green.
Climatic range. A, B, H, M, Mts, P, S.

PAEÒNIA

Derived from Paion, the physician to the gods in Greek mythology, implying praise for something of exceptional quality.

Paeony or Peony; Moutan.

Paeoniaceae, the Paeony family; formerly included in Ranunculaceae.

Generic description. A family of a single genus comprising 33 species scattered throughout the northern temperate zone. Most are herbaceous, dying to the thickened roots during winter, but several species have persistent, woody stems forming shrubby growth. *Paeonia suffruticosa*, described in detail below, is the principal parent of the many cultivars offered by nurseries. They are highly prized in cool-climate gardens in Australia, grown specifically for their ornamental foliage and huge flowers with a good variety of colours.

Propagation. The paucity of the Moutan Paeony in local gardens is partly due to its difficulty of propagation. The early nurseries imported their plants directly from the English and Dutch growers, very few bothering to grow their own. One leading Sydney nursery listed 15 varieties in 1940, but stocks are rather more difficult to locate now.

a) Seeds saved from clonal stock are unlikely to reproduce the qualities of their parent plant, but certainly should be grown to flowering stage for critical evaluation before being discarded. Seeds should be sown as soon as possible after harvesting, in an approved mixture, and placed in a warm, moist atmosphere.

b) Apical-grafting is almost always used in the northern hemisphere (whip-and-tongue, spliced or cleft-grafts are the most common forms); seedling understocks of any of the herbaceous species are used. When planted out, the graft-union is buried 8–10 cm below soil level to encourage the scion to initiate its own roots and become independent of the understock.

Modern facilities and new methods — cuttings, tissue-culture, etc. — may well overcome many of the earlier difficulties in propagation sufficiently so to restore the Paeony to its former popular status.

Cultivation. The best soils are the deep, fertile 'mountain' soils of basaltic origin, heavily fed annually with well-prepared compost fortified with mild organic manure or fertilizer, and not allowed to dry out excessively during droughts. Places with a reliably cool winter, free of wide fluctuations of temperature in spring, especially late frosts, provide the plants with the long dormant period they need to flower well in spring. Protection from strong wind and scorching sun is essential; a lightly-shaded position on a cool southerly slope is ideal, especially if mulched well to reduce soil temperature in summer.

Pruning. Removal of spent flowers and dead or misplaced shoots is the only pruning necessary, unless seeds are required for the production of understocks when seed follicles should be allowed to develop and ripen naturally.

Species and cultivars

Paeònia suffruticòsa (Latin 'having a low, shrubby habit of growth'): Moutan Paeony: NW China, on the foothills of the Tibetan plateau and westward to Bhutan on the southern slopes of the Himalayas.

Habit. A deciduous shrub to 1–2 m tall and as broad, with persistent, stout woody stems arising from a short trunk, forming a roughly hemispherical crown.

Leaves. Alternate, compound, bipinnate, 20–30 cm long usually 3- to 5-cleft, variously cut and lobed among the cultivars, borne on stout petioles 8–10 cm long; apices acute to acuminate; mostly glabrous but sometimes hairy on the midrib beneath; dark green above, but some forms reddish while young, all changing to brown in autumn.

Flowers. Solitary at the terminals of the new season's shoots with a single or double row of 5–10 petals in the wild plants, but much fuller in cultivated stock, forming a large open flower to 20–25 cm across, the petals fluted and frilled at the edges in reds, pinks, whites and violets, many with a purplish blotch near the base; a few are slightly fragrant.

Flowering season is mid-spring, usually from late September to early November.

Nursery catalogues should be consulted for availability and detailed descriptions of the many cultivars.

Fruit. A group of papery follicles with numerous black seeds.

Climatic range. H, M, Mts, and on cool, elevated sites in A, P, S.

PÉNTAS

Derived from the Greek *pente* 'five', describing the floral parts.
Pentas.
Rubiaceae, the Madder family.

Generic description. A small genus of soft-wooded shrubs, some herbaceous, mostly from Central Africa and neighbouring countries, used popularly in gardens for their rapid growth and brightly coloured flowers produced over an extended season.

Propagation. Soft-tip cuttings, taken in spring to early autumn, strike easily in a sand/peat mixture in a glass-house or frame.

Cultivation. Pentas is easy to cultivate but prefers a frost-free, humid position with a well-drained soil of reasonable fertility.

Pruning. Young plants should be tip-pruned to develop a dense, twiggy growth but in established plants the current season's flowered stems should be shortened slightly in early spring.

Species and cultivars

Péntas lanceolàta (Latin 'with lance-like leaves') (syn. *P. carnea*) tropical Africa, especially around Uganda and Ethiopia.
Habit. An evergreen shrub to about 1 m tall and wide, with erect, hairy stems forming a rounded bush, eventually woody at the base.
Leaves. Simple, opposite, the blade lanceolate to elliptical, 10–15 cm long and 4–5 cm wide; apex acuminate; margin entire; midrib and main laterals prominent beneath; dark green and dull above, paler beneath, all parts pubescent.
Flowers. Inflorescence a terminal corymb, 6–8 cm across, comprising several small cymes; flowers numerous; calyx campanulate, with 5 spreading sepals; corolla salverform to 2 cm long, the tube slender below; limb 5-lobed to 1.5 cm wide, the lobes ovate, surrounding a white disc and rim of white down, the throat and 5 stamens almost obscured; style exserted, the stigma bifurcate; flower colour variable, typically pale rosy-purple, but also red, purple-red, white, and mauve, flowering abundantly from early November to winter.
Fruit. Capsular, with numerous fine seeds.
Other distinguishing features. Upper stems squarish, green to purplish, pubescent.
Climatic range. B, P, S, T, on warm, sheltered sites only in marginal areas.

PHEBÀLIUM

Derived from the ancient name for the Myrtle which several of the species resemble.
Phebalium.
Rutaceae, the Rue family.

Generic description. A small indigenous genus of about 30 species, mostly of eastern Australia, several becoming increasingly popular for their attractive spring flowers. Leaves are simple, alternate, discolorous, often heavily dotted with oil glands and sometimes scurfy scales; flowers are borne terminally or in the upper leaf axils in small umbels or dense racemes, the 5 stellate petals meeting at their edges or only slightly overlapped, the apices inflexed, mostly white to yellow, flowering abundantly between late winter and early summer.

Propagation. a) Seeds, collected before dispersal, and sown in a friable material in late spring, germinate satisfactorily.
b) Soft-tip cuttings are also widely used, taken in late spring and planted in a sand/peat mixture in a humid atmosphere.

Cultivation. Phebaliums grow on well-drained, sandy or light loamy soils within the limits of their climatic range, but additional irrigation may be required in dry times. The species described are hardy to $-2°C$.

Pruning. By shortening the leading shoots slightly, immediately after the spring flowering, pruning should aim to thicken the plants' normally loose growth habit by the development of twiggy laterals.

Species and cultivars

Phebàlium dentàtum (Latin 'toothed'): coastal gullies of the Hawkesbury sandstone areas.
Habit. An evergreen, open shrub to 2–3 m tall in the wild but responding to cultivation and pruning with a more regular, twiggy form.
Leaves. Linear, 5–7 cm long and 4–5 mm wide; apex obtuse; margin shallowly and indistinctly dentate, the edge recurved; midrib prominent below; glabrous, but heavily dotted with pale-green oil glands; dark-green and shiny above, white and finely tomentose beneath.
Flowers. Inflorescence an axillary umbel of 6–12 flowers, clustered on a 30 cm length of stem just below the terminals; flowers greenish in the ovoid bud, the 5 calyx lobes very short; petals 5, broad-lanceolate, forming a stellate flower 7–8 mm across, deep cream, flowering

between August and October; stamens 10, exserted, filaments white, anthers cream.

Fruit. A dehiscent capsule of 5 cells with lustrous, black seeds.

Other distinguishing features. Twigs brown-green, with a fine stellate pubescence.

Climatic range. B, M, P, S, and on warm lower elevations of Mts.

Phebàlium diósmeum (Latin 'with leaves like *Diosma*'): coastal plain and lower slopes of the tablelands of southern NSW and eastern Victoria.

Habit. An erect shrub to 1.5 m, with reddish, pubescent upper branchlets issuing from a crowded base to form an irregularly globose bush.

Leaves. Narrowly linear to 1.2 cm long, lying closely against and partly concealing the slender branchlets; apex obtuse; base broad, sessile; margin entire, recurved; surface rough and puberulent; dark green above, paler beneath.

Flowers. In a dense, terminal umbel on short axillary spurs from the upper 1-year old shoots; calyx with 5 linear sepals to 4 mm long; corolla of 5 lanceolate petals to 8 mm long in stellate form, bright yellow; stamens 10, exserted beyond the petals, the cream, pubescent filaments with golden-yellow anthers; flowering season from mid-winter to late October.

Fruit. Not seen.

Climatic range. B, M, P, S, and on warm, sheltered sites on lower Mts.

Phebàlium glandulòsum (Latin 'bearing glands'): Desert Phebalium: eastern Australia, mainly in the 300–600 mm annual rainfall region.

Habit. A small evergreen shrub to about 1 m tall, with numerous branchlets supporting a rounded crown about 1.5 m across, but occasionally almost tree-like in moist gullies.

Leaves. Simple, alternate, linear-oblong, 1.5–3.0 cm long and 2–3 mm wide, borne on silver-scaly twigs; apex truncate to bilobed; margin recurved and notched by green translucent glands; upper surface dark green and glandular; lower surface scaly.

Flowers. In a small terminal umbel of 10–12 flowers, many together almost covering the crown of the plant, all parts silver-scaly and glandular; flowers stellate, 4 mm across, pale yellow, with 10 paler filaments and deep yellow anthers; flowers abundant in spring.

Fruit. Not seen.

Climatic range. A, H, I, M, P, S, and on warm sites in Mts.

Phebàlium squàmeum (Latin 'bearing scales'): Scaly Phebalium (syn. *P. billardieri*) eastern Australian coastal plain and lower slopes of the Great Dividing Range, mainly in moist, sheltered gullies.

Habit. Usually seen as a small tree to 4 m or so on a short, single trunk in sheltered places, but often reduced to open shrubby form on poor sandy sites in the heathlands or scrubby, hind-dune forests.

Leaves. Linear to lanceolate or narrowly elliptic, 8–10 cm long and 1.5–3.0 cm wide; petiole to 5–6 mm long; apex acuminate; base tapered; margin entire, but slightly recurved; midrib prominent beneath; glabrous, mid-green and slightly shiny above, grey-white and scaly beneath; glandular and aromatic.

Flowers. In small, round corymbs of up to 20 or so flowers on white, scaly peduncles arising from the upper axils; flowers stellate, 8–10 mm across, the 5 linear petals creamy-white; stamens 10, exserted as long as the petals, the filaments white, anthers cream; flowering season from late winter to early summer.

Fruit. Not seen.

Other distinguishing features. Upper twigs and branchlets rough, pale brown and finely scaly, with angular ridges running decurrently below the leaves.

'Illumination' is slightly smaller in stature and has leaves with a conspicuous margin of creamy-yellow around the irregular central patch of green.

Climatic range. B, M, P, S, T, and on warm sheltered sites on lower Mts.

Phebàlium squamulòsum subsp. *squamulòsum* (Latin 'bearing small scales'): NSW and eastern Vic. on sandy heathlands and sandstone ridges between the coast and the lower tablelands.

Habit. A shrub to 2.5–3.0 m tall, based on a short trunk, soon dividing into many ascending scaly branches, forming a handsome rounded bush when brought into cultivation and pruned annually.

Leaves. Alternate, but often nearly opposite, linear-oblong, 2.5–5.5 cm long, 4–6 mm wide; petiole to 3 mm long, scaly; apex obtuse-mucronate; margin entire but slightly recurved; midrib prominently raised beneath; dark green, dull and minutely warted above, whitish with brown spots beneath, and covered with fine scales.

Flowers. Inflorescence a terminal, umbellate corymb of 15–20 flowers on slender 4 mm long pedicels, all parts whitish, glandular and scaly; calyx to 1.5 mm across; corolla stellate, 4–5 mm across, of 5 acute petals, deep cream; stamens 10, the slender filaments cream, anthers large; style exserted, longer than the petals and stamens, pale cream; flowers lightly fragrant, flowering from early September to late October.

Fruit. A soft-wooded capsule splitting into 5 cells at the apex to release the solitary round, smooth seeds.

Other distinguishing features. Upper twigs yellowish-brown, roughened by the small flaky scales.

Climatic range. B, M, P, S, and on warm sheltered sites on the lower Mts.

Phebàlium whitei (commemorating Cyril T. White, one-time Queensland Government Botanist): Granite Phebalium: SE Qld and northern NSW on the granite belt of the Great Dividing Range.

Habit. An evergreen shrub about 1 m tall and as broad with a mass of slender branchlets from the base.

Leaves. Simple, alternate, linear-oblong, 5–6 cm long, 6–10 mm wide; apex obtuse; base cuneate; margin finely undulate, irregularly glandular-roughened; midrib prominent beneath; glabrous, dark green and dotted with translucent glands above, silvery-white and heavily scaly beneath, the glands dark brown, giving the leaves an attractive bicoloured effect.

Flowers. In small terminal umbels of 4–6, many together forming a 15–30 cm long spray; flowers stellate, 1.5 cm across, the 3–4 mm cup-shaped calyx supporting the ovoid buds; petals lanceolate, 7–8 mm long, yellow inside, tan-scaly outside; stamens 10, with yellow anthers; style 1, long exserted; flowering in spring.

Fruit. Not seen.

Other distinguishing features. Upper twigs with tan scales, aging to nearly black in the first year.

Climatic range. A, H, M, Mts, P, S.

PHILADÉLPHUS

A name of uncertain origin, said by some authors to derive from Ptolemy Philadelphus, King of Egypt in pre-Christian times, whose connection with the genus is not clear; others quote the Greek *phileo* 'love', and *adelphos* 'brother', as the derivation.

Mock Orange, referring to its use in bridal bouquets as a substitute for genuine orange blossom. Philadelphaceae, the Philadelphus family; formerly included in Saxifragaceae.

Generic description. A genus of mostly deciduous shrubs native of Europe, Asia, the Orient and North America, popular in Australia for their late spring and early summer flowers. Leaves are simple, opposite, often pubescent or strigose, with 3 or 5 nearly parallel veins from the base; flowers are crucifom or open funnelform in shape, sometimes semi or fully double in the cultivars, pure white or with a small purplish blotch at the base of the petals, borne singly or in small clusters of mostly 3, but sometimes up to 7 or 9, at the ends of short laterals arising from the main erect stems at a wide angle; flower parts are in fours, but with numerous showy stamens with yellow anthers; fruit is a small, soft-wooded capsule dehiscing into 4 cells to release the many small seeds.

Propagation. a) Soft-tip or semi-hardwood cuttings taken in summer and autumn strike readily in a warm, humid atmosphere.
b) Hardwood cuttings of about 12–15 cm from the fully-matured wood, taken in mid-winter, root well if planted deeply in prepared open-ground beds or in containers in a sheltered shade house.

Cultivation. Full sun exposure, wind protection, free drainage and a rich friable soil are the essential requirements for strong, healthy growth.

Pruning. Flowered laterals should be reduced to the lowest pair of growth buds immediately after the flowering period; several of the oldest basal shoots should be removed entirely each year at the same time, thinning out the congested base to make way for new water-shoots. The remaining basal shoots should not be shortened but may be tipped when nearly fully grown to induce the stronger growth of laterals. Pruning should *not* be carried out in winter.

Species and cultivars

Philadélphus coronàrius (Latin 'crowned with flowers'): Common European Mock Orange: southern Europe to Turkey and the Caucasus.
Habit. A deciduous shrub to 3–4 m tall, with many stems from the crowded base, erect at first, but developing laterals to form a broad rounded crown to 2–3 m wide.
Leaves. Narrowly elliptic to ovate-oblong, 6–9 cm long and 3–5 cm wide; petiole to 1 cm long, pubescent; apex acuminate; base obtuse to acute; margin with a few coarse, serrate-dentate notches, and finely denticulate in the upper half; venation reticulate between the 3 or 5 main veins, slightly pubescent beneath in the axils; mostly glabrous otherwise, bright green when young, becoming dark green above, paler beneath, changing to dull-yellow in autumn.
Flowers. In terminal racemes, on short lateral shoots carrying about 7 flowers about 3.5 cm across, on puberulent pedicels to 8–10 mm long, the obovate to ovate petals about 1 cm wide, white, heavily fragrant, flowering in late spring; stamens numerous, the filaments white, anthers creamy-yellow.
Fruit. A small, brown, 4-celled capsule with numerous fine seeds.
Other distinguishing features. Young shoots green, smooth-barked but somewhat angular, becoming mid-brown when mature, then flaking and peeling longitudinally.
Climatic range. A, H, M, Mts, P, S.

Philadélphus x cymòsus (Latin 'with flowers in a cyme'): interspecific hybrid between *P. x lemòinei* and *P. inodòrus* var. *glandiflòrus*, comprising several cultivars, represented mainly in Australia by the following:
'**Conquette**' (designated as the type of the hybrid)
Habit. A slender shrub to about 1 m tall, with many erect shoots arching outwards near the apex to form a rounded bush to 1.5 m across.
Leaves. Broadly lanceolate to 6–8 cm long and 2.5–3.5 cm wide; apex acuminate; base broadly cuneate to rounded; margin sparsely serrate-dentate; dark green and glabrous above, paler and pubescent, especially on the veins beneath.
Flowers. In a terminal cymose cluster of 3 to about 7, the corolla open funnelform to cruciform, 4–5 cm across, the outer petals narrow-obovate, the inner petals oblong when semi-double, petaloids filling in the centre, pure white, sweetly fragrant, flowering in late spring.

'**Rosace**' is somewhat similar but is taller to 1.5 m or so, with larger lanceolate leaves, 9–10 cm long, and large, semi-double, pure white flowers to 5–6 cm across in terminal, cymose clusters of 3 or 5, perfumed, and flowering in late spring.
Climatic range. A, H, M, Mts, P, S.

Philadélphus x lemoìnei (commemorating Victor Lemoine, eminent horticulturist and hybridist of Nancy, France): interspecific hybrid between *P. coronàrius* and *P. microphýllus* comprising several well-regarded cultivars, one 'Lemoinei', designated as the type.
'**Lemoìnei**' : Lemoine Mock Orange
Habit. A shrub to 1.75–2.0 m tall with slender, erect stems arching outwards near the tip to form a rounded crown.
Leaves. Broad-lanceolate to ovate to 7–8 cm long on water-shoots, but 3–5 cm elsewhere; apex slightly acuminate; base obtuse; margin entire or with a few remote denticulate teeth; finely strigose and dark green above, paler and pubescent at least on the main veins below.
Flowers. In teminal racemes of 5 or 7, on short axillary spurs arising from the erect branches; flowers cruciform to crateriform to 3 cm across, on 4–5 mm pedicels, pure white, the numerous stamens with golden-yellow anthers; sweetly perfumed, flowering in October and November.
'**Avalanche**' is a large bush to about 2 m, with somewhat pendulous, vase-shaped branching pattern, lanceolate-elliptic, entire leaves to 2.5 cm long and 8–10 mm wide, and heavy masses of single, cup-shaped flowers about 3 cm across in terminal clusters of about 5 or 7, milky white, with a cluster of golden-yellow stamens.
'**Boule d'Argent**' is a shrub to 1.5 m tall with outward-arching branches, the laterals carrying the abundant, large double flowers to 5–6 cm across in dense panicles of 5 or 7, pure white, but with little perfume.
'**Innocence**' has large, single, pure white, fragrant flowers of open funnelform shape to 3.5–4.0 cm across, in panicles of 5 to 7 on short laterals, borne in great profusion, covering the crown of the attractive rounded shrub to 1.5–2.0 m tall, some leaves departing from the normal dark green with an occasional cream variegation.
Climatic range. All A, B, H, M, Mts, P, S.

Philadélphus mexicànus (Latin 'from Mexico'): Mexican Mock Orange: mountain regions of southern Mexico and Guatemala.

Habit. An evergreen shrub to 2 m or so, with numerous, slender ascending shoots from the base, arching outwards to form a loose, open crown.

Leaves. Broad-lanceolate to ovate, 3–6 cm long and 1.5–2.5 cm wide, the petiole 5–8 mm long, pale-green, pubescent, grooved above; apex acuminate; base rounded to broadly acute; margin with 3 to 5 remote serrations, sharp and gland-tipped; finely reticulate between the midrib and 2 other main laterals, all densely strigose below; texture soft; upper surface puberulent and bright green; rough and strigose beneath.

Flowers. Solitary, or in terminal clusters of 3, on lateral shoots from the upper branches; calyx pubescent; corolla funnelform to 4 cm across, the broadly obovate petals creamy-white and slightly puberulent, sweetly perfumed, flowering abundantly in late spring; stamens numerous, with white filaments and yellow anthers.

Fruit. Capsules ovoid to 1 cm long, the style with 4-branched stigma.

Other distinguishing features. Upper twigs slender, mid brown, densely pubescent.

Climatic range. A, B, M, P, S.

Philadélphus microphýllus (Greek 'with small leaves'): Small-leafed Mock Orange: low rainfall areas of south-western USA, mainly on the lower levels of the southern Rocky Mountains.

Habit. A deciduous shrub to 1.0–1.5 m tall, with many slender pubescent branches from a crowded base, forming an open, lax bush to 1.5 m wide, the bark of the older stems decorticating in reddish-brown strips.

Leaves. Lanceolate to ovate, 1.5–2.0 cm long and 7–8 mm wide on a petiole of 1–2 mm; apex acute to shortly acuminate; base acute; margin ciliate but otherwise entire; glabrous or only finely puberulent and dark green above, glaucous-green and strigose beneath.

Flowers. Solitary or occasionally in threes, borne terminally on short laterals to 4–5 cm long; corolla funnelform to cruciform to 3.5 cm across, the 4 obovate petals white; stamens numerous, with yellow anthers; flowers sweetly fragrant, flowering in late spring.

Fruit. Capsules broadly ovoid, to 1 cm long and 7–8 mm wide.

Other distinguishing features. Young twigs softly pubescent at first but becoming glabrous, smooth and lustrous chocolate-red.

Climatic range. A, H, M, Mts, and on cool, elevated sites in P and S.

Philadélphus x *purpùreo-maculàtus* (Latin 'purple-spotted'): interspecific hybrid between *P.* x *lemoinei* and *P. mexicanus* var. *coulteri* ? raised by Victor Lemoine of Nancy, France; appears to be represented in Australia by a single but now well-known cultivar, described below.

'**Belle Etoile**' is a strong-growing shrub to 1.5–2.0 m tall, with an open rounded form about as wide; leaves are ovate to 4.0–5.0 cm long and 1.5–2.5 cm wide, strongly 3-nerved, coarsely but sparsely toothed, the apex abruptly acuminate, pubescent on both surfaces, dark green above; flowers are borne singly or in terminal clusters of 3 to 9, the calyx funnelform with lanceolate, pubescent sepals to 1 cm long, an open funnelform corolla to 5 cm across, somewhat squarish at the base, the ovate-oblong, glabrous petals centrally channelled and often shallowly notched at the edges, white, with a rosy-purple stain at the base, strongly fragrant; stamens numerous, showy, the filaments white with yellow anthers; flowering season from mid spring to early summer.

Climatic range. A, H, M, Mts, P, S.

Philadélphus x *virginàlis* (Latin 'white or pure'): interspecific hybrid between *P.* x *lemoinei* and *P.* x *nivàlis*, comprising several cultivars, '**Virginal**' the best-known Mock Orange in Australian gardens being designated as the type of the hybrid.

'**Virginal**' grows to about 2.5 m tall, with many erect shoots from the base, arching above to form an open crown about 2 m across, the bark mid brown and peeling and shredding in strips from the 2-year old and older shoots; leaves ovate to elliptic to 6–8 cm long and 3–5 cm wide, apex shortly acuminate, margin coarsely serrate-dentate, the ciliate edge often denticulate, venation 3-nerved, upper surface nearly glabrous, dark green, lower surface paler and strigose, the leaves changing to dull yellow in autumn; flowers semi- to fully double to 4.5 cm across, in terminal racemes of 5 to 7, the corolla with broad-obovate outer petals and slightly laciniate inner petaloids, sweetly perfumed, flowering abundantly in late spring and early summer.

'**Enchantment**' is somewhat similar, as an erect shrub to about 2 m, with unusually heavily flowered laterals carrying up to 7 or 9 double flowers, each to 3 cm across, in a crowded raceme, pure white and strongly perfumed, the inner petaloids irregularly arranged, with a few abortive stamens.

Climatic range. A, H, M, Mts, P, S.

PHILODÉNDRON

Derived from the Greek, meaning 'tree-loving', referring to the support provided for many of the climbing species.

The generic name is commonly used. No other common name is generally recognised.

Araceae, the Arum family.

Generic description. A large and varied genus of soft-wooded plants numbering over 200 species, mostly from tropical South America, Central America, Mexico and the West Indies. Many are of climbing habit with aerial roots, some popularly grown as indoor plants. Other non-climbing species, of more or less shrub-like form are grown in sheltered, outdoor positions, mainly for the beauty of their leaves. The species treated below is probably the most common example of these.

Propagation. a) Seeds are planted 4–5 mm deep in a good sowing mix, placed in a warm, humid atmosphere, and potted on when large enough to handle.

b) Stem cuttings are also used, each short length having at least one node from which the new shoot will emerge. The cuttings are planted in a bed of sand and peat, kept moist in a warm atmosphere, and potted on when roots appear

Cultivation. A mild climate such as coastal NSW and Qld is ideal. The plant performs best in a lightly-shaded, warm corner protected from strong salty winds, thriving in almost any friable soil with moderate drainage, but responds vigorously to additional feeding and water during spring and summer.

Pruning. Old decrepit leaves should be removed as they decline. A few of the aerial roots should be allowed to reach the soil to stabilise the heavy crown, but the surplus should be removed.

Species and cultivars

Philodéndron sellòum (commemorating Friedrich Sellow, 1789–1831, German botanical collector in Brazil): tropical and warm-temperate South America, chiefly Brazil and Paraguay.

Habit. An evergreen foliage shrub growing to 2–3 m tall and sometimes a little broader, the stout, erect stem with numerous thick aerial roots reaching downwards to connect with the surface soil.

Leaves. Simple, scattered in a rosette-like cluster from the apex of the trunk; petiole to 1 m or more splayed at the base, ridged and flattened above; blade to 40–60 cm long and nearly as wide, deeply pinnatisect, the 10–12 primary segments on each side of the midrib irregularly pinnate, dividing again into secondary segments of extremely diverse shape and arrangement; all dark green and glossy when well-grown, the main veins broad and sometimes yellowish-green, very prominent beneath.

Flowers. Arum-like, typical of the family, the stout spadix enclosed at first, but eventually exposed by the opening of the fleshy, boat-shaped spathe about 25–35 cm long and 6–8 cm thick, maturing in summer, then creamy-yellow inside, dull green outside.

Other distinguishing features. Leaf scars transversely oval, 4–6 cm across, making a bicoloured pattern on the main trunk.

Climatic range. B, P, S, T, under outdoor conditions, but in conservatories elsewhere.

PHÒRMIUM

Derived from the Greek *phormion* 'a kind of fibrous plant', alluding to its use by the Maoris for weaving baskets, mats etc.

New Zealand Flax.

Agavaceae, the Agave family.

Generic description. An evergreen plant, virtually stemless, but grown for its long, sword-shaped leaves of various colours, forming a leafy clump 1.5 to 3.0 m tall and as wide, often restricted from spreading by being planted in containers or troughs. An important feature-plant, especially when associated with water gardens.

Propagation. The green-leafed species are easily raised by seeds, collected before dispersal by wind in autumn and sown in a warm, humid atmosphere; cultivars are grown by separation of an old clump in winter, each short piece of rhizome being sufficient to start a new colony.

Cultivation. An open, sunny aspect is best, especially for the coloured-leafed sorts, in a fertile soil, well supplied with water but not water-logged. Hardy to cold to at least −5°C but risky in more severe climates.

Pruning. Pruning consists of removal of spent inflorescences when no longer decorative and also old leaves shredded by wind or by natural deterioration by age.

Species and cultivars

Phòrmium ténax (Latin 'to hold securely' referring to the toughness of the leaf fibres): New Zealand Flax: both islands of New Zealand.

Habit. A radical-leafed plant, 1.5–2.5 m tall, developing from a thick, fibrous rhizome, spreading laterally to form a leafy clump 1–2 m wide, the drooping leaves appearing to make the clump broader.

Leaves. Ensiform, arranged in 2 overlapping ranks at the base but soon separating, to 1.5–2.5 m long and 5–12 cm wide; apex long-attenuate; base sheathed by neighbouring leaves; margin entire; texture smooth but fibrous, tough and stringy; glabrous; venation parallel-striate; mostly erect and stiff, but less so and drooping in some forms; dark green above, glaucous beneath, but of various colours in the many cultivars.

Flowers. Inflorescence a tall, leafless scape 3 to 5 m tall, bare at the base but with 10 to 20 or so paniculate branches towards the apex, brownish-red, the stems tough and fibrous; flowers in a terminal panicle 25–35 cm long, with numerous flowers, pedicels 2 cm long, the perianth tubulate, reddish, the inner series of 3 segments long and spreading at the apex; stamens 6, long-exserted; flowering from November to February.

Fruit. Capsules 8–10 cm long, erect, falcate, 3-ribbed on the outside, 3-celled inside; capsule drying to pale brown, tough and fibrous, mature in autumn and persisting throughout winter; seeds glossy, black, 8–9 mm long and 3 mm wide, crimped and winged, easily dispersed by wind.

'Purpùreum' has leaves 1.5 to 2.0 m long, erect and stiff, purplish-bronze, with slightly glaucous reverse.

'Variegàtum' resembles 'Purpureum' in general habit but the dark green, glossy leaves are striped longitudinally with creamy-yellow in a variety of patterns, at least one broad cream stripe superior to the others, and with several minor stripes towards the margin which is bright tan for about 1 mm wide; glaucous beneath, with the other colours somewhat muted. Other variations of this form appear in gardens, the main difference being the width and arrangement of the creamy-yellow stripes.

'Rùbrum' is thought to be distinct from the P. tenax group and may be a hybrid; the growth habit is shorter to 1.0–1.5 m, the leaves less stiff and somewhat inclined to droop over near the middle when fully or over-mature, purplish-red, more intense at the margin, but slightly grey-purple beneath. A favourite tub plant for terrace or patio planting.
Climatic range. All A, B, H, M, Mts, P, S, T.

Phòrmium cookiànum 'Trícolor' is somewhat similar to P. tenax but has leaves rather more drooping and arching outwards gracefully; leaves are bright green in the middle, with several cream stripes within 1.0–1.5 cm of the outer edges, and margined with a 2–3 mm wide stripe of rosy-crimson; strikingly beautiful when used with judgement as an accent plant.
Climatic range. A, B, H, M, Mts, P, S, T.

PHOTÍNIA

Derived from the Greek, describing the glabrous, lustrous leaves.
Photinia; Chinese Hawthorn; etc.
Rosaceae, sub-family Pomoideae (Rose family, Pome sub-family).

Generic description. A small genus of both evergreen and deciduous shrubs and trees from the Orient, with simple, alternate, toothed leaves, some richly coloured in spring, others equally so in autumn, white flowers in flattish, corymbose panicles, and fruit a small, reddish pome. The cultivars listed below are grown for their brilliant red leaves and are popular as hedges and screens, while P. serratifolia is admired most for its handsome fruits.

Propagation. a) P. serratifolia reproduces reliably by seeds sown in spring, the better for having spent the winter in just-damp sphagnum moss at 4°–5°C.
b) The cultivars listed are mostly propagated by semi-hardwood, heeled tip cuttings taken in autumn-winter and placed in a humid atmosphere.

Cultivation. Free drainage is an essential cultural requirement. All species thrive on the better class volcanic soils, especially in the tablelands where they are safe to at least −10°C. Grown well in a sun-exposed position, and with adequate food and water, the photinias are among the most spectacular of all foliage plants, especially when used for tall hedging.

PLATE 25

▲ Schefflera venulosa
◄ Sedum praealtum
▼ Senecio petasitis

▼ Raphiolepis x delacourii

▼ Rhododendron Azalea Mollis 'Dr M. Oosthoek'

▼ Syringa x vulgaris 'Katherine Havemeyer'

▼ Rhododendron Azalea Ghent Hybrid

▼ Streptosolen jamesonii

PLATE 26

▲ Syringa vulgaris 'Vulcan'

▲ Telopea speciosissima

▼ Tibouchina lepidota

▲ Spiraea cantoniensis 'Lanceata'
◄ Tibouchina lepidota
▼ Spartium junceum

▼ Thryptomene saxicola

▼ Viburnum opulus 'Sterile'

Pruning. *P. serratifolia* is seldom pruned except to restrict its growth. *P. x fraseri* is often used as a tall hedge or as a street tree and needs some shaping in both capacities. *P. glabra* 'Rubens' is the most suitable hedging plant; after the basic shape of the hedge has been established, several flushes of coloured leaves may be attained throughout the growing part of the year by trimming the plants when the leaves turn green, and where necessary, by the addition of food and water. Any major pruning is best done in late winter before the new growth starts.

Species and cultivars

Photínia **x** *fràseri* The interspecific hybrid group derived from crossing *P. glabra* with *P. serratifolia.*

'Robústa' (Latin, *robur* 'an Oak', signifying strength — hence robust).

Habit. A large, evergreen shrub, 4–5 m tall, with many stems from the short trunk forming a top-shaped bush, but frequently seen as a single-stemmed tree as the result of pruning.

Leaves. Oblong-obovate, 8–12 cm long and 4–6 cm wide; petiole to 3 cm; apex shortly acuminate; margin finely serrate, the teeth with incurved points; glabrous, soft at first, becoming coriaceous; young leaves crimson to copper-red, becoming progressively greener as they mature, at length dark green and lustrous, a few turning crimson in autumn.

Flowers. Inflorescence a terminal, corymbose panicle, 12–15 cm across, above the upper leaves; flowers rotate, to 1 cm across, with 5 obovate white petals; calyx whitish with 5 short teeth; stamens about 20, with white filaments and cream anthers; styles 2; flowers white when fresh, but aging to brown, flowering from October to late November and intermittently through summer.

Fruit. Not seen; the plant may be sterile like many other hybrids.

Other distinguishing features. Youngest twigs crimson at first, becoming chocolate-red with a silver cuticle.

'Red Robin' is a New Zealand raised cultivar of the same parentage with similar habit of growth but with deeper ruby-red young leaves.

Climatic range. A, H, M, Mts, P, S.

Photinia glàbra (Latin 'smooth', referring to the leaves): Japan.

Habit. A small evergreen tree, 4–5 m tall, with a short trunk and ascending branches forming a narrow-domed crown.

Leaves. Simple, alternate, elliptic-ovate to oblanceolate, 6–10 cm long and 3–4 cm wide; petiole to 1.2 cm; apex shortly acuminate; base acute; margin serrulate; glabrous; reddish when young but aging to dark green.

Flowers. Inflorescence a terminal, corymbose panicle, 10–15 cm across; calyx campanulate to 1–2 mm, reddish, with 5 acute teeth; corolla rotate to 7–8 mm diameter, with 5 obovate petals, white; stamens about 20, with white filaments and brown anthers; flowers from September to late November.

Fruit. A fleshy, ovoid drupe to 5 mm, green at first, then red, the teeth of the calyx persisting at the apex; fruit ripens in autumn, lasting throughout winter.

'Rùbens' is somewhat smaller in all main parts and has brilliant red young leaves which gradually age to green, to be followed by successive flushes of growth throughout spring and summer, all producing red leaves. One of the most popular plants for hedging in cool, moist climates.

Climatic range. A, H, M, Mts, P, S.

Photínia serratifòlia (Latin *serra*, 'a saw', referring to the margin) (syn. *serrulata*) Chinese Hawthorn: China.

Habit. A small evergreen tree to 5–8 m, with a short trunk and a broad-domed crown but often reduced to shrubby form by pruning.

Leaves. Simple, alternate, oblong-obovate, 10–15 cm long; apex shortly acuminate; margin finely serrate; glabrous and coriaceous; reddish at first, becoming lustrous green with a few red leaves in autumn.

Flowers. Inflorescence a terminal, corymbose panicle, 15–20 cm across; flowers very numerous, rotate, to 1 cm across, with 5 white, orbicular petals, flowering in October to December.

Fruit. A 4-seeded, fleshy pome 4–6 mm across, orange-red, with persistent, grey calyx lobes, borne abundantly from April to July.

Other distinguishing features. Leaf scars broad, forming conspicuous ring-like ridges.

Climatic range. A, H, M, Mts, P, S.

PHYGÈLIUS

Derivation obscure.
Cape Fuchsia.
Scrophulariaceae, the Figwort family.

Generic description. A South African genus of

2 species, one grown in eastern Australia for its rapid growth and showy fuchsia-like flowers, described in detail under specific notes below.

Propagation. Soft-tip cuttings, taken between spring and autumn, strike readily in a sand/peat mixture in a warm, humid atmosphere.

Cultivation. A fertile, light-textured soil, with a high organic content and with free drainage, is ideal; the plant enjoys dappled shade or a fully sun-exposed position, but is brittle and needs protection from wind.

Pruning. Frequent tip-pruning is desirable in the early years. Established plants may have about half the annual growth removed in late winter-early spring.

Species and cultivars

Phygèlius capénsis (Latin 'from Cape of Good Hope'): Cape Fuchsia: eastern Cape of South Africa, usually near permanent streams, often at elevations of up to 1000 m.

Habit. An evergreen shrub to about 1 m tall, with soft, succulent, squarish stems, eventually hardening near the base, and twiggy, leafy growth forming an upright bush about 1 m wide.

Leaves. Simple, opposite, ovate, 4–8 cm long and 2.5–3.5 cm wide; petiole 1.5–2.0 cm long, purplish, slightly winged and grooved above, auriculate at the base; apex rounded to acute; base sub-cordate; margin crenate; midrib and main veins prominent beneath; dark green above, pale glaucescent-green below.

Flowers. Inflorescence a terminal panicle, 30–45 cm long, carrying small clusters of 3–4 flowers, drooping from the reddish peduncles; flowers tubulate to 4–5 cm long, curved near the 5-lobed, spreading limb, supported by a shallowly campulate, green calyx with 5 acute lobes; corolla bright coral-scarlet outside, yellow inside; stamens 4, exserted, with red filaments and green anthers; flowers borne abundantly from late October to autumn.

Fruit. An ovoid capsule, green at first but ripening to mid brown, with the style persisting; seeds numerous.

Other distinguishing features. Stems soft and succulent, decurrently ridged, purplish-green.

Climatic range. A, B, M, P, S, T, and in mild microclimates in Mts.

PHYSOCÀRPUS (syn. *Neillia, Spiraea*)

Derived from the Greek words describing the bladder-like seed follicles.
Ninebark.
Rosaceae, sub-family Spiraeoideae (Rose family, Spiraea sub-family).

Generic description. A small genus of deciduous shrubs, mainly from USA, one species and its yellow-foliaged cultivar used in Australian gardens for their showy leaves and spring flowers, the plants usually being well placed in the front rows of a shrub border to display their attractive, pendulous form.

Propagation. Hardwood stem cuttings, 10–15 cm long, taken from the winter prunings, strike readily in sheltered open-ground beds or in individual containers in a shade-house.

Cultivation. A fertile, well-drained soil, and an open sun-exposed position are essential to bring out the best yellow colour in the cultivar, but the plants must be protected from harsh drying winds which desiccate and spoil the leaves. A cool, temperate climate is best. Hardy to cold of at least −10°C.

Pruning. The plants should be grown in their natural form and not 'trimmed' into a geometrical shape; about one-third of the basal shoots should be completely removed each winter to make way for more vigorous, leafy shoots with a better flowering display in spring.

Species and cultivars

Physocàrpus opulifòlius (Latin 'with leaves like *Viburnum opulus*', especially in the shape of the lobes): Common Ninebark: eastern USA.

Habit. A spirea-like shrub to 2.5–3.0 m tall and 3–4 m wide, the branches arching outwards to form a broad, rounded crown, the branchlets drooping.

Leaves. Simple, alternate, broad-ovate, 3–6 cm long and as wide, with 3 main rounded lobes and often 2 smaller lobes; leaves usually larger on vigorous spring growth; petiole 1–2 cm, slender; apex obtuse to acuminate; margin irregularly to doubly crenate-dentate; venation trinerved at the base; glabrous; pale green at first, maturing to dark green above, paler to slightly glaucous-green and sometimes finely pubescent beneath, changing to dull yellow in autumn.

Flowers. Inflorescence a terminal corymb to 4–5 cm across on short, leafy, lateral twigs from the previous year's shoots; flowers rotate to 1 cm across; calyx campanulate, with 5 green sepals; petals 5, nearly orbicular, white, but often flushed with pink outside; stamens numerous, with purplish anthers; flowering season October and early November.

Fruit. A cluster of about 3 red-brown, inflated, non-woody follicles, splitting along 2 sides to release the few yellowish seeds in autumn.

Other distinguishing features. Upper twigs angular, striate, pale to dark brown, peeling when mature.

'Lùteus' (syn. *'Aureus'*) has bright butter-yellow leaves in spring, becoming a somewhat dull bronze-yellow by summer.

Climatic range. A, H, M, Mts, P, S.

PIÈRIS (syn. *Andromeda*)

Derived from Pieria, a district on the slopes of Mount Olympus in Macedonia, the birthplace of the daughters of Jupiter, the Muses of Greek mythology.

Pearl-flower or Andromeda. (Not Lily-of-the-valley which correctly belongs to *Convallaria*, and sometimes applied to *Clethra*).

Ericaceae, the Erica family.

Generic description. A small but important genus of highly decorative shrubs from the northern temperate zone with simple, alternate, evergreen leaves, sometimes brightly coloured; mostly white or pink urceolate flowers in pendulous, terminal panicles or clustered racemes; and fruit a 5-celled, soft-wooded capsule. *Pieris* is a popular shrub in Australian gardens, grown mostly in the cool, humid climates for its attractive flowers and foliage.

Propagation. a) Seeds, collected in autumn before the capsules split to release their contents, and sown in early spring, germinate readily in a coarse, sterile sand and shredded sphagnum-moss mixture, the seeds barely covered with the same material and placed in a warm, humid atmosphere, preferably in a lightly shaded part of a glass-house.

b) Semi-hardwood, leafy tip cuttings may be used for clonal stock, planted in coarse sand and peat in the proportion of 1:3, in an atmosphere of warmth and high humidity; heeled cuttings are sometimes preferred and root-promoting treatments are beneficial, the best period being from early summer to mid-autumn.

Cultivation. The best soil is a mildly acid (5.0–6.0 pH), sandy or porous loam with a high organic content, kept cool and uniformly moist by the addition of a coarse surface mulch. Free aeration and drainage in the soil are essential. Fresh manure should not be used. A cool, dapple-shaded position makes for the best floral display extended over a longer season. The species listed are hardy to low temperatures of about –5°C or –6°C but the early flowers may be seriously damaged by more severe cold.

Pruning. Removal of the spent inflorescences to keep the plant tidy is the only pruning required; the pleasantly irregular, natural form of the plant is rarely improved by pruning and is best left undisturbed.

Species and cultivars

Pièris japónica (Latin 'from Japan'): Pearl-flower or Japanese Andromeda: main islands of Japan, mainly in the foothills of the mountains.

Habit. An evergreen shrub to 2–3 m tall, of somewhat indeterminate shape, founded on a short trunk with several low branches supporting a dense, leafy crown.

Leaves. Simple, alternate but often appearing to be whorled at the growth junctions, lanceolate to oblanceolate, 6–10 cm long, 1.0–2.5 cm wide; petiole 1.5 cm long, terete but grooved above, pale green; apex acute to acuminate; margin shallowly crenate-serrate, slightly thickened at the edge; venation reticulate, the yellowish-green midrib prominent; glabrous and coriaceous; young leaves reddish at first but maturing to dark green and lustrous above, paler beneath.

Flowers. Inflorescence a spreading cluster of up to 8 or 10 slender, drooping racemes, forming a terminal panicle 12–15 cm long; calyx of 5 acute, lanceolate sepals, grey-green; corolla urceolate, 7–8 mm long, externally ridged with 5 rounded ribs, the corolla-lobes very short, broad and blunt; flowers waxy-white, sometimes stained or streaked with red near the rim; flowering season late winter to mid spring; stamens 10, deep inside the corolla, filaments 2 mm long, white, pubescent, anthers reddish-brown.

Fruit. A rounded, globular capsule to 6 mm across, pale brown, with 5 dehiscent cells enclosing the roughened seeds.

Other distinguishing features. Upper twigs green, slightly angular by the decurrent ridges below the leaf bases.

'**Bert Chandler**' (commemorating the leading Victorian nurseryman of that name): included here as a cultivar of *P. japonica* in deference to the raiser's classification, but considered by at least two other prominent plantsmen to be either a seedling variant of *P. formosa* var. *forrestii*, or an interspecific hybrid between that plant and *P. japonica*; the plant is more vigorous in growth habit than *P. japonica*, the young leaves bright coral-pink at first, gradually becoming cream and finally bright green, all colours being present together during the spring and early summer period at least. An unusual and very beautiful shrub deserving of careful placement in the garden to ensure its best display and protection against strong sunlight and harsh drying winds.

'**Flamingo**' has red flowers opening to pale pink, but is otherwise similar to the parent species.

'**Variegàta**' is a smaller-growing sort with pinkish-green early leaves, becoming lustrous dark green, with a distinct margin of creamy-white.

Climatic range. H, M, Mts (in sheltered microclimates only) and on cool, elevated sites in A, P, and S. Also occasionally planted is:

Pièris formòsa (Latin 'beautiful'): China and eastern Himalayas. A tall evergreen shrub, 4 to 8 m, with a somewhat erect form, large, lanceolate-elliptic, lustrous green leaves and urceolate, white flowers in pendulous racemes, clustered together to form a large terminal panicle, flowering in spring, mainly September to November.

var. fórrestii (after George Forrest, Scottish botanical collector in the Orient): SW China.

An evergreen shrub, 2.5–3.5 m tall, low and broad at first, but eventually with narrow upright form about 2 m wide; leaves are larger than those of the species, to 10–12 cm long and 3 cm wide, bright crimson when young, changing to creamy-pink, then pure cream, pale green, and finally lustrous green, the duration of the colour change extending throughout spring to mid-summer; flowers are urceolate, ivory-white, waxy, somewhat more conspicuously ribbed than in other species, borne in heavy panicles in late September and October. A number of clonal forms showing minor variations have been isolated and awarded cultivarietal names.

Climatic range. H, M, Mts (in sheltered microclimates only), and on cool, elevated sites in A, P, and S.

PIMÈLIA

Derived from the Greek *pimele* 'fat', descriptive of the oily seeds.
Rice-flower (various).
Thymelaeaceae, the Mezereum family.

Generic description. A large genus of evergreen shrubs with mostly simple, opposite, but occasionally alternate leaves; flowers are salverform or campanulate in terminal heads, subtended by coloured, leafy involucral bracts, but sometimes solitary or racemose, in a variety of colours, mainly white, yellow, pink, or red.
A few species have been brought into cultivation, the two listed below, grown especially for their showy flowers, being the most important.

Propagation. Soft or semi-hardwood tip cuttings, taken while the plants are in active growth, root satisfactorily in a warm, humid atmosphere.

Cultivation. A loose, open soil — ideally sandy with a generous organic component — is best, in a sun-exposed position in a mild climate, with low temperatures remaining above –5°C.

Pruning. Early tip-pruning is beneficial; mature plants should be lightly pruned immediately after flowering to maintain the plant in good shape.

Species and cultivars

Pimèlia ferrugínea (Latin 'rust-coloured') (syn. *P. decussata*) Pink Rice-flower: south-west WA.

Habit. A dense evergreen shrub to 1 m tall and about as wide, with a rounded crown of attractive foliage.

Leaves. Simple, opposite, elliptic to 1 cm long and 5 mm wide, almost sessile; apex obtuse; base rounded; margin entire but recurved, the extreme edge translucent; venation obscure except for the broad midrib; glabrous; shiny and bright green above, pale grey-green below.

Flowers. Inflorescence a dense, umbellate head about 2.5–3.0 cm across, at the terminals of the 1-year old twigs, subtended by a whorl of green or brown, ovate involucral scales to 7–8 mm long; flowers numerous, salverform to 1 cm long, the slender tube densely white-pubescent, pale blush-pink, the limb expanded to 7–8 mm with 4 broad-ovate, rose-pink lobes; stamens 2, slightly longer than the petals, with white filaments and bright-orange anthers; flowers produced over most of the spring season from early September to December,

Fruit. A small, rounded drupe.

Other distinguishing features. Youngest twigs whitish-green, becoming dull orange and eventually nearly black, and somewhat square in section.

A useful and decorative little plant for exposed sites near the coast, especially on dry sandy soils. 'Bonne Petite' is a registered cultivar chosen as the 'Shrub of the Year 1980'. It has a compact growth habit with densely-leafed twigs, and flowers in heads about 2.5 cm across, pale pink, fading to white.

'Magenta Mist' from WA, is also registered as a cultivar; its neat, low growth habit is well-leafed and covered with rosy-magenta flowers in a loose, open head to 3 cm across.

Climatic range. A, M, P, S.

Pimèlia linifòlia (Latin 'with *Linum*-like leaves' but not *Reinwardtia*): Flax-leafed Rice-flower or Slender Rice-flower: coastal NSW, SA, Vic., Tas and southern Qld, on sandy heathland and gravelly ridges, especially on Hawkesbury sandstones in NSW.

Habit. An evergreen shrub to 1 m or so, of irregular erect form in its native habitat but responsive to pruning and cultivation, then more attractive as a rounded, densely foliaged bush to 0.75 m tall and wide.

Leaves. Simple, opposite, linear-oblanceolate to narrow-oblong, 1.0–2.5 cm long and 3–6 mm wide; petiole 1 mm long; apex acute; margin entire; venation indistinct except for the midrib; glabrous; pale green at first, deepening to dark green but slightly glaucescent beneath.

Flowers. Inflorescence a terminal head of about 20 flowers, enclosed at first by 4 persistent, green involucral scales; flowers salverform with a slender tube to 1 cm long and 1 mm or less wide, with 4 spreading lobes to 7–8 mm wide, creamy-white, pubescent, flowering abundantly in late winter and spring, but then intermittently throughout the year; stamens 2, with slender white filaments, the anthers orange, standing 3 mm clear of the limb.

Fruit. A small, thin-walled hairy drupe with a single, ovoid seed.

Other distinguishing features. Upper twigs pale reddish-brown, the bark becoming darker with age.

Climatic range. A, B, M, P, S.

PLECTRÁNTHUS

Derived from the Greek, descriptive of the spur-like base of the corolla.
Spur-flower or Flowering Coleus.
Lamiaceae, the Mint family; formerly Labiatae.

Generic description. A genus of tender, soft-wooded plants, mostly shrubs or herbs, with simple, opposite, evergreen leaves, and terminal or axillary showy flowers in panicles or racemes, mostly tubulate and lipped, some with a sac-like spur at the base, grown for their attractive flowers and ease of culture.

Propagation. Soft-tip cuttings strike readily in a sand/peat mixture in a warm, humid atmosphere, in spring and summer; semi-hardwood cuttings are also used in late autumn and winter, preferably over a bottom-heated bench.

Cultivation. A warm, frost-free climate is essential, preferably with protection from harsh winds. The plants are tolerant of a little shade, but flowers are more brilliant when seen in a sunny position. Average soils will suit, provided drainage is free.

Pruning. Spent flower stems should be removed and the plant shaped to its natural hemispherical form in late winter.

Species and cultivars

Plectránthus écklonii (commemorating Christian F. Ecklon, nineteenth-century German botanist in South Africa): SE South Africa, in warm, sheltered places close to the coast.

Habit. An evergreen shrub, soft-wooded but not herbaceous, of globular or hemispherical shape to 2 m tall, with many twiggy branches from the base, the stems squarish and somewhat fleshy.

Leaves. Ovate to 10 cm long and 4–5 cm wide; petiole 1.5–2.0 cm long, channelled above; apex acute; margin crenate; main veins prominent and heavily white-tomentose beneath; mid green and dull above, paler beneath; minty-aromatic when crushed.

Flowers. Inflorescence a terminal panicle 15–18 cm tall, erect and standing well clear of the leaves; flowers labiate, to 2 cm long, the tube slender, opening to a single-lipped, lower limb over which the exserted stamens curl, leaving the style free; pedicels, calyx and corolla deep violet-blue, flowering freely from February to May.

Climatic range. B, P, S, T, and in warm sheltered parts of M.

Plectránthus saccátus (Latin 'with saccate flowers'): warm, sheltered sites in coastal South Africa.

Habit. A low spreading, soft-wooded, evergreen shrub to 0.75 m tall and 1.0 m wide, with horizontally inclined branches, forming a dense, leafy bush useful for sheltered, shady sites.

Leaves. Broadly ovate to triangular, 2–4 cm long and as broad; petiole soft-succulent, grooved above, about as long as the blade, sparsely pilose; apex acute; base truncate; margin coarsely dentate or doubly so, venation reticulate, the main veins prominent beneath; pubescent; upper surface rugose and bright green, pale green beneath; aromatic when bruised.

Flowers. Inflorescence a short terminal raceme to 5–6 cm long, the 8–10 flowers on 5 mm purplish pedicels, in pairs or in threes, from the nodes of the green rachis; calyx campanulate to 3 mm long, with 1 broad lobe and 4 narrowly acute, purplish teeth; corolla about 1.5 cm long, the upper lip orbicular, about 1.3 cm across, the lower folded together in boat-shaped fashion, all deep violet in the bud, opening to lavender-blue, the throat paling to glistening white, flowers borne freely over the crown of the plant from early February to mid-autumn.

Fruit. Not seen.

Other distinguishing features. Stems squarish, pilose, dull green.

Climatic range. B, P, S, T, and in warm microclimates in M.

PLUMBÀGO

Derived from the Latin *plumbum* 'lead', describing the colour of the flowers of some of the species.
Leadwort.
Plumbaginaceae, the Leadwort family.

Generic description. A small genus of shrubs or part-climbers mainly from tropical Central America, southern Asia, and Africa, with evergreen, alternate, simple leaves, and mostly blue, white, or purplish flowers in racemes at the end of long, trailing shoots. The species treated here is a useful plant for specimen, walling or informal hedging, on account of its good foliage and flowers.

Propagation. a) Soft-tip cuttings taken in spring to autumn strike readily in a sand/peat mixture in a warm, humid atmosphere.

b) Semi-hardwood cuttings taken in winter are also used, struck under mist.

Cultivation. The plant grows well in freely drained soil of moderate fertility in a warm locality, with minimum temperatures not much lower than –3°C, preferably with full exposure to sunlight. When planted alternately in an informal hedge, the two coloured forms provide an attractive contrast.

Pruning. In most cases, annual pruning is necessary to control the vigorous growth. Since the flowers are borne on the new season's growth, the long stems may be pruned quite severely in late winter to the desired shape.

Species and cultivars

Plumbàgo auriculàta (Latin 'with an ear', referring to the stipulate leaves) (syn. *P. capensis*) South Africa, from Eastern Cape to Natal.

Habit. An evergreen shrub to 3 m tall, with loose, spreading habit but of dense, leafy growth when pruned to shrub, espalier, or hedge form.

Leaves. Oblong to oblanceolate, 8–10 cm long and 3.5 cm wide; apex acute or obtuse; base cuneate; margin entire; glabrous but with a white glandular dusting beneath; dull green; small stipules at the base.

Flowers. Inflorescence a terminal, umbel-like raceme on short laterals towards the end of the branchlets; calyx slender to 1 cm long, with 5 small teeth at the apex, and 40–50 slender-stalked, viscous glands on the upper half; corolla salverform, 3–4 cm long, with a slender tube and a 5-lobed, expanded limb to 2.5 cm across, pale blue, but slightly deeper towards the centre; stamens 5, with deep-blue anthers; pistil 1, 5-pronged at the apex; flowering between November and June, with the peak period in February and March.

Fruit. Not seen.

Other distinguishing features. Young stems channelled, mid green, but with white glandular dust.

'Álba' has white flowers but is otherwise identical.

Climatic range. B, M, P, S, T, and on warm sheltered sites in A.

PODALÝRIA

Commemorating Podalyrius, son of Aesculapius, the God of Medicine in Greek mythology.
Sweet-pea Bush or Satin Bush.
Fabaceae, the Pea family.

Generic description. A small genus of ever-green shrubs from South Africa, with simple, alternate, mostly silky-pubescent leaves; the fragrant, pea-shaped flowers are solitary or in small axillary clusters, blooming mainly in winter and spring; and fruit is an inflated legume.

Propagation. a) Seeds germinate readily if soaked in warm water for 24 hours soon after ripening, and then sown in a coarse, friable mixture in a warm atmosphere.
b) Soft-tip cuttings, taken in spring and summer, strike with some difficulty in a warm, humid glass-house.

Cultivation. A coarse sandy or gravelly soil with free aeration and drainage is the ideal, the plants being especially well adapted to the hot, dry summers of the hinterland, remote from the heavy rainfall and high atmospheric humidity of the coastal regions. Both species are hardy to low temperatures to about −3°C but are liable to injury in more severe climates.

Pruning. Young plants should be tip-pruned frequently in their first few years, and in later years moderately, to reduce the length of the 1-year-old shoots, immediately after the flowering period.

Species and cultivars

Podalýria calyptràta (Greek 'having a calyptra', a hood-like covering over the flower buds) (syn. *P. grandiflora*) Sweet-pea Bush: South Africa, near the Cape of Good Hope, often in exposed places on coarse, open soils.
Habit. An evergreen shrub, 2–3 m tall, densely foliaged into a rounded bush to 3 m wide, or rarely, trained as a small tree on a single stem.
Leaves. Oval to slightly obovate, 4.5–5.0 cm long and 2.0–2.5 cm wide, the petiole 5 mm long; apex acute-mucronate; base acute; margin entire; venation reticulate; finely silky-pubescent and silvery-green on both surfaces, the youngest leaves whitish-silver.
Flowers. Solitary in the upper axils, on pedicels 2.5 cm long, with 6 to 12 flowers together; flowers pea-shaped to 4 cm across; calyx 5-lobed, about 1.3 cm long, silky-pubescent, purplish, the sepals lanceolate, acute, reflexing fully; corolla

with a broad standard, partly split in the middle, pink-mauve with a white base; wings smaller, slightly deeper in colour and white at the base; keel beaked, with a tinge of mauve on the tip; flowers sweetly perfumed, flowering from early September to late December.
Fruit. An ovoid-oblong, inflated legume, pale silvery-green.
Other distinguishing features. Young twigs covered with silvery pubescence.
'Álba' is similar but has white flowers.
Climatic range. A, M, P, and on elevated, well-drained sites in S.

Podalýria serícea (Latin 'silky'): Silver Sweet-pea Bush or South Africa Satin Bush: South Africa, on the Cape of Good Hope Peninsula, mostly on dry gravelly or sandy soils.
Habit. An evergreen shrub to 1 m or so, the lower stems procumbent, the remainder ascending to form a dense, hemispherical bush.
Leaves. Oval or obovate, 2–3 cm long and 1.5–2.0 cm wide; apex obtuse; margin entire; midrib prominent below; densely silky pubescent, silvery-grey, more so when young.
Flowers. Solitary in the upper axils on short pedicels; flowers pea-shaped to 2.0–2.5 cm, across, the standard sub-orbicular, emarginate at the apex, the obovate wings smaller, the keel broadly obovate; all parts mauve-pink, flowering from June to October.
Fruit. An inflated legume, pale green but with silvery silky-pubescent covering.
Other distinguishing features. Upper twigs and branchlets finely silky-pubescent.
Climatic range. A, M, P, and on elevated, well-drained sites in S.

POLÝGALA

From the Greek *polus* 'much', and *gala* 'milk', referring to the supposed use as a lactic stimulant.
Polygala or Milkwort.
Polygalaceae, the Milkwort family.

Generic description. A large genus of mostly herbs but with a few woody species, from warm climatic zones, mostly South Africa, with simple, alternate, evergreen leaves and showy pea-like flowers, the posterior petal extended into a brush-like tuft. The two species listed below are popular as showy border plants with a long flowering season.

Propagation. a) Seeds germinate readily if sown in a warm, humid place in spring or early summer.

b) Soft-tip cuttings taken in summer and autumn strike satisfactorily in a sand/peat mixture in a glass-house with mist and bottom heat.

Cultivation. A warm, sunny exposure in a mild climate with minimum temperatures remaining above −5°C is most suitable. The ideal soil is light and open with free drainage.

Pruning. A moderate pruning of the flowered shoots is desirable, immediately after the main flowering season, to thicken the growth habit.

Species and cultivars

Polýgala myrtifòlia (Latin 'with Myrtle-like leaves'): South Africa, from South-West Cape to Natal.

Habit. An evergreen shrub, 1.5–2.5 m tall, with several main stems from the base, dividing early into a mass of small twiggy branchlets carrying the abundant leaves and flowers.

Leaves. Narrowly elliptic to oval or obovate, 3–4 cm long and 1–2 cm wide; petiole 2–3 mm long, pubescent; apex broadly acute with a short, purplish mucro; margin entire; texture soft and thin; glabrous; bright green and slightly shiny above, paler beneath.

Flowers. Inflorescence a short, terminal raceme of several to about 10 flowers, irregular, somewhat pea-shaped, on purplish-green pedicels to about 1 cm long; calyx of 5 dissimilar sepals; petals 3, the 2 smallest lateral petals wing-like, 1 cm long, purple and white, the larger posterior petal to 1.5 cm long, strongly keeled on the lower edge into a brush-like extension, the bristles to 5 mm long, purplish-white, the body of the petal imperial-purple, with a large whitish patch near the keel, heavily veined with deep purple, enclosing the curved staminal tube; stamens 8, fused together with the exserted pistil, all purplish-white with yellow anthers; flowers measure about 2 cm across when fully developed, flowering from mid winter to summer, then somewhat sparsely throughout autumn.

Fruit. An irregularly obovoid capsule, 6–8 mm long.

Other distinguishing features. Upper twigs slightly puberulent, purplish-green.

Climatic range. A, B, M, P, S, T, and on warm sites in lower Mts.

Polýgala virgàta (Latin *virga*, 'a rod', referring to the wand-like leafless stems of the lower parts of the plant): southern coast of South Africa.

Habit. An evergreen shrub to about 2 m or so, with thin, reed-like stems, loose and open in character, but improved by annual pruning to form a compact bush of globose shape.

Leaves. Linear to narrow-oblanceolate, 4–5 cm long and 5–6 mm wide; apex acute-mucronate; margin entire; texture soft and slightly succulent; finely puberulent; bright green above, paler beneath.

Flowers. Inflorescence a terminal raceme, 15–20 cm long, of 30 to 50 or more flowers; calyx of 5 dissimilar sepals, the 2 laterals petaloid and nearly orbicular, pale violet, with deep purple veins, the other sepals concave, elliptical, greenish with a purplish margin; petals 3, purplish, with deeper veins; the 2 lateral, clasping, wing-like petals to 7 mm long, the largest posterior petal about 1 cm long, folded deeply into a hood-like envelope enclosing the sexual parts, its spine expanded into a bifid, imperial-purple tassel 6–8 mm long; stamens 8, in a claw-like bundle, the filaments white, anthers yellow; flowers are borne freely from late winter to summer.

Fruit. A flattened, obovate, winged capsule to 8–9 mm long, 2-celled, containing 2 ovoid, blackish seeds, ripening in late autumn.

Other distinguishing features. Stems hollow, rod-like, and glabrous apart from some fine pubescence on the youngest twigs.

Climatic range. A, B, M, P, S, T.

POSOQUÈRIA

The Latinised form of the native vernacular name of one of the species.

Posoqueria or Needle-flower Tree.

Rubiaceae, the Madder family.

Generic description. A genus of evergreen, flowering shrubs and small trees from Mexico, Central America and the warmer parts of South America, with simple, entire, opposite leaves with large interpetiolar stipules and mostly white, perfumed flowers produced in summer. One species is occasionally grown in warm coastal gardens for its handsome foliage and flowers.

Propagation. Ripened, semi-hardwood cuttings taken between late summer and early spring strike well in a warm, humid atmosphere.

Cultivation. Posoqueria grows well in a light-textured soil with free drainage, preferably in a warm, frost-free climate in an open, sun-exposed position.

Pruning. Young plants should be tip-pruned during the first 2 or 3 years to build up a dense, leafy growth habit, but thereafter a light shaping in late winter is the only pruning required.

Species and cultivars

Posoquèria multiflòra (Latin 'many-flowered'): Brazil.

Habit. An evergreen shrub of rounded bun-shape to 1.5–2.0 m tall but often slightly broader when mature, the lower branches decumbent.

Leaves. Elliptic to broadly oblong, 8–12 cm long and 4–8 cm across; petiole to 1 cm; interpetiolar stipules broadly ovate to 8–9 mm long and wide; apex shortly acute; base obtuse; margin entire but thickened and slightly recurved; venation reticulate, yellow-green beneath; glabrous; dark green and shiny above, yellowish-green and dull beneath; texture somewhat brittle and easily fractured.

Flowers. Inflorescence a terminal corymb of several to about 12–15 flowers; calyx tube campanulate to 4 mm wide, with 5 acute, apical teeth; corolla salverform, about 10 cm long, the tube slender to 3 mm wide, pale green at the base, creamy-white towards the apex; limb of 5 revolute lobes to 1.5 cm long and 6 mm wide, fully reflexed upon opening, creamy-white, densely pubescent in the throat; stamens 5, with white filaments and boat-shaped, brown anthers; pistil 1, deeply inserted in the tube; flowers sweetly perfumed, flowering from early December to autumn.

Fruit. Not seen, local plants apparently denied an effective means of pollination.

Other distinguishing features. Upper stems slightly compressed and squared at the enlarged nodes.

Climatic range. B, S, T, and in warm microclimates in M and P.

PROSTANTHÈRA

Derived from the Greek words describing the linear appendages on the anthers of the stamens. Mint-bush (various).
Lamiaceae, the Mint family; formerly Labiatae.

Generic description. A large and important genus of Australian shrubs with evergreen, simple, opposite, aromatic, green leaves; labiate flowers, solitary or in mostly terminal racemes and panicles, the calyx and corolla both 2-lipped, the corolla campanulate in white, violet, blue, or purple; and small nut-like fruits.

The species described below represent a sample of the 60 or more species, especially popular for their rapid growth and wealth of flowers in spring.

Propagation. a) The natural method of propagation is by seeds, often dispersed widely by moving water.

b) In cultivation, firm-tip cuttings are mostly preferred by growers, taken in summer and autumn and struck in a coarse, gritty sand in a warm, moist environment; The National Botanic Gardens reports success in apical grafting on understocks of *Westringia fruticosa* to reduce or eliminate losses caused by soil-borne root diseases such as *Phytophthora cinnamomii*.

Cultivation. Most Mint-bushes reach their best development on well-drained sandy or gravelly soils enriched with leaf-mould or other coarse, fibrous organic matter to improve aeration; many are mountain plants, hardy in low temperatures to at least −5°C but need protection from violent winds by being closely planted among other plants. They must not want for water during spring and summer. A mulch of pebbles or large flat 'floater' stones is beneficial in conserving soil water in dry times and in maintaining an even temperature in the root zone, especially in mid summer.

Pruning. All species are improved by early tip-pruning for the first 2 or 3 years until a dense, leafy plant is established, then pruned annually after flowering, into current season's growth only.

Species and cultivars

Prostanthèra caerùlea (Latin 'blue', referring to the flower colour): NSW Central Tablelands, usually in cool, sheltered localities on better-class soils; common near Bilpin and the neighbouring mountain slopes.

Habit. An evergreen shrub, 2–3 m tall, with several erect main trunks and many smaller twiggy lateral branches and abundant foliage, forming a medium-wide cone of more regular shape than most other species.

Leaves. Narrow-ovate to lanceolate, 2.5–4.5 cm long and 5–8 mm wide; apex acute; margin serrate, occasional leaves nearly entire; venation with 3 or 4 clearly defined laterals on either side of the midrib; finely glandular on both surfaces, and aromatic when bruised; dark green but not shiny above, paler beneath.

Flowers. Inflorescence a terminal raceme of about 10–15 flowers in opposite pairs, many such racemes forming a large panicle; calyx 2-lipped, 6 mm across, purplish-green, glandular; corolla with broad, shallow, campanulate tube, 1.3 cm across, opening to 5 lobes of unequal size, violet-blue, deeper towards the base, flowering abundantly from early September to November; stamens 4, the curved filaments violet, the purple-black anthers with 2 bifid appendages; pistil bifid, curved, exserted, pale lavender.

Other distinguishing features. Upper twigs 4-sided, grooved, glandular and finely pubescent.

Climatic range. H, M, Mts, and on cool, moist sheltered sites on the elevated parts of S.

Prostanthèra cuneàta (Latin 'wedge-shaped' referring to the leaf-shape): Alpine Mint-bush: NSW Snowy Mts and at similar elevations in Vic. and Tas, usually above 1000 m.

Habit. A shrub of about 1 m tall and 1.5 m broad, sometimes almost prostrate in its alpine habitat, but becoming taller at lower elevations.

Leaves. Broadly obovate-orbicular, 6–8 mm long and 5–6 mm wide, densely-crowded to almost conceal the twigs; thick; apex obtuse to retuse; base tapered; margin entire; glandular and highly aromatic when disturbed; dark green above, paler beneath.

Flowers. Solitary or a few together in the upper axils; corolla campanulate-bilabiate, 2 cm across, the upper lobe hooded, the lower trilobed, the margins frilled and waved; white to pale mauve, with deep violet spots in the throat and an orange blotch on the lower lobe; flowering in the short alpine summer during January and February.

Fruit. Not seen.

Other distinguishing features. Upper twigs whitish, glandular.

'Alpine Gold' is a registered cultivar from the Victorian highlands with yellow-variegated young leaves over the crown of the plant.

Climatic range. H, M, Mts.

Prostanthèra incàna (Latin 'hoary and grey'): Hairy-leafed Mint-bush: sheltered gullies of NSW Central Tablelands and lower North Coast.

Habit. An evergreen shrub, 1.5–2.0 m tall, irregular globose form to about 2 m wide.

Leaves. Broadly ovate to 1.8 cm long and 1 cm wide; petioles 2–4 mm long, densely pubescent; apex obtuse; margin crenate-ciliate, recurved; venation distinctly depressed above; finely silky-pubescent and dark green above, densely white-pubescent and paler beneath; aromatic when bruised.

Flowers. In a 10- to 12-flowered raceme at the ends of the youngest shoots, the flowers densely clustered together, the upper pairs subtended by broad-ovate, lobed, purplish bracts about 3 mm long; calyx 5 mm long, bi-lobed, purplish, pubescent; corolla campanulate-labiate 1.3 cm across, the upper lip deeply emarginate, the lower lip 3-lobed, lavender-violet, flowering from early September to late October; stamens 4, pale violet, anthers blackish-violet.

Other distinguishing features. Upper twigs squarish, heavily white-pubescent, green but reddish beneath.

Climatic range. H, M, Mts, and on cool, moist sites on the upper levels of P and S.

Prostanthèra incìsa (Latin 'with irregularly cut leaf margins'): Cut-leafed Mint-bush; moist, sheltered gullies of NSW Central Coast, and lower levels of Blue Mountains.

Habit. An evergreen shrub of variable character but usually seen as a slender, twiggy shrub, 1.5–2.0 m tall, with abundant foliage.

Leaves. Narrowly ovate, 1.5–2.0 cm long; apex acute to obtuse; base narrowly cuneate and slightly winged; margin rarely entire, mostly with several serrate notches on each side, usually above the middle; glandular and strongly aromatic; dark green and dull above, the veins obscure, paler beneath, the midrib distinct; pubescent.

Flowers. In the axils of the upper shoots, forming a slender raceme of 10 or more flowers on 4 mm purplish pedicels; calyx cup shape, 3 mm deep and 5 mm across the unequally bi-lobed mouth, deep purple, glandular; corolla funnelform-labiate to 1 cm long, the upper lip reflexed, the lower lip 3-lobed, lilac to deep violet, but variable in colour, flowering during September and October; stamens 4, the filaments pale mauve, the anthers blackish-violet.

Other distinguishing features. Young twigs square, puberulent, mid-green, with purplish shadings.
Climatic range. B, M, P, S and in warm microclimates in lower levels of Mts.

Prostanthèra lasiánthos (Latin 'with hairy flowers'): Victorian Christmas Bush: moist coastal and elevated gullies in Tas, Vic. and the Southern and Central Tablelands of NSW.
Habit. A tall shrub or open-branched, small tree, 3–5 m tall, with a short trunk and spreading branches, often used as a screen plant for more tender species.
Leaves. Lanceolate, 5–12 cm long and 1.0–2.5 cm wide; apex acute to slightly acuminate; margin coarsely to shallowly serrate, the edge slightly recurved; midrib and main veins prominent beneath; glabrous; glandular-dotted and aromatic; bright to dark green above, paler and often slightly glaucescent-green beneath.
Flowers. Inflorescence a terminal panicle made up of several racemes, the rachis square; corolla campanulate-funnelform to 1.8 cm long, the lower lobes broad and spreading, mostly white but stained or suffused with violet-blue, or rarely pinkish-mauve, with purplish and orange spots in the hairy throat, all parts pubescent; mildly fragrant, flowering from late September to mid-summer.
Other distinguishing features. Upper shoots squarish, shallowly grooved.
'Kallista Pink' is a registered cultivar developed in the Victorian Dandenongs, near Kallista. It is distinct in its clear pink flowers.
Climatic range. H, M, Mts, and on cool, moist, sheltered sites in P and S.

Prostanthèra nívea (Latin 'snow-white'): Snowy Mint-bush: found mostly on coarse gravels and other free-draining soils on the Western Slopes of the Great Dividing Range in NSW, also on similar sites in Vic. and Qld.
Habit. A shrub to about 2.5 m tall, with an irregularly rounded form, densely clothed with foliage and flowers.
Leaves. Slender-linear, 2.5–3.0 cm long and 1–2 mm wide, almost sessile, the petiole broadened to partly clasp the stem; apex acute; margin entire; glabrous; midrib prominent below; dark green and dull; aromatic when bruised.
Flowers. Solitary in the upper axils, forming a racemose spray to 10 cm long, 12 or more together, becoming paniculate; calyx campanulate-funnelform, labiate, the upper lip the

larger and erect, slightly flared outwards, the lower lip smaller and incurved, corolla campanulate-labiate to 1.5 cm long, the upper lip emarginate, the larger lower lip with 3 lobes; pure white but with 6 to 8 yellowish-brown spots in the throat; some forms pale blue; flowering in September and October; stamens 4, the filaments white, anthers violet; style white, with a bifid stigma.
Other distinguishing features. Upper twigs slightly square, pale green and smooth.
var. *indùta* (Latin 'with a hairy covering') from elevated, rocky sites on the Western Slopes of the Blue Mountains: has narrower, greyish leaves and larger, pale-lilac flowers.
Climatic range. H, M, Mts, and on cool sites in P and S.

Prostanthèra ovalifòlia (Latin 'with oval leaves'): Purple Mint-bush: on sheltered sites in gullies, or on the elevated margins of streams along the NSW coastal plateaus, Tablelands and Western Slopes, and in similar habitats on the southern Qld coastal plain and mountains, mainly on better class soils.
Habit. A shrub to 3 m or so, with a short trunk, branching low to form a broadly conical bush when young, but later becoming sparse and of irregular form.
Leaves. Narrowly oval to ovate-lanceolate, 1.5–3.5 cm long and 7–11 mm wide but usually smaller in plants in their native habitat; apex acute to obtuse; base cuneate but tapered into the pubescent 3–5 mm petiole; margin entire or shallowly serrate; both surfaces densely glandular, and aromatic when bruised; dull, dark green above, pale green beneath.
Flowers. Inflorescence a 12- to 16-flowered terminal raceme, sometimes paniculate, the rachis squarish and densely white-tomentose; pedicels slender, 3–5 mm long, glandular, purplish; calyx shallowly crateriform, with 2 broad lobes, glandular, purplish; corolla labiate, the upper, shorter lip erect and split into 2 broad, recurved lobes, the lower lip spreading, divided into 3 long, broad lobes, the whole 1.5–1.8 cm across; colour variable from violet-blue to mauve-purple and occasionally rosy-mauve, flowering abundantly from early September to late October; stamens 4, the curved filaments mauve, the anthers whitish-purple; pistil exserted, curved, bifid, rosy-purple.
Other distinguishing features. Upper twigs squarish, purple, but with a dense, short whitish pubescence.

var. *latifòlia* (Latin 'with broad leaves'): is the form occurring on the Hawkesbury sandstone plateaux, especially in the valleys of Berowra and Cowan Creeks. It is distinct in its broader leaf-blade with an irregularly-serrated margin.

'**Variegàta**' is a cultivar whose leaves have a yellow margin of varying width, the central panel dull-green.

Climatic range. H, M, Mts, S, and on cool, moist sites in A, B, and P.

Prostanthèra rotundifòlia (Latin 'with round leaves'): Round-leafed Mint-bush: NSW Tablelands, Western Slopes and in deep coastal valleys, also in eastern Tas, eastern Vic. and Southern Qld, usually on well-drained, better class soils.

Habit. A shrub to 2.5 m tall, of open, irregular habit in the wild, but improved by cultivation and annual pruning to become dense and leafy.

Leaves. Broadly obovate to nearly orbicular to 1 cm across; apex obtuse; margin mostly entire or with a few irregular notches; midrib slightly raised beneath; finely glandular-dotted, and strongly aromatic; dark green and only moderately shiny above; paler beneath.

Flowers. Inflorescence a small terminal raceme of up to 12–15 flowers in opposite pairs, many racemes forming a panicle on the upper 30–40 cm of the previous season's shoots; pedicels 1–2 mm long, purplish, with a pair of small leafy bracts at the base of the funnelform, 4 mm long calyx; broadly rounded calyx lobes glandular, purplish; corolla broadly funnelform, the 2 upper lobes smaller and recurved, the lower 3 lobes larger and spreading, campanula violet, but varying to mauve, pale lilac, or nearly white, flowering heavily from early September to late November.

Other distinguishing features. Upper twigs terete, purplish, but greyed by fine white tomentum.

'**Ròsea**' has mauve-pink flowers but is otherwise similar.

Climatic range. H, M, Mts, and in cool, moist microclimates in A, P, and S.

Prostanthèra sièberi (commemorating F. W. Sieber, Czechoslovakian botanical explorer and author of several species of this genus): mainly from the sheltered coastal and mountain gullies in the Central NSW region.

Habit. A shrub of indefinite shape in its native habitat, but becoming more regular in cultivation, globose to 2.5–3.0 m tall, dense and twiggy.

Leaves. Variable in shape, narrow-elliptic, ovate-lanceolate to rhombic 2–3 cm long and 8–15 mm wide; base tapered into a slightly-winged, channelled petiole 5–8 mm long; apex acute to obtuse; base slenderly cuneate; margin rarely entire, usually with 1 to 3 shallow crenate-serrate notches on each side, mostly above the middle; midrib alone prominent beneath; glabrous except for some fine down on the petiole; glandular-dotted on both surfaces, and strongly aromatic; dark green and dull above, paler beneath.

Flowers. Inflorescence a short terminal panicle of 20–30 flowers on slender, 3 mm, purplish pedicels; calyx campanulate to 5 mm long, bi-lobed, purplish-green, glandular; corolla campanulate-labiate to 1.2 cm across, the lips distinctly lobed, amethyst-violet, slightly deeper in the throat, flowering thinly but daintily from late September to November.

Other distinguishing features. Upper twigs squarish, with shallow, decurrent, internodal ridges, the green surface roughened by the numerous glands.

Climatic range. H, M, Mts, and on cool, part-shaded, sheltered sites in A, P, and S.

Prostanthèra violàcea (Latin 'with violet flowers'): Violet Mint-bush: NSW, mainly on the eastern slopes of the Blue Mts and in the Nepean River valley.

Habit. A shapely shrub to 1.5 m tall, mostly of erect, leafy growth, responding well to light annual pruning.

Leaves. Broadly ovate to obovate, 4–6 mm long; pubescent; margin shallowly crenate and slightly recurved; mid-green; glandular and aromatic when disturbed.

Flowers. Borne in a panicle of terminal racemes over the crown of the plant; calyx 2-lipped, pubescent; corolla about 6 mm long, mostly violet but variable in colour; flowering period from September to December.

var. *albiflòra* (Latin 'with white flowers'): is a localised form in the lower Blue Mts, with white flowers.

Climatic range. H, M, Mts, and on cool, sheltered sites in A, P, S.

PRÒTEA

Commemorating Proteus, Greek God of the Sea, to whom Neptune assigned the power to alter form, a reference to the diversity of the many species.

Protea (various); South African Sugar Bush; Cape Honey Flower; and other common names of local regional significance.

Proteaceae, the Protea family.

Generic description. A large genus of over 100 species of evergreen shrubs and small trees from South Africa, with simple leaves and bisexual flowers in a cone-like head surrounded by an involucre of leaf-like coloured bracts, flowering mostly between autumn and late spring. Fruit is a small nut tipped with long hairs as an aid to seed dispersal.

Although somewhat demanding in their preferences as to climate, soil type and cultivational management, the proteas are becoming widely grown in southern Australia both as garden ornaments and for cut-flower production for which their long-lasting qualities are outstanding.

Propagation. a) Seeds should be sown in individual containers as soon as fully ripe, ideally in a friable mixture pasteurised against weeds, insect pests and disease organisms, and placed in a well-ventilated frame or glasshouse. The seedlings are best raised in a slightly dry atmosphere with a moderately low water ration.

b) Semi-hardwood leafy cuttings taken from ripened terminal shoots in early summer are also used. A hormone type dust or dip is usually beneficial. The preferred media are clean, sharp sand, perlite or vermiculite mixed with an equal volume of peat-moss. The cuttings, in individual containers, are struck under glass, preferably with intermittent mist adjusted to the lowest setting of the water cycle.

c) Budding and grafting methods are sometimes practised with kinds that perform better on the rootstocks of another closely-related species.

Cultivation. Proteas have long been regarded, perhaps unfairly, as difficult to grow in Australia, but where satisfactory growth conditions are provided, good results are often seen. The most favourable climates prevail in near-coastal Victoria and South Australia, south-west WA, northern Tasmania and on the slopes of the tablelands in NSW, all regions with predominantly winter or uniform seasonal rains, and where winter temperatures remain above –3°C to –5°C, with low humidity levels in summer. Proteas perform best in the open, preferably in full sunlight with free air circulation.

Heavy, slow-draining clay soils must be avoided in favour of coarse, free-draining sands, open sandy-loams or gravelly loams with low phosphorus levels, and of moderately acid reaction, although a few species are tolerant of neutral or mildly alkaline soils.

Once plants are installed, the surface of the soil should be left undisturbed, but preferably heavily mulched with coarse vegetative matter. Some growers apply a small ration of blood and bone fertiliser in late winter just in advance of the spring growth. A reliable water supply is essential. During droughts, additional water should be applied at weekly intervals to the root area, not over the foliage which is best kept dry. Proteas will tolerate brief periods of heavy rainfall provided the water soon drains away, but like most other plants, are more likely to suffer from an excess, rather than a deficiency of water.

Pruning. Regular pruning of the plants should commence after the first flowering and continued throughout the plants' life. The flowered stems should be reduced to within 5–6 cm of their bases so as to induce replacement shoots for the next flowering.

Species and cultivars

Pròtea aristàta (Latin 'awned or terminated with a stiff bristle'): Pine Sugar Bush; Ladysmith Protea: Christmas Protea: mountain slopes of Cape Province.

Habit. A shrub of roughly globular form to about 1.5 m tall, made denser in growth and more leafy by regular annual pruning.

Leaves. Linear, flat, with a recurved tip, all pointing forward to nearly cover the reddish-brown twigs, grey-green.

Flowers. Heads compactly cone-shaped, rosy-crimson to pink with pink hairs, the involucral bracts of similar colour towards the apex, the lower bracts smaller and dark sooty-crimson, all softly pubescent; flowering period early to mid-summer.

Pròtea compácta (Latin 'closely packed together', referring to the overlapped leaves): Bot River Protea; South Coast of Cape Province.

Habit. An erect, somewhat sparse bush to 2.5 m

or so, but developing denser growth with regular annual pruning.

Leaves. Variable, from narrowly elliptic to orbicular, to 8–10 cm long, green to glaucous, with a red-orange ciliate edge.

Flowers. Heads about 10–12 cm long, rose-pink, in a slender cone partly enclosed by the rosy-carmine bracts with their silky-white ciliate margins; flowering period in autumn and winter.

Pròtea cynaroïdes (Latin 'resembling *Cynara*, the European artichoke'): King Protea, the national flower of South Africa: south-coastal sandy heathlands and lower mountain slopes of Cape Province.

Habit. One of the best-known and most impressive species with squat shrubby form to about 2 m, developing from an underground ligno-tuber like that of the mallee eucalypts, by which means it recovers from fires and other damage to the aerial parts. The plant needs regular pruning to produce denser foliage and more abundant flowers.

Leaves. Scattered, ovate to obovate, 6–8 cm long and 4–6 cm wide, on a stout, red, channelled petiole 5–8 cm long; apex rounded or shortly tipped; base obtuse; margin entire, slightly thickened and often red or yellow; glabrous; bright green at first, grey-green in age.

Flowers. Heads often 20–25 cm across, densely packed in a flattish cone with a shallow central peak, the anthers silky-white on yellow filaments; bracts linear-lanceolate, spreading widely to form a shallow cup, variable but mostly rose-pink, tipped with silky-white hairs; flowering period variable between mid-winter and early summer.

Pròtea grándiceps (Latin 'large-headed'): Peach Protea: the lower levels of the coastal ranges of Cape Province.

Habit. A dense shrub to 1–2 m tall, often a little broader to irregular hemispherical form.

Leaves. Scattered, sessile, elliptic to obovate, 10 cm long and 6–7 cm wide; apex rounded; base sub-cordate; margin entire, with a red edge; midrib and main laterals yellowish; upper leaves forming a rosette cup beneath the flowers: grey-green.

Flowers. Heads broadly obovoid to 10 cm tall, the flowers almost hidden by the white-woolly crown; bracts spathulate, peach-pink to light scarlet, margined with silky hairs varying from white to red or brown; flowering period variable between autumn and spring.

Pròtea magnífica (Latin 'great', referring to the large flowers) (syn. *P. barbígera*) Bearded or Queen Protea or Giant Woolly-beard: lower slopes of the mountains of Cape Province.

Habit. A spreading, open shrub to about 1.5 m tall and as broad, but variable in both shape and size.

Leaves. Oblanceolate to obovate, flat or undulate, grey-green with a narrow red edge and yellowish midrib.

Flowers. Heads 15–20 cm across in a globose cone, each flower tipped with silky-white hairs, the centre flowers with black-tipped hairs, the perianth segments varying in colour from yellow to pink to rose-red; involucral bracts lanceolate, as long as the flower head, varying in colour as in the segments, each tipped with a tuft of white cottony hairs; flowering period mid-winter to late spring.

Pròtea neriifòlia (Latin 'with Nerium-like leaves'): Oleander-leafed Protea: mountain slopes of the South Coast of Cape Province.

Habit. Perhaps the most common protea grown in Australia, forming an erect shrub to 2 m or more, improved in shape and density by regular annual pruning.

Leaves. Linear-oblong, 12–15 cm long and 2–3 cm wide; apex obtuse or notched; base tapered; margin entire, with a yellowish-edge; midrib distinct, pale yellow; glabrous; mid-green.

Flowers. Heads obovoid, 12–15 cm long and 6–8 cm broad; involucral bracts slightly longer and partly concealing the flower heads, varying in colour from cream and pink to rosy-crimson, the apices with tufts of blackish or sooty-brown hairs; flowering period between early autumn and spring.

This species grows best on neutral to slightly-acid soils.

Pròtea obtusifòlia (Latin 'with blunt leaves'): Blunt-leafed Protea: South Coast of Cape Province.

Habit. A leafy bush of irregular hemispherical form to 2 m or so when properly managed, but taller and of sparse growth if left unpruned.

Leaves. Oblanceolate, 10–12 cm long and 2–4 cm wide; apex obtuse, mucronate at the tip; base cuneate; margin entire, reddish at the edge;

midrib thick, prominent, yellowish, with a red base; glabrous; coriaceous; dark green.
Flowers. Heads slenderly conical in the buds, but becoming obovoid to 10 cm long, the white-woolly tipped flowers forming a blunt apex; bracts lanceolate, about 12 cm long, forming a coronet around the flower head; bracts yellow-green below, tipped with pink to crimson; flowering period from late autumn to early spring.
This species grows best on neutral to slightly alkaline, coarse soils.

Pròtea rèpens (Latin 'of low, creeping growth') (syn. *P. mellífera*) Honey Protea or Sugar-Bush Protea, referring to the abundance of nectar secreted by the flowers: mountain slopes of South Coast, Cape Province. One of the earliest and most successful proteas to be introduced into Australian gardens.
Habit. An erect bush of 2.5 m or so, with a short trunk and open framework of slender branches, more compact in growth, with improved foliage and flowers when pruned regularly.
Leaves. Scattered on reddish-brown branchlets; linear to slenderly oblanceolate, 8–12 cm long and 1–2 cm wide; apex acute, with a short, recurved point; margin entire, the edge yellowish; midrib distinct, pale yellow; glabrous; grey-green.
Flowers. Heads slenderly ovoid, about 10 cm long, the individual flowers greenish-white to pale pink, with a white-woolly tip; bracts lanceolate, white or yellowish, with rosy-crimson or yellow tips; flowering period variable between early autumn and winter, and spring at higher elevations.
A species with a preference for neutral or slightly acid sandy loams.

Pròtea scolymocéphala (Latin 'with flower heads like the Spanish Golden Thistle, *Scólymus hispánicus*'): Green Protea or Green Button Protea: slopes of the western mountain ranges, Cape Province.
Habit. A small shrub of about 1 m or so, with an irregular, spikey habit of growth, improved by regular pruning.
Leaves. Scattered on the reddish branchlets, linear-falcate, 5–7 cm long and 1 cm wide; apex acute, with a short, hard point; base tapered to the reddish petiole; margin entire, often reddish yellow; texture thick and somewhat stiff; glabrous; mid-green.

Flowers. Heads broadly ovoid, 2 cm across, shorter than the uppermost leaves, the unopened bracts of the involucre forming an attractive mosaic of red and white; heads greenish when expanded to about 3.5 cm across, tipped with whitish-woolly anthers, set in a cupped ring of bracts about 4 cm across, yellow-green inside, reddish outside, with a silvery edge; flowering period from early winter to spring.

Pròtea speciòsa (Latin 'showy'): Brown-beard Protea: mountain ranges of the Cape Province.
Habit. A leafy shrub of about 1 m with a roughly-rounded crown.
Leaves. Scattered, spathulate to obovate, 10–12 cm long and 3–5 cm wide; apex rounded with a shallow notch; margin undulate, the edges red; coriaceous; midrib alone distinct, yellowish; glabrous, mid- to dark-green.
Flowers. Heads ovoid, 12–15 cm long and 6–8 cm broad, the apex all but concealed by the enveloping bracts, but with a small tuft of creamy-white hairs still visible; bracts elliptical, varying from white to cream to deep rose-pink, the edges ciliate with fine hairs, the apices with a large tuft of tan-brown or white hairs; flowering period mainly in spring.
Climatic range. All A, H, M, P, S, and on lower levels of Mts.

PRÙNUS

The ancient Latin name of the European Plum. The Stone Fruits (the flowering forms only are treated here).
Rosaceae, the Rose family.

Generic description. A large and widely varied genus of about 400 species, including many important fruiting and ornamental plants, mostly deciduous trees or shrubs with simple, alternate leaves, some of the deciduous kinds colouring their leaves attractively in autumn; flowers are solitary or in various clustered inflorescences, mainly racemes or corymbs, the floral parts typically in fives, the colours white, pink, or red; the single-stoned, drupaceous fruits vary widely in size and colour and include the valuable food crops, almond, apricot, cherry, plum, peach, nectarine, etc. The genus rates among the most common and popularly grown groups in Australian gardens because of its handsome foliage, especially in autumn, often spectacular floral display, and sometimes attractive fruits.

See 'Ornamental Flowering Trees in Australia' for taller, tree-like species.

Propagation. a) Seeds may be used to propagate the single-flowered species, *P. glandulosa*. They are collected as soon as ripe, cleaned of the fleshy pulp, and stored for about 90 days in just-moist sphagnum moss or coarse sand at 4°–5°C, then sown in a warm, sheltered place.

b) Root cuttings are usually preferred for the cultivars. The parent plant is lifted in winter, young, undamaged roots about 4–5 mm thick are removed, cut into lengths of 2–3 cm and planted in individual containers placed in a warm, sheltered place.

Cultivation. Tractable in cultivation, most species of *Prunus* thrive in freely-drained soils of moderate fertility but give their best performance where soils are rich, deep, and not allowed to dry out excessively, especially during the flowering and growth seasons. They enjoy a sun-exposed position but need protection from strong winds, otherwise, much of the flower crop is lost.

Propagation. In *P. glandulosa* the 1-year old flowered shoots are usually pruned severely to within 10 cm or so of ground level to encourage the development of suckers and new watershoots that flower abundantly in the following spring over their full length of 1 m or more; they may be cut for interior decoration during the flowering season or immediately after the flowers have fallen.

Species and cultivars

Prunus glandulòsa (Latin 'glandular'): Chinese Bush Cherry: central and northern China, and Japan.

Habit. A deciduous shrub to 1.5 m tall, of erect slender growth with suckers from the roots, forming a clump 1–2 m broad, possibly more when pruned heavily as is customary in Australia.

Leaves. Narrowly elliptic to lanceolate, 8–10 cm long and 2.5–4.0 cm wide; petiole about 5 mm, reddish and grooved above; stipules linear, laciniate, with fine, glandular-bristly teeth; apex acuminate; margin serrate to biserrate; glabrous or puberulent on the midrib and main veins beneath: bright green above, paler beneath, changing to dull crimson-red in autumn.

Flowers. Either solitary or mostly in pairs at the nodes of the 1- and 2-year-old shoots, before the leaves; calyx cup-shaped, 3 mm deep and 1 cm across the 5 spreading, reflexed, green lobes; corolla rotate to 2 cm across, with 5 obovate petals varying in colour from pale-pink to white among seedlings; stamens 25–30, 6–8 mm long, with pale pink filaments and yellow anthers; flowering from late August to late September.

Fruit. A fleshy, red, globular drupe with flat base and mucronate apex, 1.2 cm long, succulent when ripe in early summer, with a single ovoid stone.

'**Alba Plèna**' (Latin 'double white') has the growth habit of the parent species but the flowers are double, with numerous petals forming an almost globular flower to 2.5–3.0 cm across, the stamens modified into additional petals, the flowers pure white, flowering about one week later then the parent species and 'Rosea Plena'.

'**Rosea Plena**' (syn. 'Sinensis') is like 'Alba Plena' but has rose-pink flowers, paler towards the centre, with a few stamens, the filaments pale pink and the anthers yellow, flowering in September.

Climatic range. All A, H, M, Mts, P, S.

PSORÀLEA

Derived from the Greek *psoralios* 'scurfy', referring to the scales subtending the calyx.

Scurfy Pea Bush.

Fabaceae, the Pea family.

Generic description. A large genus of shrubs and herbs from the warmer regions of several continents, with compound leaves, pea-shaped flowers in spring, commonly white, blue, or purple, and leguminous fruits. The species described below, imported from South Africa, is a popular plant in Australia, but is inclined to escape from cultivation through its prolific seeding habit.

Propagation. a) Seeds sown as soon as ripe in summer and autumn germinate readily.

b) Soft-tip cuttings taken in autumn and planted in a sand/peat mixture in a warm, humid atmosphere strike satisfactorily.

Cultivation. *P. affinis* is best grown in an open, sunny position under somewhat austere conditions of food- and water-supply to restrict its aggressive growth; sandy or gravelly soils are suitable. The ideal climate is mild, with only light frosts.

PLATE 27

▲ Sambucus canadensis 'Aurea'
▼ Viburnum rhytidophyllum

▼ Viburnum tinus

▼ Vitex agnus-castus

▲ Templetonia retusa *Photo by Bro. P. Stanley*

▲ Tibouchina heteromalla

▲ Tetratheca ericifolia *Photo by Bro. P. Stanley*

▲ Verticordia grandis *Photo by Bro. P. Stanley*

PLATE 28

▲ Weigela florida 'Aureo-variegata'

▲ Tibouchina mutabilis
◄ Weigela 'Styriaca'
▼ Viburnum opulus 'Sterile'

▼ Viburnum macrocephalum 'Sterile'

▼ Viburnum plicatum var. tomentosum

▼ Tibouchina macrantha

Pruning. Pruning consists of tip-pruning frequently in the first 2 or 3 years to establish a dense, compact form, then annually, by shortening the newly-flowered shoots by about half, cutting into new-season's wood only, immediately after flowering time, to restrict the development of seeds.

Species and cultivars

Psoralea affínis (Latin 'related', application obscure): Scurfy Pea Bush: South Africa, from around Table Mountain, along the coastal strip to Natal and inland to Transvaal.
Habit. A dense, evergreen shrub to 3 m or so when grown in the open, but occasionally taller to 4 m, then with a single, lanky, angular stem.
Leaves. Compound, alternate, imparipinnate, with 5 to 9 linear leaflets arranged in opposite pairs on a slender rachis; leaflets 2.5 cm long, 1 mm wide; apex acute; margin entire; bright green, heavily dotted with blackish, translucent glands; slightly aromatic when bruised.
Flowers. Inflorescence a cluster of flowers at the terminals of the upper shoots; flowers to 1.5 cm across, the hirsute, campanulate calyx 7–8 mm long, with 5 acute teeth; standard orbicular, folded backwards over the calyx, violet-blue with 2 wing-like, white patches near the base; wings erect, broad-obovate, white with a violet-blue recurved rim; keel erect, white, with a swollen violet patch near the apex; flowering abundantly from early September to November.
Fruit. A small green legume, ovoid, pubescent, with a single seed.
Climatic range. A, B, M, P, S, T, and on warm, sheltered sites in H and Mts.

PULTENAÈA

Commemorating Richard Pulteney, 1730–1801, British botanical and historical author.
Bush-pea.
Fabaceae, the Pea family.

Generic description. A large Australian native genus of evergreen shrubs with simple, alternate, stipulate leaves, and mostly yellow, pea-shaped flowers, sometimes solitary in the upper axils but more commonly in dense clusters at the end of the 1-year-old shoots, each flower subtended by a pair of green or brownish bracteoles beneath or attached to the calyx, flowering abundantly in spring; seeds are ovoid or kidney-shaped, in a small, sometimes inflated, legume.

Propagation. Seeds are collected as soon as ripe and held until spring in a cool, dry place, then immersed in warm water and allowed to soak for 24 hours; sowings are made at once in a friable material in a warm, humid atmosphere.
Cultivation. The bush-peas are easily grown on a well-drained sandy soil, with coarse organic material added for improved aeration. They must not be neglected for water in spring and summer. The species listed are hardy to at least −3°C but enjoy the protection afforded by tall, overhead trees.
Pruning. Young plants are best occasionally tip-pruned in the early years to thicken their growth, then subsequently pruned lightly into the young wood, after the flowering season each year.

Species and cultivars

Pultenaèa altíssima (Latin 'tallest') (syn. *P. obovata*) Tall Bush-pea or Balloon Bush-pea: NE Vic. and NSW, mainly on well-drained sites on the Blue Mts.
Habit. An evergreen shrub to 2–3 m tall and as broad, with erect, spreading stems from the base and a dense rounded canopy of foliage.
Leaves. Obovate to oblanceolate, about 5–6 mm long and 2 mm broad; petiole slender, 1 mm: apex obtuse; base narrowly cuneate; margin entire, slightly recurved; mid-green above, paler beneath.
Flowers. In small umbellate clusters over the crown of the plant; calyx campulate, the 5 acute lobes 3 mm long; corolla pea-shaped, 7 mm long, deep yellow with reddish veins, the orbicular standard petal the largest; stamens 5 mm long, pale yellow; flowering period in spring, the peak in September-October.
Fruit. Not seen.
Climatic range. H, M, Mts, P, S, and on cool, elevated sites in A.

Pultenaèa daphnoídes (Latin 'like a *Daphne*'): Large-leafed Bush-pea: eastern Australia, on a variety of sites from the gravelly or rocky ridges of the Hawkesbury sandstones to better class loams near permanent streams, in the shelter of taller trees.
Habit. An evergreen shrub to 2 m or so, of somewhat indefinite upright form in its native habitat but more densely globose when brought into cultivation with regular pruning.
Leaves. Spathulate to oblanceolate, 1.5–3.5 cm

long and 8–15 mm wide; apex broadly obtuse; margin entire; slightly concave above; midrib pubescent and prominent; glabrous and coriaceous; dark green above, pale grey-green beneath.

Flowers. In a dense terminal cluster about 3.5 cm across, at the end of the youngest shoots; flowers sessile, subtended by imbricate bracts and the upper leaves; calyx 6–7 mm long, pubescent and bracteolate; standard petal 1.0–1.5 cm long, the margin incurved, yellow, with a few reddish streaks at the base; wing petals oblong to 9–12 mm long, yellow; keel shorter, incurved, dull purplish-red, enclosing the 10 free stamens, flowering abundantly through September and October.

Fruit. An ovoid legume to 7–8 mm long, ripening in autumn.

Other distinguishing features. Upper twigs pubescent, ridged longitudinally.

Climatic range. A, H, M, Mts, P, S.

Pultenaèa fléxilis (Latin 'flexible', referring to the twigs): Yellow Bush-pea: NSW and southern Qld, mainly on rocky land between the coast and the lower tablelands, abundant on the Hawkesbury plateaus and lower Blue Mountains.

Habit. An evergreen shrub to 3 m or more, with a short trunk and several low branches supporting a fine-textured, twiggy crown but sometimes taller and of tree-like form by pruning or in especially favourable growth conditions.

Leaves. Linear to narrowly oblanceolate, 1.0–2.5 cm long and 1.5–3.0 mm wide, the petiole 1 mm long; apex acute-mucronate; base tapered, with very fine, 2 mm long stipules; margin entire; midrib distinct beneath; dark blue-green above, bright green and slightly shiny beneath; glabrous and finely glandular-dotted.

Flowers. In 2 cm long, racemose clusters of a few to about 8, forming a large panicle; bracteoles 1 mm long, acute, attached to the tube; calyx 3–5 mm with 5 ciliate lobes; standard petal orbicular to 8–9 mm across, emarginate and slightly folded, golden-yellow, with a reddish fan at the base; wing petals oblanceolate, yellow; keel yellowish-green, enclosing the 10 stamens; slightly fragrant, flowering from early September to late October.

Fruit. A 6–7 mm long legume, ovate-elliptic, ripening in summer.

Other distinguishing features. Upper twigs slender, reddish-green with prominent leaf-bases.

Climatic range. A, B, H, M, P, S, and in warm microclimates in Mts.

Pultenaèa stipuláris (Latin 'bearing stipules'): NSW, mainly on sandy or gravelly heathlands, or rocky plateaus between the coast and mountains.

Habit. A shrub to 2 m tall, of upright habit, the branches somewhat sparse.

Leaves. Linear, 2–3 cm long and 2–3 mm wide, densely crowded, pointing forward and nearly covering the stems, subtended by brown, papery stipules 1 cm long; apex acute, with a slender point; margin entire; sparsely hairy; mid green.

Flowers. About 20 together at the terminals; calyx tubulate to 1 cm, green with reddish shadings; bracteoles subulate to 1 cm, standard orbicular to 1.3 cm, yellow, with reddish fan at the base; wings oblong, yellow; keel oblanceolate to 1.3 cm, greenish-yellow; stamens 10; flowering from September to October.

Climatic range. A, B, H, M, P, S, and in warm microclimates in the lower Mts.

Pultenaèa villòsa (Latin 'shaggy'): Bronze Bush-pea: eastern Australia, mostly on loamy soils on the coastal plains; abundant along the Pacific Highway between the Hunter and Hastings Rivers.

Habit. A shrub to 1.5 m tall and as broad, with ascending branches drooping at the ends to form an arching, vase-shaped bush.

Leaves. Alternate or scattered, linear to oblanceolate, 4–6 mm long, 1–2 mm wide, stipular at the base; apex acute; base cuneate; blades concave, the margin incurved; dark green, tubercular and villous beneath, nearly glabrous and mid-green above.

Flowers. Solitary in the upper axils, sometimes several together; bracteoles 2, slenderly linear, 3–4 mm long; calyx campanulate, 6–7 mm long, the sepals villous; corolla pea-shaped, 8–10 mm across, the erect standard nearly orbicular, with smaller wings and incurved keel petals, all deep yellow with a small red fan at the base; stamens 10, free, as long as the standard; flowering period from early September to late October.

Fruit. A silky, ovate legume 5–7 mm long, containing 2 seeds, ripening in summer.

Climatic range. B, P, S, and on warm sites in A, M, and lower Mts.

PÙNICA

Derived from *Malum punicum*, the name used by the ancient Carthaginians (near the present Tunis in North Africa) for the fruit.

Pomegranate; or the ancient name, Apple of Carthage.

Punicaceae, the Pomegranate family.

Generic description. Of the two species in the genus, the one described below is a popular decorative plant in Australia, with its simple lanceolate leaves, scarlet flowers, and reddish-yellow, apple-shaped fruits. Both the single and double-flowered forms are attractive.

Propagation. a) Seeds sown in spring reproduce the parent species fairly reliably.

b) Soft-tip and semi-hardwood cuttings taken between spring and autumn strike readily in a sand/peat mixture in a warm, humid atmosphere.

c) Hardwood cuttings, with heels of older wood, are also taken in winter.

Cultivation. Among the hardiest ornamentals used in Australia, the Pomegranate will tolerate low temperatures to −8°C, as well as sustained high temperatures with low humidity, but responds favourably to a well-aerated, coarse-textured soil of moderate fertility, preferably enriched with organic matter and with additional water in dry times. Well-grown specimens may be seen at Broken Hill, Alice Springs and other inland towns.

Pruning. Light pruning of the current year's growth is desirable in late winter just before resumption of growth to maintain a dense, leafy habit.

Species and cultivars

Pùnica granàtum (Latin *granum* 'a grain', descriptive of the tightly packed seeds in the fleshy pericarp): Common Pomegranate: Eastern Mediterranean, North Africa, Afghanistan and Iran.

Habit. A deciduous small tree in its native habitat, reaching about 7–8 m tall with a single trunk and a broad-domed crown, and a common sight in the Middle Eastern villages, but in Australia usually seen as a large, irregular but generally erect shrub to 4 m or so with several trunks. Short, hard thorns occur on the ends of the lateral shoots.

Leaves. Opposite on young vigorous shoots but appearing to be whorled on undeveloped lateral spurs; broadly lanceolate or elliptic-obovate, 4–8 cm long and 1.5–3.0 cm wide, with a 3 mm reddish petiole; apex acute to retuse, often reflexed, margin entire but sometimes undulate, midrib and main veins translucent; spring leaves are often reddish but become bright green, glabrous and shiny, changing to yellow in late April.

Flowers. Solitary or in few-flowered clusters at the ends of the young branchlets; calyx campanulate to 2 cm long, the lobes 5 to 8, bright scarlet and succulent; corolla 3 to 5 cm across, of 5 to 8 obovate petals, spreading, crepe-like, scarlet; stamens many, filaments scarlet 4–5 mm long, anthers yellow; flowering from early November to February.

Fruit. Globose, fleshy berry to about 10 cm diameter, with persistent calyx lobes at the apex; seeds many, embedded in the edible, reddish, jelly-like pulp; the fruit is green at first, becoming yellow, ripening with a heavy red shading; fruiting season from February to June.

Other distinguishing features. Upper twigs squared in cross-section by the 4 soft, papery wings.

'**Alboplèna**' (syn. '*Multiplex*') has the normal habit of growth of the parent species but has creamy-white, double flowers and therefore does not produce fruit.

'**Legrelliae**' has a similar habit of growth, but the double flowers are salmon-scarlet, with a white edge to each petal, and no fruit.

'**Nàna**' is a dwarf form to 1 m or less, with smaller leaves, single scarlet flowers to 3 cm across, and abundantly produced fruits to 4 cm across with the yellow-scarlet colouring of the parent.

'**Nàna Plèna**' is the double-flowered form of 'Nana' but has no fruit.

'**Plèna**' (syn. 'Pleniflora', 'Flore Pleno') has the normal habit of growth of the parent species, with the flowers bearing many crepe-like petals forming a double scarlet flower to 5–7 cm across, but no fruit.

Climatic range. A, H, I, M, Mts, P, S.

PYRACÁNTHA

From Greek *pyr* 'fire', and *akanthos* 'thorn'.
Firethorn.
Rosaceae, sub-family Pomoideae; the Rose
family, the Pome sub-family.

Generic description. A small genus of evergreen shrubs mostly from eastern Asia, with
simple, alternate leaves, mostly toothed at the
margins, whitish flowers in corymbose clusters
in spring, followed by heavy crops of showy
fruits in autumn, and with short, hard thorns at
the ends of the laterals. Among the most useful
plants for garden display, especially in harsh climates, as are fruiting branches for decoration.

Propagation. a) Where strict uniformity of type
is not important, the quickest and easiest method
of propagation is by seeds sown as soon as ripe
(but not allowed to dry out), in autumn or winter
when germination may be expected within 2 or
3 weeks in the protection of a warm glass-house.
b) Clonal material is kept true to type by vegetative propatation, preferably by semi-hardwood,
tip cuttings, 5–8 cm long, taken in autumn or
winter; mild bottom heat and mist useful.

Cultivation. Pyracanthas enjoy a fully exposed,
sunny position, preferably in a cool, moist climate. They perform well, with heavier crops of
larger berries, in a rich, well-drained soil,
although they are tolerant of austere conditions
of soil and water-supply better than most plants.
They are seen in almost every part of Australia,
including the dry towns of the interior, as well as
the severely cold parts of the tablelands.

Pruning. Pruning is not an essential requirement to fruit production; indeed, better crops are
seen on plants that are never pruned. Training
for hedging or walling should begin in the first
year or so.

Species and cultivars

Pyracántha angustifòlia (Latin *angustus*
'narrow', and *folium* 'a leaf', referring to the
slender leaf outline): Narrow-leafed Firethorn:
SW China.
Habit. A shrub to 3–5 m tall, with an irregular
globose shape, somewhat inclined to the horizontal in the pattern of branches.
Leaves. Alternate on young, vigorous shoots,
but clustered in whorls on the short, lateral
spurs, oblong-lanceolate, 4–7 cm long and 7–10
mm wide, but often smaller; apex obtuse-
mucronate or slightly emarginate; margin entire

but occasionally with a few vestigial notches
near the apex, the edge slightly recurved; midrib
prominent beneath; dark green, glabrous and
shiny above, grey-green beneath, with a dense
whitish tomentum.
Flowers. Inflorescence a terminal corymb of up
to 30 flowers or more, borne on short, leafy laterals towards the ends of the 1- and 2-year-old
shoots; calyx campanulate; tomentose; flowers
crateriform to 8–12 mm across, petals 5, nearly
orbicular, white, stamens about 20, filaments
white, anthers becoming dark brown; flowering
in November and December.
Fruit. A fleshy flattened-globose pome, borne in
corymbose clusters of a few to about 30 or more,
on short lateral shoots; fruits 7–10 mm across
and 5–8 mm deep, conspicuously depressed at
both poles, the distal end partly covered by the
persistent, grey calyx lobes; pedicels slender, 5–
10 mm long, densely tomentose; seeds 5, angular, embedded in floury, yellow pulp; fruit
yellow at first, but ripening to bright orange with
a glossy skin in April, and lasting well until early
August, finally becoming deep reddish-brown
before falling.
Other distinguishing features. Thorns at the
end of the short laterals; 5–8 mm long, woody,
sharp, dark mahogany-red; youngest twigs
reddish-green, white woolly-tomentose, but
soon becoming glabrous, reddish and shiny,
with prominent brown lenticels.
Climatic range. A, B, H, I, M, Mts, P, S.

Pyracántha atalantioìdes (Latin 'resembling
Atalantia', a genus of the family Rutaceae) (syn.
P. gibbsii) southern and western China.
Habit. An evergreen shrub to 4–5 m tall, with
many erect shoots from the base, arching outwards gracefully to form a vase-shaped crown.
Leaves. Alternate, or whorled on the spurs,
broad-elliptic to oval, 4–7 cm long and 1.5–2.5
cm wide; petiole about 5 mm, grooved and
tomentulose; apex obtuse to sub-acute, sometimes with a fine mucro; base obtuse; margin
shallowly serrate, or often entire, the edge
recurved; midrib prominent below; reddish-
green with a red margin, and covered with a
tawny-yellow tomentum while young, but soon
becoming glabrous, dark green and glossy
above, paler and somewhat glaucous-green
beneath.
Flowers. Inflorescence a dense corymb of up to
20 flowers, borne on short peduncles close to the
stems; petals 5, white, the crateriform-rotate

flowers 9–10 mm across, flowering in November-December.

Fruit. A fleshy pome, 7–9 mm across and 5 mm deep, in dense corymbose clusters of 15–20 on short lateral spurs carried close to the slender, arching, 1-year-old shoots; fruit oblate, the distal end with 5 persistent calyx lobes; fruit deep crimson-red when fully coloured by early April, lasting until late August; outer skin only slightly glossy; seeds 5, angular, black, embedded in soft, creamy-yellow pulp.

Other distinguishing features. Thorns few or entirely absent on some plants; young shoots reddish with tawny-yellow tomentum, aging to dark metallic-green with grey tomentum, but eventually glabrous in the second year, with pale brown, elliptical lenticels.

Climatic range. A, H, I, M, Mts, P, S.

Pyracántha coccinea 'Lalándei' (Latin 'scarlet'; commemorating M. Lalande, nurseryman of Angers, France who selected the clone from a batch of seedlings of *P. coccinea*): Lalande Firethorn; the parent species is native to southern Europe, to Middle East and Western Himalayas.

Habit. An evergreen, erect shrub to 5–6 m tall, slender at first but broadening to 3–4 m wide, the main stems remaining upright and producing the horizontal and drooping fruiting wood.

Leaves. Alternate or in small whorls at the base of the thorns, elliptic to 4–6 cm long and 1.5–2.0 cm wide; apex sharply acute-mucronate; base obtuse; margin crenulate-serrulate; slightly downy at first but becoming glabrous, dark green and somewhat shiny above, paler and duller beneath.

Flowers. Inflorescence a corymb of up to 30 or more flowers on the 1-year-old laterals from the main branches; flowers crateriform-rotate to 9–12 mm across, the 5 rounded petals white; stamens numerous; flowering from early October to late November.

Fruit. A fleshy pome in corymbose clusters of about 30 berries, on short axillary spurs 4–5 cm long arising from the 60–70 cm long laterals; fruits globose, 8–9 mm broad and 7–8 mm deep, only slightly flattened at the poles, dark brown calyx lobes persisting; fruits bright orange-red, glossy, abundant from late February to April; seeds 5, angular, dark brown; flesh soft, cream.

Other distinguishing features. Thorns sharp, woody, straight, 1.5–2.0 cm long; fruiting shoots dark metallic-green with pale brown lenticels.

Climatic range. A, H, I, M, Mts, P, S.

Pyracántha crenulàta (Latin *crena*, 'a notch', referring to the leaf margins): southern slopes of the Himalayas in Nepal.

Habit. An erect, evergreen shrub to 3–4 m tall, the main basal stems arching outwards to form a distinctly vase-shaped outline.

Leaves. Alternate, or seemingly whorled, oblong-lanceolate to 5–7 cm long and 1.3 cm wide, broadest near the middle; apex rounded to acute-mucronate; petiole to 6–7 mm long; margin crenulate to serrulate; midrib prominent beneath; glabrous; dark green and glossy above, paler beneath.

Flowers. Inflorescence a corymb of up to 30 crateriform, 5-petalled white flowers with numerous stamens, flowering from early November to late December.

Fruit. A fleshy pome in a corymbose cluster of 10 to 30; fruits 9 mm across, 6–7 mm deep, flattened at the poles; fruit colour variable in the cultivars, most local stock being glossy dark-red to bright crimson, fully coloured by April and lasting until June; seeds 5, angular, black, 3 mm long, in a soft-yellowish pulp.

Other distinguishing features. Thorns sharp, strong, 7–10 mm long; upper twigs finely pubescent at first, becoming glabrous, reddish where exposed to the sun.

Climatic range. A, B, H, M, Mts, P, S.

Pyracántha fortuneàna (commemorating Robert Fortune, botanical explorer in China and Japan in the mid-1800s) (syn. *P. crenato-serrata*, *P. yunnanensis*) central and western China.

Habit. An evergreen shrub to about 3 m tall, spreading to about 4 m when well grown, the main branch pattern being horizontally inclined.

Leaves. Alternate, narrowly obovate 3.5–6.0 cm long and 1.0–1.5 cm wide, but frequently smaller; petiole 3–4 mm; apex broadly obtuse, but occasionally emarginate or with a small mucro; margin entire or crenate-serrate, the coarse notches mostly above the middle; upper surface concave; glabrous, dark green and glossy above, paler beneath.

Flowers. Inflorescence a small corymb, the 30–60 flowers crateriform, with 5 rounded petals, white, the stamens numerous, flowering abundantly from late October to early December.

Fruit. A fleshy pome, 9–10 mm broad and 5–6 mm deep, flattened at the poles, borne in a crowded corymbose cluster of 30–60 berries, the black calyx lobes persisting at the apex; the berries scarlet when fully ripe in April, deepening to crimson and lasting well to August.

Other distinguishing features. The short leafy shoots are mostly terminated by sharp, woody thorns 5–6 mm long.

Climatic range. A, H, I, M, Mts, P, S.

Pyracántha koidzùmii (commemorating Genichi Koidzumi, 1883–1953, Japanese botanical author) (syn. *P. formosana*) Taiwan.

Habit. An evergreen shrub to 4–5 m tall, with several main trunks and an irregular, open crown, somewhat vase-shaped.

Leaves. Alternate or in rosette-like whorls on the short lateral spurs; oblanceolate to narrowly obovate to 5–6 cm long and 1–2 cm wide, but often smaller; apex emarginate; base cuneate to the 4–6 mm petiole; margin entire, apart from an occasional vestigial irregularity; glabrous, except for some fine tomentum on the lower midrib; dark green and glossy above, paler beneath.

Flowers. Inflorescence a small corymb of 10–15 rotate flowers on short, leafy lateral spurs; calyx brown-tomentose; petals 5, broadly ovate, white, the flower 9–10 mm across; stamens about 20, filaments white, anthers brown; flowering in November and December.

Fruit. A small, fleshy pome to 10–12 mm across and 7–9 mm deep, flattened conspicuously at the distal pole, less so at the proximal end, borne in a loose cluster of several to about 15, on short leafy laterals; fruits variable from orange-red to crimson-red when fully ripe in early April, falling by mid June; seeds 5, angular, black, embedded in soft yellowish pulp.

Other distinguishing features. Thorns hard and sharp, 5–10 mm long, mostly at the ends of the laterals; twigs metallic-green, shiny, with blackish lenticels.

Climatic range. A, B, H, M, P, S, and in mild parts of Mts.

Pyracántha rogersiàna (commemorating Charles Rogers, English botanical author) (syn. *P. crenulata* 'Rogersiana') SW China.

Habit. An evergreen shrub to 3.5 m tall, of generally upright habit in youth, the main branches arching outwards to form a vase-shaped shrub with a broader top than base but becoming broadly bun-shaped in age.

Leaves. Alternate but seemingly whorled at the end of the short spurs; spathulate to narrow-obovate 2.5–4.0 cm long and 1.5 cm wide; apex obtuse; base cuneate to the 5–8 mm petiole; margin crenulate, mostly above the middle, the glandular teeth largest near the apex; most leaves concave; venation reticulate, glabrous; mid-green and glossy above, paler beneath.

Flowers. Inflorescence a 10- to 15-flowered corymb, mostly on short spurs from the 2-year-old branches; flowers crateriform to 8–9 mm across, the petals broad to nearly orbiculate, white, stamens about 20; flowering abundantly from late October to December.

Fruit. A fleshy pome, 9–10 mm across and 5–7 mm deep, borne in corymbose clusters of 10–15 berries; fruit orange-red but variable when grown by seeds to orange and various tones of yellow, fully developed and coloured by early April and lasting until late July; calyx lobes persisting at the distal end; seeds 5, small, angular, black. Some of the colour variants have individual cultivarietal names: 'Aurantiàca' has large, orange-yellow fruit; 'Flàva' is the best-known cultivar, with butter-yellow fruit.

Other distinguishing features. All have sharp, woody thorns to 1 cm long, mostly at the end of the fruiting spurs.

Climatic range. A, H, I, M, Mts, P, S.

New Hybrids. A number of new hybrids are appearing in USA and in Great Britain, most as a result of research and experimental breeding by the Crops Research Division of the US National Arboretum. The main objective is to develop resistance to disease, especially fireblight and scab, both serious diseases of Rosaceae, as well as to extend the plants' limits of hardiness as evergreens. So far, several good cultivars have beeen isolated and named commemoratively for the North American Indian tribes, 'Mohave' and 'Shawnee', the former the progeny of a cross between *P. koidzumii* and *P. coccinea*, the other from *P. fortuneana* and *P. koidzumii*. Selections from the extremely variable *P. coccinea*, as well as from *P. fortuneana* and *P. koidzumii*, are commonly seen in the USA.

RAPHIÓLEPIS (also spelt *Rhaphiolepis*)

Derived from the Greek *raphis* a 'needle', and *lepis* 'a scale', referring to the slender, chaffy bracts at the base of each flower.

Indian Hawthorn.

Rosaceae, sub-family Pomoideae; the Rose family, the Pome sub-family.

Generic description. Dense, leafy, evergreen shrubs from eastern Asia having simple alternate, coriaceous leaves, and white or pinkish flowers in short terminal panicles or corymbs, followed by clusters of red or black fruits, often with a bluish bloom. The species listed below are useful specimen plants, especially handsome in cool, temperate climates and often used as uncut hedges.

Propagation. a) Seeds germinate readily if sown in autumn when ripe, or held over until spring in just-moist sphagnum moss at 4° or 5°C.
b) Cultivars and hybrids such as R. x *delacourii* and R. x *fergusonii* must be propagated vegetatively to preserve their clonal character, ideally by short, firm-tip cuttings taken in autumn or winter, and struck in a sand/peat mixture, preferably in a warm, moist atmosphere.

Cultivation. Best growth is made on loamy or sandy soils, well supplied with water in summer, but adequately drained against poor soil aeration, in any of the cooler Australian climates.

Pruning. Young plants benefit from a light trim of the vigorous terminal shoots to induce lateral branching, but otherwise little pruning is needed. Hedges are best shaped in summer, after the main flowering season when pruning scars are soon overgrown by new growth.

Raphiólepis x *delacoùrii* (the collective name given to the interspecific hybrid progeny of the cross between R. *indica* and R. *umbellata*, commemorating its raiser, M. Delacour of Cannes, France): the progeny show the typical clonal variations of interspecific hybrids and vegetative propagation is essential to maintain the character of a selected clone; a typical clone is described hereunder.
Habit. An evergreen shrub of about 1.5 m tall with a dense, leafy habit of hemispherical shape to 2 m broad, suitable as specimen or hedging.
Leaves. Alternate, elliptic to obovate, 4–6 cm long and 2.5–4.0 cm wide; apex variable from retuse to obtuse, acute or shortly acuminate; base more or less cuneate to the 1 cm petiole; margin crenate-serrate, mostly above the middle; midrib prominent and yellowish beneath; coriaceous; bronze-green at first in spring, maturing to glossy dark green above, paler and dull beneath.
Flowers. Inflorescence a terminal panicle standing clear of the upper leaves; peduncles, pedicels and calyces with a fine rufous tomentum; calyx campanulate to 1 cm long, with 5 acute, spreading, deep-red sepals; corolla rotate to 2 cm across, with 5 obovate, spreading petals, the edges ciliate, rose-pink, paling towards the centre; stamens 15–20, filaments white, anthers yellow, styles 2; flowering abundantly over the top of the plant from August to November.
Fruit. A fleshy, 1-seeded black pome, globose to 1 cm across, pruinose, with cream pulp and a globose, chocolate-brown seed, ripening in autumn and persisting through winter.
Other distinguishing features. Upper twigs, especially in the inflorescence, reddish with a fine silky pubescence.
Climatic range. A, B, H, M, Mts, P, S.

Raphiólepis x *fergusonii* (commemorating Bruce Ferguson, a prominent Sydney nurseryman of the 1930–50 period, in whose nursery the plant originated, probably as an interspecific hybrid).
Habit. A low-growing evergreen bush to 1 m tall, with a broad bun shape to 1.5–2.0 m wide, always neat and attractive in form.
Leaves. Alternate, oblanceolate to narrow-elliptic, 5–8 cm long and 2 cm wide, the petiole 2–5 mm long; apex acute; base cuneate; margin shallowly serrate-crenate but entire towards the base; glabrous and coriaceous; dark green and lustrous above, paler beneath.
Flowers. Inflorescence a terminal panicle or cluster of axillary panicles; calyx reddish, tubulate to 5 mm long, with 5 acute lobes; corolla rotate to 2 cm across, the 5 petals oval to ovate, flesh-pink in the pointed buds but opening to pure white, with pink shadings on the reverse; stamens 17 to 20, filaments white, anthers yellow; flowers abundant from mid-September to November.
Fruit. A small globose to ellipsoidal pome, green at first but ripening to black in autumn and persisting until winter.
Other distinguishing features. Upper twigs grey-brown, with large round lenticels; rachis of the inflorescence silky-pubescent.
Climatic range. A, B, H, M, Mts, P, S.

Raphiólepis indíca (Latin 'of Indian origin', but not necessarily only of the Indian region): Indian Hawthorn: temperate southern China.
Habit. An evergreen shrub to 2–3 m tall, usually based on a short main trunk, dividing into numerous spreading branches to form a densely rounded bush 3–4 m broad.

Leaves. Simple, or occasionally apparently whorled at the growth junctions, broadly oblanceolate to obovate, 4–7 cm long and 2–3 cm wide; petiole flattened 4–6 mm long; apex variable from obtuse to abruptly acuminate; margin serrate, mostly above the middle; midrib and main laterals yellowish and translucent; pubescent when young but later glabrous and coriaceous; reddish at first, but aging to lustrous dark green above, paler and duller beneath.

Flowers. Inflorescence a terminal panicle 6–8 cm tall, of many tomentose racemes; floral bracts subulate, brown-chaffy, 5–8 mm long, soon deciduous; calyx pubescent, the campanulate tube 4 mm long, with 5 subulate sepals 7–8 mm long, reddish; petals 5, oblanceolate to obovate, acute, to 1 cm long, forming a stellate flower 2 cm across, white but with crimson staining on the edges of the petals at the base; stamens about 3 mm long, filaments white to crimson, anthers cream; styles 2; only slightly fragrant; flowering from August to October.

Fruit. A globose pome to 1 cm, ripening to blue-black in autumn and persisting until winter.

Other distinguishing features. Upper twigs tomentose, chocolate-brown at first, becoming glabrous and greyish with brown lenticels.

Climatic range. A, B, H, M, Mts, P, S.

Raphiólepis umbellàta (Latin *umbella*, 'a little shade', referring to the shape of the inflorescence): Japan, Korea and neighbouring islands.

Habit. An evergreen shrub to 2–3 m tall, the trunk stout and multi-branched near the base to form a broad bush 3–4 m wide.

Leaves. Simple, alternate on vigorous shoots, but appearing to be whorled on the short, stubby growths near the apex; broadly elliptic to obovate, the blade 4–8 cm long and 2–4 cm wide, the petiole 1 cm long; apex acute to obtuse; margin shallowly serrate above the middle or nearly entire, recurved; glabrous and coriaceous; dark green and shiny above, paler and dull beneath.

Flowers. Inflorescence a terminal panicle of umbellate form 5–12 cm across; calyx funnelform, with 5 slender lobes, pubescent; corolla rotate, the petals 5, obovate, 10–12 mm long, white, with pale pink staining outside; lightly fragrant; flowering abundantly from September to early summer, then intermittently until late autumn.

Fruit. A globose pome to 1 cm, slightly flattened at the poles, borne in umbellate clusters of 10 to 20 on short terminals from the upper branchlets, ripening to blue-black in autumn.

Other distinguishing features. Young twigs pubescent at first, with pale-brown lenticels, becoming roughened by vertical ridges and widely triangular leaf-scars.

'Ovata' has broadly ovate to obovate leaves, the marginal indentations less evident or quite absent, the margin more recurved.

Climatic range. A, B, H, M, Mts, P, S.

REINWÁRDTIA (syn. *Linum*)

Commemorating Prof. Kaspar Reinwardt, Director of the Botanic Gardens at Leiden, Holland.
Yellow Flax or Linum.
Linaceae, the Flax family.

Generic description. A small genus of sub-shrubs with soft-wooded stems, evergreen only in warm climates, with simple, alternate leaves and yellow salverform flowers.

Propagation. a) Soft-tip cuttings taken from the young growth in early spring, preferably from a severely pruned stock-plant, root satisfactorily in a sand/peat mixture in a warm, moist atmosphere.

b) An established clump may be divided into several new plants in winter.

Cultivation. The plant is best grown in a light-fibrous soil with free drainage, in a warm, wind-sheltered position, preferably with the protection of other neighbouring shrubs.

Pruning. Pruning should be severe, almost to half-height, in late winter after the flowering season, to encourage suckering from the base. A mulch of fertilised compost is beneficial, followed by deep watering.

Species and cultivars

Reinwárdtia índica (Latin 'of India') (syn. *Linum trigynum*) Yellow Flax: Northern India, mostly from the foothills of the Himalayas.

Habit. A small evergreen shrub to 1 m or less, with soft-wooded, erect stems, suckering from the base into a broad clump.

Leaves. Elliptic to obovate, 4–8 cm long and 2–4 cm wide; apex acute-cuspidate; margin entire or shallowly serrulate; texture soft and thin; glabrous; bright green and slightly dull, paler beneath, occasionally yellowish in winter.

Flowers. Solitary or in few-flowered clusters in the upper axils, on 5–10 mm pedicels; calyx tubulate-campanulate to 1 cm long, with 5 acute lanceolate sepals, green, glabrous; corolla salverform-funnelform, the 5 broadly obovate petals spirally folded in the bud, but spreading when open to form a circular limb about 5 cm across, bright butter-yellow, flowering abundantly from May to August but falling quickly; stamens 5, with cream filaments and yellow anthers; styles 3, as long as the tube, the stems white, the stigmas bright green.

Fruit. Not seen.

Other distinguishing features. Upper twigs glabrous, terete, but with a few indistinct ridges and large, crescentic leaf-scars.

Climatic range. B, P, S, T, and in warm, sheltered localities in A and M.

RETÀMA (formerly included in *Genista*)

Derived from the Arabic vernacular name for the plant.

White Weeping Broom or Bridal-wreath Broom. Fabaceae, the Pea family.

Generic description. A small genus, now separated from *Genista* because of its inflated legumes, mainly represented in Australia by the species described below. In flower, it is a very beautiful plant deserving of greater use in gardens, ideally placed at the back of a shrub border, its somewhat bare base hidden by suitably low, front-row material.

Propagation. Seeds are collected as soon as ripe in autumn and stored in a cool, dry place until spring, then sown in individual containers to minimise root disturbance when potting on. Pretreatment in warm water is beneficial.

Cultivation. Like the *Genistas*, the White Weeping Broom grows well in a freely drained, open sandy or gravelly soil, but is responsive to better class soils also, with more rapid growth. It is hardy to low temperatures to about –3°C without distress.

Pruning. 'Trimming' spoils the plant's very attractive pendulous form; however, removal of the spent flowers is beneficial unless wanted for seeds.

Retàma monospèrma (Greek 'one-seeded'): White Weeping Broom: southern Portugal and Spain and North Africa: the cultivarietal name 'Pendula' is sometimes added in nursery terminology, but appears to be invalid.

Habit. A shrub to 2–3 m tall, with a short main trunk and many slender stems, erect at first but becoming pendulous, the almost leafless, green twigs adopting the photosynthetic role of leaves.

Leaves. Very sparse, simple, alternate, linear, 1–2 cm long, silky-pubescent and silver-green when young, becoming glabrous and green.

Flowers. Inflorescence a lateral raceme to 2.5–3.5 cm long, with 10 to 15 flowers on a silky-pubescent peduncle, the racemes numerous in a loose cluster near the terminals of the 1-year-old shoots; calyx campanulate to 3–4 mm long, 3-lobed, the middle one trifid, deep-purple, enclosed at first by a pair of silky deciduous bracts; flowers pea-shaped, the standard orbicular, ridged centrally into 2 equal halves, white, but with purple splashes on the inner base; wings narrow-oblong, pure white; keel narrowly elliptical, with a pointed beak at the apex, pure white; flowers measure about 7–9 mm in all directions; all parts silky-pubescent; sweetly-perfumed; flowering abundantly from late July to September.

Fruit. A rugose, obliquely ovoid to obovoid legume 1.2 cm long and 7–8 mm broad, shortly mucronate, yellowish-green, mostly 1-seeded.

Other distinguishing features. Upper stems shallowly grooved, green and pubescent but with faint stomatic lines, giving a slightly greyish appearance.

Climatic range. A, B, M, P, S, T, and in warm microclimates on the lower levels of Mts.

RHODODÉNDRON: subgenera EURHODODÉNDRON and AZALEÁSTRUM

Derived from the Greek *rhodon* 'a rose', and *dendron* 'a tree'.

Rhododendron and Azalea (various). Ericaceae, the Erica family.

Generic description. A very large and important genus of showy-flowered, evergreen and deciduous shrubs or small trees, mainly from the northern temperate zone, with several from the highlands of Papua New Guinea and one from Australia, but the majority from southern Asia, especially in the Himalayan region and the Orient, and a score or two of important species from North America.

Leaves are simple and alternate, with an entire,

sometimes recurved margin, the deciduous kinds occasionally colouring well in autumn. Flowers are rarely solitary but usually in a terminal inflorescence as an umbellate raceme, the gamopetalous flowers mostly funnelform or campanulate. Flowers are normally single but sometimes, notably in the Kurume Azaleas, have an additional corolla set within the first, forming a 'hose-in-hose' flower. Stamens are from 5 to 20, exserted nearly to the mouth of or beyond the corolla, the single style slightly longer. Fruit is a septicidal capsule, splitting when ripe to release the numerous fine seeds. Almost all flower in late winter, spring or early summer and rate amongst the most spectacular of flowering plants.

At least 800 species are recognised, as well as countless hybrids and cultivars. Specialist nursery catalogues should be consulted for details and the full range of the main groups grown in Australia. The following brief treatment merely outlines the main types, with a representative sampling of the floral forms and colours in the many cultivars available, selected for reliability of performance under the environmental conditions described in paragraph 7 below.

Propagation. a) Seed propagation is practised mainly by hybridists in the quest for new and improved plants by cross-pollination of existing selected parents. The very small seeds are usually sown on a bed of sterile, coarse sand and granulated peat and barely covered with finely shredded sphagnum moss. A shaded, moderately warm, humid atmosphere in a frame or glass-house is required, preferably with an additional cover of clear plastic sheeting to maintain a uniform water status in the soil. Germination is usually rapid if fresh seeds are used, sown in early spring.

b) Semi-hardwood, leafy tip cuttings are mostly used to reproduce clonal material reliably. The cuttings vary in size with the type of plant, from about 3–4 cm in the smaller-growing Kurume Azaleas, to 10–12 cm in the larger Broad-leafed Rhododendrons. The most favoured time is between early summer and mid autumn, the best material being taken from the tips of the partly matured, current year's growth. Various rooting media are used, granulated peat mixed with coarse gritty river sand in the proportions of 1:1 to 3:1 being customary. A high level of atmospheric humidity is desirable, preferably controlled by mechanical means, such as mist

and electronic leaf, with a uniform temperature between 18° and 24°C. The use of root-promoting dusts, applied to a shallowly wounded base is an advantage.

Very young, leafy tip cuttings are used to increase the Ghent, Mollis and Knap Hill types, with high atmospheric humidity, bottom heat and mist irrigation overhead.

c) Simple layers, or modified trench-layers are often used where only a few new plants are required, 1- and 2-year-old stems being shallowly wounded on the lower side of the stem, which is then pegged-down horizontally and covered with a peat/sand mixture and mulched heavily until roots are well established, then severed and lifted, preferably in cool, humid weather in autumn.

Cultivation. The ideal soil for Rhododendrons and Azaleas is a mildly acid (pH 5–6), light, well-drained, sandy or porous loam to which is added organic matter in the form of well-prepared compost, granulated peat or leaf mould. The lighter soils require more organic matter than the loams. Fresh manure or lime should not be used. The moisture content of the soil should remain fairly constant by addition of thick mulches of litter, compost or granulated peat; the plants themselves contribute to this mulch with dropped leaves and flowers. Mulching helps to moderate wide fluctuations in surface soil temperatures, a point of importance in the cultivation of fibrous, surface-rooting plants. Disturbance of the surface with digging tools is therefore unnecessary and even detrimental. The ideal aspect is one in which the plants are protected from the heat of the afternoon sun, and from strong, dry winds. They grow moderately well, however, in open sunny positions on the cooler southerly and easterly slopes, provided their water requirements in hot dry times are adequately catered for. Such open-grown plants often flower better but are more readily damaged by sun and wind. They are perhaps at their best as an under-storey to taller, small-leafed trees; the subdued light makes for brilliant colour effects, especially if the deciduous types, such as Mollis and Ghent Azaleas, and other spring-flowering shrubs are used in association. The evergreen Azaleas are sensitive to cold below about −2° or −3°C and are suitable in cold climates only with adequate overhead protection, or when grown in portable containers and brought indoors when temperatures fall below their normal limits.

Pruning. Pruning is necessary only to control wayward growth or to contain aggressive growers to their allotted space; when performed it should follow the flowering period.

Broad-leafed Rhododendrons

The Broad-leafed Rhododendrons, commonly referred to in Australia simply as 'rhododendrons', comprise the LEPIDOTE group, with scaly and often hairy leaves, and the ELEPIDOTE group, without scales on the leaves but commonly with a hairy undersurface. They are distinguished by:

a) Their often larger growth habit, old plants of some species reaching to 10–12 m or more, although others, and many of the hybrids and cultivars, are much smaller.

b) Almost all are wholly evergreen, except for a few genuinely deciduous, or others that in very severe climates discard some or all of their leaves.

c) The very large leaves that occur in some species, sometimes measuring 35–45 cm long; leaves are usually smooth above, either glossy or dull, but may be scaly or heavily pubescent beneath, often with conspicuously recurved margins.

d) Flowers are sometimes very large, up to 12 cm across, mostly in terminal umbellate heads of a few to as many as 20 flowers in tubulate, funnelform, campanulate or urceolate form, or rarely salverform, the stamens 5 to 25, the floral colour range extremely wide in the red, pink, white, cream, yellow, orange, mauve, lavender, and purple range, flowering from late winter through spring, with a few lasting until early summer; some are fragrant.

Climatic range. Successful plantings are almost wholly confined to the cool, moist, humid climates with mild summer temperatures, where winters are cold enough to induce full dormancy; the distribution and amount of rainfall provide for high atmospheric humidity and an unfailing supply of water in the soil; and where the soils are mildly acid, well aerated and generously furnished with organic matter.

A few districts in SE Australia, well known for their rhododendron displays, are favoured almost ideally by these environmental conditions. All suffer occasional periods of heat-wave weather, usually accompanied by scorching winds and very low humidity, but such times are mercifully of short duration. The basaltic 'caps' of the central Blue Mountains, such as Mt Wilson, and the Bowral-Exeter districts in NSW, the Dandenong and Macedon areas in Victoria, and the northern, central and eastern parts of Tasmania are good examples, all with celebrated collections of Broad-leafed Rhododendrons in public and private gardens. Significantly, almost all the rhododendron nurseries in Australia are located in these districts, offering a wide range of the best species, hybrids and cultivars suitable to the local conditions. In these regions, at least as far south as 40°S the weather can be quite hot in October, temperatures of 35° to 38°C being not uncommon. Late flowering kinds are often damaged by such heat, the buds failing to open or flowers being scorched and fading readily. Since in the relatively mild Australian winters, the risk of plants or buds being destroyed by severe cold is minimal, it is wise to make the basic plantings at least with early-flowering kinds.

Few Broad-leafed Rhododendrons are suitable for low-elevation, warm climates such as Sydney, the two most dependable being the old-established 'Broùghtonii' and *pónticum* 'Grandiflòrum' many fine specimens of which may be seen in the hilly parts of Sydney during September and October.

Broad-leafed Rhododendrons: sample list of species, hybrids and cultivars available in Australian nurseries, selected for reliability of performance

Cultivar name	Flowering Time	Height	Colour
'Alice'	M	3 m	Deep pink, with paler pink centre
arbòreum	E–M	6 m+	'Album' white 'Blood Red' crimson 'Roseum' mid-pink
augustìnii	E–M	3 m+	Lavender to violet-blue
'Avalanche'	E–M	3 m	Pale pink, opening to white, rosy-crimson throat
'Beauty of Littleworth'	E–M	3 m+	White with crimson spots; slightly fragrant

Cultivar name	Flowering Time	Height	Colour
'Beauty of Tremough'	E	3 m+	Pale pink with deeper pink margin
'Blue Diamond'	E	1 m	Deep violet-blue flowers, small but prolific
'Blue Peter'	M	1.5 m	Lavender-blue with whitish-blue throat; frilled edge
'Blue Tit'	E	0.75 m	Pale lavender-blue
'Britannia'	M	1.5–2 m	Glowing crimson-red, paler in the centre
'Brocade'	E–M	1.5–2 m	Rosy-carmine in the bud, opening to rose-pink
'Bròughtonii'	E–M	3 m+	Rosy-crimson; hardy and suitable for hills of Sydney
'C. B. van Nes'	M	3 m	Dark scarlet in large conical head; prolific
'Christmas Cheer'	E	1.5–2 m	Blush-pink in the bud, opening to nearly white
'Cornish Cross'	E–M	2 m+	Carmine-pink outside, paler inside; large bell-shaped
'Cornubia'	E	4–5 m	Glowing waxy-scarlet, bell-shaped; large conical heads
'Countess of Athlone'	E–M	3 m+	Rosy-violet in the bud opening to light-mauve; frilled
'Countess of Derby'	E–M	3 m+	Large open flowers of carmine-pink, paler at the edges
'Countess of Haddington'	E	1.5–2 m	Palest pink, flushed rose, fading to almost white; fragrant
'Cynthia'	M	3 m+	Large rosy-crimson, shaded magenta with crimson markings
decòrum	E–M	4 m+	Blush-pink to white with yellow-green shadings; fragrant
'Earl of Athlone'	M	2 m+	Deep glowing crimson; large bell-shaped flowers
'Elizabeth'	E–M	1.5 m	Bright vermilion-red; large funnelform flowers
x *fragrantíssimum*	E–M	2.5–3 m	Blush-pink in the bud, opening to waxy-white; fragrant
'Goldsworth Yellow'	E–M	2 m+	Apricot buds opening to primrose-yellow; deeper markings
gránde	M	3 m+	Blush to creamy-white, reddish throat; large handsome leaves
'Lionel's Triumph'	E–M	2 m+	Deep-yellow, red throat; large campanulate flowers
lóchiae (n. Australian)	E	1 m	Deep rosy-red campanulate flowers in drooping heads
x *lòderi*	M	3 m+	White, cream or pink; large; fragrant; large conical heads
x *lòderi* 'King George'	M	3 m+	Pale pink in the bud, opening to glistening white
x *lòderi* 'Venus'	M	3 m+	Carmine buds opening to pale-pink; yellow-green throat
x *lòderi* 'White Diamond'	M	3 m+	Buds flesh pink opening to glistening white
'Loder's White'	M	3 m+	Blush-pink buds opening to pure white; large conical head

Cultivar name	Flowering Time	Height	Colour
macabeànum	E–M	5 m+	Butter-yellow, reddish-purple throat; large conical heads
'Madame de Bruin'	M	3 m+	Large cerise-red, shaded carmine; large flowers
'Mrs. E. C. Stirling'	M	3 m+	Carmine-pink buds opening to blush, tinted lilac
'Naomi'	M	3 m	A hybrid group with large, fragrant, open flowers in soft pinks with lilac, green or yellow throat
x *nobleànum*	E	4 m+	Red to pink funnelform flowers with white throat
x *nobleanum* **'Álbum'**	E	3 m+	Buds bluish-pink opening to white; greenish
x *nobleanum* **'Coccíneum'**	E	3 m+	Bright rosy-scarlet, spotted crimson in the throat
'Penjerrick Cream'	E	2 m+	Large open heads; deep-cream, campanulate, fragrant flowers
'Pink Pearl'	E–M	3 m+	Rose-pink buds opening to blush; large funnelform
pónticum **'Grandiflòrum'**	M	4 m+	Mauve to lavender-blue; small heads; prolific; hardy
'President Roosevelt'	M	2 m+	Bright rosy-crimson with white throat; creamy-yellow variegated foliage
'Prince Camille de Rohan'	E–M	3 m+	Rosy-pink; prolific medium-sized heads; hardy
'Professor Hugo de Vries'	M	3 m+	Clear rose-pink in large globular heads
'Purple Splendour'	E–M	2 m+	Deep-purple with dark-violet spots on upper petal
'Sappho'	M	3–4 m	White, the upper petal heavily spotted purplish-black
'Unknown Warrior'	E–M	2–3 m	Buds bright rosy-crimson maturing to deep rose-pink
'White Pearl'	M	3 m+	Pale-pink in the bud opening to glistening white, suffused with blush-pink

E = Early-flowering, mainly during July to early September. E-M = Early-midseason, mainly between late September and early October. M = Mid-season, mainly between late October and early November. Climatic range: All H, M, Mts.

Azaleas

Belgian-Indian Azaleas

This, the most numerous group of the evergreen Azaleas, is derived principally from the Chinese species, *Rhododendron simsii*, with several other species contributing various characteristics. The bulk of the Azaleas grown by the Dutch and Belgian nurserymen for indoor use as forced, potted ornamentals, belong here. In the milder Australian climates they are grown as outdoor shrubs, usually massed together with other spring material such as maples, crab-apples, Prunus, Forsythias, Spireas, Viburnums and Weigelas and often backed by their taller counterparts, the Tall Single Indica Azaleas. Growth habit is either dwarf (0.5 m to 0.75 m), or medium (0.75 m to 1.0 m), compact and of somewhat spreading shape with dense, attractive, evergreen foliage. Flowers are a) single, the flattish, funnelform corolla 5-lobed, 6–9 cm across, and often ruffled or crinkled at the edge; b) semi-double, similar but with a cluster of small petaloids in the centre, the stamens mostly modified or distorted; or c) fully-double, the centre more or less filled with petals, with few or no stamens showing.

The colours are in the white, pink, red, mauve, and violet range in a wide variety of self and multiple-colour combinations, flowering mainly in spring but many starting to flower in late autumn or winter and continuing to flower intermittently in less quantity throughout the early summer.

They are tolerant of cold to –2°C or –3°C but may be injured by more severe conditions. Most will flower well with full sun exposure, but the best results are achieved in dappled shade, preferably within the shelter of tall overhead trees, or at least protected from hot, dry winds and northerly or westerly sun.

Dwarf Growth Habit (0.5 m to 0.75 m)
Note: Abbreviations used for Azaleas are:S = single; S/D = semi-double; D = double; HH = hose-in-hose.
'**Advent Bells**': S/D bright glowing red.
'**Balsaminiflorum**': S/D clear salmon-pink.
'**Deutsche Perle**': D white, with pale-green throat.
'**Leopold Astrid**': D white, suffused with rose, bordered deep rosy-red; margin frilled.
'**Madame August van Damme**': S/D pale lavender-pink, with white margin.
'**Phoebus**': D deep salmon-red, with magenta shading.
'**Sweet Sixteen**': D pale pink, ruffled and frilled edge.
'**Vervaeneànum**': D soft pink, with rosy-red streaks and cerise spots, bordered white.
'**Vervaeneanum Album**': D white, with yellow-green shading at the base.

Medium Growth Habit (0.75 to 1.0 m)
'**Agnes Neale**': S/D amaranth-pink, with darker spots. '**Albert Elizabeth**': S/D white, bordered rosy-vermilion.
'**Avenir**': D apricot-salmon, shaded orange-red.
'**Ballerina**': D white, with rosy-mauve margin.
'**Blushing Bride**': S/D soft pink, with carmine spots.
'**Bonnie McKee**': D large, deep rosy-mauve.
'**Elsa Karga**': D bright glowing red.
'**Eri Schame**': S/D salmon-rose, bordered white.
'**Firedance**': D glowing red, with frilled edge.
'**Gloria**': S/D salmon to pale pink; waved and frilled.
'**Gretel**': D white, with rosy-red;ruffled edge.
'**James Belton**': S large pale pink, grading to lavender.
'**Maves**': S dark glowing red.
'**Paul Schame**': S/D clear salmon-red.
'**Pavlova**': D pale lavender-pink; frilled.

'**Pink Pearl**': S/D pale pink, with salmon shadings.
'**Pink Ruffles**': D phlox pink, margined white, waved edge.
'**Red Ruffles**': D deep salmon-red; waved and frilled.
'**Rosa Belton**': S white, with rosy-lavender margin.
'**Ruth Kirk**': S pale vermilion-pink, with white markings.
'**Saidee Kirk**': D large shell-pink, with greenish centre.
'**Temperance**': S/D clear mauve.
'**Theodorus**': S brilliant red, with crimson spots.
'**Violaceum**': D violet-purple.

Tall Single Indica Azaleas

This group is often included with the Belgian-Indian Azaleas but is considered to be worthy of separation on account of its different genetic background, having derived mainly from *R. mucronatum* and R. 'Phoeniceum', later to be crossed with many of the Belgian-Indian cultivars. Their taller growth, to 1.5–2.5 m, together with a dense, leafy habit makes them useful for large-scale plantings, especially if planted boldly as foundation plants around large buildings, or as the back-row material to other shorter kinds. They are hardy to low temperatures of at least –2°C to –3°C but could suffer injury in more severe conditions. They are ideally placed in the mild, humid climates of the Sydney hills and lower tablelands. Flowers are produced in abundance in the main flush between late August and early November.

Climatic range. A, M, P, S, and in warm, sheltered microclimates in H and Mts.

'**Alba Magna**' large white, suffused with green in the throat
'**Alphonse Anderson**' light orchid-pink, paler at the edge, rosy-pink in the throat
'**Exquisite**' light lilac-pink, with darker rosy blotch
'**Jean Alexandra**' peach-pink, with paler margin and occasional central petaloids
'**Lady Poltimore**' white, with greenish throat; perfumed
'**Magnificum**' large rosy-purple
'**Mauve Schryderi**' pale mauve, with spotted lilac throat
'**Mortii**' large white, with yellowish-green throat
'**Orange Brilliant**' bright scarlet
'**Phoeniceum**' deep rosy-purple, with deeper spots

'**Roi de Hollande**' crimson, with deeper spots
'**Schryderi**' large white, with lilac spots; fragrant
'**Splendens**' (syn. *Salmonea*) rosy salmon-pink, with magenta spots
'**Victoria**' salmon-orange, with deeper spots
'**William Wylum**' large rosy-purple

Kurume Azaleas

The principal parents of this type are the Kyushu Azalea, *R. kiusiànum*, and the Kaempfer Azalea, *R. káempferi*.

They resemble the Belgian-Indian Azaleas in some features but are more variable in growth habit, some dwarf to 0.5 m tall, others to 2 m tall, the majority between these limits, usually at about 1.0–1.5 m tall, and at least as wide when well grown, with room to spread laterally. Their leaves are generally smaller, on more twiggy branchlets, making for greater density of growth, ideal for the shrub border, for hedging or for massing in large-scale plantings. Flowers vary in size and shape, some being almost tubular, others flatter, almost rotate, the great majority funnelform, either single, or 'hose-in-hose' with an additional corolla within the first. A few have solitary flowers but most are borne in small umbellate clusters at the end of the preceding year's growth. The wide colour range covers white, pink, red, lavender, purple, and mauve, either as pure self-colours, or gradated from one colour to another. Flowers are produced in great abundance, some cultivars starting in early August, the main season being from late August to early November, with the peak period in September.

They thrive in the usual conditions prescribed for Rhododendrons and Azaleas but are probably more tolerant of poverty in soil and water-supply than other types. Temperatures below −4°C are likely to cause distress and may damage the spring flower buds. They are at their best in a moist, humid climate with mild winters such as in the Sydney hills, Central and Southern Tablelands of NSW, and the Victorian Dandenongs. Many hundreds of clonal selections have been made by the Japanese nurserymen, some so closely resembling others as to be scarcely deserving of separate identity. The celebrated 'Wilson's Fifty', selected in Japan in 1914 by E. H. Wilson of the Arnold Arboretum, includes many whose popular appeal has been maintained for over 75 years, but it is unlikely that a complete collection of the 'Fifty' could now be assembled in Australia. The first of the following lists includes those known to have been imported into Australia, and many of these are probably still reliably labelled in some public or private collections. In the second list are some of more recent introduction or release, all selected for general quality.

Climatic range. A, H, M, P, S, and in warm, sheltered microclimates in Mts.

A Selection of the 'Wilson's Fifty'
Kurume Azaleas

Wilson number	Valid name and English synonym	Brief description of flowers
43	'**Aioi**' (Fairy Queen)	HH almond-blossom pink
14	'**Asa-Gasumi**' (Rosy Morn)	HH rosy carmine-pink
16	'**Azuma-Kagami**' (Pink Pearl)	HH rose-pink and salmon
35	'**Fudesute-yama**' (Poppy)	S light salmon-red
42	'**Hinode-giri**' (Red Hussar)	S cerise-crimson
9	'**Ho-o**' (Apple Blossom)	S rose-pink and carmine
36	'**Ima-shojo**' (Christmas Cheer)	HH bright crimson-red
8	'**Iro-hayama**' (Dainty)	S white, edged lavender
32	'**Kasane-kagaribi**' (Rosita)	S dull salmon-red
22	'**Kirin**' (Daybreak)	HH silvery-rose
29	'**Kumo-no-uye**' (Salmon Prince)	S deep salmon-pink
40	'**Kurai-no-himo**' (Carmine Queen)	HH deep carmine-pink
25	'**Oi-no-mezame**' (Melody)	S silvery-rose
26	'**Omoine**' (Dame Lavender)	S lavender to white
17	'**Osaraku**' (Penelope)	S white, edged lavender
37	'**Rasho-mon**' (Meteor)	S scarlet-red
21	'**Saotome**' (Peach Blossom)	S rosy lavender-pink
1	'**Seikai**' (Madonna)	HH white
20	'**Shintoki-no-hagasane**' (Rose Taffeta)	HH rose and silver pink

Wilson number	Valid name and English synonym	Brief description of flowers
34	'Suetsumu' (Flame)	S crimson-red
10	'Sui-yohi' (Sprite)	S pink, edged salmon
11	'Takasago' (Cherry Blossom)	HH rosy-lilac, spotted red
6	'Tancho' (Seraphim)	HH pink, edged rose
38	'Waka-kayede' (Red Robin)	S bright cerise-red
39	'Yaye-hiryu' (Scarlet Prince)	HH scarlet-red

Other Kurume Azaleas and Kurume Hybrids

'Addy Wery'	S	bright vermilion-red
'Adonis'	HH	white
'Aladdin'	S	bright orange-scarlet
'Betty Cuthbert'	HH	soft silver-pink
'Blaauw's Pink'	HH	rosy-salmon; dwarf habit
'Debutante'	S/D	salmon-pink with paler centre
'Duke of Connought'	HH	flame-red
'Elizabeth Belton'	HH	rose-pink with paler edge
'Esmeralda'	S/D	pale pink; dwarf habit
'Flora'	S/D	rosy salmon-pink
'Fred Colbert'	S/D	bright red
'Hatsu-giri'	S	bright mauve-purple
'Hexe'	HH	bright carmine-crimson
'Hinamoyo'	S	soft phlox-pink
'Jill Seymour'	HH	pink with red streaks
'Roseate'	S/D	large deep rose-pink
'Salmon Beauty'	HH	salmon-rose with red spots
'Scarlet Gem'	HH	orange-scarlet
'Suga-no-ito'	S/D	lavender-pink
'Violetta'	S/D	light violet-purple

Ghent Hybrid Azaleas

A mixed race derived from *R. luteum*, from Eastern Europe, and the North American species, *R. calendulaceum* and *R. periclymenoides*. They have woody, twiggy stems forming a mostly-erect bush to 1.5 m tall, the young stems pubescent. Leaves are deciduous, simple, alternate, lanceolate to oblanceolate-oblong or narrowly elliptic, green but often colouring well in autumn. Flowers are in large umbellate heads of up to 15 or so, appearing before or with the early leaves from early October to early November. Single flowers are funnelform to 4–6 cm across, the 5 lobes broad and reflexed when fully developed, with 5 stamens exserted to or beyond the corolla lobes; the doubles have an additional corolla inserted, at the expense of stamens. Colours are mainly in the strong yellows, oranges and scarlets, with a few salmon and pink; all are more or less fragrant. They are hardy to at least −8°C and are best in a cool, moist, tablelands climate on deep fibrous-loamy soils, but are generally unsatisfactory in warm lowland climates.

Climatic range. H, M, Mts.

'Bouquet de Flore': S carmine-pink, deeper at the edge, with a yellowish blotch in the throat.
'Coccinea Speciosa': S brilliant orange-red, blotched orange-yellow.
'Corneille': D bright pink, with cream centre.
'Fanny': S large magenta-pink, blotched yellow.
'Gloria Mundi': S orange-red, yellow shadings.
'Nancy Waterer': S large golden-yellow; good autumn foliage.
'Narcissiflorum': D pale sulphur-yellow; fragrant.
'Pallas': S deep orange-red, with yellow blotch.
'Unique': S large tangerine-orange, flushed yellow.
'Willem III': S orange-red, yellow shadings.

Mollis Hybrids

The Japanese species *R. japónicum*, and the yellow Chinese Azalea, *R. mólle* (syn. *R. sinénse*) are the principal parents of the modern cultivars, the early ones originating in the Netherlands but since duplicated, more or less, in several other centres, using the same or closely-related genetic combinations.

They have stiff, woody stems arising from a common base, forming an erect or globose bush to 1.0 m or so tall. Leaves are deciduous, lanceolate to oblanceolate or oblong-elliptic, 5–10 cm long, mostly finely pubescent at least while young, bright green at first, some colouring to deep red in autumn. Flowers are in globular, umbellate heads of up to 12 or so, funnelform to 5–6 cm across, the 5 lobes not usually reflexing, the 5 stamens and single style shorter than the corolla. Colours are clear and bright in the yellow, orange, scarlet, deep red, and salmon range, with a few salmon-pinks and an occasional cream, flowering with or before the early leaves from early October to late October or early November. Some are slightly fragrant, although this is not a pronounced feature.

Climatic range. H, M, Mts.

'**Altaclarense**': yellowish-orange, orange-blotched.
'**Anthony Koster**': large bright golden-yellow.
'**Comte de Gomer**': phlox-pink, yellow-blotched.
'**Directeur Moerlands**': deep golden-yellow.
'**Dr M. Oosthoek**': large reddish-orange.
'**Dr Reichenbach**': salmon-orange.
'**Hortulanus H. Witte**': reddish-orange buds, opening to orange-yellow.
'**Hugo Koster**': reddish-vermilion.
'**J. C. van Tol**': large bright crimson-red.
'**Koster's Brilliant Red**': large bright blood-red.
'**Nicolaas Beets**': orange-yellow, tinged bright red.

Knap Hill and Exbury Hybrids

The Knap Hill strain of deciduous Azaleas was first developed in England by Anthony Waterer of Knap Hill Nursery in the 1860s with *R. calendulaceum*, *R. mòlle*, *R. occidentàle* and *R. arboréscens* as the main breeding stocks. The development was continued and extended at Exbury by Lionel de Rothschild to give rise to a somewhat similar group known as Exbury Hybrids. A few cultivars are presently available in Australia. Another fine strain, from the same parentage but clearly much improved in size of flower and vigour, has been developed in New Zealand and named Ilam Hybrids. A score or more of named cultivars are available in New Zealand but are not yet listed in Australia.

All are similar in general character to the Mollis Azaleas but have larger, flatter flowers, sometimes 6–8 cm across, in globular heads of up to 12 or 15 together. They flower slightly later than the Mollis and Ghent Hybrids, starting in mid-October and lasting until mid-November, unless destroyed by adverse weather. Like the others, they are best grown in an open woodland situation with early sun, but with protection from the harsh afternoon light and from strong wind. A cool root-run beneath a generous mulch of organic matter is desirable.

Climatic range. H, M, Mts.

'**Cecile**': large carmine-pink, with deep yellow blotch.
'**Gibraltar**': deep-scarlet buds, opening to orange.
'**Gog**': tangerine-orange, with yellowish blotch.
'**Harvest Moon**': pale yellow, with deeper blotch.
'**Homebush**': semi-double, deep carmine pink.
'**Satan**': bright geranium red.

RÌBES

Derivation uncertain.
Flowering Currant.
Grossulariaceae, the Gooseberry family (formerly included in Saxifragaceae)

Generic description. A large genus of mostly deciduous shrubs, many with edible fruits, notably the Black and Red Currants, one species grown in the cooler parts of Australia for its attractive flowers produced in spring.

Propagation. Semi-hardwood tip cuttings, taken during the growing season, strike readily in a sand/peat mixture in a cool, humid atmosphere; some growers prefer hardwood cuttings taken during the dormant period in winter.

Cultivation. The Red-flowering Currant grows well in a soil of moderate fertility in an open, sun-exposed position and is best suited to cool, moist climates; it is undamaged by an occasional low temperature of −10°C.

Pruning. Several of the oldest shoots should be removed at the base each year to encourage the growth of new water-shoots; removal of the spent inflorescences, immediately after flowering, keeps the plant tidy.

Species and cultivars

Ribes sanguíneum (Latin 'blood red'): Red-flowering Currant: SW Canada and NW USA.
Habit. A deciduous shrub to 2 m or so, with many erect stems arising from the base, forming a nearly globose bush 1.5–2.0 cm wide.
Leaves. Simple, alternate, palmately-lobed or ovate-reniform, with 3 main and 2 minor lobes, the blade 7–8 cm across; petiole 2–3 cm long, pubescent; apex acute to obtuse; base cordate; margin biserrate; venation based on 3 main radiating veins; aromatic when bruised; dark-green, rugose and puberulent above, paler and white-tomentose beneath.
Flowers. Inflorescence a 15- to 40-flowered raceme, to 10 cm long, on a reddish, pubescent

rachis borne on the new season's leafy shoots; pedicels slender, 5–10 mm long, with an oblanceolate bract at the base; calyx tubulate to 1 cm, with an expanded 5-lobed limb, red at first, opening to deep-rose pink; petals 5, forming a short cylinder exserted to 4 mm or so beyond the calyx tube, white, pink, or red; stamens 5, as long as the petals, the filaments and anthers white; flowers prolific from late September to late October.

Fruit. A many-sided, rounded berry about 1 cm across, purplish-black, with a bluish bloom in summer.

'**Album**' is similar, but has white flowers.
'**Carneum**' has deep-pink flowers.
'**King Edward VII**' has crimson flowers.
'**Plenum**' has double, rosy-red flowers.

Climatic range. All A, H, M, Mts, P. S.

RICINOCÀRPOS

Derived from the Greek 'with seeds like those of *Ricinus*', the Castor Bean.
Wedding Bush (various).
Euphorbiaceae, the Spurge family.

Generic description. An Australian native genus of evergreen shrubs, several planted ornamentally for their showy flowers and in some, sweet fragrance. Leaves are alternate, simple, flat or nearly terete by the rolling of the margins; flowers rotate, with 4–6 white or pink petals, unisexual, both sexes appearing together in the terminal inflorescence, followed by a bristly globular capsule containing the mottled seeds which give the plant its generic name.

Propagation. a) Seeds are hard to germinate because of their impervious testa; light scarification or soaking in warm water for 24 hours helps the process of water imbibition. Planting should follow at once in a warm, humid atmosphere.
b) Soft-tip cuttings treated with hormone rooting material and placed under mist have met with some success.

Cultivation. The requirements vary with the species but all those treated here belong to well-drained, sandy or gravelly soils in sunny places with hot, dry summers and cool winters. Wherever possible, these conditions should be provided but plants should not be pampered unduly.

Pruning. Tip-pruning of the youngest shoots during the early years is beneficial.

Species and cultivars

Ricinocàrpos bòwmanii (commemorating Edward McArthur Bowman, 1826–72, Sydney-born author of the species): Pink Wedding Bush: Qld and NSW, mainly on the sandy soils along the inland slopes of the Great Dividing Range in the 400–500 mm rainfall zone.

Habit. A bushy shrub, usually 1 m or so tall and as broad, stiff and open in the wild but improved by regular pruning in cultivation.

Leaves. Linear, 1.0–2.5 cm long, almost sessile on pubescent twigs; margin incurved; apex blunt; surface rough, often pubescent beneath; bright green, sometimes with a reddish cast.

Flowers. Rotate, about 2.5 cm across the mostly 5 broad-ovate petals, pale pink at first, later pure white; male flowers in terminal clusters of about 6 the females fewer, even singly, among the males; calyx slender-campanulate with 4–6 distinct lobes; male flowers with reddish stamens, females with 3 red styles divided to near the base; flowering period from September to November, with a few at other times.

Fruit. A nearly-globose, 3-celled capsule about 8 mm long, bristly, containing 3 smooth oblong seeds.

Climatic range. A, M, P, S, and on warm sites in lower Mts.

Ricinocàrpos pinifòlius (Latin 'pine-leafed'): Wedding Bush: eastern Australia, mainly on sandy or rocky sites near the sea or on coastal plateaus or lower tablelands.

Habit. A shrub to 1.5–2.0 m tall, of irregular, open form in the wild but with denser foliage and improved form in cultivation.

Leaves. Scattered, pointing upwards, partly concealing the stems; linear, 2.0–4.5 cm long, 1–2 mm wide; apex acute, with a sharp, not horny point; margin revolute; glabrous; dark green.

Flowers. In terminal clusters of up to 10, on slender green pedicels about 1.5 cm long; calyx campanulate; female flowers in a minority of about 1:5, with a red, 3-celled ovary and 3 branched styles; male flowers numerous, with an erect cluster of stamens; petals 4 to 6, oblanceolate, forming a stellate flower to 2.5 cm across, pure white, abundant, delicately perfumed, flowering from mid-August to November, the peak period in September.

Fruit. An ovoid-globular capsule on a thickened peduncle the surface densely covered with blackish-green bristles.

Climatic range. A, B, H, M, P, S, and on warm sites on lower Mts.

Ricinocarpos tuberculàtus (Latin 'with pimple-like swellings'): West Australian Wedding Bush: south-west WA, mainly on rocky sites on the inland slopes of the Darling and Stirling Ranges, and adjacent wheatbelt country.
Habit. A spreading shrub to 2 m tall and as broad, sparse in the wild but improved in density by regular late-summer pruning.
Leaves. Linear, 1.5–2.0 cm long, almost terete, the margins fully revolute; apex finely acute; closely set on the upper shoots, nearly covering the stems; dark green.
Flowers. Stellate to 2.5 cm across, of 5 spreading, oblanceolate petals; unisexual, the males predominating by about 6:1 in showy terminal clusters, the waxy-white flowers carried on slender 2 cm pedicels, supported by a 5-lobed greenish calyx; flowering period in November and December, almost covering the crown of the plant.
Fruit. A narrowly-ovoid capsule about 1 cm long, with 3 cells containing the 3 seeds, the exterior of the capsule heavily tuberculate.
Climatic range. A, H, M, P, S, and on warm sites in Mts.

RONDELÈTIA

Commemorating Prof. Guillaume Rondelet, sixteenth-century French naturalist.
Rondeletia.
Rubiaceae, the Madder family.

Generic description. Evergreen shrubs and small trees from tropical America, with opposite leaves, mostly stipulate, and terminal or axillary inflorescences of tubulate flowers rich in nectar and attractive to small birds, the species described here popular for their long flowering season.

Propagation. Semi-hardwood, leafy tip cuttings, 5–10 cm long, are taken in October or November just as the green-barked twigs turn brown, and struck in a sand/peat mixture, preferably over bottom heat and with high humidity. The leaves may be reduced in size to facilitate mass planting.

Cultivation. In the Sydney climate the plants require the warmest aspect possible, preferably facing north or north-east and in full sun. The soil should be light and friable with free drainage. In low-lying gardens where cold air may collect, plants are sometimes damaged by frost, resulting in a serious loss of flower.

Pruning. *R. amoena* is best pruned with moderate severity in November-December when the flowers have faded, reducing the flowered shoots to within several nodes of the past season's growth and shaping the bush into hemispherical form, but allowing a few twiggy, unflowered growths to remain unpruned to relieve the severely-pruned appearance. *R. strigosa* and *R. odorata* should be thinned annually in late winter by removing some of the oldest shoots from the base to make way for new vigorous growth.

Species and cultivars

Rondelètia amoèna (Latin 'lovely'): Central America.
Habit. An evergreen shrub of globose form to about 3 m, with many erect stems from the base carrying the dense foliage and abundant flowers.
Leaves. Simple, opposite, ovate, 10–12 cm long and 5–7 cm wide, the petiole to 5 mm, with 2 triangular stipules to 1 cm long at the base; base obtuse to slightly cordate; apex acute; margin entire; midrib and main veins prominent beneath, pubescent; pale bronze-green at first in spring but aging to dark glossy green above, paler, dull and pubescent beneath.
Flowers. Inflorescence a terminal corymbose cyme, 8–15 cm across, with many flowers, the tubulate buds clavate, opening to salverform, to 1.5 cm long and 7–9 mm across, with 4 or 5 broad lobes; the tube deep salmon-pink, the limb pale salmon with a cluster of yellow bristles in the throat, partially concealing the stamens; perfume faint; flowering from early August to late October.
Fruit. Not seen.
Other distinguishing features. Upper stems dark brown, with whitish lenticels.
Climatic range. B, S, T, and in frost-free localities in M and P.

Rondelètia odoràta (Latin 'fragrant') (syn. *R. speciòsa*) Sweet-scented Rondeletia: Central America.
Habit. A small evergreen shrub to about 1.5 m, with many erect stems from a crowded base, forming an upright vase-shaped bush about 1 m wide.
Leaves. Simple, opposite, elliptic-ovate, 3–5 cm long and 3–4 cm wide, sessile or with very short petiole; apex acute; base cuneate to sub-cordate;

margin entire but slightly recurved; venation reticulate, the reddish midrib and main laterals prominent and pubescent beneath; dark velvety-green above, reddish-green beneath.

Flowers. Inflorescence a terminal cymose cluster of 10 to about 20 salverform flowers on reddish, pubescent pedicels, the slender tube to 2 cm long, expanding into a 5-lobed rotate limb to 1.2 cm across, orange-scarlet to crimson, with a bright yellow throat in the tube; sweetly fragrant; flowering season late summer and autumn.

Fruit. Not seen.

Other distinguishing features. Upper twigs red, and densely pubescent with reddish hairs.

Climatic range. B, P, S, T.

Rondelètia strigòsa (Latin 'having short, stiff hairs') (syn. *R. anómala*) Guatemala.

Habit. An evergreen shrub to 1.5 m or so, with slender, erect or arching shoots arising from the common base to form an open, vase-shaped bush.

Leaves. Simple, opposite or 3-whorled, broad-ovate, 3–4 cm long and 2.0–2.5 cm wide; the petiole 1–2 mm; apex acuminate; base obtuse or rounded; margin finely ciliate; midrib and the 3 to 5 main laterals prominent beneath; both surfaces strigose; bright green above, paler beneath.

Flowers. Inflorescence a small terminal cyme of 1 to 3 flowers at the ends of the leading and lateral shoots; calyx strigose, reddish, the receptacle clavate to 6 mm, the slender 5 (or rarely 6) lobes stellate to 2 cm across; corolla salverform, to about 2 cm long, the tube 2 mm wide, swollen near the apex, opening to the 5- or 6-lobed limb; lobes obovate, issuing from a circular rim; flowers glowing crimson; stamens 5, just clear of the tube; flowering season from early December to late April but more or less continually in climates warmer than that of Sydney.

Fruit. An ovoid capsule with 2 seeds, ripening in late autumn.

Other distinguishing features. Upper twigs terete, dark green, of somewhat pebbly texture and finely strigose.

Climatic range. B, T, and in warm localities in S.

ROSMARÌNUS

Derived from the Latin, referring to the plant's maritime habitat.
Rosemary.
Lamiaceae, the Mint family; (formerly Labiatae).

Generic description. A genus of two species of the Mediterranean coastal region, with evergreen, aromatic leaves and small blue flowers, one species a shrub with dense, leafy habit, the other a prostrate, trailing plant of special value as a wall or rock-garden subject. They are grown for their ease of culture on a wide variety of soils and climates, and as a token of remembrance.

Propagation. Firm tip cuttings, taken from late summer to winter, strike readily in a sand/peat mixture in a cool, humid environment.

Cultivation. The plants thrive in a well-drained soil, preferably somewhat dry and of only moderate fertility, in an open sunny position, even close to the sea; tolerant of low temperatures to −5°C when acclimatised.

Pruning. Immediately after the main flowering season, a light annual pruning is beneficial in maintaining the dense, leafy habit.

Species and cultivars

Rosmarìnus officinàlis (Latin 'used in a shop', especially in an apothecary, alluding to its use by the ancient herbalists): Rosemary: southern Europe to Turkey, especially around the Mediterranean coast.

Habit. An evergreen shrub to 1.5–2.0 m tall, with a spreading habit to 2.5 m, the dense, leafy branches forming a somewhat spiky outline.

Leaves. Simple, opposite, linear, 2.0–3.5 cm long and 2–4 mm wide; apex obtuse; base slightly tapered; margin entire, recurved; central vein alone prominent; dark green above, whitish and finely tomentose below; strongly aromatic when crushed.

Flowers. Inflorescence an axillary raceme of 15–20 flowers; calyx campanulate, 3–4 mm long, green, with white tomentum; corolla bilabiate to 8–10 mm long, pale whitish-lavender, heavily spotted and splashed with deep violet-blue, flowering from early August to October.

Fruit. Not seen.

Other distinguishing features. Upper twigs squarish, nut-brown but densely white-tomentose.

Rosmarìnus lavandulàceus (Latin 'like *Lavandula*') is somewhat similar in foliage and flowers but has a prostrate, spreading habit ideal for large-scale rock gardens or over walls.

Climatic range. Both A, B, M, P, S, and on the lower, warmer levels of Mts.

ROYÈNA

Commemorating Adrian van Royen, 1704–79, Dutch botanist of Leyden, Netherlands.South African Snowdrop Bush; Shiny-leafed Snowdrop Bush.
Ebenaceae, the Ebony family.

Generic description. A genus of about twenty, mostly African, trees and shrubs, one species grown in Australian gardens for its handsome foliage. For details, see specific notes below.

Propagation. Semi-hardwood cuttings, taken in late autumn to winter strike readily in a friable medium in a warm, humid atmosphere.

Cultivation. A fully sun-exposed site is best, in a moderately rich soil of open texture and free drainage; the plant is tolerant of cold to about −3°C and of wind, except the harsh salt-laden winds of the coast.

Pruning. A light trimming of the leading shoots during the early years is beneficial to shape the plant as required; thereafter, pruning is necessary only to control size.

Species and cultivars

Royèna lùcida (Latin 'to shine', referring to the glossy leaves): South African Snowdrop Bush: South Africa.

Habit. An evergreen shrub to about 3 m, dense and twiggy when grown well but a little taller when pruned to tree form; ideally suited to hedging, preferably with only infrequent trimming so as to fully display the beauty of the leaves.

Leaves. Simple, alternate, broadly ovate to nearly orbicular, 2–3 cm long, 2.0–2.5 cm wide, on a reflexed petiole of 2–4 mm; apex acutecuspidate; base auriculate; margin entire but undulate; venation not conspicuous, but the midrib more so beneath; glabrous except for whitish down on the margins and midrib while young, a few bristles persisting into maturity.

Flowers. Solitary or in few-flowered clusters in the upper leaf axils, borne on a 5–15 mm pedicel, subtended by two pale green stipules about 3 mm long; calyx 4–5 mm long, conical in the bud but opening with 5 ovate hairy sepals; corolla urceolate, 5–6 mm long, the flat limb 10 mm across with 5 ovate creamy-white segments; flowering season late winter and early spring.

Fruit. A fleshy berry, globular to ovoid, 2–3 cm long, reddish, ripening in summer.

Other distinguishing features. Bark of main branches dark brown, reddish on the young twigs.

Climatic range. A, B, M, P, S, and in sheltered parts of H and lower Mts.

RUÉLLIA

Commemorating the French botanist, J. de la Ruelle.
Ruellia.
Acanthaceae, the Acanthus family.

Generic description. A large genus of soft-wooded plants, mostly from the warmer parts of South and Central America, with evergreen, opposite, often succulent leaves, sometimes handsomely veined, and funnelform or campanulate flowers in the blue, white, red, or purplish colour range, valued for their winter flowers in frost-free climates.

Propagation. a) Soft-tip cuttings taken in spring or summer root readily in a peat/sand mixture in a warm, humid atmosphere.
b) Semi-hardwood, nodal cuttings may also be used in autumn-winter, with the leaves removed or reduced proportionally with the level of atmospheric humidity attainable.

Cultivation. The species treated below is frost-tender and fragile; it needs a warm, humid, wind-sheltered site with a rich, fibrous, well-drained soil, not wanting for additional water in dry, hot weather.

Pruning. A light pruning of the lanky, erect stems is desirable after the last of the spring flowers, to maintain the density of growth and quality of foliage and flowering wood.

Species and cultivars

Ruéllia macrántha (Greek 'with large flowers'): margins of the forest-lands of tropical Brazil.

Habit. An evergreen shrub to 1.5–2.0 m, with erect, jointed stems, forming a vase-shaped bush.

Leaves. Simple, opposite, narrowly ovate, 12–18 cm long and 4–6 cm wide; petiole 2–3 cm long; apex acuminate; base cuneate; margin entire, midrib and laterals prominent beneath; succulent but slightly scabrous; dark green and barely shiny above, paler and dull beneath.

Flowers. Solitary in the upper axils, several close together forming a loose panicle; calyx to

2.5 cm, green, of 5 linear-lanceolate sepals; corolla funnelform-campanulate, 8–10 cm long, the lower tube slender, expanding into a 5-lobed limb to 7–8 cm across, the lobes slightly reflexed, cyclamen-purple, paler in the throat and with darker veins; stamens 4, as long as the tube, filaments yellow-brown, anthers nut-brown; pistil 1, purplish, with bifurcate stigma; flowers borne abundantly from early winter to October.

Climatic range. B, T, and on warm, sheltered sites in S.

RUSSÉLIA

Commemorating Alexander Russell, eighteenth-century physician and author.
Russelia; Coral-Plant.
Scrophulariaceae, the Figwort family.

Generic description. A small genus of tender shrubs from Central America with slender, rush-like stems, opposite or whorled leaves, sometimes little more than scales, clustered at the nodes, and tubulate flowers borne freely over an extended period beginning in spring.

Propagation. Firmwood cuttings of the almost leafless stems strike readily in a sand/peat mixture in a warm, moist environment.

Cultivation. The species described are best grown in a warm, sheltered position, in a locality where minimum temperatures remain above −2°C. A well-drained, moderately fertile soil is suitable.

Pruning. Several of the oldest shoots should be removed at the base each year to make way for new water-shoots which soon develop into full flowering quality. The flowered shoots may be reduced slightly to remove the spent inflorescences, preferably in late winter before the new growth.

Species and cultivars

Russélia equisetifòrmis (Latin from 'Equisetum', the Horse-tails, descriptive of the tail-like form of the branches) (syn. *R. juncea*) Coral-Plant: Mexico.

Habit. An evergreen shrub of loose, open growth to 1.5 m, of indefinite form but with many slender, arching branches from the base.

Leaves. Simple, 5- or 6-whorled on the larger stems but often opposite on the flowering stems; ovate-lanceolate to 1 cm but frequently reduced to scales; petiole 3–4 mm; apex acute; margin irregular, entire to remotely serrate; bronze to bright green.

Flowers. Inflorescence a loose, elongate panicle 20–40 cm long, at the end of the rush-like stems; calyx campanulate to 3 mm diameter, purplish, the 5 teeth shallow but acute; corolla scarlet, tubulate to 2 cm long and 4 mm wide, opening to the 5-parted limb; stamens 4, filaments cream, anthers yellowish; pistil solitary, pink; flowers abundant from October to March.

Fruit. Not seen.

Other distinguishing features. Stems marked longitudinally, between the somewhat distant nodes, with 5 or 6 parallel ridges, green or slightly bronze.

Climatic range. B, P, S, T, and in warm, sheltered microclimates in A and M.

Russélia sarmentòsa (Latin 'bearing prostrate stems or sarments'): Mexico and Central America.

Habit. An evergreen, leafy shrub to 1.5 m tall but often broader because of the many spreading, almost-prostrate lateral stems.

Leaves. Simple, ovate, opposite, 6–8 cm long and 5–6 cm wide on young vigorous shoots but reduced to 2.5 cm long and 1.5 cm wide and 3-whorled on the flowering shoots; petiole 2–3 mm long and as broad; apex acute to acuminate; base broadly cuneate to truncate; margin crenate-serrate; midrib and main laterals very prominent beneath, dotted with translucent glands; glabrous; mid green and slightly shiny above, paler beneath.

Flowers. Inflorescence a small cyme, 3-whorled in the upper axils of the erect shoots, with about 10 flowers in each cyme; flowers tubulate, 1.0–1.5 cm long, on slender 5–6 mm pedicels; calyx urceolate to 4 mm, with a short tube and 5 long slender sepals, reddish-green; corolla to 3 mm wide near the 5-lobed apex, scarlet, lined densely inside with short yellow hairs, flowering abundantly from October to late March, and later in very warm areas.

Fruit. Not seen.

Other distinguishing features. Stems conspicuously angular, with 4 or 6 longitudinal, knife-like ridges running decurrently below the pubescent leaf bases.

Climatic range. B, S, T, and in sheltered microclimates in A, M, and P.

SAMBÙCUS

Latin name for the Elder, said to be from *sambuca*, a zither-like instrument made from the wood.
Elder.
Caprifoliaceae, the Honeysuckle family.

Generic description. A genus of deciduous shrubs and small trees from Asia, Europe, and North America, with compound leaves, some colouring well in autumn, white flowers in large terminal corymbs or panicles, and colourful drupaceous fruit. Two species grown in Australia for their variegated-leafed cultivars.

Propagation. a) Soft-tip cuttings taken in spring or early summer root readily if placed in a warm, humid atmosphere.
b) Hardwood cuttings, taken at pruning time in winter and planted deeply in a friable medium, preferably in individual containers.

Cultivation. A moderately rich, moist soil with reliable water supply in summer, in a sunny exposure, is ideal. When grown in dry soils, in summer the tender leaves of the coloured cultivars are inclined to burn but when grown in shade, much of their colour is lost.

Pruning. A well-grown shrub is best pruned back in winter by one-third of its size to develop density of growth and to improve the quality and size of the leaves; the hemispherical shape of the plant should be preserved.

Species and cultivars

Sambùcus canadénsis (Latin 'from Canada'): American Elder: SE Canada and USA.
Habit. A deciduous, strong-growing shrub to 3.5 m tall, of irregular, broad outline with many stout branches arching outwards from the base.
Leaves. Compound, opposite, imparipinnate, to 20–30 cm long, with mostly 7 or 9 leaflets arranged in opposite pairs, the main rachis grooved on the upper surface; terminal leaflet oblanceolate, only slightly larger than the others; leaflets almost sessile, lanceolate to narrow-ovate to 10 cm long and 2–4 cm wide, the lower leaflets occasionally laciniate or with small sub-leaflets; apex acuminate; base obtuse, often slightly oblique; margin sharply serrate, but entire near the base; midrib prominent beneath; glabrous except for fine pubescence on the midrib above and on all veins beneath; bright green above, paler beneath, changing to yellow in autumn, the better in cool, moist climates.
Flowers. Inflorescence a nearly flat, terminal, compound, 5-rayed cyme to 20 cm across, the individual flowers numerous, 8 mm across, rotate, with 5 ovate lobes, pure white, flowering in November and December; stamens 5, to 3 mm long, filaments white, anthers golden-yellow.
Fruit. A mostly 5-seeded, fleshy drupe to 4–5 mm across, globular, on slender 3–5 mm pedicels, borne in a broad cymose head well clear of the upper leaves; fruits green at first but ripening in May to dark claret-red.
Other distinguishing features. Upper twigs green, becoming brownish, with sparse brown lenticels and a thick central core of white pith.
'Aùrea': Golden American Elder: has greenish-yellow leaves when grown in shade but colouring richly to butter-yellow when grown in sun in spring and autumn especially. An extremely showy plant if treated generously to food and additional water in dry times.
Climatic range. A, H, M, Mts, P, S.

Sambùcus nigra (Latin, *niger*, black, descriptive of the black berries): European Elder: Europe, western Asia and North Africa.
Habit. A somewhat tree-like plant to 8 m tall in its native habitat but mostly shrubby to 4–5 m tall and as wide in Australia.
Leaves. Compound, opposite, imparipinnate, the leaflets mostly 5 but occasionally 7, the terminal leaflet with a 1.5 cm petiolule, the others shorter; leaflets elliptic to ovate 6–10 cm long and 3–4 cm broad; apex acute; base obtuse or cuneate; margin serrate, the lower half entire or nearly so; midrib prominent below and finely tomentose, otherwise glabrous; mid-green above, paler beneath, turning yellow in autumn; leaves have an unpleasant smell when bruised.
Flowers. Inflorescence a terminal, 5-rayed compound cyme, 12–18 cm across, the flowers creamy-white, with a strong, disagreeable odour, flowering from late October to December.
Fruit. A small fleshy drupe 6–8 mm across, black and glossy, borne in a large cymose cluster well clear of the upper leaves in late summer and autumn.
Other distinguishing features. Upper branchlets pale grey or yellowish-green, with shallow longitudinal grooves and prominent brown lenticels.
'Álbo-variegàta' has smaller leaves with an irregular margin of creamy-white in spring, paling in summer to almost pure white. A smaller plant, rarely more than 2 m tall and as wide.

'Aùreo-variegàta' has an irregular yellow margin but is otherwise of similar habit.
Both cultivars should be grown in full sun to produce effective colour of foliage but must not be allowed to become dry at the roots, otherwise the foliage will burn.
Climatic range. A, H, M, Mts, P, S.

Sambùcus racemòsa (Latin 'with flowers in a raceme'): Red-berried Elder or European Red Elder: Europe to western Asia.
Habit. A large deciduous shrub to about 3 m tall, the crown usually hemispherical to 3–4 m across.
Leaves. Imparipinnate, with 5 or 7 ovate-elliptic leaflets 5–8 cm long, the terminal leaflet larger; apex acuminate; base obtuse to cuneate; margin serrate; glabrous; pale green at first, maturing to deep green in summer and changing to clear yellow in autumn.
Flowers. Inflorescence a domed terminal panicle about 8–10 cm tall and 5–6 cm wide, the small stellate flowers creamy-white, flowering on the upper new shoots during September and October.
Fruit. A dense, rounded cluster of drupes each 5–6 mm across, bright crimson, fully coloured in November and lasting until taken by birds.
'Plumòsa Aùrea' is slightly smaller in growth, the leaves with deeply-cut margins, often half-way to the midrib, butter-yellow, the colour improved in plants grown in fertile, moist soils with protection from harsh, drying winds.
Climatic range. H, M, Mts, and in cool, sheltered microclimates in A, P, and S.

SCHEFFLÈRA (Sometimes included in Brassaia)

Commemorating the Polish botanist, G. C. Scheffler, botanical explorer in many tropical countries; died in Uganda in 1910.
Queensland Umbrella Tree.
Araliaceae, the Ginseng family.

Generic description. A large tropical genus of more than 100 species of evergreen trees and shrubs with mostly digitately compound leaves and racemose or paniculate flowers; several species are used extensively as indoor or terrace plants, at least while young, and later as garden, street, or park trees, the two species listed below popular in warm climates along the eastern Australian coastal strip.

Propagation. a) Seeds are collected as soon as ripe, cleaned and sown at once in a friable sowing mixture in a warm, humid atmosphere. b) Short hardwood cuttings are taken in autumn-winter and struck in individual containers, preferably in a controlled glass-house.

Cultivation. Both species make rapid growth in any moderately fertile soil with free drainage but with adequate summer water; the ideal position is warm and sunny, with protection from violent or cold wind, but lightly shaded sites are also suitable. Both are hardy to mild frosts when fully acclimatised but are easily damaged by more severe cold.

Pruning. The only pruning necessary is the removal of spent inflorescences immediately after flowering, or of the occasional misplaced shoot. *S. actinophylla*, when grown as a tree in the open, should have competing leaders removed; *S. venulosa* is usually grown as a large shrub, sometimes needing restraint where space is limited.

Species and cultivars

Schefflèra actinophýlla (from the Greek *actis* 'a ray', and *phullon* 'a leaf', referring to the radially arranged leaflets): Queensland Umbrella Tree (syn. *Brassaia actinophylla*) Northern Qld coastal region and neighbouring islands.
Habit. An evergreen shrub attaining 12–15 m tall in the moist, humid forest lands of its native habitat, but elsewhere usually seen as a multi-stemmed specimen plant to 5–6 m tall, of erect growth with stems of about equal size carrying an abundance of handsome foliage.
Leaves. Compound, alternate, digitate, with 7 to 15 radially arranged leaflets; petiole 15–35 cm long and 4–8 mm thick, terete and tough, the base flared broadly; petiolules 5–9 cm long, 2–3 mm thick, slightly grooved above, green to brownish; leaflets oblong-elliptic, 15–30 cm long, 5–10 cm wide; apices shortly acuminate; bases obtuse to cuneate; margins entire, thickened; midrib and main veins yellow-green; texture coriaceous; glabrous; bright green and lustrous above, paler and somewhat dull beneath.
Flowers. Inflorescence a broad cluster of slender racemes, several to 20 or so together from the upper terminals; flowers sessile in small dense heads to 1.5 cm across, closely clustered on 1 cm long, reddish-peduncles scattered along the rachides; flowers deep-crimson, with conspicu-

ous cream stamens; flowers rich in nectar; flowering season from February to August.
Fruit. A reddish, 1-seeded, fleshy drupe ripening in winter and spring.
Other distinguishing features. Upper stems bright green, marked with large leaf-bases and pale-brown lenticels.
Climatic range. B, P, S, T, and in warm, sheltered microclimates in A and M.

Schefflèra venulòsa (Latin 'with small veins'): India, South-East Asia, Indonesia and Northern Qld.
Habit. An evergreen shrub of indefinite form to 3 m or more tall, with several to many cane-like trunks supporting the leafy crown.
Leaves. Compound, alternate, digitate, borne on a stout terete petiole 15–25 cm long, the shallowly channelled petiolules 3–4 cm long, glabrous, yellow-green; leaflets 5 to 7, variable in shape but mostly elliptic-ovate, 10–18 cm long and 5–7 cm wide; apices acuminate; bases rounded; margins entire, the edges translucent; midrib alone raised beneath; glabrous; lustrous green above, paler beneath.
Flowers. In a chain of umbels 30–35 cm long, the main rachis and minor rachides terete, deep ruby-red, forming a pendulous raceme; umbels of 10–20 flowers, greenish to nearly white; flowering season, spring to early summer.
Fruit. A small globose drupe to 4 mm wide, borne in a symmetrical umbel of 10–20 fruits; greenish at first, becoming dull orange to reddish-brown in late summer, usually at their best in February.
Climatic range. B, P, S, T.

SÈDUM

The ancient Latin name for the Stone-crop, *Sedum acre*, a common plant around the Mediterranean region.
Mexican Sedum.
Crassulaceae, the Orpine family.

Generic description. Mostly succulent, perennial low shrubs or herbs with alternate, opposite or whorled leaves, sometimes with a notched margin; flowers are borne in cymose clusters in a variety of colours, the floral parts 4- or 5-merous. A large genus of over 250 species, native to the northern temperate zone, with a few from colder parts.

Propagation. Almost any kind of stem material

will root easily in a sand/peat medium, kept somewhat drier than the normal propagating conditions.

Cultivation. A well-drained sandy soil in a warm, sunny position is ideal. While tolerant of dry stony ground in its native habitat, the species described below responds favourably to better soils and regular watering in dry times. Safe to 0°C but damaged by frost in severe climates.

Pruning. Removal of spent flower stems is sufficient to keep the plant from becoming unkempt; an occasional light tip-pruning of lanky stems may also be necessary when the plant is growing too strongly.

Species and cultivars
Sèdum praeáltum (Latin 'very tall', in contrast with the lower, ground-covering species): Mexican Sedum: Mexico.
Habit. An evergreen shrub to 0.75 m tall, but of sprawling habit, forming a wide, bun-shaped bush 1.0–1.5 m across, the lower stems decumbent.
Leaves. Simple, alternate, oblanceolate, to 7 cm long and 2 cm wide, fleshy and about 5 mm thick; apex slightly acute; base tapering to the fleshy stem without a distinct petiole; margin entire; glabrous; venation indistinct; bright green on both surfaces often edged with red.
Flowers. Inflorescence a terminal cyme, 10–15 cm tall and as wide; calyx crateriform to 4–5 mm across, fleshy, green, with 5 claw-shaped sepals; petals 5, forming a stellate corolla to 2 cm across, butter-yellow, flowering in spring, mainly September to early November; stamens 10, the greenish-yellow filaments nearly as long as the petals.
Fruit. Not seen — plant possibly sterile.
Other distinguishing features. Upper fleshy stems becoming yellowish within the inflorescence, otherwise green.
Climatic range. B, I, M, P, S, T.

SENÈCIO

Derived from the Latin, *senescere* 'to age', alluding to the white bristly hairs of the pappus.
Dusty Miller: Velvet Groundsel.
Asteraceae, the Aster family; (formerly Compositae, the Composite family).

Generic description. An extensive and varied

genus of over 2000 species of annuals, perennials, climbers and shrubs. The representative species listed here are evergreen woody plants with simple, alternate leaves, yellow flowers in broad corymbose clusters over the crown of the plant, and fruit a pappus-bearing achene.

Propagation. Semi-hardwood cuttings, with most of the leaves removed, strike well in a warm, humid atmosphere, preferably in individual containers to minimise root disturbance when moving on or planting out.

Cultivation. The senecios are vigorous plants, easily grown in any moderately fertile soil with free drainage. *S. cineraria* is tolerant of light frosts to −2° or −3°C, but the others are more sensitive and should be confined to warm, coastal gardens.

Pruning. All species need frequent tip-pruning while young to build up a dense leafy growth but once established should be pruned moderately, immediately after flowering, to remove spent inflorescences and to encourage new lateral shoots.

Species and cultivars

Senècio cinerària (Latin 'ash-coloured') (syn. *Cineraria maritima*) Dusty Miller: northern Mediterranean countries.
Habit. An evergreen shrub to 1 m or less, with soft, weak branches, forming an open bush about 1 m or more wide, the lower stems decumbent.
Leaves. Shallowly to deeply pinnatisect, 10–15 cm long, 5–7 cm wide; petiole 4–5 cm long, grooved above, finely white-tomentose; blade divided, often deeply to within 1–3 mm of the midrib, into 5–7 pairs of lobes, themselves irregularly bi- or tri-lobed in the outer half; apices of lobes obtuse to rounded; midrib and main veins prominent beneath; dark green above but made silvery-grey by the dense white-tomentose cover, almost pure white beneath.
Flowers. Inflorescence a flattish cyme over the crown of the plant, the individual flowers radiate, to 2–3 cm across, bright yellow, flowering mainly in late spring and summer but otherwise intermittent.
Fruit. A slender elongate achene, with a pappus of whitish hairs attached at the apex, ripening in autumn.
Other distinguishing features. Handsome in foliage and especially useful to provide variety of colour in a predominantly green garden.

Climatic range. A, M, P, S, and in warm microclimates on lower elevations of Mts.

Senècio grandifòlius (Latin 'with large leaves'): tropical Southern Mexico.
Habit. An evergreen shrub to 2.5–3.5 m tall and as broad, with many strong shoots from the base when well managed, forming a densely foliaged, globose bush.
Leaves. Broadly elliptic to oblong-ovate, 15 to about 45 cm long and 10 to 30 cm wide; petiole 15–25 cm long, 5–10 mm thick; apex acute; base rounded to subcordate; margin dentate with glandular tips, between the larger, coarsely sinuate lobes; midrib and main laterals prominent beneath; texture soft and waxy; dark velvety-green on the upper surface, paler and pubescent beneath.
Flowers. Inflorescence a broad, corymbose mass of small cymes, the whole to 35–45 cm across, borne clearly above the leaves; pedicels 5–10 mm, on soft, green, fleshy peduncles; involucre cylindrical, 6–7 mm long, 2–3 mm wide, ribbed, green; flowers radiate to 1.5 cm across, the 5 ray-florets narrowly oblong, 5 mm long and 2 mm wide, yellow; disc-florets 6–8, greenish-yellow; flowering season late summer to winter, in mild climates extending into spring.
Fruit. An elongate achene, with whitish bristly pappus attached.
Other distinguishing features. Lower stems and trunk buff-coloured, upper stems dark metallic-green with pale lenticels.
Climatic range. B, P, S, T, and in warm, sheltered microclimates in M.

Senècio petasitis (Greek *petasitos*, 'a broad-brimmed hat', worn by the ancient Greeks, referring to the large plate-like leaves): Velvet Groundsel: southern Mexico.
Habit. An evergreen shrub to 2–3 m tall, broadly rounded to 3 m wide, with erect stems from the base carrying the abundant foliage and flowers.
Leaves. Broadly ovate-cordate, 12–18 cm long and 15–20 cm wide; petiole about as long as the blade; 5–8 mm thick, dark reddish-brown; apex acute; base cordate; margin with 9 to 13 large sinuate dentate lobes, the edge ciliate and minutely glandular; main veins prominent beneath; finely pubescent on all parts; yellowish-green and dull above, paler beneath, with a whitish, nap-like, velvety surface.
Flowers. Inflorescence a terminal panicle 20–30

cm across and as deep, the rachis thick, fleshy and reddish; flowers radiate, the involucre a campanulate, ribbed tube, purplish-red and bristly; ray-florets 5, lanceolate; disc-florets 10–15, tubulate with reflexed lobes, the flowers 2.0–2.5 cm across, yellow, flowering from early July to late September.

Fruit. An achene, with a white bristly pappus.

Other distinguishing features. Upper stems thick and fleshy, pale green, pubescent, with transversely-crescentic leaf scars to 1 cm across.

Climatic range. B, M, P, S,T.

SERÍSSA

Derived from the vernacular name in its native region.
Serissa.
Rubiaceae, the Madder family.

Generic description. A monotypic genus from India and South-East Asia, the single species forming a low spreading shrub, the foliage with an unpleasant odour when crushed, the small white flowers borne across the top of the plant throughout the year. The plant is seen mostly in the variegated-leafed form chosen by the Australian Federation of Nurserymen as the 1971 'Shrub of the Year'.

Propagation. Soft-tip cuttings taken in spring and summer strike readily in a warm, humid atmosphere; older wood is also used in autumn and winter.

Cultivation. A moderately fertile, coarse-textured soil in a warm, sunny position suits the plant well. It is tolerant of light frosts to about –2°C.

Pruning. Light pruning annually in late winter is beneficial.

Species and cultivars

Seríssa japónica (Latin 'from Japan') (syn. *S. foetida*): South-East Asia.

Habit. An evergreen shrub to 1 m or so tall, with an open, spreading habit usually wider than tall; useful for topiary and tub-culture.

Leaves. Simple, opposite, ovate-elliptic, to 2 cm long and 7–8 mm wide; apex acute-cuspidate; margin serrulate; stipules subulate, about 2 mm long, 3 on each side of the nodes; venation reticulate between the 4–5 pairs of lateral veins; glabrous except for the tomentose veins on the lower side; fetid when crushed; dark green and shiny above, paler beneath.

Flowers. Solitary or in small clusters near the ends of the upper twigs; calyx stellate, to 3 mm across, green; corolla funnelform to 1 cm long, the tube slender, expanded to 1.5 cm across the 5–6 lobes, rosy-heliotrope in the bud, opening to nearly pure white inside but with a fine stain of colour along the midrib of each lobe and on the outer tips, the throat and inner surface white-pilose; stamens 4–6, as long as the tube, the anthers white, the exserted white style bifurcate; flowering season extended over most of the year but more abundant in summer and autumn.

Fruit. Not seen.

Other distinguishing features. Upper twigs puberulent, deep violet-purple, becoming pale green, then grey-green in maturity.

'Variegata' (syn. 'Snowleaves') has leaves margined with creamy-yellow to 0.5 mm wide but is otherwise similar to the parent species.

Climatic range. A, B, M, P, S, T.

SPÀRTIUM

Derived from the ancient Greek name.
Spanish Broom.
Fabaceae, the Pea family.

Generic description. A genus of one species, with almost leafless, rush-like branches, simple, alternate or occasionally opposite, evergreen leaves, pea-shaped yellow flowers, and leguminous fruit. The plant is well known throughout the temperate countries and is commonly seen in shrub borders in Australia, used principally for its long flowering season and brightly coloured, perfumed flowers.

Propagation. Seeds are sown in spring under outdoor conditions, or in autumn-winter in a warm, moist atmosphere; pre-treatment in warm water for 24 hours is an advantage in accelerating germination.

Cultivation. The plant is very hardy and thrives in all Australian climates. The best soil is a friable, fertile loam with free drainage. Any open aspect with full sun exposure is suitable. Tolerant of cold to –10°C.

Pruning. Moderate pruning of the newly grown wood after the flowers have fallen prevents the plant from becoming thin and top-heavy.

Species and cultivars

Spàrtium júnceum (Latin, *juncus* 'a rush', referring to the sparsely leafed, rush-like twigs):

Spanish Broom: Mediterranean countries and islands.

Habit. An evergreen shrub to 3 m or so, forming a dense, rounded bush when pruned occasionally but sometimes seen as a small tree.

Leaves. Sparse, simple, mostly alternate, linear to lanceolate, 3.5 cm long; apex acute; margin entire; silky pubescent when young but becoming glabrous; glaucous-green above, paler beneath.

Flowers. Inflorescence a terminal raceme, occasionally to 25–30 cm long, with about 20–30 flowers, calyx a slender, green papery tube; corolla pea-shaped, the standard almost orbicular to 2.5 cm across, bright yellow, with a few faint reddish-brown streaks; wings elliptical, yellow; keel lanceolate, yellow; stamens hooked, in a curved bundle of 10; flowering from late September to early December; sweetly perfumed.

Fruit. A legume 5–7 cm long and 6–7 mm wide, silvery-silky at first, ripening to brown in summer to split and release the 10–12 shiny, disc-shaped, 3 mm seeds.

Climatic range. A, B, H, M, Mts, P, S, and inland where water is available.

SPIRAÈA

Derived from the Greek word for 'wreath', the flowering branches being used for garlands.
Spirea (not 'May' which belongs to *Crataegus*).
Rosaceae, the Rose family.

Generic description. A large genus of deciduous flowering shrubs from the northern temperate zone, particularly America and the Orient, valued as garden plants on account of their superior flowering and foliage qualities. Leaves are simple, alternate, variously toothed or lobed, flowers are mostly corymbs, panicles or umbels in white, pink, or red, abundant in spring or summer. The species described below are popular subjects for landscape planting, or lawn or border specimens but must be allowed sufficient space to display their natural form without being spoiled by injudicious pruning.

Propagation. a) Soft-tip or firmwood cuttings taken in summer, strike readily when planted in a sand/peat mixture in a warm, moist environment.
b) Some species strike well as hardwood cuttings taken in winter, preferably pre-callused in a warm place before being planted in the open or in containers.

Cultivation. Most species are hardy in the milder Australian climates but are at their best where conditions are cool and moist, and when grown in fertile soils that drain well. The species listed are tolerant of low temperatures to at least −8°C.

Pruning. To achieve the best flowering results, pruning must be performed correctly and at the proper time. Some of the oldest, less-productive stems should be removed completely at the base each year immediately after flowering, to make way for new vigorous water-shoot growth. The remaining stems should not be cut back to a geometrical shape but spent inflorescences may be removed to keep the plant tidy.

Species and cultivars

Spiraèa x *argùta* (Latin 'with a sharply toothed margin'): an interspecific hybrid between *S. thunbergii* and *S. multiflora*: Bridal Wreath.

Habit. A deciduous shrub to 1.5–2.0 m tall, with many erect stems arising from the crowded base, arching outwards at the top to form an attractive round-headed crown.

Leaves. Broadly oblanceolate to 4–5 cm long and 1.0–1.5 cm wide; apex acute; margin sharply serrate above the middle; midrib and main veins whitish-translucent; silky-pubescent and pale green when young but soon glabrous and dark green above, paler beneath, a few leaves colouring to orange-yellow and red in autumn.

Flowers. Inflorescence a 3- to 8-flowered umbel in the axils of the leafy 1-year-old shoots; calyx broadly campanulate to 6 mm wide, with 5 acute green sepals; corolla rotate, 8–12 mm across, with 5 orbicular, white petals; stamens about 20, the filaments whitish with yellow anthers; flowers produced from late September to mid-October.

Fruit. Not seen — probably sterile.

Other distinguishing features. Youngest twigs silky-pubescent and angular by the 2 decurrent ridges below the leaf bases, pale green at first, becoming reddish-brown.

Climatic range. A, H, M, Mts, P, S.

Spiraèa x *bìlliardii* (commemorating the French hybridist and nurseryman, L. C. B. Billiard): hybrid between *Spiraea douglasii* and *Spiraea salicifolia*: Billiard's Spirea:

Habit. A shrub to about 2 m tall, with a mass of upright brownish-pubescent shoots from a congested base.

Leaves. Oblong-lanceolate, 5–8 cm long and

2–3 cm wide; apex acute; base cuneate; margin serrulate; midrib and main lateral veins prominent; glabrous and bright green above, grey-green below.

Flowers. In a spire-like terminal panicle 15–18 cm tall, broadening at the base; individual flowers with conspicuous fluffy stamens, bright rose-pink, flowering from October to late December.

Fruit. None produced — the plant is a sterile hybrid.

'**Triumphans**' is the cultivar most seen in gardens, with prolific cyclamen-pink flowers.

Climatic range. A, B, H, M, Mts, P, S.

Spiraèa blùmei (commemorating K. L. Blume, German botanical author) (syn. *S. trilobata*): main islands of Japan, mostly on elevated land.

Habit. A deciduous shrub to 2 m tall, with many twiggy branches arising from the base and arching outwards to form a broad, hemispherical bush to 3 m across.

Leaves. Broadly ovate to rhombic-obovate, 2.0–4.0 cm long and 2.0–2.5 cm wide; apex rounded; margin with 2–3 pairs of crenate lobes, the lower third entire; midrib and main laterals pale yellow and prominent below; surface glabrous but rugose; dark green above, glaucous beneath, a few leaves changing to orange-yellow and scarlet in autumn before falling.

Flowers. Inflorescence a small terminal umbel of 15–20 flowers borne on leafy lateral shoots, flowers rotate, 6–9 mm across, with 5 white, orbicular petals, the stamens pale-green with cream anthers; flowering in September and October.

Other distinguishing features. Branchlets slender, flexuous, with shredding bark and prominent winter buds.

Climatic range. A, H, M, Mts, P, S.

Spiraèa x *bumálda* '**Anthony Waterer**' (commemorating a member of the English nursery family of Bagshot, Surrey): a cultivar of the interspecific hybrid between *S. japonica* and *S. albiflora*.

Habit. A deciduous shrub to 1 m or less, with erect branches issuing from a dense clump, the stems leafy and terminated in late spring and summer with broad panicles of showy flowers.

Leaves. Lanceolate, 6–7 cm long and 1.5–2.0 cm wide; apex finely acute; margin sharply and sometimes doubly serrate; main veins prominent beneath; glabrous; dark green above, glaucous beneath, occasional leaves marked with or wholly pale yellow with some pink shadings, especially towards the terminals.

Flowers. Inflorescence a corymb-like, flattened panicle to 10 cm across, borne freely at the terminals of the current season's growth; calyx broadly funnelform, purplish-red; corolla crateriform to 4 mm across, of 5 broadly ovate petals, deep crimson; stamens numerous, the filaments crimson, the anthers darker; flowers produced abundantly from late October to late December, then intermittently until winter.

Other distinguishing features. Upper twigs green and pubescent at first, becoming tan, and finally dark chocolate-brown, with a few longitudinal paler stripes.

Climatic range. A, H, M, Mts, P, S.

Spiraèa cantoniénsis (Latin 'from Canton') (syn. *S. reevesiana*): SE China.

Habit. A deciduous shrub to about 2.5 m tall, with a dense mass of erect stems arching upwards and outwards to form a round-headed shrub with the outer shoots drooping to ground-level.

Leaves. Lanceolate to broad-oblanceolate, about 5–7 cm long on the smaller twigs but 9–10 cm long on strong shoots; apex acute; margin serrate and doubly serrate, sometimes with 3 fairly distinct lobes in the upper half; midrib prominently raised beneath; glabrous; dark green and moderately shiny above, pale glaucous-green beneath.

Flowers. Inflorescence a 20- to 25-flowered umbel, borne at the terminals of leafy shoots 4–5 cm long, issuing from the past year's wood for a length of 40–50 cm; flowers rotate, about 1 cm across, calyx to 6 mm across, with 5 ovate-acute green sepals; petals typically 5 but occasionally 7, overlapped at the edges to form a nearly circular flower, pure white, flowering abundantly in September and early October; stamens about 25, shorter than the petals, filaments white, anthers yellow, then brown; pistils 5, in a central column, whitish.

Other distinguishing features. Winter buds ovoid with sharply acute apex, covered with loose brown scales; upper twigs chocolate-brown, with slightly shredding bark; wood very hard, the stems with a central core of pith.

'**Lanceàta**' (Latin 'shaped like a lance'): syn. *S. reevesiana florepleno* is similar but flowers are fully double to 1.5 cm across, with white petals slightly greenish at the base, the long unpruned 1-year-old shoots drooping beneath the mass of

flowers, giving the plant a very attractive appearance. Regarded popularly as one of the best white-flowering plants grown in Australian gardens.
Climatic range. A, H, M, Mts, P, S.

Spiraèa dóuglasii (commemorating David Douglas, Scottish botanical explorer in north-west USA): Douglas Spirea: Washington, Oregon and Northern California, mainly on the slopes of the Coast and Cascade Ranges.
Habit. A shrub to 1.5–2.0 m tall, with many erect stems, developing a few suckers from the base, the younger growths tomentose, older shoots smooth and reddish-brown.
Leaves. Elliptic-oblong, 5–10 cm long, 2–3 cm wide; petiole 3–4 mm long; apex acute; base rounded; margin serrate, the lower half entire; midrib prominent; dark green and smooth above, whitish-tomentose below.
Flowers. In a terminal, cylindrical panicle, 12–18 cm tall; flowers numerous, rotate with 5 spreading obovate petals, deep rose-red; stamens numerous, about twice the length of the petals; flowering period from October to December.
Fruit. A small, 1-celled follicle with several seeds.
Other distinguishing features. Young shoots green, pubescent, developing slightly shaggy, reddish-brown bark in age.
Climatic range. A, H, M, Mts, P, S.

Spiraèa prunifòlia '**Plèna**' (Latin 'with leaves like *Prunus*' and 'full', referring to the double flowers): Bridal-wreath Spirea: China and Korea.
Habit. A deciduous shrub to about 2 m tall, with a mass of slender, erect stems from the base, forming a rounded bush, 1.5–2.0 m wide.
Leaves. Broad-elliptic to ovate, to 3.5 cm long or larger when well grown; apex acute; margin serrulate; venation reticulate; glabrous and somewhat shiny green above, paler and pubescent beneath, colouring to orange and red in autumn.
Flowers. Inflorescence a few-flowered umbel of up to 7 or 8 flowers; calyx about 5 mm wide, of 5 rounded lobes, petals many, broadly obovate, pure-white, forming a double-rotate flower 8–10 mm across, flowering on 1- to 3-year old wood from early September to late October.
Other distinguishing features. Upper twigs somewhat angled, with prominent winter buds, dark reddish-grey when mature.

Climatic range. A, H, M, Mts, P, S.

Spiraèa thúnbergii (commemorating the Swedish systematic botanist, Carl Pehr Thunberg, 1743–1828, author of *Flora Japonica*) (syn. *S. gracilis*): Thunberg Spirea: China, but naturalised in the principal islands of Japan.
Habit. A deciduous shrub to about 1.5 m tall, with many slender branches arching gracefully outwards from the crowded base.
Leaves. Linear-lanceolate, 3.5–4.5 cm long and 5–6 mm wide; apex acute to slightly acuminate; margin finely serrulate; venation reticulate, the veins whitish-green; glabrous; pale green at first, becoming darker then changing to orange-yellow and scarlet in autumn.
Flowers. Inflorescence a 2- to 6-flowered umbel, borne at the nodes of the 1-year-old shoots, often 30–40 cm long; calyx with 5 erect, nearly orbicular teeth; petals 5, obovate, spreading, forming a rotate flower about 1 cm across, pure white; flowering from early September to mid October; stamens short, about 20, on the rim of the receptacle; flowers pleasantly fragrant.
Other distinguishing features. Youngest twigs slightly ridged longitudinally, finely pubescent.
Climatic range. A, H, M, Mts, P, S.

STACHYÙRUS

Derived from the Greek *stachys* and *oura* describing the tail-like racemes.
Early Stachyurus.
Stachyuraceae, the Stachyurus family.

Generic description. A small genus of shrubs from the Orient and Himalaya region with simple, alternate leaves, and mostly yellow campanulate flowers in axillary racemes. The species described in detail below is somewhat uncommon in gardens but worthy of greater attention by growers who seek the unusual.

Propagation. Firm tip-cuttings taken in late summer and autumn strike readily in a sand/peat mixture in a warm, humid glass-house, with mist and bottom-heat an advantage.

Cultivation. A plant from the cool, well-drained soils of the Japanese highlands, it thrives in a fertile loam, preferably with high organic content and not wanting for summer water. It is safe in light frosts to −3°C but is better for the protection of neighbouring taller plants, otherwise the flower buds may be injured.

Pruning. The only pruning required is the removal of spent inflorescences, after the flowers have faded, and untidy or badly-placed stems.

Species and cultivars

Stachyùrus praècox (Latin 'very early', referring to the flowering season): main islands of Japan, mostly in the lower mountains.

Habit. A deciduous shrub to 2–3 m tall, with an open habit of long arching stems forming a loose bush 2.5–3.5 m wide.

Leaves. Simple, alternate, elliptic-ovate to broad-ovate, 10–12 cm long and 4–8 cm wide; petiole to 3 cm long, terete but grooved, red in autumn-winter, like the midrib and 7–9 pairs of main lateral veins; apex acuminate; base rounded or sub-cordate; margin serrate; glabrous, apart from some fine hair on the veins beneath; venation reticulate, translucent; bright green at first, deepening when mature, slightly dulled above by the glaucous bloom, the lower surface shiny; leaves change in late autumn to a spectacular range of yellow, tan-orange and bright scarlet.

Flowers. Inflorescence a pendulous raceme to 18 cm long from the upper nodes; flower buds enclosed in red-brown scales; sepals and petals 4-merous, corolla campanulate, 7–8 mm long, open at the mouth but not reflexed, pale yellow-green in late winter and spring; stamens 8, yellowish, style 1, with large green stigma.

Fruit. A fleshy berry to 1.5 cm long and 8 mm wide, separating into 4 equally partitioned cells with numerous small brown seeds.

Other distinguishing features. Upper branchlets coppery-green, shallowly ridged and heavily dotted with rounded whitish lenticels, the bark copper-red in summer.

Climatic range. A, H, M, P, S, and on warm sites on the lower levels of Mts.

STRANVAÈSIA

Commemorating William Thomas Horner Fox-Strangways, nineteenth-century Earl of Ilchester and amateur botanist.
Stranvaesia.
Rosaceae, the Rose family.

Generic description. A small genus of ever-green shrubs from the Orient and the eastern Himalayas, strongly resembling several of the larger Cotoneasters, grown for their showy fruits in autumn. See specific notes below for detailed description of the leading species.

Propagation. a) Seeds are collected as soon as ripe in autumn, cleaned and stored in just-moist sphagnum moss at 4°–5°C until spring, then sown in a friable material in a warm, humid atmosphere.

b) Leafy tip cuttings are also used, taken in late summer and struck in a sand/peat mixture in controlled environmental conditions.

Cultivation. Stranvaesias are easily grown in a well-drained soil of moderate fertility, in a cool-temperate climate with winter temperatures not below −15°C.

Pruning. The plant described is more or less self-shaping and performs well without pruning; old neglected specimens may benefit from severe pruning in late winter, followed by additional feeding and watering.

Species and cultivars

Stranvaèsia davidiàna (commemorating Abbé Armand David, nineteenth-century French missionary, naturalist and botanical collector in China): western China.

Habit. An evergreen shrub to 3–5 m, with a short main trunk and spreading branches, forming a broad hemispherical crown to 3–5 m across.

Leaves. Simple, alternate, narrowly elliptic to oblanceolate, 3–10 cm long and 1.2–2.5 cm wide; petiole to 1.5 cm long, puberulent, creamy-green to red; apex acute-mucronate; margin entire-undulate; downy midrib prominent beneath; puberulent when young but soon glabrous; pinkish at first, maturing to dark green above, paler and slightly glaucous beneath, some leaves changing to scarlet and persisting through winter to spring.

Flowers. Inflorescence a leafy, terminal panicle to 8–9 cm across; flowers numerous, rotate, 9–10 mm across, 5-petalled, white, the petals obovate to nearly orbicular; stamens 15–25, 5 mm long, with white filaments and reddish anthers; flowers borne freely between October and December.

Fruit. A small globose pome 6–8 mm across, green at first, ripening in autumn to coral-scarlet and persisting throughout winter.

Climatic range. A, H, M, Mts, P, S.

STRELÍTZIA

After Charlotte Sophia of Mecklenburgh-Strelitz, a patron of botany who married King George III.
Bird's Tongue Flower or Crane Flower.
Strelitziaceae, the Strelitzia family; (formerly included in Musaceae).

Generic description. A small genus of 5 species of soft-wooded plants, grown for their remarkable flowers and large leaves, and used as accent plants or for special foliage effects. The species are mostly low in growth to 2 m or so, without a visible stem, the leaves developing from underground rhizomes, but with 2 tall exceptions in *S. alba* and *S. nicolai*. Leaves vary from those with a rush-like petiole and spoon-shaped blade to those with a pronounced blade 30 to 60 cm long and a petiole to 60 cm or more. Flowers are borne either at the top of a long leafless scape, or, in the woody species, from the upper leaf axils, carried in a sheath-like bract, the flowers 4 to about 10 in each. The floral parts are erect and spiky, in mostly white, pale-blue, yellow, orange, and deep violet-blue, standing above the spathe, the flowers opening in succession.

Propagation. a) Seeds sown as soon as ripe in late spring germinate readily in a warm, humid atmosphere; the flowers are usually cross-pollinated manually as an aid to fertilization.
b) An established clump may be lifted and separated into a number of new rhizome divisions in late winter, the new pieces being re-established for several months in a sheltered frame or glass-house.

Cultivation. The Strelitzias enjoy a freely drained soil, ideally light and friable, with the addition of coarse compost. An abundant water-supply is essential during hot, dry weather. A warm, sun-exposed aspect, sheltered from strong or cold wind is preferred.

Pruning. The only pruning necessary is the regular removal of old disfigured leaves as they deteriorate, and spent flower stems.

Species and cultivars
Strelítzia regìnae (Latin 'of the Queen'): Bird's Tongue Flower or Crane Flower, *not* Bird of Paradise Flower: south-eastern coastal South Africa.
Habit. An evergreen plant to about 1.2 m tall, gradually spreading to 2–3 m wide, composed of a trunkless clump of banana-like leaves and leafless flower scapes.

Leaves. Simple, radical, to 1 m long, the oblong-ovate blade to 50 cm long and 20 cm broad; petiole to nearly 1 m long, oval in section and about 2 cm thick, glaucous-green, smooth, finely striate; apex acute and cuspidate; base obtuse; margin entire; venation finely striate, the central vein prominent beneath, the blade dark green and glossy above, paler and glaucous below.

Flowers. Borne on a long, solid scape to 1.2 m, terminating in a boat-shaped spathe 20 cm long, mostly purplish-green; the flowers, 4 to about 10, issue in succession from the top of the spathe and comprise 3 bright-orange, boat-shaped sepals to 10 cm long, enclosing the violet-blue petals, one small and ovate, the other two united into a 10 cm spear-like, vertical shaft, complete with barb and bristle-like point; flowering season from late April to November.

Fruit. A 3-celled, soft-wooded capsule ripening the many seeds in summer.

Other distinguishing features. A strikingly handsome species much in demand by florists for its long-lasting flowers.

Climatic range. A, B, M, P, S, T.

Other species less commonly planted are:

Strelítzia x parvifòlia (Latin 'with small leaves'): Small-leafed Strelitzia: is a plant of similar style to *S. reginae*, excepting that the foliage texture is finer, the blade being spatula-like or oblanceolate, to 15–18 cm long and 4–5 cm wide, the petiole to 1 m long.

Strelítzia júncea (Latin 'rush-like'): has the leaf blade further reduced to 6–8 cm long and 3–4 cm wide, to resemble a long slender spoon.

Two other species are occasionally seen, mostly in botanical collections, both much taller than the foregoing, to at least 6 m or so, forming a coarse-foliaged, open clump with erect, woody stems, the flowers carried high on the upper stems:

Strelítzia álba (Latin 'white') (syn. *S. augústa*) has white flowers with purplish pedicels, the boat-shaped spathe deep purple, on a short peduncle.

Strelítzia nícolai (commemorating Czar Nicholas): has white flowers, stained with pale mauve-blue, usually several together on a short peduncle.

Climatic range. All A, B, M, P, S, T.

STREPTOSÒLEN

Derived from the Greek, describing the curiously twisted corolla tube.

Orange Browallia; Orange Marmalade-bush in South Africa.

Solanaceae, the Potato family.

Generic description. A monotypic evergreen species from tropical South America, popular in Australian gardens for its spectacular floral display. See specific notes below for details.

Propagation. Soft-tip cuttings taken in late spring and summer strike readily in a warm, moist atmosphere, as do semi-hardwood cuttings in autumn or winter, with bottom heat then an advantage.

Cultivation. The most suitable position is in full sun with shelter from cold and boisterous winds; the ideal soil is light, fibrous and freely drained but should be kept well supplied with water in dry times. The plant is not tolerant of frost.

Pruning. Frequent tip-pruning in the first year or two will develop a densely foliaged bush; thereafter regular light pruning after the flowering period will maintain its quality.

Species and cultivars

Streptosòlen jámesonii (commemorating William Jameson, Professor of Natural Sciences at the University of Quito, Ecuador) (syn. *Browallia jamesonii*): Ecuador, Colombia and northern Peru.

Habit. An evergreen shrub to 2 m tall and 1.5 m wide, the flexible branches responding to training over a support or fanning on a wall.

Leaves. Simple, alternate, ovate to 2–4 cm long and 1.0–2.5 cm wide; petiole 4–5 mm, grooved above, pubescent; apex acute; margin entire; midrib and main laterals prominent beneath; finely pubescent on all surfaces; dark green and slightly shiny above, paler beneath.

Flowers. Inflorescence a dense, corymbose panicle of 20–30 flowers, borne at the terminals of the young shoots; pedicels 7–8 mm, slender; calyx tubulate-campanulate to 1 cm long, 3–4 mm wide, the tube dark green and pubescent, with 5 black ribs; corolla salver-funnelform, the twisted, curved tube to 2.5 cm long, the limb expanded to 2.0–2.5 cm across the 5 broad, unequal lobes, all parts finely pubescent. Two floral forms are available, the more common with a colourful mixture of yellows and reds to tangerine-orange and nasturtium-red; the other form has pure yellow flowers; both flower abundantly from late August to late November, then intermittently throughout the year, some winter flowers being seen in warm microclimates; stamens 4, the longer pair as long as the tube; filaments and anthers yellow; pistil 1, with large green stigma.

Fruit. Seeds not seen.

Climatic range. B, S, T, and in warm, frost-free microclimates in M.

STROBILÁNTHES (syn. *Goldfussia* in part)

Derived from the Greek words describing the cone-like inflorescence.

Purple-leafed Strobilanthes; Goldfussia.

Acanthaceae, the Acanthus family.

Generic description. A large genus of tender, mostly soft-wooded plants from tropical Asia and the Orient with simple, opposite leaves sometimes handsomely coloured, and white, blue, or purple flowers in terminal spikes. The species listed below are grown in warm, sheltered gardens in humid climates, mainly along the eastern Australian coastal strip.

Propagation. Soft-tip or semi-hardwood stem cuttings taken between late summer and winter strike readily in a sand/peat mixture in a warm, humid atmosphere.

Cultivation. A fertile, light-textured soil is best, preferably in a warm, wind-sheltered environment.

Pruning. The plants need to be tip-pruned frequently in the early years to build up a dense, leafy habit; thereafter an annual shortening of the strong leading shoots and removal of spent flowers is beneficial.

Species and cultivars

Strobilánthes anisophýllus (Greek 'with leaves of unequal size'): India, mainly Assam (syn. *Goldfussia anisophylla*).

Habit. An evergreen shrub to 1.5 m tall, conical at first, but becoming globose, with many erect, brittle stems from the base.

Leaves. Simple, opposite, lanceolate, each pair unequal in size, the larger leaves to 8–12 cm long and 2 cm wide, the smaller leaves to 5–7 cm long and 1 cm wide; petiole 5–7 mm long, winged at the edges; apex attenuate; margin shallowly serrulate; veins prominent above;

glabrous; dark green above, paler beneath, stained blackish-purple on both sides.

Flowers. Inflorescence a spike of 1 to about 6 flowers, often forming a panicle; flowers subtended by purplish bracts 4–8 mm long; calyx tubulate, 5-lobed, pubescent, greenish-white, with purplish tips; corolla funnelform-campanulate to 2 cm long, widening to 1.3 cm at the mouth, the 5 lobes equal and emarginate; corolla whitish at first, maturing to lavender at the mouth with white and violet veins inside; stamens 4, filaments white, anthers cream; flowering mainly in spring but intermittently throughout the year, rarely without a few flowers.

Other distinguishing features. Upper shoots somewhat flexuose, squared in section by the decurrent ridges below the leaves, the stems swollen conspicuously just above the nodes; stems green to blackish-purple.

Climatic range. B, S, T, and in warm, sheltered microclimates in A, M, and P.

Strobilánthes dyerànus (commemorating an early Director of the Royal Botanic Garden, Kew, William Thiselton-Dyer): tropical South-East Asia, especially Burma.

Habit. An evergreen, soft-wooded shrub to 1 m or so, with erect, leafy shoots from the base, somewhat thin and leggy unless regularly pruned.

Leaves. Simple, in opposite pairs, 12–24 cm long, 4–10 cm wide, narrowly elliptic; sessile; apex acuminate; base tapered, sub-cordate to auriculate, the wings partly clasping the stem; margin serrulate and finely puckered; venation finely reticulate, the rugose surface with raised midrib and main laterals, prominently so beneath; bristly and metallic purplish-green above, with a pair of somewhat irregular, nearly parallel bands of rosy-purple extending from base to apex midway between the midrib and margin, glabrous and dark beetroot-purple beneath.

Flowers. Inflorescence an erect terminal spike, 5–10 cm tall and clear of the upper leaves; calyx with 5 linear lobes; corolla tubulate, 3–4 cm long, the 5-lobed limb rotate, the lobes recurved, pale rosy-violet, flowering in spring and summer.

Other distinguishing features. Upper stems dull metallic-green, squarish, with swollen nodes, heavily pubescent, grooved on decussately opposite internodes, less so on the others.

Climatic range. B, P, S, T, and in warm, sheltered microclimates in A and M.

STYPHÈLIA

Derived from the Greek, *styphelos* 'rigid', thought to refer to the stiff, spiky habit of the plants.

Five-corners (various).

Epacridaceae, the Epacris family.

Generic description. An Australian genus of small evergreen shrubs with simple, alternate leaves and tubulate flowers borne in the upper axils. For details, see specific notes below.

Propagation. When available, seeds are the easiest means of propagation, being sown in a warm, humid atmosphere as soon as possible after collection. Otherwise, soft-tip cuttings are taken in early summer.

Cultivation. Coarse sands and loams are the most suitable soil types, preferably kept moderately moist and cool with a thick vegetative mulch. Partial over-head shade is desirable but not essential.

Pruning. Early tip-pruning helps to develop a densely leafed bush, with improved flowering performance.

Species and cultivars

Styphèlia triflòra (Latin 'three-flowered'): Three-flowered or Pink Five-corners: eastern Australia, mainly on sandy heathlands on the coastal plains and open forests.

Habit. A thin shrub of indeterminate form to about 1 m tall.

Leaves. Oblong-lanceolate, 2–3 cm long, 5–6 mm wide; apex acute, with a sharp tip; margin entire; surface flat or shallowly concave; glabrous; pale glaucous-green.

Flowers. Pendulous, in small clusters in the upper axils; calyx tubulate, 1 cm long, with 5 overlapped sepals and chaffy bracts, glaucous-pink; corolla tube to 2 cm long, with 5 recurved lobes, densely hairy within, pink to rosy red at the base, shading to yellow at the mouth; stamens 5, exserted; pistil 1; flowering from August to November.

Fruit. A succulent drupe, 5-celled, with a single seed in each.

Climatic range. A, B, H, M, Mts, P, S.

SYMPHORICARPOS

Derived from the Greek words describing the clustered fruits.
Snowberry; Coral-berry; Indian Currant.
Caprifoliaceae, the Honeysuckle family.

Generic description. A small genus of deciduous shrubs, mainly from North America, with simple, opposite leaves, campanulate or funnel-form flowers in the axils of the upper shoots of the previous year's growth, and globose drupaceous fruits, either white or reddish, containing 2 flattish seeds. The species listed below are occasionally grown in Australia mainly for their showy fruits or variegated foliage.

Propagation. a) Semi-hardwood leafy cuttings taken between late spring and early autumn strike readily in a cool, moist atmosphere in a sand/peat mixture.
b) Hardwood cuttings taken in winter are more commonly used, sometimes planted directly in the open but preferably first established in individual containers in a cool, sheltered shade-house.

Cultivation. A moderately fertile soil, with good aeration and free drainage, is satisfactory, ideally in a cool, moist climate with a plentiful summer rainfall. The species listed are hardy in severe conditions of cold. They are seen at their best along the tablelands on the better class soils.

Pruning. Pruning should be confined to the removal of several of the oldest basal shoots in winter each year to make way for the growth of new watershoots.

Species and cultivars

Symphoricàrpos álbus (Latin 'white', referring to the fruit) (syn. *S. racemosus*) Common Snowberry: North America, east of the Rocky Mountains.
Habit. A deciduous shrub to about 1 m tall, with slender, erect, arching shoots arising from a central clump, forming a globose bush.
Leaves. Simple, opposite, the blade elliptic to broad-obovate, 4–5 cm long and 3–4 cm wide, the petiole 5–6 mm long; apex rounded; base bluntly obtuse; margin entire or sometimes sinuate with about 2 to 4 lobes on each side, the sinuses 5 to 10 mm deep; midrib and main laterals prominent beneath; glabrous, slightly shiny and bright green above, paler, finely pubescent and dull beneath.

Flowers. Inflorescence a cluster of flowers at the ends and in the upper axils of the 1-year-old shoots; corolla campanulate, 6–7 mm long, pubescent inside, pale coral-pink, flowering in October and November.
Fruit. A white drupe to 1 cm across, globose or slightly obovoid, soft and succulent, containing 2 white, flat-sided seeds 3–4 mm long, the fruits borne in terminal and axillary clusters of 10 to 30, abundant in April-May, especially striking in a typical autumn landscape of brightly coloured leaves and green grass.
Other distinguishing features. Upper twigs thin, wiry, shiny but finely pubescent.
Climatic range. A, H, M, Mts, P, S.

Symphoricàrpos rivulàris (Latin 'from the margin of a rivulet'): (syn. *S. albus* var. *laevigatus*) Garden Snowberry: is a larger, more vigorous grower to 1.5–2.0 m tall, forming a mass of erect, suckering shoots, the foliage and flowers larger, but otherwise similar to those of *S. albus*, and with larger white fruits to at least 1.3 cm across, very showy in autumn. This is probably the most commonly planted species of Snowberry in Australian gardens.

Symphoricàrpos orbiculàtus (Latin 'spherical', referring to the globose fruits): Indian Currant or Coral-berry: USA, east of the Rocky Mountains.
Habit. A small deciduous shrub to 2 m tall, with many slender shoots issuing from a crowded base and arching outwards to form a rounded crown.
Leaves. Simple, opposite, broadly elliptic-ovate, to 3.5 cm long and 2.0 cm wide; petiole 2–3 mm long, pubescent, grooved above; apex obtuse to acute-mucronate; base rounded; margin entire but undulate and finely ciliate; midrib and main veins prominent beneath; mid-green and glabrous but not shiny above, glaucous and finely pubescent beneath, becoming deep red in late autumn and persisting into winter.
Flowers. In clusters at the end of the 1-year-old shoots; corolla campanulate, about 5–6 mm long, with 4 shallow lobes at the mouth, whitish, faintly suffused with pink, pubescent inside, flowering in October and November.
Fruit. A globose, berry-like drupe about 5 mm across, clustered in the upper axils along the slender, flexible shoots for up to 30 cm or more, deep coral-pink to carmine-rose or slightly purplish-red in autumn and persisting into winter.

Other distinguishing features. Upper twigs yellowish-brown and finely pubescent.

'**Variegàtus**' has bright green leaves, margined and sometimes irregularly stippled with creamy-yellow, the colour often extending into the midrib and occupying about half the blade area. Handsome in foliage but easily damaged by hot, dry conditions in neglect and better suited to a lightly shaded, somewhat moist situation.

Climatic range. A, H, M, Mts, P, S.

SYRÍNGA

Derived from *syrinx*, the Greek word for 'pipe', on account of the hollow, pith-filled stems of *Philadelphus* to which the name was first applied.

Lilac (various).

Oleaceae, the Olive family.

Generic description. An important genus of deciduous shrubs and small trees, mostly from southern Europe, southern Asia and China, with simple, opposite leaves, sometimes deeply cut on the margin, paniculate, sweetly-perfumed flowers produced in spring on new shoots issuing from the previous year's terminals, and capsular fruits ripening in autumn and winter to release the small, winged seeds. One of the best-known plants in southern Australia, the lilac is grown extensively for its wide colour range and fragrant flowers which are often used as cut material.

Propagation. a) Seeds, collected as soon as the capsules show signs of splitting to release and disperse the winged seeds, are best over-wintered in moist sphagnum moss at 4°–5°C, and sown in a friable material in August-September. Seedlings often take 7 to 10 years to flower, and do not reproduce cultivarietal or interspecific hybrid parents reliably and are therefore seldom used except for the propagation of pure species, or by hybridists and other experimenters seeking to produce new forms.

b) Suckers from the root system of an established plant are sometimes used, but unless the parent plant is growing on its own roots, that is, not budded or grafted on a foreign understock, the suckers will be quite different and probably inferior to the parent.

c) Nurserymen commonly work cultivars and interspecific hybrids on understocks of one of the strong-growing privets, mostly *Ligustrum*
lucidum or *L. ovalifolium*. The privet understocks are sufficiently compatible with the lilac to take scions readily by grafting in late winter, or by shield-budding in summer, and to soon develop a vigorous, but somewhat short-lived, response in the new scions. If planted deeply, however, with the graft or bud-union 5 to 6 cm below soil level, the scion soon develops its own roots to become independent of the privet, which thereafter usually dies. Clonal material worked in this manner may sucker, as lilacs are inclined to do, but the suckers have the same identity as the original scion, and if detached and established independently, will behave similarly as to growth habit, foliage, and floral type.

d) Firm tip cuttings taken in late spring or early summer are often used, struck in a sand/peat mixture in a cool, humid glass-house, preferably under mist, and treated with a root-promoting material.

Cultivation. Lilacs grow well in a wide range of soil types but are most prolific in deep, friable loams of 6.0–6.5 pH, enriched with organic matter or well-prepared compost. They prefer slightly moister soil and atmospheric conditions than most plants, and are at their best in the more humid parts of the tablelands with a moderately high annual rainfall. They enjoy full exposure to the sun but are best protected from violent winds.

Pruning. A well-managed lilac makes strong watershoot growths from near the base and these should be encouraged as replacement material for old, almost-stagnant growths, some of which are best removed each year. The result of such pruning, carried out only after flowering has finished in late spring, is the development of younger, more vigorous shoots which carry larger and more abundant crops of flowers. To prevent the formation of the unsightly seed capsules, spent inflorescences should be removed as soon as the flowers have finished. Excessive sucker growth on the perimeter of an old plant may be removed with a sharp spade.

Species and cultivars

Syrínga vulgàris (Latin from *vulgus*, 'common' or 'general', referring to its wide distribution): Common Lilac: SE Europe.

Habit. A deciduous shrub to about 2.5 m tall, with strong, upright growth, eventually developing a broadly rounded crown; very old plants are larger, sometimes assuming a tree-like growth habit.

Leaves. Simple, opposite, narrowly to broadly ovate, 6–12 cm long and 5–10 cm wide, occasionally larger on water-shoots; petiole 2–4 cm long, terete, but deeply grooved above; apex acute to acuminate; base bluntly cuneate to sub-cordate; margin entire; glabrous; thin and soft in texture; dark green and dull above, paler beneath, colouring to dull yellow in autumn, but not spectacular.

Flowers. Inflorescence a terminal panicle, often in pairs, usually 12–18 cm long but occasionally larger in the modern cultivars, issuing from the previous year's wood, in advance or with the earliest leaves; calyx campanulate to 2–3 mm broad; corolla salverform, the tube about 1 cm long and 2 mm wide, the limb of 4 spreading lobes, rotate when single but with an additional corolla surmounting the first in the double forms, 2.5–3.0 cm across, in a variety of colours from white, through pale mauve, blue, violet, purple, and pink to carmine-red, flowering from early October to mid November; flowers sweetly perfumed.

Fruit. A 2-celled capsule to 1.5 cm long, splitting from the apex to release the winged seeds in late autumn and winter.

Other distinguishing features. Youngest twigs squarish, puberulent, green or dark plum-coloured.

Climatic range. A, H, M, Mts, and on cool, elevated sites in P and S.

The cultivars available from nurseries have originated mostly in France, England and USA, with the species *S. vulgaris* and *S. oblata* being the principal breeding stocks. The name of Lemoine, Pierre Louis Victor (1823–1911) and Emile (1862–1942) of Nancy, NE France, appears prominently in the genealogy of the modern cultivars. Both father and son made seedling selections from *S. vulgaris*, and hybrids with *S. oblata*, the interspecific brood being designated *S. x hyacinthiflòra* by Victor Lemoine in 1876. Other breeders, notably W. B. Clarke of USA, have since added a number of improved cultivars with very large flowers, many of which have superseded the older sorts in nursery lists. Hundreds of cultivars are now available, with frequent new additions. The following table represents a good sample of the range, but nursery catalogues should be consulted for a more comprehensive treatment.

Cultivars of *Syringa vulgaris*, the Common Lilac

Abel Carriere	D	violet-blue
Ambassadeur	S	lilac
Condorcet	D	lavender-blue
Cora Brandt	D	white
Edward Andre	D	pink
Hugo Koster	S	reddish-violet
Katherine Havemeyer	D	lilac
Mrs Edward Harding	D	claret-red
Monge	S	reddish-violet
President Fallieres	D	mauve-pink
President Grevy	D	lilac-blue
Souvenir de Louis Spaeth	S	claret-red
Vauban	D	mauve-blue
Vestale	S	white

Cultivars of *S. x hyacinthiflora*, the Lemoine Lilac

Alice Eastwood	D	rosy-purple
Blue Hyacinth	S	mauve-blue
Buffon	S	mauve-pink
Clarke's Giant	S	lilac-blue
Esther Staley	S	pink
Sunset	D	reddish-violet

Several other species are sometimes grown, but are comparatively uncommon.

Syrínga x chinénsis: an interspecific hybrid between *S. persica* and *S. vulgaris*, originating in Rouen, France in the eighteenth century: Rouen Lilac.

Habit: A vigorous, upright shrub to 2–3 m, eventually broadening to globose form.

Leaves: Oval to ovate-lanceolate, 6–8 cm long, 2–4 cm broad, more pointed at both ends than *S. vulgaris*; green, changing to dull yellow in autumn.

Flowers: Borne in larger, slightly-drooping panicles in pairs at the terminals of the 1-year-old growths in late September and October; lilac-purple, fragrant; several different coloured forms are available.

Climatic range: A, H, M, Mts, P, S.

Syrínga mèyeri 'Palibin' (commemorating Ivan Vladimirovitch Palibin, 1872–1949, Russian botanist and author on the flora of Korea): provenance obscure, but believed to be from North China or Korea.

Habit: A small deciduous shrub of about 1 m tall and as wide, globose to hemispherical, the lower branches resting on the ground.

Leaves: Simple, obovate to nearly orbicular,

about 4 cm long and as broad; glabrous, but main veins pubescent beneath; mid-green.

Flowers: Inflorescence a dense panicle to about 8 cm tall and 5 cm broad; corolla tube to 1 cm long, rosy-purple, flowering freely over the crown and sides of the bush in October/November.

Fruit: Not seen.

Climatic range: A, H, M, Mts, P, S.

Syrínga pèrsica: Northern Iran (formerly Persia), from Turkey to Afghanistan: considered by some authorities to be an interspecific hybrid between *S. laciniata* and *S. vulgaris*.

Habit. An attractive deciduous shrub to 2–3 m tall, slender and arching at first, but eventually becoming almost globular.

Leaves. Lanceolate to 5–6 cm long and 1–2 cm wide, the apex acuminate; mid-green.

Flowers. Borne in a slender, loose panicle, many almost covering the top and sides of the bush in October and early November; soft lilac, fragrant.

'Alba' has white to very pale blush-pink flowers.

'Laciniata' has leaves divided pinnately into about 5 to 9 lobes, but flowers like the parent species, and all parts are slightly smaller in scale.

Climatic range. A, H, M, Mts, P, S.

Syrínga wólfii (commemorating Egbert Ludvigovich Wolf, 1860–1931, Russian dendrologist at the university of St Petersburg (now Leningrad), one-time botanical explorer in Northern China and Manchuria): Wolf's Lilac: Korea and Manchuria.

Habit. A deciduous shrub to 4 m or so with a mass of erect branches arising from the short main trunk to form a loose, open crown.

Leaves. Elliptic, 8–15 cm long and 5–6 cm wide on a 1.5 cm petiole; apex acuminate; base cuneate; margin entire but hairy; lower veins hairy, otherwise glabrous; mid-green above, grey-green beneath.

Flowers. An erect, terminal panicle 20–30 cm tall, or numerous purplish-pink, funnelform flowers, sweetly scented; abundant over the upper and lateral branchlets in October and November.

Fruit. Not seen.

Climatic range. A, H, M, Mts, P, S.

TECOMÀRIA

A generic name derived from the old *Tecoma*.
Cape Honeysuckle.
Bignoniaceae, the Bignonia family.

Generic description. A small genus of tender plants from Central America and South Africa, formerly united with *Tecoma*. Leaves are imparipinnate with up to 13 leaflets, and flowers are in terminal racemes, often several together forming a panicle, campanulate-funnelform, yellow, orange, or scarlet and grown mainly for that feature. The species described is versatile, being seen as a walling plant, as a hedge, shrub specimen, or as a trained climber.

Propagation. Soft-tip or semi-hardwood tip cuttings taken at any time of the year strike readily in a sand/peat mixture in a warm, moist environment.

Cultivation. A well-drained soil of moderate fertility in a warm, sunny position sheltered from frost is ideal, although when acclimatised and mature the plant will tolerate mild frosts to −1° or −2°C.

Pruning. When grown as a shrub specimen, the plant should be pruned annually to restrain the long trailing growths and induce a dense, leafy habit.

Species and cultivars

Tecomària capénsis (Latin 'from the Cape of Good Hope'): Cape Honeysuckle: SE coast of South Africa to Natal, Transvaal and central East Africa.

Habit. A part climbing, evergreen shrub with weak basal stems that trail along the ground and root readily at the nodes.

Leaves. Compound, opposite, imparipinnate, to 15 cm long, the main rachis channelled above by 2 longitudinal wings; leaflets 7 to 11, broadly ovate to oval, to 4 cm long; apex acute; base broadly cuneate; margins serrate above the middle; sessile or with very short petiolules; both surfaces glabrous; dark green above, paler beneath.

Flowers. Inflorescence a terminal raceme of 10 to 12 flowers; calyx campanulate, 5-toothed, green; corolla funnelform-tubulate to 5 cm long, curved, the 4-lobed limb to 3 cm across, the upper lobe cleft to half its length; bright orange-red to scarlet, flowering freely from February to May; stamens 4, filaments cream, anthers brown; style longer than the stamens, persisting after the flowers.

Other distinguishing features. Young shoots pale green but becoming dark grey, with brown lenticels.

'**Aùrea**' has golden-yellow flowers, but is otherwise identical.

Climatic range. A, B, M, P, S, T.

TELÌNE (formerly included in *Genista* and *Cytisus*)

Derivation obscure.
Madeira Broom.
Fabaceae, the Pea family.

Generic description. A small genus, now separate from the other brooms, important for at least one popular garden plant described below, the main characters of which are typical of the genus.

Propagation. Seeds sown in autumn or as soon as ripe germinate readily in a friable sowing mixture; germination may be accelerated by treatment in warm (40°C) water for 24 hours prior to sowing.

Cultivation. Any mildly-acid friable soil will suit, not necessarily of high fertility but with free drainage and in a sun-exposed position, preferably sheltered from frost. As an island plant, it will tolerate the salty winds of the coast moderately well, but needs protection while young.

Pruning. The current flowering wood should be shortened slightly to just below the lowest flowers, immediately after the flowers have fallen. Heavier pruning into old trunk and branches is often detrimental, even fatal.

Species and cultivars

Teline maderénsis var. *magnifoliòsis* (Latin 'from Madeira' and 'with large leaves'): Madeira Broom: formerly confused with *Cytisus stenopetalus*: Madeira.

Habit. An evergreen shrub, 3–4 m tall of erect irregular form, or a small tree to 4–5 m tall, with a single trunk and bushy head to 3 m wide.

Leaves. Compound, alternate, trifoliolate; leaflets elliptical to obovate to 3.0 cm long, the terminal slightly larger; apices acute, with short mucro; bases cuneate; margins entire; bright green and sparsely pubescent above, paler and silky-hairy beneath.

Flowers. Inflorescence a terminal raceme, 5–8

cm long, of 20–25 flowers at the ends of the leafy axillary shoots; calyx campanulate to 5 mm long, silky-pubescent, 2-lipped; corolla pea-shaped, the standard 1 cm across, nearly orbicular, wings obovate to 1 cm long, keel falcate, folded into twin halves to 8–9 mm long, all parts yellow; lightly perfumed; 10 stamens and a single style in an exserted bundle; flowering season from early September to late October.

Fruit. A silvery-grey, pubescent legume about 3 cm long and 5 mm wide, slightly falcate and flattened, with constrictions between the 4 or 5 ellipsoidal, black seeds about 3 mm long; fruit ripens in summer.

Other distinguishing features. Upper twigs vertically grooved and silky pubescent.

Climatic range. A, B, M, P, S, T.

TELÒPEA

Derived from the Greek *telopos* 'seen from afar', referring to their striking appearance in the bush.
Waratah.
Proteaceae, the Protea family.

Generic description. A small Australian genus of 4 species, all evergreen shrubs or small trees with simple, alternate, leathery leaves, and flowers in dense, terminal, head-like racemes, opening in succession from the base and subtended by an involucre of red floral bracts. The structure of the flowers is typical of the family, with hooked perianth segments, the red styles held captive until the pollen is ripe, then more or less straightening. Fruit is a follicle, becoming brown and woody when ripe and splitting to release the winged seeds.

Propagation. Seeds are sown in late winter in a coarse material such as gritty sand mixed with peat-moss, to which is added a small amount of leaf-mould and surface soil from the base of an established proteaceous plant to provide the mycorrhizal fungus essential to the successful development of roots. Individual containers should be used to avoid later root disturbance when potting on or planting out.

Chemical fertilisers, especially those high in phosphorus or potassium should not be used. Some growers apply a light ration of blood and bone in advance of the main growing period.

Cultivation. The NSW Waratah occurs naturally on a variety of soils, all moderately well-drained and mostly deep sandy loams of low fertility. Growth performance in such soils is improved by the addition of a thick mulch of coarse vegetative matter such as forest litter, leaf mould, peat, shredded bark, coarse compost, etc. This appears to favour the development of proteoid roots, the dense clusters of small roots occurring on proteaceous plants responsible for increased absorption of water and nutrients from the soil. A surface layer of flat 'floater' stones helps also to provide a cool root-run. A fully sun-exposed or partly shaded position will suit, preferably in a mild climate with winter temperatures not lower than −8°C. The other species listed occur on heavier soils in cooler climates with a moderately-high rainfall.

Pruning. Young plants should be tip-pruned for several years to increase the number of growth terminals; flowered plants should have about half or more of the annual growth reduced when flowers are cut.

Species and cultivars

Telòpea speciosíssima (Latin 'very showy'): NSW Waratah: the official floral emblem of the State of NSW: found mainly on the NSW coastal plains and tablelands, mostly on deep, sandy loam soils between the Clyde River and the mid-North Coast.

Habit. An evergreen shrub of erect, cane-like growth to about 3 m, the woody stems issuing from a woody lignotuber at the base.
Leaves. Narrowly obovate to spathulate, 15–25 cm long and 4–6 cm wide; apex obtuse; base tapered; margin dentate-serrate, with a few small irregular lobes; midrib yellow, prominent; glabrous and coriaceous; dark or reddish-green above, mid-green beneath.
Flowers. A dense, broadly-conical head-like raceme to 10–12 cm deep and wide, borne terminally on the long, erect canes; involucral bracts lanceolate, 4–6 cm long, bright red; perianths and styles rosy-crimson; flowering period September to November.
Fruit. A woody, recurved follicle about 12 cm long and 2 cm thick, with 15–20 winged seeds.
'Wirrimbirra White' is a registered cultivar from the Southern Tablelands of NSW near Robertson, with creamy-white flowers on a somewhat less vigorous plant than the parent species.
Climatic range. A, M, P, S, and on the warmer, lower levels of Mts.

Telòpea mongaénsis (Latin 'from Monga'): Monga or Braidwood Waratah: native of the Clyde Mountain, high-rainfall forest country near Braidwood, NSW.
Habit. An evergreen shrub to about 2 m tall, with a few large branches arising from the basal mallee-like clump, soon dividing into stiff branchlets, forming a broad open bush of hemispherical form.
Leaves. Simple, alternate, narrowly oblanceolate, 8–18 cm long and 1.5–2.5 cm wide, occasionally lobed above the middle; apex acute; base attenuate; margin entire; dark green above, paler and slightly glaucescent beneath.
Flowers. Inflorescence like that of the NSW Waratah but shorter and flatter to 8–10 cm across, with 50 to 60 flowers, the involucral bracts 5 mm to 2 cm long, rufous-ciliate at the edges; perianths and styles crimson, flowering from mid October to early summer.
Fruit. To 6–8 cm long, the style woody and persistent at the apex, with 12 to 20 winged seeds to 2.5 cm long.
Other distinguishing features. Upper twigs reddish-brown, softly pubescent, with brown lenticels.
Climatic range. H, M, Mts, and on elevated, cool, moist sites in P and S.

Telòpea 'Braidwood Brilliant' is a registered cultivar developed as a hybrid between *T. mongaensis* (pollen parent) and *T. speciosissima* (seed parent) by the staff of the Research Section of the Australian National Botanic Gardens.
Its growth habit is shrubby to about 2 m tall and as broad, compact and well-furnished with leaves; the flowers resemble those of *T. speciosissima*, are large and bright crimson, borne abundantly over the crown of the plant in spring.
The new hybrid is likely to be planted extensively in cool climate gardens where its frost resistance, derived mainly from the Monga Waratah, will prove to be a great advantage.
Climatic range. H, M, Mts and on cool, elevated sites in A, P, S.

Telòpea oreàdes (Latin 'from a mountain habitat'): Gippsland Waratah: SE NSW and eastern Vic. in the sheltered gullies and forests of the east-flowing streams.
Habit. Shrubby when young with a few erect, straight stems from a crowded base, but tree-like

when mature with one to several dominant leaders to 6–8 m or more and a mass of minor stems forming a lower storey of foliage.

Leaves. Simple, alternate, oblanceolate, 12–25 cm long and 3.0–4.5 cm wide; petiole scarcely distinguishable from the blade but swollen to 5–6 mm wide; apex acute to abruptly acuminate; base slenderly attenuate; margin entire; venation coarsely reticulate and slightly translucent, the midrib prominent below; glabrous and coriaceous; dull dark green above, paler and slightly glaucous beneath.

Flowers. Inflorescence a terminal condensed raceme of about 50 spreading flowers, subtended by 10–15 reddish or green involucral bracts 1–3 cm long, ovate to oblong, with ciliate margins; pedicels deep rosy-crimson; perianth 2–3 cm long, deep crimson, slightly curved, the limb globose at first but splitting into 4 fully recurved segments when ripe and then soon deciduous; style terete to 4.5 cm long, curved, crimson, the stigma 5 mm long, oval, convex, lustrous crimson; flowers produced abundantly from early October to late November.

Fruit. A woody follicle on a hard, curved peduncle 2–3 cm long; follicle boat-shaped, 6–7 cm long, split on the upper edge, the woody style persisting; seeds 10–12, elongate, winged.

Climatic range. H, M, Mts, and on cool, moist sheltered sites in P and S.

TEMPLETÒNIA

Commemorating John Templeton, eighteenth-century Irish taxonomic botanist.
Templetonia; Cockies' Tongues.
Fabaceae, the Pea family.

Generic description. A small genus of Australian native shrubs with simple, alternate, entire leaves, colourful pea-shaped flowers from the axils of the upper shoots of the previous year's growth, and flattened, elongate leguminous fruits. The species described below is a popular flowering plant in native gardens, especially near the sea.

Propagation. Seeds germinate readily if soaked in warm water for 24 hours, then planted at once in a warm, humid place.

Cultivation. Templetonias thrive in an open, sun-exposed position in a mild coastal climate with minimum temperatures remaining above –3°C. Native to coastal limestone sands, the species treated here is adaptable to any well-drained, coarse-textured soil, the better for the addition of fibrous organic matter and a mulch of floater stones or gravel. It is tolerant of seaside conditions, preferably with shelter from violent, salt-laden winds.

Pruning. Moderate shortening of the flowered shoots during or immediately after the flowering season is beneficial; pruning is best confined to the youngest shoots only.

Species and cultivars

Templetònia retùsa (Latin 'having a leaf apex with a shallow terminal notch'): Red-flowered or Common Templetonia: west- and south-coastal plains of WA, and the Flinders Ranges in SA.

Habit. An evergreen shrub to 1.0–1.5 m tall, of erect but somewhat loose form in the wild but improved in foliage and floral quality by cultivation and regular pruning.

Leaves. Oblanceolate to narrowly obovate, 2–4 cm long and 5–15 mm wide; petiole 1–2 mm long, stout; apex retuse to obtuse-mucronate; base cuneate; margin entire; venation indistinct apart from the prominent midrib; glabrous; coriaceous; dark grey-green above, paler beneath.

Flowers. Solitary or in twos and threes in the upper axils, on pedicels of 8–10 mm, thickened near the apex; calyx campanulate, with 4 short acute lobes and 1 longer acuminate lower lobe, glabrous, pale green; corolla pea-shaped, the standard petal broadly oblong to obovate, dorsally folded to the acute apex, drooping downward; wing and keel petals folded together to form an erect, falcate sheath enclosing the 10 united stamens; all corolla parts dull scarlet to brick-red; flowering season from early July to early November.

Fruit. A flattened, elongate legume to 5 cm long, with a short-acuminate, curved apex.

Other distinguishing features. Upper twigs shallowly furrowed; yellow-green to brownish.

Climatic range. A, B, M, P, S, and in warm microclimates in lower Mts.

TETRATHÈCA

Derived from the Greek, referring to the 4-celled anthers.
Black-eyed Susan or Pink Bells.
Tremandraceae, the Tremandra family.

Generic description. An Australian native genus of about 25 evergreen shrubs and herbs, mainly from the south-eastern states. Leaves are simple, variable, alternate, opposite or whorled and from scale-like to lanceolate or broadly obovate; flowers are rotate, mostly pink or red, with 4 widely-spaced petals and a central cluster of 8 stamens. Several species are commonly grown in native gardens, especially for their handsome flowers.

Propagation. Seeds germinate readily in a warm, humid atmosphere. Improved clonal material needs to be grown by firm tip cuttings, preferably under mist irrigation.

Cultivation. All species perform best in a lightly shaded position sheltered from harsh winds, preferably on an open textured, sandy or loamy soil with a liberal organic content and a surface mulch of vegetative litter.

Pruning. Shortening the shoots after the last flowers is beneficial in maintaining a dense, leafy growth habit.

Species and cultivars

Tetrathèca ciliàta (Latin 'fringed with hairs'): Pink Bells: south-eastern Australia, mostly in elevated, open woodland on sandy or rocky soils.
Habit. A low shrub to 30–45 cm tall, the slender branches more or less erect.
Leaves. Mostly 3-whorled, ovate to nearly orbicular, about 1 cm long, bristly pubescent, especially on the margins; dark green.
Flowers. Rotate, to about 20 mm across, solitary in the upper axils, drooping on slender reddish pedicels, but sometimes crowded together in a racemose cluster; calyx squat, with reflexed reddish sepals; petals 4, oblong-lanceolate to 1 cm long, spreading, lilac-pink, flowering in late winter and spring.
Fruit. A small capsule with hairy seeds.
'Alba' is similar but with white flowers.
Climatic range. A, B, M, P, S, and on sheltered sites in Mts.

Tetrathèca ericifòlia (Latin 'with Erica-like leaves'): Heath-leafed Pink Bells: south-eastern Australia, mainly on sandy or rocky sites on the lower tablelands.
Habit. A broad, spreading bush to 30–50 cm tall and about as broad.
Leaves. Almost sessile, widely-angled, 4-whorled on the slender pubescent upper stems; acicular to linear, 4–10 mm long; apex acute

with a short reddish point; margin entire but strongly recurved; midrib distinct dark green and glandular above, whitish-green beneath.
Flowers. Solitary in the upper axils, rotate to about 2 cm across, on slender red pedicels to 1–2 cm long; calyx of 4 red glandular hairy sepals; petals 4, oblanceolate, rosy-magenta, the stamens with blackish anthers; flowering from early spring to mid-summer.
Fruit. Not seen.
Climatic range. A, B, H, M, P, S, and on lower levels of Mts.

Tetrathèca thymifòlia (Latin 'with Thyme-like leaves'): Black-eyed Susan; Thyme Pink Bells; Pink Eyes; south-eastern Australia, mostly on well-drained, low fertility soils in the coastal heathlands and rocky slopes of the tablelands, usually on partly-shaded, sheltered sites.
Habit. A low shrub to 50 cm, of thin, open growth to about 75 cm wide.
Leaves. 3- or 4-whorled, variable, but mostly ovate, 8–15 mm long, on a broad, hairy 1 mm petiole; apex acute; margin entire, revolute but conspicuously ciliate; dark green and tuberculate, paler and hairy beneath; occasional leaves colour to orange and scarlet before falling.
Flowers. Solitary or in small clusters, pendant on crimson, white-hairy pedicels to 1 cm long; calyx red, the pointed sepals glandular-pubescent; petals 4, oblanceolate to oblong, to 1.5 cm long, spreading widely, variable in colour from pale lilac-pink to deep magenta-pink, with a few deeper radial lines; stamens in a blunt cone, the anthers reddish-black; flowering season from early September to December, then sporadically until late summer.
Fruit. A flattened, broadly-obovate, 2-celled capsule about 4–5 mm long, hairy, bright green or reddish, the style persisting at the blunt apex.
Other distinguishing features. Upper twigs stiff, hairy, reddish above.
'Bicentennial Belle' is a registered cultivar from the South Coast of NSW, more compact in growth habit than the species, about 45 cm tall and 75 cm broad, flowering mainly in spring and early summer but with a few flowers at odd times; the mauve-pink flowers are somewhat larger than those of the parent.
Climatic range. A, B, H, M, P, S, and on sheltered parts of Mts.

TEÙCRIUM

Commemorating Teucer, a Trojan king whose apothecaries used the herbaceous sorts medicinally.
Germander.
Lamiaceae, the Mint family; (formerly Labiatae).

Generic description. A large and varied genus of over 100 species of herbaceous and evergreen shrubs, all with the characteristically squarish stems, opposite twigs and leaves, and labiate flowers in whorls. The species described below is a useful garden plant mainly for its decorative leaves and flowers.

Propagation. Soft-tip cuttings taken in spring and summer strike readily in a sand/peat mixture in a warm atmosphere, as do semi-hardwood cuttings taken in autumn and winter.

Cultivation. The species is from the dry climates around the Mediterranean Sea and will tolerate the dry heat of the inland but is better in the Sydney climate for a well-drained, open soil from which prolonged rain drains freely. Light frosts to −2°C are endured without injury.

Pruning. A light pruning of the ends of the branchlets to remove the spent inflorescences and to stimulate development of laterals is beneficial, immediately after the summer flowering period.

Species and cultivars

Teùcrium frùticans (Latin 'shrubby'): Shrubby Germander: Mediterranean region.
Habit. An evergreen shrub, 1.5–2.5 m tall, of broad open shape to 2 m wide, dense and leafy if pruned regularly, open and sparse if neglected.
Leaves. Simple, opposite, ovate-elliptic to 3–4 cm long and 2–3 cm wide; apex acutely rounded; margin entire, slightly recurved; main veins prominent beneath; softly coriaceous; aromatic when bruised; dark green and shiny above, densely white-tomentose and dull beneath.
Flowers. Inflorescence a few-flowered raceme terminating the upper shoots and axillary laterals; flowers labiate, the main lip extended to 2 cm, all parts lavender-blue, with deep violet-blue veins, flowering from September to late summer; stamens 4, with pale-violet filaments and brown anthers, long exserted to 1.5 cm.
Fruit. Of 4 small obovoid nutlets, ripening in late summer and autumn.

Other distinguishing features. Youngest stems squarish, white-tomentose, the outer bark leathery, some older shoots hexagonal, the lateral twigs in whorls of 3.
Climatic range. A, H, I, M, P, S, and on warm, sheltered slopes of lower Mts.

THEVÈTIA

Commemorating the sixteenth-century French monk, André Thevet.
Yellow Oleander.
Apocynaceae, the Dogbane family.

Generic description. A small genus of evergreen trees and shrubs from tropical America, with simple, alternate leaves, and showy yellowish flowers borne freely during summer. The species described below is poisonous and every precaution should be taken against accidental ingestion, especially by children attracted by the curious fruit.

Propagation. a) Seeds sown in spring in a warm environment germinate satisfactorily.
b) Soft-tip cuttings taken in spring, or semi-hardwood cuttings taken in autumn and winter, strike readily in a heated, misted glass-house.

Cultivation. Thevetia responds favourably to a light, fibrous soil with free drainage but with plenty of water during summer, especially when in flower; the plant is tolerant of several degrees of frost if not over-indulged with liberal treatments but allowed to adapt naturally to the prevailing conditions.

Pruning. Removal of spent flower stems shortly behind the inflorescence, in late autumn at the end of the flowering season, maintains a dense, attractive shape; more severe pruning may be necessary to control size of the plant every 3–4 years or so, and is best done in late winter.

Species and cultivars

Thevètia peruviàna (Latin 'from Peru') (syn. *T. neriifolia*) Yellow Oleander: Central America, Peru and West Indies.
Habit. A large evergreen shrub to 2–3 m tall, of hemispherical shape with many erect, arching stems from the base.
Leaves. Linear, 10–12 cm long and 8 mm wide; finely tapered to apex and base; margin entire but recurved; central vein prominent; glabrous; dark green and lustrous above, paler and duller beneath.

Flowers. Borne on 3 cm pedicels, singly or in few-flowered clusters at the terminals; calyx stellate to 1.5 cm across the 5 narrow-triangular, acute lobes; corolla funnelform to 5 cm long, the 5 lobes oblanceolate but with a single dentate point on the left margin where the extension of the greenish tube terminates; slightly fragrant; pale orange or clear-yellow, flowering from November to May.

Fruit. An oddly shaped fleshy drupe, 3.5–5.0 cm long, roughly globose in outline but with a pronounced ridge; green in autumn, changing to yellow, then to black when fully ripe; seeds 1 to several.

Other distinguishing features. Stems and petioles exude a white, milky sap when the bark is broken. All parts of the plant are poisonous.

Climatic range. A, B, I, M, P, S, T,

THRÝPTOMENE

Derived from the Greek, referring to the small scale of the floral parts.

Heath-myrtle (various).

Myrtaceae, the Myrtle family.

Generic description. An Australian native genus of evergreen shrubs with opposite, simple leaves, small cup-shaped flowers with 5 rounded petals and either 5 or 10 stamens, flowering mainly in winter and spring, and popularly used as dwarf garden shrubs or by florists for their cut flowers.

Propagation. Seeds may be raised with some difficulty and are seldom used when soft-tip or semi-hardwood cuttings are available; the cuttings should be struck in a sand/peat mixture in a warm, moist environment, between late spring and winter. Hormone rooting-powder is beneficial.

Cultivation. The species treated here are tough little plants thriving in any well-drained soil of reasonable quality but preferring full sun exposure with shelter from violent winds; hardy to −3°C but liable to injury in more severe conditions.

Pruning. Moderate pruning of the flowered shoots during or immediately after flowering is helpful in maintaining a dense, twiggy growth habit.

Species and cultivars

Thrýptomene calycina (Latin 'calyx-like' referring to the similarity between sepals and petals): Grampians Heath-myrtle or Bushy Heath-myrtle: The Grampians in western Vic.

Habit. A dense bush to about 1.5 m, forming an irregularly-round bush up to 2 m wide.

Leaves. Oblanceolate, about 1 cm long and 3–4 mm wide; apex shortly acute; margin entire; glandular; dark green; aromatic when crushed.

Flowers. Rotate to 6–7 mm wide, profuse in the upper axils, almost concealing the twigs; calyx of 5 sepals alternating with and resembling the 5 rounded petals, both floral parts glistening white; stamens 5, in a tight central cluster, the yellow anthers turning reddish when fully mature; flowering period from late June to October.

Fruit. A vase-shaped green nut, ripening in summer.

Other distinguishing features. The plant is used extensively in the floral trade, especially valued for its durability as a cut flower.

Climatic range. A, H, M, Mts, P, S.

Thrýptomene saxícola (Latin 'growing among rocks'): southern coast of WA.

Habit. An evergreen shrub with short trunk and many arching branches, forming a round topped plant about 1 m tall and 1.5 m wide.

Leaves. Opposite in neat decussate pattern, elliptic to obovate, 3–8 mm long, 2–3 mm wide; petiole 1 mm or less; apex acute to obtuse; base cuneate; margin entire; venation indistinct, but surface minutely glandular; dark green; aromatic when bruised.

Flowers. Solitary or in pairs in the upper axils, on glandular pedicels 2–3 mm long, forming a slender racemose cluster, many together in a panicle; calyx a shallow cup 2–3 mm across, green, glandular-pitted but not ribbed, the 5 lobes 1 mm across, pale pink; corolla cup-shaped to 3 mm across, with 5 orbicular petals curving inwards over the stamens, white but faintly stained with pink, scentless; stamens 10, to 1 mm long, the filaments pale pink, anthers black; flowers abundant from early July to late September, persisting and fading to brown.

Fruit. A vase-shaped, green receptacle, ripening in summer.

Other distinguishing features. Upper twigs square, the edges sharply defined.

'Payne's Hybrid' belongs here (syn. *T. paynei*) a plant of apparently uncertain origin but very similar to *T. saxicola* in all major features, especially in its 10 stamens which separates it from *T. calycina* with 5 stamens, to which it is often attributed.

Climatic range. A, B, M, P, S, and on warm sites in lower Mts.

TIBOUCHÌNA (syn. *Lasiandra, Pleroma*)

The ancient aboriginal name of one of the many species from South America.

Glory-bush; Lasiandra; Quaresma.

Melastomataceae, the Melastome family.

Generic description. A large genus of mostly shrubs or small trees, now understood to have more than 300 species, mainly from the higher slopes of the Amazon Basin in NW South America, and from SE Brazil within the latitudes of 10° north and about 30° south. The genus is easily recognised. It has large, evergreen, prominently veined, hairy leaves borne on the mostly square stems; the 5-petalled flowers are borne singly or in terminal panicles, most commonly purplish, pink, or white; the globose buds are enclosed in 2 to about 6 bracts; and the 10 prominent stamens occur in 2 series, each of 5 of dissimilar length. The blooms are short-lived, but the plants remain in flower sometimes for several months, often almost concealing the foliage in their abundance.

Propagation. a) Seeds germinate readily in a friable medium in a warm, humid atmosphere.

b) Soft-tip leafy cuttings strike at almost any time of the year, preferably in a heated glasshouse with humidity control.

Cultivation. The Glory-bushes enjoy a light, friable soil, at least moderately fertile, with plenty of moisture in the growing season, preferably in a frost-free climate, with shelter from cold or violent winds. Well-acclimatised plants are tolerant of the light frosts of the lower tablelands without serious injury. Planting is best carried out in early summer, not during the colder months.

Pruning. The summer and autumn-flowering species such as *T. granulosa* and *T. urvilleana* benefit from an annual light pruning of the current year's wood in late winter, before the onset of new growth, to encourage the development of dense, twiggy growth. Should an occasional heavy frost cause damage to the upper leaves and twigs, the injured material should not be pruned at once but retained until all risk of frost is over to help prevent more serious damage to the older wood. *T. macrantha* is resentful of heavy pruning but responds favourably to occasional tip-pruning during the main growing period between spring and late summer.

Species and cultivars

Tibouchìna clavàta (Latin 'club-shaped') (syn. *T. holosericea*) Brazil.

Habit. An evergreen shrub to 1.5 m or so tall, with erect stems from the basal trunk, forming a rounded, leafy bush about 1.5–2.0 m broad.

Leaves. Broadly elliptic to ovate, 5–10 cm long and 4–5 cm wide; apex obtuse with a short, acute point; base sub-cordate; margin entire but densely ciliate; main veins 5, prominent and densely pubescent beneath, converging at the base and apex, 2 lesser intramarginal veins evident from the base to about halfway to the apex; texture silky and soft; silvery-green above, paler beneath, the young leaves silver-white.

Flowers. In a terminal panicle to 15–20 cm tall, each flower enclosed in a pair of elliptic-ovate bracts 8–9 mm long, silky-pubescent; calyx tube 10–12 mm long, silky-pubescent; corolla of 5 obovate petals forming a rotate flower to 4.5 cm across, varying from violet-purple to pink and white; stamens with purple anthers; flowering season mainly in spring but intermittently at other times in warm microclimates.

Fruit. Capsules ovoid, to 1 cm long, brown-pubescent, with numerous fine cochleate seeds.

'Alba' has white flowers, with mauve anthers.

Climatic range. B, M, P, S, T, and in warm microclimates in A and lower Mts.

Tibouchìna granulòsa (Latin 'from *granulum*, 'a small grain', referring to the gritty texture of the leaves): Purple Glory-bush: widespread in SE Brazil.

Habit. A small evergreen tree to about 10–12 m tall when grown on a single trunk, and then suitable for street or shade planting, but more usually seen as a large bush to 4–5 m tall and as broad, with branches radiating more or less uniformly from the short, central trunk.

Leaves. Oblong-lanceolate to narrowly ovate to

15–20 cm long and 5–7 cm wide; apex finely acute to acuminate; margin ciliate, with long strigose bristles; petiole stout, 1.5–3.0 cm long; dark green, shiny but shortly strigose above, bright green beneath and densely strigose, especially on the prominent veins.

Flowers. Inflorescence a terminal panicle 20–40 cm long, the branches square, pubescent and prominently winged; bracts 2; calyx tube ovoid-campanulate to 2 cm long; corolla rotate to 6–8 cm across, the 5 rhombic-obovate petals with an abruptly acuminate apex, narrowly-tapered base and ciliate margin; flowers variable in colour from violet-purple to rosy-purple and pink, several distinctly coloured clones bearing cultivarietal names; most stock in Australia is vegetatively propagated from a clone with royal-purple flowers fading to pale-violet, with deeper violet veins radiating from the centre, flowering abundantly from late summer until early winter; stamens 10, in 2 series, the 5 long to 2 cm, and the 5 short to 1 cm, all conspicuously jointed at about the middle, the anthers purple, the filaments with shaggy, purplish hairs; pistil 1, whitish-mauve.

Fruit. A 5-valved capsule, dull red, with a dense coat of silky-brown pubescence; seeds numerous, dark brown.

Other distinguishing features. Young shoots prominently 4-winged.

'Rosea' is of similar growth habit but with somewhat smaller flowers, averaging 5–6 cm across, with narrower petals, varying in colour from mallow-purple to rosy-magenta, with deeper veins radiating from the base; flowers abundant during the March to May period.

Climatic range. A, B, M, P, S, T, and on warm sites on lower Mts.

Tibouchìna heteromálla (Greek 'with the leaves turned in different directions'): SE Brazil, mainly in the provinces of Minas Gerais and Sao Paulo.

Habit. An evergreen shrub usually about 1 m tall and 1–2 m broad, with many erect stems arising from a somewhat crowded base.

Leaves. Broadly ovate, 10–15 cm long and 6–10 cm wide, the short internodes accentuating the decussate arrangement; petiole 2–5 cm long, 5–6 mm thick, pubescent, slightly grooved above; apex obtuse; base subcordate; margin ciliate; venation with 3 main veins and 2 pairs of smaller intramarginal veins converging at base and apex, very prominent below and finely white-pubescent; blade surface bright green of velvety texture, finely strigose, the grain following the direction of the veins, the lower surface whitish-green with a soft-woolly texture.

Flowers. In an erect terminal panicle, 10–20 cm tall, the branches densely pilose; bracts ovate-oblong, the apices acute; calyx tube 6–7 mm long, with erect sepals 3–5 mm long; corolla rotate to 4–6 cm across, the 5 broad-ovate petals deep violet-purple, flowering from December to early autumn, or beyond in warm localities.

Fruit. An ovoid capsule 8–10 mm long and 6–7 mm wide, whitish-brown.

Climatic range. B, P, S, T, and in warm microclimates in A, M, and lower Mts.

Tibouchìna 'Jules' (a cultivar name used provisionally pending authentic identification).

Habit. A small shrub to about 1 m tall and somewhat broader, with many slender, squarish stems spreading widely from the base.

Leaves. Narrowly-ovate to elliptic, 5–8 cm long and 2–3 cm wide on a 5–6 mm petiole; all parts densely hairy; apex acute; margin entire-ciliate; venation 5-nerved, prominent and densely hairy beneath; dark green above, paler below.

Flowers. Borne in a terminal panicle 10–12 cm tall, of 5 to 9 flowers on 2 cm pedicels; bracts 2, rosy-red; calyx tube to 1 cm long; petals obliquely obovate, 3 cm long and 2 cm wide, opening to a rotate flower 5–6 cm across, violet-purple, with deeper veins; stamens 10, with pale-violet filaments and dark violet anthers; flowering period March to May.

Fruit. Not seen.

Other distinguishing features. Upper twigs conspicuously hairy, especially along the ridges.

Climatic range. B, M, P, S, T, and on sheltered sites in A and on lower levels of Mts.

Tibouchìna láxa (Latin 'of loose, open form') (syn. *T. sarmentòsa*, *Pleròma sarmentòsa*) tropical parts of Peru and Ecuador.

Habit. An evergreen shrub to 1.5 m tall, the branches thin, weak and somewhat sarmentose, but more densely twiggy if tip-pruned frequently while young, then self-supporting and of attractive, shrubby habit.

Leaves. Broadly ovate 3–6 cm long and 2.5–4.0 cm wide; petiole 5–15 mm long, channelled above, pilose, crimson; apex acute to shortly acuminate; base rounded to subcordate; margin serrulate-ciliate; venation reticulate, the prominent midrib and 4 main veins converging at base and apex, prominent and whitish beneath; upper surface bright green, whitish-strigose, the lower surface pale green.

Flowers. In a mostly 3-flowered, cymose cluster at the terminals of the young shoots; calyx tube ovoid, 7–9 mm long, green with dense red hairs; corolla rotate, 4–5 cm across, of 5 broadly obovate, deep violet-purple petals; stamens in 2 dissimilar series, the filaments pale rosy-purple; style to 1.5 cm long, bright-cyclamen; flowering season autumn and winter, extending to spring in warm localities.

Fruit. Capsules soft-wooded, about 1 cm long, ovoid with truncate apex.

Other distinguishing features. Upper stems squarish, pale green, shaded crimson where sun-exposed, heavily pubescent with red hairs.

Climatic range. B, P, S, T, on warm, frost-free sites only.

Tibouchìna lepidòta (Latin 'scaly'): Ecuador and Colombia.

Habit. A dense leafy shrub to 4 m or so tall, usually with a short trunk and low branches, but occasionally tree-like to 8–15 m tall in its native habitat, then with a distinct trunk and rounded crown.

Leaves. Ovate-oblong to oblong-lanceolate, 8–10 cm long and 3–5 cm wide; apex acute to slightly acuminate; margin serrulate-ciliate, slightly recurved; venation reticulate between the 5 main veins, the 3 middle veins converging at the base, the outermost minor pair joining with the innermost pair 3–4 mm from the base, prominent and strigose beneath; upper surface dark green, slightly shiny, with broad lines of strigose hairs separating the main veins; lower surface paler and finely strigose

Flowers. Inflorescence a terminal panicle to 12–15 cm tall; bracts deeply concave, 2 cm long and 1 cm wide, pinkish, silky-pubescent, soon deciduous; calyx tube urceolate, reddish, densely strigose, the 5 sepals obliquely oblong, magenta, pubescent outside; corolla rotate to 8 cm across, the 5 broadly obovate petals to 3.5 cm long and 2.5–3.0 cm wide, violet-purple with deeper veins, stamens 10, violet-purple; style curved, to 2.5 cm long, rosy-magenta; flowering season from late summer to early winter.

Fruit. A soft-wooded capsule of ovoid shape to 8–9 mm long.

Other distinguishing features. Stems square, with pronounced wing-like ridges at the corners, 1.5 mm deep, sparsely reddish-hairy.

Climatic range. A, B, M, P, S, T, and on warm sites in lower Mts.

Tibouchìna macrántha (Latin 'with large flowers') (syn. *T. semidecándra* 'Grandiflora') Large-flowered Glory-bush: Brazil.

Habit. An evergreen shrub or small tree to 2–3 m tall, usually with a short main trunk and several low branches forming a somewhat open, rounded bush about 2 m wide, more leafy and dense when tip-pruned frequently during the growing period.

Leaves. Elliptic-ovate, 6–10 cm long and 3–5 cm wide; apex acuminate; margin ciliate; venation reticulate, with 3 main greenish-white veins converging with the petiole, and 2 smaller intramarginal veins joining the outer pair 5 mm or so from the base, all prominent and whitish-strigose beneath; upper surface with a fine, pebbly texture, dark green, but paler beneath, and finely strigose on both surfaces.

Flowers. Solitary or in few-flowered, paniculate clusters with a terminal flower and several in the adjacent axils; buds globose to broadly conical, apiculate, enclosed in 6 concave bracts 2 cm long and 1.5 cm wide, whitish-green, with red stains outside; calyx tube urceolate; corolla crateriform to 10–14 cm across, of 5 broadly obovate, oblique petals 5–7 cm long and 5 cm wide, royal-purple, with a reddish-magenta centre and darker veins radiating from the base; stamens 10, in 2 series, the longer 5 strongly falcate, with blackish-purple anthers, the shorter 5 with white-tipped anthers, all filaments 2.0–2.5 cm long, white-pubescent; style carmine-red with a white stigma, persisting after the fall of petals and sepals; flowering season from March to spring.

Fruit. An ovoid, 5-valved capsule to 2 cm long, silky-pubescent, green at first, but ripening to brown in late winter; seeds numerous, small, orange-brown.

Other distinguishing features. Youngest twigs green with reddish hairs, the nodes swollen with a conspicuous, transverse ridge connecting the opposite leaf bases; stems square, at least for several years, but becoming terete.

Climatic range. A, B, M, P, S, T, and on warm, sheltered sites in lower Mts.

Tibouchìna mutábilis (Latin *mutare* 'to change', referring to the colour of the flowers): SE Brazil, in the provinces of Sao Paulo and Minas Gerais.

Habit. An evergreen tall shrub or small tree up

to 4 to 7 m tall, usually with a short trunk and vase-shaped branch pattern, supporting a rounded crown of dense twigs and foliage.

Leaves. Lanceolate-elliptic, 8–10 cm long and 2–3 cm wide on a densely brown-hairy petiole 1.5 cm long; apex and base acute; margin entire but sparsely ciliate; venation finely reticulate, the 3 main veins depressed above, prominent beneath, with 2 fine marginal veins 1 mm or so from the edges; glabrous or nearly so and bright green above, paler ashy-green beneath, the lower veins with pale hairs pointing forwards.

Flowers. Solitary or in few-flowered clusters at the terminals of the outer twigs; bracts 4, concave, 1.5 cm long, 6–8 mm wide, nearly glabrous; calyx campanulate about 1 cm long; petals 5, broadly obovate to 3–4 cm long, with a slightly-eccentric rounded or retuse apex, the base narrowed to a slender claw, with clear sinuses between; opening white, then changing to rose-pink and aging to reddish-violet, with crimson radial veins; stamens 10, violet-purple, about 1.5 cm long, with purple anthers; flowering period in late spring and early summer.

Fruit. Not seen.

Other distinguishing features. Upper twigs obscurely 4-angled beneath the densely pubescent thatch, pinkish above at first, becoming brownish-green when mature; the leaves show no trace of the bronze colouration at the base of the leaves of several other species such as *T. pulchra*.

Climatic range. B, M, P, S, T, and on warm, sheltered sites in A and lower Mts.

Tibouchìna urvilleàna (commemorating Capt Dumont d'Urville, French botanical explorer and author): Santa Caterina, SE Brazil.

(The species is commonly represented in Australian gardens by a form called '**Edwardsii**', the origin of which is somewhat uncertain, but reputed to be a cross between *T. urvilleana* and *T. macrantha* made by the Melbourne nursery propagator, Edward Edwards. It appears to be not greatly different from the species but is claimed to have larger flowers; the following description refers to the widely planted cultivar.)

Habit. An evergreen shrub to 3–4 m tall, with a short trunk and several heavy branches from near the base, forming a densely foliaged, rounded bush.

Leaves. Ovate, 8–12 cm long and 4–6 cm wide; apex acute to slightly acuminate; margin

rufous-ciliate; venation 5-nerved, prominent beneath; dark green and finely strigose above, paler and silky beneath.

Flowers. Solitary, or in few-flowered, paniculate clusters; buds to about 3 cm long, narrowly ovoid, enclosed in ovate involucral scales, hairy and reddish; calyx-tube to 1.5 cm long and 8 mm wide at the apex, pale green, the 5 sepals ovate-lanceolate, all parts silky-strigose; corolla rotate, about 8 cm across, the 5 petals broadly obovate to 3.5–4.0 cm long and as wide, overlapped and finely ciliate on the edge, royal-purple, shaded reddish-magenta in the centre, with darker veins radiating from the base; stamens 10, in 2 series, the longer 5 with dark-purple, falcate anthers, the shorter 5 with violet and white, falcate anthers; style curved, to about 2.5 cm long, glabrous, carmine-red with a white stigma; flowers abundant from early December until late May, with a few intermittent flowers during winter and spring in warm localities.

Fruit. An urceolate, 5-valved capsule to 1.5–2.0 cm long, ripening to brown, the surface strigose; seeds numerous.

Other distinguishing features. Young twigs and upper stems square, covered with soft red hairs, becoming brown on the older wood.

'**Robústa**' is somewhat similar, but has larger flowers and more vigorous growth; in the early stages of growth at least, it is distinctly more hirsute than 'Edwardsii'.

Climatic range. A, B, M, P, S, T, and on warm, sheltered sites in lower Mts.

ÙLEX

The ancient Latin name, originally applied to *U. europaeus*.

Gorse, Furze or Whin.

Fabaceae, the Pea family.

Generic description. A genus of evergreen shrubs with the true leaves compound and trifoliolate but mostly reduced to a sharp-tipped spine, actually a modified petiole, and pea-shaped flowers borne in the leaf axils.

Propagation. a) The single-flowered *U. europaeus* is easily propagated by seeds sown as soon as ripe.

b) Cultivars are grown by firm tip-cuttings, 4–5 cm long, taken in autumn and struck in a sandy medium in a cool, humid atmosphere.

Cultivation. Gorse usually performs better on a

well-drained, mildly acid, sandy or gravelly soil than on improved, more fertile garden soils. It is tolerant of winds and is safe in the coldest Australian climates to at least −15°C.

Pruning. Some light pruning of the flowered shoots in early November, after the flowers have faded, is desirable to restrict the vigorous growth to reasonable limits. Pruning should be performed annually to obviate the need for heavy lopping which the plant often resents by its failure to regenerate from the old wood.

Species and cultivars

Ùlex europàeus (Latin 'from Europe'): Gorse, Furze or Whin: the single-flowered species is indigenous to Europe and North Africa but is now naturalised in almost every temperate country and a weedy pest in most; the double-flowered form is sterile and therefore not objectionable.

Habit. An evergreen, low-branched, broad mound to 1–2 m tall and usually much wider unless pruned to shape, of impenetrably dense growth, its barrier value enhanced by the sharp foliar spines.

Leaves. Modified to sharp-tipped, squarish spines at the terminals and axils of the lateral shoots, the primary spine with several secondary spines; dark green, the spines reddish-brown, horny, 2–3 mm long and extremely sharp.

Flowers. Solitary, or in twos or threes, on 8–10 mm petioles from the upper spiny shoots, enclosed in 2 ovate, grey-green floral bracts; calyx to 9–10 mm, pubescent, with 2 yellowish sepals; corolla pea-shaped, with a typical standard, wings and keel, the whole 1.8 cm long, buttercup-yellow, sweetly perfumed; flowering from late April to October.

Fruit. A densely pubescent legume, ellipsoidal to ovoid, to 1.5 cm long, greenish-brown, containing several dark-brown seeds, exploding when ripe.

'**Plenus**': as above, but with additional wings and keels, forming a double flower of larger size, which is sterile and unproductive of fruits.

Climatic range. A, H, I, M, Mts, P, S.

VERTICOÌDIA

Derivation uncertain.
Feather-flower.
Myrtaceae, the Myrtle family.

Generic description. A genus of predominantly WA native evergreen shrubs with opposite entire leaves, showy flowers borne singly in the upper axils of the young shoots from the previous year's growth or in terminal corymbose clusters, the floral parts 5-merous, the petals and sepals conspicuously fringed. While not yet commonly grown in eastern Australia, the species described below, with their interesting foliage and colourful flowers make an attractive addition to any garden able to provide satisfactory growth conditions.

Propagation. a) Seeds sown as soon as fully ripe germinate somewhat erratically.
b) Semi-hardwood, leafy tip cuttings, taken after the young shoots ripen slightly in summer and autumn, root readily in a warm, humid atmosphere; root-promoting dust and mist humidification are beneficial.

Cultivation. Native to sandy heathlands and gravelly hillsides close to the WA coast, the Verticordias are sensitive to their environment and should be attempted only where similar conditions prevail. Well-drained, deep sandy soils are best, in a mild climate with minimum temperatures remaining above −3°C. An undisturbed mulch of coarse organic litter or of flat 'floater' stones is an advantage in maintaining an even temperature and water status in the root zone.

Pruning. Annual pruning of the youngest shoots during or immediately after the flowering season is beneficial in thickening the growth habit and extending the life span.

Species and cultivars

Verticoìrdia gràndis (Latin 'great', referring to the profusion of flowers): Scarlet Feather-flower: coast of WA, mainly between the Swan and Murchison Rivers.

Habit. A shrub to 1.0–1.5 m tall, with erect but open habit in the wild, made denser and more floriferous by cultivation and regular pruning.

Leaves. Orbicular or nearly so, 1.0–1.5 cm across, in opposite pairs, the sessile bases partly enclosing the stems; apex rounded or bluntly obtuse; base cordate; margin entire; venation indistinct apart from the more prominent midrib and several main veins; glabrous; glaucous-green.

Flowers. Solitary in the upper axils, on slender reddish pedicels to 1.0 cm long; calyx cup-shaped to 8–9 mm long, with 5 lobes, each with a fine plumose fringe of hairs; petals 5, orbicular, similarly fringed but with shorter hairs, scarlet, forming an attractive colour contrast with the greyish foliage, main flowering season early to mid-summer, with a few flowers at other times.

Verticordia insignis (Latin 'remarkable', 'outstanding'): coast of WA, mainly on deep sandy soils in the Swan River region.
A shrub of smaller stature, usually less than 1 m tall, dense and upright when well grown; the grey-green fleshy leaves are elliptic to ovate to 9–10 mm long and 4–6 mm wide; flowers are borne singly on slender pedicels to 2.5 cm long, from the axils of the upper twigs; calyx 5-lobed, with ciliate margin; petals 5, similarly fringed, both floral parts pale to mid-pink, flowering mostly in late spring.

Verticordia monadelpha (Greek *mono*, 'one', and *adelphos*, 'brother', referring to fusion of the stamen filaments into a single column): Pink Woolly Feather-flower: coast of WA, mainly on sandy, semi-desert country in the Geraldton region.
A shrub to 1 m or so, with many erect slender branches from a crowded base, the plant becoming denser and more leafy when cultivated; leaves linear, 1–2 cm long and 2–3 mm wide; flowers in terminal corymbs of about 10–12, with ciliate sepals and petals, each flower to about 1.5 cm across, deep rose-pink, flowering mostly in spring.

Verticordia nitens (Latin 'shining'): Morrison Feather-flower: western slopes of the Darling Range in WA.
A shrub of about 1 m, with a mass of slender twigs arising from the base; leaves slenderly linear, 1.0–2.5 cm long and 1–2 mm wide, dark green; flowers borne in flattish, terminal corymbs covering the crown of the plant, deep yellowish-orange, flowering very profusely in early summer.
Climatic range. All A, M, P, S, and lower levels of Mts, on well-drained, deep sandy or gravelly soils only.

VIBURNUM

The ancient Latin aboriginal name for one of the species, *V. lantana*, the Wayfaring Tree of Europe and western Asia.
Viburnum (various).

Caprifoliaceae, the Honey-suckle family.

Generic description. A large and important genus of evergreen and deciduous shrubs, a few becoming tree-like, mostly from the northern temperate zone of Asia, America and Europe, and grown extensively for their handsome leaves, flowers and fruits. The leaves are simple, opposite, sometimes lobed, a few colouring well in autumn; flowers are in terminal cymes or panicles, the sterile-flowered sorts with large round heads, mostly white but often with a pink reverse, some sweetly perfumed; and the fruits are borne in flattish clusters over the crown of the plant, the colours red, blue, yellow, or black, some very decorative in autumn or persisting into winter to enhance the bare branches.

Propagation. a) Seeds may be used for the species which reproduce reliably by this means.
b) Most species strike readily by semi-hardwood, leafy cuttings taken in summer, autumn or winter, placed in a warm, humid atmosphere with bottom heat an advantage in winter.
c) Some of the deciduous species are grown by hardwood cuttings in winter, preferably in a warm, moist atmosphere, e.g. *V. opulus*.

Cultivation. Although sometimes seen growing under harsh conditions of climate and soil, the Viburnums respond best to light soils of modern fertility with free drainage, and with adequate water in spring and summer. All enjoy full exposure to sun. All are hardy in the main horticultural centres, but in the more severe climates should be planted in warm, sheltered microclimates only, to obviate the risk of losing flowers by late-frost injury.

Pruning. When given space and light to develop their natural form, there is little reason to prune most species at all. However, several are inclined to become congested by the bountiful growth in the centre of the bush, and should be thinned by complete removal of a few of the oldest shoots every year immediately after flowering in spring, to make way for more productive, new water-shoot growth from the base. Examples are *V. x burkwoodii*, *V. carlesii*, *V. x carlcephalum*, *V. fragrans*, *V. opulus* and *V. rhytidophyllum*.
Evergreen species such as *V. japonicum*, *V. suspensum* and *V. tinus* may be restricted in size if necessary by shortening the longest shoots appropriately but should never be denied their attractive natural form by being clipped closely.

Species and cultivars

Viburnum x *búrkwoodii* (commemorating the raiser, Albert Burkwood, principal of a well-known English nursery firm): an interspecific hybrid between *V. carlesii* and *V. utile*.

Habit. A partly-deciduous shrub to 2–3 m tall, with a mass of ascending shoots arching outward to form a twiggy shrub of globose form to 2 m or so wide. In warm climates it is virtually evergreen.

Leaves. Narrowly to broadly ovate, or elliptical, the blade 7–12 cm long and 2.5–5.0 cm wide; petiole 5–10 mm long; apex acute to acuminate; base rounded to sub-cordate; margin irregularly dentate-serrate, and usually entire on the lowest third; midrib and main laterals prominent beneath; glossy dark green above, whitish grey-green beneath, densely stellate-pubescent; some leaves colour to yellow, scarlet, or crimson in autumn.

Flowers. Inflorescence an umbellate cyme about 6–8 cm across, borne at the ends of the young 1-year-old shoots; corolla salverform, the limb spreading to 1.3 cm wide, pink outside, pure white inside, sweetly and strongly perfumed, flowering from late August to late October.

Fruit. Occasionally produced; fruits are fleshy ellipsoidal drupes about 8 mm long and 6 mm wide, ripening to red in autumn.

Other distinguishing features. Upper twigs brownish-green, with dense stellate tomentum, becoming smooth and grey in the second year. 'Anne Russell' belongs here as a hybrid between *V.* x *burkwoodii* and *V. carlesii*. Semi-deciduous in the mild Sydney climate, growing to 2 m tall and a little broader, with glossy dark-green leaves and sweetly-perfumed flowers in terminal cymose clusters 6–8 cm across over the crown of the plant, the individual flowers reddish in the bud, maturing to pure white.

Climatic range. A, H, M, Mts, P, S.

Vibúrnum x *carlcéphalum:* the interspecific cross between *V. carlesii* and *V. macrocephalum*.

Habit. A partly or fully deciduous shrub of globose shape to 2–3 m tall; retains most leaves in warm climates but autumn colour is then inferior.

Leaves. Broadly oval to ovate, 6–10 cm long and 5–6 cm wide; apex acute or shortly acuminate; base rounded; margin shallowly dentate; midrib and main laterals prominent beneath; glabrous and slightly shiny above, finely stellate-pubescent beneath, maturing to dark green, changing to orange and crimson in autumn.

Flowers. Inflorescence an umbellate cyme 9–12 cm across, at the terminals of the outer 1-year-old shoots; flowers salver-funnelform to 1.5 cm across; calyx 2 mm across, with 5 oval lobes; corolla 5-lobed, the segments broadly ovate, pink in the bud but opening to pure white; stamens 5, as long as the corolla, filaments white, anthers yellow; flowers sweetly and heavily perfumed, flowering from early August to late October.

Other distinguishing features. Upper twigs and buds pale brown, stellate-pubescent, older wood becoming glabrous and greyish in colour, with brown lenticels.

Climatic range. H, M, Mts, S (hills) and on cool, elevated sites in A and P.

Vibúrnum cárlesii (commemorating the British diplomat and amateur plant collector, W. R. Carles, who discovered the plant): Korea and Japan.

Habit. A deciduous shrub to 1.5–2.0 m tall, the many erect shoots forming an irregularly globose bush with heavily stellate-pubescent branchlets and inflorescences.

Leaves. Ovate to broad-elliptic, 5–9 cm long and 4–7 cm wide; apex acute or abruptly acuminate; base obtuse to sub-cordate; margin irregularly serrate-dentate; midrib and the 4–7 pairs of lateral veins prominent beneath and ending in the teeth; dark-green above, whitish-green beneath; stellate-pubescent; some leaves colour to yellow or red in autumn but are usually not spectacular.

Flowers. Inflorescence a hemispheric cyme 7–8 cm across; flowers salverform, the slender tube 1.3 cm long, supported by a short red 5-toothed calyx, the 5-lobed, rotate limb expanded to 1.5 cm across; unopened buds carmine, the tube rose-pink, and the inside of the corolla pure white; heavily and sweetly perfumed, flowering with the first leaves from mid September to early November.

Fruit. A 1-seeded, ellipsoidal drupe 7–10 mm long, red at first, becoming black in autumn.

Other distinguishing features. One of the most beautiful plants grown in Australia and deserving of a choice, sheltered part of the garden.

Climatic range. H, M, Mts, and on cool, well-attended sites in A, P, and S.

Vibúrnum **x** *júddii* (commemorating the raiser, William H. Judd, plant breeder at the Arnold Arboretum, Boston): a hybrid of *V. carlesii* and *V. bitchiuense*.

A newly-imported Viburnum resembling its seed parent *V. carlesii* in its abundant, sweetly perfumed white flowers, lightly stained pink when opening in spring, and handsome dark green leaves until autumn when some turn to yellow, orange and scarlet.

Climatic range. H, M, Mts, and on cool sites in A, P, S.

Vibúrnum davidii (commemorating Abbé Armand David, nineteenth-century French missionary and plant collector in the Orient): western China.

Habit. An evergreen shrub to 1.0–1.5 m tall, but often 2 m or more broad.

Leaves. Narrowly elliptic to obovate, 10–15 cm long and 5–8 cm across; petiole stout 1.0–2.5 cm, terete but grooved and bright crimson above, green beneath; apex acuminate; base cuneate, often oblique and with several small glands; margin shallowly dentate; venation reticulate, the 3 main longitudinal veins converging at the base; dark green, slightly shiny, glabrous and somewhat bullate above, paler below, with axillary tufts of villous hair.

Flowers. Inflorescence a dense cyme about 6–10 cm across; flowers salver-funnelform, 5 mm across at the limb, white, with 5 exserted stamens, flowering in October and November.

Fruit. Elliptic to ovoid, 5–8 mm long and 4–5 mm broad, turquoise-blue, in flattish clusters in autumn; (group-planting ensures better pollination and more abundant fruits).

Other distinguishing features. Upper twigs glabrous, somewhat 4-angled, pale-green, with reddish lenticels, becoming chocolate-brown and rougher in the second year.

Climatic range. A, H, M, Mts, P, S.

Vibúrnum fràgrans (Latin 'with fragrant flowers') (syn. *V. farreri*) northern China and Korea.

Habit. A deciduous shrub to 3–4 m tall, the many erect shoots from the base forming a hemispherical outline.

Leaves. Elliptic to obovate, 5–7 cm long, 3–4 cm wide; apex acute to shortly acuminate; margin sharply serrate; midrib and 5–7 pairs of laterals prominent beneath; pubescent when young, later glabrous; bronze-green at first, becoming dark green above, purplish-green beneath, changing to dull red in autumn.

Flowers. Inflorescence a panicle of 20–40 flowers, at the terminals of the young shoots; flowers salverform, the carmine buds to 1.3 cm long, opening to the flattish limb 1.0 cm wide, with 5 spreading, orbicular lobes with ruffled edges, the corolla white inside with a pink flush on the outside; sweetly perfumed; flowering from early June to late August.

Other distinguishing features. Young twigs reddish-green, stellate-pubescent at first but later smooth and glabrous, the older bark exfoliating in irregular vertical sheets and strings in late autumn; lenticels pale-brown.

Climatic range. A, H, M, Mts, P, S.

Vibúrnum japónicum (Latin 'from Japan'): Japanese Viburnum: Japan and Taiwan.

Habit. An evergreen shrub to 2–3 m tall, of globose form to 3 m wide, densely and attractively foliaged.

Leaves. Elliptic-ovate to rhombic, 8–12 cm long and 4–6 cm wide; petiole 1.5–2.5 cm long, channelled above, glabrous, reddish in autumn; apex acuminate; margin shallowly serrate-dentate, the teeth terminating the main lateral veins, but entire below the middle; veins prominent below; glabrous; bright green and lustrous above, paler and finely glandular-dotted beneath, some leaves changing to red in autumn.

Flowers. Inflorescence a compound cyme to 10 cm across; flowers salverform-rotate, white, sweetly perfumed, flowering in October and November.

Fruit. A 1-seeded drupe, 5–6 mm long, the calyx teeth persisting at the apex, lustrous, crimson, abundant in April and May, in mild areas persisting into winter; seeds cream, flattened on one side.

Other distinguishing features. Young twigs purplish-brown, with shallow longitudinal ridges; lenticels sparse, brown; leaf-scars as wide as the twigs but shallow.

Climatic range. A, H, M, Mts, P, S, and on cool sites in B.

Vibúrnum macrocéphalum 'Stérile' (Greek 'large-headed'): Chinese Snowball-Tree: China.
Habit. A shrub of globose form to 3–4 m tall, mostly deciduous but more evergreen in temperate climates; main trunk short, with many erect spreading branches.
Leaves. Elliptic to ovate, rarely broad-obovate, 4–8 cm long, 3–5 cm wide; petiole 7–12 mm long, stellate-pubescent, channelled above; apex obtuse; base rounded; margin denticulate; midrib and main laterals prominent and yellowish beneath; dark green and slightly scabrous above, paler, dull and densely stellate-pubescent beneath.
Flowers. Inflorescence a terminal, globose compound cyme, 15–20 cm across, the numerous sterile flowers 3.0–3.5 cm across; corolla with 5 broadly obovate to orbicular lobes, pea-green at first, paling to pure white by early October and lasting until November.
Fruit. None produced.
Other distinguishing features. Upper twigs grey-brown, densely stellate-pubescent, becoming warty by the numerous close leaf bases.
This is one of the aristocrats of the plant world, the huge balls of white flowers producing a fine display in the spring garden.
Climatic range. A, H, M, Mts, P, S.

Vibúrnum ópulus 'Stérile' ('Opulus' once the generic name for the Guelder Roses but now used only for a taxonomic section of the genus *Viburnum*): Guelder Rose or Common Snowball Bush: Europe, North Africa and western Asia.
Habit. A deciduous shrub to 3 m tall and 2.5 m wide, the many erect stems arising from a thick-based clump to form a rounded bush.
Leaves. Broadly ovate to 15 cm across, maple-like, with 3 large lobes and several smaller lobes; petiole to 3 cm long, grooved above, with a cluster of 4–12 glands on the upper edge, the stipules at the base aristate or often leafy; apices of the lobes acute; base truncate to sub-cordate; margin coarsely dentate; main veins prominent and pubescent beneath; dark green, changing to deep purple-red in autumn, better in cool, moist climates.
Flowers. Inflorescence a globose, umbellate, compound cyme 6–10 cm across, the flowers all sterile, rotate, 5-petalled to 2.5 cm across, pea-green at first but maturing to pure white, flowering from early October to late November.
Fruit. None produced by 'Sterile' but abundant and handsome in the species.

Other distinguishing features. Young shoots green, with prominent brown lenticels; older stems pale grey; all stems angular with hexagonal cross-section.
'**Nànum**' has a dense, dwarf habit but flowers very sparsely.
'**Notcutt's Variety**' is a well-regarded cultivar in Britain, recently introduced to Australian gardens. Of stronger growth than the parent species, it forms a hemispherical bush about 4 m tall and as broad, with large heads of inner fertile flowers, surrounded by a ring of white sterile flowers in spring, followed by bright-red globose fruits and red foliage in autumn.
Climatic range. A, H, M, Mts, P, S.

Vibúrnum plicàtum var. *plicàtum* (Latin *plicare*, 'to fold', referring to the peculiar folded appearance of the emerging new leaves) (syn. *V. tomentosum* var. *sterile*, *V. tomentosum* var. *plicatum*) Japanese Snowball Bush: southern islands of Japan, also in China and Taiwan.
Habit. A deciduous shrub to 3 m tall, with a few large branches arising from the base and developing a horizontal branching pattern to 3 m wide, the outer stems weighed down by the flowers.
Leaves. Elliptical to broadly ovate, 8–12 cm long, 4–8 cm wide; petiole 2.5–3.5 cm long, channelled above; apex acute to shortly acuminate; base obtuse; margin dentate-serrate; sparsely stellate-pubescent; midrib and 10–14 lateral veins on each side densely pubescent, and prominent below; bright green and slightly shiny above, paler and dull beneath, changing to deep coppery-red in autumn, intensely so in cool, moist climates.
Flowers. Inflorescence a terminal, globose, 2-tiered cyme, 8–10 cm across, borne on new shoots in opposite pairs from the previous year's wood; individual florets sterile, rotate, the 4–5 petals broadly obovate or orbicular, the edges slightly overlapped, the flowers arranged in varying planes; pea-green at first, maturing to pure white, flowering abundantly from early October to mid November.
Fruit. Not produced — all flowers sterile.
Other distinguishing features. Upper twigs metallic-brown with sparse but conspicuous lenticels.
'**Grandiflòrum**' is similar in most respects but has larger florets, in larger, globose heads, becoming slightly pinkish at the edges as the flowers age.

Vibúrnum plicàtum var. *tomentòsum* (Latin 'covered with woolly hairs'): Double-file Viburnum: the wild form of *V. plicatum*, found natively in the principal islands of Japan, and in China, Korea and Taiwan.

Habit. As for *V. plicatum*.

Leaves. As for *V. plicatum*.

Flowers. Inflorescence a flattened, umbellate, compound cyme, about 8 cm across, the marginal flowers sterile, forming a fringe around the inner fertile flowers, all supported by 7-branched, green, stellate-pubescent, 5 cm long peduncles; sterile flowers about 3 cm across, rotate, with 5 unequal petals, the largest towards the outer rim of the inflorescence, the innermost very small, pure white; fertile flowers broadly funnelform to 5 mm across, with 5 reflexed cream-white petals and 5 exserted stamens with white filaments and cream anthers, flowering from early October to mid November.

Fruit. A 1-seeded drupe, green at first, ripening in summer to red, then aging to black, 4–6 mm long, ovoid but somewhat flattish.

Other distinguishing features. Upper twigs as for *V. plicatum*.

'Lanarth' and 'Mariesii' are strong-growing variations with slightly larger florets around the inner fertile flowers, in larger heads.

'Pink Beauty' is slightly smaller than the parent variety, with a dense mass of foliage on spreading horizontal branches, the flowers white at first, but maturing to pale pink.

Climatic range. H, M, Mts, P, S, and on cool, well-managed sites in A, P, and S.

Vibúrnum prunifòlium (Latin 'with leaves resembling *Prunus*'): Black-haw Viburnum: eastern USA.

Habit. A deciduous species to 5 m tall, with a short main trunk and conical head when well grown but otherwise likely to be shrubby or of indeterminate form.

Leaves. Elliptic to ovate, 5–10 cm long and 4–6 cm wide; petiole to 2 cm long, reddish and slightly flanged at the edges; apex acute to obtuse; base broadly cuneate; margin serrulate; veins prominent below; downy at first but soon glabrous; dark green above, paler beneath, changing to orange and scarlet in autumn.

Flowers. Inflorescence a terminal cyme to 10 cm across, the rotate flowers 8–10 mm across, white, with 5 broad, nearly-round petals and 5 prominent stamens, flowering from September to late October.

Fruit. A flattened cluster of 1-seeded, ellipsoidal drupes to 1.3 cm long, green at first but becoming blue-black with a whitish bloom, ripening in autumn, then sweet and attractive to birds.

Other distinguishing features. Young shoots reddish-green, the trunk becoming grey, with irregularly fissured ridges.

Climatic range. A, H, M, Mts, P, S.

Vibúrnum rhytidophýllum (from the Greek words, describing the rough, irregular surface of the leaves): central and western China.

Habit. An evergreen shrub to 2.5–3.0 m tall, with an irregularly globose form.

Leaves. Narrow-ovate to oblong, 15–20 cm long and 3–6 cm wide; petiole to 3.5 cm long, rusty-tomentose; apex acute to obtuse; base obtuse to sub-cordate; margin minutely denticulate; surface rugose, the midrib and main veins prominent beneath; dark green and shiny above, whitish-green and dull beneath, stellate-pubescent.

Flowers. Inflorescence a flat, terminal cyme, 15–18 cm across, the main rachis 5–6 cm long, densely stellate-tomentose, dividing into mostly-7 radial branches carrying the cymes; flowers all fertile, rotate, 5–6 mm across, the buds greenish at first, opening to white in October and lasting into December.

Fruit. A fleshy, usually flattened drupe, ovoid, 5–6 mm long, green at first, changing to red in summer, then maturing to black in autumn and persisting until winter.

Other distinguishing features. Winter buds, petioles and upper twigs rusty stellate-pubescent.

Climatic range. A, H, M, Mts, P, S.

Vibúrnum suspénsum (Latin 'to hang', the application obscure here, although the branchlets are somewhat pendulous): the islands to the south of Japan, mainly the Ryukyus and Taiwan.

Habit. An evergreen shrub, 2–3 m tall, the main branches ascending and spreading to 3 m or so, the smaller branchlets drooping at the ends.

Leaves. Ovate to broadly elliptic, 7–10 cm long, 3.0–4.5 cm wide; petiole 7–10 mm long, apex bluntly pointed or round; base cuneate to obtuse; margin entire or remotely and sparsely toothed above the middle; midrib and 3 to 5 pairs of laterals prominent beneath; glabrous except for a few hairs in the lower axils of the veins; dark green and glossy above, paler beneath.

Flowers. Inflorescence a terminal panicle, 5–6 cm tall, at the ends of the young shoots; calyx slender, tubulate, 5-toothed; corolla salverform to 1 cm long, the tube slender, the limb rotate to 6–8 mm across, pink outside, white inside, sweetly perfumed, flowering from late September to mid-November.

Fruit. An ellipsoidal drupe to 5–6 mm long, in terminal clusters over the crown of the plant, bright-red in autumn.

Other distinguishing features. Branchlets reddish-warty, tomentulose when young but soon glabrous.

Climatic range. A, M, P, S, and in mild, sheltered microclimates in H and Mts.

Vibúrnum tínus (the ancient Latin name for the species): Laurustinus: southern Europe.

Habit. An evergreen shrub, 2–3 m tall and 3 m wide, forming a dense, globose bush with abundant flowers covering the top of the plant.

Leaves. Narrowly elliptic to ovate, 6–10 cm long, 2–3 cm wide; petiole to 1.5 cm long, grooved and hairy on the upper edge only; apex acuminate; base obtuse; margin entire but coarsely undulate; midrib and main laterals prominent beneath, and densely villous in the vein axils; coriaceous, dark green and slightly shiny above, paler and dull beneath.

Flowers. Inflorescence a terminal compound cyme, 8–10 cm across; calyx tubulate at the base, with 5 short spreading sepals; corolla clavate at first and rosy-carmine, opening to a funnelform-rotate, white flower 7–8 mm across, the 5 lobes broadly ovate; stamens 5, exserted; the single pistil shorter than the tube; flowering season from May to October.

Fruit. A 1-seeded ovoid drupe, red at first, becoming turquoise-blue, then ripening in late autumn to blue-black.

Other distinguishing features. Peduncles angular, reddish; flowers faintly perfumed.

var. *lúcidum* is somewhat similar, but the larger leaves are glabrous and dark shining green, the midrib and 3–4 main veins on each side yellowish and prominent beneath, with dense, villous tufts in the axils of the main veins; the inflorescence is larger, to 10–12 cm across, the peduncles and pedicels bright reddish; flowers are larger to 1.3 cm across, pure white inside, often flushed with pink outside, mildly fragrant;

fruit is larger to 7–8 mm long, red, then blue, ripening to blue-black, the calyx lobes persisting at the end.

Climatic range. A, H, M, Mts, P, S.

VÌTEX

The ancient Latin name for the Chaste-Tree, a popular ornamental plant around the Mediterranean since earliest times.

Chaste-Tree or Hemp-Tree.

Verbenaceae, the Verbena family.

Generic description. A large genus of diverse character, with both evergreen and deciduous trees and shrubs inhabiting the warmer parts of the temperate zone. (See specific notes below for the differences between the two main species used in Australia.)

Propagation. a) The species may be grown by seeds sown in spring in a warm place.

b) The species and/or cultivars may be grown by soft-tip cuttings of the young shoots, or by semi-hardwood cuttings from the older wood in autumn in a heated, humidified glass-house.

c) Hardwood cuttings from the prunings of the deciduous *V. agnus-castus* in late winter in a cool, humid atmosphere.

Cultivation. Both species are easy to cultivate in a well-drained, fertile soil and an open, sunny position with adequate water in summer. *V. agnus-castus* is the hardier species, tolerant of cold to −5°C without serious injury.

Pruning. *V. agnus-castus* has its spent inflorescences removed in late summer and is pruned hard in late winter to remove at least half of the past year's growth, to shape the plant into globose form. *V. trifolia* is pruned lightly across the top of the plant in late winter.

Species and cultivars

Vìtex agnus-cástus (Latin *agnus*, 'a lamb', and *castus*, 'pure'; a name of obscure application but with a probable religious significance): Chaste-Tree: southern Europe, especially around the Mediterranean Sea.

Habit. A deciduous, globose shrub to 3 m or so, based on a low-branched short trunk, the branches spreading widely.

Leaves. Compound, opposite, digitately palmate, 15–20 cm long, the 5 to mostly 7, lanceolate leaflets increasing in size from petiole to apex from 5 to 15 cm long, on terete, pubescent petioles to 3–4 cm long; apex of leaflets acuminate; bases cuneate to the 1 cm long petiolules; margins entire; midrib prominent; glabrous and dark green above, finely puberulent and grey-green beneath; aromatic when crushed.

Flowers. Inflorescence a terminal mass of 7 to 9 slender, cymose panicles, varying in length from 10 to 20 cm; cymes of 40–50 flowers; calyx campanulate 3–4 mm long, with 5 short triangular teeth, grey-green; corolla funnelform, the tube about 8 mm long, pubescent inside, the limb 5-lobed, reflexed, violet-blue, paler on the outside; stamens 4, filaments pale violet, anthers dark violet and white; lightly perfumed, flowering abundantly from early December to late February and intermittently throughout autumn.

Fruit. A small, berry-like drupe to 3 mm, obovoid, green at first, then purple-brown, in March and April.

Other distinguishing features. Upper twigs somewhat squarish, puberulent, bright to copper-green.

'Alba' has white flowers, but is otherwise identical with the parent.

Climatic range. A, B, H, M, P, S, and on warm, sheltered sites in Mts.

Vìtex trifòlia (Latin 'having compound leaves of 3 leaflets'): North Coast of NSW and the coast of Queensland, through Indonesia to South-East Asia.

Habit. An evergreen, globose shrub to 2–3 m, usually with a short trunk dividing early into several nearly equal stems.

Leaves. Compound or simple, opposite, trifoliolate or simple-ovate; petiole to 3 cm, finely pubescent; the simple leaves 6–8 cm long and 3–4 cm wide; trifoliolate leaves 6–8 cm long, the terminal leaflet the largest, the others about 4–5 cm long, all sessile, narrow elliptic-ovate; apex acute to acuminate; base rounded when simple, attenuate when trifoliolate; margin mostly entire; midrib and main laterals prominent beneath; glabrous or finely puberulent and bright green above, white-canescent below.

Flowers. Inflorescence a short terminal panicle, all parts white pubescent; calyx tubulate to 3 mm, with 5 short acute teeth; corolla tubulate-labiate, 7 mm long, the limb with 4 equal ovate lobes and an enlarged pubescent fifth, all lavender-blue with a violet throat; stamens 4, exserted, filaments white, anthers blackish-

brown; flowers are borne on young growth from late spring to autumn.

Fruit. A globular drupe to 1 cm across, black, succulent at first, but splitting into 2 valves when ripe in late autumn.

Other distinguishing features. Upper young stems somewhat squarish, puberulent at first but becoming glabrous and dusky-green, with pale brown lenticels.

'Purpurea' has leaves purplish beneath and often with a purplish cast above.

'Variegata' has bright green leaves with an irregular, often very narrow, margin of pale creamy-yellow, occasionally extending to the midrib, or wholly green.

Climatic range. B, P, S, T, and in warm microclimates in M.

WEIGÈLA (formerly included with a somewhat similar genus, *Diervilla*, found only in North America, but now distinct)

Commemorating Prof. Christian E. von Weigel, 1748–1831, German botanical author.
Weigela.
Caprifoliaceae, the Honeysuckle family.

Generic description. A small genus of deciduous shrubs from the Orient, highly regarded by Australian gardeners for their rapid growth, hardiness, and abundance of showy flowers in spring. Leaves are simple, opposite or occasionally 3-whorled, mostly elliptic to ovate, from 5 to 10 cm long and 3–5 cm wide, with acute to acuminate apex, cuneate to obtuse base, finely serrate margin, either glabrous or pubescent, at least on the lower veins, mainly green but with a few coloured or variegated sorts. Inflorescence is a 1- to 5-flowered cyme borne on short leafy lateral twigs issuing from the previous year's branches, the flowers tubulate/funnelform, narrow in the lower half but expanding above to a broad, spreading 5-lobed limb in white, pink, or red; there are 5 stamens, the filaments mostly white, the anthers cream, the single style with a broad white stigma. Flowers are borne freely from late September to early November. Fruit is a slender soft-wooded, 2-valved, dehiscent capsule, 1–3 cm long, with fine seeds, ripening in early autumn.

Propagation. a) Soft-tip cuttings, taken from the

freshly developing shoots when 6–8 cm long in spring, strike readily in a sand/peat mixture in a warm, moist atmosphere, bottom-heat and mist are beneficial.

b) Hardwood cuttings are also used, taken in winter from fully mature dormant wood, mostly 1-year-old, and planted in individual containers in a sheltered shade-house.

Cultivation. Weigelas thrive in a fertile, well-drained soil, fully exposed to sun but preferably protected from harsh winds. They are hardy to low temperatures of at least −10°C.

Pruning. Since the flowers are produced on short leafy twigs arising from the previous year's wood, pruning must be delayed until flowering time or shortly afterwards. The flowering branches may be cut for interior use, being especially effective in large-scale floral arrangements. The best method of pruning involves the removal of about one-third or one-half of the plant each year, cutting out the oldest flowered branches right to their base. This thinning allows the next year's growth to develop freely and with enough space to flower prolifically. Flowered branches should not be merely shortened, as this encourages top growth, which ruins the graceful arching appearance of the plant.

Species and cultivars

The Weigelas grown in Australian gardens are almost all cultivars or hybrids of the main Oriental species, *W. coraeënsis, floribunda, florida, hortensis, japonica* and *praecox.* Distinct in minor morphological detail, the species are relatively unimportant here, the pure species being seen only rarely in collections at botanic gardens and arboreta.

Although the modern nurseries stock only a small representative range, the following cultivars are known to have been imported into Australia and are probably still available. All are worth a place in gardens and municipal parks.

Weigèla '**Abel Carriere**' flowers purplish-carmine in the bud, opening to rosy-carmine, with a yellow spot in the throat.

Weigèla '**Avalanche**' flowers large, pure white; early flowering.

Weigèla '**Bristol Ruby**' flowers ruby-red, larger and deeper in colour than those of its parent 'Eva Rathke'.

Weigèla '**Conquette**' flowers very large, deep rosy-pink, fading to soft shell-pink when mature; vigorous habit, tall to 3 m.

Weigèla '**Esperance**' flowers rosy-salmon, paler within the floral tube, early flowering.

Weigèla '**Eva Rathke**' flowers crimson, with pale-cream exserted anthers, the growth dwarf and compact to 2 m.

Weigèla flórida '**Argénteo marginàta**' has green leaves irregularly margined with white, and a fine serrate edge of rosy-crimson, the intermediate areas grey-green; flowers are rosy-magenta, shading to soft-pink on the outer lobes.

Weigèla flórida '**Aùreo-variegàta**' has flowers as above but the leaves have a creamy-yellow margin at first, fading to creamy-white as they mature; the two cultivars are distinct.

Weigèla flórida '**Fòliis-purpùreis**' has flowers as above but the leaves are suffused with purplish-green, of deeper colour when young but less distinctive by summer.

Weigèla '**Mont Blanc**' flowers large, pure white; plant vigorous to 3 m.

Weigèla '**Newport Red**' flowers bright ruby-red, large and very prolific.

Weigèla '**Styriaca**' flowers are carmine-pink to pale rose-pink on a medium-vigorous, prolific plant.

Climatic range. All A, H, M, Mts, P, S.

WESTRÍNGIA

Commemorating Dr Johann P. Westring, physician to the Swedish royal court and botanical author.

Coast Rosemary.

Lamiaceae, the Mint family (formerly Labiatae).

Generic description. A wholly Australian genus of about 25 species of evergreen shrubs with whorled leaves, and small axillary flowers borne over a long season.

Propagation. a) Short-soft-tip cuttings of 4–5 cm, taken in the active growing seasons, root easily in a sand/peat mixture in a warm, moist atmosphere.

b) Semi-hardwood cuttings taken in autumn and winter are also satisfactory.

Cultivation. The ideal conditions for growth comprise an open sunny position with a light, well-drained soil, preferably enriched with fertilised compost, and with adequate summer water. Westringias tolerate the salty winds of the east coast, often being seen at the extreme edge of the land. Safe in temperatures as low as −5°C but risky in colder places.

Pruning. Regular annual pruning after the flowering season helps to develop and maintain a dense, leafy growth habit in both species. Westringia is ideal for hedging, for tub-planting, or as a protective plant to more fragile material in exposed situations, especially along the coast.

Species and cultivars

Westríngia fruticòsa (Latin *frutex*, 'a shrub', descriptive of the low growth) (syn. *W. rosmariniformis*) Coast Rosemary: NSW coastal heathland, and rocky headlands of the Hawkesbury-Port Jackson area, but also south to Vic and north to Qld.
Habit. A low evergreen shrub to 2 m or so tall and 2 m wide, broadly bun-shaped, but often prostrate when exposed to violent, salty winds.
Leaves. Simple, 4-whorled, with regular internodes, linear-lanceolate, 1.0–2.5 cm long and 3–4 mm wide; apex acute; petiole 1 mm long, purplish; margin entire but recurved; midrib distinct; dark glossy green and glandular above, white-tomentose beneath.
Flowers. Sessile, solitary in the upper leaf axils thus appearing to be 4-whorled; calyx campanulate, 5 mm long, the 5 sharply acute teeth, densely tomentose; corolla bilabiate, the flower 1.8–2.0 cm across, tomentose, white, with a few reddish-purple spots on the lower lobe; flowers abundant from September to December but also intermittent throughout the year.
Fruit. Of 4 nutlets within the calyx-tube, dispersed by wind when ripe.
Other distinguishing features. Upper twigs pubescent and conspicuously ridged between the nodes.
'**Morning Light**' has variegated leaves.
Climatic range. A, B, M, P, S, T, and on warm sites at lower elevations of Mts.

Westríngia glàbra (Latin 'smooth', referring to the leaves): Violet Westringia: Eastern Australia, mainly on the coastal plateaus and adjacent tablelands.
Habit. A bushy shrub to 1.5 m tall, sparse on poor soils, but improved in cultivation, especially on partly-shaded sites.
Leaves. Variable from linear-lanceolate to ovate or obovate to 2 cm long, in whorls of mostly 3, thick and coriaceous, glabrous, dark green and glossy above, dull and paler below.
Flowers. Solitary or in small clusters in the upper axils, abundant, pale lilac to violet-purple,

borne mainly in spring and sporadically throughout the growing period.
Fruit. Not seen.
Other distinguishing features. Young shoots conspicuously angular and sometimes silky.
Climatic range. A, B, M, Mts, P, S.

Westríngia longifòlia (Latin 'with long leaves'): Long-leafed Westringia: eastern Vic. and central NSW coastal strip on coarse sandy or gravelly soils with free drainage, mostly in sheltered gullies between the sea and the lower tablelands.
Habit. An evergreen shrub to about 3 m or so, with an irregular, erect but somewhat spiky form.
Leaves. Simple, 3-whorled, narrowly linear, 2.0–3.5 cm long and 2 mm wide; petiole 1–2 mm; apex acute-mucronate; margin entire, recurved; midrib raised beneath; both surfaces roughened by numerous fine oil glands; mildly aromatic when crushed; dark green and dull above, paler beneath.
Flowers. Solitary, or in twos or threes in the upper leaf axils; calyx campanulate to 3–4 mm long, with 5 sharp teeth, bright green, corolla funnelform-labiate to 1 cm long, white-pubescent inside, pale hyacinth-blue, the middle lobe with 10–12 reddish-brown spots; stamens 4; style 1, white, bifid at the stigma; flowering season, September to November.
Fruit. A 4-celled schizocarp held until ripe by the green persistent calyx tube.
Other distinguishing features. Upper twigs hexagonally ridged, finely pubescent, bright green.
Climatic range. A, B, M, P, S, and in sheltered microclimates in lower Mts.

Westríngia ráleighii (commemorating Raleigh Adelbert Black, 1880–1963, Tasmanian botanical collector): formerly classified as a variety of the Short-leafed Westringia, *W. brevifolia*: Tasmania.
Habit. A twiggy shrub to 1–2 m tall, spreading wider, the upper shoots squarish, finely pubescent, violet-purple above, green beneath.
Leaves. Simple, mostly 4-whorled; petioles 1–2 mm long, whitish-pubescent, blades to 1.5 cm long and 2–3 mm wide, oblong-lanceolate; apex a short, abrupt point; margin revolute; finely glandular and dark green above, white-pubescent beneath.
Flowers. In the upper axils in whorls of 2 to 4; calyx 7–9 mm long, with slender, acute lobes half as long, densely white-pubescent; corolla about 1.5 cm across, varying from nearly white

to lavender, with a few reddish-orange spots near the base of the lobes, the throat with a few sparse hairs; flowering mainly from mid-winter to late spring, with a few at other times.

Fruit. Not seen.

Climatic range. A, B, H, M, Mts, P, S.

'**Wynyabbie Gem**': a hybrid of *W. erimicola* and *W. fruticosa*.

Habit. A densely-leafed shrub to about 1.5 m tall and a litle broader, with strong, erect stems, the young shoots angular and purplish-green.

Leaves. Linear, 2–3 cm long, bright green above, silvery-felted beneath.

Flowers. In axillary clusters at the ends of the upper laterals, pale mauve, flowering mainly in spring and early summer.

Climatic range. A, B, M, P, S, T, and on warmer parts of H, Mts.

YÚCCA

Derived from the native Haitian name for a plant of close resemblance.

Adam's Needle; Spanish Bayonet; Joshua Tree; and other common names for various species.

Agavaceae, the Agave family.

Generic description. A genus of about 30 evergreen species from southern USA and Mexico, most species developing from a stout woody trunk, often short and partly concealed by the stiff narrow leaves, armed with a sharp point; the flowers are borne in a panicle carried on an erect spike sometimes 2–3 m tall, the perianth cup-shaped, mostly white, cream or greenish; and fruit is either a fleshy or dry capsule containing numerous seeds which vary widely in form according to species.

Propagation. a) Seeds sown as soon as ripe germinate freely in an approved sowing mixture kept in a warm, moist atmosphere;
b) Off-sets from the main stem(s) may be detached in early spring and treated as cuttings;
c) Root cuttings are cut into short lengths and laid horizontally on a bed of potting mix kept in a warm, moist atmosphere.

Cultivation. An open coarse soil with free drainage is essential to simulate the somewhat arid conditions of the native habitat, but the species treated here adapt well to a wide range of soils and climates.

Pruning. Removal of the spent inflorescences and old, damaged leaves is the only pruning necessary.

Species and cultivars

Yúcca aloifòlia (Latin 'with Aloe-like leaves'): Spanish Bayonet or Dagger Plant: southern USA, Mexico and West Indies.

Habit. An evergreen plant with a slender, erect trunk to 2–3 m or more, simple or branched, the foliage confined to the apices of short off-shoots.

Leaves. Simple, spirally-arranged, straight, sword-shaped, 45–50 cm long, 3–5 cm wide, tapered to the splayed base and sharp-spined acuminate apex; margin denticulate with minute teeth; light green in the species, but with other colour variations in the cultivars.

Flowers. Pendulous, on drooping pedicels, in an erect panicle to 50 cm long; individual flowers cup-shaped, the 3 petals and 3 sepals of similar form, all creamy-white, with a purplish flush at the base; flowering period in summer.

Fruit. A fleshy, obovoid capsule about 5–6 cm long, 3-celled, green, ripening to purplish-black.

'**Marginàta**' has leaves bordered with yellow.

'**Trícolor**' has yellow or whitish stripes in the middle of the leaves and yellow on the edges.

'**Variegàta**' has yellowish-white stripes.

Climatic range. A, I, M, P, S.

Yúcca filamentòsa (Latin 'bearing cotton-like threads', referring to the appendages on the leaf margins): Adam's Needle: south-east USA, mainly around the Gulf of Mexico.

Habit. A striking foliage plant with a short main stem supporting a rosette-like mass of erect leaves, and developing laterals by off-sets from the base.

Leaves. Simple, arranged spirally at the base, sword-shaped to 50–60 cm long and 3–5 cm wide; apex ending in a sharp, woody spine, the base splayed widely; margin entire but with curling, whitish threads; surface striate; glabrous; dull green.

Flowers. Inflorescence a spire-like panicle to 3 m or more tall, of numerous creamy-white flowers, bell-shaped in the bud but petals and sepals opening to irregular form to 5–6 cm across; slightly perfumed, especially at night; flowering period in summer and autumn.

Fruit. A dry dehiscent capsule with blackish seeds.

'**Variegàta**' is similar except for its yellow-striped leaves.

Climatic range. A, B, M, I, P, S, T, and on lower levels of Mts.

Bibliography

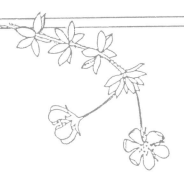

The author wishes to acknowledge the value of reference to the following publications, mainly to verify the identity of the plant material treated.

Anderson R.H. *The Trees of NSW* NSW Government Printer Sydney

Australian Hibiscus Society *Hibiscus Nomenclature, A Guide to the Growing and Culture of Hibiscus* Published by the Society

Australian National Botanic Gardens *Growing Native Plants* vols 1–14 AGPS Canberra

Bailey F.M. *The Queensland Flora* Queensland Government Printer

Bailey L.H. Hortorium, Cornell University *Hortus Third* Macmillan New York

Bailey L.H. Hortorium, Cornell University *Baileya* New York

Beadle N.C.W. Evans O.D. and Carolin R.C. *Flora of the Sydney Region* Reed Books Sydney

Blakely W.F. *A Key to the Eucalypts* Forestry and Timber Bureau Canberra

Blombery A.M. *A Guide to Native Australian Plants* Angus & Robertson Sydney

Brown A. and Hall N. *Growing Trees on Australian Farms* Department of National Development, Forestry and Timber Bureau Canberra

Bruggeman L. *Tropical Plants* Thames and Hudson London

Chippendale G.M. *Eucalypts of the Western Australian Goldfields* AGPS Canberra

———— *Eucalypts Buds and Fruits* Department of Primary Industry Forestry and Timber Bureau Canberra

Chittenden F. *The Royal Horticultural Society Dictionary of Gardening* OUP UK

Cochrane G.R. and others *Flowers and Plants of Victoria and Tasmania* Reed Books Sydney

Costermans L.F. *Trees of Victoria* Costermans Melbourne

———— *Native Trees and Shrubs of South-eastern Australia* Rigby Adelaide

den Boer A. *Flowering Crabapples* American Association of Nurseryman Washington

Eagle A.L. *Trees and Shrubs of New Zealand in Colour* Collins Auckland

Enari L. *Ornamental Shrubs of California* Ward Ritchie Press USA

Erickson R. and others *Flowers and Plants of Western Australia* Reed Books Sydney

Forests Department of Western Australia *Selected Flowering Eucalypts of Western Australia* Forests Department of Western Australia Perth

Francis W.D. *Australian Rain-forest Trees* Forestry and Timber Bureau Commonwealth of Australia

Galbraith J. *Collins Field Guide to the Wild Flowers of South-East Australia* Collins Sydney

Hall N. and others *The Use of Trees and Shrubs in the Dry Country of Australia* Department of

National Development Forestry and Timber Bureau Canberra

Hall N. Johnston R.D. and Chippendale G.M. *Forest Trees of Australia* AGPS Canberra

Harden G. ed *Flora of New South Wales Vol 1* New South Wales University Press Sydney

Harrison R.E. and C.R. *Trees and Shrubs* A.H. and A.W. Reed New Zealand

Hillier and Sons *Hillier's Manual of Trees and Shrubs* Hillier and Sons UK

Hosie R.C. *Native Trees of Canada* Department of the Environment Government of Canada

Hu S.Y. 'The Genus Philadelphus': *Journal of the Arnold Arboretum* vols 35, 36, 37

Jones D.L. *Ornamental Rainforest Plants in Australia* Reed Books Sydney

Kelly S. *Eucalypts* Nelson Melbourne

la Croix T.P. *Rhododendrons and Azaleas* Reed Books Sydney

Lancaster R. *Trees for Your Garden* Floraprint UK

Lee F.P. *The Azalea Book* van Nostrand USA

The Macquarie Dictionary of Trees and Shrubs Macquarie Library Sydney

Metcalf L.J. *The Cultivation of New Zealand Trees and Shrubs* A.H. and A.W. Reed New Zealand

Millet M.R.O. *Native Trees of Australia* Lansdowne Press Melbourne

Morley B.D. and Toelken H.R. *Flowering Plants in Australia* Rigby Adelaide

National Herbarium, Royal Botanic Gardens Sydney *Contributions* NSW Department of Agriculture Sydney

——— *Telopea* NSW Department of Agriculture Sydney

Ohwi J. *Flora of Japan* Smithsonian Institute Washington DC

Penfold A.R. and Willis J.L. *The Eucalypts* Leonard Hill London

Phillips R. *Trees of North America and Europe* Pan Books UK

Polunin O. and Huxley A. *Flowers of the Mediterranean* Houghton Mifflin USA

Pryor L.D. *Trees in Canberra* Department of the Interior Canberra

Rehder A. *Manual of Cultivated Trees and Shrubs* Macmillan New York

Rotherham E.R. and others *Flowers and Plants of New South Wales And Southern Queensland* Reed Books Sydney

Royal Horticultural Society *The R.H.S. Colour Chart* The Royal Horticultural Society London; *The Journal* various authors

Salmon J.T. *New Zealand Flowers and Plants in Colour* A.H. and A.W. Reed New Zealand

Seabrook P. *Shrubs for your Garden* Editions Floraisse France

Smith I.L.L. Smith A.W. and Stearn W.T. *A Gardener's Dictionary of Plant Names* Cassell Sydney

Society for Growing Australian Plants *Australian Plants* Published by the Society

——— *Native Plants for N.S.W.* Published by the Society

Urban Services Department Hong Kong *Hong Kong Trees* Government Printer Hong Kong

Vines R. *Trees, Shrubs and Woody Vines of the Southwest* University of Texas Press USA

West Australian Newspapers and Gardner C.A. *West Australian Wildflowers* W.A. Newspapers Perth

Murdock J.J. *Melastomataceae of Santa Caterina* Herbario Barbosa Rodrigues Brazil

Wyman D. *Trees for American Gardens* Macmillan New York

Glossary

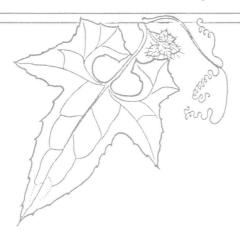

a-: a prefix in Greek compound words, indicating that parts are missing, e.g. 'apetalous', without petals.

ab-: Latin prefix meaning 'away', 'from' or 'off'.

abaxial: the dorsal or reverse side of an organ facing away from the axis.

aberrant: departing from the normal, as in the sudden appearance of variegated leaves in a normally green plant.

abortive: imperfect; improperly developed.

abrupt: occurring suddenly, as in a shortly-acuminate leaf-apex.

acarpous: without fruit; sterile; barren.

-aceae: the typical modern ending in the names of plant families, meaning 'belonging to'.

-aceous: Latin suffix meaning 'like' or 'resembling'.

achene: a dry, one-seeded fruit, which does not split open when ripe.

acicular: needle-shaped, with a slender, stiff point.

acorn: the fruit of *Quercus,* the Oak.

aculeate: armed with prickles, not thorns.

acuminate: the long-pointed, tapering apex of a leaf as in *Prunus serrulata.*

acute: a leaf-apex ending in a sharp point, as in *Plumeria acutifolia.*

ad-: Latin prefix meaning 'to' or 'toward'.

adnate: said of the connection of a smaller structure to a larger, e.g. the fusion of filaments to the inside of a corolla.

adventitious: said of roots or shoots arising in an irregular place, such as the roots developed by cuttings or the buds developed on old stems subjected to damage or heavy pruning.

aerial: the above-ground parts of a plant; aerial roots are those growing from the upper branches as in *Ficus.*

aestivation: the arrangement of the floral parts, especially petals, in the bud.

aggregate: a fruit consisting of a cluster of ripened ovaries.

alate: with projecting wing-like outgrowths as in *Euonymus alatus.*

alternate: the arrangement of leaves or other parts when not opposite or whorled on the stem, e.g. *Camellia japonica.*

ament, amentum: a catkin; an elongate spike of small flowers carried on scale-like bracts, e.g. *Betula pendula.*

amplexicaul: stem-clasping, the base of the leaf partly enveloping the stem as in some juvenile-leafed *Eucalyptus* species.

anastomosed: said of veins which join into a connected network, usually near the margins.

andro-: Greek prefix meaning 'man' or 'male'.

androecium: the pollen-producing part of the flower; the stamens.

Angiosperm: a flowering plant whose seeds are enclosed in an ovary.

annual: a plant which grows to maturity in one vegetative year, e.g. *Zinnia elegans.*

annular: shaped like a ring.

angusti-: Latin prefix meaning 'narrow'.

ant-, anti-: Greek prefixes meaning 'against' or 'opposed to'.

ante-: Latin prefix meaning 'before'.

anterior: the front, as distinct from 'posterior'.

anther: the distal part of a stamen, bearing the pollen.

anthesis: the life period of a flower beginning with the opening of the perianth.

apetalous: lacking in petals.

apex, apices (pl), *apical* (adj): the top or summit of a leaf, inflorescence, petal, sepal, or even the plant itself.

aphyllous: lacking in leaves, or with leaves modified, e.g. *Tamarix aphylla.*

apicula, apiculate (adj): a short, sharp but not rigid or stiff point; usually but not always applied to leaves.

appendage: a secondary outgrowth or attachment, not an essential, integral part.

appressed, adpressed: pressed flatly and closely against but not wholly connected with, e.g. *Cotoneaster adpressus.*

aquatic: plants whose natural habitat is water.

arbor: Latin for 'tree'; hence *arboraceous* — tree-like; *aborescent* — becoming tree-like or growing like a tree; *arboretum* — a collection of trees planted for botanical purposes; *arboriculture* — the cultivation and scientific management of trees.

areole: a small clear space between the veins of a leaf.

aril: an enlarged modification of the small stalk (funicle) of a seed.

aristate: terminating with an awn or stiff bristle.

armed: equipped or provided with thorns, prickles or spines as a means of defence, as in some *Acacias, Pyracanthas, Berberis,* etc.

aromatic: fragrant in flowers, or more commonly, foliage.

articulate: provided with joints such as nodes or parts which meet naturally, e.g. petioles to stems.

ascending: said of branches or stems whose general direction is upward, even though the inner, proximal part may point in another direction.

asexual: reproduction without use of sexual parts; said mostly of propagation by vegetative means, not by seeds.

asymmetrical: irregular, without a symmetrical plane of division in any direction. Especially relevant to the shapes of flowers.

attenuate: slenderly tapered, as in the apices or bases of leaves, e.g. *Persoonia attenuata.*

auricle, auriculate (adj): an ear-shaped appendage often found at the junction of blade and sheath or petiole of some leaves, as in *Plumbago auriculata.*

awl-shaped: subulate; tapered uniformly from base to apex, terminating in a sharp point.

awn: a long, stiff, usually terminal bristle.

axil, axillary (adj): the upper angle formed by the junction of one plant part with another, e.g. leaf petiole and stem.

axis, axes (pl): the main stem of a plant or organ, such as an inflorescence or the rachis of a pinnate leaf.

baccate: berry-like, usually fleshy.

bark: the softer, outer covering of a stem or root as distinct from the wood from which it may be peeled, varying sufficiently in colour, texture and general appearance as to form an important means of distinguishing between species.

base, basal (adj): the lower end of a plant part such as a leaf.

beak: a protruding outgrowth from a fruit or other plant part, e.g. the beaked follicles of *Hakeas.*

beard: having a tuft of hair.

berry: a succulent, indehiscent fruit, mostly of rounded form, containing one or usually many seeds, as in *Fuchsia.*

bi-, bis-: Latin prefix, meaning 'two' or 'twice'.

biennial: a plant requiring two years to grow, flower and die.

bifarious: arranged in a double row on opposite sides of a central axis.

bifid: forked into two prongs or lobes.

bifoliate: having two leaves from the same node.

bifoliolate: a compound leaf with a single pair of opposite leaflets.

bifurcate: forked into two branches, as in some stigmas.

bilabiate: having two lips, as in the flowers of the family *Lamiaceae.*

bilobed: having two lobes, as in the leaves of *Bauhinia.*

bipinnate: twice-pinnate, the paired pinnae being again divided, e.g. *Acacia baileyana.*

bipinnatisect: twice-pinnately divided, the sinuses extending to the midrib.

biserrate: a margin whose teeth bear minor or secondary serrations, usually on the longer, proximal side.

bisexual: said of flowers having both male and female parts in the same flower.

biternate: a leaf which is twice divided into three divisions, as in *Grevillea biternata.*

blade: the lamina, or distal, expanded part of a leaf, beyond the point of connection with the petiole.

bloom: a fine white or bluish powder occurring on plant parts, mostly stems, leaves and fruits, easily removed by rubbing.

boss: a prominence, often pointed, found in the centre of a flat surface such as the female scales of a conifer cone.

brachy-: Greek prefix meaning 'short'.

bract: a modified leaf often found at the base of a flower or pedicel; in *Euphorbia pulcherrima* the bracts are the larger, more colourful part of the inflorescence.

bracteole: small secondary bracts usually found on the pedicel close to and directly beneath the flower as in *Hibiscus.*

bristle: a seta or erect (or nearly so) stiff hair.

bud: the undeveloped stage of a shoot, flower or leaf; *bud-scales* often provide protection against extreme cold.

budding: a form of graftage employing a single growth bud as the scion, inserted beneath the bark of a compatible understock and tied in place.

bulb: a modified shoot in the dormant stage, being made up of a short, disc-like plate from which emerge the roots, and a series of fleshy closely pressed scales with axillary buds between.

bulbil: a small aerial bulb found in the axils of the leaves of *Liliums.*

bulblets: small, partly grown bulbs found among the feeding roots of *Liliums.*

bullate: a roughly blistered surface between the veins of a leaf, as in *Cotoneaster bullatus.*

bush: a plant of low, shrub-like growth, lacking the single trunk of a tree.

caducous: prematurely deciduous as in the bracts of *Magnolia* flowers.

caespitose, cespitose: of tufted growth with many closely arranged shoots from a common base.

calcar, calcarate (adj): a spur-like appendage at the base of a petal or sepal, as in *Delphinium.*

calceolate: shaped like the toe of a slipper, as in *Calceolaria.*

callus tissue: the whitish cell tissue developing at the base of a cutting or other wound.

calyptra: a hood-like covering on certain flowers or fruits, e.g. *Podalyria calyptrata.*

calyx, calyces (pl): the outer whorl of sepals enclosing the corolla.

cambium: a layer of rapidly dividing cells located between the wood and bark of woody stems and roots, responsible for their growth in diameter and the healing of wounds; of special importance in grafting.

campanulate: bell-shaped, as in the flowers of *Campanula.*

canaliculate: channelled or furrowed longitudinally, as in many petioles.

canescent: hoary or so finely pubescent as to make the individual hairs indistinct; usually greyish.

capillary: very slender, like a hair; usually applied to vascular tissue.

capitate: having a head-like form, as in the inflorescence of *Cornus capitata.*

capitulum: an inflorescence composed of many flowers arranged densely together in a flat or mounded disc, as in the family Asteraceae.

capsule: a dry, dehiscent fruit of more than one carpel, opening either at the apex or at the side when ripe, e.g. *Eucalyptus.*

carinate: keeled with a strengthening ridge usually on the lower surface, especially in leaves.

carpel: the female part of a flower bearing the ovule(s) at the base and elongated into the style and stigma.

carpo-, -carp: Greek prefix and suffix referring to 'fruit'.

caryo-: Greek prefix referring to 'nut'.

catkin: a slender, often pendulous, inflorescence bearing many sessile, unisexual flowers lacking in petals, e.g. *Salix.*

caul-, -caul: Latin prefix and suffix meaning 'stem'.

cauline: pertaining to the stem.

chloro-: Greek prefix meaning 'light green'.

chlorophyll: the minutely-granular, green colouring matter in plants.

cilium, cilia (pl), *ciliate* (adj): a short, fine hair; a margin fringed with such hairs as in many *Tibouchina* spp.

cinereous: ashy-grey coloured as in *Eucalyptus cinerea.*

circinate: rolled into a circular coil with the tip innermost, as in an unfolding frond of a fern.

circum-: Latin prefix meaning 'around'.

cladode: a green, flattened, modified stem performing the function of a leaf.

clasping: amplexicaul; said of a leaf base which partly or wholly surrounds the stem.

clavate: club-shaped, like an Indian club, with a slender base but thickening towards the apex; usually applied to flower buds and fruits.

cleft: said of leaves whose margins are cut or divided into lobes with sinuses short of the midrib.

clone, clonal (adj): a group of plants composed of individuals derived in a direct line from a single original plant and kept true-to-type in cultivation by vegetative propagation; the term applies equally to any single individual of a clone.

coalescent: plant parts fused or grown together.

cochleate: coiled spirally like a snail's shell.

columnar: applied to the shape of plants when their form is that of a column or erect pillar, with nearly-vertical, parallel sides.

complete flower: one with all parts present.

composite: a plant species of the old family Compositae, now Asteraceae.

compound: not simple; in compound leaves, leaflets are arranged along a central axis or rachis as in *Cassia,* or radially as in *Aesculus.*

compressed: flattened; mostly applied to stems or fruits normally rounded.

concave: hollowed inwards.

concolorous: having a single uniform colour throughout.

cone: a collection of flowers or fruits arranged on a central axis, usually elongated, e.g. conifers and *Casuarina.*

conical: a term applied to solid, three-dimensional bodies (not flat) and applicable especially to the shape of trees with a circular base and slender, tapering apex, like a young plant of *Cedrus.* (Trees are *not* pyramidal unless clipped to that shape.)

confluent: parts running together to unite with others, as in the cone-scales of Junipers.

connate: parts joined together, usually at the base, as in petals.

connective: the link joining the two cells of an anther together.

constricted: a part drawn together or narrowed as between the seeds of a cylindrical legume, as in *Sophora japonica.*

contorted: twisted out of the normal shape, as in *Salix matsudana* 'Contorta'.

convex: curved or arched outward; the antonym of 'concave'.

convolute: rolled up lengthwise, with overlapping edges.

coppice: used generally to designate a small grove of trees, but technically referring to a group of trees periodically cut or felled for various purposes, such as the provision of fuel.

cordate: having a heart-shaped base with two rounded lobes, the leaf shape usually being broadly ovate as in *Tilia cordata.*

coriaceous: having a tough, leathery texture; mainly applied to leaves.

corm: a solid bulb-like storage organ with growth buds at the apex and giving rise to roots at the base, e.g. *Gladiolus.*

cornicle, corniculate (adj): a small horn-like protuberance as seen on the capsules of *Parrotia persica.*

corolla: the inner whorl of floral parts made up of petals which may be united or free, usually alternating with the sepals in the whorl below.

corrugate: wrinkled into regular ridges, as at the branch junctions of many of the smooth-barked *Eucalyptus* spp. e.g. *E. rossii.*

corymb, corymbose (adj): an inflorescence in which the pedicels are longer towards the base of the central axis, thus bringing the flowers to much the same level, the outer flowers opening first, e.g. *Luculia gratissima.*

costa, costate (adj): a rib of thickened tissue to provide strength or support as in the capsular ribs of *Angophora costata.*

cottony: tomentose; covered with a dense mat of short, soft, whitish hairs.

cotyledon: a primary leaf in the embryo of a seed, a single leaf in Monocotyledons, an opposite pair in Dicotyledons.

crateriform: shaped like a volcanic crater; saucer-shaped.

creeping: said of stems that remain close to the ground surface and often develop roots at the nodes as in the prostrate *Grevilleas.*

crenate: a leaf-margin with shallow dentate teeth, bluntly rounded at the points.

crenulate: diminutive of the above; finely or minutely crenate.

crescentic: shaped like a first-quarter moon; strongly falcate.

crisped, crispate (adj): regularly wrinkled or puckered at the margin as in *Ardisia crispa.*

crown: the head or top of a tree.

crustaceous: having a dry, brittle texture.

culcullate: hood-shaped.

cultivar: The International Code of Nomenclature for Cultivated Plants (1961) Article 5 states . . . 'The term cultivar, abbreviated cv., denotes an assemblage of cultivated individuals which is distinguished by any characters (morphological, physiological, cytological, chemical, or others) significant for the purposes of agriculture, forestry, or horticulture, and which, when reproduced (sexually or asexually), retains its distinguishing features.'

cultrate, cultriform: sharp-edged like a knife, as in *Acacia cultriformis.*

cuneate: wedge-shaped at the base.

cupule, cupulate (adj): a cup-shaped structure, as in the base of the acorn in *Quercus.*

cusp, cuspidate (adj): a sharp, rigid point, mainly applied to leaf-apices.

cutting: a severed portion of stem, leaf or root used in propagation.

cyano-: Greek prefix meaning 'blue'.

cyathium, cyathiform (adj): the cup-shaped involucre peculiar to the inflorescence of *Euphorbia.*

cylindrical: an elongate structure with circular cross-section.

cyme, cymose (adj): a broad, flattish, determinate inflorescence in which the central terminal flower opens first, others developing from the forked lateral branches; the branching may be symmetrical or irregular.

de-: Latin prefix meaning 'down', 'from' or 'away'.

deca-: Greek prefix meaning 'ten'; *decem-:* Latin prefix meaning 'ten'.

deciduous: not persistent; falling off, as in leaves, bracts or scales, not necessarily associated with autumn.

declined: turned or bent downwards, as in leaf-apices, stamens, etc.

decorticate: to shed or peel off the outer bark of a tree, as in many of the smooth-barked Eucalypts.

decumbent: said of branches lying on the ground but with ascending ends.

decurrent: running down the stem and attached for part of its length, as in the leaves of *Acacia decurrens.*

decurved, deflexed: curved or bent downwards.

decussate: the arrangement of opposite leaves on a stem, adjacent pairs being at right angles to each other forming four equal longitudinal rows, e.g. *Melaleuca decussata.*

dehiscent (adj): said of a fruit that opens or splits when ripe to free seeds.

deliquescent: said of a tree whose leading stem is lost among the branches; antonym of 'excurrent' (q.v.) e.g. *Jacaranda mimosifolia, Ulmus parvifolia, Sapium sebiferum.*

deltoid: shaped like a delta; triangular, as in the leaves of *Populus deltoides.*

dendri-, dendro-, -dendron: Greek prefixes and suffix meaning 'tree'.

dentate: a leaf-margin having sharp teeth directed outwards, not upwards.

denticulate: diminutive of above; finely dentate.

depressed: flattened or pressed down; sunken as in veins.

derma-: Greek prefix meaning 'skin'.

determinate: having a definite limit; usually applied to inflorescences which do not lengthen indefinitely, e.g. umbel or corymb.

di-, dis-: Greek prefixes meaning 'two' or 'twice'.

dich-, dicho-: Greek prefixes meaning 'apart' or 'divided into two'.

dichotomous: branches or other organs which divide regularly into pairs.

Dicotyledon: an Angiosperm whose seed-leaves are in an opposite pair.

didynamous: having two pairs of stamens of different length.

diffuse: with spreading or loose, open growth habit.

digitate: radiating like fingers; said of an arrangement of parts such as leaflets which arise from a common central point, as in *Schefflera actinophylla.*

dimorphic, dimorphous: having two markedly different growth forms or types of leaves, as in the juvenile and adult forms of foliage in *Eucalyptus* spp.

dioecious: having unisexual, male and female flowers on different plants, as in *Acer negundo.*

disc: the centre or tubulate flowers of Asteraceae (formerly Compositae) as distinct from the outer, expanded ray florets, e.g. *Felicia.*

discolorous: having two distinct colours, as in the upper and lower leaf surfaces of many of the *Cotoneaster* spp.

dissected: deeply cut, but not separated, into many narrow segments, as in *Acer palmatum* 'Dissectum'.

distal: at the outer end, farthest from the point of attachment; the antonym of 'proximal' (q.v.).

distended: swollen or inflated.

distichous: arranged in two opposite vertical ranks, e.g. the leaves of *Lonicera nitida.*

diurnal: opening during or lasting only a day, as in most *Hibiscus* flowers.

divaricate: branching or spreading widely.

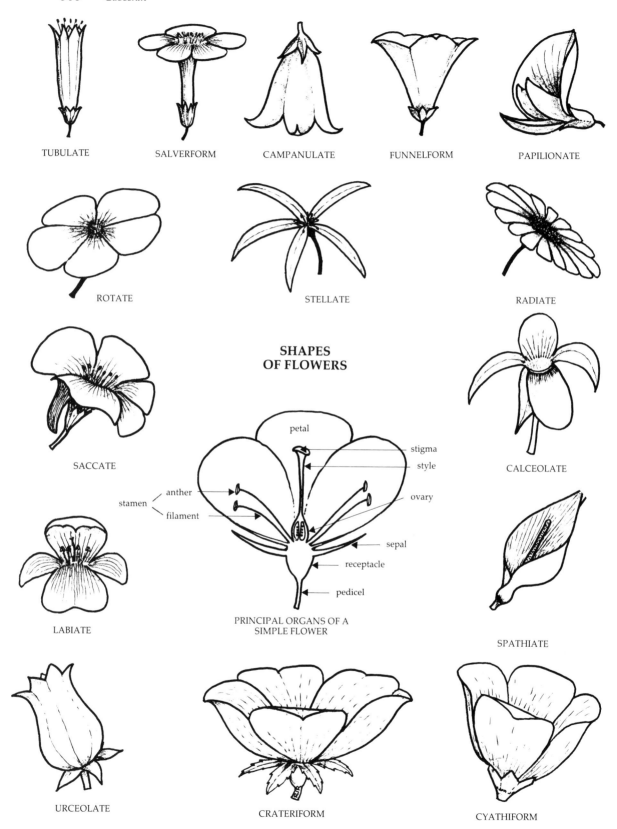

TUBULATE

SALVERFORM

CAMPANULATE

FUNNELFORM

PAPILIONATE

ROTATE

STELLATE

RADIATE

SHAPES OF FLOWERS

SACCATE

CALCEOLATE

petal

stigma

style

ovary

anther

stamen

filament

sepal

receptacle

LABIATE

pedicel

PRINCIPAL ORGANS OF A
SIMPLE FLOWER

SPATHIATE

URCEOLATE

CRATERIFORM

CYATHIFORM

divided: said of a leaf whose margin is lobed to or near the rachis.

division: a method of propagating perennials which form suckering or tillering offshoots, each new plant having a sound crown and some roots.

dorsal (adj): pertaining to the back of a leaf or other organ.

dorsi-, dorso-: Latin prefixes meaning the 'back'.

double: applied to flowers with petals increased in number beyond the norm, often by modification of stamens.

downy: having a surface with short, soft hairs.

drupe: a fleshy, indehiscent fruit with a hard kernel containing a solitary seed, e.g. peach, cherry, plum, apricot.

drupelet, drupel: a small drupe, usually one of the individual seeds in an aggregate fruit like a blackberry or strawberry.

e-, ex-: Latin prefixes meaning 'not', 'beyond', 'out of', 'out from' or 'without', indicating that parts are missing, e.g. *ecostate* — without ribs, *exstipulate* — without stipules.

eccentric: not centrally located, as in the midrib of a leaf or the point of attachment with the petiole in a peltate leaf.

echinate: a surface with sharp pimply swellings of narrow conical shape.

ellipsoid, ellipsoidal (adj): pertaining to a solid structure with the shape of an ellipse, applied generally to fruits of that shape.

elliptic, elliptical: shaped like an ellipse, but of plane surfaces such as leaves, not solids such as fruits.

emarginate: a leaf-margin with a distinct notch at the apex.

embryo: the undeveloped plant within the seed-coat.

endo-: Greek prefix meaning 'within' or 'inside'.

ennea: Greek prefix meaning 'nine'.

ensiform: sword-shaped; said of leaves with a long narrow blade and fine point, e.g. *Phormium tenax.*

entire: a margin free of any indentation, e.g. *Ligustrum lucidum.*

epi-: Greek prefix meaning 'on' or 'upon'.

epicormic: said of strong-growing shoots developing from the woody trunk of a plant, especially if heavily lopped.

epidermis: the outer skin of plant parts such as leaves.

epigynous: having floral organs, petals, sepals and stamens above the ovary.

epipetalous: occurring on the petals or corolla.

epiphyte: an 'air' plant, growing on for support, but not parasitising, another host plant.

erose: a margin with a jagged, irregular edge.

estuarine: pertaining to an estuary; the flora of such a habitat.

evergreen: a plant remaining in foliage throughout the year.

excurrent: a plant form in which the main axis is clearly dominant from base to apex; antonym of 'deliquescent' (q.v.); e.g. *Liquidambar styraciflua.*

exfoliate: to shed the outer surface or layer of bark by flaking or peeling.

exotic: foreign, not native; introduced from another country.

exserted: projected beyond, as of stamens which extend beyond the mouth of the corolla.

exude, exudation: to release fluids, resins, etc. from a plant, e.g. kino from the trunk of *Eucalyptus* spp.

eye: a growth bud used in 'budding'; a spot or ring of contrasting colour in the centre of a flower.

facial: the plane surface facing the observer rather than the lateral or dorsal surfaces or edges.

falcate: crescentic or sickle-shaped, as in the leaves of many *Eucalyptus* spp.

family: the taxon immediately subordinate to the order; a group of closely related genera. Modern family names end in -aceae.

farinose, farinaceous: mealy; a surface covered with hairs so short that they appear to be a whitish dust and are easily removed.

fasciation: a plant abnormality in which stems grow together to assume a laterally flattened form.

fascicle: a cluster of flowers, leaves, etc.

fastigiate: having erect, slender growth as in *Quercus robur* 'Fastigiata'.

faveolate: with a surface resembling the cells of a honey-comb.

female: a plant or flower bearing pistils but lacking in stamens.

fenestrate: having transparent or translucent spots or patches in an otherwise opaque structure such as a leaf.

-ferous; Latin suffix meaning 'bearing'.

ferruginous: of rust-red colour.

fertile: having the capacity to bear seeds or fruits; also said of pollen-bearing anthers.

fetid, foetid: having a strong, unpleasant odour.

fibrilla, fibrillose (adj): a fine, hair-like filament or fibre; said of an organ such as a leaf or sepal with a fringed edge of such fibres.

-fid: Latin suffix meaning 'split', 'cleft' or 'divided'.

filament: the elongate, slender part of a stamen supporting the anther.

fili-: Latin prefix meaning 'thread'.

filiform: long and slender, like a thread.

fimbriate: fringed, as in the petals of *Camellia japonica* 'Fimbriata'.

fistula, fistulate (adj), *fistulose* (adj): an elongate, hollow, cylindrical structure like a pipe, e.g. *Cassia fistula* capsules.

flabellate: fan-shaped.

flaccid: soft, weak, flexible, especially in relation to leaves.

flavi-: Latin prefix meaning 'yellow'.

flexuose, flexuous: bent from side to side in zigzag fashion, as in the stems of *Agonis flexuosa*.

floccose: woolly, especially when easily removed as in the leaves of *Populus alba*.

flora: the plants of a particular locality; a descriptive book or list of those plants.

floral: pertaining to flowers.

floral leaves: leaves immediately beneath the flowers.

floret: a small flower of a larger inflorescence such as the disc- and ray-florets of Asteraceae (formerly Compositae).

flori-, -florous: Latin prefix and suffix meaning 'flower'.

floriculture: the commercial cultivation of flowering plants.

floriferous: abundant in flowers.

floury: covered with a white, dust-like coating; also said of pome fruits with a dry, soft-textured flesh.

flower: the term to cover the structure bearing the sexual parts, either staminate or pistillate, or both, when it is a 'perfect' flower, as well as the perianth parts such as calyx and corolla, which if both present, make the flower 'complete'.

foliaceous: said of other parts such as sepals, bracts or stipules that resemble leaves.

-foliate: in compound words, 'having leaves', e.g. *trifoliate* — 3-leafed.

folio-: Latin prefix meaning 'leaf'.

-foliolate: in compound words, 'having leaflets', e.g. *trifoliolate* — with 3 leaflets.

follicle: a dry, dehiscent fruit with usually many seeds, splitting along one side only when fully ripe as in *Brachychiton*.

forest: land occupied by a plant community consisting mainly of trees, either natural or cultivated; said also of the plants themselves.

form, forma, formae (pl): the lowest taxon in the plant classification system, immediately subordinate to the botanical variety or varietas, used mainly to distinguish plants showing only a minor departure from the norm, e.g. size or colour of flowers or foliage.

foveolate: pitted with small depressions.

fragrance, fragrant (adj): a pleasant perfume as in *Viburnum fragrans*.

free: separate and independent, not united in a group or attached to other parts.

fructi-: Latin prefix meaning 'fruit'.

fruit: the seed-bearing part of a plant, consisting of ovary and fertilised seeds.

frutescent: becoming shrubby or woody.

fruticose: shrubby, with woody stems as in *Westringia fruticosa*.

fulvous: of a dull yellowish colour.

funicle: the small stalk connecting a seed to the ovary.

funnelform: a flower shape with a gradual widening of the corolla from base to mouth, e.g. *Plumeria*.

furcate: branched or forked.

furrowed: having longitudinal grooves, as in leaves and bark.

fusiform: a solid body tapered at both ends like a spindle, e.g. the cigar-shaped follicles of *Nerium oleander*.

galeate: helmet-shaped.

gamo-, -gamous: Greek prefix and suffix meaning 'united'.

gamopetalous: having the petals united.

gamosepalous: having the sepals united.

geniculate: with an abrupt bend, like the knee joint.

genus: a group of closely related species; the taxon immediately subordinate to the family. Generic names are always capitalised.

germination: the process of growth of a seed to become independently established.

gibbous: with convex swellings, usually at the base of a structure, e.g. the corolla of *Enkianthus perulatus*.

glabrous: smooth, not hairy, e.g. *Photinia glabra*.

gladiate: sword-shaped; applied mainly to long, slender leaves, as in *Gladiolus* spp.

gland: an appendage or part normally dry but sometimes containing a substance such as oil or resin.

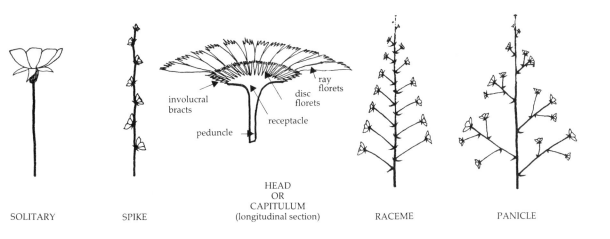

SOLITARY   SPIKE

involucral
bracts

ray
florets

disc
florets

receptacle

peduncle

HEAD
OR
CAPITULUM
(longitudinal section)

RACEME   PANICLE

INFLORESCENCES

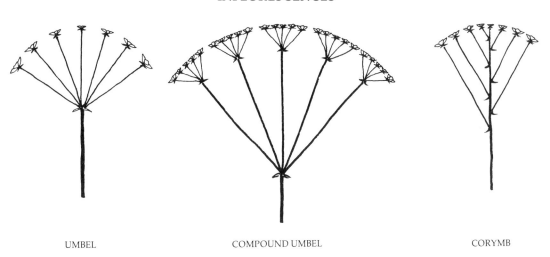

UMBEL   COMPOUND UMBEL   CORYMB

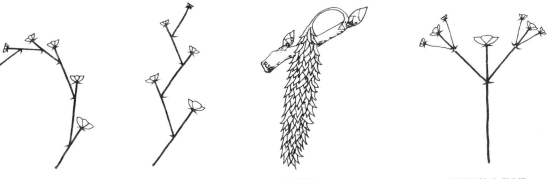

MONOCHASIAL CYMES   CATKIN   DICHASIAL CYME

glaucous, glaucescent: covered with a bluish-white bloom, or of this colour; becoming so coloured, e.g. *Acacia glaucescens.*

globose, globular: globe-shaped or spherical or nearly so.

glomerule: a dense cluster of flowers, e.g. *Syncarpia glomulifera.*

glumes: the chaffy, usually-sterile bracts enclosing the base of the flowers in grasses.

glutinous: sticky, usually as the result of exudation as in *Alnus glutinosa.*

grafting: the process of uniting a part of one plant (scion) with the stem or roots of another (understock). The principal methods are approach-, apical-, side-, bud-, and bridge-grafting.

granular, granulous: with minute grains on a plane surface, e.g. *Tibouchina granulosa.*

guttation: the exudation of droplets of water from leaves in excessively humid conditions.

Gymnosperm: a plant of the subdivision Gymnospermae whose seeds are not enclosed in an ovary but lie naked on the female cone-scales as in conifers and cycads.

gynoecium: the female part of a flower.

habit: the style of growth of a plant referring particularly to the pattern of its main branches.

habitat: the locality and environment conditions to which a plant is indigenous.

hastate: arrow-shaped but with the two basal lobes standing out at a horizontal or wide angle.

head: a capitulum; a dense cluster of sessile flowers.

heath, heathland: land, sometimes adjacent to the seashore, but also seen at higher, even alpine elevations, occupied mainly by low, shrubby plants in a wide variety of species; the growth habit is conditioned mainly by severe climate, nutritional and drainage factors as well as by the occurrence of frequent bushfires.

heel: the basal end of a cutting with a small portion of older wood attached as would occur when a lateral branch is pulled outward and downward.

helio-: Greek prefix meaning 'sun'.

hemi-: Greek prefix meaning 'half'.

hepta: Greek prefix meaning 'seven'.

herbaceous: said of plant stems which are usually soft, and die to the roots or main stems each year, e.g. Perennial Phlox.

hermaphrodite: bisexual; a flower with both sexes present.

hetero-: Greek prefix meaning 'different', 'various' or 'diverse'.

hex-, hexa-: Greek prefixes meaning 'six'.

hilum: the small scar on a seed marking its original point of attachment with the seed vessel.

hip: contraction of hypanthium (q.v.): the fruit of the rose.

hirsute: having a coarsely hairy surface.

hirsutulous: diminutive of above; slightly hairy.

hirtellous: softly hairy.

hispid: having a surface covered with short, stiff hairs.

hispidulous: diminutive of above; minutely hispid.

hoary: canescent (q.v.)

homo-: Greek prefix meaning 'similar' or 'alike'.

hook: an accessory organ, mostly a modified stem, like a slender, backward pointing prickle used as a climbing aid, e.g. *Bougainvillea.*

husk: the outer, often non-fleshy covering of certain fruits; e.g. Coconut.

hybrid: a plant resulting from the crossing of two different species, or their subordinate taxa, subspecies, varieties or forms; plants so produced are designated with a small 'x' preceding the specific epithet, e.g. *Magnolia* x *soulangiana.*

hypanthium: the calyx tube or cup developed from the fusion of other organs such as sepals and androecium as in the genus *Rosa.*

hyper-: Greek prefix meaning 'above', 'beyond' or 'over'.

hypo-: Greek prefix meaning 'below', 'less' or 'under'.

hypogynous: having the calyx, corolla and androecium placed on the receptacle beneath the ovary.

imbibition: absorption of water by a seed as a preliminary to germination.

imbricate: overlapping in regular fashion like roofing shingles.

imparipinnate: said of a pinnate leaf having an odd number of leaflets, that is, with a single terminal leaflet, e.g. *Fraxinus* spp.

imperfect: lacking essential sexual organs, either stamens or pistils.

impressed: sunken below the general plane, as in sunken veins.

il-, im-, in-, ir-: Latin prefixes indicating 'not'.

incanous: with a grey or whitish pubescence as in *Alnus incanus.*

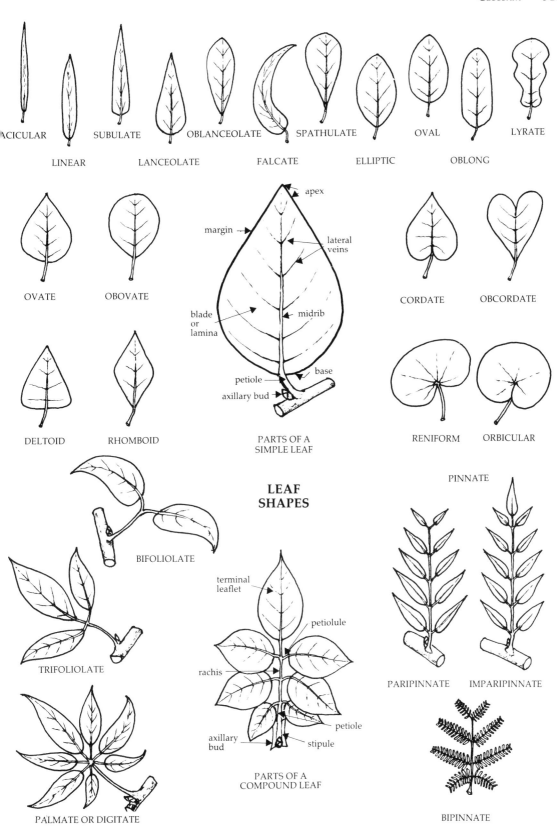

ACICULAR LINEAR SUBULATE LANCEOLATE OBLANCEOLATE FALCATE SPATHULATE ELLIPTIC OVAL OBLONG LYRATE

OVATE OBOVATE

apex

margin

lateral veins

blade or lamina midrib

base

petiole

axillary bud

PARTS OF A SIMPLE LEAF

CORDATE OBCORDATE

DELTOID RHOMBOID

RENIFORM ORBICULAR

LEAF SHAPES

BIFOLIOLATE

TRIFOLIOLATE

PINNATE

terminal leaflet

petiolule

rachis

axillary bud

petiole

stipule

PARTS OF A COMPOUND LEAF

PARIPINNATE IMPARIPINNATE

PALMATE OR DIGITATE

BIPINNATE

incised: deeply and irregularly cut, referring mainly to leaves, sepals, petals or stipules.

included: said of parts set wholly within a structure such as stamens shorter than the corolla; the antonym of 'exserted'(q.v.).

indehiscent: a fruit that does not open or split when mature.

indeterminate: an inflorescence whose axis is not limited by terminal flowers, e.g. the spike of *Callistemon.*

indigenous: native of a particular region.

indumentum: any form of hairy or woolly covering in a plant.

induplicate: with margins rolled inwards.

inferior: of lower or subordinate rank or position.

infertile: barren or non-productive.

inflated: distended like a bladder.

inflorescence: the arrangement of flowers in a cluster, or the cluster of flowers itself rather than the arrangement.

infra-: Latin prefix meaning 'below', 'beneath' or 'under'; hence, *infraspecific* — below the rank of species.

infundibular: funnelform (q.v.).

inodorous: scentless; without odour or perfume.

inserted: an organ growing out of or on another structure, as in stamens attached to the corolla.

inter-: Latin prefix meaning 'between'; hence *interspecific* — between species, a term commonly used for hybrids.

interjugary: the spaces on the rachis of a pinnate or bipinnate leaf between the leaflets or pinnae; glands occur in this position in some *Acacia* spp.

internode: the part of a stem between adjacent nodes or joints.

interpetiolar: found on stems between the bases of opposite petioles, e.g. stipules in *Rondeletia* spp.

interveinal: the spaces between the main veins.

intra-: Latin prefix meaning 'within' or 'inside'; hence *intraspecific* — within the species, a term commonly used to designate the close scion-understock relationship in grafting when a cultivar is grafted to an understock of its own species or to another cultivar within the species.

intramarginal: a vein just within and following the margin closely; characteristic of *Eucalyptus* leaves.

introduced: not native but brought in from another region; exotic.

involucre, involucral (adj): a whorl of mostly leafy bracts just below a flower or cluster, e.g. *Hibiscus* spp.

involute: rolled inwards along the edges.

irregular: flowers that are asymmetrical on the main axis.

iso-: Greek prefix meaning 'equal'.

jointed: articulate or bearing nodes, as in stems.

jugate: with paired leaflets, usually prefixed numerically as 'multijugate'.

juncous: like a rush; of the order Juncaceae, as in *Spartium junceum.*

juvenile: said of plants or parts differing significantly between their early, immature and, later, mature forms; as in leaves of many *Eucalyptus* spp.

keel: the ridge formed on the lower side of some leaves by the thickening and strengthening of the midrib; the two lowest petals of a pea-shaped flower.

key: a samara; usually applied to the fruits of *Acer* and *Fraxinus* spp.

kino: the reddish gum exuded from the bark of *Eucalyptus* spp., especially the Bloodwoods.

labiate: having a lipped calyx or corolla, as in family Lamiaceae, formerly Labiatae.

lacerate: irregularly divided or cut.

laciniate: cut into narrow, pointed lobes as in *Alnus incana* 'Laciniata'.

lacti-: Latin prefix meaning 'milky'.

lamellate: composed of transversely arranged partitions or thin plates, e.g. the core of the stems of *Forsythia* and *Juglans* spp.

lamina: a leaf blade.

lamini-, lamelli-: Latin prefixes meaning 'plate-like' or 'leaf-like'.

lanate: loosely woolly.

lanceolate: lance-shaped, as in leaves, the length being 4 to 6 times the width, e.g. *Azara lanceolata.*

lanuginose: covered with soft, fine woolly hair.

lat-, lati-: Latin prefixes meaning 'broad'.

lateral: on the side or edge, not front or rear.

latex: the usually white, milky sap of certain genera such as *Plumeria, Euphorbia* and *Ficus* spp.

lax: of irregular, loose, open growth habit, e.g. *Tibouchina laxa.*

leaf: the usually green, flat organ attached to a stem by a petiole and responsible for the

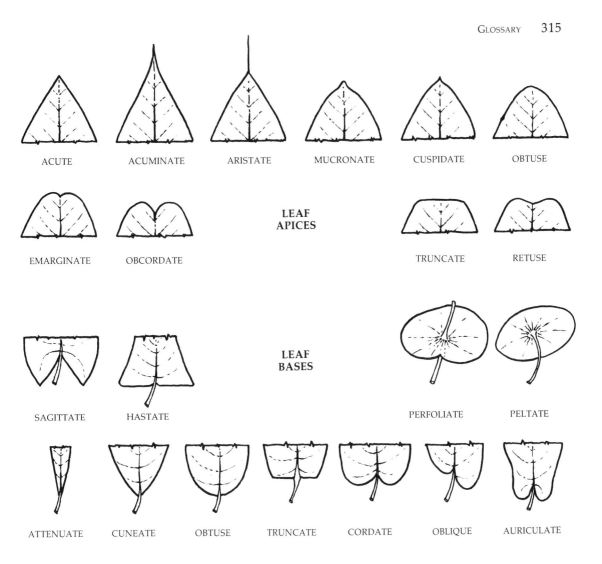

ACUTE   ACUMINATE   ARISTATE   MUCRONATE   CUSPIDATE   OBTUSE

LEAF APICES

EMARGINATE   OBCORDATE   TRUNCATE   RETUSE

LEAF BASES

SAGITTATE   HASTATE   PERFOLIATE   PELTATE

ATTENUATE   CUNEATE   OBTUSE   TRUNCATE   CORDATE   OBLIQUE   AURICULATE

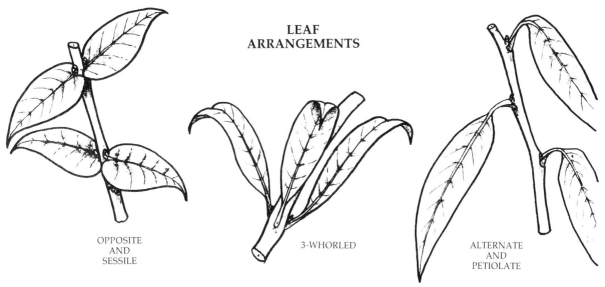

LEAF ARRANGEMENTS

OPPOSITE AND SESSILE   3-WHORLED   ALTERNATE AND PETIOLATE

manufacture of plant food by the process of photosynthesis. Leaf dimensions apply to the blade only, not the petiole.

leaflet: a secondary part of a compound leaf; a pinna or pinnule.

leaf-bud sinus: a small window-like aperture between the lower edges of leaves of the youngest growth buds in *Hebe* spp.

leaf-stalk: a petiole.

legume: a pod or dry, dehiscent fruit splitting along both lateral sutures; the fruits of the plant families Caesalpiniaceae, Mimosaceae and Fabaceae (formerly united in Leguminosae).

lemma: in the grasses, the inner chaffy bracts enclosing the flowers.

lenticel: a small corky pore in the bark of the plant.

lepi-: Greek prefix meaning 'scale'.

lepidote: covered with fine stellate-hairy scales as on the wings of a butterfly, e.g. *Tibouchina lepidota.*

ligni-, ligno-: Latin prefixes meaning 'woody', hence *ligneous* — woody.

lignotuber: the woody basal swelling at the root-crown of some *Eucalyptus* spp., mainly the mallees, from which regrowth is initiated from dormant adventitious buds following destruction of the aerial parts by bushfires.

ligule, ligulate (adj): an outgrowth or projection located at the top of the leaf sheath in grasses; strap-shaped as in the slender ray-florets of composite flowers.

limb: the outer expanded part of a corolla.

linear: line-like; long and narrow with parallel sides, as in the leaves of *Callistemon linearis.*

lingulate: tongue-shaped.

lip: one of the parts of a divided corolla or calyx, especially in the flowers of Lamiaceae, the Labiate family.

littoral: used generally to refer to the foreshores and the plants of that habitat. Technically, between the low and high tidal levels.

lobe, lobule (dimin): a rounded or pointed division of a leaf or other organ, e.g. the lobes of the twin leaves of *Bauhinia* spp.

locule: a cavity of an anther, ovary or fruit.

loculicidal (dehiscence): the splitting of a fruit such as a capsule, from the apex to the base into separate valves.

longi-: Latin prefix meaning 'long'.

lorate: thong or strap-shaped.

lunate: shaped like a crescentic, quarter moon.

lustrous: glossy; gleaming bright.

lyrate: shaped like a lyre, i.e. pinnatifid with a large terminal lobe and several other lesser lobes, as in the leaves of *Quercus macrocarpa.*

macerate: to soften by soaking; often used to clean seeds of their outer pulp.

macro-: Greek, prefix meaning 'large'.

magna-, magni-: Latin prefixes meaning 'great'.

malic swellings: the small bulges, usually 5, at the calyx end of the fruits of some Malus spp.

mallee: a form of growth habit in Eucalypts, common in arid and alpine regions, the plants developing a thicket of several to many stunted stems from a swollen lignotuber.

margin: the edge of a leaf or other organ, sometimes entire (unbroken) or variously notched.

marginate: edged or bordered with a distinct margin, usually of contrasting colour.

maritime: pertaining to the sea or adjacent shores and the plants of that habitat.

marlock: a form of growth applied to several *Eucalyptus* spp. with a dwarf tree-like habit, usually with a single stem arising from a swollen base or lignotuber.

mealy: covered with a white, floury dust.

membranous: said of tissue that is thin and almost transparent.

medi-, medio-: Latin prefixes meaning 'middle' or 'medium'.

mega-: Latin prefix meaning 'great'.

melano-: Greek prefix meaning 'black'.

mericarp: the dehiscent halves of a schizocarp (q.v.).

-merous: Greek suffix indicating number of parts; hence 4-, 5- or 6-merous.

micro-: Greek prefix meaning 'small'.

midrib: the main vein or rib of a leaf or other flat structure.

moniliform: resembling a string of beads; often applied to legumes with deep regular constrictions between the seeds, e.g. *Sophora japonica.*

mono-: Greek prefix meaning 'one'.

Monocotyledon: an Angiosperm having a single cotyledon in the embryo.

monoecious: with unisexual flowers of both sexes on the same plant, e.g. *Juglans, Betula, Quercus* and *Buxus.*

monotypic: said of a genus with a single species.

morpho-, -morphic: Greek prefix and suffix meaning 'shape' or 'form'.

mucro, mucronate (adj), *mucronulate* (dimin): a short, sharp point, as in the apex of some leaves when the midrib is extended beyond the apex.

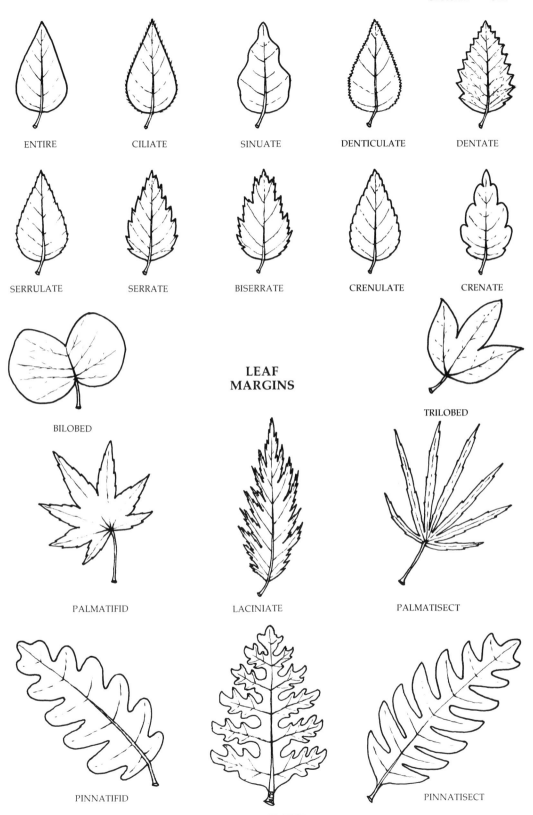

ENTIRE CILIATE SINUATE DENTICULATE DENTATE

SERRULATE SERRATE BISERRATE CRENULATE CRENATE

BILOBED

LEAF MARGINS

TRILOBED

PALMATIFID LACINIATE PALMATISECT

PINNATIFID PINNATISECT

BIPINNATIFID

multi-: Latin prefix meaning 'many'.

muricate: a surface, usually of leaves or stems, with small prickly tubercles.

mutant, mutation: an abrupt and inexplicable variation from the norm, such as doubleness in flowers, changes of colour, habit of growth; when confined to a single shoot, then termed a 'bud-sport'.

mycorrhiza: literally 'fungus root'; a fungus/ higher plant association of mutual benefit.

naked: usually applied to (a) seeds not borne in an ovary as in the Gymnosperms; (b) flowers lacking a showy corolla; (c) a glabrous, hairless surface.

nema-, nemato-: Greek prefixes meaning 'thread'.

nerve: a slender vein, especially if unbranched.

netted, net-veined: said of the venation of a leaf when the veins form a network; reticulate.

nocturnal: night-flowering.

nodding: pendulous.

node: a joint in a stem from which may issue leaves and buds.

novem-: Latin prefix meaning 'nine'.

nut: a dry, indehiscent fruit having one seed and a hard woody exterior.

nutlet: a small nut.

ob-: Latin prefix signifying inversion of a part.

obconical: a solid body, inversely tapered to 'conical', i.e. with the pointed end at the base.

obcordate: inversely cordate or heart-shaped.

oblanceolate: inversely lanceolate, with the broadest part near the apex.

oblate: spheroidal like the Earth; globular but flattened at the poles.

oblique: asymmetrically arranged on an axis; having odd sides.

oblong: said of leaves whose sides are longer than the width, and nearly parallel; roughly rectangular.

obovate: an inversely-ovate plane surface, i.e. with the broadest part nearer the apex.

obovoid: an inversely ovoid solid body such as a fruit.

obpyriform: inversely pear-shaped.

obsolete: a plant part now lost or only present in vestigial or rudimentary form.

obtuse: with blunt or rounded apex or base.

ochro-: Greek prefix meaning 'yellow'.

octo-: Latin and Greek prefix meaning 'eight'.

odd-pinnate: imparipinnate (q.v.).

offset: a short lateral shoot arising from near the base of the parent plant.

-oid: Latin suffix meaning 'like'.

operculum: a lid or covering over a flower, as in *Eucalyptus*.

opposite: said of leaves and branches when they occur in pairs, one on each side of the stem at the same node.

orbicular: circular in outline as in the leaves of *Symphoricarpus orbiculatus*.

order: the taxon immediately superior to and comprising closely related families. Modern order names end with 'ales'.

organ: a plant part having an independent and special role, e.g. leaf, root.

ortho-: Greek prefix meaning 'straight'.

-ose: Latin suffix meaning 'with', 'like' or 'containing'.

osier: a long, flexible shoot like that of a willow; used in basket-making.

ov-, ovi-: Latin prefix meaning 'egg'.

oval: a leaf shape wherein the length is nearly twice the width and the ends are rounded.

ovary: the part of the carpel bearing the ovule which, after fertilisation, becomes the fruit.

ovate: an egg-shaped part with the larger end toward the base, e.g. leaf.

ovoid: an egg-shaped solid body such as a fruit.

palmate: a compound leaf divided radially into 3 or more leaflets issuing from a common petiole, e.g. *Schefflera actinophylla*.

palmately-lobed or *palmatifid:* a simple leaf whose lobes occur in palmate fashion with the sinuses about half way to the middle, e.g. *Acer palmatum* and other simple-leafed Maples.

palmatisect: a simple leaf, cut to the midrib in palmate fashion, but not having separate leaflets, e.g. *Acer palmatum* 'Dissectum'.

panicle, paniculate (adj): a compound inflorescence in which the central axis is branched into racemes of more than one flower each, e.g. *Hydrangea paniculata*.

pannose: with a fine felt-like tomentum, e.g. *Cotoneaster pannosus*.

papilionaceous: having a pea-shaped corolla; members of the family Fabaceae (formerly Papilionaceae), the Pea family.

papilionate: literally 'butterfly-like' but applied to plants of the Pea family above.

pappus: a modification of the calyx limb in some composite flowers, having scales or hairs which assist in seed dispersal.

parallel: said of veins which extend separately and side-by-side, from the base of a leaf to the apex.

parasite: a plant which relies on another, the host plant, for support and sustenance; some are only hemisparasitic, such as Mistletoe, which is not wholly dependent upon its host.

paripinnate: a compound, pinnate leaf with an even number of leaflets, usually in regular pairs, but lacking a terminal leaflet.

parted: cut or divided almost to the base, as in some leaves.

patho-: Greek prefix meaning 'disease'.

pectinate: in a pinnatifid leaf when the lateral segments are closely set like the teeth of a comb, and in much the same plane.

ped-: Latin prefix meaning 'foot'.

pedicel, pedicellate (adj): the stalk of one flower in an inflorescence.

peduncle, pedunculate (adj): the main stalk of an inflorescence or of a solitary flower.

pellucid: translucent or nearly transparent.

peltate: a leaf shape wherein the petiole joins the blade inside the margin, e.g. Nasturtium.

pendent, pendulous: having a hanging or drooping habit, e.g. *Betula pendula.*

penninerved: nerves or veins arising evenly from the midrib, as in a feather.

penta-: Greek prefix meaning 'five'.

pentamerous: with parts in fives; often written as 5-merous.

perennial: a plant lasting for more than two years; correctly included are hard-wooded trees and shrubs with persistent aerial parts. Herbaceous perennials have annual aerial parts but persistent roots.

perfect: said of flowers having both male and female sexual parts.

perfoliate: a leaf whose margin encloses the stem; a pair of such leaves occurring oppositely on a stem, e.g. some *Eucalyptus* juvenile leaves.

perforate: leaves with scattered, irregularly shaped holes, as in *Monstera.*

perianth: the calyx and corolla as a single unit, the parts then termed segments.

perigynous: having floral organs (calyx, corolla and stamens) borne around the rim of a concave receptacle arising below the base of the gynoecium.

persistent: not deciduous but remaining attached, e.g. sepals persisting until the fruit is fully ripe; evergreen leaves are persistent for a number of years.

petal: one of the segments of a corolla, usually brightly coloured.

petalloid (adj): resembling a petal in shape and colour, used to describe the modified stamens of some *Camellia* cultivars.

petiole, petiolate (adj): the stalk of a leaf connecting the blade with the stem; when absent, a leaf is sessile.

petiolule: the stalk of a leaflet or pinnule.

philo-, -phile: Greek prefix and suffix meaning 'loving'.

photo-: Greek prefix meaning 'light'.

phyllo-, -phyll: Greek prefix and suffix meaning 'leaf'.

phyllode, phyllodal (adj): a modified petiole performing the function of a leaf, as seen in the non-bipinnate *Acacia* spp., e.g. *Acacia glaucescens, longifolia, prominens,* etc.

phyto-, -phyte: Greek prefix and suffix meaning 'plant'.

pilose: having long soft hairs, not densely crowded together.

pinna, pinnae (pl): (a) a primary leaflet in a pinnately-compound leaf; (b) in decompound leaves, the primary or secondary axes or rachillae are pinnae, carrying the ultimate leaflets or pinnules (q.v.).

pinnate: a compound leaf with leaflets placed laterally along the rachis, either oppositely or alternately; when the leaflets are even in number the leaf is paripinnate, but when a terminal leaflet occurs the leaf is imparipinnate.

pinnatifid: a simple leaf whose lobes occur in pinnate fashion, being cut about half way to the midrib.

pinnatisect: a simple leaf cut to the midrib or nearly so, but not into separate leaflets.

pinni-: Greek prefix meaning 'feather'.

pinnule: a secondary pinna or leaflet in a bipinnate leaf, e.g. *Acacia baileyana.*

pisiform: pea-shaped; from *Pisum,* the generic name of the Pea.

pistil: the female or seed-bearing part of a flower, made up of ovary, style and stigma.

pistillate: bearing a pistil but no stamens; a female flower.

pith: the central core of a stem, composed of soft, white, cellular tissue.

pitted: with a dimpled surface of irregular depressions.

plane: a flat surface with a single direction.

platy-: Greek prefix meaning 'broad'.

pleated, plicate: creased or folded lengthwise.

plumo-: Latin prefix meaning 'feathery'; hence *plumose* — having soft, fine hairs arranged laterally on opposite sides of a rachis.

pluri-: Latin prefix meaning 'many'.

pneumatophore: a small, erect breathing organ developed from the roots of certain aquatic plants for respiration, e.g. Mangrove.

pod: a legume; the dry, dehiscent, multi-seeded fruit of the leguminous plant families, *Caesalpiniaceae*, *Mimosaceae* and *Fabaceae*.

pollard: to restrict the upper growth of a tree by pruning, or to shape it to perform a particular function such as to provide shade in streets, courtyards, or plazas, or for the production of osiers by the various *Salix* spp.

pollen: the powdery, usually yellow, pollinating grains borne by an anther.

pollination: the introduction of male pollen grains to the receptive female stigma as a preliminary to fertilisation.

poly-: Greek prefix meaning 'many'.

polyandrous: with many stamens.

polygamous: bearing bisexual and unisexual flowers on the same plant.

polymorphic: many-formed, usually applied to plants bearing leaves of distinct shape on the same plant.

pome: a mostly globose fruit having fleshy pulp surrounding the several carpels containing the seeds, e.g. apple, pear, quince.

posterior: the rearmost part; in a flower, usually the part such as the standard petal in a papilionate flower, towards the axis.

prickle: a hard-wooded, sharp outgrowth from the bark of a stem, either straight or curved, occurring at random, e.g. Rose.

pro-: Latin or Greek prefix meaning 'before', 'for', 'forward', 'in front of'.

procumbent: of trailing habit.

prostrate: lying on the ground or nearly so.

proto-: Greek prefix meaning 'first' or 'original'.

provenance: the place of origin or native habitat of a plant.

proximal: at the inner end, closest to the point of attachment; the antonym of 'distal' (q.v.).

pruinose: covered with a glistening, whitish or bluish bloom.

pseudo-: Greek prefix meaning 'false'.

puberulent: finely pubescent.

pubescent: downy; having a surface with short, soft hairs.

pulvinus, *pulvini* (pl), *pulvinate* (adj): a small peg- or cushion-like structure, as in the persistent petiolar base of *Picea* spp.

punctate: dotted with translucent or coloured spots or pits.

pungent: sharp or biting to the taste; ending in a stiff, sharp tip.

pustule, *pustulate* (adj): a small, pimple-like swelling or blister.

pyriform: pear-shaped, from *Pyrus*, the pear.

quadri-: Latin prefix meaning 'four'.

quinque-: Latin prefix meaning 'five'.

raceme, *racemose* (adj): an indeterminate inflorescence having a simple, unbranched rachis from which arise the pedicelled flowers, e.g. *Wisteria floribunda*, *Cassia fistula*.

rachilla, *rachillae* (pl): a minor or secondary axis of an inflorescence or decompound leaf. Also spelt 'rhachilla', 'rhachillae'.

rachis, *rachides* (pl): the main axis of an inflorescence or of a compound leaf. Also spelt 'rhachis', 'rhachides'.

radiate: spreading out from a common centre, as in the ray-florets in the family Asteraceae (formerly Compositae).

radical: said of leaves and flowers which issue from ground level, near the roots.

radicle: the primary root issuing from a germinating seedling.

rainforest: an area of high rainfall and atmospheric humidity, mostly on the 'wet' side of the mountain ranges, supporting a mixed community of tall 'top-storey' trees, several intermediate layers of miscellaneous material and a 'ground-floor' of ferns, mosses, etc.

rami-: Latin prefix meaning 'branch'.

ramus, *rami* (pl): a branch or twig borne on a larger structure; hence *ramiform* — like a branch, and *ramose* — branched.

ray: the outer, flattened flowers of the family Asteraceae (formerly Compositae).

re-: Latin prefix meaning 'again' or 'back'.

receptacle: the often enlarged top of a stem on which the floral parts are supported.

reclining: bent or curved towards the base.

recurved: curving backwards or outwards; also 'reflexed'.

regular: said of a flower with each series of floral parts uniform; i.e. petals with similar shape, size and placement.

reniform: kidney-shaped, applicable to flat, single-planed parts like leaves or to solid bodies like fruits, e.g. the seed of the bean.

resinous: having a coating or exudation of resin or gum as in the buds and twigs of *Populus balsamifera*.

reti-, reticuli-: Latin prefixes meaning 'netted'; hence 'reticulate'.

retrorse: bent or pointing backwards, opposed to the normal pattern.

retuse: said of a rounded or truncate leaf-apex with a shallow terminal notch or depression.

revolute: a margin which is rolled backwards to the lower side; e.g. leaves of *Pittosporum revolutum.*

rhizome: a creeping, slightly- or wholly-underground, modified stem; e.g. Tall Bearded Iris.

rhom, rhombic (adj), *rhombiform* (adj), *rhomboidal* (adj): diamond-shaped or with the shape of a rhombus, e.g. *Pittosporum rhombifolium.*

rib: the prominent veins in a leaf or fruit, usually the main vein.

riverine: pertaining to a river or its valley; the flora of such a habitat.

rogue: to eliminate weak or non-conforming seedlings by weeding-out.

root: the mostly underground part of a plant, responsible for anchorage and the absorption of water and nutrients from the soil.

rostrum, rostrate (adj): having a beak-like point, e.g. fruits of *Hakea sericea.*

rotate: with a wheel-shaped corolla, with regularly spreading petals.

rudimentary: vestigial; a part much reduced in size or shape by improper development or abortion.

rufous: of brownish-red colour; applied mainly to hairs or bristles.

rugose: having a wrinkled surface.

runcinate: a leaf whose lobes or leaflets point backwards towards the base.

runner: a sarment; an elongated, prostrate, stoloniferous stem forming roots at the nodes in contact with the ground.

saccate: said of irregular-shaped flowers whose lowest petal is spurred and modified into a small, rounded sac or pouch, e.g. *Plectranthus saccatus.*

sagittate: arrow-shaped, with the basal lobes pointing downwards.

salverform: a corolla shape in which the slender cylindrical lower part expands at the mouth into a flat, rotate limb, e.g. *Luculia gratissima.*

samara: a one-seeded, indehiscent, winged fruit as in *Fraxinus,* made up of a nut, and a wing for aerial dispersal; sometimes seen as a twin samara with two seeds joined together, the wings forming a variety of angles, e.g. *Acer* spp.

sapro-: Greek prefix meaning 'rotten'.

sarment, sarmentose (adj): a long, weak stem of a shrubby plant, in need of support but lacking visible climbing aids.

saxicolous: growing among rocks, e.g. *Thryptomene saxicola.*

scaber-: Latin prefix meaning 'rough'; hence *scabrid, scabrous* — having a rough surface, as in *Deutzia scabra.*

scaberulous: diminutive of above; minutely scabrous.

scale: a very small rudimentary leaf as in *Casuarina* spp., or the flat, closely pressed leaves of *Hebe cupressoides;* sometimes used to describe the roughly plated bark of trunks or branches.

scandent: of climbing habit, e.g. *Cobaea scandens.*

scape: a leafless flower stem arising from a foliage clump as in the elongated peduncle of *Strelitzia reginae.*

scarious: leaves, scales or bracts, usually thin and membranous, with a dry, stiff and brittle texture.

scattered: leaves that occur in random manner on the stem, not in regular opposite, alternate or whorled arrangement.

schizo-: Greek prefix meaning 'split' or 'separated'.

schizocarp: a dry, dehiscent fruit of two or more carpels, splitting when ripe into individual 1-seeded mericarps.

scion: the aerial part of a graft combination, induced by various methods to unite with a compatible understock.

sclero-: Greek prefix meaning 'hard'; hence *sclerotic* — hardened.

sclerophyll, sclerophyllous (adj): plants with harsh-textured, tough leaves as in *Eucalyptus sclerophylla.* The 'sclerophyll' forests, both 'wet' and 'dry' are composed mainly of plants of this type.

scrambler: a climbing plant armed with backward pointing hooks, e.g. *Bougainvillea.*

scree-soils: a coarse mixture of decomposed rock and organic matter accumulated at the base of a slope or among rocks.

scurfy: covered with small, dry scales.

sect-: Latin prefix meaning 'cut' or 'separated'.

seed: the ripening ovule containing the embryo, enclosed in a testa or seed-coat.

seedling: a young plantlet resulting from the germination of a seed.

segment: a part of a leaf that is divided into lobes or divisions but is not properly compound; a unit of a perianth (q.v.).

self-pollination: the introduction of pollen from the stamens to the pistil of the same flower.

semi-: Latin prefix meaning 'half'.

sepal: one of the segments of the calyx.

sepaloid: resembling a sepal.

separation: a form of vegetative propagation by use of parts that are either naturally detachable or can be induced to part readily, e.g. bulb separation in *Narcissus.*

septem-: Latin prefix meaning 'seven'.

septi-: Latin prefix meaning 'partition'; hence *septate* — partitioned.

septum: a partition between parts, especially in fruits.

sericate, sericeous: covered with soft, straight, silky hairs.

serrate: a leaf-margin with sharp teeth like those of a rip-saw, pointing slightly forward as in *Banksia serrata.*

serrulate: diminutive of above; minutely serrate, e.g. *Boronia serrulata.*

sessile: stalkless, the petiole absent.

seta: a bristle.

setose, setulose (dimin): covered with stiff, erect, straight bristles.

sex-: Latin prefix meaning 'six'.

sheath: a plant part enfolded around another as in the leaf sheath of grasses or of *Ficus elastica.*

shrub: a woody plant of perennial character with several or many stems from the base and not a single main trunk as in a tree.

siliqua: a dry, dehiscent fruit in which the outer parts, the pericarp, separate from the inner wall, the false septum, to which the seeds are attached, e.g. fruit of the family Brassicaceae (Cruciferae).

silky: covered with fine soft hairs.

silvi-, silva-: Latin prefixes meaning 'forest'; hence *silviculture* — the cultivation of trees in a forest.

simili-: Latin prefix meaning 'alike' or 'similar'.

simple: a leaf that is not compound, even though the margin may be lobed.

sinuate: a leaf-margin with a wavy outline composed of broad, shallow indentations.

sinus: the space between the lobes of a leaf.

smooth: a surface, like a leaf's, that is not rough or scabrous.

solitary: flowers or fruits borne singly, not in clusters.

spadix: a fleshy, spike-like inflorescence enclosed partly by an envelope called a spathe; the yellow, finger-like organ in Arum Lily.

spathe: the bracteate envelope enclosing a spadix; it may be coloured and showy as in *Calla.*

spathulate, spatulate: shaped like a spatula; a leaf of slender-obovate shape, tapering from the rounded apex to a narrow base.

species (sing and pl): a group of plants essentially alike when grown under similar conditions and which normally breed freely and truly amongst their own kind; the taxon immediately subordinate to the genus, constituting the principal unit in the system of plant classification. In modern nomenclatural practice, specific epithets (species names) are not capitalised, regardless of their derivation.

spherical: a solid plant form with the shape of a globe.

spike, spicate (adj): a compact, indeterminate inflorescence of sessile flowers as in the 'bottlebrush' of *Callistemon.*

spikelet: a secondary spike.

spine, spinose (adj), *spinous* (adj): a sharp-pointed outgrowth resulting from modification to (a) leaves, as in *Cacti, Ilex, Ulex* and the spinose *Acacias,* (b) stipules, as in *Robinia,* and (c) branchlets, as in *Gleditsia.*

spinule: diminutive of above; a small or minute spine.

spore: the sexual reproductive body of ferns and other lower-order plants.

sporo-, -spore: Greek prefix and suffix meaning 'seed'.

spur: a sac-like floral extension, often secreting nectar, e.g. *Delphinium.*

squama, squamae (pl): a scale; hence *squamate, squamose* — bearing scales.

squarrose: overlapping scales or leaves with spreading, projecting or recurving edges.

stalk: the elongated support of a flower or fruit (pedicel or peduncle) or leaf (petiole).

stamen: the male part of a flower comprising the elongate 'filament' and the pollen-bearing 'anther'.

staminal column: an elongate column formed by the fusion of filaments, e.g. *Hibiscus* spp.

staminate: a male flower or inflorescence, having stamens but no pistil.

staminode: an abortive and sterile stamen, as in *Jacaranda mimosifolia.*

standard: the broad posterior petal in a pea-shaped flower; the 3 upright petals in Tall

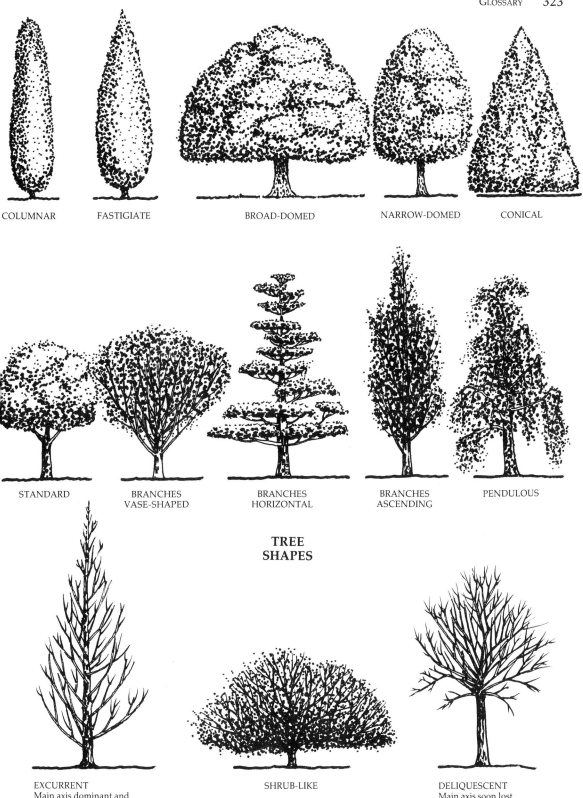

COLUMNAR   FASTIGIATE   BROAD-DOMED   NARROW-DOMED   CONICAL

STANDARD   BRANCHES VASE-SHAPED   BRANCHES HORIZONTAL   BRANCHES ASCENDING   PENDULOUS

TREE SHAPES

EXCURRENT
Main axis dominant and
clearly defined throughout

SHRUB-LIKE

DELIQUESCENT
Main axis soon lost
amongst the branches

Bearded Iris; a mostly artificially induced plant shape with a single, erect trunk and a rounded head.

stellate: star-shaped, as in the flowers of *Magnolia stellata;* a cluster of hairs radiating from the centre, or hairs branched radially.

stem: the principal axis of a plant; applied also to flower stems.

sterile: barren; lacking in one or both essential sexual parts.

stigma: the upper distal part of a pistil comprising the receptive surface for the transfer of pollen.

stipel, stipellae (pl): a stipule of a leaflet in a compound leaf.

stipule, stipulate (adj): a leafy outgrowth sometimes occurring at the base of a petiole.

stolon, stoloniferous (adj): a trailing shoot, usually on the soil surface, rooting and shooting at the nodes, as in couch-grass.

stoma, stomata (pl): minute opening in the surface of leaves allowing the interchange of gases.

stoma-, stomati-: Greek prefixes meaning 'mouth'.

stone-fruits: said of the single-stoned species of *Prunus,* e.g. peach, plum, apricot, cherry, nectarine, almond.

striate: bearing fine longitudinal grooves or marks.

strigose, strigillose (dimin): a surface with stiff, short hairs, mostly with a swollen base, lying closely and in one direction, e.g. *Rondeletia strigosa.*

strobile: a cone-like axis with closely-imbricate scales carrying the fertilised seeds, e.g. *Alnus* spp.

style: the elongate part of the pistil connecting the ovary and the stigma.

sub-: Latin prefix meaning 'below', 'nearly', or 'under'; hence, *sub-cordate* — nearly cordate, *sub-orbicular* — almost round.

subtend: the placement of a structure such as a stipule or bract immediately beneath a flower, petiole or twig.

subulate: awl-shaped; narrowing to a fine point as in the leaflets of *Boronia subulifolia.*

succulent: soft and juicy as in the leaves of *Sedum praealtum.*

sucker: adventitious shoots developing from a plant's roots or from below the union in grafted plants.

suffruticose: having a low, shrubby growth habit.

sulcate: a surface, usually leaf or bark, with longitudinal parallel ridges; more pronounced than 'striate' but less than 'costate'.

super-: Latin prefix meaning 'above', 'over', or 'on'.

supra-: Latin prefix meaning 'above', 'beyond', or 'over'.

suture: a line or ridge along which a seed-vessel dehisces, or where two parts unite.

sym-: Greek prefix meaning 'with' or 'together'.

symmetrical: said of a regular flower having the same number of sepals, petals, etc in each whorl; also used to describe plants of very regular habit such as Norfolk Island Pine.

sympetalous: gamopetalous; with petals joined together.

syncarp, syncarpous (adj): an aggregated fruit with several or many individuals coalesced, e.g. *Magnolia* and *Syncarpia.*

synonym (abbreviated to 'syn.'): in plant nomenclature an invalid plant name set aside in favour of an earlier valid name.

taproot: the strong, main-axis root of a plant from which secondary roots develop.

taxo-, taxis: Greek prefixes meaning 'arrangement'; hence *taxonomy* — the science of classification.

taxon, taxa (pl): the term used to refer to any of the taxonomic groups in the classification system of plants.

tendril: a modified stem, leaf or petiole having a thread-like form sensitive to physical contact, whose purpose is to support the stems of climbing plants.

tepal: petals and sepals so alike as to be scarcely distinguishable, e.g. *Magnolia* and *Michelia* spp.

terete: said of round stems or other parts circular in cross-section, having a generally cylindrical form although some taper may be present.

terminal: placed at the apex or end.

ternate: parts arranged in groups of three, as in leaves from the same node on one side of a stem only; compound leaves with three leaflets are better described as 'trifoliolate'.

terrestrial: plants which grow in the ground, not in water (aquatics) or air (epiphytes).

tessellate: said of a surface with a squared or checkered pattern, as in the bark of some *Eucalyptus* spp.

testa: the usually hard, outer coat of a seed.

tetra-: Greek prefix meaning 'four'; hence

tetramerous — with parts in fours, *tetragonal* — four-angled.

thorn: a stem modified into a hard, sharp-pointed spur as in *Crataegus*.

throat: the opening of a corolla or perianth.

thyrse: a narrowly conical paniculate inflorescence in which the main axis is indeterminate, and the lateral axes, mostly small cymes, are determinate.

tomentum, tomentose (adj), *tomentulose* (dimin): short, soft, dense hairs usually matted together to form a felt-like surface, e.g. *Cassia tomentosa*.

topiary: the pruning of plants into various ornamental or geometrical shapes, usually at the expense of flower and fruit production.

tortuous: irregularly twisted or bent, e.g. *Salix matsudana* 'Tortuosa'.

torulose: a cylindrical structure marked at irregular intervals by swellings or constrictions, e.g. *Casuarina torulosa*.

trans-: Latin prefix meaning 'across' or 'over'.

translucent: semi-transparent.

tree: a perennial plant with a single woody trunk and a more or less distinct and elevated head, the main criterion being 'form' rather than 'size', e.g. a tree grown by Bonsai culture does not become a shrub merely because of its reduced size.

tri-: Latin and Greek prefix meaning 'three', hence *trimerous* — with parts in threes.

trichotomous: branches or other parts which divide regularly into 3 parts, e.g. the upper stems of *Gardenia thunbergia*.

trifid: cut into 3 lobes, about half way to the midrib.

trifoliate: with leaves borne in threes.

trifoliolate: a leaf having 3 leaflets as in *Ceratopetalum gummiferum*.

tripinnate: thrice pinnate as in the leaves of *Nandina domestica*, which may also be bipinnate and quadripinnate.

-tropic: Greek suffix meaning 'to turn'; hence *heliotropic* — to turn towards the sun.

truncate: a leaf-apex or base which ends abruptly as if cut straight across.

tuber: a modified underground stem usually acting as a storage organ, having buds on the body from which new shoots develop, e.g. potato.

tubercle, tuberculate (adj): small, round or pointed, pimple-like swellings.

tubulate: shaped like a hollow tube, not necessarily with regular parallel sides, applied mostly to corollas.

tumid: enlarged, swollen, turgid.

tunic, tunicate (adj): the papery outer covering of a bulb or other storage organ.

turbinate: shaped like a spinning-top; obconical.

turgid: swollen or distended; said of healthy, fully developed cells.

twig: a young branchlet of the outermost parts of a plant.

twiner: a climbing plant in which the entire stem coils around the support, as in *Wisteria*: some turn clockwise, others counter-clockwise.

ultimate: the outermost or finally-distal part of a structure, e.g. twigs.

umbel, umbellate (adj): an inflorescence in which the pedicels are of much the same length and arise from the same point on the peduncle, each carrying a single flower as in *Agapanthus*; when the pedicels arise from a number of peduncles, the inflorescence is a 'compound umbel' as in Parsley, the secondary umbels being termed 'umbellets' or 'umbellules'.

umbilicate: a surface with one or more small round depressions, usually as the result of the separation of other parts, e.g. leaf-scars.

umbo, umbonate (adj): a small central protuberance, commonly seen on the cone-scales of conifers.

umbrageous: shade-giving; usually said of trees with a broad spreading crown, such as *Ulmus parvifolia*.

uncinate: hooked, like the leaf-apices of *Chamelaucium uncinatum*.

undulate: having a wavy surface as in the leaves of *Pittosporum undulatum*.

uni-: Latin prefix meaning 'one'; hence *uniflora* — one-flowered.

unijugate: a pinnate leaf with a single pair of leaflets.

unilateral: one-sided, as the inflorescence of some *Grevilleas*.

unisexual: of one sex only, either staminate or pistillate.

urceolate: shaped like an urn, being narrowed at the mouth and globose below, as in the fruits of many of the *Eucalyptus* spp.

valvate: meeting but not overlapping at the edges, as in sepals or petals.

valve: a cell or compartment in a fully matured capsule.

variety or *varietas, varietates* (pl): the taxon immediately subordinate to the species, used to designate plants occurring in the wild, exhibiting clearly defined but minor variations from the specific norm which are not usually lost when the plant is grown from seeds. Many taxonomic botanists now prefer to use the taxon 'subspecies' for such material.

variegated: irregularly marked with blotches or patches of another colour.

vein, venation: the nerves or vascular tubes in a leaf that give it a peculiar netted, parallel or anastomosed arrangement.

ventral: anterior; towards the main axis; the antonym of 'dorsal' (q.v.).

verrucose: covered with warty protuberances as in *Eriostemon verrucosus.*

versatile: said of an anther attached dorsally and at about the middle to the tip of the filament, allowing it to move freely.

verticil, verticillate (adj): a whorl of twigs or leaves from a node.

vestigial: a rudimentary trace of an organ or part, once more evident.

viable, viability: the ability of a seed or other plant part to grow and live.

villous: having long, soft hairs.

virgate: having long straight, wand-like twigs as in *Polygala virgata.*

viscid, viscous: having a sticky surface from an exuded gum or resin.

warted: a surface covered with small round protuberances, especially in leaves and twigs, as in *Eriostemon myoporoides.*

water-shoot: an erect, strong-growing or epicormic shoot developing from near the base of a shrub or tree, but distinct from 'sucker' (q.v.).

weeping: a plant form having pendulous branches, e.g. Weeping Willow.

whorl: a ring of 3 or more parts around an axis, as in leaves, petals, etc.

wing: a thin membranous extension of an organ, as in the papery wings of the samaras of *Acer* and *Fraxinus;* the lateral petals of a pea flower.

woolly: lanate; having long, soft, matted hair.

xantho-: Greek prefix meaning 'yellow'.

xero-: Greek prefix meaning 'dry'.

xerophyte: a plant growing in or tolerant of dry conditions.

Index of Plant Names